3770

WITHDRAWN

Index to
BOOK REVIEWS
IN
HISTORICAL PERIODICALS
1977

by

John W. Brewster

and

Deborah Gentry

The Scarecrow Press, Inc.
Metuchen, N.J. & London
1979

Ref
Index/
Abstr.
D
/
B73
1977

ISBN: 0-8108-1192-8
LC: 75-18992

INTRODUCTION

The Index to Book Reviews in Historical Periodicals has developed out of a recognized need for aid in locating reviews of books assigned for class readings. The present volume includes 96 of the better known scholarly journals and historical society organs. Although the reviews concentrate more heavily upon U.S. history, an effort has been made to include materials relating to other countries as well. The index includes only English-language periodicals. Books written in foreign languages are included if the review is in English. The original title is indicated except where a translation is given, in which case the English version is used. In some periodicals, works are included which stress other disciplines as well as history. These are included for the sake of completeness, such entries comprise a very small minority of the total index.

In most cases, the complete title of the work is indicated although in the case of an exceptionally long title, an abridged form may appear. In all cases, the policy has been to include enough of the title to enable the researcher to identify the work. In regard to imprint, the editors have endeavored to provide enough information to identify the work clearly. Well-known publishers whose works appear frequently are cited by abbreviations (a key to academic press abbreviations begins on page x). States are included only when needed to identify a city.

Although designed primarily as a tool for locating book reviews, because the index includes some 3000 titles, most of which are current publications, it may also serve as a bibliographic guide in history. As nearly as possible, the editors have used the format of the University of Chicago Style Manual. Standardized abbreviations for months and seasons are used. In most cases where reviewers' entries conflict, Books in Print has been followed.

The editors present this work with the belief that it will be a useful tool for the scholar, the student, and the general reader with an interest in history.

John W. Brewster
Deborah G. Gentry

December 1978

ACKNOWLEDGEMENTS

The authors of the index recognize that their efforts have been made much easier by the indulgence and cooperation of others. Special thanks go to Carol McLeod and Rena Gallego for their assistance in the compilation and typing of this volume. Appreciation also goes to Bruce Hodges and Pam Brewster for their role as sounding boards, a role which afforded us much indulgence and commiseration.

PERIODICALS INDEXED (1977)

EEQ	East European Quarterly
EHR	English Historical Review
E-I	Eire-Ireland
ESR	European Studies Review
ETHJ	East Texas Historical Journal
FCHQ	Filson Club History Quarterly
FHQ	Florida Historical Quarterly
GHQ	Georgia Historical Quarterly
GR	Georgia Review
H & T	History & Theory
HAHR	The Hispanic American Historical Review
Historian	Historian
History	History
HJ	Historical Journal
HRNB	History: Review of New Books
HT	History Teacher
HTo	History Today
InHi	Indian Historian
IQ	India Quarterly
JAAS	Journal of Asian and African Studies
JAH	Journal of American History
JAmS	Journal of American Studies
JAriH	Journal of Arizona History
JAS	Journal of Asian Studies
JEH	Journal of Economic History
JIH	Journal of Interdisciplinary History
JLAS	Journal of Latin American Studies
JMH	Journal of Modern History
JMiH	Journal of Mississippi History
JNES	Journal of Near Eastern Studies
JNH	Journal of Negro History
JOW	Journal of the West
JSH	Journal of Southern History
LaH	Louisiana History
Mankind	Mankind

MAS	Modern Asian Studies
MHM	Maryland Historical Magazine
MHR	Missouri Historical Review
MiA	Mid America
MichH	Michigan History
MinnH	Minnesota History
NCHR	North Carolina Historical Review
NDH	North Dakota History
NEQ	New England Quarterly
NMHR	New Mexico Historical Review
NYHSQ	New York Historical Society Quarterly
OH	Ohio History
OHQ	Ohio Historical Quarterly
OrHQ	Oregon Historical Quarterly
PH	Pennsylvania History
PHR	Pacific Historical Review
PNQ	Pacific Northwest Quarterly
RAH	Reviews in American History
SCHM	South Carolina Historical Magazine
SCQ	Southern California Quarterly
SS	Social Studies
SWHQ	Southwestern Historical Quarterly
TAm	The Americas
Texana	Texana
UHQ	Utah Historical Quarterly
VH	Vermont History
VMHB	Virginia Magazine of History and Biography
WHQ	Western Historical Quarterly
WMH	Wisconsin Magazine of History
WMQ	William and Mary Quarterly
WVH	West Virginia History

ABBREVIATIONS OF PUBLISHERS

Standard abbreviations are used for commercial publishers. The following abbreviations are used for university presses and educational presses:

Cam U Press	Cambridge University Press, Cambridge, England
Cath U Amer Press	Catholic University of America Press, Washington, D. C.
Coll and U Press	College and University Press, New Haven, Conn.
Cor U Press	Cornell University Press, Ithaca, N.Y.
CWRU Press	Case Western Reserve University Press, Cleveland, Ohio
Edin U Press	Edinburgh Univ. Press, Edinburgh, Scotland
Fla St U Press	Florida State Univ. Press, Tallahassee, Fla.
Har U Press	Harvard University Press, Cambridge, Mass.
Heb Union Coll Press	Hebrew Union College Press, Cincinnati, Ohio
Huntington	Huntington Library, San Marino, California
Ia St U Press	Iowa State University Press, Ames, Ia.
Ind U Press	Indiana University Press, Bloomington, Indiana
JHU Press	Johns Hopkins University Press, Baltimore, Md.
LSU Press	Louisiana State University Press, Baton Rouge, La.
MHS	Maryland Historical Society, Baltimore, Maryland
MIT	Massachusetts Institute of Technology Press, Cambridge, Mass.

N Ill U Press	Northern Illinois University Press, DeKalb, Ill.
NW St U La Press	Northwest State University of Louisiana, Natchitoches, La.
NWU Press	Northwestern University Press, Evanston, Ill.
NYU Press	New York University Press, New York, N.Y.
PHMC	Pennsylvania Historical and Museum Commission
Prin U Press	Princeton University Press, Princeton, N.J.
S Ill U Press	Southern Illinois University Press, Carbondale, Ill.
Stan U Press	Stanford University Press, Stanford, California
Syr U Press	Syracuse University Press, Syracuse, N.Y.
TCU Press	Texas Christian University Press, Ft. Worth, Texas
U and Coll Press Miss	University and College Press of Mississippi, Hattiesburg, Mississippi
UBC Press	University of British Columbia Press, Vancouver, B.C.
U Cal Press	University of California Press, Berkeley and Los Angeles
U Chi Press	University of Chicago Press, Chicago, Illinois
U Ga Press	University of Georgia Press, Athens, Georgia
U Ia Press	University of Iowa Press, Iowa City, Iowa
U Ill Press	University of Illinois Press, Urbana, Ill.
U Kan Press	University of Kansas Press, Lawrence, Kansas
U Mich Press	University of Michigan Press, Ann Arbor, Michigan
U Minn Press	University of Minnesota Press, Minneapolis, Minn.
U Mo Press	University of Missouri Press, Columbia, Mo.
U Mont Press	University of Montana Press, Missoula, Mont.

Abbreviations of Publishers   xii

UNC	University of North Carolina Press, Chapel Hill, N.C.
U NMex Press	University of New Mexico Press, Albuquerque, N.M.
U Okla Press	University of Oklahoma Press, Norman, Oklahoma
U Press Ky	University Press of Kentucky, Lexington, Ky.
U Press NE	University Press of New England, Hanover, Vt.
U Press Va	University Press of Virginia, Charlottesville, Va.
USC Press	University of South Carolina Press, Columbia, S.C.
USNI	United States Naval Institute, Annapolis, Md.
U Tenn Press	University of Tennessee Press, Knoxville, Tenn.
U Tor Press	University of Toronto Press, Toronto
U Tx Press	University of Texas Press, Austin, Texas
U Utah Press	University of Utah Press, Salt Lake City, Utah
U Wash Press	University of Washington Press, Seattle, Washington
U Wis Press	University of Wisconsin Press, Madison, Wisconsin
Van U Press	Vanderbilt University Press, Nashville, Tenn.
W St U Press	Wayne State University Press, Detroit, Mich.
Wes U Press	Wesleyan University Press, Middletown, Conn.

THE INDEX: 1977

Abbazia, Patrick. Mr. Roosevelt's Navy: The Private War of the
U. S. Atlantic Fleet, 1939-1942. Annapolis: Naval Inst. Press,
1975. Rev. by R. W. Leopold, AHR, 81(Dec 1976):1279.

Abbott, Carl. Colorado: A History of the Centennial State. Boulder: Colorado Associated U Press, 1976. Rev. by L. E.
Leyendecker, NMHR, 52(Jan 1977):85-6; R. C. Sims, PNQ,
68(Oct 1977):192-3; M. Sprague, WHQ, 8(Apr 1977):212.

Abbott, Nabia. Studies in Arabic Literary Papyri, III, Language
and Literature. Chicago: U Chi Press, 1969. Rev. by
R. B. Serjeant, JNES, 36(Jan 1977):57-8.

Abel, Wilhelm. Massenarmut und Hungerkrisen im vorindustriellen
Europa: Versuch einer Synopsis. Hamburg: Verlag Paul
Parey, 1974. Rev. by R. Gottfried, AHR, 82(Feb 1977):84-5.

Abernethy, Francis Edward, ed. What's Going On? (In Modern
Texas Folklore). Austin: Encino Press, 1976. Rev. by B.
Groce, ETHJ, 15(No. 2, 1977):64-5.

Abler, Thomas S. , Douglas Sanders, and Sally M. Weaver. A
Canadian Indian Bibliography, 1960-1970. Toronto: U Toronto
Press, 1974. Rev. by G. F. G. Stanley, AIQ, 3(Spring 1977):
54-6.

Abramor, S. Zalman. Perpetual Dilemma: Jewish Religion in the
Jewish State. n. l.: Fairleigh Dickinson Press, n. d. Rev.
by H. M. Sachar, Comm, 64(Oct 1977):84-6.

Abs, Hermann J. Lebensfragen der Wirtschaft. Dusseldorf and
Vienna: Econ Verlag, 1976. Rev. by J. P. McKay, JEH,
37(Sep 1977):769.

Acton, Harold see Shang-jen, K'ung

Adamolekun, Ladipo. Sekou Toure's Guinea: An Experiment in
Nation Building. N. Y.: Barnes and Noble, 1976. Rev. by
V. Thompson, AHR, 82(Apr 1977):407.

Adams, Ansel. Photographs of the Southwest. Boston: New York
Graphic Society, 1976. Rev. by A. T. Row, JAriH, 18(Sum
1977):220-1.

Adams, Ramon F. The Adams One-Fifty: A Checklist of the 150
    Most Important Books on Western Outlaws and Lawmen. Aus-
    tin: Remberton Press, 1976. Rev. by A. C. Ashcraft, JOW,
    16(Jl 1977):101-102.

Adams, Richard E. W., ed. The Origins of Maya Civilization.
    Albuquerque: U NM Press, 1977. Rev. by E. B. McCluney,
    History, 6(Nov/Dec 1977):34-5.

Adams, William Howard, ed. The Eye of Thomas Jefferson. Wash-
    ington: National Gallery of Art, 1976. Rev. by J. Kukla,
    VMHB, 85(July 1977):366-7.

Addison, Paul. The Road to 1945: British Politics and the Second
    World War. London: Jonathan Cape, 1975. Rev. by H.
    Pelling, History, 62(Feb 1977):150-1.

Addy, John. The Textile Revolution. New York: Longman, 1976.
    Rev. by D. C. Anderson, HT, 10(Aug 1977):638-9.

Agulla, Juan Carlos. Eclipse of an Aristocracy: An Investigation
    of the Ruling Elites of the City of Córdoba. University, Ala-
    bama: U Ala Press, 1976. Rev. by J. R. Scobie, TAm, 34
    (Jl 1977):140-1.

Airs, Malcolm. The Making of the English Country House 1500-
    1640. London: Architectural Press, 1975. Rev. by H. M.
    Colvin, EHR, 92(Oct 77):894; A. H. Smith, History, 62(Feb
    1977):112-3.

Aitken, Hugh G. J. Syntony and Spark: The Origins of Radio.
    New York: John Wiley, 1976. Rev. by B. S. Finn, JEH,
    37(Je 1977):477-8.

Akerblom, Lars. Sir Samuel Hoare och Etiopienkonflikten, 1935.
    Stockholm: Alquist and Wiksell International, 1976. Rev. by
    H. P. Krosby, AHR, 82(Oct 1977):974-5.

Akerman, Joe A., Jr. Florida Cowman, A History of Florida Cat-
    tle Raising. Kissimee: Florida Cattlemen's Association, 1976.
    Rev. by C. W. Tebeau, FHQ, 55(Jan 1977):366-8.

Akers, Samuel Luttrell. The First Hundred Years of Wesleyan Col-
    lege. Macon: Wesleyan College, 1976. Rev. by A. F.
    Scott, GHQ, 51(Win 1977):357-9.

Akhtar, Shahid. Health Care in the People's Republic of China: A
    Bibliography with Abstracts. Ottawa: International Develop-
    ment Research Center, 1975. Rev. by P. S. Heller, CQ,
    No. 69(Mar 1977):179-81.

Akinari, Ueda. Ugetsu Monogatari: Tales of Moonlight and Rain.
    Vancouver: U Brit Col Press, 1974. Rev. by L. Rogers,
    JAS, 36(May 1977):564-5.

Akioka, Lorena M. and Carolyn S. Hudgins, ed. Georgia Statistical
    Abstract, 1976. Athens, Ga.: University of Georgia, 1976.
    Rev. by P. Spalding, GHQ, 51(Sum 1977):191-2.

Akrigg, G. P. V. and Helen Akrigg. British Columbia Chronicle,
    1778-1846: Adventures by Sea and Land. Vancouver: Dis-
    covery Press, 1975. Rev. by G. F. G. Stanley, AHR, 82
    (Apr 1977):475; P. E. Roy, PNQ, 68(Jan 1977):43.

Akrigg, Helen B. see Akrigg, G. P. V.

Alatas, Syed Hussein. The Myth of the Lazy Native: A Study of
    the Image of the Malays, Filipinos and Javanese from the 16th
    to the 20th Century and Its Function in the Ideology of Colon-
    ial Capitalism. Totowa, N. J.: Frank Cass & Co., 1977.
    Rev. by W. P. Strauss, History, 6(Nov/Dec 1977):40.

Albanese, Anthony Gerald. The Plantation School. New York:
    Vantage Press, 1976. Rev. by E. M. Steel, Jr., JSH, 43
    (May 1977):294-5.

Aldred, Cyril. Tutankhamun's Egypt. London: British Broadcast-
    ing Corporation, 1972. Rev. by E. R. Russmann, JNES, 36
    (Oct 1977):312-3.

Aleksandrov, V. A. The Village Commune in Russia from the
    Seventeenth to the Beginning of the Nineteenth Century. Mos-
    cow: Izdatil'stvo "Nauka," 1976. Rev. by D. Field, AHR,
    82(Je 1977):692-3.

Alexander, Charles C. Holding the Line: The Eisenhower Era,
    1952-1961. Bloomington: Indiana U Press, 1975. Rev. by
    W. M. Simons, PH, 45(July 1977):275-6.

Alexander, Edward Porter. Military Memoirs of a Confederate, A
    Critical Narrative. Dayton, Ohio: Morningside Press, 1977.
    Rev. by D. Evans, GHQ, 51(Sum 1977):205-6.

Alexander, J. J. G., ed. and M. T. Gibson, ed. Medieval Learn-
    ing and Literature. N. Y.: Oxford U Press, 1976. Rev. by
    R. W. Pfaff, AHR, 82(Feb 1977):73-4; D. Luscombe, EHR,
    92(Oct 1977):883-4; D. Hay, History, 62(Feb 1977):102-3.

Alexander, John. Yugoslavia Before the Roman Conquest. N. Y.:
    Praeger, 1972. Rev. by D. W. Wade, AHR, 82(Feb 1977):69.

Alexander, Michael Van Cleave. Charles I's Lord Treasurer: Sir
    Richard Weston, Earl of Portland (1577-1635). Chapel Hill:
    U NC Press, 1975. Rev. by R. W. Kenny, AHR, 82(Apr
    1977):352-3.

Alexander, Nancy. Father of Texas Geology: Robert T. Hill.
    Dallas: SMU Press, 1976. Rev. by M. L. Aldrich, AHR,

82(Apr 1977):451-2; J. R. Jameson, A&W, 19(Sum 1977):164-5; A. P. McDonald, ETHJ, 15(Spr 1977):60-1; R. A. Bartlett, JSH, 43(May 1977):331.

Alexander, Thomas G. Essays on the American West, 1974-1975. Provo: Brigham Young U Press, 1976. Rev. by M. P. Malone, NMHR, 52(Jan 1977):84-5; V. C. Dahl, PHR, 46 (Feb 1977):136-8.

Alfoldi, Andreas and Elisabeth Alfoldi. Die Kontorniat-Medaillons. Berlin: Walter de Gruyter, 1976. Rev. by W. E. Metcalf, AJA, 81(Sum 1977):406-7.

Alfoldi, Elisabeth see Alfoldi, Andreas

Alföldy, Géza. Die römischen Inshriften von Tarraco. New York: Walter de Gruyter, 1975. Rev. by J. H. Oliver, AJA, 81 (Win 1977):126-7.

Algar, Hamid. Mirza Malkum Khan: A Study in the History of Iranian Modernism. Berkeley and Los Angeles: U Cal Press, 1973. Rev. by J. R. Perry, JNES, 36(Jl 1977):233-5.

Alho, Olli. The Religion of the Slaves: A Study of the Religious Tradition and Behaviour of Plantation Slaves in the United States 1830-1865. Helsinki, Finland: Suomalainen Tiedeakatemi, Academia Scientiarum Fennica, 1976. Rev. by J. T. O'Brien, JSH, 43(Nov 1977):615-6.

Aliano, Richard A. American Defense Policy from Eisenhower to Kennedy: The Politics of Changing Military Requirements, 1957-1961. Athens: Ohio U Press, 1975. Rev. by B. Brodie, PHR, 46(Aug 1977):533-4.

All, Sheikh Rustum. Saudi Arabia and Oil Diplomacy. New York: Praeger, 1976. Rev. by A. Z. Rubinstein, CurH, 72(Jan 1977):28.

Allen, Frederick S., et al. The University of Colorado, 1876-1976. New York: Harcourt Brace Jovanovich, 1976. Rev. by G. W. Chessman, AHR, 82(Je 1977):774.

Allen, H. C. ed., and Roger Thompson, ed. Contrast and Connection: Bicentennial Essays in Anglo-American History. London: G. Bell, 1976. Rev. by J. J. McCusker, EHR, 92(Oct 1977):913-4, R. Berthoff, JSH, 43(Aug 1977): 486-8.

Allen, James B. and Glen M. Leonard. The Story of the Latter-Day Saints. Salt Lake City: Deseret Book Company, 1976. Rev. by E. L. Schapsmeier, JOW, 16(Jan 1977):74-5; R. W. Paul, WHQ, 8(Jl 1977):351-3.

Allen, John Logan. Passage Through the Garden: Lewis and Clark and the Image of the American Northwest. Urbana: U Ill Press, 1975. Rev. by R. A. Bartlett, AHR, 82(Apr 1977): 439-40; A. P. Nasatir, PHR, 46(Feb 1977):123-4; M. G. Burlingame, PNQ, 68(Jl 1977):143-4.

Allen, Richard, ed. Social Gospel in Canada: Papers of the Inter-disciplinary Conference on the Social Gospel in Canada, March 21-24, 1973 at the University of Regina. Ottawa: National Museum of Man, 1975. Rev. T. Copp, CHR, 58(Mar 1977): 70-2.

Alley, Rovert S. Television: Ethics for Hire? Nashville: Abingdon, 1977. Rev. by D. Thorburn, GR, 31(Fall 1977):775-8.

Allinson, Gary D. Japanese Urbanism: Industry and Politics in Kariya, 1872-1972. Berkeley: U Cal Press, 1975. Rev. by B. K. Marshall, AHR, 82(Feb 1977):162-3; K. Yamamura, JEH, 35(Je 1977):478-9.

Allison, K. J., ed. The Victoria History of the County of York, East Riding, Vol. III. London: Ox U Press, 1976. Rev. by B. Dobson, EHR, 92(Oct 1977):939-40; J. C. Beckett, History, 62(Feb 1977):85-6.

Allmand, C. T., ed. War, Literature, and Politics in the Late Middle Ages. N.Y.: Barnes and Noble, 1976. Rev. by M. R. Powicke, AHR, 82(Je 1977):618.

Almqvist, Bo, et al., ed. Hereditas: Essays and Studies Presented to Professor Seámus O Duilearga. Dublin: Folklore of Ireland Society, 1975. Rev. by J. Stewart, E-1, 12(Spr 1977):152-4.

Alper, M. Victor. America's Freedom Trail (Massachusetts, New York, New Jersey, Pennsylvania): A Tour Guide to Historical Sites of the Colonial and Revolutionary War Period. New York: Macmillan, 1976. Rev. by F. D. Klein, AHI, 11(Jan 1977):49.

_____. America's Heritage Trail (South Carolina, North Carolina, Virginia). New York: Macmillan, 1976. Rev. by F. S. Klein, AHI, 11(Jan 1977):49.

Altbach, Philip T. Publishing in India: An Analysis. Delhi: Ox U Press, 1976. Rev. by N. G. Barrier, JAS, 36(May 1977): 575-6.

Aluko, Olajide. Ghana and Nigeria, 1957-70: A Study in Inter-African Discord. New York: Barnes and Noble, 1976. Rev. by E. Bustin, AHR, 82(Oct 1977):1034-5.

Alvarez, Manuel Fernández. Charles V: Elected Emperor and Hereditary Ruler. London: Thames and Hudson, 1975. Rev.

by R. J. Knecht, History, 62(Je 1977):319-20; W. D. Phillips, HAHR, 57(May 1977):325-6; H. G. Koenigsberger, AHR, 82 (Oct 1977):946-8.

Alzinger, Wilhelm. Augusteische Architektur in Ephesos. Vienna, 1974. Rev. by J. Russell, AJA, 81(Spr 1977):259.

Aman, Jacques. Les officiers bleus dans la marine française au XVIIIe siècle. Geneva: Librairie Droz, 1976. Rev. by D. C. Baxter, AHR, 82(Apr 1977):366-7.

Amann, Peter H. Revolution and Mass Democracy: The Paris Club Movement in 1848. Princeton: Princeton U Press, 1975. Rev. by I. Collins, ESR, 7(Jan 1977):112-13.

Ambrose, Stephen E. Crazy Horse and Custer: The Parallel Lives of Two American Warriors. Garden City, N.Y.: Doubleday, 1975. Rev. by R. C. Carriker, PHR, 46(Aug 1977):504-6; L. M. Hauptman, PNQ, 68(Apr 1977):101.

Amelotti, Mario and Giorgio Costamagna. Alle origini del notariato italiano. Rome: Consiglio Nazionale del Notariato, 1975. Rev. by R. A. Goldthwaithe, AHR, 82(Oct 1977):940.

American Acupuncture Anesthesia Study Group. Acupuncture Anesthesia in the People's Republic of China. Washington, D. C.: National Academy of Sciences, 1976. Rev. by V. H. Li, CQ, No. 71(Sep 1977):631-3.

The American War of Independence 1775-83: A Commemorative Exhibition Organized by the Map Library and the Department of Manuscripts of the British Library Reference Division. London: Museum Publications Limited, 1975. Rev. by M. M. Roberts, NEQ, 50(Je 1977):374-6.

Ameringer, Charles D. The Democratic Left in Exile: The Antidictatorial Struggle in the Caribbean, 1945-1959. Coral Gables: U Miami Press, 1974. Rev. by J. E. Fagg, AHR, 82(Feb 1977): 228.

Ames, Susie M., ed. County Court Records of Accomack-Northampton, Virginia, 1640-1645. Charlottesville, Va.: U Press Va for the Virginia Historical Society, 1973. Rev. by H. A. Johnson, WMQ, 34(Jl 1977):501-3.

Amin, Samir, ed. Modern Migrations in West Africa. London: Oxford U Press, 1974. Rev. by R. M. Prothero, Africa, 47(No. 1, 1977):118-19.

Amos, Keith. The Guard Movement, 1931-1935. Melbourne: Melbourne U Press, 1976. Rev. by F. C. Clarke, AHR, 82(Feb 1977):167-8.

Amyx, D. A. and Patricia Lawrence. Corinth VII, Part II, Archaic Pottery and the Anaploga Well. Princeton: American School of Classical Studies at Athens, 1975. Rev. by H. Geagan, AJA, 81(Spr 1977):245-6.

Andaya, Leonard Y. The Kingdom of John, 1641-1728. London: Ox U Press, 1975. Rev. by H. R. C. Wright, AHR, 82(Apr 1977):426; B. Harrison, Historian, 39(Feb 1977):363-4; C. R. Boxer, History, 62(Je 1977):298; M. C. Ricklefs, JAS, 36 (Feb 1977):385-6.

Anders, Leslie. The Twenty-First Missouri: From Home Guard to Union Regiment. Westport, Conn.: Greenwood, 1975. Rev. by W. Rundell, Jr., AS, 18(Fall 1977):110; W. L. Burton, JISHS, 70(Feb 1977):95-6.

Anderson, Arthur J. O., et al. Beyond the Codices: The Nahua View of Colonial Mexico. Berkeley: U Cal Press, 1976. Rev. by W. Borah, AHR, 82(Oct 1977):1103-4; C. Gibson, HAHR, 57(May 1977):327-8; M. León-Portilla, TAM, 34(Oct 1977):307-9.

Anderson, Chester G., ed. Growing Up in Minnesota: Ten Writers Remember Their Childhoods. Minneapolis: U Minn Press, 1976. Rev. by G. Keillor, MinnH, 45(Sum 1977):253-4.

Anderson, Frederick, ed., Michael B. Frank, ed., and Kenneth M. Sanderson, ed. Mark Twain's Notebooks and Journals, Volume I: 1855-1873. Berkeley: U Cal Press, 1975. Rev. by D. C. Grover, WHQ, 8(Jan 1977):55-6.

Anderson, Gregory. Victorian Clerks. Manchester: Manchester U Press, 1976. Rev. by R. Silverstone, BH, 19(Jl 1977): 226-7; M. A. Crowther, HJ, 20(No. 4, 1977):991-9.

Anderson, Irvine H., Jr. The Standard-Vacuum Oil Company and United States East Asian Policy, 1933-1941. Princeton: Prin U Press, 1975. Rev. by N. H. Pugach, AHR, 81(Dec 1976): 1274-75.

Anderson, John A., Eugene Buechel, and Don Doll. Crying for A Vision: A Rosebud Sioux Trilogy, 1886-1976. Dobbs Ferry, N.Y.: Morgan and Morgan, 1976. Rev. by D. L. Beaulieu, MinnH, 45(Fall 1977):301-2.

Anderson, John M., and Charles Jones, eds. Historical Linguistics. Amsterdam: North-Holland Publishing, 1974. Rev. by N. H. Zide, JAS, 36(May 1977):537.

Anderson, R. D. Education in France, 1848-1870. Oxford: Clarendon Press, 1975. Rev. by R. Gibson, ESR, 7(Oct 1977): 458-64.

Anderson, Rodney D. Outcasts in Their Own Land: Mexican Indus-
trial Workers, 1906-1911. DeKalb: No Ill U Press, 1976.
Rev. by J. Womack, Jr., AHR, 82(Je 1977):781; S. R. Ross,
HAHR, 57(May 1977):346-8.

Anderson, Terry Lee. The Economic Growth of Seventeenth-
Century New England: A Measurement of Regional Income.
New York: Arno Press, 1975. Rev. by B. C. Daniels,
WMQ, 34(Jan 1977):160-2.

Andrew, John A., III. Rebuilding the Christian Commonwealth:
New England Congregationalists and Foreign Missions, 1800-
1830. Lexington: U Press Ky, 1976. Rev. by J. M. Bum-
sted, AHR, 82(Je 1977):741-2; R. D. Shiels, NEQ, 50(Je
1977):376-8; L. W. Banner, WMQ, 34(Apr 1977):350-1.

Andrews, G. F. Maya Cities: Place Making and Urbanization.
Norman: U Oklahoma Press, 1975. Rev. by B. G. Trigger,
JAAS, 12(Jan/Oct 1977):303-4.

Andrews, J. Richard. Introduction to Classical Najuatl. Austin:
U Texas Press, 1975. Rev. by A. Beidler, AIQ, 3(Aut 1977):
265-6.

Angelo, Frank. Yesterday's Michigan. Miami, Florida: E. A.
Seeman Publishing, n.d. Rev. by H. Kelsey, MichH, 61(Spr
1977):93-4.

Angermann, Erich, Marie-Louise Frings, and Hermann Ellenreuther,
eds. New Wine in Old Skins: A Comparative View of Socio-
Political Structures and Values Affecting the American Revolution. Stuttgart, Germany: Ernst Klett Verlag, 1976. Rev.
by I. H. Polishook, JSH, 43(Nov 1977):609-10.

Ansari, J. see H. Singer

Anstey, Roger. The Atlantic Slave Trade and British Abolition
1760-1810. Atlantic Highlands, N.J.: Humanities Press,
1975. Rev. by R. C. Reinders, CHR, 58(Mar 1977):93-4;
P. Jupp, HJ, 20(No. 3, 1977):771-3; J. B. Stewart, Historian, 39(Feb 1977):329-31; D. K. Fieldhouse, History, 62
(Feb 1977):88-9; J. A. Rawley, JSH, 43(Aug 1977):434-6.

Anuario de Estudios Americanos. Vol. XXX. Sevilla: Escuela
de Estudios Hispano-Americanos, 1973. Rev. by D. C.
Cutter, JOW, 16(Jl 1977):94.

Appelt, Heinrich and Rainer Maria Herkenrath, et al., eds. Die
Urkunden der deutschen Könige und Kaiser. Vol. 10, Pt. 1:
Die Urkunden Friedrichs I., 1152-1158. Hanover: Hahnsche
Buchhandlung, 1975. Rev. by M. B. Dick, AHR, 82(Apr
1977):345.

Appleman, Roy E. with Robert G. Ferris. Lewis and Clark: His-
    toric Places Associated with Their Transcontinental Exploration
    (1804-06). Washington, D. C.: U. S. Department of the Interior,
    National Park Service, National Survey of Historic Sites and
    Buildings, 1975. Rev. by M. G. Burlingame, PNQ, 68(Jl
    1977):143-4; L. D. Ball, ChOk, 55(Sum 1977):238-9.

Aptheker, Herbert, ed. The Correspondence of W. E. B. Du Bois.
    Volume II: Selections 1934-1944. Amherst: U Mass Press,
    1976. Rev. by C. G. Contee, JSH, 43(May 1977):320-1.

_____. Early Years of the Republic from the End of the Revo-
    lution to the First Administration of Washington 1783-1793.
    New York: International Publishers, 1976. Rev. by H.
    Ohline, WMQ, 34(Oct 1977):675-6.

Ara, Angelo. L'Austria-Ungheria nella politica Americana durante
    la prima guerra mondiale. Rome: Edizioni dell'Ateneo,
    1973. Rev. by C. F. Delzell, AHR, 82(Feb 1977):200-1.

Archdeacon, Thomas J. New York City, 1664-1710: Conquest and
    Change. Ithaca: Cornell U Press, 1976. Rev. by G. B. Nash,
    JIH, 8(Sum 1977):164-7; M. Zuckerman, WMH, 60(Spr 1977):
    240-1; E. Countryman, WMQ, 34(Jl 1977):491-2.

Archer, W. G. Visions of Courtly India. The Archer Collection
    of Pahari Miniatures. n.l.: Sotheby Parke Bernet, n.d.
    Rev. by F. Watson, HTo, 27(Mar 1977):199-201.

Archivo de Sucre. Caracas: Fundacion Vicente Lecuna and Banco
    de Venezuela, 1974. Rev. by J. P. Hoover, TAm, 34(Jl
    1977):150-2.

Are, Giuseppe. Economia E Politica Nell'itatia Liberale (1890-
    1915). Bologna: il Mulino, 1974. Rev. by S. J. Woolf,
    History, 62(Feb 1977):164-5.

Aresvik, Oddvar. The Agricultural Development of Turkey. New
    York: Praeger, 1975. Rev. by M. E. Kurtzig, AgH, 51
    (Jan 1977):280-1.

Argersinger, Peter H. Populism and Politics: William Alfred
    Peffer and the People's Party. Lexington: U Press Ky,
    1974. Rev. by G. Clanton, AHR, 82(Feb 1977):198-9; H.
    W. Morgan, JSH, 43(May 1977):312-3.

Arkin, Marcus. Aspects of Jewish Economic History. Philadelphia:
    Jewish Publication Society of America, 1975. Rev. by B.
    Ravid, JEH, 37(Je 1977):479-81.

Armstrong, Ellis L., ed. History of Public Works in the United
    States. Chicago: American Public Works Association, 1976.
    Rev. by C. Curran, JEH, 37(Je 1977):481-2.

Armstrong, Terence, ed. Yermak's Campaign in Siberia: A Selection of Documents. London: Hakluyt Society, 1975. Rev. by E. V. Leonard, AHR, 82(Feb 1977):147-8.

Arndt, Karl J. R., ed. A Documentary History of the Indiana Decade of the Harmony Society, 1814-1824: Volume I: 1814-1819. Indianapolis: Indiana Historical Society, 1975. Rev. by D. R. Wrone, JISHS, 70(May 1977):168-9.

Arnold, Morris S., ed. Year Books of Richard II, 1378-9. Cambridge, Mass: Ames Foundation, 1975. Rev. by J. R. Maddicott, EHR, 92(Oct 1977):889.

Aron, Raymond. Penser la guerre, Clausewitz. I, L'age européen. II, L'age planétaire. Paris: Gallimard, 1976. Rev. by P. Paret, JIH, 8(Aut 1977):369-72.

Arrington, Leonard J. Charles C. Rich: Mormon General and Western Frontiersman. Provo: Brigham Young U Press, 1974. Rev. by M. Wells, PNQ, 68(Jan 1977):43.

_____. From Quaker to Latter-Day Saint: Bishop Edwin D. Woolley. Salt Lake City: Deseret Book Co., 1976. Rev. by L. Foster, AHR, 82(Oct 1977):1072-3.

_____, et al. Building the City of God: Community and Cooperation Among the Mormons. Salt Lake City: Deseret Book Co., 1976. Rev. by M. S. de Pillis, AHR, 82(Oct 1977): 1071; C. Bryson, JAriH, 18(Sum 1977):225-6; J. L. Dodson, JOW, 16(Jl 1977):97-8; M. S. Snow, UHQ, 45(Sum 1977):313-4; R. W. Paul, WHQ, 8(Jl 1977):351-3.

_____, ed. see also Wilkinson, Ernest L., ed.

Arrom, Silvia M. La mujer mexicana ante el divorcio eclestástico: 1800-1857. Mexico: SepSetentas, 1976. Rev. by A. Lavrin, HAHR, 57(Aug 1977):542-3.

Artibise, Alan F. J. Winnipeg: A Social History of Urban Growth, 1874-1914. Montreal: McGill-Queen's U Press, 1975. Rev. by W. A. McKay, AHR, 82(Feb 1977):219-20.

Arutiunov, G. A. The Workers' Movement in Russia in the Period of the New Revolutionary Upsurge, 1910-1914. Moscow: Izdatel'stvo "Nauka," 1975. Rev. by W. Gleason, AHR, 82 (Je 1977):700-1.

Ashagun, Fray Bernardino. Florentine Codex, General History of the Things of New Spain: Book 12--The Conquest of Mexico. Sante Fe: The School of American Research and Salt Lake City: U Utah Press, 1975. Rev. by H. Hewitt, WHQ, 8 (Apr 1977):214-5.

Ashbee, Paul. Ancient Scilly: from the Farmers to the Early
    Christians. Newton Abbot, London: David and Charles,
    1974. Rev. by B. Wailes, Antiquity, 51(Jl 1977):156-7.

Ashby, LeRoy and Bruce M. Stave, eds. The Discontented Society:
    Interpretations of Twentieth Century American Protest.
    Chicago: Rand McNally, 1972. Rev. by J. A. Gazell, JISHS,
    70(May 1977):164-5.

Ashe, Geoffrey. The Virgin. London: Routledge and Kegan Paul,
    1976. Rev. by A. Collard, AHR, 82(Oct 1977):920-1.

Ashkenasi, Abraham. Modern German Nationalism. New York:
    Halsted Press, 1976. Rev. by R. G. L. Waite, JIH, 8(Aut
    1977):380-2.

Ashtor, E. A Social and Economic History of the Near East in the
    Middle Ages. London: Collins, 1976. Rev. by W. M. Watt,
    History, 62(Feb 1977):97-8; M. G. Morony, JEH, 37(Sep 1977):
    770-1.

Asmani, J. O. Index Africanus. Stanford: Hoover Institution
    Press, 1975. Rev. by J. M. Janzen, JAAS, 12(Jan/Oct
    1977):289-90.

Assante, Franca. Città e campagne nella Puglia del secolo XIX.
    Vol. 4. Geneva: Librairie Droz, 1975. Rev. by E. Argento,
    AHR, 82(Apr 1977):384.

Association d'Etudes du Sud-Est Européen. Structure sociale et
    développement culturel des villes Sud-Est européenes et
    adriatiques aux XVIIᵉ-XVIIIᵉ siècles. Bucharest: Assoc.
    Internationale d'Etudes du Sut-Est Européen, 1975. Rev. by
    S. M. Stuard, AHR, 82(Apr 1977):390-1.

Astorquia, Madeline, et al. Guide des sources de l'histoire des
    Etats-Unis dans les Archives Francais. Rockefeller Plaza,
    New York: Clearwater, 1976. Rev. by S. Turner, AmArc,
    40(Apr 1977):237-8.

Athearn, Robert G. The Coloradans. Albuquerque: U NM Press,
    1976. Rev. by R. W. Larson, NMHR, 52(Jl 1977):251-2; E.
    H. Berwanger, PHR, 46(Aug 1977):509-10; W. T. Eagan,
    WHQ, 8(Oct 1977):459-60.

Atkinson, James. An Account of the State of Agriculture and Gra-
    zing in New South Wales. Sydney: Sydney U Press, 1975.
    Rev. by P. Perry, AgH, 51(Apr 1977):478-9.

Auerbach, Jerold S. Unequal Justice: Lawyers and Social Change
    in America. New York: Oxford U Press, 1976. Rev. by
    R. Wilkinson, JAmS, 11(Dec 1977):407-8.

Augé, Marc, et al. Prophétisme et thérapeutique: Albert Atcho et la communauté de Bregbo. Paris: Hermann, 1975. Rev. by A. Alland, Jr., Africa, 47(No. 3, 1977):326-7.

Aurigemma, Luigi. Le signe zodiacal du Scorpion dans les traditions occidentales de l'Antiquite greco-latine a la Renaissance. Paris: Mouton, 1976. Rev. by B. P. Copenhaver, AHR, 82 (Je 1977):607-8.

Austin, D. and R. Luckham, eds. Politicians and Soldiers in Ghana, 1962-1972. London: Frank Cass, 1975. Rev. by R. Crook, AfAf, 76(Jl 1977):408-9.

Austin, Reginald. Racism and Apartheid in Southern Africa: Rhodesia. UNESCO Press, 1975. Rev. by E. Windrich, AfAf, 76(Jan 1977):119-22.

Auty, Phyllis and Richard Clogg, eds. British Policy Towards Wartime Resistance in Yugoslavia and Greece. New York: Barnes and Noble, 1975. Rev. by H. Cliadakis, AHR, 82(Je 1977):644; W. H. McNeill, JMH, 49(Mar 1977):147-51.

AviYonah, Michael, ed. The World History of the Jewish People. New Brunswick: Rutgers U Press, 1975. Rev. by M. Smith, AHR, 82(Je 1977):705-6.

Axelos, Kostas. Alienation, Praxis, and Techne in the Thought of Karl Marx. Austin: U Tex Press, 1976. Rev. by D. Gross, AHR, 82(Oct 1977):923-4.

Axelsson, Arne. The Links in the Chain: Isolation and Interdependence in Nathaniel Hawthorne's Fictional Characters. Uppsala: Act Universitas Upsaliensis, Studia Anglistica Upsaliensia 17, 1974. Rev. by C. S. B. Swann, JAmS, 11(Dec 1977):417-20.

Axelsson, Sun see Silva, Raul

Axford, Faye Acton, ed. The Journals of Thomas Hubbard Hobbs: A Contemporary Record of an Aristocrat from Athens, Alabama, Written Between 1840, When the Diarist Was Fourteen Years Old, and 1862, When He Died Serving the Confederate States of America. University, Ala.: U Ala Press, 1976. Rev. by L. G. Cleveland, JSH, 43(Aug 1977):454-5; W. W. Rogers, CWH, 23(Mar 1977):89-90.

Axford, H. William. Gilpin County Gold: Peter McFarlane, 1848-1929, Mining Entrepreneur in Central City, Colorado. Chicago: Swallow Press, 1976. Rev. by B. F. Gilbert, JOW, 16(Jan 1977):73-4.

Axon, Gordon V. The California Gold Rush. New York: Mason/ Charter, 1976. Rev. by G. F. Gilbert, JOW, 16(Jan 1977): 72.

Ayling, Stanley. The Elder Pitt, Earl of Chatham. New York:
David McKay, 1976. Rev. by G. B. Cooper, AHR, 82(Oct
1977):964; P. D. G. Thomas, History, 62(Feb 1977):132-3.

Azu, D. G. The Ga Family and Social Change. Cambridge: African Studies Center, 1974. Rev. by C. Oppong, Africa, 47
(No. 3, 1977):329-30.

Baaklini, Abdo I. Legislative and Political Development: Lebanon,
1842-1972. Durham, N.C.: Duke U Press, 1976. Rev. by
C. E. Dawn, AHR, 82(Je 1977):706-7.

Babb, Lawrence A. The Divine Hierarchy: Popular Hinduism in
Central India. New York: Col U Press, 1975. Rev. by D.
McGilvray, JAS, 36(May 1977):567-9.

Babcock, Robert H. Gompers in Canada: A Study in American
Continentalism Before the First World War. Buffalo, N.Y.:
U Tor Press, 1974. Rev. by R. C. Brown, AHR, 82(Feb
1977):221.

Bachrack, Stanley D. The Committee of One Million: "China
Lobby" Politics, 1953-1971. New York: Col U Press, 1976.
Rev. by R. D. Bukite, AHR, 82(Je 1977):772-3.

Badash, Lawrence. Rutherford Correspondence Catalog. New York:
Center for History of Physics, American Institute of Physics,
1974. Rev. by S. A. Morris, AmArc, 39(Jl 1977):359-60.

Badcock, C. R. Levi-Strauss: Structuralism and Sociological
Theory. London: Hutchinson, 1975. Rev. by F. C. T.
Moore, History, 62(Feb 1977):71.

Bady, Paul, tr. see She, Lao

Baechler, Jean. The Origins of Capitalism. Oxford: Basil Blackwell, 1975. Rev. by V. G. Kiernan, History, 62(Feb 1977):
78-9.

_____. Revolution. Oxford: Basil Blackwell, 1975. Rev. by
P. Calvert, History, 62(Feb 1977):92-3.

Baerwald, Hans H. Japan's Parliament: An Introduction. New
York: Cambridge University Press, 1974. Rev. by M. W.
Donnelly, JAS, 37(Nov 1977):137-9.

Bagdasarian, Nicholas der. The Austro-German Rapprochement,
1870-1879: From the Battle of Sedan to the Dual Alliance.
Cranbury, N.J.: Fairleigh Dickinson, 1976. Rev. by J.
Rogainis, AHR, 82(Je 1977):673-4.

Baglole, Harry and David Weale, eds. Cornelius Howatt: Superstar!
Belfast: William & Crue, 1974. Rev. by D. Alexander, CHR,
58(Je 1977):227-8.

Bagnall, Roger S. The Florida Ostraka: Documents from the Roman Army in Upper Egypt. Durham: Duke U, 1976. Rev. by R. K. Sherk, AHR, 82(Oct 1977):931.

Bahl, Kali Charan. Studies in the Semantic Structure of Hindi. Delhi: Motilal Bararsidass, 1974. Rev. by P. E. Hook, JAS, 36(Feb 1977):369-70.

Bailey, Consuelo Northrop. Leaves Before the Wind. Burlington: author, 1976. Rev. by C. A. Gravel, VH, 45(Sum 1977): 180-1.

Bailey, Kenneth P. Christopher Gist: Colonial Frontiersman, Explorer, and Indian Agent. Hamden, Conn.: Archon Books, 1976. Rev. by D. E. Leach, AHR, 82(Feb 1977):171; B. E. Steiner, JSH, 43(Feb 1977):109-10; N. B. Wainwright, WMQ, 34(Jan 1977):177-9.

_____, ed. see Marin, Joseph

Bailey, Thomas A. Voices of America: The Nation's Story in Slogans, Sayings, and Songs. New York: Free Press, 1976. Rev. by M. Plesur, AHR, 82(Je 1977):727.

_____ and Paul B. Ryan. The Lusitania Disaster: The Real Answers Behind the World's Most Controversial Sea Tragedy. New York: Free Press, n.d. Rev. by R. D. Burns, Mankind, 5(No. 11, 1977):5.

Bailyn, Bernard. The Ordeal of Thomas Hutchinson. Cambridge, Mass.: Har U Press, 1974. Rev. by B. W. Sheehan, AHR, 82(Je 1977):735-6; J. M. Nelson, HJ, 20(No. 3, 1977):741-9.

Bairoch, Paul. Commerce exterieur et developpement economique de l'Europe au XIXe siecle. Paris: Mouton, 1976. Rev. by R. Cameron, AHR, 82(Oct 1977):951-2.

Baklanoff, Eric N. Expropriation of U. S. Investments in Cuba, Mexico and Chile. New York: Praeger, 1975. Rev. by J. L. Payne, HAHR, 57(Aug 1977):561-2.

Bakunin, Jack. Pierre Leroux and the Birth of Democratic Socialism, 1797-1848. New York: Revisionist Press, 1976. Rev. by R. L. Hoffman, AHR, 82(Oct 1977):982.

Balans, J. L., C. Coulon and J. M. Gastellu. Autonomie Locale et Integration Nationale au Senegal. Editions Pedone, 1975. Rev. by D. C. O'Brien, AfAf, 76(Apr 1977):264-5.

Balawyder, Aloysius. Canadian-Soviet Relations Between the World Wars. Toronto: U Tor Press, 1972. Rev. by G. F. G. Stanley, AHR, 82(Feb 1977):220-1.

Balderston, Marion and David Syrett, eds. The Lost War: Letters
    from British Officers during the American Revolution. New
    York: Horizon Press, 1976. Rev. by C. R. Ferguson, WMQ,
    34(Jan 1977):147-8.

Baldwin, Alice Blackwood. An Army Wife on the Frontier: The
    Memoirs of Alice Blackwood Baldwin, 1867-1877. Ed. by
    Robert C. and Eleanor R. Carriker. U of Utah Tanner Trust
    Fund, 1975. Rev. by G. Riley, Al, 44(Fall 1977):156-8.

Baldwin, Robert E. The Philippines. New York and London: Col
    U Press for the National Bureau of Economic Research, 1975.
    Rev. by K. M. Langley, JEH, 37(Je 1977):482-5.

Balseiro, Jose Agustin, ed. Presencia Hispanica en La Florida,
    Ayer y Hoy: 1513-1976. Miami: Ediciones Universal, 1976.
    Rev. by B. S. Chappell, FHQ, 55(Apr 1977):486-7.

Bandopadhyaya, Manik. Padma River Boatman. Tr. by Barbara
    Painter and Yann Lovelock. New York: U Queensland Press,
    1973. Rev. by C. Seely, JAS, 37(Nov 1977):152-3.

Barden, Thomas E., ed. see Perdue, Charles L., Jr., ed.

Barger, Bob see Nava, Julian

Barghoorn, Frederick C. Detente and the Democratic Movement in
    the USSR. New York: Free Press, 1976. Rev. by A. Z.
    Rubinstein, CurH, 73(Oct 1977):128.

Barker, Elisabeth. Austria 1918-1972. Coral Gables, Fla.: U
    Miami Press, 1973. Rev. by R. J. Roth, Historian, 39(May
    1977):560-1.

_____. British Policy in Southeast Europe in the Second World
    War. New York: Barnes and Noble, 1976. Rev. by G.
    Augustinos, AHR, 82(Je 1977):643-4; A. J. P. Taylor, EHR,
    92(Oct 1977):934.

Barker, Lucius J. and Jesse J. McCorry. Black Americans and
    the Political System. Cambridge, Mass.: Winthrop, 1976.
    Rev. by M. F. Rice, JNH, 62(Apr 1977):187-9.

Barker, Michael. Gladstone and Radicalism: The Reconstruction
    of Liberal Policy, 1835-94. New York: Barnes and Noble,
    1975. Rev. by R. K. Webb, AHR, 82(Je 1977):635-7.

Barker, Thomas M. The Military Intellectual and Battle: Raimondo
    Montecuccoli and the Thirty Years War. Albany, N.Y.: SUNY
    Press, 1975. Rev. by D. McKay, History, 62(Feb 1977):
    125.

Bar-Kochva, Bezalel. The Seleucid Army: Organization and Tactics in the Great Campaigns. New York: Cam U Press, 1976. Rev. by W. McLeod, AHR, 82(Feb 1977):69-70.

Barnard, T. C. Cromwellian Ireland: English Government and Reform in Ireland, 1649-1660. Oxford: Ox U Press, 1975. Rev. by T. D. Dow, History, 62(Feb 1977):121-2.

Barnes, James J. Authors, Publishers and Politicians: The Quest for an Anglo-American Copyright Agreement 1815-1854. Columbus: Ohio St U Press, n.d. Rev. by J. E. Walsh, AHR, 82(Feb 1977):186-7.

Barnes, Peter. The People's Land: A Reader on Land Reforms in the United States. Emmaus, Pa.: Rodale, 1975. Rev. by J. M. Petulla, AgH, 51(Jan 1977):268-9.

Barnett, A. Doak. China Policy. Washington, D. C.: Brookings Institution, 1977. Rev. by O. E. S., CurH, 72(Sep 1977): 84-5.

Barnum, Priscilla Heath, ed. Dives and Pauper. Vol. 1, pt. 1. New York: Ox U Press, 1976. Rev. by W. J. Mulligan, AHR, 82(Je 1977):619-20.

Baron, Salo W., et al. Economic History of the Jews. New York: Schocken Books, 1975. Rev. by H. Freudenberger, AHR, 82 (Apr 1977):333-4.

Barraclough, Geoffrey. The Crucible of Europe: The Ninth and Tenth Centuries in European History. London: Thames and Hudson, 1976. Rev. by P. McGurk, History, 62(Je 1977): 311.

Barratt, Glynn. M. S. Lunin: Catholic Decembrist. The Hague: Mouton, 1976. Rev. by D. Hardy, AHR, 82(Apr 1977):401-2.

Barratt, John, David S. Collier, Kurt Glaser, and Herman Monnig, eds. Strategy for Development. London: Macmillan, 1975. Rev. by A. Kuper, AfAf, 76(Apr 1977):274-5.

Barrow, Elfrida DeRenne. In the Calendar's Shadow, Selected Poems. Ed. by Malcolm Bell III. Darien, Ga.: Ashantilly Press, 1976. Rev. by B. Vanstory, GHQ, 51(Sum 1977): 193-4.

Barth, Gunther. Instant Cities: Urbanization and the Rise of San Francisco and Denver. New York: Ox U Press, 1975. Rev. by C. M. Frank, WHQ, 8(Jan 1977):72-3; C. Abbott, AHR, 81(Dec 1976):1245-6.

Bartlett, Richard A. The New Country: A Social History of the American Frontier, 1776-1890. New York: Ox U Press, 1974. Rev. by S. B. Hilliard, AgH, 51(Jan 1977):266-7.

Bartley, Nunan V. and Hugh D. Graham. Southern Politics and the Second Reconstruction. Baltimore: JHU Press, 1975. Rev. by J. M. Kousser, AHR, 82(Feb 1977):217; P. J. Zingo, MiA, 59(Oct 1977):206-7.

Barton, H. Arnold. Count Hans Axel von Fersen: Aristocrat in the Age of Revolution. Boston: Twayne, 1975. Rev. by C. Gold, AHR, 82(Feb 1977):121-2.

_____, ed. Letters from the Promised Land: Swedes in America, 1840-1914. Minneapolis: U Minn Press, Swedish Pioneer Historical Society, 1975. Rev. by W. Johnson, PNQ, 68(Jan 1977):37-8; C. Erickson, NYHSQ, 61(Jan/Apr 1977): 91-2.

Barton, Josef J. Peasants and Strangers: Italians, Rumanians, and Slovaks in an American City, 1890-1950. Cambridge, Mass.: Har U Press, 1975. Rev. by J. R. Webster, PNQ, 68(Jl 1977):147-8.

Barudio, Günter. Absolutismus--Zerstörung der "Libertären Verfassung". Wiesbaden: Franz Steiner Verlag, 1976. Rev. by H. P. Liebel, AHR, 82(Oct 1977):992-3.

Basadre, Jorge. La Vida y La Historia. Ensayos sobre Personas, lugares y problemas. Lima: Fondo del Libro del Banco Industrial del Peru, 1975. Rev. by F. Bronner, TAm, 33(Apr 1977):691-2.

Basham, A. L., ed. A Cultural History of India. Oxford: Ox U Press, 1975. Rev. by R. Inden, JAS, 36(Feb 1977):363-4.

Basini, Gian Luigi. Sul mercato di Modena tra cinque e seicento: Prezzi e salari. Milan: A. Giuffrè Editore, 1974. Rev. by R. A. Goldthwaite, AHR, 82(Oct 1977):1011.

Bass, Jack and Walter DeVries. The Transformation of Southern Politics: Social Change and Political Consequence Since 1945. New York: Basic Books, 1976. Rev. by D. W. Grantham, JSH, 43(Aug 1977):476-7.

Bastias, John C. see Christopoulos, George A., ed.

Basu, Dilip. Nineteenth Century China: Five Imperialist Perspectives. Ed. by Rhoads Murphey. Ann Arbor: Center for Chinese Studies, U Michigan, 1972. Rev. by J. G. Lutz, JAAS, 12(Jan/Oct 1977):278-9.

Bataillon, Claude and Helene Riviere D'Arc. La Ciudad de México. Mexico: SepSetentas, 1973. Rev. by R. W. Wilkie, HAHR, 57(May 1977):349.

Batchelor, John H. see Preston, Antony

Bates, James H. St. Petersburg: Industrialization and Change.
Montreal: McGill-Queen's U Press, 1976. Rev. by R. E.
Zelnik, AHR, 82(Oct 1977):1025-6.

Bates, Robert H. Rural Responses to Industrialization: A Study of
Village Zambia. New Haven: Yale U Press, 1976. Rev. by
A. Roberts, AfAf, 76(Apr 1977):271-2; E. L. Berger, JEH,
37(Sep 1977):771-2.

Battista, Anna Maria. Lo Spirito liberale e lo spirito religioso:
Tocqueville nel dibattito sulla scuola. Milan: Jaca Book,
1976. Rev. by E. T. Gargan, AHR, 81(Apr 1977):334-5.

Battles of the Civil War, 1861-1865: The Complete Kurz & Allison
Prints. Birmingham, Ala: Oxmoor House, 1976. Rev. by
R. D. Hoffsommer, CWTI, 16(Oct 1977):49-50.

Bauer, Arnold J. Chilean Rural Society from the Spanish Conquest
to 1930. New York: Cam U Press, 1975. Rev. by R.
McCaa, AgH 51(Jl 1977):605-7; B. Loveman, AHR, 82(Oct
1977):1108; J. P. Harrison, JEH, 37(Je 1977):485-6; C. Kay,
JLAS, 9(May 1977):164-5; W. F. Sater, TAm, 33(Jan 1977):
549-51.

Bauer, Josef. Altsumerische Wirtschaftstexte aus Lagasch. Rome:
Bilical Institute Press, 1972. Rev. by R. D. Biggs, JNES,
36(Oct 1977):305-6.

Baum, Walter and Eberhard Weichold. Der Krieg der "achsenmachte"
im Mittelmeer-Raum. Göttingen: Muster-Schmidt, 1973. Rev.
by D. S. Detwiler, AHR, 82(Feb 1977):132.

Baumgart, Winfried. Der Imperialismus. Idee und Wirklichkeit der
englischen und franzosischen Kolonial-expansion 1880-1914.
Wiesbaden: Franz Steiner, 1975. Rev. by P. M. Kennedy,
HJ, 20(No. 3, 1977):761-9.

Bawden, Liz-Anne, ed. Oxford Companion to Film. London: Ox
U Press, 1976. Rev. by D. J. Wenden, EHR, 92(Oct 1977):
930-2.

Bay, Edna G., ed. see McCall, Daniel F., ed.

Bayly, C. A. The Local Roots of Indian Politics: Allahabad, 1880-
1920. New York: Ox U Press, 1975. Rev. by B. N. Ram-
usak, AHR, 82(Apr 1977):421-2; J. M. Brown, History, 62(Je
1977):283-4.

Baym, Nina. The Shape of Hawthorne's Career. Ithaca: Cornell U
Press, 1976. Rev. by C. S. B. Swann, JAmS, 11(Dec 1977):
417-20.

Bazant, Jan. Los bienes de la Iglesia en Mexico (1856-1875):

economicos y sociales de la Revolucion liberal. Mexico City:
El Colegio de Mexico, 1971. Rev. by R. J. Knowlton, AHR,
82(Apr 1977):478.

_____. Cinco haciendas mexicanas: Tres siglos de vida rural
en San Luis Potosi (1600-1910). Mexico, D. F.: El Colegio
de Mexico, 1975. Rev. by C. Gibson, AHR, 81(Dec 1976):
1284-85; D. A. Brading, JLAS, 9(May 1977):156-9.

Beachey, R. W. A Collection of Documents on the Slave Trade of
Eastern Africa. New York: Barnes and Noble, 1976. Rev.
by M. E. Page, AHR, 82(Je 1977):712-3.

_____. The Slave Trade of Eastern Africa. New York: Barnes
and Noble, 1976. Rev. by M. E. Page, AHR, 82(Je 1977):
712-3.

Beaglehole, J. C. The Life of Captain James Cook. London: A.
and C. Black, 1974. Rev. by A. N. Ryan, History, 62(Je
1977):302-3.

Beals, Ralph L. The Peasant Marketing System of Oaxaca, Mexico.
Los Angeles and London: U Cal Press, 1975. Rev. by R. J.
Bromley, JLAS, 9(May 1977):181-3.

Beatty, David and Robert O. Beatty. Nevada: Land of Discovery.
Reno: First National Bank of Nevada, 1976. Rev. by W. S.
Shepperson, WHQ, 8(Oct 1977):461.

Beatty, William K. see Marks, Geoffrey

Beauchamp, Edward R. An American Teacher in Early Meiji Japan.
Honolulu: U Press Hawaii, 1976. Rev. by J. F. Howes, AHR,
82(Apr 1977):417-8; L. A. Makela, JAS, 36(Aug 1977):761-3.

Beauclair, Indez de, ed. Neglected Formosa: A Translation from
the Dutch of Frederic Coyett's Verwaerloosde   Formosa.
San Francisco: Chinese Materials and Research Aides Service
Center, 1975. Rev. by W. M . Speidel, JAS, 36(May 1977):
561.

Bebey, Francis. African Music: A People's Art. Tr. by Josephine
Bennett. New York: Lawrence Hill, 1975. Rev. by C. E.
Robertson-De Carbo, JAAS, 12(Jan/Oct 1977):290-1.

Bechtold, Peter K. Politics in the Sudan: Parliamentary and Military Rule in an Emerging African Nation. New York: Praeger,
1976. Rev. by A. Z. Rubinstein, CurH, 72(Feb 1977):80; P.
Woodward, AfAf, 76(Apr 1977):270-1.

Beck, Thomas D. French Legislators, 1800-1834. Berkeley: U
Cal Press, 1974. Rev. by R. Forster, JIH, 7(Win 1977):
539-42.

Becker, Jillian. Hitler's Children: The Story of the Baader-Meinhof Terrorist Gang. Boston: Lippincott, 1977. Rev. by E. M. Breindel, Comm, 64(Nov 1977):71-5.

Becker, Robert A., ed. see Jensen, Merrill, ed.

Bedarida, Francois and Jean Maitron, eds. Christianisme et Monde Ouvrier. Paris: Editions Ouvrier, 1975. Rev. by R. Magraw, History, 62(Feb 1977):156-7.

Bedini, Silvio A. Thinkers and Tinkers. New York: Charles Scribner's Sons, 1975. Rev. by H. L. Peterson, AHI, 12(Jl 1977):49.

Begnal, Michael H. and Grace Eckley. Narrator and Character in Finnegans Wake. Lewisburg, Pa.: Bucknell U Press, 1975. Rev. by W. R. Evans, E-I, 12(Win 1977):151-3.

Beguin, Hubert. L'organisation de l'espace au Maroc. Brussels: Académie Royale des Sciences d'Outre-Mer, 1974. Rev. by D. F. Eickelman, Africa, 47(No. 1, 1977):120-1.

Behnen, Michael, ed. see Ebel, Gerhard ed.

Behrends, Frederick, ed. and trans. The Letters and Poems of Fulbert of Chartres. New York: Oxford U Press, 1976. Rev. by E. Peters, AHR, 82(Apr 1977):342.

Beilharz, Edwin A. and Carlos U. Lopez, eds. We Were 49ers! Chilean Accounts of the California Gold Rush. Pasadena: Ward Ritchie Press, 1976. Rev. by A. P. Nasatir, CHQ, 56(Apr 1977):88-9; B. F. Gilbert, JOW, 16(Jan 1977):72-3.

Beliaev, Viktor M. Central Asian Music (Essays in the History of the Music of the Peoples of the U.S.S.R.). Middletown: Wesleyan U Press, 1975. Rev. by L. Sakata, JAS, 36(May 1977):542-3.

Belk, Fred Richard. The Great Trek of the Russian Mennonites to Central Asia, 1880-1884. Scottdale, Pa.: Herald Press, 1976. Rev. by J. C. Juhnke, Historian, 39(Feb 1977):357-8.

Bell, J. Bowyer. On Revolt: Strategies of National Liberation. Cambridge, Mass.: Har U Press, 1976. Rev. by D. Wilkinson, AHR, 82(Je 1977):609-10.

_____. Terror Out of Zion: Irgun Zvai Leumi, LEHI, and the Palestine Underground, 1929-1949. New York: St. Martin's Press, 1977. Rev. by J. Jankowski, History, 6(Nov/Dec 1977):36-7.

Bell, Jonathan Wesley, ed. The Kansas Art Reader. Lawrence: U Kansas, 1976. Rev. by E. F. Grier, AS, 18(Fall 1977): 112-13.

Bell, Malcolm, III, ed. see Barrow, Elfrida DeRenne

Bell, Whitfield J., Jr. The Colonial Physician & Other Essays.
New York: Science History Publications, 1975. Rev. by L.
S. King, PH, 45(Jan 1977):80-1.

Bellah, Robert. Beyond Belief: Essays on Religion in a Post-Traditional World. New York: Harper and Row, 1970. Rev. by
S. E. Ahlstrom, AHR, 82(Oct 1977):1057.

_____. The Broken Covenant: American Civil Religion in Time
of Trial. New York: Harper and Row, 1975. Rev. by S. E.
Ahlstrom, AHR, 82(Oct 1977):1057.

Bellardo, Lewis, Jr., ed. see Nunn, Louie B.

Bellush, Bernard. The Failure of the NRA. New York: W. W.
Norton, 1975. Rev. by B. Sternsher, Historian, 39(May
1977):586-7.

Belz, Herman. A New Birth of Freedom: The Republican Party
and Freedmen's Rights, 1861 to 1866. Westport, Conn.:
Greenwood Press, 1976. Rev. by D. E. Fehrenbacher,
JSH, 43(Nov 1977):621-2.

Bence-Jones, Mark. The Cavaliers. n.l.: Constable, n.d. Rev.
by M. Ashley, HTo, 27(Jan 1977):58-9.

Bender, Barbara. Farming in Prehistory. New York: St. Martin's
Press, 1975. Rev. by B. M. Fagan, JIH, 7(Win 1977):531-2.

Bender, Lynn Darrell. The Politics of Hostility--Castro's Revolution
and United States Policy. Hato Rey, Puerto Rico: Inter-American U Press, 1975. Rev. by C. Abel, JLAS, 9(May 1977):
177-8.

Bender, Thomas. Toward an Urban Vision: Ideas and Institutions
in Nineteenth Century America. Lexington: U Press Ken,
1975. Rev. by J. D. Bennett, WHQ, 8(Jan 1977):69-70.

Benjamin, Philip S. The Philadelphia Quakers in the Industrial Age,
1865-1920. Philadelphia: Temple U Press, 1976. Rev. by P.
A. Carter, AHR, 82(Apr 1977):457; E. P. Duggan, JEH, 37
(Sep 1977):772-3.

Bennett, Adrian A., comp. Research Guide to the Chiao-bui bsin-
pao (The Church News), 1868-1874. San Francisco: Chinese
Materials Center, 1975. Rev. by J. K. Fairbank, JAS, 36
(Aug 1977):719-20.

_____, comp. Research Guide to the Wan-kuo kung-pao ("The
Globe Magazine"), 1874-1883. San Francisco: Chinese
Materials Center, 1976. Rev. by J. K. Fairbank, JAS, 36
(Aug 1977):719-20.

Bennett, Edward M., ed. see Burns, Richard Dean, ed.

Bennett, G. V. The Tory Crisis in Church and State, 1688-1730: The Career of Frances Atterbury, Bishop of Rochester. Oxford: Clarendon Press, 1975. Rev. by R. E. Boyer, AHR, 82(Oct 1977):961-2.

Bennett, Josephine, tr. see Bebey, Francis

Benson, Elizabeth P., ed. Death and the Afterlife in Pre-Columbian America. Washington, D. C.: Dumbarton Oaks Research Library and Collections, 1975. Rev. by W. Bray, Antiquity, 51 (Mar 1977):77.

Bentinck-Smith, William. Building a Great Library: The Coolidge Years at Harvard. Cambridge: Har U Press, 1976. Rev. by P. J. McNiff, NEQ, 50(Je 1977):370-2.

Bercovitch, Sacvan. The Puritan Origins of the American Self. New Haven: Yale U Press, 1975. Rev. by R. C. Simmons, EHR, 92(Oct 1977):904; D. Minter, GR, 31(Fall 1977):708-11; J. V. Metzgar, Historian, 39(Feb 1977):365-6.

Berdan, Frances, ed. see Anderson, Arthur J. O., ed.

Bereday, George Z. F. and Shigeo Masui. American Education Through Japanese Eyes. Honolulu: U Press of Hawaii, 1973. Rev. by C. Burgess, JAAS, 12(Jan/Oct 1977):283-4.

Berger, Carl. Broadsides & Bayonets: The Propaganda War of the American Revolution. San Rafael, Ca.: Presidio Press, 1977. Rev. by J. B. Whisker, History, 6(Nov/Dec 1977):27.

Berger, Elena L. Labour, Race and Colonial Rule: The Copperbelt from 1924 to Independence. London: Ox U Press, 1974. Rev. by D. M. P. McCarthy, JEH, 37(Je 1977):486-9.

Berger, Ernst. Die Geburt der Athena im Ostgiebel des Parthenon. Archäologischer Verlag Basel, 1974. Rev. by E. B. Harrison, AJA, 81(Win 1977):118-20.

Berger, Gordon Mark. Parties Out of Power in Japan, 1931-1941. Princeton, N.J.: Prin U Press, 1977. Rev. by A. D. Coox, History, 6(Oct 1977):14.

Berger, Raoul. Government by Judiciary: The Transformation of the Fourteenth Amendment. Cambridge, Mass.: Har U Press, 1977. Rev. by E. Abrams, Comm, 64(Dec 1977):84-6.

Berkh, Vasilii N. A Chronological History of the Discovery of the Aleutian Islands or the Exploits of Russian Merchants. Kingston, Ontario: Limestone Press, 1974. Rev. by M. E. Wheeler, AHR, 82(Apr 1977):401; M. C. Mangusso, PNQ, 68 (Jl 1977):150.

Berkin, Carol. Jonathan Sewall. Odyssey of an American Loyalist.
New York: Columbia U Press, 1974. Rev. by J. M. Nelson,
HJ, 20(No. 3, 1977):741-9.

Berlanstein, Lenard R. The Barristers of Toulouse in the Eighteenth Century (1740-1793). Baltimore: JHU Press, 1975.
Rev. by R. E. Giesey, AHR, 82(Oct 1977):980-1.

Berlin, Ira. Slaves Without Masters: The Free Negro in the Antebellum South. New York: Pantheon Books, 1974. Rev. by
D. L. Smiley, FHQ, 55(Jan 1977):380-2.

Berlin, Isaiah. Vico and Herder. Two Studies in the History of
Ideas. New York: Viking, 1976. Rev. by P. Gardiner, H&
T, 16(Feb 1977):45-51.

Berman, Paul. Revolutionary Organization: Institution-Building
within the People's Liberation Armed Forces. Lexington,
Mass.: Lexington Books, 1974. Rev. by C. A. Thayer,
JAS, 36(Feb 1977):382.

Bernal, Martin. Chinese Socialism to 1907. Ithaca: Cornell U
Press, 1976. Rev. by H. Z. Schiffrin, CQ, No. 69(Mar
1977):155-7.

Berner, Beol. China's Science Through Visitors' Eyes. Lund:
Research Policy Program, 1975. Rev. by R. Conroy, CQ
No. 71(Sep 1977):633-4.

Bernhard, M., ed. Goswin Kempgyn de Nussia Trivita studentium.
Munich: Arbeo-Gesellschaft, 1976. Rev. by A. B. Cobban,
EHR, 92(Oct 1977):890-1.

Bernhard, Marie-Louise. Corpus Vasorum Antiquorum, Poland 9,
Warsaw, National Museum 6. Warsaw: Panstwowe Wydawn-
ictwo Naukowe, 1976. Rev. by M. A. Del Chairo, AJA, 81
(Spr 1977):252-3.

Berninger, Dieter George. La Inmigración en México (1821-1857).
Mexico: SepSentas, 1974. Rev. by H. Sims, HAHR, 57(Feb
1977):130-1.

Berns, Walter. The First Amendment and the Future of American
Democracy. n.l.: Basic Books, n.d. Rev. by W. J. Bennett,
Comm, 63(May 1977):79-84.

Bernstein, David A. New Jersey Archives. Third Series, Vol. 1:
Minutes of the Governor's Privy Council, 1777-1789. Trenton:
New Jersey State Library, 1974. Rev. by R. L. Becker, Am
Arc, 39(Jl 1976):358-9.

Berrington, Hugh. Backbench Opinion in the House of Commons,
1945-55. Oxford: Pergamon, 1974. Rev. by T. Lloyd, CHR,
58(Je 1977):242-3.

Berry, Mary Frances. Military Necessity and Civil Rights Policy:
Black Citizenship and the Construction, 1861-1868. Port Wash-
ington, N.Y.: Kennikat Press, 1977. Rev. by A. M. Kraut,
History, 6(Oct 1977):5.

Berryman, John. The Freedom of the Poet. London: Faber &
Faber, 1977; Rev. by I. F. A. Bell JAmS, 11(Dec 1977):
395-8.

Berthe, Maurice. Le comté de Bigorre: Un milieu rural au bas
moyen âge. Paris: Sevpen, 1976. Rev. by K. Kennelly,
AHR 82(Apr 1977):343.

Bertin, Jacques, et al. Atlas of Food Crops. Paris and the
Hague: Mouton, 1971. Rev. by P. M. Roup, AgH, 51(Jan
1977):257-9.

Bertino, Belvina Williamson. The Scissorbills: A True Story of
Montana's Homesteaders. New York: Vantage Press, 1976.
Rev. by A. R. Anderson, WHQ 8(Apr 1977):213-4.

Berton, Pierre. Hollywood's Canada: The Americanization of Our
National Image. Toronto: McClelland & Stewart, 1975. Rev.
by M. Vipond, CHR, 58(Je 1977):231-2.

Beskrovnyi, L. G. The Russian Army and Navy in the Nineteenth
Century: Russia's Military Economic Potential. Moscow:
Izdatel'stvo "Nauka," 1973. Rev. by J. W. Kipp, AHR, 82
(Je 1977):694.

_____, et al., eds. Early Russian Principalities in the Tenth
through the Thirteenth Centuries. Moscow: Izdatel'stvo
"Nauka," 1975. Rev. by G. P. Majeska, AHR, 82(Je 1977):
691-2.

Besouchet, Lidia. Exilio e morte do Imperador. Rio de Janeiro:
Editora Nova Fronteira, 1975. Rev. by E. Pang, HAHR, 57
(Feb 1977):139-41.

Best, Gary Dean. The Politics of American Individualism: Herbert
Hoover in Transition, 1918-1921. Westport, Conn.: Greenwood
Press, 1975. Rev. by E. W. Hawley, AgH, 51(Apr 1977):459-
60; J. H. Wilson, Historian, 39(May 1977):585-6; R. Daniels,
PNQ, 68(Apr 1977):101-2.

Betancourt, Romulo. Venezuela Dueña de su petroleo. Caracas:
Ediciones Centauro, 1975. Rev. by W. J. Burggraaff, HAHR,
57(Feb 1977):138-9.

Beteille, Andre, ed. and T. N. Madan, ed. Encounter and Experience: Personal Accounts of Fieldwork. Honolulu: U Press
Hawaii, 1975. Rev. by M. J. Wheeler-Smith, JAS, 36(Aug
1977):775-7.

Betenson, Lula Parker. Butch Cassidy, My Brother as told to Dora
   Flack. Provo: BYU Press, 1975. Rev. by G. L. Roberts,
   A&W, 19(Sum 1977):186-7.

Bettelheim, Charles. Class Struggles in the U. S. S. R. : First Period, 1917-1923. New York: Monthly Review Press, 1976.
   Rev. by O. Hayward, JEH, 37(Sep 1977):773-5.

Betts, Raymond F. The False Dawn, European Imperialism in the
   Nineteenth Century. Minneapolis: U Minnesota Press, 1976.
   Rev. by P. M. Kennedy, HJ, 20(No. 3, 1977):761-9; L. J.
   Brack, Historian, 39(Feb 1977):335-6.

Beuf, Ann H. Red Children in White America. Philadelphia: U
   Pennsylvania Press, 1977. Rev. by C. K. W. , AS, 18(Fall
   1977):112.

Beyer, Stephan. The Cult of Tara: Magic and Ritual in Tibet.
   Berkeley: U California Press, 1974. Rev. by T. V. Wylie,
   JAAS, 12(Jan/Oct 1977):294-6.

Beyerly, Elizabeth. The Europecentric Historiography of Russia,
   An Analysis of the Contribution by Russian Emigre Historians
   in the U. S. A. , 1925-1955 Concerning 19th Century Russian
   History. The Hague-Paris: Mouton, 1973. Rev. by A.
   Gerschenkron, CSSH, 19(Jan 1977):108-23.

Bhagwati, Jagdish N. and T. N. Srinivasan. India. New York and
   London: Col U Press for the National Bureau of Economic
   Research, 1975. Rev. by K. M. Langley, JEH, 37(Je 1977):
   482-5.

Bhana, Surenda. The United States and the Development of the
   Puerto Rico Status Question, 1936-1968. Lawrence: U Press
   Kan, 1975. Rev. by D. M. Pletcher, AHR, 82(Feb 1977):
   39-59.

Biaudet, Jean-Charles and Marie-Claude Jequier, eds. Mémoires
   du Landamman Monod pour servir à l'histoire de la Suisse en
   1815. 3 vols. Bern: Selbstverlag der Allgemeinen Geschich-
   tsforschenden Gesellschaft der Schweiz, Stadt- und Universit-
   ätsbibliothek, 1975. Rev. by H. F. Young, AHR, 82(Je 1977):
   678.

Bibliographical Series: Newberry Library Center for the History of
   The American Indian Bibliographical Series. Bloomington: Ind
   U Press, n. d. Rev. by J. Henry, InHi, 10(Sum 1977):46.

Bicha, Karel D. Western Populism. Lawrence, Kan. : Coronado,
   1976. Rev. by P. H. Argersinger, AHR, 82(Je 1977):754-5.

Bick, Thomas D. French Legislators 1800-1834: A Study in Quantitative History. London: U Cal Press, 1975. Rev. by P.
   Pilbeam, History, 62(Feb 1977):155.

Bickford, Charlene Bangs, ed. see De Pauw, Linda Grant, ed.

Bielinski, Stefan. Abraham Yates, Jr., and the New Political Order
in Revolutional New York. Albany: New York State American
Revolution Bicentennial Commission, 1975. Rev. by M. O.
English, NYHSQ, 61(Jan/Apr 1977):83-4.

Bierbrauer, Volker. Die Ostgotischen Grab-und Schatzfunde in
Italien. Spoleto: Centro Italiano di studi sull'alto medioevo,
1975. Rev. by S. C. Hawkes, Antiquity, 51(Nov 1977):244.

Bigler, Gene see Fernández, Anibal

Bilbao, Jon see Douglass, William A.

Bilger, Harald R. Südafrika in Geschichte und Gegenwart. Konstanz: Verlagsanstalt Konstanz, 1976. Rev. by L. H. Gann,
AHR, 82(Apr 1977):408-9.

Billias, George Athan. Elbridge Gerry: Founding Father and Republican Statesman. New York: McGraw-Hill, 1976. Rev.
by C. E. Prince, AHR, 82(Je 1977):737; R. A. Brown, NEQ,
50(Mar 1977):160-3; G. Clarfield, WMQ, 34(Oct 1977):672-3.

Billington, Ray Allen, ed. Allan Nevins on History. New York:
Scribner's, 1975. Rev. by R. Luker, PH, 45(Jl 1977):287-8.

Binion, Rudolph. Hitler Among the Germans. New York: Elsevier,
1976. Rev. by G. Cocks, AHR, 82(Oct 1977):1009-10; R. G.
Waite, JIH, 8(Aut 1977):380-2.

Biondi, Albano, et al. Eresia e Riforma nell'Italia del Cinquecento.
DeKalb: No Ill U Press, 1974. Rev. by M. P. Gilmore,
AHR, 82(Feb 1977):139-40.

Biraben, Jean-Noël. Les Hommes et la peste en France et dans
les pays européens et méditerranéens. Vol. 1, La peste
dans l'histoire. Paris: Mouton, 1975. Rev. by V. J. Knapp,
AHR, 82(Feb 1977):93; V. J. Knapp, AHR, 82(Oct 1977):936.

Bird, E. et al., tr. The Songs of Seydou Camara. Vol. I. Kambili.
Bloomington: Indiana U, 1974. Rev. by H. Dinwiddy, AfAf,
76(Jan 1977):127-9.

Birk, Douglas A. see Wheeler, Robert C.

Birnberg, Thomas B. and Stephen A. Resnick. Colonial Development:
An Econometric Study. New Haven: Yale U Press, 1975. Rev.
by L. E. Davis, JEH, 37(Je 1977):489-91.

Bischoff, William N. We Were Not Summer Soldiers: The Indian
War Diary of Plympton J. Kelly. Tacoma: Washington State
Historical Society, 1976. Rev. by G. Thomas Edwards, 78
(Je 1977):179-80.

Bish, Robert L. et al. Coastal Resource Use: Decisions on Puget Sound. Seattle: U Wash Press, 1975. Rev. by K. A. Murray, PNQ, 68(Jan 1977):44.

Bishop, Elizabeth. Geography III. New York: Farrar, Straus & Giroux, 1976. Rev. by A. Corn, GR, 31(Sum 1977):533-41.

Bitterli, Urs. Die "Wilden" und die "zivilisierten". Munich: Verlag C. H. Beck, 1976. Rev. by R. G. Cole, AHR, 82 (Apr 1977):347-8.

Black, Cyril E., et al. The Modernization of Japan and Russia: A Comparative Study. London: Collier-Macmillian, 1976. Rev. by D. H. Aldcroft, History, 62(Feb 1977):92.

Black, Earl. Southern Governors and Civil Rights: Racial Segregation as a Campaign Issue in the Second Reconstruction. Cambridge: Har U Press, 1976. Rev. by M. Billington, AHR, 82(Feb 1977):217-8; D. R. Colburn, FHQ, 55(Apr 1977):505-6; R. W. Murray, JSH, 43(Feb 1977):144-5.

Black, J. L. Nicholas Karamsin and Russian Society in the Nineteenth Century: A Study in Russian Political and Historical Thought. Toronto: U Tor Press, 1975. Rev. by R. A. H. Robinson, History, 62(Feb 1977):154-5.

Black, Nancy B. and Weidman, Bette S., eds. White on Red: Images of the American Indian. Port Washington: Kennikat, 1976. Rev. by S. Peterson, JOW, 16(Jl 1977):91.

Black, Stephen A. Whitman's Journeys into Chaos: A Psychoanalytic Study of the Poetic Process. Princeton: Prin U Press, 1976. Rev. by D. M. Wyatt, GR, 31(Spr 1977):243-8.

Blackburn, Thomas C., ed. December's Child: A Book of Chumash Oral Narratives. Berkeley: U Cal Press, 1976. Rev. by C. B. Kroeber, PHR, 46(Aug 1977):512-3.

Blacker, Carmen. The Catalpa Bow: A Study of Shamanistic Practices in Japan. London: George Allen & Unwin, 1975. Rev. by J. M. Kitagawa, JAS, 36(Feb 1977):359-61.

_____, and Michael Loewe, eds. Ancient Cosmologies. Totowa, N.J.: Rowman and Littlefield, 1975. Rev. by J. J. Peradotto, AHR, 81(Dec 1976):1078.

Blackey, Robert and Clifford Paynton. Revolution and the Revolutionary Ideal. Cambridge: Schenkman, 1976. Rev. by L. Kaplan, AHR, 82(Apr 1977):335-6.

Blackford, Mansel G. The Politics of Business in California, 1890-1920. Columbus: Ohio St U Press, 1977. Rev. by R. Batman, WHQ, 8(Oct 1977):479-80.

Blackmer, Donald L. M. and Sidney Tarrow, eds.   Communism in Italy and France. Princeton: Prin U Press, 1976. Rev. by M. L. Silsby, AHR, 82(Oct 1977):955-6; A. Z. Rubinstein, CurH, 72(Apr 1977):176-7.

Blaich, Fritz. Der Trustkampf (1901-1915): Ein Beitrag zum Verhalten der Ministerialbürokratie gegenüben Verbandsinteressen im Wilhelminischen Deutschland. Berlin: Duncker and Humblot, 1975. Rev. by C. Medalen, AHR, 82(Feb 1977):128.

Blaikie, Piers M. Family Planning in India: Diffusion and Policy. New York: Holmes & Meier, 1975. Rev. by J. E. Kivlin, JAS, 37(Nov 1977):164-5.

Blainey, Geoffrey. Triumph of the Nomads: A History of Aboriginal Australia. Woodstock, N.Y.: Overlook Press, 1976. Rev. by S. C. McCulloch, AHR, 82(Apr 1977):427; London: Macmillan, 1976. Rev. by S. Glynn, History, 62(Je 1977):304.

Blair, Peter Hunter. Northumbria in the days of Bede. London: Gollancz, 1976. Rev. by B. Hope-Taylor, Antiquity, 51(Jl 1977):165-6.

Blaiser, Cole. The Hovering Giant: U. S. Responses to Revolutionary Change in Latin America. Pittsburgh: U Pitt Press, 1976. Rev. by J. F. Petras, JEH, 37(Sep 1977):775-6; R. F. Smith, AHR, 82(Feb 1977):213; L. D. Langley, HAHR, 57(May 1977): 321-2.

Blake, N. F. Caxton: England's First Publisher. London: Osprey, 1976. Rev. by N. Orme, History, 62(Je 1977):313.

Blakemore, Harold. British Nitrates and Chilean Politics 1886-1896: Balmaceda and North. London: Athlone Press, 1974. Rev. by R. H. Chilcote, HAHR, 57(Feb 1977):149-51.

Blakey, Arch Frederic. Parade of Memories: A History of Clay County, Florida. Jacksonville: Clay County Bicentennial Steering Committee, 1976. Rev. by G. E. Buker, FHQ, 55 (Apr 1977):487-9.

Blanco, Richard L. Wellington's Surgeon General: Sir James McGregor. Durham: Duke U Press, 1974. Rev. by R. J. T. Joy, AHR, 82(Feb 1977):103-4.

Blanco, Rómulo et al. Un hombre llamado Rómulo Betancourt. Caracas: Ediciones Centauro, 1975. Rev. by W. J. Burggraaff, HAHR, 57(Feb 1977):138-9.

Blancpain, Jean-Pierre. Les Allemands au Chili (1816-1945). Cologne: Bohlau Verlag, 1974. Rev. by A. J. Bauer, AHR, 81(Dec 1976):1286-87.

Blanshie, Sarah Rubin. Perugia, 1260-1340: Conflict and Change in a Medieval Italian Urban Society. Philadelphia: American Philosophical Society, 1976. Rev. by R. Schumann, AHR, 82 (Feb 1977):79-80.

Bleek, W. Marriage, Inheritance and Witchcraft: A Case Study of a Rural Ghanaian Family. Leiden: Afrika-Studjecentrum, 1975. Rev. by A. Alland, Jr., Afrika, 47(No. 3, 1977): 326-7.

Blickle, Peter, ed. Revolts und Revolution in Europa. Munich: R. Oldenbourg, 1975. Rev. by H. J. Cohn, EHR, 92(Oct 1977):855-8.

Blidstein, Gerald. Honor Thy Father and Mother. n.l.: Ktar, n.d. Rev. by D. Singer, Comm, 64(Dec 1977):90-3.

Blinkhorn, Martin. Carlism and Crisis in Spain, 1931-1939. New York and London: Cam U Press, 1975. Rev. by R. W. Kern, JMH, 49(Je 1977):318-9; J. M. Sanchez, Historian, 39(Feb 1977):348-9.

Bloch, Sidney and Peter Reddaway. Psychiatric Terror: How Soviet Psychiatry Is Used to Suppress Dissent. New York: Basic Books, 1977. Rev. by O. E. S., CurH, 73(Oct 1977): 128.

Block, W. T. A History of Jefferson County, Texas, from Wilderness to Reconstruction. Nederland: Nederland Publishing, 1976. Rev. by H. L. Sundefer, ETHJ, 15(Spr 1977):51.

Blocker, Jack S., Jr. Retreat from Reform: The Prohibition Movement in the United States, 1890-1913. Westport, Conn.: Greenwood, 1976. Rev. by D. J. Pivar, AHR, 82(Oct 1977): 1089; J. J. Rumbarger, JSH, 43(Aug 1977):469-71.

Bloesch, Paul. Das Anniversarbuch des Basler Domstifts, 1334/8-1610. Basel: Kommissionsverlag Friedrich Reinhardt, 1975. Rev. by H. S. Offler, EHR, 92(Oct 1977):889-90.

Blom, J. C. H. The Mutiny on "The Seven Provinces". Bussum: Unieboek, B. B., 1975. Rev. by L. D. Stokes, AHR, 82(Apr 1977):377.

Bloom, Harold. Figures of Capable Imagination. New York: Seabury Press, 1976. Rev. by A. Wordsworth, GR, 31(Sum 1977): 528-33.

Bloom, John Porter, ed. The Territorial Papers of the United States. Volume 28: The Territory of Wisconsin, 1839-1848. Washington, D. C.: National Archives and Records Service, General Services Administration, 1975. Rev. by A. E. Smith, PNQ, 68(Jan 1977):46.

Bloomfield, Maxwell. American Lawyers in a Changing Society, 1776-1876. Cambridge, Mass.: Har U Press, 1976. Rev. by N. Brockman, AHR, 82(Feb 1977):175-6; A. H. Schechter, JIH, 8(Sum 1977):177-9; P. L. Murphy, JSH, 43(Feb 1977): 115-6; J. E. Viator, Jr., WMQ, 34(Apr 1977):320-2.

Blouet, Brian W. and Merlin P. Lawson, eds. Images of the Plains: The Role of Human Nature in Settlement. Lincoln, U Neb Press, 1975. Rev. by D. H. Breen, AgH, 51(Jan 1977):270-1.

Blue, Frederick J. The Free Soilers, Third Party Politics 1848-54. Urbana: U Ill Press, 1973. Rev. by D. J. MacLeod, EHR, 92(Oct 1977):922-3.

Blum, John Morton. V Was for Victory: Politics and American Culture during World War II. New York: Harcourt Brace Jovanovich, 1976. Rev. by J. F. Heath, AHR, 82(Apr 1977): 466-7.

Blumenthal, Henry. American and French Culture, 1800-1900: Interchange in Art, Science, Literature, and Society. Baton Rouge: LSU Press, 1975. Rev. by E. Weber, LaH, 18(Spr 1977):252-3.

Blumin, Stuart, M. The Urban Threshold: Growth and Change in a Nineteenth-Century American Community. Chicago: U Chi Press, 1976. Rev. by D. R. Esslinger, AHR, 82(Apr 1977): 442; C. D. Goldin, JEH, 37(Sep 1977):777-8; V. Yans-Mc-Laughlin, JIH, 8(Sum 1977):175-7.

Boardman, John. Athenian Red Figure Vases. The Archaic Period. London: Thames and Hudson, 1975. Rev. by C. G. Boulter, AJA, 81(Win 1977):121.

Bobo, Benjamin F. , Alfred E. Osborne, Jr. and Harold Kassarjian. Emerging Issues in Black Economic Development. Lexington: D. C. Heath, 1977. Rev. by M. S. Miller, Crisis, 84(Apr 1977):155-7.

Bodde, Derk. Festivals in Classical China: New Year and Other Annual Observances During the Han Dynasty, 206 B.C. - A.D. 220. Princeton: Prin U Press, 1975. Rev. by W. Eberhard, AHR, 82(Feb 1977):158-9.

Bode, Frederick A. Protestantism and the New South: North Carolina Baptists and Methodists in Political Crisis, 1894-1903. Charlottesville: U Press Va, 1976. Rev. by K. K. Bailey, AHR, 81(Dec 1976):1272; T. E. Terrill, JSH, 43(Feb 1977): 139-40.

Bödy, Paul. Joseph Eötvös and the Modernization of Hungary, 1840-1879. Philadelphia: American Philosophical Society, 1972. Rev. by S. B. Vardy, AHR, 82(Apr 1977):394-5.

Boesen, Victor see Graybill, Florence Curtis.

Bogue, Allan G. and Robert Taylor, eds. The University of Wisconsin: One Hundred and Twenty-Five Years. Madison: U Wis Press, 1975. Rev. by G. J. Clifford, AHR, 81(Dec 1977):1270-71.

Boia, Lucian. Evolution of Romanian Historiography. Bucharest: Universitatea din Bucures i, Facultatea de istorie, 1976. Rev. by K. Hitchins, AHR, 82(Je 1977):685-6.

Bois, Guy. Crise du féodalisme: Economie rurale et démographie en Normandie orientale du début du 14e siècle au milieu du 16e siècle. Paris: Presses de la Fondation Nationale des Sciences Politiques, 1976. Rev. by T. Evergates, AHR, 82 (Oct 1977):938-9.

Boisselier, Jean. The Heritage of Thai Sculpture. New York: Weatherhill, 1975. Rev. by S. J. O'Connor, JAS, 36(May 1977):589-91.

Boitani, Francesca, Maria Cataldi, and Marinella Pasquinucci. Etruscan cities. Ed. by Filippo Coarelli. London: Cassell, 1075. Rev. by D. Ridgway, Antiquity, 51(Jl 1977):166-8.

Boles, John B. Religion in Antebellum Kentucky. Lexington: U Press Ken, 1976. Rev. by J. C. Dann, WMQ, 34(Oct 1977): 688-9; R. W. Long, WVH, 38(Apr 1977):240-2.

Bolkhovitinov, Nikolai N. The Beginnings of Russian-American Relations, 1775-1815. Cambridge, Mass.: Har U Press, 1975. Rev. by J. T. Alexander, AHR, 82(Feb 1977):148-9.

_____. Russia and the American Revolution. Tallahassee, Fla.: Diplomatic Press, 1976. Rev. by M. S. Anderson, History, 62(Feb 1977):138-9; S. A. Zenkovsky, History, 6(Oct 1977):3.

Bolkosky, Sidney M. The Distorted Image: German Jewish Perceptions of Germans and Germany 1918-1935. New York: Elsevier Scientific Publ. Co., 1975. Rev. by R. Hilberg, AHR, 82(Oct 1977):952-4; L. Kochan, History, 62(Feb 1977): 162-3.

Bolshakoff, Sergius. Russian Mystics. Kalamazoo, Mich.: Cistercian Publications, 1977. Rev. by C. A. Frazee, AHR, 82(Oct 1977):1023-4.

Boltho, Andrea. Japan: An Economic Survey. London: Ox U Press, 1975. Rev. by M. Bronfenbrenner, JAS, 36(Feb 1977):353-4.

Bona, Istvan. Die Mittlere Bronzezeit Ungarns und Ihre Sudostlichen Bezichungen. Budapest: Akademiai Kiado, 1975. Rev. by H. L. Thomas, AJA, 81(Sum 1977):392.

Bonavia, Duccio. Ricchata Quelliccani, Pinturas Murales Prehispanicas. Lima: Fondo del Libro del Banco Industrial del
Peru, 1974. Rev. by R. P. Schaedel, Antiquity, 42(Jan 1977):
133-4.

Bond, Horace Mann. Education for Freedom: A History of Lincoln
University, Pennsylvania. Princeton: Prin U Press, 1976.
Rev. by J. O. Patton, JNH, 62(Jl 1977):307-9.

Bond, M. F., ed. The Diaries and Papers of Sir Edward Dering,
2nd Bart., 1644 to 1684. London: HMSO, n.d. Rev. by A.
L. Rowse, HTo, 27(Je 1977):406-7.

Bond, Maurice, ed. see Dering, Edward

Bondanella, Peter E. Francesco Guicciardini. Boston: Twayne,
1976. Rev. by R. Starn, AHR, 82(Feb 1977):139.

Bondurant, Joan V., ed. Harijan: Collected Issues of Gandhi's
Journal, 1933-1955. New York: Garland Publishing, 1973.
Rev. by D. Dalton, JAS, 36(May 1977):570-2.

Bonfante, Larissa. Etruscan Dress. Baltimore: JHU Press, 1976.
Rev. by J. P. Small, AJA, 81(Spr 1977):253-4; D. Ridgway,
Antiquity, 51(Jl 1977):166-8.

Bongiovanni, Bruno and Fabio Levi. L'Università di Torino durante
il fascismo: Le Facoltà umanistiche e il Politecnico. Turin:
G. Giappichelli Editore, 1976. Rev. by E. Argento, AHR, 82
(Oct 1977):1012-13.

Bonilla, Heradio, comp. Gran Bretaña y el Peru: Informes de los
cónsules británicos. Lima: Instituto de Estudios Peruanos,
1975. Rev. by T. M. Bader, HAHR, 57(Aug 1977):557-9.

Bonini, Irma Valetti. Le Communità di valle in epoca signorile.
Milan: Università Cattolica del Sacro Cuore, 1976. Rev. by
K. Casey, AHR, 82(Je 1977):622-3.

Bonjean, Charles M., Louis Schneider, and Robert L. Lineberry,
eds. Social Science in America: The First Two Hundred
Years. Austin: U T Press, 1976. Rev. by C. D. Goodwin,
JEH, 37(Sep 1977):778-80.

Bonnassie, Pierre. La Catalogne du milieu du Xe à la fin du XIe
siècle: Croissance et mutations d'une société. 2 vols.
Toulouse: Assoc. des Publications de l'Universite de Toul-
ouse--le Mirail, 1975. Rev. by J. N. Hillgarth, AHR, 82
(Apr 1977):343-4.

Bonner, Gerald, ed. Famulus Christi: Essays in Commemoration
of the Thirteenth Centenary of the Birth of the Venerable Bede.
London: S. P. C. K., 1976. Rev. by R. A. Markus, History, 62(Je 1977):308-9.

Bonwick, Colin. English Radicals and the American Revolution.
Chapel Hill: UNC Press, 1977. Rev. by H. F. Rankin,
History, 6(Oct 1977):3-4.

Bookchin, Murray. The Spanish Anarchists: The Heroic Years,
1868-1936. New York: Free Life Editions, 1977. Rev. by
L. H. Nelson, History, 6(Nov/Dec 1977):44.

Boorstin, Daniel J. The Exploring Spirit: America & the World
Then and Now. New York: Random House, 1976. Rev. by
M. Klein, AHI, 12(Aug 1977):49-50; W. H. Goetzmann, WHQ,
8(Apr 1977):203-4.

Borah, Woodrow see Cook, Sherburne F.

Borbándi, Gyula. Der Ungarische Populismus. Munich: Ungar-
isches Institut München, 1976. Rev. by I. Deák, AHR, 82
(Oct 1977):1019-20.

Borchardt, Jurgen. Die Bauskultur des Heroons Von Limyra.
Berlin: Gebr. Mann, 1976. Rev. by W. A. P. Childs, AJA,
81(Sum 1977):399-400.

Bordley, James III and A. McGehee Harvey. Two Centuries of
American Medicine, 1776-1976. Philadelphia: W. B. Saunders
Co., 1976. Rev. by M. Kaufman, AHR, 82(Je 1977):728-9.

Borger, Rykle. Handbuch der Keilschriftlituratur. Berlin: Walter
de Gruyter, 1975. Rev. by R. D. Biggs, JNES, 36(Oct 1977):
304-5.

Bori, Pier Cesare. Chiesa Primitiva: L'immagine della comunità
delle origini Atti, 2, 42-47; 4, 32-37--nella storia della chiesa
antica. Brescia: Paideia Editrice, 1974. Rev. by R. E. A.
Palmer, AHR, 82(Apr 1977)340-1.

Bortoli, Georges. The Death of Stalin. New York: Praeger,
1975. Rev. by J. M. Thompson, Historian, 39(Feb 1977):
360-1.

Boscaro, Adriana. Sixteenth Century European Printed Works on
the First Japanese Mission to Europe: A Descriptive Bibliography. Leiden, Holland: E. J. Brill, 1973. Rev. by R.
K. Sakai, JAAS, 12(Jan/Oct 1977):281-3.

Bossard, Maurice and Louis Junod, eds. Chroniqueurs du XVIe
siècle: Bonivard, Pierrefleur, Jeanne de Jussie, Fromment.
Lausanne: Bibliotheque romande, 1974. Rev. by D. Nugent,
AHR, 82(Feb 1977):85-6.

Bossuet, Jacques-Benigne. Discourse on Universal History. Chicago: U Chi Press, 1976. Rev. by J. C. Rule, AHR, 82
(Je 1977):607.

Botz, Gerhard. Gewalt in der Politik. Munich: Wilhelm Fink
    Verlag, 1976. Rev. by D. Large, AHR, 82(Je 1977):675-6.

_____. Wohnungspolitik und Judendeportation in Wien 1938-
    1945. Wien-Salzburg: Geyer, 1975. Rev. by H. Delfiner,
    EEQ, 11(March 1977):127-8.

Boulnois, L. Bibliographie du Nepal. Paris: Centre National de
    la Recherche Scientifique 1975. Rev. by L. E. Rose, JAS,
    36(Aug 1977):787-8.

Bouloiseau, Marc. La république jacobine, 10 aôut 1792-9 thermidor
    an II. Paris: Editions du Seuil, 1972. Rev. by J. I. Shulim,
    AHR, 82(Feb. 1977):20-38.

Boussard, Jacques. Nouvelle histoire de Paris: De la fin du
    siège de 885-886 à la mort de Philippe Auguste. Paris:
    Hachette, 1976. Rev. by G. M. Spiegel, AHR, 82(Oct 1977):
    938.

Bowen, James. A History of Western Education. London: Methuen,
    1972; 1975. Rev. by R. R. Bolgar, History, 62(Feb 1977):
    80-1.

Bower, Donald E. Fred Rosenstock: A Legend in Books & Art.
    Flagstaff, Arizona: Northland Press, 1976. Rev. by D. Rus-
    sell WHQ, 18(Jl 1977):347.

Bowers, William L. The Country Life Movement in America, 1900-
    1920. Port Washington: New York: Kennikat Press, 1974.
    Rev. by R. H. Pells, AHR, 81(Dec 1976):1269-70; W. E. Dav-
    ies, PH, 45(Jl 1977):271.

Bowler, Peter J. Fossils and Progress: Paleontology and the Idea
    of Progressive Evolution in the Nineteenth Century. New York:
    Science History Publications, 1976. Rev. by M. Ruse, AHR,
    82(Je 1977):608.

Bowler, R. Arthur. Logistics and the Failure of the British Army
    in America, 1775-1783. Princeton: Prin U Press, 1975.
    Rev. by J. M. Coleman, AHR, 82(Apr 1977):435-6.

Bowles, Samuel and Herbert Gintis. Schooling in Capitalist America:
    Educational Reform and the Contradictions of Economic Life.
    New York: Basic Books, 1976. Rev. by A. J. Field, JEH,
    37(Je 1977):491-2.

Bowman, Larry G. Captive Americans: Prisoners during the Amer-
    ican Revolution. Athens: Ohio U Press, 1977. Rev. by J. K.
    Alexander, AHR, 82(Oct 1977):1065; J. Edwin Hendricks, JSH,
    43(Nov 1977):610-1.

Bowser, Frederick P. The African Slave in Colonial Peru, 1524-

1650. Stanford: Stanford U Press, 1974. Rev. by M. J.
Echenberg, JAAS, 12(Jan/Oct 1977):291-2.

Boxer, C. R. Women in Iberian Expansion Overseas, 1415-1815.
Some Facts, Fancies and Personalities. New York: Ox U
Press, 1975. Rev. by J. H. Parry, HAHR, 57(Feb 1977):
126-7.

Boyd, Doug. Swami. New York: Random House (in association
with Robert Briggs), 1976. Rev. by A. Bharati, JAS, 36
(Aug 1977):779-80.

Boyd, Julian P., ed. The Jefferson Papers of the University of
Virginia. Charlottesville: U Press Virginia, 1973. Rev. by
J. E. Selby, PH, 45(Jan 1977):83-4.

Boyers, Robert. Excursions: Selected Literary Essays. Port
Washington: Kennikat Press, 1977. Rev. by C. Molesworth,
GR, 31(Sum 1977):522-5.

Brack, Gene M. Mexico Views Manifest Destiny, 1821-1846: An
Essay on the Origin of the Mexican War. Albuquerque:
UNM Press, 1975. Rev. by W. F. Trimble, A&W, 19(Sum
1977):167-169; D. M. Pletcher, AHR, 82(Feb 1977):39-59;
O. B. Faulk, Historian, 39(Feb 1977):385; O. B. Faulk, WHQ,
8(Jan 1977):75.

Brading, David A. Los Origenes de Nacionalismo Mexicano. Mexico: SepSetentas, 1973. Rev. by H. M. Hamill, HAHR,
57(Feb 1977):118-21.

Bradley, Ian. The Call to Seriousness: The Evangelical Impact on
the Victorians. New York: Macmillan, 1976. Rev. by L. E.
Grugel, AHR, 82(Je 1977):638-9; S. Meacham, JIH, 8(Aut
1977):365-6.

Bradley, John. Civil War in Russia, 1917-1920. New York: St.
Martin's Press, 1975. Rev. by S. W. Page, Historian, 39
(Feb 1977):359-60.

Bradshaw, Herbert Clarence. History of Hampden-Sydney College.
Volume I, From the Beginnings to the Year 1856. Durham,
N.C.: privately printed, 1976. Rev. by J. L. Bugg, Jr.,
VMHB, 85(Jl 1977):369-71.

Braeman, John, Robert H. Bremmer and David Brody, eds. The
New Deal, Vol. I: The National Level; Vol. 2: The State and
Local Levels. Columbus: Ohio St U Press, 1975. Rev. by
T. Saloutos, PHR, 46(May 1977):310-1.

Braestrup, Peter. Big Story: How the American Press and Television Reported and Interpreted the Crisis of Tet 1968 in Vietnam and Washington. n.l.: Westview, 1977. Rev. by P. H.
Weaver, Comm, 64(Nov 1977):64-8.

Branca, Patricia. Silent Sisterhood: Middle Class Women in the
      Victorian Home. Pittsburg: Carnegie-Mellon U Press, 1975.
      Rev. by J. N. Burstyn, AHR, 82(Feb 1977):105; L. Gordon,
      JMH, 49(Je 1977):308-10.

Branco, Carlos Castello. Introducão à revolucão de 1964. Rio de
      Janeiro: Editora Artenova, 1975. Rev. by R. E. Poppino,
      HAHR, 57(Feb 1977):141-2.

Brandeis, Louis D. Letters of Louis D. Brandeis, Volume IV
      (1916-1921): Mr. Justice Brandeis. Ed. by Melvin I. Urof-
      sky and David W. Levy. Albany: State U New York Press,
      1975. Rev. by M. K. B. Tachau, FCHQ, 51(Apr 1977):202-4.

Brandes, Stuart D. American Welfare Capitalism, 1880-1940. Chi-
      cago: U Chi Press, 1976. Rev. by M. Heald, AHR, 81(Dec
      1976):1261; W. O. Wagnon, JEH, 37(Sep 1977):778-80; J. B.
      Thomas, JSH, 43(May 1977):311-2; L. R. Kunkel, WMH, 60
      (Sum 1977):349-50.

Branigan, Keith. Aegean Metalwork of the Early and Middle Bronze
      Age. Oxford: At the Clarendon Press, 1974. Rev. by J. D.
      Muhly, JNES, 36(Jan 1977):153-7.

Branson, Noreen. Britain in the Nineteen Twenties. Minneapolis:
      U Minn Press, 1976. Rev. by D. Lammers, Historian, 39
      (Feb 1977):336-7.

Braudel, Fernand and Ernest Labrousse, eds. Histoire économique
      et sociale de la France. Vol. 3, L'avènement de l'ère indus-
      trielle. Paris: Presses Universitaires de France, 1976.
      Rev. by E. B. Ackerman, AHR, 82(Oct 1977):982-3.

Bray, Edmund C. and Martha Coleman Bray, eds. Joseph N. Nic-
      ollet on the Plains and Prairies: The Expeditions of 1838-39
      with Journals, Letters, and Notes on the Dakota Indians. St.
      Paul: Minnesota Historical Society Press, 1976. Rev. by R.
      E. Ehrenberg, MinnH, 45(Sum 1977):250-1; M. L. Spence,
      WHQ, 8(Oct 1977):456-7.

Bray, Martha Coleman, ed. see Bray, Edmund C. , ed.

Breakell, Mike see Rowley, Trevor, ed.

Bream, Howard N. , Ralph D. Heim and Carey A. Moore, eds. A
      Light Unto My Path: Old Testament Studies in Honor of Jacob
      M. Myers. Philadelphia: Temple U Press, 1974. Rev. by
      D. Pardee, JNES, 36(Jl 1977):317-8.

Breeden, James O. Joseph Jones, M. D. , Scientist of the Old South.
      Lexington: U Press Ken, 1975. Rev. by W. Stanton, Histor-
      ian, 39(Feb 1977):372-3.

Bremer, Francis J. The Puritan Experiment: New England Society from Bradford to Edwards. New York: St. Martin's Press, 1976. Rev. by J. W. T. Youngs, Jr., WMQ, 34(Jan 1977): 165-6.

Bremmer, Robert H., ed. see Braeman, John, ed.

Brereton, Geoffrey. French Tragic Drama in the Sixteenth & Seventeenth Centuries. London: Methuen, 1973. Rev. by F. K. Dawson, ESR, 7(Oct 1977):450-3.

Brett, M. The English Church Under Henry I. New York: Ox U Press, 1975. Rev. by R. V. Turner, AHR, 82(Feb 1977):76.

Brewer, Elizabeth D. see Youngs, J. William T., Jr.

Brewer, Frank S. see Youngs, J. William T., Jr.

Brewer, John. Party Ideology and Popular Politics at the Accession of George III. New York: Cam U Press, 1976. Rev. by D. E. Ginter, AHR, 82(Apr 1977):356-7; J. Dinwiddy, HJ, 20(No. 4, 1977):983-9; J. Cannon, History, 62(Feb. 1977):133.

Brichford, Maynard J. et al. Manuscripts Guide to Collections at the University of Illinois at Urbana-Champaign. Urbana: U Ill Press, 1976. Rev. by K. Jacklin, AmArc, 40(Jan 1977): 79-81.

Bridbury, A. R. Historians and the Open Society. London: Routledge and Kegan Paul, 1972. Rev. by N. Tyacke, History, 62(Feb 1977):73.

Bridenbaugh, Carl. Fat Mutton and Liberty of Conscience: Society in Rhode Island. Providence, R. I.: Brown U Press, 1974. Rev. by J. P. Greene, JIH, 8(Aut 1977):385-7; R. J. Champagne, WMH, 60(Spr 1977):242.

_____. The Spirit of '76: The Growth of American Patriotism Before Independence. New York: Ox U Press, 1975. Rev. by J. W. T. Youngs, Jr., PNQ, 68(Jan 1977):33.

Bridenthal, Renate and Claudia Konnz, eds. Becoming Visible: Women in European History. Boston: Houghton Mifflin, 1977. Rev. by C. M. Prelinger, History, 6(Oct 1977):20-1.

Briggs, Walter. Without Noise of Arms: The 1776 Dominguez-Escalante Search for a Route From Sante Fe to Monterey. Flagstaff, Arizona: Northland Press, 1976. Rev. by T. E. Treutlein, A&W, 19(Spr 1977):95-96; T. J. Warner, WHQ, 8(Apr 1977):228-9.

Britt, Albert S., Jr., ed. see Hawes, Lilla Mills

Brock, Leslie V.   The Currency of the American Colonies, 1700-
    1764:   A Study in Colonial Finance and Imperial Relations.
    New York: Arno Press, 1975.   Rev. by J. R. Morrill, III,
    WMQ, 34(Jl 1977):494-6.

Brock, Peter.   The Slovak National Awakening: An Essay in the
    Intellectual History of East Central Europe.   Buffalo: U Tor
    Press, 1976.   Rev. by R. Szporluk, AHR, 82(Oct 1977):1022.

Brock, William R.   The United States, 1789-1890.   Ithaca: Cor U
    Press, 1975.   Rev. by N C. Burckel, AHR, 82(Feb 1977):
    177-8; W. L. Joyce, AmArc, 39(Jl 1976):362-3.

Brody, David, ed.   see   Braeman, John, ed.

Brooke, Christopher.   London 800-1215:   The Shaping of a City.
    Berkeley: U Cal Press, 1975.   Rev. by B. Hobley, Archae-
    ology, 30(Mar 1977):137-9; J. Le Patourel, History, 62(Je
    1977):311-2.

Brower, Daniel R.   Training the Nihilists: Education and Radical-
    ism in Tsarist Russia.   Ithaca, N.Y.:   Cor U Press, 1975.
    Rev. by P. L. Alston, AHR, 82(Feb 1977):150-1; S. H. All-
    ister, JMH, 49(Je 1977):341-3.

Brown, Alexander Crosby.   The Good Ships of Newport News: An
    Informal Account of Ships, Shipping and Shipbuilding in the
    Lower Chesapeake Bay Region Together With the Story of the
    Last Terrible Voyage of the Yarmouth Castle.   Cambridge,
    Maryland: Tidewater Publishers, 1976.   Rev. by J. A. Gold-
    enberg, VMHB, 85(Apr 1977):213-14.

Brown, David, ed.   see   Strong, Donald, ed.

Brown, Emily C.   Har Dayal, Hindu Revolutionary and Rationalist.
    Tucson: U Arizona Press, 1975.   Rev. by A. R. H. Copley,
    History, 62(Je 1977):284-5.

Brown, Judith M.   Gandhi and Civil Disobedience: The Mahatma in
    Indian Policies, 1928-34.   New York: Cam U Press, 1977.
    Rev. by B. N. Ramusack, History, 6(Nov/Dec 1977):38.

Brown, Kenneth L.   People of Salé: Tradition and Change in a
    Moroccan City, 1830-1930.   Cambridge, Mass.:   Har U Press,
    1976.   Rev. by A. A. Heggoy, AHR, 82(Oct 1977):1032-3.

Brown, L. Carl.   The Tunisia of Ahmad Bey, 1837-1855.   Princeton:
    Prin U Press, 1974.   Rev. by C. C. Stewart, Historian, 39
    (May 1977):563-4; F. X. Paz, JNES, 36(Jl 1977):240-1.

Brown, MacAlister, ed.   see   Zasloff, Joseph J., ed.

Brown, Peter Lancaster.   Megaliths, Myths and Men: An Introduc-
    tion to Astro-Archaeology.   Poole: Blandford Press, 1976.
    Rev. by R. J. C. Atkinson, Antiquity, 51(Mar 1977):81.

Brown, Ralph Adams. The Presidency of John Adams. Lawrence:
University Press of Kansas, 1975. Rev. by M. R. Zahniser,
PNQ, 68(Jan 1977):34.

Brown, Richard D. Modernization: The Transformation of American
Life, 1600-1865. New York: Hill and Wang, 1976. Rev. by
R. H. Brown, WMQ, 34(Oct 1977):656-7.

Brown, Richard Maxwell. Strain of Violence: Historical Studies of
American Violence and Vigilantism. New York: Ox U Press,
1975. Rev. by J. Caughey, PNQ, 68(Oct 1977):191.

Brown, Robert Craig. Robert Laird Borden: A Biography. Vol.
1, 1854-1914. Toronto: Macmillan of Canada, 1975. Rev.
by C. Miller, AHR, 82(Je 1977):777-8.

Brown, Sanborn C., ed. see Oleson, Alexandra, ed.

Brown, Weldon A. 'The Last Chopper: The Denouement of the
American Role in Vietnam, 1963-1975. Port Washington,
N.Y.: Kennikat Press, 1976. Rev. by R. P. Stebbins, AHR,
82(Apr 1977):474; J. H. Libby, MiA, 59(Jan 1977):65-6.

_____. Prelude to Disaster: The American Role in Vietnam,
1940-1963. n.p.: Kennikat Press, 1975. Rev. by J. H.
Libby, MiA, 59(Jan 1977):65-6.

Brown, William A. and Urgunge Onon, tr. History of the Mongolian People's Republic. Cambridge: Harvard U Press, 1976.
Rev. by C. R. Bawden, CQ, No. 71(Sep 1977):624-6.

Browne, Pat, ed. see Landrum, Larry N., ed.

Browne, Ray B., ed. see Landrum, Larry N., ed.

Brownell, Blaine A. The Urban Ethos in the South, 1920-1930.
Baton Rouge, La.: LSU Press, 1976. Rev. by L. W. Dor-
sett, AHR, 81(Dec 1976):1272-73; J. C. Klotter, ChOk, 54
(Win 1976-77):537-8; J. S. Ezell, FHQ, 55(Jan 1977):390-1;
T. Howell, LaH, 18(Sum 1977):352-3.

_____, and David R. Goldfield, eds. The City in Southern
History: The Growth of Urban Civilization in the South.
Port Washington, N.Y.: Kennikat, 1977. Rev. by Z. L.
Miller, AHR, 82(Je 1977):760-1; R. H. Haunton, GHQ, 51
(Sum 1977):201-2; E. J. Watts, JSH, 43(Aug 1977):479-81;
J. A. Williams, WVH, 38(Jl 1977):334-5.

Browning, Reed. The Duke of Newcastle. New Haven: Yale U
Press, 1975. Rev. by J. McKelvey, 82(Je 1977):634.

Browning, Robert. The Emperor Julian. Berkeley: U Cal Press,
1976. Rev. by J. Bregman, Historian, 39(May 1977):535-6;
A. E. Astin, History, 62(Je 1977):306-7.

Bruce, Dickson D., Jr. And They All Sang Hallelujah; Plain-folk
     Camp-meeting Religion, 1800-1845. Knoxville: U Tenn Press,
     1974. Rev. by M. Wittenberg, ETHJ, 15(Spr 1977):50-1.

Bruce-Mitford, Rupert. Recent Archaeological Excavations in Eu-
     rope. Boston: Routledge and Kegan Paul, 1975. Rev. by
     H. L. Thomas, Archaeology, 30(May 1977):210-2.

_____. The Sutton Hoo Ship-Burial. Vol. 1. London: British
     Museum Publ., 1975. Rev. by J. N. L. Myres, EHR, 92
     (Oct 1977):847-51; J. Graham-Campbell, Antiquity, 51(Mar
     1977):79-80.

Brucker, Gene. The Civic World of Early Renaissance Florence.
     Princeton: Prin U Press, 1977. Rev. by A. R. Lewis,
     History, 6(Oct 1977):21-2.

Brugge, David M. and Raymond Wilson. Administrative History,
     Canyon De Chelly National Monument, Arizona. Washington:
     National Park Service, 1974. Rev. by D. L. Parman, NMHR,
     52(Apr 1977):157-9.

Brugger, Bill. Contemporary China. New York: Barnes & Noble
     Books, 1977. Rev. by CurH, 73(Sep 1977):89.

Brugger, William. Democracy and Organisation in the Chinese In-
     dustrial Enterprise, 1948-1953. London: Contemporary China
     Institute Publications, Cam U Press, 1976. Rev. by A. G.
     Walder, JAS, 36(Aug 1977):732-3.

Brun, Ellen and Jacques Hersh. Socialist Korea: A Case Study in
     the Strategy of Economic Development. New York: Monthly
     Review Press, 1976. Rev. by K. Chao, JEH, 37(Sep 1977):
     811-2.

Bruner, Katherine Frost, ed. see Fairbank, John King, ed.

_____, ed. see Hart, Robert

Brunhouse, Robert L. Frans Blom, Maya Explorer. Albuquerque:
     U NM Press, 1976. Rev. by M. L. Fowler, AHR, 82(Oct
     1977):1104; T. P. Culbert, HAHR, 57(Aug 1977):559-60.

Bruns, Ilse see Westphal-Hellbusch, Sigrid

Brushwood, John S. The Spanish American Novel. A Twentieth
     Century Survey. Austin: UT Press, 1975. Rev. by G. M.
     Dorn, TAm, 33(Jan 1977):547-8.

Bryan, John Morrill. An Architectural History of the South Carol-
     ina College, 1801-1855. Columbia, S.C.: U South Carolina
     Press, n.d. Rev. by W. H. J. Thomas, SCHM, 78(Oct
     1977):319-20.

Bryant, Keith L., Jr. History of the Atchison, Topeka and Santa Fe Railway. New York: Macmillan, 1974. Rev. by R. S. Maxwell, ETHJ, 15(Spr 1977):66-7; H. R. Grant, ChOk, 55 (Sum 1977):242; R. G. Athearn, PHR, 46(Feb 1977):130-2.

Bryson, Thomas A. American Diplomatic Relations with the Middle East, 1784-1975: A Survey. Metuchen: Scarecrow Press, 1977. Rev. by P. J. Zingo, MiA, 59(Oct 1977):205-6.

Bryson, W. H. The Equity Side of the Exchequer: Its Jurisdiction, Administration, Procedures and Records. New York: Cam U Press, 1975. Rev. by C. Carlton, AHR, 82(Feb 1977):91-2.

Buchanan, A. Russell. Black Americans in World War II. Santa Barbara: ABC-CLIO Press, 1977. Rev. by M. M. Kranz, History, 6(Oct 1977):6.

Buchman, Randall, ed. The Historic Indians of Ohio. Columbus: Ohio Historical Society, 1976. Rev. in JISHS, 70(Aug 1977): 252-3.

Buchstab, Günter. Reichsstädte, Städtekurie und Westfälischer Friedenskongress: Zusammenhänge von Sozialstruktur, Rechtsstatus und Wirtschaftskraft. Münster: Verlag Aschendorff, 1976. Rev. by S. W. Rowan, AHR, 82(Je 1977):660-1.

Buck, James H., ed. The Modern Japanese Military System. Beverly Hills: Sage Publications, 1975. Rev. by G. O. Totten, III, JAS, 37(Nov 1977):139-40.

Buckland, Patrick. Irish Unionism, 1885-1922. Dublin: Gill and Macmillan, 1972-73. Rev. by A. MacIntyre, EHR, 92(Oct 1977):866-8.

Buckman, Peter. Lafayette. n.l.: Paddington Press, n.d. Rev. by J. Richardson, HTo, 27(Je 1977):408.

Buechel, Eugene see Anderson, John A.

Bueno, Patricia, comp. see Maciel, David, comp.

Buisseret, David see Pawson, Michael

Bullough, Vern L. Sexual Variance in Society and History. New York: Wiley, 1976. Rev. by M. Goodich, AHR, 82(Oct 1977): 921.

Bumgardner, Georgia B., ed. see Lowrance, Mason I., ed.

Bundgaard, J. A. Parthenon and the Mycenaen City on the Heights. Copenhagen: National Museum of Denmark, 1976. Rev. by H. Plommer, Antiquity, 51(Nov 1977):245-6.

Bunselmeyer, Robert E. The Cost of War, 1914-1919: British
Economic War Aims and the Origins of Reparation. Hamden,
Conn.: Archon Books, 1975. Rev. by A. W. Coats, AHR,
82(Feb 1977):107; J. M. McEwen, Historian, 39(May 1977):
548-9.

Bunzl, John. Klassenkampf in Der Diaspora: Geschichte Der
Judischen Arbeiterbewengung. Vienna: Europa Verlag, 1975.
Rev. by R. J. Crampton, History, 62(Feb 1977):161-2.

Burbank, Garin. When Farmers Voted Red: The Gospel of Socialism in the Oklahoma Countryside, 1910-1924. Westport, Conn.
& London: Greenwood Press, 1976. Rev. by C. H. Martin,
JSH, 43(Nov 1977):630-2; E. Pessen, History, 6(Nov/Dec
1977):26.

Burchfield, Joe D. Lord Kelvin and the Age of the Earth. New
York: Science History Publications, 1975. Rev. by S. F.
Cannon, AHR, 82(Oct 1977):971.

Burdick, Charles B. The Japanese Siege of Tsingtare: World War
I in Asia. Hamden, Conn.: Archon Books, 1976. Rev. by
R. Dingman, AHR, 82(Oct 1977):1051.

Burg, B. R. Richard Mather of Dorchester. Lexington: U Press
Ky, 1976. Rev. by R. Middlekauff, AHR, 82(Oct 1977):1059;
R. Thompson, JAmS, 11(Dec 1977):386-7.

Burg, David F. Chicago's White City of 1893. Lexington: U Press
Ky, 1976. Rev. by T. S. Hines, AHR, 82(Feb 1977):194-5;
M. G. Holli, JISHS, 70(May 1977):167-8.

Burge, Beverly see Studt, Ward B.

Burke, Edmund III. Prelude to Protectorate in Morocco: Precolonial Protest and Resistance, 1860-1912. Chicago: U Chi Press,
1977. Rev. by J. J. Cooke, AHR, 82(Oct 1977):1033-4.

Burke, S. M. Mainsprings of Indian and Pakistani Foreign Policies.
Minneapolis: U Minnesota Press, 1974. Rev. by M. Brecher,
JAAS, 12(Jan/Oct 1977):297-8.

Burnes, James MacGregor. Edward Kennedy and the Camelot Legacy. New York: Norton, 1976. Rev. by J. F. Heath, AHR,
82(Feb 1977):218.

Burns, P. L., ed. The Journals of J. W. W. Birch, First British
Resident to Perak, 1874-1875. Oxford: Ox U Press, 1976.
Rev. by I. G. Brown, History, 62(Je 1977):299; W. D. Mc-
Intyre, JAS, 36(May 1977):594-6.

_____, and C. D. Cowan, eds. Sir Frank Swettenham's Malayan
Journals, 1874-1876. Kuala Lumpur: Ox U Press, 1975.
Rev. by W. D. McIntyre, JAS, 36(May 1977):594-6.

Burns, Rex. Success in America: The Yeoman Dream and the Industrial Revolution. Amherst: U Mass Press, 1976. Rev. by R. Weiss, AHR, 82(Apr 1977):443.

Burns, Richard Dean and Edward M. Bennett, eds. Diplomats in Crisis: United States-Chinese-Japanese Relations, 1919-1941. Oxford: ABC-Clio Press, 1974. Rev. by I. Nish, History, 62(Je 1977):297.

Burrows, John, ed. Kenya: Into the Second Decade. Baltimore: JHU Press, 1975. Rev. by O. E. S., CurH, 72(Apr 1977): 177.

Burton, Anthony. Josiah Wedgwood, A Biography. n.l.: Andre Deutsch, n.d. Rev. by P. Holberton, HTo, 27(Jan 1977): 64-5.

Bury, J. P. T. Gambretta and the Making of the Third Republic. London: Longman, 1973. Rev. by R. Gibson, ESR, 7(Oct 1977):458-64.

Bury, T. T. Coloured Views on the Liverpool and Manchester Railway. n.l.: Aveyard, Broadbent, n.d. Rev. by P. Quennell, HTo, 27(Feb 1977):132-3.

Busch, Briton Cooper. Mudros to Lausanne: Britain's Frontier in West Asia, 1918-1923. Albany: SUNY Press, 1976. Rev. by R. Adelson, AHR, 82(Je 1977):641-2.

Bush, M. L. The Government Policy of Protector Somerset. Montreal: McGill-Queen's U Press, 1975. Rev. by L. B. Smith, AHR, 82(Feb 1977):93-4.

Bushman, Claudia L., ed. Morman Sisters: Women in Early Utah. Cambridge, Mass.: Emmeline Press, 1976. Rev. by P. S. Deemer, UHQ, 45(Sum 1977):312-3.

Bushman, Richard L. see Greene, Jack P.

Busse, Heribert. History of Persia under Qajar Rule: Translated from the Persian of Hasan-e Fasai's Farsnama-ye Naseri. New York and London: Col U Press, 1972. Rev. by J. R. Perry, JNES, 36(Jl 1977):239-40.

Butler, David L. Retrospect at a Tenth Anniversary: Southern Illinois University at Edwardsville. Carbondale: So Ill U Press, 1976. Rev. by B. Whitney, JISHS, 70(Aug 1977): 252.

Butler, Jeffrey, ed. see Thompson, Leonard

Butterfield, L. H., Marc Friedlaender and Mary Jo Kline, eds. The Book of Abigail and John: Selected Letters of the Adams

Family, 1762-1784. Cambridge, Mass.: Har U Press, 1975. Rev. by C. Berkin, WMQ, 34(Jan 1977):149-50.

————, ed. see also Friedlaender, Marc, ed.

Buttmann, Gunther. The Shadow of the Telescope: A Biography of John Herschel. Guildford: Butterworth Press, 1974. Rev. by E. G. Forbes, History, 62(Feb 1977):76-7.

Buxbaum, Melvin H. Benjamin Franklin and the Zealous Presbyterians. University Park: Penn State U Press, 1975. Rev. by C. C. Gelbach, PH, 45(Jan 1977):82-3.

Byrne, F. J., ed. see Moody, T. W., ed.

Byrnes, Robert F. Soviet-American Academic Exchanges, 1958-1975. Bloomington: Ind U Press, 1976. Rev. by A. Kassof, AHR, 82(Je 1977):773-4; A. Z. Rubinstein, CurH, 72(Apr 1977):176.

Cairncross, Sir Alec. Inflation, Growth and International Finance. Albany: State U New York Press, 1975. Rev. by M. Edelstein, JEH, 37(Je 1977):492-3.

Calder, Kenneth J. Britain and the Origins of the New Europe 1914-1918. Cambridge: Cam U Press, 1976. Rev. by W. V. Wallace, History, 62(Je 1977):343-4.

Calhoon, John C. The Papers of John C. Calhoon. Volume IX, 1824-1825. Ed. by W. Edwin Hemphill. Columbia, S.C.: U South Carolina Press, 1976. Rev. by D. Rison, SCHM, 78(Jl 1977):244.

Calhoon, Robert McCluer. The Loyalists in Revolutionary America, 1760-1781. New York: Harcourt Brace & Jovanovich, 1973. Rev. by J. M. Nelson, HJ, 20(No. 3, 1977):741-9.

Calhoun, Daniel F. The United Front: The TUC and the Russians, 1923-1928. New York: Cam U Press, 1976. Rev. by R. K. Debo, AHR, 82(Apr 1977):404.

Calhoun, John C. The Papers of John C. Calhoun, 1824-1825, Vol. IX. Ed. by W. Edwin Hemphill. Columbia, S.C.: U South Carolina Press, 1976. Rev. by J. E. Simpson, GHQ, 51 (Win 1977):363-4.

Calhoun, Richard J., ed. see Lander, Ernest M., Jr., ed.

Callahan, Helen see Rowland, A. Ray

Cambell, Charles S. The Transformation of American Foreign Relations, 1865-1900. New York: Harper and Row, 1976. Rev. by B. Perkins, AHR, 82(Apr 1977):455-6.

45 CAMERANI

Camerani, Sergio, ed. Carteggi di Bettino Ricasoli. Vol. 26. 1
gennaio 1870 - 31 dicembre 1872. Rome: Instituto Storico
Italiano per l'Età Moderna e Contemporanea, 1974. Rev. by
E. P. Noether, AHR, 82(Oct 1977):1011-12.

Caminos, Ricardo A. The New Kingdom Temples of Buhen. London: Egypt Exploration Society, 1974. Rev. by B. Williams,
JNES, 36(Oct 1977):308-10.

Cammarosano, Paolo. La Famiglia de Berardengi: Contributo alla
storia della società senese nei secoli XI-XIII. Spoleto: Centro Italiano di Studi sull'Alto Medioevo, 1974. Rev. by D. O.
Hughes, AHR, 82(Je 1977):621-2.

Campbell, F. Gregory. Confrontation in Central Europe: Weimar
Germany and Czechoslovakia. Chicago: U Chi Press, 1975.
Rev. by D. Horna-Perman, AHR, 82(Feb 1977):145-6.

Campbell, John. Lloyd George. The Goat in the Wilderness, 1922-
1931. n.l.: Cape, n.d. Rev. by J. Richardson, HTo, 27
(Sep 1977):617-20.

Campbell, Mavis Christin. The Dynamics of Change in a Slave Society: A Sociopolitical History of the Free Coloreds of Jamaica,
1800-1865. Rutherford, N.J.: Fairleigh Dickinson U Press,
1976. Rev. by F. W. Knight, AHR, 82(Apr 1977):479.

Campion, Harvey. The New Transkei. Sandton, South Africa:
Valiant, 1976. Rev. by R. Blausten, AfAf, 76(Jl 1977):416-
18.

Camus, Raoul F. Military Music of the American Revolution. Chapel Hill: U NC Press, 1976. Rev. by F. R. Rossiter, AHR,
82(Apr 1977):437; R. B. Harwell, JSH, 43(May 1977):286-7;
J. W. Molinar, WMQ, 34(Jl 1977):503-4.

Canadian Historic Sites: Occasional Papers in Archaeology and History, No. 14. Ottawa: Ministry of Indian and Northern Affairs, 1975. Rev. by J. Parker, WMH, 60(Spr 1977):237-8.

Cancellieri, Girolamo Ganucci. Pistoia nell XIII secolo: Saggio
storico sulla stirpe dei Cancellieri di Pistoia. Florence: Leo
S. Olschki, 1975. Rev. by D. Herlihy, AHR, 82(Je 1977):
622.

Canciani, Fulvio. Corpus Vasorum Antiquorum, Italy LV, Tarquinia,
Museo Archeologico Nazionale III. Rome: Bretschneider, 1974.
Rev. by E. E. Bell, AJA, 81(Win 1977):121-2.

Canedo, Lino Gomez. La Provincia Franciscana de Santa Cruz de
Caracas. Cuerpo de documentos para su historia 1513-1837.
Caracas: Biblioteca de la Academia Nacional de la Historia.,
1974. Rev. by D. Ramos, TAm, 33(Jan 1977):563-5.

Cannistraro, Philip F., et al, ed. Poland and the Coming of the Second World War: The Diplomatic Papers of A. J. Drexel Biddle, Jr., United States Ambassador to Poland, 1937-1939. Columbus: Ohio St U Press, 1976. Rev. by E. D. Wynot, Jr., AHR, 82(Apr 1977):398-9.

Cannistraro, Philip V. La fabbrica del consenso: Fascismo e mass media. Bari: Laterza, 1975. Rev. by R. Rosengarten, AHR, 82(Apr 1977):388-9.

Canny, Nicholas P. The Elizabethan Conquest of Ireland: A Pattern Established, 1565-76. New York: Barnes and Noble, 1976. Rev. by D. R. Quinn, AHR, 82(Oct 1977):957-8; B. Bradshaw, HJ, 20(No. 1, 1977):258-9; A. L. Rowse, HTo, 27(Jl 1977):476-8.

Canovan, Margaret. The Political Thought of Hannah Arendt. London: Dent, 1974. Rev. by G. P. Heather, ESR, 7(Apr 1977): 240-4.

Cappon, Lester J., et al, ed. Atlas of Early American History: The Revolutionary Era, 1760-1790. Princeton: Prin U Press, 1976. Rev. by J. R. Alden, AHR, 82(Apr 1977):432; R. M. Judd, VH, 45(Fall 1977):247-9; C. Earle, WMQ, 34(Apr 1977): 310-2.

Caputo, Philip. A Rumor of War. n.l.: Holt, Rinehart, & Winston, n.d. Rev. by W. J. Bennett, Comm, 64(Oct 1977): 86-8.

Caraman, Philip. The Lost Paradise: The Jesuit Republic in South America. New York: Seabury Press, 1976. Rev. by C. J. Fleener, AHR, 82(Oct 1977):1105-6; J. H. Williams, TAm, 34(Jl 1977):149-50.

Carbelli, Giancarlo. Tolandiana Materiali bibliografici per lo studio dell'opera e della fortuna di John Toland (1670-1722). Florence: La Nuova Italia, 1975. Rev. by J. Redwood, EHR, 92(Oct 1977):906-7.

Carbonell, Charles-Olivier. Histoire et Historiens: Une mutation idéologique des historiens francais, 1865-1885. Toulouse: Privat Editeur, 1976. Rev. by W. R. Keylor, JMH, 49(Sep 1977):481-2.

Carey, George G. A Sailor's Songbag: An American Rebel in an English Prison, 1777-1779. Amherst: U Mass Press, 1976. Rev. by J. W. Molinar, WMQ, 34(Jl 1977):503-4.

Carleton, Mark T., Perry H. Howard, and Joseph B. Parker, eds. Readings in Louisiana Politics. Baton Rouge: M. J. Schott, 18(Win 1977):124-5.

Carr, Barry. El Movimiento obrero y la Política en México, 1910-1929. Mexico: SepSetentas, 1976. Rev. by R. E. Ruiz, HAHR, 57(Aug 1977):538-9.

Carr, Lois Green, ed. see Land, Aubrey C., ed.

Carr, Raymond. English Fox Hunting: A History. London: Weidenfeld and Nicolson, 1976. Rev. by F. M. L. Thompson, History, 62(Je 1977):330-2.

Carrier, Fred J. The Third World Revolution. Amsterdam: B. R. Gruner, 1976. Rev. by H. S. Ferns, History, 62(Feb 1977):263.

Carriker, Eleanor R., ed. see Baldwin, Alice Blackwood

_____, ed. see Carriker, Robert C., ed.

Carriker, Robert C., ed. and Eleanor R. Carriker. An Army Wife on the Frontier: The Memoirs of Alice Blackwood Baldwin, 1867-1877. Salt Lake City: U Utah Library, 1975. Rev. by J. E. Fell, Jr., PHR, 46(Aug 1977):503-4; B. D. Blumell, PNQ, 68(Jl 1977):144-5.

_____, ed. see also Baldwin, Alice Blackwood

Carrington, Ulrich S., ed. see Sealsfield, Charles

Carrion, Benjamin. José Carlos Mariátegui: El Precursor, el anticipador, el suscitador. Mexico: SepSetentas, 1976. Rev. by J. Chavarria, HAHR, 57(May 1977):363-4.

Carroll, Berenice A., ed. Liberating Women's History: Theoretical and Critical Essays. Urbana, Illinois: U Ill Press, 1976. Rev. by M. J. Oates, JEH, 37(Je 1977):494.

Carroll, Charles. The Journal of Charles Carroll of Carrollton. Ed. by Allan S. Everest. Fort Ticonderoga, N.Y.: Champlain-Upper Hudson Bicentennial Committee, 1976. Rev. by M. Wade, VH, 45(Spr 1977):120-2.

Carroll, John M., ed. The Papers of the Order of Indian Wars. Fort Collins, Colo.: Old Army Press, 1975. Rev. by R. H. Ellis, AHR, 82(Feb 1977):193.

_____, and Lawrence A. Frost, eds. Private Theodore Ewert's Diary of the Black Hills Expedition of 1874. Piscataway, New Jersey: Consultant Resources, Inc., 1976. Rev. by D. A. Bishop, WHQ, 8(Oct 1977):463.

Carson, Ciaran. The New Estate. Belfast: Blackstaff Press, 1976. Rev. by S. M. Bogorad, E-1, 12(Fall 1977):100-8.

Carson, Jane. Bacon's Rebellion, 1676-1976. Jamestown, Va.:
Jamestown Foundation, 1976. Rev. by R. B. Davis, VMHB,
85(Jan 1977):101-3.

Carsten, F. L. Revolution in Central Europe, 1918-1919. London:
Temple Smith, 1972. Rev. by F. B. M. Fowkes, ESR, 7
(Jan 1977):115-17.

Carter, Edward C., II, Robert Forster, and Joseph N. Moody, eds.
Enterprise and Entrepreneurs in Nineteenth- and Twentieth-
Century France. Baltimore: JHU Press, 1976. Rev. by R.
W. Reichert, Historian, 39(May 1977):553-5; M. S. Smith,
AHR, 82(Apr 1977):372; R. Roehl, JEH, 37(Sep 1977):781-2.

Carter, Hilda R. and John R. Jenswold. The University of Wis-
consin-Eau Claire, A History, 1916-1976. Eau Claire, Wisconsin: Eau Claire Foundation, 1976. Rev. by R. E. Bel-
ding, Al, 44(Fall 1977):149-50.

Carter, Joseph Coleman. The Sculpture of Taras. Philadelphia:
The American Philosophical Society, 1975. Rev. by A. Hermann, AJA, (Sum 1977):401-3.

Carter, Paul A. Another Part of the Twenties. New York: Columbia U Press, 1977. Rev. by W. French, AS, 18(Fall
1977):110; D. Snowman, JAmS, 11(Dec 1977):420-1.

Carter, Samuel III. Cherokee Sunset: A Nation Betrayed. A Narrative of Travail and Triumph, Persecution and Exile. Garden City, N.Y.: Doubleday, 1976. Rev. by T. A. Zwink,
ArkHQ, 36(Aut 1977):291-2; J. E. Kleber, ChOk, 55(Spr
1977):107-8; P. B. McGuigan, JOW, 16(Jl 1977):91-2; B. W.
Sheehan, JSH, 43(May 1977):398-9.

Cartwright, Joseph H. The Triumph of Jim Crow: Tennessee
Race Relations in the 1880s. Knoxville: U Tenn Press, 1976.
Rev. by G. B. McKinney, JSH, 43(Nov 1977):625-7.

Caruthers, J. Wade. Octavius Brooks Frothingham: Gentle Radical.
University: U Alabama, 1977. Rev. by J. P. Walsh, History, 6(Nov/Dec 1977):28.

Casanova, Antonio G. Matteotti: Una vita per il socialismo. Milan:
Casa Ed. Bompiani, 1974. Rev. by C. F. Dellzell, JMH, 49
(Je 1977):321-6.

Casbier, Dennis G., comp. The Mojave Road in Newspapers. Nor-
co, California: Tales of the Mojave Road Publishing Co.,
1976. Rev. by D. L. Thrapp, A&W, 19(Sum 1977):171-73.

Case, Lynn M. Edouard Thouvenel et la diplomatie du Second Empire. Paris: Editions A. Pedone, n.d. Rev. by W. F.
Spencer, AHR, 82(Je 1977):652-3.

Casey, William J. Where and How the War Was Fought: An Arm-
    chair Tour of the American Revolution. New York: William
    Morrow and Co. , 1976. Rev. by F. S. Klein, AHI, 11(Jan
    1977):49.

Cashin, Edward J. A History of Augusta College. Augusta, Ga.:
    Augusta College Press, 1976. Rev. by J. C. Stephens, GHQ,
    51(Spr 1977):96-97.

Cassara, Ernest. The Enlightenment in America. Boston: Twayne,
    1975. Rev. by C. W. Akers, WMQ, 34(Jan 1977):176-7.

Cassinelli, C. W. Total Revolution: A Comparative Study of Ger-
    many under Hitler, the Soviet Union under Stalin, and China
    under Mao. Santa Barbara, Calif.: Clio Books, 1976. Rev.
    by J. W. Cranston, AHR, 82(Apr 1977):337.

Castillo, Edward D. see Heizer, Robert F.

Cataldi, Maria see Boitani, Francesca

Catlin, George. Letters and Notes on the North American Indians.
    New York: Clarkson N. Potter, 1976. Rev. by W. E. Wash-
    burn, AHR, 81(Dec 1976):1243.

Catton, Bruce. Michigan: A Bicentennial History. New York:
    Norton, 1976. Rev. by R. D. Averitt, III, MichH, 61(Fall
    1977):251-3.

Caughey, John and LaRee Caughey, ed. Los Angeles: Biography
    of a City. Los Angeles: U Cal Press, 1976. Rev. by K.
    A. Rowley, JAmS, 11(Dec 1977):387-8; R. W. Barsness,
    WHQ, 8(Jl 1977):338-9.

Caughey, LaRee see Caughey, John

Caukwell, T. and J. M. Smith. World Encyclopedia of Film. Lon-
    don: Studio Vista, 1972. Rev. by D. J. Wenden, EHR, 92
    (Oct 1977):930-2.

Cavallie, James. Fran fred till krig: De finansiella problemen
    kring krigsutbrottet or 1700. Uppsala: Universitetsbiblio-
    teket Uppsala, 1975. Rev. by H. A. Barton, AHR, 82(Je
    1977):658.

Caves, Richard E. and Masu Uekusa. Industrial Organization in
    Japan. Washington, D.C.: The Brookings Institution, 1976.
    Rev. by E. Rotwein, JEH, 37(Sep 1977):782-4.

Cecco, Marcello de. Money and Empire: The International Gold
    Standard, 1890-1914. Totowa, N.J.: Rowman & Littlefield,
    1975. Rev. by A. J. Schwartz, JMH, 49(Sep 1977):490-1.

Cecil, Lamar. The German Diplomatic Service, 1871-1914. Princeton, N.J.: Prin U Press, 1976. Rev. by H. H. Herwig, AHR, 82(Oct 1977):1002-3.

Cecil, Robert. Hitler's Decision to Invade Russia, 1941. London: Davis-Poynter, 1975. Rev. by B. van Everen, AHR, 82(Apr 1977):381; M. L. Dockrill, History, 62(Feb. 1977):168.

Censer, Jack Richard. Prelude to Power: The Parisian Radical Press, 1789-1791. Baltimore: JHU Press, 1976. Rev. by I. Woloch, AHR, 82(Oct 1977):981-2; G. T. Pendleton, JEH, 37(Sep 1977):784-5.

The Central Records of the Church of England. A Report and Survey Presented to the Pilgrim and Radcliffe Trustees. London: CIO Publishing, 1976. Rev. by V. N. Bellamy, Am Arc, 40(Jan 1977):88-9.

Centre National de la Recherche Scientifique. La libération de la France: Actes du Colloque International tenu à Paris du 28 au 31 octobre 1974. Paris: Centre National de la Recherche Scientifique, 1976. Rev. by S. P. Kramer, AHR, 82(Oct 1977):986-7.

Cervenka, Z., ed. Landlocked Countries of Africa. Uppsala: Scandinavian Institute of African Studies, 1973. Rev. by S. C. Nolutshungu, AfAf, 76(Jan 1977):113.

Chadwick, John. The Mycenaean World. New York: Cam U Press, 1976. Rev. by E. Vermeule, AHR, 82(Apr 1977):338-9; M. L. Lang, AJA, 81(Win 1977):116-7.

Chadwick, Nora. The British Heroic Age. Cardiff: U Wales Press, 1976. Rev. by W. Davies, History, 62(Je 1977): 307-8.

Chae-jin Lee see Dae-Sook Suh

Chaffee, Dorcas, ed. see Goodwin, Del

Chakravarti, Anand. Contradiction and Change: Emerging Patterns of Authority in a Rajasthan Village. Delhi: Ox U Press, 1976. Rev. by B. Michie, JAS, 36(Feb 1977):377-8.

Chalfont, Alun. Montgomery of Alamein. New York: Atheneum, 1976. Rev. by R. Higham, AHR, 82(Je 1977):644-5.

Chamberlin, J. E. The Harrowing of Eden: White Attitudes Toward Native Americans. New York: Seabury Press, 1975. Rev. by G. B. Nash, AHR, 82(Feb 1977):206; C. J. Jaenen, CHR, 58(Mar 1977):64-8; L. O. Saum, PHR, 46(May 1977): 284-5.

Chametzky, Jules. From the Ghetto: The Fiction of Abraham Cahan. Amherst: U Massachusetts Press, 1977. Rev. by J. Zanger, AS, 18(Fall 1977):108.

Champagne, Roger J. Alexander McDougall and the American Revolution in New York. Schenectady, N.Y.: Union College Press, 1975. Rev. by B. Mason, WMH, 60(Sum 1977):341-2.

Chandler, David. The Art of Warfare in the Age of Marlborough. London: Batsford, 1976. Rev. by D. McKay, History, 62 (Feb 1977):130-1.

Chang, I-Lok see Silverstein, Martin Elliot

Chang, K. C. Early Chinese Civilization: Anthropological Perspectives. Cambridge, Mass.: Har U Press, 1976. Rev. by N. T. Price, AgH, 51(Jl 1977):600-2; P. Wheatley, JAS, 36(May 1977):543-5.

Chaplin, David, ed. Peruvian Nationalism: A Corporatist Revolution. New Brunswick, N.J.: Transaction Books, 1976. Rev. by P. F. Klaren, HAHR, 57(May 1977):362-3.

_____. Revolution. New Brunswick, N.J.: Transaction Books, 1976. Rev. by O.E.S., CurH, 72(Feb 1977):79.

Chapman, Hester. Four Fine Gentlemen. n.l.: Constable, n.d. Rev. by M. Ashley, HTo, 27(Oct 1977):687-8.

Chapman, John Gresham. La Construcción del Ferrocarril Mexicano (1837-1880). Mexico: SepSetentas, 1975. Rev. by J. Coatsworth, HAHR, 57(Feb 1977):129-30.

Charbonneau, Hubert. Vie et mort de nos ancêtres: Etude démographique. Montréal: Les Presses de l'Université de Montréal, 1975. Rev. by R. V. Wells, WMQ, 34(Jl 1977):489-91.

Chard, Chester S. Northeast Asia in Prehistory. Madison: U Wis Press, 1974. Rev. by R. K. Beardsley, JAS, 36(May 1977):561-4.

Chartier, Roger, Marie-Madeleine Compère, and Dominique Julia. L'education en France du XVIe au XVIIIe siècle. Paris: Societe d'edition d'enseignement superieur, 1976. Rev. by R. R. Palmer, JMH, 49(Je 1977):315-8; R. L. Kagan, AHR, 82(Je 1977):648.

Chase, Allan. The Legacy of Malthus: The Social Costs of the New Scientific Racism. New York: Knopf, 1977. Rev. by L. J. Friedman, AHR, 82(Oct 1977):923.

Chaves, Jonathan. Heaven My Blanket, Earth My Pillow: Poems

CHAVES   52

from Sung Dynasty China. New York: Weatherhill, 1975.
Rev. by R. J. Lynn, JAS, 36(May 1977):551-4.

_____. Mei Yao-ch'en and the Development of Early Sung Poe-
try. New York: Columbia U Press, 1976. Rev. by R. J.
Lynn, JAS, 36(May 1977):551-4.

Checkland, S. G. Scottish Banking: A History, 1695-1973. Glasgow: Collins Publishers, 1975. Rev. by J. P. Judd, AHR,
82(Feb 1977):112; R. S. Sayers, BH, 19(Jan 1977):93-4.

Chen, Chi-yun. Hsün Yüeh (A.D. 148-209): The Life and Reflec-
tions of an Early Medieval Confucian. New York: Cam U
Press, 1975. Rev. by Ying-shi Yu, AHR, 82(Je 1977):718;
A. E. Dien, JAS, 37(Nov 1977):111-2.

Chen, Theodore Hsi-en. The Maoist Educational Revolution. New
York: Praeger, 1974. Rev. by S. L. Shirk, CQ, No. 70
(Je 1977):428-30.

Cheney, Cora. Vermont: The State with the Storybook Past.
Brattleboro, Vt.: Stephen Greene Press, 1976. Rev. by E.
J. Urie, VH, 45(Win 1977):44-5.

Cheng, Chu-yuan. China's Petroleum Industry: Output Growth and
Export Potential. New York: Praeger, 1976. Rev. by J.
Williams, CQ, No. 69(Mar 1977):164-6.

Chesnutt, David R., ed. see Rogers, George C., Jr., ed.

Chesnutt, Margaret. Studies in the Short Stories of William Carleton. Göteborg, Sweden: Acta Universitatis Gothoburgensis,
1976. Rev. by D. O. Cathasaigh, E-1, 12(Win 1977):142-3.

Chester, Edward W. Sectionalism, Politics and American Diplomacy. Metuchen, N.J.: Scarecrow Press, 1975. Rev. by
P. S. Holbo, PNQ, 68(Jan 1977):33-4.

Chester, Sir Norman. The Nationalisation of British Industry
1945-51. London: HMSO, 1975. Rev. by B. W. E. Alford,
History, 62(Feb 1977):151-2.

Cheswick Center. Underused Church Properties--a Variety of Sol-
utions. Cambridge; Cheswick Center, 1975. Rev. by G.
Kramer, CHIQ, 50(Sum 1977):94-5.

Chevigny, Bell Gale. The Woman and the Myth: Margaret Fuller's
Life and Writings. Old Westbury, N.Y.: Feminist Press,
1977. Rev. by M. V. Allen, AS, 18(Fall 1977):109.

Ch'i, Hsi-sheng. Warlord Politics in China, 1916-1928. Stanford:
Stan U Press, 1976. Rev. by D. G. Gillin, JAS, 36(May
1977):547-8.

Chiapelli, Fredi, ed. First Images of America: The Impact of the
    New World on the Old. Berkeley: U Cal Press, 1976. Rev.
    by J. L. Stokesbury, AHI, 11(Jan 1977):50; J. J. Lang, AHR,
    82(Je 1977):724-6; M. Grennhalgh, HTo, 27(Apr 1977):265-6;
    J. R. Hebert, WHQ, 8(Apr 1977):207-8.

Chickering, Roger. Imperial Germany and a World Without War:
    The Peace Movement and German Society, 1892-1914. Lon-
    don: Prin U Press, 1975. Rev. by V. R. Berghahn, His-
    tory, 62(Feb 1977):163-4.

Chierichetti, David. Hollywood Costume Design. New York:
    Crown Publishers, 1976. Rev. by A. Hollander, GR, 31(Fall
    1977):712-7.

Childs, Edmund. William Caxton: A Portrait in a Background.
    London: Northwood Publications, 1976. Rev. by N. Orme,
    History, 62(Je 1977):313.

Childs, John. The Army of Charles II. Buffalo: U Tor Press,
    1976. Rev. by J. R. Dull, AHR, 82(Feb 1977):97-8; J. S.
    Morrill, HJ, 20(No. 4, 1977):961-70; D. Allen, History, 62
    (Feb 1977):122-3.

Chinn, George M. Kentucky: Settlement and Statehood, 1750-1800.
    Frankfort: Kentucky Historical Society, 1975. Rev. by J.
    Walton, FCHQ, 51(Jan 1977):49-51.

Chirenje, J. Mutero. A History of Northern Botswana, 1850-1910.
    Cranbury, N.J.: Associated University Presses, 1977. Rev.
    by F. N. Okoye, HT, 10(Aug 1977):634-5.

Chirot, Daniel. Social Change in a Peripheral Society: The Crea-
    tion of a Balkan Colony. New York: Academic Press, 1976.
    Rev. by L. Olson, AHR, 82(Oct 1977):1018-9.

Chisholm Archibald H. T. The First Kuwait Oil Concession Agree-
    ment: A Record of Negotiations, 1911-34. London: Frank
    Cass, 1975. Rev. by R. W. Hidy, JEH, 37(Je 1977):494-5.

Chitnis, Anand C. The Scottish Enlightenment: A Social History.
    Totowa, N.J.: Rowman and Littlefield, 1976. Rev. by A.
    Donovan, AHR, 82(Oct 1977):976.

Chittick, H. Neville. Kilwa: An Islamic Trading City on the East
    African Coast. 2 vols. Nairobi: British Institute in Eastern
    Africa, 1974. Rev. by G. S. P. Freeman-Grenville, AHR,
    82(Apr 1977):407-8; T. Shaw, Antiquity, 51(Nov 1977):252-5.

_____, and Robert I. Rotberg, ed. East Africa and the Orient:
    Cultural Synthesis in Pre-Colonial Times. New York: Africana
    Publishing Co., 1975. Rev. by T. Shaw, Antiquity, 51(Nov
    1977):252-5; P. S. Garlake, History, 62(Je 1977):274-5.

Choi, C. Y. Chinese Migration and Settlement in Australia. Portland, Ore.: International Scholarly Book Service, 1975. Rev. by E. Wickberg, AHR, 82(Oct 1977):1056-7; W. E. Willmott, CQ, 70(Je 1977):432-4.

Chomsky, Noam. The Arabs in Israel. New York: Monthly Review Press, 1976. Rev. by A. Z. Rubinstein, CurH, 72(Jan 1977):28.

Choudhury, G. W. India, Pakistan, Bangladesh and the Major Powers: Politics of a Divided Subcontinent. New York: the Free Press, 1975. Rev. by R. LaPorte, Jr., JAS, 36(May 1977): 586-7.

_____. The Last Days of United Pakistan. Bloomington: Ind U Press, 1975. Rev. by K. B. Sayeed, AHR, 82(Oct 1977): 1054-5.

Christie, Ian R. and Benjamin W. Labaree. Empire or Independence 1760-1776: A British-American Dialogue on the Coming of the American Independence. Oxford: Phaidon Press, 1976. Rev. by P. D. G. Thomas, EHR, 92(Oct 1977):912-3; J. J. Hecht, NEQ, 50(Mar 1977):186-9; J. Sainsbury, WMQ, 34(Oct 1977): 657-9.

Christopher, Maurice. Black Americans in Congress. New York: Thomas Y. Crowell, 1976. Rev. by C. Vincent, JNH, 62(Jl 1977):304-6.

Christopoulos, George A. and John C. Bastias, ed. The Archaic Period. History of the Hellenic World, Vol. 2. Athens, 1975. Rev. by A. Andrewes, Antiquity, 51(Nov 1977):249-51.

Chuan, Han-Sheng and Richard A. Kraus. Mid-Ch'ing Rice Markets and Trade: An Essay in Price History. Cambridge: Har U Press, 1975. Rev. by R. P. Gardella, JAS, 36(Aug 1977): 722-3.

Chung, William K. see Denison, Edward F.

Church, Robert L. and Michael W. Sedlak. Education in the United States: An Interpretive History. New York: Free Press, 1976. Rev. by M. Lazerson, AHR, 82(Feb 1977):170; P. A. Kalisch, JSH, 43(May 1977):327-8; W. J. Reese, PNQ, 58(Jl 1977):146.

Church, William F. Louis XIV in Historical Thought: From Voltaire to the Annales School. New York: Norton, 1975. Rev. by R. Mettam, History, 62(Feb 1977):127-9.

_____. Richelieu and Reason of State. Princeton: Princeton U Press, 1973. Rev. by J. H. Shennan, ESR, 7(Oct 1977):453-4.

Chūsei, Suzuki. Chūgoku shi ni okeru kakumei to shūkyo (Revolution
and religion in Chinese History). Tokyo: Tokyo U Press,
1974. Rev. by Ch'en Yung-fa, JAS, 36(Feb 1977):339-42.

Chye, Goh Thean. Modern Chinese Literature in Malaysia and
Singapore: A Classified Bibliography of Books in Chinese.
Kuala Lumpur: University of Malaya Chinese Department,
1975. Rev. by W. Dolby, CQ, No. 70(Je 1977):438-9.

Cipolla, Carlo M. Before the Industrial Revolution: European
Society and Economy 1000-1700. London: Methuen, 1976.
Rev. by R. H. Hilton, History, 62(Feb 1977):108-9; C. H.
Wilson, Historian, 39(May 1977):538-9; E. L. Jones, JEH,
37(Je 1977):495-6.

_____, ed. The Fontana Economic History of Europe. Vol. III:
The Industrial Revolution. Vol. IV: The Emergence of Industrial Societies. London: Collins, 1973. Rev. by C. Trebilcock, HJ, 20(No. 3, 1977):751-60; D. F. Good, JEH, 37(Je
1977):497-9.

_____. Public Health and the Medical Profession in the Renais-
sance. New York: Cam U Press, 1976. Rev. by D. G.
Bates, AHR, 82(Feb 1977):138; G. Packer, History, 62(Feb
1977):110.

Clapham, Christopher. Liberia and Sierra Leone: An Essay in Comparative Politics. Cambridge U Press, n.d. Rev. by R. Jefferies, AfAf, 76(Apr 1977):265-7; C. Fyfe, AHR, 82(Je 1977):
710-1.

Clark, Malcolm, Jr., ed. Pharisee Among Philistines: The Diary
of Judge Matthew P. Deady, 1871-1892. Portland: Oregon
Historical Society, 1975. Rev. by T. D. Morris, PNQ, 68
(Jl 1977):145-6.

Clark, Norman H. Deliver Us From Evil: An Interpretation of
American Prohibition. New York: Norton, 1976. Rev. by
K. A. Kerr, AHR, 82(Je 1977):761-2.

_____. Washington: A Bicentennial History. New York: Nor-
ton and Nashville: American Association for State and Local
History, 1976. Rev. by C. B. Coulter, WHQ, 8(Jl 1977):
335.

Clark, Patricia P., ed. see Graf, LeRoy P., ed.

_____, ed. see Jackson, Andrew, ed.

Clark, Peggy J., ed. see Laurens, Henry, ed.

_____, ed. see Rogers, George C., Jr., ed.

Clark, Peter and Paul Slack. English Towns in Transition, 1500-1700. New York: Ox U Press, 1976. Rev. by R. M. Berger, JEH, 37(Sep 1977):785-6.

Clark, Thomas D., ed. The Great American Frontier: A Story of Western Pioneering. Indianapolis: Bobbs-Merrill, 1975. Rev. by R. H. Hurt, AgH, 51(Jan 1977):267-8.

_____, ed. Off at Sunrise: The Overland Journal of Charles Glass Gray. San Marino: Huntington Library, 1976. Rev. by J. J. Rawls, CHQ, 56(Sum 1977):183; F. H. Hayes, WHQ, 8(Oct 1977):457-8.

Clark, Truman R. Puerto Rico and the United States, 1917-1933. n.l.: U Pitt, 1975. Rev. by A. C. Wilgus, PHR, 46(Feb 1977):142-3.

Clarke, Austin. Collected Poems. Dublin: Dolmen Press, 1974. Rev. by R. F. Garratt, E-1, 12(Win 1977):133-8.

_____. Selected Poems. Ed. by Thomas Kinsella. Winston-Salem, N.C.: Wake Forest U Press, 1976. Rev. by R. F. Garratt, E-1, 12(Win 1977):133-8.

Clarke, Colin G. Kingston, Jamaica: Urban Development and Social Change, 1692-1962. Berkeley: U Cal Press, 1976. Rev. by E. L. Farley, AHR, 82(Feb 1977): 227-8; R. C. Batie, JEH, 37(Sep 1977):786-7.

Clarkson, Leslie. Death, Disease and Famine in Pre-Industrial England. Dublin: Gill and Macmillan, 1975. Rev. by P. Slack, History, 62(Feb 1977):112.

Claudin, Fernando. The Communist Movement: From Comintern to Cominform. Part I & II. New York: Monthly Review Press, 1976. Rev. by S. M. Poppel, AHR, 82(Feb 1977): 65-6; M. Perrie, History, 62(Feb 1977):167; R. Wohl, JMH, 49(Je 1977):305-7.

_____, et al. Problemi di storia dell'Internazionale Comunista (1919-1939). Turin: Fondazione Luigi Einaudi, 1974. Rev. by J. M. Cammett, AHR, 82(Apr 1977):350-1.

Clausewitz, Carl von. On War. Princeton: Prin U Press, 1976. Rev. by M. M. Lowenthal, AHR, 82(Je 1977):608-9.

Clay, Grady. Close-Up: How to Read the American City. New York: Praeger, 1973. Rev. by C. E. Kramer, FCHQ, 51 (Jl 1977):284-6.

Cleaveland, George J., et al. Up from Independence: The Episcopal Church in Virginia. Norfolk: Interdiocesan Bicentennial Committee of the Virginias, 1976. Rev. by S. A. Riggs, VMHB, 85(Jan 1977):106-7.

Cleaver, Charles Grinnell. Japanese and Americans: Cultural Parallels and Paradoxes. Minneapolis: U Minn Press, 1976. Rev.
by J. H. Bailey, JAS, 36(Aug 1977):763-4.

Cleaves, Peter S. Bureaucratic Politics and Administration in Chile.
Berkeley: U Cal Press, 1974. Rev. by P. Peppe, HAHR, 57
(May 1977):360-1; D. Skidmore, JLAS, 9(May 1977):172-3.

Clecak, Peter. Crooked Paths: Reflections on Socialism, Conservatism, and the Welfare State. New York: Harper & Row,
n.d. Rev. by S. Miller, Comm, 63(Mar 1977):94-6.

Cleland, Charles E., ed. Cultural Change and Continuity: Essays
in Honor of James Bennett Griffin. New York: Academic
Press, 1976. Rev. by J. R. Halsey, MichH, 61(Fall 1977):
254-6.

_____, ed. For the Director: Research Essays in Honor of
James B. Griffin. Ann Arbor: University of Michigan, 1977.
Rev. by J. R. Halsey, MichH, 61(Fall 1977):254-6.

Cleland, Robert Glass. The Reckless Breed of Men: The Trappers
and Fur Traders of the Southwest. Albuquerque: U NM Press,
1976. Rev. by T. E. Chavez, ChOk, 55(Spr 1977):104.

Clemoes, P., ed. Anglo-Saxon England, IV. Cambridge: Cam U
Press, 1975. Rev. by J. L. Nelson, History, 62(Feb 1977):
98.

Cline, Platt. They Came to the Mountain: The Story of Flagstaff's
Beginnings. Flagstaff, Arizona: Northland Press, 1976. Rev.
by B. Luckingham, A&W, 19(Sum 1977):180-82.

Clinton, Kevin. The Sacred Officials of the Eleusinian Mysteries.
Philadelphia: American Philosophical Society, 1974. Rev. by
R. O. Hubbe, AHR, 82(Feb 1977):68; M. H. Jameson, AJA,
81(Spr 1977):248-50.

Clissold, Stephen. The Barbary Slaves. n.l.: Paul Elek, n.d.
Rev. by Alan Hodge, HTo, 27(May 1977):342-3.

Clogg, Richard, ed. see Auty, Phyllis, ed.

Clough, Cecil, H., ed. Cultural Aspects of the Italian Renaissance:
Essays in Honour of Paul Oskar Kristeller. Manchester: Man
U Press, 1976. Rev. by D. Hay, History, 62(Je 1977):
314-5.

Clymer, Kenton J. John Hay: The Gentleman as Diplomat. Ann
Arbor: U Mich Press, 1975. Rev. by R. W. Leopold, AHR,
82(Feb 1977):194.

Coarelli, Filippo, ed. see Boitani, Francesca

Coatsworth, John H. El impacto económico de los ferrocarriles en el Porfirato: Crecimiento y desarollo. Mexico: Sep Setentas, 1976. Rev. by D. M. Pletcher, HAHR, 57(Aug 1977):541-2.

Cobb, Richard. Paris and Its Provinces, 1792-1802. London: Ox U Press, 1975. Rev. by M. Lyons, ESR, 7(Jan 1977):110-12.

Cochran, Thomas C. 200 Years of American Business. New York: Basic Books, 1977. Rev. by E. W. Hawley, JSH, 43 (Nov 1977):634-5.

Cochrane, Willard W. and Mary E. Ryan. American Farm Policy, 1948-1973. Minneapolis: U Minn Press, 1976. Rev. by E. L. Schapsmeier, JSH, 43(May 1977):322-4; R. C. Loehr, MinnH, 45(Win 1977):161-2.

Cockerell, H. A. L. and Edwin Green. The British Insurance Business, 1547-1970: An Introduction and Guide to Historical Records in the United Kingdom. London: Heinemann Educational Books, 1976. Rev. by B. W. E. Alford, JEH, 37(Sep 1977):787-8.

Codere, Helen. The biography of an African society, Rwanda, 1900-1960, based on forty-eight Rwandan autobiographies. Tervuren: Musee royal de l'Afrique central, 1973. Rev. by J. Beattie, Africa, 47(No. 1 1977):110-11.

Codex Vaticanus 3773 (Codex Baticanus B) Biblioteca Apostolica Vaticana. Graz, Austria: Akademische Druck-und Verlagsanstalt, 1972. Rev. by W. R. Ruwett, TAm, 33(Jan 1977):337-8.

Coen, Rena Neumann. Painting and Sculpture in Minnesota, 1820-1914. Minneapolis: U Minn Press, 1976. Rev. by P. Hills, MinnH, 45(Fall 1977):297-8.

Coffey, Joseph I. Arms Control and European Security. New York: Praeger, 1977. Rev. by O. E. S., CurH, 73(Nov 1977):174.

Coffin, Tristram Potter. The Female Hero in Folklore and Legend. n.l.: Seabury Press, 1975. Rev. by H. Prado, Mankind, 5 (No. 11, 1977):5,58.

Cohen, Colin. Watermark 74. London: Wiggins Teape, 1974. Rev. by L. Papport, AmArc, 40(Jan 1977):77-8.

Cohen, David W., ed. and Jack P. Greene, ed. Neither Slave Nor Free: The Freedmen of African Descent in the Societies of the New World. London: JHU Press, 1973. Rev. by H. Temperley, History, 62(Feb 1977):87-8.

Cohen, Edward H. Ebenezer Cooke: The Sot-Weed Canon. Athens:

U Ga Press, 1975. Rev. by C. Dolmetsch, WMQ, 34(Jl 1977):
507-8.

Cohen, Myron L. House United, House Divided: The Chinese Family in Taiwan. New York: Columbia U Press, 1976. Rev. by S. Harrell, JAS, 36(Feb 1977):352-3.

Cohen, Paul A. and John E. Schrecker, ed. Reform in Nineteenth-Century China. Cambridge: Harvard U Press, 1976. Rev. by A. Rosenbaum, JAS, 37(Nov 1977):116-7.

Cohen, Ralph. New Directions in Literary History. Baltimore: JHU Press, 1974. Rev. by R. W. Etulain, PHR, 46(May 1977):280-1.

Cohn, Bernard S. India: The Social Anthropology of a Civilization. Englewood Cliffs, N.J.: Prentice-Hall, 1971. Rev. by A. Ostör, AHR, 82(Oct 1977):1051-2.

Cohn, Victor. Sister Kenny: The Woman Who Challenged the Doctors. Minneapolis: U Minn Press, 1976. Rev. by R. A. Wengler, MinnH, 45(Win 1977):160.

Cole, A. O. C., ed. Illustrated Historical Atlas of Peterborough County, 1825-1875. Peterborough: Peterborough Historical Atlas Foundation, 1975. Rev. by J. M. S. Careless, CJR, 58(Mar 1977):68-70.

Cole, J. P. Latin America: An Economic and Social Geography. Totowa, N.J.: Rowman and Littlefield, 1975. Rev. by N. R. Stewart, HAHR, 57(Aug 1977):563-4.

Coleman, D. C. Industry in Tudor and Stuart England. New York: Macmillan, 1975. Rev. by M. W. Flinn, BH, 19(Jan 1977): 98-9.

Coleman, J. Winston, Jr. The Squire's Memoirs. Lexington: Keystone Printery, 1975. Rev. by R. L. Hagy, FCHQ, 51 (Apr 1977):210-1.

Coleman, John F. The Disruption on the Pennsylvania Democracy, 1848-1860. Harrisburg: Pennsylvania Historical and Museum Commission, 1975. Rev. by R. L. Bloom, PH, 45(Jl 1977): 285-6.

Coleman, John M. Thomas McKean: Forgotten Leader of the Revolution. Rockaway, N.J.: American Faculty Press, 1975. Rev. by B. H. Newcomb, WMQ, 34(Oct 1977):673-5.

Coleman, Kenneth. Colonial Georgia: A History. New York: Charles Scribner's Sons, 1976. Rev. by B. I. Wiley, AHI, 11(Feb 1977):49-50; G. C. Rogers, Jr., AHR, 82(Feb 1977): 173-4; R. P. Thomson, JSH, 43(Feb 1977):106-7; J. E. Selby, VMHB, 85(Jan 1977):100-1; B. Wood, WMQ, 34(Jl 1977):308-11.

_____, and Milton Ready, eds. Colonial Records of the State of Georgia: Original Papers of Governors Reynolds, Ellis, Wright, and Others, 1757-1763. Athens, Ga.: U Ga Press, 1976. Rev. by H. T. Lefler, JSH, 43(Feb 1977):107-8.

Collier, David. Squatters and Oligarchs: Authoritarian Rule and Policy Change in Peru. Baltimore: JHU Press, 1976. Rev. by F. La Mond Tullis, HAHR, 57(May 1977):368-9.

Collier, David S. see John Barratt

Collier, George A. Fields of the Tzotzil: The Ecological Bases of Tradition in Highland Chiapas. Austin: UT Press, 1975. Rev. by G. Primov, AgH, 51(Jan 1977):275-6; J. Nash, TAm, 34(Oct 1977):309-10.

Collins, Doreen. The European Communities: The Social Policy of the First Phase. Vol. I: The European Coal and Steel Community 1951-70. London: Martin Robertson, 1976. Rev. by R. W. Heywood, AHR, 83(Je 1977):628-9; A. Hartley, JEH, 37(Sep 1977):788-9.

Collins, Robert F. A History of the Daniel Boone National Forest, 1770-1970. Winchester, Kentucky: Daniel Boone National Forest, 1976. Rev. by H. L. Wallace, FCHQ, 51(Oct 1977): 364-6.

Colliva, Paolo, intro. Acta Germanica. Vol. 1: Statuta Nationis Germanicae Universitatis Bononiae (1292-1750). Bologna: Associazione Italo-Tedesca, 1975. Rev. by D. Williman, AHR, 82(Apr 1977):344-5.

Cometti, Elizabeth, ed. see Enys, John

Commager, H. S. see Morison, S. E.

Commager, Henry Steele. Jefferson, Nationalism, and the Enlightenment. New York: George Braziller, 1975. Rev. by R. McColley, PH, 45(Jan 1977):84-6.

Compère, Marie-Madeleine see Chartier, Roger

Conciani, Fulvio. Corpus Vasorum Antiquorum. Rome: "L'Erma" di Britschneider, 1974. Rev. by E. E. Bell, AJA, 81(Win 1977):121-2.

Concise Dictionary of American Biography. New York: Charles Scribner's Sons, 1977. Rev. by R. O. Barney, WHQ, 8(Jl 1977):327-8.

Confalonieri, Antonio. Banca e industria in Italia, 1894-1906. Vol. 2: Il sistema bancario tra due crisi. Milan: Banca Commerciale Italiana, 1975. Rev. by F. J. Coppa, AHR, 82 (Apr 1977):385-6; J. S. Cohen, JEH, 37(Je 1977):499-501.

Conjoncture économique structures sociales: Hommage â Ernest
Labrousse. Paris-La Haye: Mouton, 1974. Rev. by T. Le
Goff, CHR, 58(Je 1977):218-20.

Connell-Smith, Gordon. The United States and Latin America, An
Historical Analysis of Inter-American Relations. New York:
Wiley, 1974. Rev. by D. M. Fletcher, AHR, 82(Feb 1977):
39-59.

Connor, Seymour V. Texas in 1776. Austin: Jenkins, 1975.
Rev. by D. S. Chandler, ETHJ, 15(Spr 1977):45.

Conoco: The First One Hundred Years. Building on the Past for
the Future. New York: Dell, 1975. Rev. by H. C. Arbuckle, III, ETHJ, 15(Spr 1977):61.

Conrat, Maisie and Richard Conrat. The American Farm: A
Photographic History. San Francisco: California Historical
Society/Boston: Houghton Mifflin, 1977. Rev. by P. S.
Taylor, AgH, 51(Je 1977):627-8; J. H. Shideler, CHQ, 56
(Sum 1977):175-6.

Conrat, Richard see Conrat, Maisie

Constantinescu, Miron, et al. Relations between the Autochthonous
Population and the Migratory Populations on the Territory of
Romania. Bucharest: Academiei Republicii Socialiste Rom-
ania, 1975. Rev. by D. W. Wade, AHR, 82(Feb 1977):69.

Constantino, Renato. A History of the Philippines: From the
Spanish Colonization to the Second World War. New York:
Monthly Review Press, 1975. Rev. by M. P. Onorato, PHR,
46(Aug 1977):519-20.

Continental Oil Company. Conoco: The First One Hundred Years.
New York: Dell, 1975. Rev. by H. C. Arbuckle, III, ETHJ,
15(No. 1, 1977):61.

Conzen, Kathleen Neils. Immigrant Milwaukee 1836-1860: Accom-
modation and Community in a Frontier City. Cambridge:
Har U Press, 1976. Rev. by A. T. Brown, AHR, 82(Apr
1977):442-3; H. P. Chudacoff, JEH, 37(Je 1977):501-2; C.
Abbott, WHQ, 8(Oct 1977):473-4.

Cook, Adrian. The Alabama Claims: American Politics and Anglo-
American Relations, 1865-1872. Ithaca: Cornell U Press,
1975. Rev. by M. Lester, AHR, 81(Dec 1976):1254; M.
Crawford, NYHSQ, 61(Jan/Apr 1977):92-3.

Cook, Chris. The Age of Alignment: Electoral Politics in Britain,
1922-1929. Buffalo: U Tor Press, 1975. Rev. by V. Bogdanor, AHR, 82(Feb 1977):108-9; P. F. Clarke, History, 62
(Feb 1977):145-6.

_____. A Short History of the Liberal Party 1900-1976. London: Macmillan, 1976. Rev. by M. Bentley, History, 62(Je 1977): 341.

_____, and John Paxton. European Political Facts 1918-73. London: Macmillan, 1975. Rev. by R. A. H. Robinson, History, 62(Feb 1977):153-4.

_____, ed. see also Peele, Gillian, ed.

_____, ed. see also Sked, Alan, ed.

Cook, D. Louise, comp. Guide to the Manuscript Collections of the Atlanta Historical Society. Atlanta: Atlanta Historical Society, 1976. Rev. by R. C. McCrary, GHQ, 51(Spr 1977):97-8.

Cook, Edward M., Jr. The Fathers of the Towns: Leadership and Community Structure in Eighteenth-Century New England. Baltimore: JHU Press, 1976. Rev. by R. D. Brown, AHR, 82 (Je 1977):731-2; G. L. Main, JEH, 37(Je 1977):501-2; D. B. Rutman, JIH, 8(Sum 1977):167-9; J. J. Waters, NEQ, 50(Sep 1977):541-4; D. L. Jones, WMQ, 34(Jl 1977):485-7.

Cook, Michael see Crone, Patricia

Cook, Noble David. Tasa de la visita general de Francisco de Toledo. Lima: Seminario de Historia Rural Andina, Universidad Nacional Mayor de San Marcos, 1975. Rev. by F. Bronner, TAm, 33(Jan 1977):562-3.

Cook, Scott, and Martin Diskin. Markets in Oaxaca. Austin: UT, 1976. Rev. by J. K. Chance, AgH, 51(Jan 1977):273-4; A. Mayhew, JEH, 37(Je 1977):503-4; C R. Berry, TAm, 33(Jan 1977):559-60.

Cook, Sherburne F. The Conflict Between the California Indian and White Civilization. Berkeley: U Cal Press, 1976. Rev. by G. H. Phillips, A&W, 19(Sum 1977):183-85; R. N. Ellis, NMHR, 52(Oct 1977):337-43.

_____. The Population of the California Indians, 1769-1970. Berkeley: U Cal Press, 1976. Rev. by G. H. Phillips, A&W, 19(Sum 1977):183-185; D. H. Ubelaker, AHR, 82(Oct 1977): 1081; A. B. Elsasser, CHQ, 56(Spr 1977):84-5; M. Mobley, JOW, 16(Jl 1977):98; R. N. Ellis, NMHR, 52(Oct 1977):337-43.

_____, and Woodrow Borah. Essays in Population History: Mexico and the Caribbean. Volume 2. Berkeley: U Cal Press, 1974. Rev. by M. J. McLeod, AHR, 82(Feb 1977):221-3.

Cook, Sylvia Jenkins. From Tobacco Road to Route 66: The Southern Poor White in Fiction. Chapel Hill: U North Carolina Press, 1976. Rev. by R. Gray, JAmS, 11(Dec 1977):402-4; P. G. Gerster, JSH, 43(Aug 1977):481-2.

Cookson, J. E. Lord Liverpool's Administration: The Crucial
Years, 1815-1822. Edinburgh: Scottish Academic Press,
1975. Rev. by M. Brock, History, 62(Je 1977):334; W. R.
Brock, JMH, 49(Mar 1977):136-7.

Cooling, Benjamin Franklin, ed. War, Business, and American
Society: Historical Perspectives on the Military-Industrial
Complex. Port Washington, N.Y.: Kennikat Press, 1977.
Rev. by C. B. Smith, History, 6(Oct 1977):10.

Coombs, Charles A. The Arena of International Finance. New
York, John Wiley, 1976. Rev. by P. Kressler, JEH, 37(Sep
1977):789-90.

Cooper, Michael, ed. This Island of Japan: Joao Rodrigues'
Account of 16th-century Japan. Tokyo: Kodansha International,
Ltd., 1973. Rev. by R. K. Sakai, JAAS, 12(Jan/Oct 1977):
281-3.

Copeland, Carolyn Faunce. Language & Time & Gertrude Stein.
Iowa City: U Iowa Press, 1975. Rev. by A. T. K. Crozier,
JAmS, 11(Dec 1977):400-1.

Copeland, Pamela C. and Richard K. Macmaster. The Five George
Masons: Patriots and Planters of Virginia and Maryland.
Charlottesville: U Press Va, 1975. Rev. by D. W. Jordan,
AHR, 82(Apr 1977):433-4.

Copeland, William R. The Uneasy Alliance: Collaboration between
the Finnish Opposition and the Russian Underground, 1899-1904.
Helsinki: Suomalainen Tiedeakatemia, 1973. Rev. by P. K.
Hamalainen, AHR, 82(Je 1977):659.

Coppejans-Desmedt, H. Guide des Archives d'Enterprises Conserees
dans les depots publics de la Belgique. Brussels: Archives
Generales du Royaume et Archives de l'Etat dans les Provinces, 1975. Rev. by F. L. Blouin, AmArc, 40(Jan 1977):
85-6.

Copper, John Franklin. China's Foreign Aid. Lexington: D. C.
Heath, 1976. Rev. by A. Z. Rubinstein, CurH, 73(Sep 1977):
85; R. F. Grow, JAS, 37(Nov 1977):130-1.

Cordell, Alexander. The Dream and the Destiny. London: Hodder
and Stoughton, 1975. Rev. by D. Lary, CQ, No. 70(Je 1977):
442-3.

Corina, Maurice. Trust in Tobacco: The Anglo American Struggle
For Power. New York: St. Martin's Press, 1975. Rev. by
J. E. Fell, Historian, 39(Feb 1977):338-9.

Cornelius, Wayne A. Politics and the Migrant Poor in Mexico City.
Stanford: Stan U Press, 1975. Rev. by E. J. Williams, HAHR,
57(May 1977):365-6; B. R. Roberts, JLAS, 9(May 1977):173-5.

Corriente, Federico. Las Muallaqat: antologia panorama de Arabia preislamica. Madrid: Instituto Hispanoarabc de Cultura, 1974. Rev. by A. G. Chejne, JNES, 36(Oct 1977):322.

Cortes, Raúl Arreola. Melchor Ocampo: Textos Politicos. México: SepSetentas, 1975. Rev. by R. J. Knowlton, HAHR, 57(May 1977):350-1.

Corvisier, André. Les Francais Et L'Armée Sous Louis XIV: D'Après Les Mémoires Des Intedants, 1697-1689. Paris: Ministère de la Defense, 1975. Rev. by R. M. Hatton, History, 62(Je 1977):324.

Cossons, Neil. The BP Book of Industrial Archaeology. Newton Abbot: David and Charles, 1975. Rev. by J. Tann, History, 62(Feb 1977):83.

Costamagna, Giorgio see Amelotti, Mario

Costeloe, Michael P. Mexico State Papers, 1744-1843. London: U London, 1976. Rev. by B. Naylor, JLAS, 9(May 1977):147-8.

_____. La Primera Republica Federal de Mexico (1824-1835). Mexico City: Fondo de Cultura Economica, 1975. Rev. by R. Sinkin, AHR, 82(Feb 1977):225-6; B. Hamnett, JLAS, 9(May 1977):159-61; H. D. Sims, TAm, 33(Jan 1977):556-8.

Cott, Nancy F. The Bonds of Womanhood: "Woman's Sphere" in New England, 1780-1835. New Haven: Yale U Press, 1977. Rev. by L. M. Maloney, History, 6(Oct 1977):11.

Coughlan, Neil. Young John Dewey: An Essay in American Intellectual History. Chicago: U Chi Press, 1975. Rev. by A. G. Wirth, AHR, 82(Feb 1977):188-9; G. Dykhuizen, VH, 45(Sum 1977):181-2.

Coulon, C. see J. L. Balans

Coulter, E. Merton. George Walton Williams: The Life of a Southern Merchant and Banker, 1820-1903. Athens, Ga.: Hibriten Press, 1976. Rev. by L. H. Harrison, AHR, 82(Apr 1977):447; M. Childs, GHQ, 51(Spr 1977):86-8; P. E. McLear, JSH, 43(Aug 1977):452-3; L. P. Jones, SCHM, 78(Jan 1977):75-6.

Courdurié, Marcel. La dette des collectivités publiques de Marseille au XVIIIe siècle. Marseilles: Institute Historique de Provence, 1974. Rev. by T. F. Sheppard, AHR, 82(Apr 1977):368-9.

Court, David and Dharam P. Ghai, eds. Education, Society and Development: New Perspectives from Kenya. Nairobi: Ox U Press, 1974. Rev. by W. T. S. Gould, Africa, 47(No. 1, 1977):116-7.

Covell, Jon and Yamada Sōbin. Zen at Daitoku-ji. Tokyo and New York: Kodansha International, 1974. Rev. by C. M. Zainie, JAS, 36(Feb 1977):361-2.

Cover, Robert M.   Justice Accused: Antislavery and the Judicial
   Process. New Haven: Yale U Press, 1975. Rev. by J. A.
   Sokolow, NEQ, 50(Sep 1977):555-6; J. M. McPherson, JIH, 7
   (Win 1977):551-3.

Coverdale, John F. Italian Intervention in the Spanish Civil War.
   Princeton: U Press, 1975. Rev. by R. Whealey, Historian,
   39(Feb 1977):347-8; G. Jackson, TAm, 33(Apr 1977):693-4.

Covert, James T. A Point of Price: The University of Portland
   Story. Portland: U Portland, n.d. Rev. by E. F. O'Meara,
   OrHQ, 78(Sep 1977):285-6.

Cowan, C. D. and O. W. Wolters, eds. Southeast Asian History
   and Historiography: Essays Presented to D. G. E. Hall.
   London: Cornell U Press, 1976. Rev. by I. G. Brown,
   History, 62(Je 1977):297-8; R. V. Niel, JAS, 36(May 1977):
   587-9.

_____, ed. see also Burns, P. L., ed.

Cowan, Ian B. The Scottish Covenanters 1660-1688. London: Gollancz, 1976. Rev. by J. S. Morrill, HJ, 20(No. 4, 1977):
   961-70; F. D. Dow, History, 62(Feb 1977):124-5.

Cowling, Clare see Pearce, Ian

Cowling, Maurice. The Impact of Hitler: British Politics and
   British Policy, 1933-1940. New York: Cam U Press, 1975.
   Rev. by T. E. Hachey, AHR, 81(Dec 1976):1117-18; O. E. S.,
   CurH, 73(Nov 1977):174-5.

Cox, Archibald. The Role of the Supreme Court in American Government. New York: Oxford U Press, 1976. Rev. by R.
   Maidment, JAmS, 11(Dec 1977):410-1.

Cox, Thomas R. Mills and Markets: A History of the Pacific
   Coast Lumber Industry to 1900. Seattle: U Washington Press,
   1975. Rev. by P. R. Shergold, JAmS, 11(Apr 1977):156-7.

Cox, Thomas S. Civil-Military Relations in Sierra Leone. Cambridge, Mass.: Harvard U Press, 1976. Rev. by J. P.
   Smaldone, AHR, 82(Feb 1977):155-6.

Cox, Tom. Damned Englishman: A Study of Erskine Childers
   (1870-1922). Hicksville, N.Y.: Exposition Press, 1975.
   Rev. by C. Townshend, History, 62(Je 1977):344.

Cramer, Howard Ross. Emigrant Trails of Southeastern Idaho.
   Washington, D. C.: U. S. Dept. of Interior, 1976. Rev. by
   D. L. Crowder, UHQ, 45(Win 1977):95.

Craton, Michael, James Walvin, and David Wright, eds. Slavery,

Abolition and Emancipation: Black Slaves and the British Empire. New York: Longman, Inc., 1977. Rev. by L. E. Tise, History, 6(Oct 1977):6-7.

Craven, Roy C., Jr. and William R. Bullard, Jr. and Michael C. Kampen. Ceremonial Centers of the Maya. Gainesville, Fla.: U Presses of Florida, 1974. Rev. by D. M. Pendergast, Archaeology, 30(Jan 1977):66.

Crawford, Charles W. Yesterday's Memphis. Miami, Fla.: E. A. Seeman Pub., 1976. Rev. by J. C. Kiger, JMiH, 39 (Feb 1977):91-2.

Crawford, James M., ed. Studies in Southeastern Indian Languages. Athens: U Ga Press, 1975. Rev. by J. Campbell, ChOK, 55 (Spr 1977):118-9.

Creel, Herrlee G. Shen Pu-Hai: A Chinese Political Philosopher of the Fourth Century B. C. Chicago: U Chi Press, 1975. Rev. by Tu Wei-ming, AHR, 82(Je 1977):716-7.

Cregier, Don M. Bounder from Wales: Lloyd George's Career before the First World War. Columbia: U Mo Press, 1976. Rev. by K. O. Morgan, AHR, 82(Apr 1977):362.

Creigh, Dorothy Weyer. A Primer for Local Historical Societies. Nashville: American Association for State and Local History, 1976. Rev. by L. Horton, Al, 44(Sum 1977):76-7; S. McArthur, CHQ, 56(Spr 1977):89.

Cremin, Lawrence A. Traditions of American Education. n.l.: Basic Books, n.d. Rev. by C. E. Finn, Comm, 63(Je 1977): 89-91.

Crespigny, R. R. C. de. China This Century. New York: St. Martin's Press, 1975. Rev. by J. H. Boyle, JAS, 36(Feb 1977):339.

Crews, Harry. A Feast of Snakes. New York: Atheneum, 1976. Rev. by G. Owen, GR, 31(Sum 1977):525-8.

Cripps, Thomas. Slow Fade to Black: The Negro in American Film, 1900-1942. New York: Ox U Press, 1977. Rev. by R. Sklar, AHR, 82(Oct 1977):1093-4.

Crisp, Olga. Studies in the Russian Economy Before 1914. New York: Barnes and Noble, 1976. Rev. by W. M. Pintner, AHR, 82(Je 1977):697-8; C. Trebilcock, HJ, 20(No. 3, 1977): 751-60; F. V. Carstensen, JEH, 37(Sep 1977):790-1; J. Metzer, JMH, 49(Sep 1977):521-4.

Critall, Elizabeth, ed. Victoria County History of Wiltshire, Volume X. Cambridge: Ox U Press for the Institute of Historical Research, 1975. Rev. by G. A. Harrison, History, 62(Feb 1977):83-4.

Crone, Patricia and Michael Cook. Hagarism: The Making of the Islamic World. New York: Cam U Press, 1977. Rev. by D.
W. Littlefield, History, 6(Nov/Dec 1977):37.

Crook, D. P. The North, the South, and the Powers, 1861-1865.
New York: John Wiley, 1974. Rev. by F. Owsley, Jr., LaH,
18(Win 1977):110-1.

Crook, J. Mordaunt. The Greek Revival: Neo-Classical Attitudes
in British Architecture 1760-1860. London: John Murray,
1972. Rev. by M. H. Port, History, 62(Feb 1977):141.

Crook, M. J. The Evolution of the Victoria Cross. Tunbridge
Wells: Midas Books, 1975. Rev. by G. Best, History, 62
(Je 1977):342.

Crosbie, Sylvia K. A Tacit Alliance: France and Israel from
Suez to the Six Day War. Princeton: Prin U Press, 1974.
Rev. by H. G. Simmons, CHR, 58(Je 1977):246-7.

Crosby, Alfred W., Jr. Epidemic and Peace, 1918. Westport,
Conn.: Greenwood Press, 1976. Rev. by J. H. Cassedy,
AHR, 82(Feb 1977):202; M. S. Pernick, JIH, 8 (Sum 1977):
161-3.

Crosby, Travis L. Sir Robert Peel's Administration, 1841-1846.
Hamden, Conn.: Archon Books, 1976. Rev. by R. W. Davis,
AHR, 82(Apr 1977):357.

Cross, Colin, ed. see Sylvester, A. J.

Cross, Frederick C., ed. Nobly They Served the Union. n. p.:
Frederick Cross, 1976. Rev. by R. D. Hoffsommer, CWTI,
16(Aug 1977):49.

Crossick, Geoffrey, ed. The Lower Middle Class in Britain, 1870-
1914. London: Croom Helm, 1976. Rev. by M. A. Crowther, HJ, 20(No. 4, 1977):991-9.

Crossman, Richard. The Diaries of a Cabinet Minister. Vol. I:
1964-1966. New York: Holt, Rinehart and Winston, 1975.
Rev. by D. Rubinstein, AHR, 82(Apr 1977):363; V. Bogdanor,
History, 62(Je 1977):344-5.

Crouch, Thomas W. A Yankee Guerrillero: Frederick Funston and
the Cuban Insurrection, 1896-1897. Memphis: Memphis St U
Press, 1975. Rev. by W. B. Gatewood, Jr., FHQ, 55(Jan
1977):388-9; D. Healy, PHR, 46(May 1977):303.

Crow, Jeffery J., ed. North Carolina in the American Revolution.
Raleigh: North Carolina Dept. of Cultural Resources, Divi-
sion of Archives and History, 1975-76. Rev. by K. Coleman,
GHQ, 51(Sum 1977):209-10.

Crowley, Frank K., ed. A New History of Australia. New York: Holmes and Meier, 1975. Rev. by F. P. King, AHR, 82(Feb 1977):166.

Crownhart-Vaughn, E. A. P. see Dmythryshyn, Basil

Cru, Jean Norton. War Books: A Study in Historical Criticism. San Diego: San Diego St U Press, 1976. Rev. by F. Field, AHR, 82(Oct 1977):984-5.

Csatári, Daniel. Dans la tourmente: Les relations hungaro-roumaines de 1940 à 1945. Budapest: Akadémiai Kiadó, 1974. Rev. by S. D. Kertesz, AHR, 82(Oct 1977):1021.

Cuff, R. D. and J. L. Granatstein. Canadian-American Relations in Wartime: From the Great War to the Cold War. Toronto: Hakkert, 1975. Rev. by R. C. Brown, CHR, 58(Je 1977): 232-3.

Culbert, David Holbrook. News for Everyman: Radio and Foreign Affairs in Thirties America. Westport, Conn.: Greenwood Press, 1976. Rev. by A. A. Offner, AHR, 82(Feb 1977):211.

Cullen, M. J. The Statistical Movement in Early Victorian Britain: The Foundations of Empirical Social Research. New York: Barnes and Noble, 1975. Rev. by J. Roebuck, AHR, 82(Feb 1977):102-3.

Cumming, Kate. The Journal of a Confederate Nurse. Ed. by Richard Harwell. Savannah, Ga.: Beehive Press, 1975. Rev. by B. J Brandon, GHQ, 51(Sum 1977):197-8.

Cummins, Cedric. The University of South Dakota, 1862-1966. Vermillion: U S. Dak Press, 1975. Rev. by J. F. Hopkins, AHR, 82(Feb 1977):187-8.

Cunliffe, Barry. Excavations at Portchester Castle: Vol. I: Roman. London: Thames and Hudson, 1975. Rev. by S. S. Frere, Antiquity, 51(Jl 1977):163-4.

_____. Iron Age Communities in Britain: An Account of England, Scotland and Wales from the Seventh Century B.C. Until the Roman Conquest. London: Routledge and Kegan Paul, 1974. Rev. by J. V. S. Megaw, AJA, 81(Spr 1977): 255-7.

Current, Richard N. The History of Wisconsin: The Civil War Era, 1848-1873, Vol. 2. Madison: State Historical Society of Wisconsin, 1977. Rev. by R. H. Jones, AHR, 82(Oct 1977):1076-7; W. D. Wyman, MinnH, 45(Fall 1977):300-1.

Currie, Harold W. Eugene V. Debs. Boston: Twayne Publ., 1976. Rev. by J. H. M. Laslett, AHR, 82(Je 1977):758.

Curtin, Phillip D. Economic Change in Precolonial Africa. Madison:
    U Wis Press, 1975. Rev. by R. Floud, JIH, 7(Win 1977):
    553-5.

Curtis, James C. Andrew Jackson and the Search for Vindication.
    Boston: Little, Brown and Company, 1976. Rev. by A
    Castel, AHI, 11(Jan 1977):50; C. M. Wiltse, AHR, 82(Je
    1977):743-4.

Cushman, Joseph D., Jr. The Sound of Bells: The Episcopal
    Church in South Florida, 1892-1969. Gainesville: U Presses
    of Florida, 1976. Rev. by H. W. Mann, JSH, 43(Nov 1977):
    629-30.

Cushner, Nicolas P. Landed Estates in the Colonial Philippines.
    New Haven: Yale U Southeast Asia Studies, Monograph Ser-
    ies 20, 1976. Rev. by P. A. Krinks, AgH, 51(Jl 1977):614-5.

Custer, George A. My Life on the Plains or, Personal Experiences
    with Indians. Norman: U Okla Press, 1976. Rev. by R. N.
    Ellis, MichH, 61(Sum 1977):171-2.

Cutright, Paul Russell. A History of the Lewis and Clark Journals.
    Norman: U Okla Press, 1976. Rev. by M. J. Maltes, AHR,
    82(Oct 1977):1069-70; W. E. Lass, MinnH, 45(Sum 1977):254;
    R. E. Lange, OrHQ, 78(Sep 1977):284-5; J. A. Caylor, WHQ,
    8(Jl 1977):348.

Czarnecki, Jan. The Goths in Ancient Poland: A Study on the His-
    torical Geography of the Odervistula Region during the First
    Two Centuries of Our Era. Coral Gables, Fla.: U Miami
    Press, 1975. Rev. by M. Gimbutas, AHR, 82(Feb 1977):72-3.

Czerny, Peter G. The Great Great Salt Lake. Provo, Ut.: Bri-
    gham Young U Press, 1976. Rev. by E. L. Cooley, UHQ,
    45(Spr 1977):202-3.

Dabney, Virginius. Richmond: The Story of a City. New York:
    Doubleday, 1976. Rev. by J. P. Cullen, AHI, 12(Aug 1977):
    49; W. H. Daniel, JSH, 43(Nov 1977):644-5; E. M. Thomas,
    VMHB, 85(Jan 1977):97-8.

Dae-Sook Suh and Chae-jin Lee. Political Leadership in Korea.
    Seattle: U Wash Press, 1976. Rev. by B. H. Hazard, AHR,
    82(Apr 1977):419-20.

D'Aguiar, Hernani. A Revolucão por Dentro. Rio de Janeiro:
    Editora Artenova, 1976. Rev. by J. W. F. Dulles, HAHR,
    57(Aug 1977):551-3.

Dahl, Edward H., ed., et al. La Ville de Quebec, 1800-1850: Un
    Inventaire de Cartes et Plans. Ottawa: National Museums of
    Canada, 1975. Rev. by A. K. Lathrop, AmArc, 40(Jan 1977):
    90-1; T. Copp, CHR, 58(Mar 1977):70-2.

Dakin, D., ed. see Medlicott, W. N., ed.

Dakyns, Janine R. The Middle Ages in French Literature, 1851-1900. London: Oxford U Press, 1973. Rev. by W. G. van Emden, ESR, 7(Oct 1977):464-6.

Dangerfield, George. The Damnable Question: A Study in Anglo-Irish Relations. Boston: Little, Brown, n.d. Rev. by G. A. Colburn, E-1, 12(Fall 1977):121-5; B. L. Solow, JEH, 37(Sep 1977):791-2.

Daniels, Jonathan. White House Witness, 1942-45. Garden City, N.Y.: Doubleday, 1975. Rev. by G. T. McJimsey, PNQ, 68(Jan 1977):39.

Daniels, Maygene, ed. Guide to Unpublished Materials of the Holocaust Period. Jerusalem: Hebrew University Institute of Contemporary Jewry, n.d. Rev. by S. Milton, AmArc, 40(Jl 1977):349-51.

Daniels, Roger. The Decision to Relocate the Japanese Americans. New York: Lippincott, 1975. Rev. by E. Uno, CHQ, 55(Win 1976-77):367-8.

Darby, H. C., ed. A New Historical Geography of England. Cambridge: Cam U Press, 1973. Rev. by J. R. Harris, History, 62(Feb 1977):82-3.

Dargo, George. Jefferson's Louisiana: Politics and the Clash of Legal Traditions. Cambridge: Har U Press, 1975. Rev. by J. W. Bardley, LaH, 18(Spr 1977):245-6.

Darilek, Richard E. A Loyal Opposition in Time of War: The Republican Party and the Politics of Foreign Policy from Pearl Harbor to Yalta. Westport: Greenwood Press, 1976. Rev. by J. T. Patterson, AHR, 82(Je 1977):767; A. Clive, MiA, 59(Oct 1977):197.

Darley, Gillian. Villages of Vision. New York: Universe Books, 1976. Rev. by D. J. Olsen, AHR, 82(Oct 1977):968-9.

Das Mexiko - Projekt der Deutschen Forschungsgemeinschoft: Eine Deutsch Mexikanische Interdisziplinare Regional-Forschung im Becken von Purbla-Tlaxcala. Wiesbaden: Franz Steiner Verlag, 1968-75. Rev. by P. Marzahl, HAHR, 57(Feb 1977): 172-6.

Dassow, Ethel see Jackson, W. H.

Dathorne, O. R. African Literature in the 20th Century. Heinemann, 1976. Rev. by C. L. Innes, AfAf, 76(Jan 1977):125-7.

Datta, V. N., ed. New Light on the Punjab Disturbances in 1919:

Volumes 6 and 7 of Disorders Inquiry Committee Evidence.
Simla: Indian Institute of Advanced Study, 1975. Rev. by J.
Barrier, AHR, 82(Oct 1977):1053-4.

Dauber, Kenneth. Rediscovering Hawthorne. Princeton: Prin U
   Press, 1977. Rev. by C. S. B. Swann, JAmS, 11(Dec 1977):
   417-20.

Davenport, John B., comp. Guide to the Orin G. Libby Manuscript
   Collection and Related Research Collections. Grand Forks,
   N.D.: n.p., 1975. Rev. by J. Newman, AmArc, 39(Jl 1976):
   356; L. Lucas, MinnH, 45(Win 1977):162-3.

Davenport, T. R. H. South Africa: A Modern History. n.l.:
   Macmillan, n.d. Rev. by G. Douds, HTo, 27(Aug 1977):
   544-5.

David, Paul A., et al. Reckoning with Slavery. New York: Ox
   U Press, 1976. Rev. by A. G. Bogue, AHR, 82(Je 1977):
   745-6; J. H. Moore, FHQ, 55(Jan 1977):382-4; R. B. Campbell, JSH, 43(May 1977):296-7.

Davidovich, A. M. Autocracy in the Age of Imperialism: The
   Class Nature and Evolution of Absolutism in Russia. Moscow:
   Izdatel'stvo "Nauka", 1975. Rev. by M. S. Conroy, AHR,
   82(Je 1977):698-9.

Davidson, Basil, Joe Slovo and Anthony R. Wilkinson. Southern
   Africa: The New Politics of Revolution. Penguin, 1976. Rev.
   by P. Wall, AfAf, 76(Jl 1977):418-20.

Davidson, H. R. Ellis. The Viking Road to Byzantium. Totowa,
   N.J.: Rowman and Littlefield, 1976. Rev. by H. E. Eller-
   sieck, AHR, 82(Apr 1977):347; D. M. Wilson, Antiquity, 51
   (Mar 1977):75-6.

Davidson, J. W. Peter Dillon of Vanikoro: Chevalier of the South
   Seas. New York: Ox U Press, 1975. Rev. by W. P.
   Strauss, AHR, 82(Feb 1977):165-6; G. Jackson, History, 62
   (Je 1977):303-4.

Davidson, James West. The Logic of Millennial Thought: Eighteenth Century New England. New Haven: Yale U Press,
   1977. Rev. by H. A. Barnes, History, 6(Oct 1977):10-11.

Davidson, Sara. Loose Change: Three Women of the Sixties. New
   York: Doubleday, n.d. Rev. by J. L. Crain, Comm, 64(Aug
   1977):70-2.

Davies, C. S. L. Peace, Print, and Protestantism 1450-1558.
   London: Hart-Davis, MacGibbon, 1976. Rev. by H. Miller,
   History, 62(Feb 1977):111-2.

Davies, E. K. G., ed. Documents of the American Revolution, 1770-
1783. Shannon: Irish U Press, 1973, 1974. Rev. by P. S.
Haffenden, EHR, 92(Oct 1977):858-60.

Davies, Horton. Worship and Theology in England: From Andrewes
to Baxter and Fox, 1603-1690, vol. 2. Princeton: Prin U
Press, 1975. Rev. by K. W. Shipps, AHR, 82(Feb 1977):
95.

Davies, P. N. Trading in West Africa. London: Croom Helm,
1976. Rev. by C. Ehrlich, BH, 19(Jl 1977):223-4; A. J. H.
Latham, History, 62(Je 1977):266.

Davies, Robert B. Peacefully Working to Conquer the World: Singer Sewing Machines in Foreign Markets, 1854-1920. New
York: Arno Press, 1976. Rev. by D. Bunting, JEH, 37(Sep
1977):792-3.

Davin, Delia. Woman-Work: Women and the Party in Revolutionary China. New York: Ox U Press, 1976. Rev. by V.
Schwarz, AHR, 82(Oct 1977):1050-1; D. Martin, CQ, 69(Mar
1977):172-4; N. Diamond, JAS, 36(May 1977):548-9.

Davis, Calvin Dearmond. The United States and the Second Hague
Peace Conference. Durham, N.C.: Duke U Press, 1976.
Rev. by R. D. Schulzinger, AHR, 82(Apr 1977):456.

Davis, Curtis Carroll. Revolution's Godchild: The Birth, Death,
and Regeneration of the Society of the Cincinnati in North
Carolina. Chapel Hill: Published for the North Carolina Society of the Cincinnati by the U NC Press, 1976. Rev. by N.
K. Risjord, JSH, 43(Nov 1977):641-2.

Davis, David Brion. The Problem of Slavery in the Age of Revolution 1770-1823. Ithaca: Cor U Press, 1975. Rev. by R.
C. Reinders, CHR, 58(Mar 1977):91-2; M. Turner, Historian,
39(May 1977):573-4; J. R. Pole, HJ, 20(No. 2, 1977):503-13.

Davis, Harold E. The Fledgling Province: Social and Cultural
Life in Colonial Georgia, 1733-1776. Chapel Hill: U NC
Press, 1976. Rev. by D. T. Morgan, AHR, 82(Je 1977):
733; H. H. Jackson, GHQ, 51(Spr 1977):84-6; R. L. Lewis,
JNH, 62(Apr 1977):191-2; L. J. Bellot, JSH, 43(Aug 1977):
429-30; B. Wood, WMQ, 34(Jl 1977):308-11.

Davis, Harold Eugene and Larmon C. Wilson. Latin American
Foreign Policies: An Analysis. Baltimore: JHU Press,
1975. Rev. by K. J. Grieb, TAm, 34(Jl 1977):135-6.

Davis, James C. A Venetian Family and Its Fortune. Philadelphia:
American Philosophical Society, 1975. Rev. by J. Kirshner,
JMH, 49(Sep 1977):505-7.

Davis, Joseph L. Sectionalism in American Politics, 1774-1787.
Madison, Wis.: U Wis Press, 1977. Rev. by R. J. Chaffin,
History, 6(Nov/Dec 1977):32.

Davis, Kenneth S. Kansas: A Bicentennial History. New York:
Norton and Nashville: American Association for State and
Local History, 1976. Rev. by P. H. Argersinger, WHQ, 8
(Jl 1977):334-5.

Davis, Levi H. see Scott, Stanley H.

Davis, Richard W. Disraeli. Boston and Toronto: Little, Brown
and Company, 1976. Rev. by T. L. Crosby, Historian, 39
(May 1977):545-6.

Davis, Thomas B. Aspects of Free Masonry in Modern Mexico:
An Example of Social Cleavage. New York: Vantage Press,
1976. Rev. by L. L. Blaisdell, HAHR, 57(Aug 1977):537-8.

Davis, Walter W. Joseph II: An Imperial Reformer for the Austrian Netherlands. The Hague: Martinus Nijhoff, 1974. Rev.
by E. Wangermann, History, 62(Feb 1977):137-8.

Davis, William C. Breckinridge: Statesman, Soldier, Symbol.
Baton Rouge: LSU Press, 1974. Rev. by E. B. Long, AHR,
81(Dec 1976):1252-53.

_____. Duel Between the First Ironclads. Garden City, N.Y.:
Doubleday, 1975. Rev. by M. B. Lucas, CWH, 23(Je 1977):
181-2.

Davison, Peter. Walking the Boundaries: Poems, 1957-74. New
York: Atheneum, 1974. Rev. by P. Stitt, GR, 31(Fall 1977):
762-71.

Dawidowicz, Lucy S., ed. A Holocaust Reader. New York: Beh-
rman House, 1976. Rev. by R. Hilberg, AHR, 82(Oct 1977):
952-4.

Dawley, Alan. Class and Community: The Industrial Revolution in
Lynn. Cambridge: Har U Press, 1976. Rev. by C. Hoffecker, AHR, 82(Je 1977):752-3; JAmS, 11(Dec 1977):
388-9.

Dayal, Rajeshwar. Mission for Hammarskjold: The Congo Crisis.
Princeton: Prin U Press, 1976. Rev. by A. T. Stephens,
AHR, 82(Je 1977):711-2.

Deaderick, Lucile, ed. Heart of the Valley: A History of Knoxville, Tennessee. Knoxville, Tenn.: East Tennessee Historical Society, 1976. Rev. by J. B. Crooks, JSH, 43(Nov 1977):
642-3.

Deagan, Kathleen A. Archaeology at the National Greek Orthodox
    Shrine, St. Augustine, Florida: Microchange in Eighteenth-
    Century Spanish Colonial Material Culture. Gainesville:
    University Presses of Florida, 1976. Rev. by A. Manucy,
    FHQ, 55(Jan 1977):371-3.

de Alarcão, Adilia Moutinho see Delgado, Manuela.

de Alarcão, Jorge. Fouilles de Conimbriga V: La céramique com-
    mune locale et régionale. Paris: Boccard, 1975. Rev. by
    H. Comfort, AJA, 81(Win 1977):125-6.

Dean, Britten. China and Great Britain: The Diplomacy of Com-
    mercial Relations, 1860-1864. Cambridge, Mass.: Har U
    Press, 1974. Rev. by S. W. Barnett, AHR, 82(Apr 1977):
    412-3.

Dean, John. Blind Ambition. New York: Simon & Schuster, n.d.
    Rev. by J. Q. Wilson, Comm, 63(Feb 1977):66-8.

Dean, Warren. Rio Claro: A Brazilian Plantation System, 1820-
    1920. Stanford: Stan U Press, 1976. Rev. by J. D. Wirth,
    AHR, 82(Apr 1977):484-5; R. Conrad. HAHR, 57(May 1977):
    353-4; T. E. Skidmore, JEH, 37(Je 1977):506-7; C. A.
    Preece, TAm, 33(Apr 1977):683-4.

De Bary, Wm. Theodore. The Unfolding of Neo-Confucianism.
    New York: Col U Press, 1975. Rev. by C. O Hucker,
    Historian, 39(Feb 1977):361-2.

de Blois, Lukas. The Policy of the Emperor Gallienus. Leiden:
    E. J. Brill, 1976. Rev. by M T. W. Arnheim, AHR, 82
    (Je 1977):614-5.

Debo, Angie. Geronimo, The Man, His Time, His Place. Norman:
    U Ok Press 1976. Rev. by D. Brown, AHI, 12(Nov 1977):47;
    P. Iverson, AHR, 82(Oct 1977):1081-2; D. L. Thrapp, JAriH,
    18(Spr 1977):99-101.

Debus, Allen G. , ed. Medicine in Seventeenth Century England: A
    Symposium. Berkeley: U Cal Press, 1974. Rev. by J.
    Duffy, AHR, 82(Feb 1977):95-6.

De Canio, Stephen J. Agriculture in the Postbellum South: The
    Economics of Production and Supply. Cambridge, Mass.:
    MIT Press, 1975. Rev. by J. R. Mandel, AgH, 51(Apr
    1977):470-2; T. Saloutos, AHR, 82(Feb 1977):186.

DeCell, Harriet and JoAnne Prichard, Yazoo: Its Legends and
    Legacies. Yazoo City, Miss.: Yazoo Delta Press, 1976.
    Rev. by B. R. Baker, JMiH, 39(Aug 1977):283-4.

De Conde, Alexander. This Affair of Louisiana. New York:

Charles Scribner's Sons, 1976. Rev. by G. G. Eggert, AHI,
12(Nov 1977):47; C. L. Egan, AHR, 82(Oct 1977):1069; S. S.
Sprague, JSH, 43(Aug 1977):450-1; G. B. Mills, VMHB, 85
(Apr 1977):208-9; G. Dargo, WMQ, 34(Oct 1977):664-6.

Dedera, Don. Navajo Rugs: How to Find, Evaluate, Buy and Care
for Them. Flagstaff: Northland Press, 1975. Rev. by C.
L. Tanner, JAriH, 18(Sum 1977):221-3.

_____, and Bob Robles. Goodbye, Garcia, Adios. Flagstaff:
Northland Press, 1976. Rev. by S. P. Brown, A&W, 19
(Sum 1977):177-79.

De Felice, Renzo. Interpretations of Fascism. Cambridge: Har
U Press, 1977. Rev. by E. P. Noether, History, 6(Nov/Dec
1977):46.

De Gennaro, Nat, ed. Statistical Abstract of Arizona, 1976. Tucson: U Arizona, 1976. Rev. by D. Bufkin, JAriH, 18(Spr
1977):103-4.

Deist, Wilhelm. Flottenpolitik und Flottenpropaganda. Stuttgart:
Deutsche Verlags-Anstalt, 1976. Rev. by A. H. Ganz, AHR,
82(Oct 1977):1004-5.

DeJong, Gerald F. The Dutch in America, 1609-1974. Boston:
Twayne, 1975. Rev. by A. P Kenny, NYHSQ, 61(Jan/Apr
1977):80-1.

De Jong, L. The Kingdom of the Netherlands in the Second World
War. Gravenhage: Martinus Nijhoff, 1975. Rev. by W.
Warmbrunn, AHR, 82(Feb 1977):120-1.

deKlerk, W. The Puritans in Africa: a story of Afrikanerdom.
Rex Collins, 1975. Rev. by S Paterson, AfAf, 76(Jan 1977):
108-11.

de la Croix, René. La France et l'Indépendance américaine: Le
livre du bicentenaire de l'Indépendance. Paris: Librairie
Académique Perrin, 1975. Rev. by W. Stinchombe, AHR, 82
(Apr 1977):434-5.

De Laet, Sigfried J., ed. Acculturation and continuity in Atlantic
Europe, mainly during the Neolithic period and the Bronze
Age. Papers presented at the IVth Atlantic Colloquium,
Ghent, 1975. Vol. XVI. Bruges: De Tempel, 1976. Rev.
by A. M. AP Simon, Antiquity, 51(Jl 1977):171.

DeLancey, Mark W. and Virginia H. DeLancey. A Bibliography of
Cameroon. New York: Africana Pub. Co., 1975. Rev. by
I. Kopytoff, JAAS, 12(Jan/Oct 1977):274.

DeLancey, Virginia H. see DeLancey, Mark W.

Delgado, Manuela, Françoise Mayet and Adília Moutinho de Alarcão. Fouilles de Conimbriga IV: Les sigilleés. Paris: Boccard, 1975. Rev. by H. Comfort, AJA, 81(Win 1977):125-6.

Dell, Christopher. Lincoln and the War Democrats: The Grand Erosion of Conservative Tradition. Rutherford: Fairleigh Dickinson U Press, 1975. Rev. by J. A. Rawley, AHR, 81 (Dec 1976):1251-52; V. B. Howard, JISHS, 70(Aug 1977):249-50.

Del Negro, Piero. Il Mito americano nella Venezia del settecento. Rome: Accademia Nazionale dei Lincei, 1975. Rev. by M. Suozzi, AHR, 82(Je 1977):680.

De Luna, Giovanni. Badoglio: Un militare al potere. Milan: Casa Editrice V. Bompiani, 1974. Rev. by C F. Delzell, AHR, 82(Je 1977):682-3.

de Mesquita, Bruce Bueno. Strategy, Risk, and Personality in Coalition Politics: The Case of India. Cambridge: Cambridge U Press, 1975. Rev. by N. D. Palmer, JAS, 37(Nov 1977): 166-7.

Dempsey, Hugh A., ed. The Best of Bob Edwards. Edmonton: Hurtig, 1975. Rev. by J. M. Gray, CHR, 58(Mar 1977):75-6.

Denevan, William M., ed. The Native Population of the Americas in 1492. Madison: U Wis Press, 1976. Rev. by N. Sanchez-Albornoz, TAm, 34(Oct 1977):294-5.

Denhardt, Robert M. Foundation Sires of the American Quarter Horse: A Digest of known information about the stallions whose descendants appear in the early volumes of the Official Stud Book of the American Quarter Horse Association, together with a brief history of the beginnings of the American Quarter Horse Association. Norman: U Ok Press, 1976. Rev. by C. W. Black, JOW, 16(Jan 1977):89.

Denison, Edward F. and William K. Chung. How Japan's Economy Grew So Fast: The Sources of Postwar Expansion. Washington, D.C.: Brookings Institution, 1976. Rev. by M. F. Loutfi, JAS, 37(Nov 1977):133-4; E. Rotwein, JEH, 37(Sep 1977):782-4.

Denzler, Georg. Das Papsttum und der Amtszölibat, 2 vols. Stuttgart: Anton Hiersemann, 1976. Rev. by E. Peters, AHR, 82 (Oct 1977):945-6.

DeOnis, José, ed. The Hispanic Contribution to the State of Colorado. Boulder, Colorado: Westview Press, 1976. Rev. by F. L. Swadesh, HAHR, 57(May 1977):372-3.

De Pauw, Linda Grant, Charlene Bangs Bickford, and La Vonne Siegel Hauptman, ed. Documentary History of the First Fed-

eral Congress of the United States of America, March 4, 1789-
March 3, 1791. Volume III, House of Representatives Journal.
Baltimore: Johns Hopkins U Press, 1977. Rev. by B. Tarter,
VMHB, 85(Jl 1977):373-4.

Derfler, Leslie. Socialism Since Marx: A Century of the European
Left. New York: St. Martin's Press, 1973. Rev. by S. B.
Ryerson, CHR, 58(Mar 1977):102-4.

Dering, Edward. The Diaries and Papers of Sir Edward Dering,
2nd Baronet, 1644-1684. Ed. by Maurice Bond. London: H.
M.S.O., 1976. Rev. by B. G. Hutton, Archives, 13(Spr 1977):
50-1.

de Rochemont, Richard see Root, Waverley.

Derrett, J. Duncan M., ed. Bharuci's Commentary on the Manusmrti. Wiesbaden: Franz Steiner Verlag, 1975. Rev. by R.
Inden, JAS, 37(Nov 1977):159.

Derry, John. English Politics and the American Revolution. London: Dent, 1976. Rev. by I. R. Christie, History, 62(Feb
1977):135.

Derry, John W. Castlereagh. London: Allen Lane, 1976. Rev.
by M. Brock, History, 62(Je 1977):334.

Des Gagniers, Jean see Karageorghis, Vassos.

De Shields, James T. Border Wars of Texas: Being An Authentic
and Popular Account, in Chronological Order, of the Long and
Bitter Conflict Waged Between Savage Indian Tribes and the
Pioneer Settlers of Texas-Wresting of a Fair Land From Savage Rule-A Red Record of Fierce Strife, Profusely Illustrated
with Spirited Battle Scenes by Special Artists, Rare Portraits
of Famous Rangers, Indian Fighters and Pioneers, Maps, etc.
Waco: Texian Press, 1976. Rev. by W. D. Hearell, ETHJ,
15(Spr 1977):56-7.

Desmond, Adrian J. The Hot-Blooded Dinosaurs: A Revolution in
Paleontology. n.l.: Dial Press, n.d. Rev. by V. Cox,
Mankind, 5(No. 11, 1977):58.

Despalatović, Elinor Murray. Ljudevit Gaj and the Illyrian Movement. New York: Columbia U Press, 1975. Rev. by J. B.
Bukowski, AHR, 82(Apr 1977):392-3.

Dessain, C. S. and T. Gornall, eds. The Letters and Diaries of
John Henry Newman. vol. XXIX and XXX. Oxford: Clarendon Press, 1976. Rev. by O. Chadwick, EHR, 92(Oct 1977):
923.

Destenay, Anne, tr. see Guillermaz, Jacques.

Dethan, Georges. The Young Mazarin. n.l.: Thames and Hudson, n.d. Rev. by J. Richardson, HTo, 27(Aug 1977):548.

de Tourtier-Bonazzi, Chantal, comp. Lafayette: Documents conservés en France. vol. 1. Paris: Archives nationales, 1976. Rev. by S. Taylor, AHR, 82(Je 1977):651.

Deventer, David E. van. The Emergence of Provincial New Hampshire, 1623-1741. Baltimore and London: JHU Press, 1976. Rev. by D. E. Ball, JEH, 37(Je 1977):566-7; J. R. Daniell, NEQ, 50(Mar 1977):170-3; S. D. Crow, WMQ, 34(Jl 1977): 511-2.

Devereux, Anthony Q. The Life and Times of Robert F. W. Allston. Georgetown, S.C.: Waccamaw Press, 1976. Rev. by D. T. Lawson, SCHM, 78(Apr 1977):150-2.

Devine, T. M The Tobacco Lords: A Study of the Tobacco Merchants of Glasgow and Their Trading Activities c. 1740-90. Edinburgh: John Donald, 1975. Rev. by S. G. Checkland, JEH, 37(Je 1977):507-8; J. H. Soltow, WMQ, 34(Jl 1977): 496-7.

Devisse, Jean. Hincmar: Archevêque de Reims, 845-882. 3 vols. Geneva: Librarie Droz, 1973. Rev. by R. E. Sullivan, AHR, 82(Je 1977):620-1.

Devlin, John F. The Ba'th Party: A History from Its Origins to 1966. Stanford: Hoover Institution Press, 1976. Rev. by S. G. Haim, AHR, 82(Oct 1977):1030.

De Vooght, Paul. L'hérésie de Jean Hus. 2 vols. Louvain: Publications Universitaires de Louvain, 1975. Rev. by H. Kaminsky, AHR, 82(Oct 1977):1021-2.

Devore, Ronald M. The Arab-Israeli Conflict: A Historical, Political, Social, and Military Bibliography. Santa Barbara, Cal.: Clio Books, 1976. Rev. by B. M. J. Wasserstein, AHR, 82 (Je 1977):708.

de Vries, Jan. Economy of Europe in an Age of Crisis, 1600-1750. New York: Cam U Press, 1976. Rev. by J. C. Riley, AHR, 82(Je 1977):623-4.

DeVylder, Stefan. Allende's Chile: The Political Economy of the Rise and Fall of the Unidad Popular. New York: Cam U Press, 1976. Rev. by F. M. Nunn, AHR, 82(Apr 1977):482-3; Q. E. S., CurH, 72(Feb 1977):80.

Dewdney, Selwyn. The Sacred Scrolls of the Southern Ojibway. Toronto: U Toronto Press, 1975. Rev. by R. H. Thompson, AIQ, 3(Sum 1977):165-7.

79   DE WILKIE

De Wilkie, Edna Monzón see Wilkie, James W.

Dhaky, M. A., ed. see Shah, U. P., ed.

Dick, Everett. Conquering the Great American Desert. Lincoln:
   Nebraska State Historical Society, 1975. Rev. by R. G.
   Bremer, AgH, 51(Apr 1977):469-70; M. W. M. Hargreaves,
   AHR, 82(Apr 1977):450; H. T. Hoover, MinnH, 45(Win 1977):
   160-1; S. N. Dicken, OrHQ, 78(Sep 1977):282-3; J. C. Olson,
   WHQ, 8(Jan 1977):73-4.

Dick, Robert C. Black Protest: Issues and Tactics. Westport,
   Conn.: Greenwood, 1974. Rev. by J. White, JAmS, 11(Apr
   1977):149-52.

Dickens, A. G., ed. The Courts of Europe: Politics, Patronage
   and Royalty 1400-1800. n.l.: Thames and Hudson, n.d.
   Rev. by A. Haynes, HTo, 27(Aug 1977):545-6.

Dickens, Roy S., Jr. Cherokee Prehistory: The Pisgah Phase in
   the Appalachian Summit Region. Knoxville: U Toronto Press,
   1976. Rev. by J. A. Walthall, AIQ, 3(Aut 1977):243-5.

Dickson, Brenton H. and Homer C. Lucas. One Town in the American Revolution. Weston: Weston Historical Society, 1976.
   Rev. by T. F. Glick, NEQ, 50(Je 1977):353-6.

Dickson, James G., Jr. Law and Politics. Manchaca, Texas:
   Sterling Swift, 1976. Rev. by T. Russell, ETHJ, 15(Spr
   1977):62-3.

Diepenthal, Wolfgang. Drei Volksdemokratien: Ein Konzept kommunistischer Machtstablisierung und seine Verwirklichung in
   Polen, der Tschechoslowakei und der Swojetischen Besatzungszone Deutschlands, 1944-1948. Cologne: Verlag Wissenschaft und Politik, 1974. Rev. by R. A. Francisco, JMH,
   49(Sep 1977):519-21.

Diggins, John P. Up from Communism: Conservative Odysseys in
   American Intellectual History. New York: Harper & Row,
   1975. Rev. by R. Nash, AHR, 82(Feb 1977):214.

Dillon, Richard. Images of Chinatown: Louis J. Stellman's Chinatown Photographs. San Francisco: Book Club of California,
   1976. Rev. by C. Wollenberg, CHQ, 56(Sum 1977):182-3.

Dimitrov, Ilcho. Bulgaro-Italian Political Relations, 1922-43. Sofia:
   Izdatelstvo nauka i izkustvo, 1976. Rev. by C. A. Moser,
   AHR, 82(Oct 1977):1018.

Dingman, Roger. Power in the Pacific: The Origins of Naval Arms
   Limitations, 1914-1922. Chicago, Ill.: U Chi Press, 1976.
   Rev. by W. R. Braisted, PHR, 46(Aug 1977):526-7.

Di Peso, Charles C. Casas Grandes: A Fallen Trading Center of
    the Gran Chichimeca. Dragoon, Arizona: Amerind Foundation,
    1974. Rev. by R. F. Heizer, AIQ, 3(Sum 1977):169-70.

Dippie, Brian W. Custer's Last Stand: The Anatomy of an Ameri-
    can Myth. Missoula: U Mon Press, 1976. Rev. by B.
    Rosenberg, AHR, 82(Je 1977):749-50; R. C. Carriker, PHR,
    46(Aug 1977):504-6; P. A. Hutton, WHQ, 8(Apr 1977):222-4.

Diskin, Martin, ed. see Cook, Scott, ed.

Dixon, Peter. Canning: Politician & Statesman. London: Weiden-
    feld & Nicolson, 1976. Rev. by E. A. Smith, EHR, 92(Oct
    1977):916; P. J. V. Rolo, History, 62(Je 1977):334-5.

Djilas, Milovan. Wartime. Boston: Harcourt, Brace & Jovano-
    vich, 1977. Rev. by S. Miller, Comm, 64(Nov 1977):75-8.

Djurfeldt, Goran and Staffan Lindberg. Pills against Poverty: A
    Study of the Introduction of Western Medicine in a Tamil Vil-
    lage. Lund: Student-litteratur, 1975. Rev. by M. Moffat,
    JAS, 36(Feb 1977):379-81.

Dmytryshyn, Basil. A History of Russia. Englewood Cliffs, N.J.:
    Prentice-Hall, 1977. Rev. by O. E. S., CurH, 73(Oct 1977):
    128.

_____, and E. A. P. Crownhart-Vaughn, eds. Colonial Russian
    America: Kyrill T. Khlebnikov's Reports, 1817-1832. Port-
    land: Oregon Historical Society, 1976. Rev. by W. Kirchner,
    AHR, 82(Oct 1977):1070; C. B. O'Brien, CHQ, 56(Sum 1977):
    178-9; J. W. Caruthers, JOW, 16(Jan 1977):71-2.

Dobbs, Betty Jo Teeter. The Foundations of Newton's Alchemy or,
    "The Hunting of the Greene Lyon." New York and London:
    Cam U Press, 1975. Rev. by H. Guerlac JMH, 49(Mar
    1977):130-3.

Dobbs, Farrell. Teamster Politics. New York: Monad Press,
    1975. Rev. by H. Berman, MinnH, 45(Spr 1977):201-2.

Dobyns, Henry F. Native American Historical Demography: A
    Critical Bibliography. Bloomington: Ind U Press, 1976.
    Rev. by R. N. Ellis, NMHR, 52(Oct 1977):337-43.

_____. Spanish Colonial Tucson: A Demographic History. Tuc-
    son: U Ariz Press, 1976. Rev. by D. J. Garr, AHR, 82
    (Je 1977):735; M. F. Doran, ChOk, 55(Spr 1977):110-2; M.
    Simmons, HAHR, 57(May 1977):336-7; J. R. Fireman, NMHR,
    52(Apr 1977):164-6; B. M. Fireman, WHQ, 8(Jl 1977):339-40.

_____, and Paul L. Doughty. Peru: A Cultural History. New
    York: Ox U Press, 1976. Rev. by F. B. Pike, AHR, 82(Je

1977):783-4; O. E. S., CurH, 72(Feb 1977):79; D. M. Gleason, HAHR, 57(Aug 1977):522-3.

Dodd, G. Days at the Factories or the Manufacturing Industry of Britain Described. E. P. Publishing Co. Ltd., 1975. Rev. by J. Tann, BH, 19(Jan 1977):106-7.

Dodge, Ernest S. Islands and Empires: Western Impact on the Pacific and East Asia. Oxford: Ox U Press, 1976. Rev. by P. M. Kennedy, History, 62(Je 1977):301.

Doerries, Reinhard R. Washington--Berlin, 1908-1917: Die Tätigkeit des Botschafters Johann Heinrich Graf von Bernstorff in Washington. Düsseldorf: Pädagogischer Verlag Schwann, 1975. Rev. by H. W. Gatzke, AHR, 82(Feb 1977):128-9.

Doetsch, Raymond N. Journey to the Green and Golden Lands: The Epic of Survival on the Wagon Trail. Port Washington: Kennikat Press, 1976. Rev. by D. A. Smith, JOW, 16(Jl 1977): 97.

Dolan, Jay P. The Immigrant Church: New York's Irish and German Catholics, 1815-1865. Baltimore: JHU Press, 1975. Rev. by H. B. Leonard, AHR, 82(Apr 1977):441; R. Ernst, NYHSQ, 61(Jan/Apr 1977):90-1.

Dolby, William. A History of Chinese Drama. London: Paul Elek, 1976. Rev. by L. Wu-chi, CQ, No. 71(Sep 1977):626-8.

D'Oliveira, Louise Destrehan Roger see Harvey, Horace

Dolkart, Ronald H., ed. see Falcoff, Mark, ed.

Doll, Don see Anderson, John A.

Donald, David Herbert, ed. Gone for a Soldier: The Civil War Memoirs of Private Alfred Bellard. Boston & Toronto: Little, Brown & Co., 1975. Rev. by J. L. Nichols, JSH, 43(Feb 1977):134-5.

Donaldson, Peter Samuel, ed. A Machiavellian Treatise by Stephen Gardiner. Cambridge: Cam U Press, 1975. Rev. by M. E. James, History, 62(Feb 1977):114-5.

Donavon, A. L. Philosophical Chemistry in the Scottish Enlightment: The Doctrines and Discoveries of William Cullen and Joseph Black. Totowa, N.J.: Biblio Distribution Center, 1976. Rev. by S. Mauskopf, AHR, 82(Feb 1977):112-3.

Donnelly, James S., Jr. The Land and the People of Nineteenth-Century Cork: The Rural Economy and the Land Question. London: Routledge and Kegan Paul, 1975. Rev. by S. H. Palmer, E-I, 12(Fall 1977):127-30.

Donnelly, Joseph P. Jean de Brébeuf, 1593-1649. Chicago: Loyola
    U Press, 1976. Rev. by C. J. Jaenen, AHR, 82(Oct 1977):
    1101-2.

Donno, E. S., ed. An Elizabethan in 1582: The Diary of Richard
    Madox, Fellow of All Souls. n.l.: Hakluyt Society, 1976.
    Rev. by A. L. Rowse, HTo, 27(Aug 1977):547-8.

Donovan, Arthur L. Philosophical Chemistry in the Scottish Enlight-
    enment: The Doctrines and Discoveries of William Cullen and
    Joseph Black. Edinburgh: Edinburgh U Press, 1976. Rev.
    by R. G. Olson, WMQ, 34(Oct 1977):681-2.

Donovan, Francis D. The New Grant: A History of Medway. Med-
    way: Town of Medway, 1976. Rev. by T. F. Glick, NEQ,
    50(Je 1977):353-6.

Donovan, Peter, Carl E. Dorris, and Lawrence R. Sullivan. Chi-
    nese Communist Materials at the Bureau of Investigation Ar-
    chives, Taiwan. Ann Arbor: U Michigan, Center for Chinese
    Studies, 1976. Rev. by D. Holm, CQ, No. 70(Je 1977):439-40.

Doran, J. E. and F. R. Hodson. Mathematics and Computers in
    Archaeology. Cambridge: Har U Press, 1975. Rev. by G.
    L. Cowgill, AmAnt, 42(Jan 1977):126-9; J. Wilcock, Antiquity,
    51(Jl 1977):158-9.

Dorig, Jose. Art Antique. Collections Privees De Suisse Romande.
    Mainz: Philipp von Zabern, 1975. Rev. by J. G. Pedley,
    AJA, 81(Spr 1977):251-2.

Dorris, Carl E. see Donovan, Peter

Dorson, Richard M. Folklore and Fakelore: Essays toward a Dis-
    cipline of Folk Studies. Cambridge: Har U Press, 1976.
    Rev. by J. Vansina, JIH, 8(Aut 1977):357-9.

Dorwart, Jeffery M. The Pigtail War: American Involvement in
    the Sino-Japanese War of 1894-1895. Amherst: U Mass Press,
    1975. Rev. by P. A. Varg, AHR, 81(Dec 1976):1266.

Doty, C. Stewart. From Cultural Rebellion to Counter-revolution:
    The Politics of Maurice Barrès. Athens: Ohio U Press,
    1976. Rev. by R. Soucy, AHR, 82(Apr 1977):372-3.

Dougan, Michael B. Confederate Arkansas: The People and Policies
    of a Frontier State in Wartime. University, Ala.: University
    of Alabama Press, 1976. Rev. by L. B. Baltimore, JSH, 43
    (Nov 1977):620-1.

Doughty, Paul L. see Dobyns, Henry F.

Douglas, Ann. The Feminization of American Culture. New York:
    Knopf, 1977. Rev. by S. Schnur, Comm, 64(Nov 1977):68-71.

Douglas, David C. The Norman Fate, 1100-1154. Berkeley: U
Cal Press, 1976. Rev. by J. W. Alexander, AHR, 81(Dec
1976):1088-89; J. W. Baldwin, Historian, 39(May 1977):536-7.

Douglas, Roy. Land, People and Politics: A History of the Land
Question in the United Kingdom, 1878-1952. London: Allison
and Busby, 1976. Rev. by F. M. L. Thompson, History, 62
(Je 1977):340.

Douglass, William A. and Jon Bilbao. Amerikanuak: Basques in
the New World. Reno: U Nev Press, 1975. Rev. by O. L.
Jones, WHQ, 8(Jan 1977):62-3.

Dove, Vee. Madison County Homes: A Collection of Pre-Civil War
Homes and Family Heritages. Madison County, Va.: author,
1975. Rev. by J. R. Fishburne, VMHB, 85(Jan 1977):112-13.

Dowling, Brendan R. see Kennedy, Kieran A.

Downey, Matthew T., ed. see Linden, Glenn M., ed.

Downs, Robert B. Books That Changed the South. Chapel Hill:
UNC Press, 1977. Rev. by W. J. Cooper, Jr., JSH, 43
(Nov 1977):638-9.

Doyle, Gerald P. Calligraphy on the Spanish Borderland. Privately
printed, 1976. Rev. by J. M. McReynolds, ETHJ, 15(No. 2,
1977):55-6.

Doyle, Lynn, pseud. see Montgomery, Leslie Alexander

Drache, Hiram M. Beyond the Furrow: Some Keys to Successful
Farming in the Twentieth Century. Danville, Ill.: Interstate
Printers and Publishers, 1976. Rev. by G. C. Fite, MinnH,
45(Fall 1977):302.

Drago, George. Jefferson's Louisiana: Politics and the Clash of
Legal Traditions. Cambridge: Har U Press, 1975. Rev.
by J. E. Eblen, PHR, 46(May 1977):281-3.

Drake, Fred W. China Charts the World: Hsü Chi-yü and His
Geography of 1848. Cambridge, Mass.: Har U Press, 1975.
Rev. by S. M. Jones, AHR, 82(Apr 1977):411-2; S. W. Barnett, CQ, 71(Sep 1977):614-6; J. K. Leonard, JAS, 37(Nov
1977):117.

Drake, H. A. In Praise of Constantine. Berkeley: U Cal Press,
1976. Rev. by J. Eadie, AHR, 82(Oct 1977):931-2.

Dralle, Lothar. Der Staat des Deutschen Ordens in Preussen nach
dem II. Thorner Frieden. Wiesbaden: Franz Steiner Verlag,
1975. Rev. by L. G. Duggan, AHR, 82(Apr 1977):345-6; T.
Scott, EHR, 92(Oct 1977):891-2.

Draxten, Nina. Kristofer Janson in America. Boston: Twayne for the Norwegian-American Historical Association, 1976. Rev. by M. Brook, MinnH, 45(Sum 1977):251-2.

Drew, Wayland see Littlejohn, Bruce

Dreyer, June Teufel. China's Forty Millions. Cambridge: Har U Press, 1976. Rev. by M. Rossabi, JAS, 37(Nov 1977):127-8.

Driskell, David C. Two Centuries of Black American Art. New York: Knopf, 1976. Rev. by J. Maas, AHR, 82(Je 1977): 726-7.

Drucker, Peter F. The Unseen Revolution: How Pension Fund Socialism Came to America. New York: Harper & Row, 1976. Rev. by J. E. Fell, Jr., JEH, 37(Sep 1977):793.

Drummond, Ian M. Imperial Economic Policy 1917-1939: Studies in Expansion and Protection. Toronto: U Tor Press, 1974. Rev. by S. Buckley, CHR, 58(Mar 1977):100-1.

Drury, Clifford M. Nine Years with the Spokane Indians: The Diary, 1838-1848, of Elkanah Walker. Glendale, Calif.: Arthur H. Clark, 1976. Rev. by J. O. Oliphant, PNQ, 68 (Oct 1977):198.

Dryden, Edgar A. Nathaniel Hawthorne: The Poetics of Enchantment. Ithaca: Cor U Press, 1977. Rev. by C. S. B. Swann, JAmS, 11(Dec 1977):417-20.

Dubay, Robert W. John Jones Pettus, Mississippi Fire-eater: His Life and Times, 1813-1867. Jackson: U Press Miss, 1975. Rev. by J. G. Tregle, Jr., AHR, 82(Feb 1977):183-4; M. S. Legan, ETHJ, 15(Spr 1977):51-2.

Dube, Leela. Sociology of Kinship: An Analytical Survey of Literature. Bombay: Popular Prakashan, 1974. Rev. by S. Vatuk, JAS, 36(Aug 1977):777.

Dubey, S. M. Social Mobility among the Professions: Study of the Professions in a Transitional Indian City. Bombay: Popular Prakashan, 1975. Rev. by A. B. Cottrell, JAS, 36(Aug 1977): 774.

Dubinsky, A. M. The Far East in the Second World War. Moscow: Izdatel'stvo "Nauka," 1972. Rev. by Y. Akashi, AHR, 82 (Apr 1977):424-5.

Du Bois, W. E. B. The Correspondence of W. E. B. Du Bois. Vol. I and II. Amherst: U Mass Press, 1973, 1976. Rev. by D. L. Lewis, AHR, 82(Apr 1977):444-5.

Duby, Georges and Armand Wallon, eds. Histoire de la France

rurale. 3 vols. Paris: Seuil, 1975. Rev. by E. Weber, AHR, 82(Feb 1977):115-7.

Ducellier, Alain. Le Drame de Byzance: Idéal et échec d'une société chretienne. Paris: Hachette, 1976. Rev. by T. E. Gregory, AHR, 82(Oct 1977):935-6.

Duckett, Kenneth W. Modern Manuscripts: A Practical Manual for Their Management, Care, and Use. Nashville: American Association for State and Local History, 1975. Rev. by R. C. Berner, PNQ, 68(Jl 1977):148-9.

Ducrey, Pierre. Gibbon Et Rome A La Lumiere De L'Historiographie Moderne. Geneve: Librairie Droz, n.d. Rev. by A. L. Rowse, HTo, 27(Oct 1977):681-2.

Duff, Ernest A. and John F. McCamant. Violence and Repression in Latin America: A Quantitative and Historical Analysis. New York: Free Press, 1976. Rev. by P. H. Smith, AHR, 82(Apr 1977):477; J. Miller, HAHR, 57(May 1977):367-8.

Duff, Wilson. Images: Stone: B.C.: Thirty Centuries of Northwest Coast Indian Sculpture. Seattle: U Wash Press, 1975. Rev. by H. J. Calkins, PNQ, 68(Oct 1977):197-8.

Duffy, John. The Healers: The Rise of the Medical Establishment. New York: McGraw-Hill, 1976. Rev. by J. H. Ellis, AHR, 82(Je 1977):728.

Duignan, Peter, and L. H. Gann, eds. Colonialism in Africa 1870-1960. Cambridge: Cam U Press, 1975. Rev. by J. F. Munro, History, 62(Je 1977):265-6; W. B. Cohen, JMH, 49 (Mar 1977):120-1.

Duiker, William J. The Rise of Nationalism in Vietnam, 1900-1941. Ithaca: Cor U Press, 1976. Rev. by J. P. Harrison, AHR, 82(Apr 1977):425; K. W. Jones, Historian, 39(May 1977):565-6; N. V. Long, JAS, 36(May 1977):592-3.

Dull, Jonathan R. The French Navy and American Independence: A Study of Arms and Diplomacy, 1774-1787. Princeton: Prin U Press, 1976. Rev. by R. J. Bauer, AHR, 82(Feb 1977):118; E. L. Asher, WMQ, 34(Jan 1977):145-7.

Duls, Louisa Desaussure. Richard II in the Early Chronicles. The Hague: Mouton, 1975. Rev. by G. B. Stow, Jr., AHR, 82(Feb 1977):78.

Dumbarton Oaks Papers, number 29. Washington, D. C.: Dumbarton Oaks Center for Byzantine Studies, 1975. Rev. by D. de F. Abrahamse, AHR, 82(Je 1977):615-6.

Duncan, Archibald A. M. Scotland: The Making of the Kingdom.

New York: Barnes and Noble, 1975. Rev. by R. D. Fiala, HT, 10(Feb 1977):339.

Duncan, Bingham. Whitelaw Reid: Journalist, Politician, Diplomat. Athens: U Ga Press, 1975. Rev. by H. W. Morgan, PHR, 46(May 1977):300-1.

Duncan-Jones, Richard. The Economy of the Roman Empire. London: Cam U Press, 1974. Rev. by W. F. Jashemski, AHR, 82(Je 1977):612-3.

Dunham, Dows and William Kelly Simpson. The Mastaba of Queen Mersyankh III G 7530-7540. Boston: Dept. of Ancient Near Eastern Art, Museum of Fine Arts, Boston, 1974. Rev. by D. P. Silverman, JNES, 36(Jan 1977):75-6.

Dunlap, Leslie W. and Fred Shelley, ed. The Publication of American Manuscripts. Iowa City: University of Iowa Libraries, 1976. Rev. by P. D. Jordan, AI, 44(Sum 1977):78-9; P. I. Chestnut, AmArc, 40(Jl 1977):352-4; D. J. Olson, MichH, 61 (Sum 1977):179-81.

Dunleavy, Gareth W. and Janet E. Dunleavy. The O'Conor Papers: A Descriptive Catalog and Surname Register of the Materials at Clonalis House. Madison: U Wis Press, 1977. Rev. by T. E. Hachey, E-I, 12(Fall 1977):125-7.

Dunleavy, Janet E. see Dunleavy, Gareth W.

Dunn, F. L. Rain-Forest Collectors and Traders: A Study of Resource Utilization in Modern and Ancient Malaya. Kuala Lumpur: Malaysian Branch of the Royal Asiatic Society, 1975. Rev. by K. L. Hutterer, JAS, 36(Aug 1977):792-3.

Dunn, Stephen. Looking for Holes in the Ceiling: Poems. Amherst: U Mass Press, 1974. Rev. by P. Stitt, GR, 31(Fall 1977):762-71.

Durden, Robert F. The Dukes of Durham, 1865-1929. Durham: Duke U Press, 1975. Rev. by J. A. Pratt, AHR, 82(Apr 1977):457-8.

Durham, Walter T. Daniel Smith, Frontier Statesman. Gallatin, Tennessee: Sumner Co. Library Board, 1976. Rev. by W. A. Walker, Jr., ArkHQ, 36(Spr 1977):91-2; R. C. Bailey, FCHQ, 51(Oct 1977):368-9; J. T. Bloom, JSH, 43(Aug 1977): 446-7; O. K. Rice, WMQ, 34(Oct 1977):687-8.

Duus, Peter. The Rise of Modern Japan. Boston: Houghton Mifflin, 1976. Rev. by G. L. Bernstein, JAS, 36(Aug 1977): 754-6.

Duval, P. M. and C. Hawkes, ed. Celtic Art in Ancient Europe.

London: Seminar Press, 1976. Rev. by S. J. de Laet, Antiquity, 51(Jl 1977):161-2.

Dworkin, Ronald. Taking Rights Seriously. n.l.: Har U, n.d.
Rev. by W. J. Bennett, Comm, 64(Aug 1977):75-8.

Dwyer, D. J., ed. Asian Urbanization: A Hong Kong Casebook.
Hong Kong: Hong Kong U Press, 1971. Rev. by T. F.
Barton, JAAS, 12(Jan/Oct 1977):269-72.

_____, ed. The City as a Centre of Change in Asia. Hong
Kong: Hong Kong U Press, 1972. Rev. by T. F. Barton,
JAAS, 12(Jan/Oct 1977):269-72.

_____, ed. The City in The Third World. New York: Harper
and Row, 1974. Rev. by T. F. Barton, JAAS, 12(Jan/Oct
1977):269-72.

_____. People and Housing in Third World Cities: Perspectives
on the Problem of Spontaneous Settlements. New York: Longman, 1975. Rev. by W. E. Reed, JAS, 36(May 1977):537-8.

Dwyer, John T. Condemned to the Mines: The Life of Eugene
O'Connell, 1815-1891, Pioneer Bishop of Northern California
and Nevada. New York: Vantage Press, 1976. Rev. by P.
T. Conmy, CHQ, 56(Sum 1977):187-8.

Dziewanowski, M. K. The Communist Party of Poland. Cambridge,
Mass.: Har U Press, 1976. Rev. by A. Bromke, AHR, 82
(Je 1977):687-8.

Earle, Carville V. The Evolution of a Tidewater Settlement System: All Hollow's Parish, Maryland, 1650-1783. Chicago:
U of Chicago Geography Research Paper 170, 1975. Rev. by
D. O. Percy, AgH, 51(Jan 1977):265-6; L. S. Walsh, WMQ,
34(Jan 1977):157-9.

Earle, John R., Dean D. Knudsen, and Donald W. Shriver, Jr.
Spindles and Spires: A Re-study of Religion and Social
Change in Gastonia. Atlanta: John Knox Press, 1976. Rev.
by G. Wolfskill, JSH, 43(May 1977):321-2.

Ebato, Akira, and Kazuo Watanabe, eds. Atlas of Japan: Physical,
Economic and Social. Tokyo: International Society for Educational Information, 1974. Rev. by R. Hall, JAS, 36(Feb 1977):
357-8.

Ebel, Gerhard and Michael Behnen, eds. Botschafter Paul Graf von
Hatzfeldt: Nachgelassene Papiere, 1838-1901. 2 vols. Boppard am Rhein: Harald Boldt Verlag, 1976. Rev. by J. S.
Mortimer, AHR, 82(Oct 1977):1001-2.

Echols, John M. and Hassan Schadily. An English-Indonesian

Dictionary. Ithaca: Cor U Press, 1975. Rev. by H. Krida-laksana, JAS, 36(Feb 1977):387-8.

Eckes, Alfred E., Jr. A Search for Solvency: Bretton Woods and the International Monetary System, 1941-1971. Austin: U Tex Press, 1975. Rev. by G. C. Herring, AHR, 82(Oct 1977): 1097-8.

Eckley, Grace see Begnal, Michael H.

Economisch-en Sociaal-Historisch Jaarboek. The Hague: Martinus Nijhoff for Het Nederlandsch Economisch-Historisch Archief, 1975. Rev. by H. R. C. Wright, JEH, 37(Je 1977):522-3; J. Mokyr, JEH, 37(Sep 1977):812-3.

Edel, Elmar, and Staffen Wenig, eds. Die Jahreszeitenreliefs aus dem Sonnenheiligtum de Konigs Ne-user-re. Berlin: Akademie-Verlag, 1974. Rev. by W. J. Murnane, JNES, 36 (Jan 1977):76.

Edelson, Marshall. Language and Interpretation in Psychoanalysis. New Haven: Yale U Press, 1975. Rev. by R. H. King, GR, 31(Spr 1977):252-8.

Edwardes, Michael. Nehru: A Political Biography. New York: Praeger, 1972. Rev. by E. Zelliot, JAAS, 12(Jan/Oct 1977): 312.

Edwards, A. C. John Petre. n.l.: Regency Press, n.d. Rev. by A. L. Rowse, HTo, 27(Feb 1977):133.

Edwards, G. Roger. Corinth VII, Part III, Corinthian Hellenistic Pottery. Princeton: American School of Classical Studies at Athens, 1975. Rev. by W. W. Rudolph, AJA, 81(Spr 1977): 246-7.

Edwards, John N. Noted Guerrillas, or The War-fare of the Border. Dayton, Ohio: Morningside Bookshop, 1976. Rev. by E. B. Long, CWTI, 16(Oct 1977):49.

Edwards, Lovett F., tr. see Sigman, Jean

Edwards, Robert, ed. The preservation of Australia's Aboriginal Heritage. Canberra: Australian Institute of Aboriginal Studies, 1975. Rev. by P. Gathercole, Antiquity, 51(Jl 1977):157-8.

Egan, Ferol. Frémont: Explorer for a Restless Nation. Garden City, N.Y.: Doubleday, 1977. Rev. by W. T. Jackson, CHQ, 56(Fall 1977):277-8; M. L. Spence, NMHR, 52(Jl 1977):253-4.

Ehrenberg, Ralph E., ed. Pattern and Progress: Research in His-torical Geography. Washington: Howard U Press, 1975. Rev. by C. V. Earle, AgH, 51(Jl 1977):597-9; D. E. Green, JSH, 43(Feb 1977):148-50.

Ehrlich, Cyril. The Piano: A History. London: J. N. Dent, 1976. Rev. by M. Wilkins, JEH, 37(Sep 1977):793-4.

Eidelman, N. Ia. Herzen against Autocracy: the Secret Political History of Russia in the 18th and 19th Centuries and the Free Press. Moscow: Izdatel'stvo "Mysl'", 1973. Rev. by A. Gleason, AHR, 82(Feb 1977):150.

Eikenberg, Wiltrud. Das Handelshaus der Runtinger zu Regensburg. Göttingen: Vandenhoeck and Ruprecht, 1976. Rev. by P. W. Strait, AHR, 82(Oct 1977):939-40.

Eisenberg, Peter L. The Sugar Industry in Pernambuco: Modernization Without Change, 1840-1910. Berkeley and Los Angeles: U Cal Press, 1974. Rev. by M. Craton, AgH, 51(Jan 1977): 276-8.

Eksteins, Modris. The Limits of Reason: The German Democratic Press and the Collapse of Weimar Democracy. Oxford: Ox U Press, 1975. Rev. by W. E. Mosse, ESR, 7(Jl 1977):355-6.

Ekwensi, Cypreian. Survive the Peace. Heinemann, 1976. Rev. by H. Dinwiddy, AfAf, 76(Jl 1977):409-10.

El-Ayouty, Yassin, ed. The Organization of African Unity After Ten Years: Comparative Perspectives. Rev. by I. Wallerstein, JAAS, 12(Jan/Oct 1977):293.

Elazar, Daniel J. Community and Polity: The Organizational Dynamics of American Jewry. n.l.: Jewish Publication Society, n.d. Rev. by J. Weinberg, Comm, 63(Je 1977): 83-8.

Eliasberg, George. Der Ruhrkrieg von 1920, Schriftenreihe des Forschungsin Forschungsinstituts der Friedrich-Ebert Stiftung, Vol. 100. Bonn: Verlag Neue Gesellschaft, 1974. Rev. by F. L. Carsten, ESR, 7(Jan 1977):118-19.

Elkins, David J. Electoral Participation in South Indian Context. Durham, N.C.: Carolina Academic Press, 1975. Rev. by R. L. Hargrave, Jr., JAS, 36(Aug 1977):769-70.

Elkins, Stanley M. Slavery: A Problem in American Institutional and Intellectual Life. Chicago: U Chicago Press, 1976. Rev. by J. White, JAmS, 11(Aug 1977):283-4.

Ellenburg, Stephen. Rousseau's Political Philosophy. Ithaca: Cor U Press, 1976. Rev. by R. Birn, AHR, 82(Je 1977):650.

Ellenreuther, Hermann, ed. see Angermann, Erich, ed.

Elliott, Emory. Power and the Pulpit in Puritan New England. Princeton: Prin U Press, 1975. Rev. by D. Weber, JIH, 8(Sum 1977): 173-4.

Elliott, Lawrence. The Long Hunter: A New Life of Daniel Boone. New York: Reader's Digest Press, 1976. Rev. by R. B. Maddox, WVH, 38(Jan 1977):171-2.

Ellis, John. The Social History of the Machine. London: Croom Helm, 1976. Rev. by G. Best, History, 62(Je 1977):342.

Ellis, Joseph and Robert Moore. School for Soldiers: West Point and the Profession of Arms. New York: Ox U Press, 1974. Rev. by C. L. Christman, AHR, 82(Apr 1977):462; W. Rundell, Jr., AS, 18(Fall 1977):110.

Ellis, Peter Beresford. Hell or Connaught!: The Cromwellian Colonisation of Ireland, 1652-1660. London: Hamish Hamilton, 1975. Rev. by F. D. Dow, History, 62(Feb 1977):121-2.

Elmen, Paul. Wheat Flour Messiah: Eric Jansson of Bishop Hill. Carbondale: So Ill U Press, 1976. Rev. by K. L. Miller, JISHS, 70(Aug 1977):255-6.

Elphick, Richard. Kraal and Castle: Khoikhoi and the Founding of White South Africa. New Haven, Conn.: Yale U Press, 1977. Rev. by B. M. Fagan, History, 6(Nov/Dec 1977):35-6.

Elvin, Mark, and G. William Skinner, eds. The Chinese City Between Two Worlds. Stanford: Stan U Press, 1974. Rev. by S. C. Lee, AHR, 82(Feb 1977):160-1.

Elwitt, Stanford. The Making of the Third Republic: Class and Politics in France, 1868-1884. Baton Rouge: LSU Press, 1975. Rev. by J. Q. Graham, Jr., JMH, 49(Mar 1977):142-3.

Elwood, Ralph Carter. Russian Social Democracy in the Underground: A Study of the RSDRP in the Ukraine, 1907-1914. Assen: Royal Vangorcum, 1974. Rev. by A. K. Wildman, JMH, 49(Sep 1977):524-6.

Ely, James W., Jr. The Crisis of Conservative Virginia: The Byrd Organization and the Politics of Massive Resistance. Knoxville: U Tenn Press, 1976. Rev. by R. L. Zangrands, AHR, 82(Apr 1977):472-3; M. V. Woodward, GHQ, 51(Sum 1977):210-1; B. A. Glasrud, JSH, 43(May 1977):324-5; J. R. Sweeney, VMHB, 85(Apr 1977):214-6.

Ely, Richard. Unto God and Caesar: Religious Issues in the Emerging Commonwealth, 1891-1906. Forest Grove, Ore.: International Scholarly Book Services, 1976. Rev. by F. G. Clarke, AHR, 82(Oct 1977):1055-6.

el Zein, Abdul Hamid M. The Sacred Meadows: A Structural Analysis of Religious Symbolism in an East African Town. Evanston: Northwestern U Press, 1974. Rev. by H. & M. Ottenheimer, JAAS, 12(Jan/Oct 1977):288-9.

Emden, A. B. A Biographical Register of the University of Oxford,
A. D. 1501-1540. Oxford: Ox U Press, 1974. Rev. by P.
Williams, History, 62(Feb 1977):114.

Emerson, Everett, ed. Letters from New England. The Massachusetts Bay Colony, 1629-1638. Amherst: U Massachusetts
Press, 1976. Rev. by R. Thompson, JAmS, 11(Aug 1977):
294-5; D. B. Rutman, NEQ, 50(Sep 1977):556-7; F. J. Bremer, WMQ, 34(Oct 1977):679-81.

Emmanuelli, François, Xavier. Pouvoir royal et vie régionale en
Provence au déclin de la monarchie. 2 vols. Lille: Université de Lille, 1974. Rev. by T. E. Hall, AHR, 82(Apr 1977):
368.

Emmison, F. G. Elizabethan Life: Home, Work and Land. Chelms-
ford: Essex County Council, 1976. Rev. by C. S. L. Davies,
EHR, 92(Oct 1977):895; J. A. Sharpe, History, 62(Je 1977):
321-2.

Ende, Stuart A. Keats and the Sublime. New Haven: Yale U Press,
1976. Rev. by F. Ferguson, GR, 31(Sum 1977):511-6.

Endicott, S. L. British China Policy 1933-37: Diplomacy and Enterprise. Manchester: Manchester U Press, 1975. Rev. by W.
E. Cheong, BH, 19(Jan 1977):103-5.

Endicott, Stephen Lyon. Diplomacy and Enterprise: British China
Policy 1933-1937. Manchester: Man U Press, 1975. Rev.
by P. Lowe, History, 62(Feb 1977):149-50.

Engel-Janosi, Friedrich, Grete Klingenstein, and Heinrich Lutz, eds.
Fürst, Bürger, Mensch: Untersuchunger Zu Politischen Und
Soziokulturellen Wandlungsprozessen Im Varrevolutionaren Europa.
Munich: R. Oldenbourg Verlag, 1975. Rev. by T. C. W.
Blanning, History, 62(Feb 1977):140-1.

Engerman, Stanley L., and Eugene M. Genovese, eds. Race and
Slavery in the Western Hemisphere: Quantitative Studies.
Princeton: Prin U Press, 1975. Rev. by C. N. Degler,
JLAS, 9(May 1977):150-2; O. M. Scruggs, PH, 45(Jl 1977):
276-9.

Englund, Karl. Workmen's Insurance in Swedish Politics, 1884-
1901. Stockholm: Almqvist and Wiksell, 1976. Rev. by P.
V. Thorson, AHR, 82(Oct 1977):994.

Engstrand, Iris Wilson. Royal Officer in Baja California, 1768-
1770: Joaquin Valázquez de León. Los Angeles: Dawson's
Book Shop, 1976. Rev. by E. A. Brilharz, WHQ, 8(Apr
1977):227-8.

Entelis, John P. Pluralism and Party Transformation in Lebanon:

Al-Kata'ib, 1936-1970. Leiden: E. J. Brill, 1974. Rev. by
W. W. Haddad, AHR, 82(Oct 1977):1029-30.

Enys, John. The American Journals of Lt. John Enys. Ed. by
    Elizabeth Cometti. Syracuse, N.Y.: Adirondack Museum,
    1976. Rev. by D. A. Donath, VH, 45(Win 1977):46-7.

Eogan, George see Herity, Michael

Epp, Frank H. Mennonites in Canada, 1786-1920: The History of
    a Separate People. Toronto: Macmillan, 1974. Rev. by P.
    K. Conkin, AHR, 81(Dec 1976):1282-83.

Epstein, Edward Jay. Agency of Fear. Boston: Putnam, 1977.
    Rev. by S. Cropsey, Comm, 64(Nov 1977):78-80.

Epstein, T. S. and D. Jackson. The Feasibility of Fertility Plan-
    ning. Oxford: Pergamon Press, 1977. Rev. by L. Mair,
    AfAf, 76(Jl 1977):413-14.

Erdoes, Richard. The Raindance People: The Pueblo Indians,
    Their Past and Present. New York: Knopf, 1976. Rev. by
    F. J. Johnston, JOW, 16(Jan 1977):86-7.

Erickson, Carolly. The Medieval Vision: Essays in History and
    Perception. Oxford: Ox U Press, 1976. Rev. by C. Morris,
    History, 62(Feb 1977):103-4.

Erickson, Erik H. Life History and the Historical Moment. New
    York: W. W. Norton, 1975. Rev. by L. R. Johnson, AmArc,
    39(Jl 1976):366-7.

Erickson, Jackson T. Indian Rights Association Papers: A Guide
    to the Microfilm Edition, 1864-1973. Glen Rock, N.J.:
    Microfilming Corp. of America, 1975. Rev. by J. R. Glenn,
    AmArc, 39(Jl 1976):356-7.

Erikson, Kai T. Everything in Its Path: Destruction of Community
    in the Buffalo Creek Flood. New York: Simon and Schuster,
    1976. Rev. by H. D. Shapiro, AS, 18(Fall 1977):111.

Ernby, Eibert. Adeln och bondjorden. Stockholm: Almqvist &
    Wiksell, 1975. Rev. by M. Roberts, EHR, 92(Oct 1977):
    904-6.

Ernst, Robert T., and Lawrence Hugg, eds. Black America:
    Geographic Perspective. Garden City, N.Y.: Doubleday,
    1976. Rev. by D. V. Taylor, MinnH, 45(Sum 1977):252-3.

Erskine-Hill, Howard. The Social Milieu of Alexander Pope: Lives,
    Example and the Poetic Response. London: Yale U Press,
    1975. Rev. by H. T. Dickinson, History, 62(Feb 1977):132.

Eschmann, Anncharlott. Das Regigiöse Geschichtsbilt Der Azteken.
    Berlin: Mann Verlag, 1976. Rev. by U. Lamb, HAHR, 57
    (Aug 1977):528-9.

Esh, Tina and Illith Rosenblum. Tourism in Developing Countries--
    Trick or Treat? A Report from the Gambia. Uppsala: Scan-
    dinavian Institute of African Studies, 1975. Rev. by E. Gillies,
    Africa, 47(No. 1, 1977):116.

Esherick, Joseph W., ed. Last Chance in China: The World War
    II Despatches of John S. Service. New York: Vintage Books,
    1974. Rev. by W. W. Toxer, PHR, 46(Aug 1977):529-31.

_____. Reform and Revolution in China: The 1911 Revolution
    in Hunan and Hubei. Berkeley: U Cal Press, 1975. Rev.
    by J. H. Fincher, JAS, 37(Nov 1977):119-20.

Euler, Robert C., ed. see Gumerman, George, ed.

Evans, Elizabeth. Weathering the Storm: Women of the American
    Revolution. New York: Charles Scribner's, 1975. Rev. by
    R. E. Berger, NYHSQ, 61(Jan/Apr 1977):82-3.

Evans, Eric J. The Contentious Tithe: The Tithe Problem and
    English Agriculture 1750-1850. London: Routledge and Kegan
    Paul, 1976. Rev. by W. R. Ward, EHR, 92(Oct 1977):911;
    J. T. Ward, History, 62(Je 1977):332.

Everest, Allan S. Moses Hazen and the Canadian Refugees in the
    American Revolution. Syracuse: Syr U Press, 1976. Rev. by
    J. R. Maguire, VH, 45(Sum 1977):175-8.

_____, ed. see also Carroll, Charles

Evers, Hans-Dieter. Monks, Priests and Peasants: A Study of
    Buddhism and Social Structure in Central Ceylon. Leiden:
    E. J. Brill, 1972. Rev. by H. L. Senviratne, JAS, 36(Feb
    1977):381-2.

Evitts, William J. A Matter of Allegiances: Maryland from 1850
    to 1861. Baltimore: JHU Press, 1974. Rev. by M. C.
    Kahl, AHR, 81(Dec 1976):1251.

Ewald, Ursula. Estudios sobre la hacienda colonial en Mexico.
    Wiesbaden: Franz Steiner Verlag, 1976. Rev. by W. B.
    Taylor, AHR, 82(Je 1977):779-80.

Ewen, Stuart. Captains of Consciousness: Advertising and the
    Social Roots of the Consumer Culture. New York: McGraw-
    Hill, 1976. Rev. by O. A. Pease, AHR, 82(Oct 1977):1092-3.

Eyll, Klara van, ed. see Kellenbenz, Hermann, ed.

Faaland, Just and J. R. Parkinson. Bangladesh: The Test Case for Development. Boulder: Westview Press, 1976. Rev. by P. J. Bertocci, JAS, 36(Aug 1977):783-4.

Fagan, B. see Oliver, R.

Fagan, John Lee. Altithermal Occupation of the Spring Sites in the Northern Great Basin. Eugene: U Oregon Press, 1974. Rev. by D. D. Fowler, Antiquity, 42(Jan 1977):140-1.

Fairbank, John, et al. The I. G. in Peking: Letters of Robert Hart, Chinese Maritime Customs, 1868-1907. Cambridge, Mass.: Har U Press, 1976. Rev. by E. G. Beal, Jr., AHR, 82(Feb 1977):159-60; J. M. Downs, PHR, 46(Aug 1977): 520-2; S. A. M. Adshead, JAS, 36(Aug 1977):720-1.

Fairbank, John K. see Kamachi, Noriko

_____, ed. see Kierman, Frank A., ed.

Fairbank, John King, ed. see Hart, Robert

Fairbank, Wilma. America's Cultural Experiment in China, 1942-1949. Washington: Department of State, 1976. Rev. by P. A. Zimmerman, AHR, 82(Apr 1977):416.

Fairchilds, Cissie C. Poverty and Charity in Aix-en-Provence, 1640-1789. Baltimore: Johns Hopkins U Press, 1976. Rev. by O. Hufton, HJ, 20(No. 4, 1977):971-6; H. M. Solomon, JEH, 37(Je 1977):508-9; E. Fox-Genovese, JIH, 8(Aug 1977): 361-3.

Fairfield, Leslie P. John Bale: Mythmaker for the English Reformation. West Lafayette, Ind.: Purdue U Press, 1976. Rev. by J. F. H. New, 82(Je 1977):631.

Fairhurst, Janet Perry. Homes of the Signers of the Declaration. New York: Hartt, 1976. Rev. by S. A. Riggs, VMHB, 85 (Jl 1977):369.

Fajn, Max. The Journal des hommes libres de tous les pays, 1792-1800. The Hague: Mouton, 1975. Rev. by R. Birn, AHR, 82(Apr 1977):370.

Falcoff, Mark and Ronald H. Dolkart, eds. Prologue to Peron: Argentina in Depression and War, 1930-1943. Berkeley: U Cal Press, 1976. Rev. by R. A. Potash, AHR, 81(Dec 1976):1286.

Falconer, Thomas. On the Discovery of the Mississippi, and on the Southwestern Oregon, and North-Western Boundary of the United States. Austin: Shoal Creek Publishers, 1975. Rev. by R. S. Weddle, LaH, 18(Win 1977):120-1.

Falk, Stanley L. Seventy Days to Singapore. New York: G. P.
Putnam, 1975. Rev. by R. Callahan, AHR, 82(Je 1977):
645-6.

Fal'kovich, S. M. The Proletariat of Russia and Poland in Their
Joint Revolutionary Struggle (1907-1912). Moscow: Izdatel'
stvo "Nauka", 1975. Rev. by R. D. Lewis, AHR, 82(Apr
1977):403-4.

Fancer, Shoshana B. Economic Nationalism in Latin America:
The Quest for Economic Independence. New York: Praeger,
1976. Rev. by W. Baer, HAHR, 57(May 1977):319-20.

Fanning, Michael, ed. France and Sherwood Anderson: "Paris
Notebook, 1921." Baton Rouge: LSU Press, 1976. Rev. by
K. Carabine, JAmS, 11(Dec 1977):409-10.

Fantel, Hans. William Penn: Apostle of Dissent. New York: Wm.
Morrow, 1974. Rev. by W. T. Parsons, AHR, 82(Je 1977):
730.

Farber, Samuel. Revolution and Reaction in Cuba, 1933-1960: A
Political Sociology from Machado to Castro. Middletown,
Conn.: Wesleyan U Press, 1976. Rev. by R. F. Smith, AHR,
82(Je 1977):782.

Farmer, Edward L. Early Ming Government: The Evolution of
Dual Capitals. Cambridge: Har U Press, 1976. Rev. by
C. O. Hucker, AHR, 82(Oct 1977):1043-4.

Farmer, John David. James Ensor. New York: George Braziller,
1977. Rev. by R. Paulson, GR, 31(Sum 1977):502-11.

Farrelly, Jill E. see Williams, Joyce G.

Farwell, Byron. The Great Boer War. n.l.: Allen Lane, n.d.
Rev. by G. Douds, HTo, 27(Jl 1977):475-6.

Fass, Paula S. The Damned and the Beautiful: American Youth in
the 1920's. New York: Ox U Press, 1977. Rev. by F.
Annunziata, History, 6(Oct 1977):8.

Faucher, Albert. Québec en Amérique au XIXe siècle: Essai sur
les caractères économiques de la Laurentie. Montreal: Fides,
1973. Rev. by I. M. Spry, JEH, 37(Je 1977):509-11.

Faulk, Odie B. The U. S. Camel Corps: An Army Experiment.
New York: Ox U Press, 1976. Rev. by W. B. Skelton,
AHR, 82(Je 1977):744; W. S. Greever, PHR, 46(Aug 1977):
502-3; R. Brandes, WHQ, 8(Jan 1977):76-7.

Fausto, Boris. Trabalho Urbano e Conflito Social (1890-1920). Rio de
Janeiro - Sao Paulo: DIFEL/Difusao Editorial S. A., 1976. Rev.
by H. Spaulding, HAHR, 57(Aug 1977):553-4.

Favreau, Marie-Luise. Studien zur Frühgeschichte des Deutschen
Ordens. Stuttgart: Ernst Klett Verlag, 1974. Rev. by L.
G. Duggan, AHR, 82(Apr 1977):345-6.

Fay, Peter Ward. The Opium War, 1840-1842: Barbarians in the
Celestial Empire in the Early Part of the Nineteenth Century
and the War by Which They Forced Her Gates Ajar. Chapel
Hill: U NC Press, 1975. Rev. by P. A. Cohen, Historian,
39(Feb 1977):362-3; I Nish, History, 62(Je 1977):291-2.

Febvre, L. and H. J. Martin. The Coming of the Book: The
Impact of Printing, 1450-1800. London: NLB, 1976. Rev.
by G. Parker, History, 62(Je 1977):316.

Feder, Ernst. Heute sprach ich mitt...: Tagebucher eines Berliner Publizisten 1926-1932. Stuttgart: Deutsche Verlags-
Anstalt, 1971. Rev. by V. L. Lidtke, AHR, 82(Feb 1977):
131.

Fehrenbacker, Don E., ed. Freedom and Its Limitations in American Life. Stanford, Calif.: Stan U Press, 1976. Rev. by
R. H. Bremner, JSH, 43(Nov 1977):601-2.

_____, ed. see also Potter, David M.

Feinstein, Estelle F. Stamford from Puritan to Patriot: The Shaping of a Connecticut Community, 1641-1774. Stamford:
Stamford Bicentennial Corp., 1976. Rev. by C. Colber, AHR,
82(Je 1977):731.

Felmly, Bradford K. see Grady, John C.

Felt, Thomas E. Researching, Writing and Publishing Local History. Nashville: American Association for State and Local
History, 1976. Rev. by S. McArthur, CHQ, 56(Spr 1977):89.

Fenley, Florence. Heart Full of Horses. San Antonio: Naylor,
n.d. Rev. by G. Lasseter, ETHJ, 15(Spr 1977):59-60.

Ferluga, Jadran, et al, eds. Glossar zur fruhmittelalterlichen
Geschichte im ostlichen Europa. Series A & B. Wiesbaden:
Franz Steiner Verlag, 1973-1975. Rev. by L. L. Blodgett,
AHR, 82(Feb 1977):81.

Ferm, Robert L. A Colonial Pastor: Jonathan Edwards the Younger, 1745-1801. Grand Rapids, Mich.: Eerdmans, 1976.
Rev. by C. C. Goen, AHR, 82(Oct 1977):1062.

_____. Jonathan Edwards the Younger, 1745-1801: A Colonial
Pastor. Grand Rapids, Mich.: Wm. B. Eerdmans, 1976.
Rev. by P. F. Gura, NEQ, 50(Mar 1977):173-6.

Fernández, Anibal, Alejo Planchart, and Gene Bigler. Modelo

demo-econo´mico de Venezuela. Caracas, Venezuela: Instituto
de Estudios Superiores de Administracion, 1975. Rev. by R.
Cowell, JEH, 37(Je 1977):511-2.

Ferrer Benimeli, Jose Antonio. Los Archivos Secretos vaticanos y
la masonería. Caracas: Universidad Cato´lica "Andres Bello",
1976. Rev. by I. M. Zavala, AHR, 82(Oct 1977):951.

Ferris, Norman B. Desperate Diplomacy: William H. Seward's
Foreign Policy, 1861. Knoxville: U Tenn Press, 1976. Rev.
by A. Castel, AHI, 12(Nov 1977):48; E. N. Paolino, AHR, 82
(Feb 1977):183; H. Jones, CWH, 23(Mar 1977):82-4; T. J.
Farnham, JSH, 43(Aug 1977):459-60.

Ferris, Robert G. see Appleman, Roy E.

Festschrift zum 150 jahrigen Bestehen des Berliner agyptischen
Museums. Berlin: Akademie-Verlag, 1974. Rev. by D.
Mueller, JNES, 36(Jan 1977):71-2.

Fetter, Bruce. The Creation of Elizabethville, 1910-1940. Stanford, Cal.: Hoover Inst. Press, 1976. Rev. by E. L. Berger, AHR, 82(Oct 1977):1034; A. Roberts, AfAf, 76(Jl 1977):
414-5; V. M. Smith, History, 6(Nov/Dec 1977):36.

Feuchtwanger, E. J. Gladstone. New York: St. Martin's Press,
1975. Rev. by R. K. Webb, AHR, 82(Je 1977):635-7; P.
Stansky, Historian, 39(Feb 1977):332-4.

Fichtenau, Heinrich. Beiträge zur Mediävistik: Ausgewählte Aufsätze. Vol. 1, Allgemeine Geschichte. Stuttgart: Anton
Hiersemann, 1975. Rev. by L. Wallach, AHR, 82(Oct 1977):
934.

Fiechter, Georges-Andre. Brazil since 1964: Modernisation Under
a Military Regime. New York: Wiley, 1975. Rev. by T. E.
Skidmore, AHR, 82(Apr 1977):486; J. D. Wirth, Historian,
39(May 1977):595-6.

Field, Daniel. The End of Serfdom: Nobility and Bureaucracy in
Russia, 1855-1861. Cambridge, Mass.: Har U Press, 1976.
Rev. by F. A. Miller, AHR, 82(Apr 1977):402.

Fields, Rona M. Society Under Siege: A Psychology of Northern
Ireland. Philadelphia: Temple U Press, 1977. Rev. by C.
Owens, E-I, 12(Fall 1977):116-17.

Filippini, Jean-Pierre, et al., eds. Dossiers sur le commerce
français en Méditerranée orientale au XVIIIᵉ siècle. Paris:
Universitaires de France, 1976. Rev. by P. W. Bamford,
AHR, 82(Apr 1977):367.

Filler, Louis. Appointment at Armageddon: Muckraking and Pro-

gressivism in the American Tradition. Westport, Conn.:
Greenwood Press, 1976. Rev. by D. W. Noble, AHR, 82
(Feb 1977):198; R. W. Schneider, AS, 18(Fall 1977):111; A.
Gutfeld, FHQ, 55(Apr 1977):503-4; R. M. Spector, JISHS, 70
(May 1977):165; R. Lora, MichH, 61(Fall 1977):256-9.

_____. The Muckrakers. University Park, Pa.: Pennsylvania
State U Press, 1976. Rev. by R. Lora, MichH, 61(Fall 1977):
256-9.

Fincher, E. B. Spanish-Americans as a Political Factor in New
Mexico, 1912-1950. New York: Arno Press, 1974. Rev. by
D. J. Weber, HAHR, 57(May 1977):371-2.

Fine, John V. A., Jr. The Bosnian Church: A New Interpretation.
New York: Columbia U Press, 1975. Rev. by G. P. Majeska, AHR, 82(Apr 1977):346-7.

Fine, Sidney. Frank Murphy: The Detroit Years. Ann Arbor: U
Mich Press, 1975. Rev. by R. D. Lunt, Historian, 39(Feb
1977):378-9.

Finlay, John L. Canada in the North Atlantic Triangle: Two Centuries of Social Change. Toronto: Ox U Press, 1975. Rev.
by W. M. Baker, CHR, (Mar 1977):67-8.

Finley, M. I., ed. Studies in Roman Property. Cambridge: Cam
U Press, 1976. Rev. by D. Hood, Historian, 39(May 1977):
534.

Finnegan, John Patrick. Against the Specter of a Dragon: The
Campaign for American Military Preparedness, 1914-1917.
Westport, Conn.: Greenwood Press, 1975. Rev. by R.
Gregory, AHR, 82(Feb 1977):201-2.

Fischer, Ernest G. Robert Potter: Founder of the Texas Navy.
Gretna: Pelican Publishing, 1976. Rev. by J. D. Hill, LaH,
18(Sum 1977):363-4.

Fischer, Leroy H. Territorial Governors of Oklahoma. Oklahoma
City: Oklahoma Historical Society, 1975. Rev. by D. E.
Green, ChOk, 55(Sum 1977):235-7.

Fisher, Allan G. B. see Nachtigal, Gustav

Fisher, Humphrey J. see Nachtigal, Gustav

Fisher, Loren R., ed. Ras Shamra Parallels: The Texts from
Ugarit and the Hebrew Bible. Rome: Pontificium Institutum
Biblicum, 1972. Rev. by D. Pardee, JNES, 36(Jan 1977):
65-8.

Fisher, Louis. Presidential Spending Power. Princeton: Prin U

Press, 1975. Rev. by H. F. Graff, AHR, 82(Je 1977):765.

Fisher, Robert C., ed. see Fodor, Eugene, ed.

Fitz, Jeno. La Pannonie sous Gallian. Brussels: Latomus, 1976.
Rev. by T. V. Buttrey, AHR, 82(Apr 1977):339-40.

Fitzgerald, E. V. K. The State and Economic Development: Peru
Since 1968. New York & London: Cam U Press, 1976. Rev.
by J. L. Dietz, JEH, 37(Je 1977):512-3.

Flack, Dora see Betenson, Lula Parker

Flack, J. Kirkpatrick. Desideratum in Washington: The Intellectual Community in the Capital City, 1870-1900. Cambridge,
Mass.: Schenkman Publishing, 1975. Rev. by G. Blodgett,
AHR, 82(Apr 1977):453; H. D. Shapiro, AS, 18(Fall 1977):
114.

Fladeland, Betty. Men and Brothers: Anglo-American Antislavery
Cooperation. London: U Ill Press, 1973. Rev. by H. Tem-
perly, History, 62(Feb 1977):87-8.

Flamant, Maurice. Histoire economique et sociale contemporaine.
Paris: Editions Montchrestien, 1976. Rev. by R. J. Barker,
JEH, 37(Sep 1977):795.

Flannery, James W. W. B. Yeats and the Idea of a Theatre. New
Haven: Yale U Press, 1976. Rev. by J D. Conway, E-I,
12(Win 1977):144-6; R. Schleifer, GR, 31(Fall 1977):736-9.

Fleming, Berry. Autobiography of a City in Arms: Augusta, Georgia, 1861-1865. Augusta, Ga.: Richmond County Historical
Society, 1976. Rev. by H. Robertson, GHQ, 51(Sum 1977):
200-1.

Fletcher, Anthony. A County Community in Peace and War. New
York: Longman, 1975. Rev. by C. Holmes, AHR, 82(Je
1977):632-3; A. L. Rowse, HTo, 27(Jan 1977):62-3; G. C. F.
Forster, History, 62(Feb 1977):119; J. S. Merrill, HJ, 20(No.
1, 1977):229-36.

Flieger, Wilhelm, and Peter C. Smith, eds. A Demographic Path
to Modernity: Patterns of Early-Transition in the Philippines.
Quezon City: Population Institute, U Philippines Press, 1975.
Rev. by B. H. Hackenberg, JAS, 36(May 1977):597-8.

Flink, James J. The Car Culture. Cambridge: MIT Press, 1975.
Rev. by G. S. May, AHR, 81(Dec 1976(:1276.

Flint, David. The Hutterites, a Study in Prejudice. Toronto: Ox
U Press, 1975. Rev. by J. H. Smylie, AHR, 82(Je 1977):
778; M. J. Penton, CHR, 58(Mar 1977):76-7.

Flood, Jeanne. Brian Moore. Lewisburg, Pa.: Bucknell U Press, 1974. Rev. by C. W. Barrow, E-I, 12(Spr 1977):154-5.

Florescu, Radu and Raymond T. McNally. Dracula: A Biography of Vlad the Impaler. New York: Hawthorn Books, 1973. Rev. by M. K. Dziewanowski, EEQ, 11(Mar 1977):126-7.

Floud, Roderick. The British Machine Tool Industry, 1850-1914. New York: Cam U Press, 1976. Rev. by R. N. Price, AHR, 82(Oct 1977):971; R. Church, History, 62(Je 1977):335-6; C. K. Hyde, JEH, 37(Je 1977):513-4; P. Uselding, JIH, 8(Aut 1977):366-9.

Flynn, George G. Roosevelt and Romanism: Catholics and American Diplomacy, 1937-1945. Westport, Conn.: Greenwood Press, 1976. Rev. by S. Adler, AHR, 82(Apr 1977):467-8.

Fockler, Herbert H., ed. see Kaufman, Harold F., ed.

Fodor, Eugene, and Robert C. Fisher, eds. Fodor's Old West. New York: David McKay, 1976. Rev. by L. J. White, JOW, 16(Jan 1977):75-6.

Fokas, Spyridonos G. The Greeks in Riverboating on the Lower Danube. Thessaloniki: Institute for Balkan Studies, 1975. Rev. by G. Augustinos, AHR, 82(Feb 1977):142-3.

Folda, Jaroslav. Crusader Manuscript Illumination at Saint-Jean D'Acre, 1275-1291. Princeton: Prin U Press, 1976. Rev. by H. E. J. Cowdrey, History, 62(Feb 1977):100-1.

Foner, Eric. Tom Paine and Revolutionary America. London, Oxford & New York: Ox U Press, 1976. Rev. by F. V. Mills, JSH, 43(Nov 1977):608-9; R. A. Rutland, WMH, 60(Spr 1977):247-8.

Foner, Philip S. American Labor Songs of the Nineteenth Century. Urbana: U Ill Press, 1975. Rev. by D. E. Schob, JISHS, 70(Feb 1977):94-5.

_____. Blacks in the American Revolution. Westport: Greenwood Press, 1976. Rev. by T. Kornweibel, Jr., NEQ, 50(Mar 1977):164-7.

_____. History of Black America: From Africa to the Emergence of the Cotton Kingdom. Westport, Conn.: Greenwood, 1075. Rev. by W. D. Jordan, AHR, 82(Feb 1977):180; R. J. Lockett, LaH, 18(Sum 1977):368-9; D. D. Waz, WMQ, 34(Jan 1977):172-4; J. White, JAmS, 11(Apr 1977):149-52.

_____. Labor and the American Revolution. Westport, Conn.: Greenwood Press, 1977. Rev. by C. S. Olton, AHR, 82(Oct 1977):1064; L. R. Gerlach, JSH, 43(Nov 1977):611-3; J. P. Greene, SCHM, 78(Oct 1977):318-9.

_____. We, the Other People. Urbana: U Ill Press, 1976. Rev. by J. A. Gazell, JISHS, 70(May 1977):164-5.

Foor, Robin see Kretschmar, Robert S.

Foot, M. R. D. and H. C. G. Matthew, eds. The Gladstone Diaries, vol. 3, 1840-1847. Vol. 4: 1848-1854. New York: Ox U Press, 1974, 1975. Rev. by R. K. Webb, AHR, 82 (Je 1977):635-7.

Foote, Shelby. The Civil War: A Narrative. Red River to Appomattox. New York: Random House, 1974. Rev. by W. A. Spedale, LaH, 18(Spr 1977):249-52.

Forbes, Duncan. Hume's Philosophical Politics. Cambridge: Cam U Press, 1975. Rev. by H. T. Dickinson, History, 62(Feb 1977):134; F. G. Whelan, HJ, 20(No. 1, 1977):259-62.

Forbes, Geraldine Hancock. Positivism in Bengal: A Case Study in the Transmission and Assimilation of an Ideology. Columbia, Mo.: South Asia Books, 1975. Rev. by J. R. McLane, JAS, 37(Nov 1977):159-60.

Forde-Johnston, J. Hillforts of the Iron Age in England and Wales. Totowa, N.J.: Rowman and Littlefield, 1976. Rev. by D. W. Harding, 82(Oct 1977):932-3.

Forrest, Alan. Society and Politics in Revolutionary Bordeaux. London: Ox U Press, 1975. Rev. by N. Hampson, ESR, 7 (Jan 1977):108-10; R. Forster, Historian, 39(Feb 1977):343-4.

Forster, Robert, ed. see Carter, Edward C., II, ed.

Fortes, Meyer and Sheila Patterson, ed. Studies in African Social Anthropology. New York: Academic Press, 1975. Rev. by R. Brown, AfAf, 76(Apr 1977):272-3.

Foster, Edward Halsey. The Civilized Wilderness: Backgrounds to American Romantic Literature, 1817-1860. New York: Free Press, 1975. Rev. by S. French, NYHSQ, 61(Jan/Apr 1977):87-8.

Foster, John. Class Struggle and the Industrial Revolution: Early Industrial Capitalism in Three English Towns. New York: St. Martin's Press, 1974. Rev. by A. Briggs, JMH, 49(Sep 1977): 500-2.

Foster, Walter Roland. The Church Before the Covenants: The Church of Scotland, 1596-1638. Edinburgh: Scottish Academic Press, 1975. Rev. by R. G. Eaves, AHR, 82(Feb 1977): 111-2.

Foucault, Michel. Surveiller et punir: Naissance de la prison.

Paris: Editions Gallimard, 1976. Rev. by H. White, AHR, 82(Je 1977):605-6.

Fouilles de Delphes, Tome II, Topographie et Architecture. Sanetuaire D'Apollon. Paris: Diffusion Boccard, 1975. Rev. by R. Scranton, AJA, 81(Sum 1977):398-9.

Fourquin, Guy. Lordship and Feudalism in the Middle Ages. New York: Pica Press, 1976. Rev. by E. A. R. Brown, AHR, 82(Je 1977):617-8.

Fowler, P. J. Recent Work in Rural Archaeology. Totowa, N.J.: Rowman and Littlefield, 1975. Rev. by E. H. Ross, Archaeology, 30(May 1977):212.

Fowler, William M., Jr. Rebels Under Sail: The American Navy During the Revolution. New York: Scribners, 1976. Rev. by W. J. Morgan, AHR, 82(Feb 1977):176-7; F. C. Mevers, JSH, 43(May 1977):285-6; N. R. Stout, VH, 45(Spr 1977): 125-7.

Fowler, William W. Woman on the American Frontier. Detroit: Gale Research Co., 1974. Rev. by J. E. Baur, AHR, 82 (Feb 1977):191-2.

Fox, Aileen. Prehistoric Maori fortifications. Auckland: Longman Paul, 1976. Rev. by P. Bellwood, Antiquity, 51(Mar 1977):77-8.

Fox, Annette Baker, Alfred O. Hero, Jr., and Joseph S. Nye, Jr., eds. Canada and the United States: Transnational and Transgovernmental Relations. New York: Col U Press, 1976. Rev. by E. McWhinney, Historian, 39(May 1977):592-3.

Fox, Feramorz Y. see Arrington, Leonard J.

Fox, Frances L. Luis Maria Peralta and His Adobe. San Jose: Smith-McKay, 1975. Rev. by O. L. Jones, JOW, 16(Jl 1977): 99.

Fox, James J. Harvest of the Palm: Ecological Change in Eastern Indonesia. Cambridge: Har U Press, 1977. Rev. by A. B. Hudson, JAS, 37(Nov 1977):176-8.

Fox-Genovese, Elizabeth. The Origins of Physiocracy: Economic Revolution and Social Order in Eighteenth-Century France. Ithaca: Cor U Press, 1976. Rev. by N. S. Hoyt, AHR, 82 (Apr 1977):367-8; O. Hufton, HJ, 20(No. 4, 1977):971-6; R. L. Meek, JEH, 27(Sep 1977):795-6; L. R. Berlanstein, WMQ, 34(Jl 1977):505-7.

Fraginals, Manuel Moreno. The Sugarmill: The Socioeconomic Complex of Sugar in Cuba, 1760-1860. New York and London:

Monthly Review Press, 1976. Rev. by S. B. Schwartz, JEH, 37(Sep 1977):797-8; B. J. Calder, AHR, 82(Je 1977):781-2.

Francis, David. The First Peninsular War, 1702-1713. London: Ernest Benn, 1975. Rev. by D. McKay, History, 62(Feb 1977):130-1.

Francis, Rell G. Cyrus E. Dallin: Let Justice Be Done. Springville, Ut.: Springville Museum of Art, 1976. Rev. by E. F. Sanguinetti, UHQ, 45(Win 1977):93.

Francis, Robert. Collected Poems, 1936-1976. Amherst: U Mass Press, 1976. Rev. by L. Leary, NEQ, 50(Je 1977):368-70.

Frandsen, Paul John. An Outline of the Late Egyptian Verbal System. Copenhagen: Akademisk Forlag, 1974. Rev. by E. F. Wente, JNES, 36(Oct 1977):310-2.

Frank, Albert J. von. Whittier: A Comprehensive Annotated Bibliography. New York and London: Garland, 1976. Rev. by L. Leary, NEQ, 50(Mar 1977):167-8.

Frank, Andre Gunder. On Capitalist Underdevelopment. Oxford: Ox U Press, 1976. Rev. by H. S. Ferns, History, 62(Feb 1977):263.

Frank, Charles R., Jr., Kwang Suk Kim, and Larry Westphal. South Korea. New York and London: Col U Press for the National Bureau of Economic Research, 1975. Rev. by K. M. Langley, JEH, 37(Je 1977):482-5.

Frank, Fedora Small. Beginnings on Market Street: Nashville and Her Jewry, 1861-1901. Nashville: Author, 1976. Rev. by A. M. Boom, JSH, 43(May 1977):299-300.

Frank, Joseph. Dostoevsky: The Seeds of Revolt, 1821-1849. Princeton, N.J.: Prin U Press, n.d. Rev. by M. Friedberg, Comm, 63(May 1977):90-4.

Frank, Michael B., ed. see Anderson, Frederick, ed.

Franklin, Benjamin. The Papers of Benjamin Franklin, Vol. 20, Jan. 1773 to Dec. 1773. Ed. by William B. Wilcox, et al. New Haven: Yale U Press, 1977. Rev. by E. Wright, JAmS, 11(Dec 1977):425-7.

Franklin, John Hope. Racial Equality in America. Chicago: U Chi Press, 1976. Rev. by C. Bolt, JAmS, 11(Dec 1977): 416-17; G. H. Watson, JISHS, 70(Aug 1977):254-5; D. L. Grant, JSH, 43(Aug 1977):455-6; W. Cohen, MichH, 61(Sum 1977):166-8.

_____. A Southern Odyssey: Travelers in the Antebellum North. Baton Rouge: LSU Press, 1976. Rev. by J. S. Ezell, AHR, 81(Dec 1976):1250; B. I. Wiley, CWTI, 16(Apr 1977):47; J. G. Taylor, FHQ, 55(Apr 1977):495-7; R. A. Wooster, JSH, 43 (Feb 1977):121-2; J. G. Tregle, Jr., LaH, 18(Sum 1977):381-2; J. W. Donnen, PNQ, 68(Apr 1977):100.

Franklin, Julian H. Jean Brodin and the Rise of Absolutist Theory. London: Cambridge U Press, 1973. Rev. by H. M. Höpfl, ESR, 7(Apr 1977):233-9.

Frantz, Joe B. Aspects of the American West: Three Essays. College Station: Texas A & M U Press, 1976. Rev. by D. M. Shockley, UHQ, 45(Sum 1977):317-8.

_____. Texas: A Bicentennial History. New York: W. W. Norton, 1976. Rev. by M. M. Sibley, JSH, 43(Aug 1977): 490-1; O. Dean, ETHJ, 15(No. 2, 1977):65-6; L. Friend, WHQ, 8(Oct 1977):460-1.

_____, et al. The Walter Prescott Webb Memorial Lectures: Essays on Walter Prescott Webb. Austin: UT Press, 1976. Rev. by L. T. Ellis, NMHR, 52(Jan 1977):82-4; R. W. Paul, PHR, 46(Aug 1977):486-8.

Fraser, Derek, ed. The New Poor Law in the Nineteenth Century. New York: St. Martin's Press, 1976. Rev. by D. Roberts, AHR, 82(Apr 1977):357-8; S. & O. Checkland, EHR, 92(Oct 1977):917-8; R. D. Fiala, HT, 10(May 1977):490-1; D. C. Moore, Historian, 39(May 1977):543-4.

_____. Urban Politics in Victorian England: The Structure of Politics in Victorian Cities. Atlantic Highlands, N.J.: Humanities Press, 1976. Rev. by T. R. Tholfsen, AHR, 82 (Oct 1977):969-70.

Frassanito, William A. Gettysburg: A Journey in Time. New York: Scribner's, 1975. Rev. by J. S. Patterson, PH, 45 (Apr 1977):187-8.

Freedman, Maurice, tr. see Granet, Marcel

Freeman, Stephen A. The Middlebury College Foreign Language Schools: The Story of a Unique Idea. Middlebury, Vt.: Middlebury College Press, 1975. Rev. by D. P. Clifford, VH, 45(Fall 1977):254-5.

Freytag, Walter P., ed. see Sinks, Julia Lee

Frias, Herman R., ed. The Arctic Diary of Russell Williams Porter. Charlottesville: U Press VA, 1976. Rev. by H. G. Jones, AmArc, 40(Apr 1977):235.

Fried, Richard M. Men Against McCarthy. New York: Columbia U Press, 1976. Rev. by J. E. Wiltz, AHR, 82(Feb 1977): 215-6; J. M. Collier, AS, 18(Fall 1977):110.

Friedlaender, Marc, and L. H. Butterfield, eds. Diary of Charles Francis Adams. Vol. V, VI Jan. 1833-June 1836. Cambridge, Mass.: Har U Press, 1974. Rev. by M. Cunliffe, EHR, 92 (Oct 1977):919.

Friedlander, Peter. The Emergence of a UAW Local, 1936-1939: A Study in Class and Culture. Pittsburgh: U Pittsburgh Press, 1975. Rev. by H. J Harris, JAmS, 11(Aug 1977): 286-9; V. J. Vogel, MichH, 61(Spr 1977):89-91.

Friedman, Bernard. Smuts: A Reappraisal. London: Allen and Unwin, 1975. Rev. by S. Marks, History, 62(Je 1977):271-2.

Friedman, Lawrence J. Inventors of the Promised Land. New York: Alfred A. Knopf, 1975. Rev. by A. C. Loveland, LaH, 18(Win 1977):122-3; M. Kammen, NYHSQ, 61(Jan/Apr 1977): 84-6.

Fries, Adelaide, Stuart Thurman Wright, and J. Edwin Hendricks, eds. Forsyth: The History of A County on the March. Chapel Hill: U NC Press, 1976. Rev. by R. E. Corlew, JSH, 43(Aug 1977):496-7.

Friis, Erik J., ed. The Scandinavian Presence in North America. New York: Harper's Magazine Press, 1976. Rev. by M. Tiblin, MinnH, 45(Win 1977):161.

Frings, Marie-Louise, ed. see Angermann, Erich, ed.

Frison, George C., ed. The Casper Site: A Hell Gap Bison Kill on the High Plains. New York: Academic Press, 1974. Rev. by E. A. Morris, Antiquity, 42(Jan 1977):136-9.

Fritz, Paul S. The English Ministers and Jacobitism Between the Rebellions of 1715 and 1745. Toronto: U Tor Press, 1975. Rev. by H. T. Dickinson, History, 62(Je 1977):325.

Frost, Lawrence A., ed. see Carroll, John M., ed.

Fry, Michael G. Freedom and Change: Essays in Honour of Lester B. Pearson. Toronto: McClelland and Stewart, 1975. Rev. by J. L. Granatstein, CHR, 58(Mar 1977):81-2.

Frye, Richard N., ed. Sasanian Remains from Qasr-i Abu Nasr: Seals, Sealings, and Coins. Cambridge, Mass.: Har U Press, 1973. Rev. by M. Gibson, JNES, 26(Jl 1977):226-8.

Fülberth, Georg and Jürgen Harrer. Die Deutsch Sozial-demokratie, 1890-1933. Darmstadt: Luchterhand, 1974. Rev. by D. K. Buse, JMH, 49(Sep 1977):516-7.

Fuller, Paul E. Laura Clay and the Woman's Rights Movement.
Lexington: U Press of Kentucky, 1975. Rev. by D. T. Cullen, FCHQ, 51(Jan 1977):52-4.

Furber, Holden. Rival Empires of Trade in the Orient, 1600-1800.
Oxford: Ox U Press, 1976. Rev. by C. R. Boxer, History,
62(Je 1977):322-3.

Fürerhaimendorf, Christoph von, ed. Contributions to the Anthropology of Nepal: Proceedings of a Symposium Held at the
School of Oriental and African Studies, University of London,
June/July 1973. Warminister: Aris & Phillips, 1974. Rev.
by D. Licter, JAS, 36(May 1977):584-6.

Furman, Necah Stewart. Walter Prescott Webb: His Life and Im-
pact. Albuquerque: UNM Press, 1976. Rev. by C. C.
Spence, A&W, 19(Sum 1977):179-80; W. R. Jacobs, AHR, 82
(Feb 1977):193-4; A. P. McDonald, ETHJ, 15(Spr 1977):60-1;
R. W. Paul, PHR, 46(Aug 1977):486-8; F. E. Vandiver, WHQ,
8(Apr 1977):206-7.

Furner, Mary O. Advocacy & Objectivity: A Crisis in the Pro-
fessionalization of American Social Science, 1865-1905. Lexington: U Press Ken, 1975. Rev. by R. A. Waller, JISHS,
70(Aug 1977):251-2.

Furth, Charlotte, ed. The Limits of Change: Essays on Conservative Alternatives in Republican China. Cambridge: Har U
Press, 1976. Rev. by M. Gasster, JAS, 36(Aug 1977):725-7.

Gabre-Sellassie, Dejjazmach Zewde. Yohannes IV of Ethiopa: A
Political Biography. Oxford: Clarendon Press, 1975. Rev.
by S. Rubenson, EHR, 92(Oct 1977):925-6.

Gagan, Brian M. see Oliver, Roland

Gagnon, Francois-Marc. La conversion par l'image: Un aspect de
la mission des jésuites auprès des indiens du Canada au XVIIe
siècle. Montreal: Las Editions Bellarmin, 1975. Rev. by J.
L. Pearl, AHR, 82(Je 1977):776.

Gains, Charles R. see Morris, John W.

Galambos, Louis. The Public Image of Big Business in America,
1880-1940: A Quantitative Study in Social Change. Baltimore:
JHU Press, 1975. Rev. by A. Raucher, AHR, 82(Feb 1977):
196-7; D. Richardson, BH, 19(Jl 1977):227-30.

Galbraith, John S. Crown and Charter: The Early Years of the
British South Africa Company. Berkeley: U Cal Press, 1974.
Rev. by D. C. Ellinwood, Jr., AHR, 82(Feb 1977):105-6; S.
Marks, Africa, 47(No. 3, 1977):330-1; R. T. Brown, JAAS,
12(Jan/Oct 1977):293-4.

Gallaher, John G. The Iron Marshal: A Biography of Louis N. Da-
vout. Carbondale: So Ill U Press, 1976. Rev. by R. S. Quim-
by, AHR, 82(Feb 1977):118.

Gallenkamp, Charles. Maya. New York: David McKay, 1976.
Rev. in CurH, 72(Feb 1977):80.

Gallo, Ezequiel. Farmers in Revolt: The Revolutions of 1893 in
the Province of Santa Fe, Argentina. Atlantic Highlands, N.
J.: Humanities Press, 1976. Rev. by W. J. Fleming, AHR,
82(Oct 1977):1110-1.

Gallo, Max. Robspierre the Incorruptible, A Psycho-Biography.
New York: Herder and Herder, 1971. Rev. by J. I. Shulim,
AHR, 82(Feb 1977):20-38.

Galmarini, Hugo Raul. Neyocios u politica en la epoca de Riva-
davia: Braulio Costa y la burguesia Comercial portena (1820-
1830). Buenos Aires: Libreria y Editorial Platero, 1974.
Rev. by J. C. Brown, HSHR, 57(Feb 1977):144-5.

Galston, William A. Kant and the Problem of History. Chicago:
U Chi Press, 1975. Rev. by U. H. Walsh, H&T, 16(May
1977):196-204; M. Despland, JMH, 49(Sep 1977):485-7.

Gambasin, Angelo. Religione e società dalle riforme napoleoniche
all'età liberale. Padua: Liviana Editrice, 1974. Rev. by
R. Grew, AHR, 82(Apr 1977):384-5.

Gambino, Richard. Vendetta: A True Story of the Worst Lynching
in America, the Mass Murder of Italian-Americans in New
Orleans in 1891, the Vicious Motivations Behind It, and the
Tragic Repercussions That Linger to This Day. New York:
Doubleday and Co., 1977. Rev. by L. Croce, JISHS, 70(Nov
1977):332; J. J. Jackson, JSH, 43(Nov 1977):628-9.

Gann, L. H., ed. see Duignan, Peter, ed.

García Cárcel, Ricardo. Orígenes de la Inquisición española: El
tribunal de Valencia, 1478-1530. Barcelona: Ediciones Peninsula, 1976. Rev. by P. J. Hauben, AHR, 82(Oct 1977):
987-8.

Garden, Maurice. Lyon et les lyonnais au XVIIIᵉ siécle. Paris:
Flammarion, 1975. Rev. by T. R. Sheppard, AHR, 82(Apr
1977):368-9.

Gardiner, C. Harvey. The Japanese and Peru, 1873-1973. Albuquerque: U NM Press, 1975. Rev. by J. E. Worrall, AHR,
82(Feb 1977):228-9; T. M. Bader, HAHR, 57(Feb 1977):156-8;
R. A. Morse, TAm, 33(Jan 1977):561-2.

Gardiner, Muriel. The Deadly Innocents: Portraits of Children

Who Kill. n.l.: Basic Books, n.d. Rev. by W. J. Bennett, Comm, 63(Jan 1977):82-4.

Gardiner, Stephen. A Machiavellian Treatise. New York: Cambridge U Press, 1976. Rev. by M. Levine, AHR, 82(Feb 1977):94.

Gardner, John. The Life and Times of Chaucer. New York: Knopf, 1977. Rev. by R. W. Hanning, GR, 31(Fall 1977): 732-5.

_____. The Poetry of Chaucer. Carbondale: So Ill U Press, 1977. Rev. by R. W. Hanning, GR, 31(Fall 1977):732-5.

Garfias, Robert. Music of a Thousand Autumns: The Togaku Style of Japanese Court Music. Berkeley: U Cal Press, 1975. Rev. by W. P. Malm, JAS, 36(May 1977):565-7.

Garlan, Yvon. War in the Ancient World: A Social History. New York: Norton, 1975. Rev. by A. Ferrill, Historian, 39(May 1977):532.

Garrett, Clarke. Respectable Folly: Millenarians and the French Revolution in England and France. Baltimore: JHU Press, 1975. Rev. by C. H. Johnson, Historian, 39(Feb 1977):344-5.

Garrone, Alessandro Galante. I radicali in Italia (1849-1925). Milan: Aldo Garzanti Editore, 1973. Rev. by C. F. Dellzell, JMH, 49(Je 1977):321-6.

Garth, Bryant G., ed. China's Changing Role in the World Economy. New York: Praeger, 1975. Rev. by R. Sinha, CQ, No. 71 (Sep 1977):618-19.

Gash, Norman. Peel. London: Longman, 1976. Rev. by M. Brock, EHR, 92(Oct 1977):916-7.

Gast, Ross H. Contentious Consul: A Biography of John Coffin Jones. Los Angeles: Dawson's Book Shop, 1976. Rev. by R. Dillon, CHQ, 56(Fall 1977):281-2.

Gastellu, J. M. see J. L. Balans

Gastil, Raymond D. Cultural Regions of the United States. Seattle: U Wash Press, 1975. Rev. by L. C. Bennion, WHQ, 8(Jan 1977):71-2.

Gates, John Morgan. Schoolbooks and Krags: The United States Army in the Philippines, 1898-1902. Westport, Conn.: Greenwood Press, 1973. Rev. by P. Herrly, WMH, 60(Spr 1977): 252-3.

Gatewood, Willard B. Black Americans and the White Man's Burden, 1898-1903. Urbana: U Ill Press, 1975. Rev. by G. Blodgett, JISHS, 70(Feb 1977):93-4; R. E. Moran, LaH, 18 (Win 1977):118-9.

Gauer, Werner. Olympische Forschungen, Band VIII, Die Tongefä-sse Aus Den Brunnen Unterm Stadion-Nordwall und im Südost-Gebiet. Berlin: Walter de Gruyter, 1975. Rev. by W. W. Rudolph, AJA, 81(Spr 1977):247-8.

Gaur, Ganesh, comp. Catalogue of Panjabi Printed Books Added to the India Office Library, 1902-1964. London: Foreign and Commonwealth Office, 1975. Rev. by N. G. Barrier, JAS, 36(May 1977):575.

Gaustad, Edwin Scott, ed. The Rise of Adventism. New York: Harper and Row, 1975. Rev. by C. Wright, AHR, 81(Dec 1976):1248.

Gay, Peter. Art and Act: On Causes in History--Manet, Gropius, Mondrian. New York: Harper & Row, 1976. Rev. by M. F. Deshmukh, AHR, 82(Feb 1977):61; P. Loewenberg, H&T, 16 (Oct 1977):354-67.

_____. Style in History. London: Jonathan Cape, 1975. Rev. by P. Burke, 62(Feb 1977):73-4.

Gayer, Arthur D., et al. The Growth and Fluctuation of the Bri-tish Economy, 1790-1850: An Historical Statistical, and Theo-retical Study of Britain's Economic Development. New York: Barnes and Noble, 1975. Rev. by F. Crouzet, JEH, 37(Sep 1977):798-801.

Geanakoplos, Deno John. Interaction of the "Sibling" Byzantine and Western Cultures in the Middle Ages and Italian Renais-sance (330-1600). New Haven: Yale U Press, 1976. Rev. by A. R. Lewis, AHR, 82(Je 1977):616-7.

Geddes, William Robert. Migrants of the Mountains: The Cultural Ecology of the Blue Miao (Hmong Njua) of Thailand. Oxford: Clarendon Press, 1976. Rev. by D. H. Marlowe, JAS, 36 (May 1977):591-2.

Geiss, Imanuel. German Foreign Policy, 1871-1914. Boston: Routledge and Kegan Paul, 1976. Rev. by L. Cecil, AHR, 82(Oct 1977):1003-4; D. W. Hendon, JEH, 37(Sep 1977):801.

Genovese, Eugene D. Roll, Jordan, Roll: The World the Slaves Made. New York: Pantheon Books, 1974. Rev. by J. G. Taylor, LaH, 18(Win 1977):114-6; L. H. Fishel, Jr., WMH, 60(Sum 1977):335-6.

Genovese, Eugene M., ed. see Engerman, Stanley L., ed.

George, Carol V. R., ed. Remember the Ladies. New Perspectives on Women in American History. Syracuse: U Syracuse
Press, 1975. Rev. by L. Masel-Walters, MichH, 61(Fall
1977):275-6.

George, W. R. P. The Making of Lloyd George. Hamden, Conn.:
Archon, 1976. Rev. by D. M. Cregier, AHR, 82(Oct 1977):
971-2.

Georgia Mothers Association. Historic Georgia Mothers, 1776-1976.
Compiled by the Bicentennial Committee, Mrs. J. Mac Bar-
ber, Chairman. Atlanta: Georgia Mothers Association, 1976.
Rev. by D. Roth-White, GHQ, 51(Sum 1977):195-6.

Georgiev, V. A. Russian Foreign Policy in the Near East from the
End of the 1830's through the Beginning of the 1840s. Moscow:
Izdatel'stvo "Moskovskogo Universiteta", 1975. Rev. by E. W.
Brooks, AHR 82(Je 1977):695.

Gerber, David A. Black Ohio and the Color Line, 1860-1915. Urbana: U Ill Press, 1977. Rev. by L. H. Fishel, Jr., AHR,
82(Oct 1977):1079-80; F. X. Blouin, Jr., MichH, 61(Fall
1977):259-61; J. H. Cartwright, JSH, 43(Nov 1977):622-3.

Gerlach, Larry R. New Jersey in the American Revolution, 1763-
1783. Trenton: New Jersey Historical Commission, 1976.
Rev. by D. L. Kemmerer, WMQ, 34(Apr 1977):329-31.

_____. Prologue to Independence: New Jersey in the Coming of
the American Revolution. New Brunswick, N.J.: Rutgers U
Press, 1976. Rev. by M. M. Klein, AHR, 82(Apr 1977):
430-1; D. L. Kemmerer, WMQ, 34(Apr 1977):329-31.

Gerlach, Russel L. Immigrants in the Ozarks: A Study in Ethnic
Geography. Columbia, Mo. and London: U MO Press, 1976.
Rev. by T. G. Jordan, JSH, 43(Nov 1977):640-1; F. C. Lue-
bke, AHR, 82(Je 1977):759-60; W. A. Schroeder, MHR, 71
(Jan 1977):359-60.

Gerow, Bert A. Co-Traditions and Convergent Trends in Prehistoric California. San Luis Obispo: San Luis Obispo County
Archaeological Society, 1974. Rev. by M. J. Moratto, Antiquity, 42(Jan 1977):145.

Gerson, Lennard D. The Secret Police in Lenin's Russia. Philadelphia: Temple U Press, 1976. Rev. by R. D. Warth, AHR,
82(Je 1977):704.

Gerth, Hans H. Bürgerliche Intelligenz um 1800: Zur Soziologie
des deutschen Frühliberalismus. Göttingen: Vandenhoeck
und Ruprecht, 1976. Rev. by P. H. Reill, AHR, 82(Oct
1977):995.

111   GESSNER

Gessner, Dieter. Agraverbände in der Weimarer Republik: Wirtschaftliche und soziale Voraussetzungen agarkonservativer
Politik vor 1933. Dusseldorf: Droste Verlag, 1976. Rev.
by C. Messman, JEH, 37(Sep 1977):801-2; A. Kovan, AHR,
82(Je 1977):669.

Ghai, Dharam P. see Court, David, ed.

Ghosh, A., ed. Jaina Art and Architecture. New Delhi: Bharatiya
Jnanpity, 1974-5. Rev. by M. W. Meister, JAS, 37(Nov 1977):
158-9.

Ghosh, Sisirkumar, tr. see Mukherji, Probhat Jumar.

Ghurye, G. S. Whither India? Bombay: Popular Prakashan, 1974.
Rev. by H. R. Isaacs, JAS, 36(Feb 1977):365-6.

Gibb, George S. see Wall, Bennett H.

Gibb, H. A. R. Saladin: Studies in Islamic History. Beirut:
Arab Institute for Research and Publishing, 1974. Rev. by
R. S. Humphreys, JNES, 36(Oct 1977):320-2.

Gibbon, Peter. The Origins of Ulster Unionism: Manchester:
Manchester U Press, 1975. Rev. by D. W. Miller, AHR,
82(Je 1977):64.

Gibbs, N. H. Grand Strategy. Vol. I, Rearmament Policy. London: MHSO, 1976. Rev. by R. P. Shay, Jr., AHR, 82(Je
1977):642; C. Thorne, EHR, 92(Oct 1977):872-7.

Gibson, Arrell Morgan, ed. America's Exiles: Indian Colonization
in Oklahoma. Oklahoma City: Oklahoma Historical Society,
1976. Rev. by A. H. DeRosier, Jr., WHQ, 8(Apr 1977):
220-1.

_____. The West in the Life of the Nation. Lexington, Mass.:
D. C. Heath, 1976. Rev. by L. H. Fischer, ChOk, 55(Sum
1977):228-9; J. Sosin, WHQ, 8(Apr 1977):204-5.

Gibson, James R. Imperial Russia in Frontier America: The
Changing Geography of Supply of Russian America, 1784-1867.
New York: Ox U Press, 1976. Rev. by R. H. Fisher, PHR,
46(Aug 1977):494-5; L. A. Rosenvall, WHQ, 8(Oct 1977):478-
9; C. M. Foust, AHR, 82(Feb 1977):178; C. B. O'Brien,
CHQ, 55(Win 1976/77):369.

Gibson, M. T., ed. see Alexander, J. J. G., ed.

Gidney, James G. see Pieper, Thomas I.

Giesey, Ralph see Hotmann, Francois.

Gilabert, Francisco Martí. La Abolición De La Inquisición En España. Pamplona: Ediciones Universidad de Navarra, 1975. Rev. by N. A. Rosenblatt, TAm, 34(Jl 1977):142-3; G. M. Addy, 82(Apr 1977):375.

Gilbert, Alan D. Religion and Society in Industrial England: Church, Chapel and Social Change 1740-1914. London: Longman, 1976. Rev. by H. McLeod, History, 62(Je 1977):332-3; T. Laqueur, AHR, 82(Je 1977):637-8.

Gilbert, Felix, ed. Bankiers, Künstler und Gelehrte: Unveröffentlichte Briefe der Familie Mendelssohn aus dem 19. Jahrhundert. Tübingen: Paul Siebeck, 1975. Rev. by W. Weber, AHR, 82(Je 1977):662-3.

Gilchrist, George, ed. Annan Parish Censuses, 1801-1821. Scottish Record Society, 1975. Rev. by R. Wall, Archives, 13 (Spr 1977):51-2.

Gildrie, Richard P. Salem, Massachusetts, 1626-1683: A Covenant Community. Charlottesville: U Press Va., 1975. Rev. by S. Nissenbaum, WMQ, 34(Jl 1977):487-9.

Gill, Brendan. Lindbergh Alone. New York & London: Harcourt, Brace Jovanovich, 1977. Rev. by N. Eubank, MinnH, 45(Fall 1977):298-9.

Gilles, Albert S., Sr. Comanche Days. Dallas: Southern Methodist U Press, 1974. Rev. by E. A. Hoebel, AIQ, 3(Sum 1977):161-2.

Gilliland, Marion Spjut. The Material Culture of Key Marco Florida. Gainesville: U Presses of Florida, 1975. Rev. by A. H. DeRosier, Jr., AIQ, 3(Spr 1977):56-8.

Gimpel, Jean. The Medieval Machine: The Industrial Revolution of the Middle Ages. New York: Holt, Rinehart, and Winston, 1976. Rev. by L. Dresbeck, AHR, 82(Oct 1977):933-4.

Ginger, Maynard, ed. As the Padres Saw Them: California Indian Life and Customs as Reported by the Franciscan Missionaries, 1813-1815. Santa Barbara: Santa Barbara Mission Archive Library, 1976. Rev. by W. M. Mathes, CHQ, 56(Sum 1977): 179-80.

Gintis, Herbert see Bowles, Samuel

Giraud, Marcel. La Louisiana après le systéme de Law, 1721-1723. Paris: Presses Universitaires de France, 1974. Rev. by J. S. Bromley, EHR, 92(Oct 1977):909-10.

Gitelman, Howard. Workingmen of Waltham: Mobility in American Urban Industrial Development, 1850-1890. Baltimore: Johns

Hopkins U Press, 1974. Rev. by R. D. Simon, PH, 45(Jl
1977):269-70.

Glanz, Rudolf. The Jewish in America: Two Female Immigrant
Generations, 1820-1829. Vol. I. New York: National Council of Jewish Women, 1976. Rev. by R. A. Rockaway, AHR,
82(Feb 1977):190; P. E. Hyman, AHR, 82(Oct 1977):1084-5.

Glaser, Kurt see John Barratt

Glassie, Henry. Folk Housing in Middle Virginia: A Structural
Analysis of Historic Artifacts. Knoxville: U Tenn Press,
1975. Rev. by J. C. Bonner, JSH, 43(Feb 1977):147-8; F.
Herman, VMHB, 85(Jan 1977):117-9.

Glassl, Horst. Das Osterreichische Einrichtungswerk in Galizien
(1772-1790). Wiesbaden: Harrassowitz, 1975. Rev. by T.
C. W. Blanning, History, 62(Je 1977):328-9.

Glauert, Earl T., and Merle H. Kunz, eds. Kittitas Frontiersmen.
Ellensburg, Wash.: Ellensburg Public Library, 1976. Rev.
by B. Mitchell, PNQ, 68(Jl 1977):149-50.

Glick, David T. Ships of the Great Lakes. Detroit: Wayne State
U Press, 1976. Rev. by L. Allin, MichH, 61(Sum 1977):
172-3.

Glover, Michael. General Burgoyne in Canada and America: Scapegoat for a System. New York: Atheneum, 1976. Rev. by I.
D. Gruber, AHR, 82(Oct 1977):1064-5.

Gluck, Sherna, ed. From Parlor to Prison: Five American Suffragists Talk About Their Lives. New York: Random, 1976.
Rev. by W. L. O'Neill, AHR, 82(Feb 1977):199-200.

Glynn, Sean and John Oxborrow. Interwar Britain: A Social and
Economic History. New York: Barnes and Noble, 1976. Rev.
by P. B. Johnson, AHR, 82(Apr 1977):362-3; P. J. Waller,
EHR, 92(Oct 1977):930.

Godfrey, E. S. The Development of English Glassmaking 1560-
1640. Oxford: Ox U Press, 1975. Rev. by G. D. Ramsay,
History, 62(Feb 1977):113-4; T. C. Barker, JEH, 37(Je
1977):514-5.

Goel, Madan Lal. Political Participation in a Developing Nation:
India. New York: Asia Publishing House, 1975. Rev. by
M. F. Katzenstein, JAS, 36(Aug 1977):768-9.

Goff, Frederick R. John Dunlap Broadside: The First Printing of
the Declaration of Independence. Washington: LC, 1976. Rev.
by L. Rapport, AmArc, 40(Jan 1977):77-8; E. L. Shepard,
VMHB, 85(Jl 1977):368-9.

Gokhale, S. D. Social Welfare: Legend and Legacy. Bombay: Popular Prakashan, 1975. Rev. by A. J. Robins, JAS, 36 (May 1977):579-80.

Goldblatt, Howard. Hsiao. Boston: Twayne, 1976. Rev. by C. T. Hsia, JAS, 37(Nov 1977):103-4.

Goldenberg, Joseph A. Shipbuilding in Colonial America. Charlottesville: Published for the Mariners Museum, Newport News, Virginia by the U Press Va., 1976. Rev. by J. C. Morton, JSH, 43(Feb 1977):108-9; L. B. Wright, VMHB, 85(Jan 1977): 104-5; W. M. Kelso, WMQ, 34(Jan 1977):175-6.

Goldfield, David R., ed. see Brownell, Blane A., ed.

Goldhurst, Richard. Pipe Clay and Drill, John J. Pershing: The Classic American Soldier. New York: Reader's Digest Press, 1977. Rev. by W. Rundell, Jr., AS, 18(Fall 1977):110.

Goldin, Claudia Dale. Urban Slavery in the American South, 1820-1860: A Quantitative History. Chicago: U Chi Press, 1976. Rev. by R. Sutch, JEH, 37(Sep 1977):803-4; D. R. Goldfield, AHR, 82(Je 1977):746-7; C. B. Dew, JSH, 43(May 1977): 297-8.

Goldin, Milton. Why They Give: American Jews and Their Philanthropies. n.l.: Macmillan, n.d. Rev. by M. L. Raphael, Comm, 64(Sep 1977):84-7.

Goldman, Irving. The Mouth of Heaven: An Introduction to Kwakuitl Religious Thought. New York: Wiley, 1975. Rev. by A. O. Wiget, AIQ, 3(Aut 1977):253-6.

Goldstein, Leon J. Historical Knowing. Austin: UT Press, 1976. Rev. by J. L. Gorman, H&T, 16(Feb 1977):66-80; M. Mandelbaum, JMH, 49(Je 1977):292-4.

Goltz, Dietlinde. Studien zur altorientalischen und griechischen Heilkunde: Therapie--Arzneibereitung--Rezeptstruktur. Wiesbaden: Franz Steiner Verlag, 1974. Rev. by R. D. Biggs, JNES, 36(Oct 1977):303-4.

Golwalkar, Alkar R. see Punekar, S. D.

Gomez-Ibanez, Daniel Alexander. The Western Pyrenees: Differential Evolution of the French and Spanish Borderland. New York: Ox U Press, 1975. Rev. by P. H. de Garmo, AgH, 51(Apr 1977):472-3.

Gomez-Martinez, Jose Luis. Americo Castro y el origen de los Espanoles: Historia de uno polemica. Madrid: Editorial Gredos, 1975. Rev. by J. F. O'Callaghan, HAHR, 57(Feb 1977):114-6.

Gongora, Mario. Studies in the Colonial History of Spanish America. New York: Cam U Press, 1975. Rev. by C. Gibson,
AHR, 81(Dec 1976):1284-85; D. Chipman, Historian, 39(Feb
1977):384-5; J. Lynch, JLAS, 9(May 1977):153-4.

González, F. Molina and E. Pareja López. Excavaciones en las
Cuesta del Negro (Purullena, Granada). Campaña de 1971.
Madrid: Excavaciones Arqueológicas en España 86, 1975.
Rev. by B. Chapman, Antiquity, 51(Nov 1977):251-2.

Goodman, J. M. see Reeves, P. D.

Goodwin, Crauford D. W. The Image of Australia: British Per-
ception of the Australian Economy from the Eighteenth to the
Twentieth Century. Durham, N.C.: Duke U Press, 1974.
Rev. by L. A. Clarkson, History, 62(Je 1977):305-6; R. A.
Shields, CHR, 58(Je 1977):222-4.

Goodwin, Del and Dorcas Chaffee, ed. Perspectives '76. Hanover,
N.H.: Regional Center for Educational Training, 1975. Rev.
by L. Coffin, VH, 45(Sum 1977):183-4.

Goodwin, Edmund P. Colonel William Fleming of Botetourt, 1728-
1795. Roanoke, Va.: Roanoke Valley Historical Society, 1976.
Rev. by A. T. Dill, VMHB, 85(Jl 1977):371-2.

Goodwin, Paul B. Los Ferrocariles briticos y la U.C.R., 1916-
1930. Buenos Aires: Ediciones La Bastilla, 1974. Rev. by
W. R. Wright, HAHR, 57(Aug 1977):546-7.

Goodwyn, Lawrence. Democratic Promise: The Populist Moment
in America. New York: Ox U Press, 1976. Rev. by K. I.
Polakoff, HT, 10(May 1977):492-5; R. C. McMath, AHR, 82
(Je 1977):753-4; M. Stokes, JAmS, 11(Dec 1977):430-2; C. A.
Cannon, JSH, 43(Aug 1977):471-2.

Goody, Jack, Joan Thirsk, and E. P. Thompson, ed. Family and
Inheritance: Rural Society in Western Europe, 1200-1800.
New York: Cambridge U Press, 1976. Rev. by P. S. Seaver,
JIH, 8(Aug 1977):359-61; J. L. Goldsmith, AHR, 82(Oct
1977):943-4.

Goodyear, Albert C., III. Hecla II and III: An Interpretive Study
of Archaeological Remains from the Lakeshore Project, South
Central Arizona. Tempe: Arizona State University, 1975.
Rev. by G. Gumerman, Antiquity, 42(Jan 1977):141-3.

Goonetileke, H. A. I. ed. Images of Sri Lanka through American
Eyes: Travellers in Ceylon in the Nineteenth and Twentieth
Centuries: A Select Anthology. Colombo, Sri Lanka: U.S.
Information Service, 1976. Rev. by K. S. Diehl, JAS, 36
(Aug 1977):788-9.

Gopal, Sarvepalli. Jawaharlal Nehru, A Biography, Volume 1:
    1889-1947. London: Jonathan Cape, 1975. Rev. by P. G.
    Robb, History, 62(Je 1977):286-7; E. R. Irschick, AHR, 82
    (Apr 1977):422-3; A. Z. Rubinstein, CurH, 72(Apr 1977):177;
    R. L. Park, JAS, 36(Aug 1977):764-5.

Gordon, Burton L. Monterey Bay Area: Natural History and Cul-
    tural Imprints. Pacific Grove, Calif.: Boxwood Press,
    1974. Rev. by C. Prentiss, JOW, 16(Jl 1977):98-9.

Gordon, Leonard A. Bengal: The Nationalist Movement, 1876-
    1940. New York: Col U Press, 1974. Rev. by F. F. Con-
    lon, JAS, 36(May 1977):569-70; M. MacMillan, CHR, 58(Je
    1977):220-2.

Gordon, Linda. Woman's Body, Woman's Right: A Social History
    of Birth Control in America. New York: Grossman Publ.,
    1976. Rev. by J. S. Lemons, AHR, 82(Oct 1977):1095.

Goriushkin, L M. Agrarian Relations in Siberia in the Period of
    Imperialism, 1900-1917. Novosibirsk: Izdatel'stvo "Nauka",
    Sibirskoe Otdelenie, 1976. Rev. by R. E. Snow, AHR, 82
    (Je 1977):698.

Gornall, T., ed. see Dessain, C. S., ed.

Goslinga, C. Ch. Curacao and Guzman Blanco. A Case Study of
    Small Power Politics in the Caribbean. 'S-Gravenhage: Mar-
    tinus Nijhoff, 1975. Rev. by J. L. Helguera, TAm, 33(Apr
    1977):697-9.

Goubert, Pierre. Clio parmi les hommes: Recueil d'articles.
    Paris: Mouton, 1976. Rev. by W. H. Beik, AHR, 82(Oct
    1977):979-80.

Gough, Barry. Canada. Englewood Cliffs, N.J.: Prentice-Hall,
    1976. Rev. by O.E.S., CurH, 72(Apr 1977):176.

Gould, W. T. S. see Masser, L.

Gourou, Pierre. Man and Land in the Far East. London: Long-
    man, 1975. Rev. by B Boxer, JAS, 36(May 1977):539-40.

Gowans, Fred R. Rocky Mountain Rendezvous: A History of the
    Fur Trade Rendezvous, 1825-1840. Provo: Brigham Young
    U Press, 1976. Rev. by J. A. Hussey, WHQ, 8(Oct 1977):
    470.

Goytia, Victor F. Episodios del siglo XX en Panama. Vol. I:
    Rumbos equivocados. Vol. II: Los decados formativas de la
    republica. Barcelona: Editorial Linosa, 1975. Rev. by C.
    D. Ameringer, HAHR, 57(May 1977):351-2.

117   GOYTIA

_____ . El siglo XIX en Panamá. (Escenarios abruptos). Barcelona: Editorial Linosa, 1975. Rev. by C. D. Ameringer,
HAHR, 57(May 1977):351-2.

Graaf, H. J. De see Pigeaud, Theodore G. Th.

Grace, John. Domestic Slavery in West Africa, with Particular
Reference to the Sierra Leone Protectorate, 1896-1927. London: Frederick Muller, 1975. Rev. by J. Davidson, History,
62(Je 1977):267-8.

Grady, John C. and Bradford K. Felmly. Suffering to Silence, 29th
Texas Cavalry CSA Regimental History. Quannah, Texas:
Nortex, 1976. Rev. by R. W. Glover, ETHJ, 15(Spr 1977):
53.

Graebner, William. Coal-Mining Safety in the Progressive Period:
The Political Economy of Reform. Lexington: U Press Ken,
1976. Rev. by W. S. Greever, JISHS, 70(Nov 1977):333; J.
W. Hevener, AHR, 82(Feb 1977):197-8; A. Hoogenboom, JSH,
43(Aug 1977):473-4.

Graetz, Heinrich. The Structure of Jewish History and Other Essays. New York: KTAV, 1975. Rev. by L. Kochan, History, 62(Feb 1977):73.

Graf, Leroy P., and Ralph W. Haskins, eds. The Papers of Andrew Johnson. Vol. 4, 1860-1861. Knoxville: U Tenn
Press, 1976. Rev. by J. N. Dickinson, AHR, 82(Oct 1977):
1075-6; T. B. Alexander, JSH, 43(Feb 1977):130-1.

_____ , ed. see also Jackson, Andrew

Graham, B. D. see Reeves, P. D.

Graham, Elizabeth. Medicine Man to Missionary: Missionaries as
Agents of Change Among the Indians of Southern Ontario,
1784-1867. Toronto: Peter Martin, 1975. Rev. by J. G.
Taylor, CHR, 68(Mar 1977):72-3.

Graham, George J., Jr., and Scarlette G. Graham, eds. Founding
Principles of American Government: Two Hundred Years of
Democracy on Trial. n.l.: n.p., 1977. Rev. by J. May,
History, 6(Nov/Dec 1977):28.

Graham, Hugh D. see Bartley Nunan V.

Graham, Ian. Corpus of Maya Hieroglyphic Inscriptions. Cambridge, Mass.: Peabody Museum of Archaeology and Eth-
nology, 1975. Rev. by D. Kelley, HAHR, 57(May 1977):
322-3.

Graham, John T. Donoso Cortés: Utopian Romanticist and Political

Realist. Columbia: U Mo Press, 1974. Rev. by I. M. Zavala, AHR, 82(Apr 1977):375-6.

Graham, Mee. Aristocratic Enterprise: The Fitzwilliam Industrial
    Undertakings 1795-1857. Blackie, 1975. Rev. by J. R Har-
    ris, BH, 19(Jl 1977):230.

Graham, Otis L., Jr. Toward a Planned Society: From Roosevelt
    to Nixon. New York: Ox U Press, 1976. Rev. by H. J.
    Harris, JAmS, 11(Dec 1977):423-4.

Graham, Richard, and Peter H. Smith, eds. New Approaches to
    Latin American History. Austin: UT Press, 1974. Rev. by
    K. J. Grieb, HT, 10(May 1977):491-2.

Graham, Scarlette, G., ed. see Graham, George J., Jr., ed.

Grandi, Alfredo, ed. Processi politici del Senato Lombardo-Ven-
    eto, 1815-1851. Rome: Istituto per la storia del Risorgi-
    mento italiano, Biblioteca scientifica, 1976. Rev by A. Pat-
    rucco, AHR, 82(Je 1977):682.

Granet, Marcel. The Religion of the Chinese People. Tr. and ed.
    by Maurice Freedman. Oxford: Basil Blackwell, 1975. Rev.
    by M. H. Fried, CQ, No. 69(Mar 1977):157-60; D. L. Over-
    myer, JAS, 37(Nov 1977):106-8.

Gransden, Antonio. Historical Writing in England, c.550 to c.1307.
    Ithaca: Cor U Press, 1974. Rev. by B. S. Bachrach, AHR,
    82(Feb 1977):75.

Grant, C. H. The Making of Modern Belize: Politics, Society and
    British Colonialism in Central America. New York: Cam U
    Press, 1976.

Grant, Campbell. The Rock Paintings of the Chumash: A Study of
    the California Indian Culture. Berkeley: U Cal Press, 1976.
    Rev. by L. J. Bean, CHQ, 56(Sum 1977):187.

Grant, Carolyn, ed. see Wakeman, Frederic, Jr., ed.

Grant, Donald L. The Anti-Lynching Movement: 1883-1932. San
    Francisco: R & E Research Associates, 1975. Rev. by R.
    F. Weston, JSH, 43(Aug 1977):467-8.

Grant, H. Roger, and L. Edward Purcell, eds. The Years of
    Struggle: The Farm Diary of Elmer G. Powers, 1931-1936.
    Ames, Iowa: Ia St U, 1976. Rev. by P..W. Gates, A&W,
    19(Sum 1977):173-75; L. Soth, AgH, 51(Apr 1977):462-3; G.
    L. Nall, ChOk, 54(Win 1976-77):529-30; J. K. Cowger,
    JISHS, 70(Nov 1977):336; J. H. Bosch, MinnH, 45(Win 1977):
    159-60.

Grant, Michael. The Fall of the Roman Empire. London: Nelson
for Annenberg School Press, 1976. Rev. by A. E. Astin,
History, 62(Je 1977):306-7.

_____. Jesus. n.l.: Weidenfeld & Nicolson, n.d. Rev. by S.
Perowne, HTo, 27(Je 1977):403-4.

_____. Saint Paul. New York: Scribners, 1976. Rev. by J.
E. Rexine, AHR, 82(Feb 1977):71-2.

Grant, Ulysses S. The Papers of Ulysses S. Grant: Volume 6:
September 1-December 8, 1972. Ed. by John Y. Simon.
Carbondale: Southern Illinois U Press, 1977. Rev. by F. A.
Dennis, JMiH, 39(Nov 1977):384-6.

Graves, Edgar B., ed. A Bibliography of English History to 1485.
Oxford: Clarendon Press, 1975. Rev. by J. S. Cook, Archives, 13(Spr 1977):49-50; A. Koren, AHR, 82(Apr 1977):341.

Gray, Dorothy. Women of the West. Millbrae: Les Femmes,
1976. Rev. by L. B. Donovan, CHQ, 56(Spr 1977):85-6.

Gray, John S. Centennial Campaign: The Sioux War of 1876.
Fort Collins: Old Army Press, 1976. Rev. by W. G. Bell,
WHQ, 8(Oct 1977):467.

Gray, Richard, ed. The Cambridge History of Africa. Vol. 4,
c. 1600-c. 1790. Cambridge: University Press, 1975. Rev.
by C. C. Stewart, Africa, 47(No. 2, 1977):224-5; C. Fyfe,
History, 62(Je 1977):264-5.

Gray, Robert Q. The Labour Aristocracy in Victorian Edinburgh.
Oxford: Clarendon Press, 1976. Rev. by T. R. Tholfsen,
AHR, 82(Apr 1977):360-1; P. L. Robertson, JEH, 37(Sep
1977):804-5.

Graybill, Florence Curtis and Victor Boesen. Edward Sheriff Curtis: Visions of a Vanishing Race. New York: Thomas Y.
Crowell, 1976. Rev. by H. A. Howard, JOW, 16(Jan 1977):
83-84.

Grayson, A. K., ed. and Donald B. Redford, ed. Papyrus and
Tablet. Englewood Cliffs, N.J.: Prentice-Hall, 1973. Rev.
by R. Harris, JNES, 36(Jl 1977):230.

Grechko, A. A., et al. History of the Second World War, 1939-
1945. 12 vols. Moscow: Voennoe Izdatel'stvo Ministerstva
Oborony SSSR, 1976. Rev. by W. J. Spahr, AHR, 82(Oct
1977):1027.

Greeg, Pauline. Black Death to Industrial Revolution: A Social and
Economic History of England. New York: Barnes & Noble,
1976. Rev. by R. B. Outhwaite, JEH, 37(Sep 1977):806-7.

Green, Edwin see Cockerell, H. A. L.

Green, William A. British Slave Emancipation: The Sugar Colo-
    nies and the Great Experiment, 1830-1865. London: Ox U
    Press, 1976. Rev. by B. W. Higman, JEH, 37(Je 1977):
    515-7; F. W. Knight, AHR, 82(Apr 1977):480.

Greenbaum, Fred. Robert Marion La Follette. Boston: Twayne
    Publ., 1975. Rev. by R. S. Maxwell, AHR, 82(Apr 1977):
    459-60.

Greenberg, Douglas. Crime and Law Enforcement in the Colony
    of New York, 1691-1776. Ithaca: Cor U Press, 1976. Rev.
    by P. U. Bonomi, AHR, 82(Je 1977):732-3; F. J Cavaioli,
    Historian, 39(May 1977):569-70; T. J. Archdeacon, WMQ, 34
    (Oct 1977):659-61.

Greenblatt, Sidney L. see Wilson Amy A.

Greene, Jack P., Richard L. Bushman, and Michael Kammen.
    Society, Freedom and Conscience: The American Revolution
    in Virginia, Massachusetts, and New York. New York: W.
    W. Norton, 1976. Rev. by J. R. Gundersen, JSH, 43(May
    1977):284-5.

Greene, Nathanael. The Papers of Nathanael Greene. Volume I.
    December 1766-December 1776. Ed. by Richard K. Showman,
    Chapel Hill: U North Carolina Press, 1976. Rev. by J. F.
    Stegeman, GHQ, 51(Spr 1977):90-2; R. Buel, NEQ, 50(Sep
    1977):548-51; P. D. Nelson, WMQ, 34(Oct 1977):668-70.

Greene, Victor. For God and Country: The Rise of Polish and
    Lithuanian Ethnic Consciousness in America 1860-1910. Mad-
    ison: St. Historical Soc. of Wis., 1975. Rev. by F. Ren-
    kiewicz, AHR, 81(Dec 1976):1259-60; J. Bodnar, PH, 45(Oct
    1977):369-70.

Greenhill, Basil, et al. Archaeology of the Boat. Middletown,
    Conn.: Wesleyan U Press, 1976. Rev. by L. Casson, AHR,
    82(Je 1977):606-7; J. R. Steffy, Archaeology, 30(Nov 1977):
    427-9.

Greenough, William C. and Francis P. King. Pension Plans and
    Public Policy. New York: Col U Press, 1976. Rev. by J.
    LaRocque, JEH, 37(Sep 1977):805-6.

Greenslade, M. W., ed. Victoria History of Stafford, volume XVII.
    Cambridge: Ox U Press for the Institute of Historical Research,
    1976. Rev. by T. Raybound, History, 62(Feb 1977):84-5.

Greenwood, Davydd J. Unrewarding Wealth: The Commercialization
    and Collapse of Agriculture in a Spanish Basque Town. New
    York: Cam U Press, 1976. Rev. by R. Pike, AgH, 51(Jl
    1977):604-5.

Gregg, Pauline. <u>Black Death to Industrial Revolution: A Social and Economic History of England</u>. New York: Barnes & Noble, 1976. Rev. by J. A. Casada, HT, 10(Aug 1977):636-7; D. B. Weiner, JIH, 8(Aug 1977):363-4.

Gregor, A. James. <u>Interpretations of Fascism</u>. Morristown, N.J.: General Learning Press, 1974. Rev. by G Allardyce, AHR, 82(Apr 1977):387-8.

Gregory, Francis W. <u>Nathan Appleton: Merchant and Entrepreneur, 1779-1861</u>. Charlottesville: U Press Va, 1975. Rev. by K. S. Kutolowski, Historian, 39(May 1977):571-3; C. W. Cheape, JEH, 37(Je 1977):517-8.

Greig, William. <u>General Report on the Gosford Estates in County Armagh, 1821</u>. Belfast: HMSO, 1976. Rev. by L. P. Curtis, Jr., AHR, 82(Oct 1977):975; B. G. Hutton, Archives, 13(Spr 1977):52-3.

Grekulov, E. F., ed. <u>Religion and the Church in Russian History</u>. Moscow: Izdatel'stvo "Mysl'," 1975. Rev. by S. A. Zenkovsky, AHR, 82(Je 1977):691.

Grele, Ronald J., ed. <u>Envelope of Sound: Six Practitioners Discuss the Method, Theory, and Practice of Oral History and Oral Testimony</u>. Chicago: Precedent Publishing, 1975. Rev. by M. F. Stein, PNQ, 68(Jan 1977):42-3.

Grendler, Marcella. <u>The "Trattato Politico-Morale" of Giovanni Cavalcanti (1381-c.1451)</u>. Geneva: Librairie Droz, 1973. Rev. by D. Nugent, AHR, 82(Feb 1977):85-6.

Grenoble University. <u>La France et l'Italie pendant la premiere guerre mondiale</u>. Grenoble: Grenoble Presses Universitaires, 1976. Rev. by J. P. J. Bury, EHR, 92(Oct 1977):929-30.

Grieb, Kenneth J. <u>The Latin American Policy of Warren G. Harding</u>. Fort Worth: TCU Press, 1976. Rev. by D. Healy, AHR, 82(Je 1977):761; R. F. Smith, HAHR, 57(May 1977): 364-5; M. T. Gilderhus, TAm, 33(Apr 1977):696-7.

Grierson, Edward. <u>King of Two Worlds: Philip II of Spain</u>. London: Collins, 1974. Rev. by G. Parker, History, 62(Feb 1977):116.

Griffin, Keith. <u>The Political Economy of Agrarian Change: An Essay on the Green Revolution</u>. Cambridge: Harvard U Press, 1974. Rev. by M. J. Frankman, JAAS, 12(Jan/Oct 1977):298-9.

Griffin, Patricia E. <u>The Chinese Communist Treatment of Counter-revolutionaires. 1924-1949</u>. Princeton: Prin U Press, n.d. Rev. by P. M. Coble, Jr., AHR, 82(Apr 1977):415-6; J. P. Harrison, JAS, 37(Nov 1977):123-4.

GRIFFITH 122

Griffith, Cyril E. The African Dream: Martin R. Delany and the emergence of Pan-African thought. University Park: Penn St U Press, 1975. Rev. by I. Duffield, AfAf, 76(Apr 1977): 267-8; J. H. Bracey, Jr., JNH, 62(Jan 1977):104-6; R. J. Cottrol, PH, 45(Jl 1977):280-1.

Griffith, Samuel B., II. In Defense of the Public Liberty. Garden City, N.Y.: Doubleday, 1976. Rev. by D. J. Pogue, AI, 44(Fall 1977):158-9; D. A. Sloan, ArkHq, 36(Spr 1977): 86-8; P. D. Nelson, JSH, 43(Aug 1977):436-7; C. R. Ferguson, WMQ, 34(Oct 1977):691-2; J. P. Cullen, AHI, 12(Jl 1977):49-50.

Grigg, John. The Young Lloyd George. Berkeley: U Cal Press, 1974. Rev. by E. Larkin, JMH, 49(Je 1977):310-1.

Grillo, R. D. Race, Class and Militancy: An African Trade Union, 1939-1965. New York: Chandler, 1974. Rev. by L. Mair, Africa, 47(No. 1, 1977):115-16.

Grime, Philip N., ed. see Lipke, William C., ed.

Grimm, Günter. Kunst der Ptolemäer- und Römerzeit im Ägyptischen Museum Kairo. Mainz: Philipp von Zabern, 1975. Rev. by R. S. Bianchi, AJA, 81(Spr 1977):257-8.

Gröbli, Fredy. Ambassador Du Luc und der Trücklibund von 1715. 2 vols. Basel: Helbing and Lichtenhahn Verlag, 1975. Rev. by W. Roosen, AHR, 82(Je 1977):677-8.

Gromyko, A., chm. of editing Commission. Dokumnty Vneshney Politiki USSR, XIX and XX, 1936, 1937. Moscow: Izdatelstvo Politicheskoy Literatury, 1974, 1976. Rev. by H. Hanak, EHR, 92(Oct 1977):877-8.

Gross, Jean-Pierre. Saint-Just, sa politique et ses missions. Paris: Bibliothèque Nationale, 1976. Rev. by M. Kennedy, AHR, 82(Apr 1977):369-70.

Gross, Nachum, ed. Economic History of the Jews. New York: Schoken Books, 1975. Rev. by B. Ravid, JEH, 37(Je 1977): 479-81.

Gross, Robert A. The Minutemen and Their World. New York: Hill and Wang, 1976. Rev. by R. P. Gildrie, AHR, 82(Apr 1977):437.

Grossman, Lawrence. The Democratic Party and the Negro: Northern and National Politics, 1868-92. Urbana: U Ill Press, 1976. Rev. by M. Les Benedict, AHR, 82(Apr 1977):443-4; B. Collins, JAmS, 11(Dec 1977):405-6; S. J. Karina, JISHS, 70(Nov 1977):335; J. G. Sproat, JSH, 43(Feb 1977):137-8.

Gruber, Carol S. Mars and Minerva: World War I and the Uses of the Higher Learning in America. Baton Rouge: LSU Press, 1976. Rev. by S. Herman, AHR, 82(Feb 1977):202.

Grugel, Lee E. George Jacob Holyoake: A Study in the Evolution of a Victorian Radical. Philadelphia: Porcupine Press, 1976. Rev. by W. L. Arnstein, AHR, 82(Apr 1977):358.

Guerrero, J. M. Briceno. America Latina en el Mundo. Caracas: Editorial Arte, 1976. Rev. by H. E. Davis, TAm, 34(Jl 1977):136-7.

Gugel, Michael. Industrieller Aufstieg und bürgerliche Herrschaft. Cologne: Pahl-Rugenstein, 1975. Rev. by W. Struve, AHR, 82(Oct 1977):998-9; J. J. Sheehan, JMH, 49(Je 1977):328-9.

Guillermaz, Jacques. The Chinese Communist Party in Power. Tr. by Anne Destenay. Boulder, Colorado: Westview Press, 1976. Rev. by J. R. Townsend, JAS, 37(Nov 1977):126-7.

Guilmartin, John Francis, Jr. Gunpowder and Galleys: Changing Technology and Mediterranean Warfare at Sea in the Sixteenth Century. Cambridge U Press, 1974. Rev. by G. V. Scammell, HJ, 20(No. 1, 1977):255-7; G. J. Marcus, JMH, 49 (Je 1977):303-5.

Guinsburg, T. N. and G. L. Renber. Perspectives on the Social Sciences in Canada. Toronto: Tor U Press, 1974. Rev. by H. J. Hanham, CHR, 58(Mar 1977):85-6.

Gumerman, George, and Robert C. Euler, eds. Papers on the Archaeology of Black Mesa, Arizona. Carbondale: So Ill U Press, 1976. Rev. by R. H. Lister, NMHR, 52(Jl 1977): 255.

Gunn, Giles. F. O. Matthiessen: The Critical Achievement. Seattle and London: U Wash Press, 1976. Rev. by D. Flower, NEQ, 50(Je 1977):359-61.

Gunther, Erna. The Permanent Collection. Vol. I: The First in a Series of Catalogs on the Permanent Collection of the Whatcom Museum of History and Art. Bellingham: Whatcom Museum of History and Art, 1975. Rev. by J. V. Powell, PNQ, 68(Oct 1977):196-7.

Guralnik, Stanley M. Science and the Ante-Bellum American College. Philadelphia: American Philosophical Society, 1975. Rev. by A. H. Dupres, AHR, 82(Je 1977):742-3; W. E. Leverette, Jr., JSH, 43(Feb 1977):128-9.

Gurian, Jay. Western American Writing: Tradition and Promise. DeLand, Fla.: Everett/Edwards, Inc., 1975. Rev. by E. R. Bingham, PHR, 46(Aug 1977):517-8.

Gurnham, Richard. A History of the Trade Union Movement in the
     Hosiery and Knitwear Industry, 1776-1976. Leicester, Eng.:
     National Union of Hosiery and Knitwear Workers, 1976. Rev.
     by R. A. Church, AHR, 82(Apr 1977):359-60.

Gusev, K. V. The SR Party: From Petit-bourgeois Revolutionism
     to Counter-Revolution. Moscow: Izdatel'stvo "Mysl", 1975.
     Rev. by M. Melancon, AHR, 82(Je 1977):703.

Gustafson, W. Eric, and Kenneth W. Jones, ed. Sources on Pun-
     jab History. Delhi: Manohar Book Service, 1975. Rev. by
     K. Sherman, JAS, 36(Feb 1977):367-8.

Gustavson, Carl G. The Mansion of History. New York: McGraw
     Hill, 1976. Rev. by L. J. Goldstein, AHR, 82(Apr 1977):
     331-2.

Guth, Delloyd J. Late-medieval England, 1377-1485. Cambridge:
     Cam U Press, 1976. Rev. by C. Richmond, History, 62(Je
     1977):312.

Gutman, Herbert G. The Black Family in Slavery and Freedom,
     1750-1925. New York: Pantheon Books, 1976. Rev. by D.
     B. Davis, AHR, 82(Je 1977):744-5; C. B. Dew, AlaR, 30(Oct
     1977):314-5; M. P. Johnson, HT, 10(Feb 1977):342-3; W. S.
     McFeely, JSH, 43(Aug 1977):432-4; E. L. Drago, SCHM, 78
     (Jl 1977):243; P. H. Wood, WMQ, 34(Jl 1977):477-9; B.
     Wyatt-Brown, Comm, 63(Jan 1977):76-8; R. L. Patterson,
     MinnH, 45(Sum 1977):254-5; J. D. Anderson, JNH, 62(Jl
     1977):389-93.

_____ . Work, Culture, and Society in Industrializing America:
     Essays in American Working-Class and Social History. New
     York: Knopf, 1976. Rev. by D. Brody, AHR, 82(Feb 1977):
     195-6; K. McQuaid, JIH, 8(Aut 1977):392-4; H. S. Nelli, JSH,
     43(May 1977):326-7.

_____   see also David, Paul A.

Gutteridge, Richard. The German Evangelical Church and the Jews,
     1879-1950. New York: Barnes and Noble, 1976. Rev. by D.
     R. Borg, AHR, 82(Oct 1977):1000-1.

Gwyn, Julian. The Enterprising Admiral: The Personal Fortune
     of Admiral Sir Peter Warren. Montreal: McGill-Queen's
     U Press, 1974. Rev. by C. R. Canedy, CHR, 58(Mar 1977):
     94-6.

_____ , ed. The Royal Navy and North America: The Warren
     Papers, 1736-1752. n.l.: Navy Records Society, n.d. Rev.
     by B. Pool, HTo, 27(Jan 1977):63-4; S. G. Morse, NEQ,
     50(Mar 1977):151-2.

Hadingham, Evan. Circles and Standing Stones: An Illustrated Exploration of the Megolith Mysteries of Early Britain. New York: Walker, 1975. Rev. by P. J. Fowler, Archaeology, 30(Jan 1977):65-6.

Hafen, Bruce C., ed. see Wilkinson, Ernest L., ed.

Haferkorn, Folkert. Soziale Vorstellungen Heinrich von Sybels. Stuttgart: Ernst Klett Verlag, 1976. Rev. by C. E. McClelland, AHR, 82(Oct 1977):999.

Haffenden, Philip S. New England in the English Nation, 1689-1713. New York: Ox U Press, 1974. Rev. by S. S. Webb, AHR, 82(Feb 1977):170-1.

Hagan, William T. United States Comanche Relations: The Reservation Years. New Haven: Yale U Press, 1976. Rev. by M. B. Husband, AgH, 51(Jl 1977):615-6; L. J. White, JOW, 16 (Jan 1977):85-6; D. J. Berthrong, NMHR, 52(Oct 1977):345-6; C. Kenner, WHQ, 8(Apr 1977):215-6.

Haimson, Leopold, ed. The Mensheviks from the Revolution of 1917 to the Second World War. Chicago: U Chi Press, 1974. Rev. by A. K. Wildman, JMH, 49(Sep 1977):524-6.

Haines, Francis. The Plains Indians. New York: Thomas Y. Crowell, 1976. Rev. by L. J. White, A & W, 19(Spr 1977): 85-86; D. J. Berthrong, NMHR, 52(Jan 1977):86-7; J. F. Yurtinus, UHQ, 45(Spr 1977):209-10; M. E. Nackman, WHQ, 8(Apr 1977):216-7.

Hair, William Ivy. Carnival of Fury: Robert Charles and the New Orleans Race Riot of 1900. Baton Rouge: LSU, 1976. Rev. by R. V. Haynes, AHR, 82(Apr 1977):460-1; J. J. Jackson, Historian, 39(May 1977):581; G. R. McNeil. JNH, 62(Jl 1977): 302-4; W. M. Tuttle, Jr., JSH, 43(May 1977):313-5; J. G. Taylor, LaH, 18(Sum 1977):382-3.

Haitani, Kanji. The Japanese Economic System: An Institutional Overview. Lexington, Mass.: Lexington Books, 1976. Rev. by R. Napier, JAS, 37(Nov 1977):134-6.

Haites, Erik F., James Mak and Gary M. Walton. Western River Transportation: The Era of Early Internal Development, 1810-1860. Baltimore: JHU Press, 1975. Rev. by D. Lindstrom, AgH, 51(Apr 1977):466-7; W. H. Adams, LaH, 18(Sum 1977): 370-1; W. D. Aeschbacher, PHR, 46(May 1977):283-4.

Halbach, Axel J. Die Südafrikanischen Bantu-Homelands. Munich: Weltforum Verlag, 1976. Rev. by L. H. Gann, AHR, 82(Oct 1977):1040-1.

Hale, J. R., ed. Renaissance Venice. n.p.: Rowman and Littlefield, 1976. Rev. by E. Muir, AHR, 82(Feb 1977):140-1.

Hale, John. Italian Renaissance Painting. n.l.: Phaidon, n.d.
Rev. by A. Haynes, HTo, 27(Jl 1977):476.

Hale, Kenneth L., ed. see Kinkade, M. Dale, ed.

Haley, Alex. Roots: The Saga of an American Family. Garden
City, N.Y.: Doubleday, 1976. Rev. by Q. Taylor, MinnH. 45(Spr
1977): 203-4; B. J. Shade, WMH, 60(Sum 1977):334-5.

Haley, James L. The Buffalo War: The History of the Red River
Indian Uprising of 1874. Garden City, N.Y.: Doubleday,
1976. Rev. by E. J. Danziger, Jr., CWH, 23(Mar 1977):
90-3; M. L. Tate, ETHJ, 15(No. 1, 1977):55-6; R. N. Ellis,
PNQ, 68(Oct 1977):193-4; W. W. Savage, WHQ, 8(Jan 1977):
66.

Hall, A. Oakley, ed. The Manhattaner in New Orleans: or,
Phases of "Crescent City" Life. Baton Rouge: LSU Press,
1976. Rev. by J. Belsom, LaH, 18(Sum 1977):375-7.

Hall, Carolyn. El Café y el desarrollo historico-geográfico de
Costa Rica. San Jose, C. R.: Editorial Costa Rica y Universidad Nacional, 1976. Rev. by J. J. Parsone, HAHR, 57(Aug
1977):543-5.

Hall, D. G. E. Henry Burney: A Political Biography. London:
U London, 1974. Rev. by B. B. Kling, AHR, 82(Feb 1977):
166-7.

Hall, Edwin S., Jr. The Eskimo Storyteller: Folktales from Noa-
tak, Alaska. Knoxville: U Tennessee Press, 1975. Rev. by
M. Lantis, AIQ, 3(Spr 1977):66-7.

Hall, Helen Gibbard see Hall Roy F.

Hall, Kermit L., ed. see Polk, James K.

Hall, Roy F. and Hellen Gibbard Hall. Collin County: Pioneering
in North Texas. Quannah, Texas: Nortex, 1975. Rev. by
J. Osburn, ETHJ, 15(Spr 1977):58.

Hall, Sharlot M. Sharlot Hall on the Arizona Strip: A Diary of a
Journey through Northern Arizona in 1911. Flagstaff, Ariz.:
Northland Press, 1975. Rev. by E. R. Carriker, PHR, 46
(Aug 1977):506-7.

Haller, John S., Jr. and Robin M. Haller. The Physician and Sexuality in Victorian America. Urbana: U Illinois Press, 1974.
Rev. by R. D. Apple, WMH, 60(Sum 1977):347-8.

Haller, Robin M. see Haller, John S.

Hallett, G. see Pieterse, C.

Halley, Donald. Uncle Sam's Farmers, The New Deal Communities
in the Lower Mississippi Valley. Urbana: U Ill Press, 1975.
Rev. by W. L. Brown, ArkHQ, 26(Spr 1977):88-90.

Hallgarten, G. and J. Radkau. Deutsche Industrie und Politik von
Bismarck bis heute. Cologne: Europäische Verlagsanstalt,
1974. Rev. by K. D. Barkin, JMH, 49(Sep 1977):512-6.

Halliburton, R. , Jr. Red Over Black: Black Slavery Among the
Cherokee Indians. Westport, Conn.: Greenwood Press, 1977.
Rev. by L. C. Kelly, History, 6(Nov/Dec 1977):29-30.

Halliday, Jon. A Political History of Japanese Capitalism. New
York: Pantheon Books, 1975. Rev. by W. B. Hauser, AHR,
82(Je 1977):722.

Hallowell, A. Irving. Contributions to Anthropology: Selected Papers of A. Irving Hallowell. Chicago: U Chicago Press, 1976.
Rev. by R. F. Heizer, AIQ, 3(Aug 1977):260-1.

Halperin-Donghi, Tulio. Politics, Economics and Society in Argentina in the Revolutionary Period. New York: Cam U Press,
1975. Rev. by R. A. Potash, AHR, 82(Feb 1977):230-1; T.
F. McGann, HAHR, 57(May 1977):340-2; P. H. Smith, JIH, 7
(Win 1977):555-7; J. Lynch, JLAS, 9(May 1977):161-2.

Hamburger, Joseph. Macaulay and the Whig Tradition. Chicago:
U Chi Press, 1976. Rev. by D. S. Goldstein, AHR, 82(Oct
1977):965; J. Clive, JMH, 49(Sep 1977):488.

Hamby, Alonzo L. Beyond the New Deal: Harry S Truman and
American Liberalism. New York: Col U Press, 1973. Rev.
by R. Dallek, PHR, 46(May 1977):314-5; D. Alden, PNQ, 58
(Jan 1977):31-2.

_____. The Imperial Years: The United States Since 1939.
New York: Weybright and Talley, 1976. Rev. by D. R.
McCoy, AHR, 82(Apr 1977):468.

Hamerly, Michael T. El Comercio del cacao de Guayaquil durante
el periodo colonial: un estudio cuanitativo. Quito: Comand-
ancia General de Marina, 1976. Rev. by M. L. Conniff, TAm,
34(Oct 1977):305.

Hamilton, Elizabeth. Henrietta Maria. London: Hamish Hamilton,
1976. Rev. by C. Russell, History, 62(Feb 1977):118.

Hamilton, Milton W. Sir William Johnson: Colonial American,
1715-1763. Port Washington, N.Y.: Kennikat Press, 1976.
Rev. by J. H. O'Donnell III, AHR, 82(Apr 1977):432; N.
Varga, WMQ, 34(Apr 1977):339-41.

Hamilton, Peter J. Colonial Mobile. Ed. by Charles G. Summersell. University: University of Alabama Press, 1976. Rev. by C. Delaney, AlaR, 30(Jan 1977):66-8.

Hammarberg, Melvyn. The Indiana Voter: The Historical Dynamics of Party Allegiance During the 1870s. Chicago: U Chi Press, 1977. Rev. by L. E. Ziewacz, History, 6(Oct 1977):9.

Hammer, Kenneth, ed. Custer in '76: Walter Camp's Notes on the Custer Fight. Provo: Brigham Young U Press, 1976. Rev. by M. B. Husband, JOW, 16(Jan 1977):84-5; R. C. Carriker, PHR, 46(Aug 1977):504-6.

Hammett, Hugh B. Hilary Abner Herbert: A Southerner Returns to the Union. Philadelphia: American Philosophical Society, 1976. Rev. by H. Hattaway, AHR, 82(Apr 1977):447-8.

Hammond, George P. Alexander Barclay: Mountain Man. Denver: Old West Publishing, 1976. Rev. by D. J. Weber, NMHR, 52 (Jan 1977):81-2; F. R. Gowans, UHQ, 45(Spr 1977):207-8; H. L. Carter, WHQ, 8(Jan 1977):58.

Hammond, Nicholas G. L. Migrations and Invasions in Greece and Adjacent Areas. Park Ridge, N.J.: Noyes Press, 1976. Rev. by M. H. Jameson, Archaeology, 30(Nov 1977):427.

Hammond-Tooke, W. D. Command or Consensus: The development of Transkeian local government. Rex Collings, 1975. Rev. by A. Kuper, AfAf, 76(Jan 1977):124-5.

Hamori, Andras. On the Art of Medieval Arabaic Literature. Princeton, N.J.: Prin U Press, 1974. Rev. by W. Heinrichs, JNES, 36(Jan 1977):60-1.

Hampe, Peter. Die "ökonomische Imperialismustheorie": Kritische Untersuchungen. Munich: Verlag C. H. Beck, 1976. Rev. by L. Schofer, JEH, 37(Sep 1977):807-8.

Hampson, Norman. The Life and Opinions of Maximilien Robespierre. London: Duckworth, 1974. Rev. by J. I. Shulim, AHR, 82(Feb 1977):20-38.

Hamscher, Albert N. The Parlement of Paris after the Fronde, 1653-1673. Pittsburgh: U Pitt Press, 1976. Rev. by S. Kettering, AHR, 82(Oct 1977):977-8.

Hanauer, Elsie. Rocks and Minerals of the Western United States. New York: A. S. Barnes & Co., 1976. Rev. by A. Probert, JOW, 16(Jan 1977):91.

Handy, Robert T. A History of the Churches in the United States and Canada. New York: Ox U Press, 1977. Rev. by H. F. Worthley, History, 6(Oct 1977):11.

Hanfmann, George M. A. and Jane C. Waldbaum. A Survey of Sardis and the Major Monuments Outside the City Walls. Cambridge, Mass.: Har U Press, 1975. Rev. by K. De Vries, AJA, 81(Sum 1977):401.

Hanham, Alison. Richard III and His Early Historians, 1483-1535. Oxford: Clarendon, 1975. Rev. by C.A.J. Armstrong, EHR, 92(Oct 1977):892-3.

Hanley, Thomas O'Brien, ed. The John Carroll Papers. 3 vols. Notre Dame: U Notre Dame Press, 1976. Rev. by J. T. Ellis, AHR, 82(Je 1977):736-7.

Hannah, Leslie. The Rise of the Corporate Economy: The British Experience. Baltimore and London: JHU Press, 1976. Rev. by G. R. Hawke, JEH, 37(Sep 1977):808-10.

Hansen, Bent and Karim Nashashibi. Egypt. New York and London: Col U Press for the National Bureau of Economic Research, 1975. Rev. by K. M. Langley, JEH, 37(Je 1977):482-5.

Hansen, Mogens Herman. Apagoge, Endeixis and Ephegesis against Kakourgoi, Atimoi and Pheugontes: A Study in the Athenian Administration of Justice in the Fourth Century B. C. Odense: Odense U Press, 1976. Rev. by R. S. Stroud, AHR, 82(Oct 1977):928-9.

_____. The Sovereignty of the People's Court in Athens in the Fourth Century B. C. and the Public Action Against Unconditional Proposals. Odense: Odense U Press, 1974. Rev. by R. S. Stroud, AHR, 82(Oct 1977):928-9.

Han-sheng, Ch'uan. Chung-kuo ching-chi-shih yen-chiu. Hong Kong: Hsin-ya yen-chiu-suo ch'u-pan, 1976. Rev. by R. H. Myers, JAS, 37(Nov 1977):110-11.

Han-Sheng Chuan and Richard A. Kraus. Mid-Ch'ing Rice Markets and Trade: An Essay in Price History. Cambridge, Mass.: Har U Press, 1975. Rev. by Chi-Ming Hou, AgH, 51(Apr 1977):476.

Hanson, Carl A. Dissertations on Iberian and Latin American History. New York: The Whitston Publishing Company, 1975. Rev. by M. L. Conniff, NMHR, 52(Jl 1977):261-2.

Hanson, James Austin. Metal Weapons, Tools, and Ornaments of the Teton Dakota Indians. Lincoln: U Nebraska Press, 1975. Rev. by J. H. Howard, AIQ, 3(Aut 1977):266-7.

Haraguchi, Torao, et al., tr. The Status System and Social Organization of Satsuma: A Translation of the Shumon Tefuda Aratame Jōmoku. Honolulu: U Presses of Hawaii, 1975. Rev. by T. M. Huber, JAS, 37(Nov 1977):141-2.

Hardach, Karl. Wirtschaftsgeschichte Deutschlands im 20. Jahrhundert. Gottingen: Vandenhoeck and Ruprecht, 1976. Rev. by M. R. Haines, JEH, 37(Sep 1977):810.

Hardeman, Nicholas Perkins. Wilderness Calling: The Hardeman Family in the American Westward Movement, 1750-1900. Knoxville: U Tenn Press, 1977. Rev. by V. G. Spence, History, 6(Nov/Dec 1977):32.

Hargreaves, John D. West Africa Partitioned, Vol. I, The Loaded Pause, 1885-1889. London: Macmillan, 1975. Rev. by P. E. H. Hair, EHR, 92(Oct 1977):868-9; R. T. Brown, JAAS, 12(Jan/Oct 1977):285-6.

Harkabi, Yehoshafat. Arab Strategies and Israel's Responses. n.l.: Free Press, n.d. Rev. by E. Grossman, Comm, 64(Oct 1977): 70-6.

Harlan, Jack R. Crops and Man. Madison, Wisc.: American Society of Agronomy and the Crop Science Society of America, 1975. Rev. by W. C. Van Deventer, AgH, 51(Jan 1977):261-2.

Harlan, Louis R., ed. see Washington, Booker T.

Harlow, Neal. Maps and Surveys of the Pueblo Lands of Los Angeles. Los Angeles: Dawson's Bookshop, 1976. Rev. by J. Caughey, PHR, 46(May 1977):291-2.

Harp, Elmer, Jr., ed. Photography in Archaeological Research. Albuquerque: U New Mexico Press, 1975. Rev. by D. R. Wilson, Antiquity, 51(Mar 1977):68-9.

Harper, George Mills, ed. Yeats and the Occult. Toronto: Macmillan, 1975. Rev. by E. Kennedy, E-I, 12(Win 1977):146-7.

Harrer, Jürgen see Fülberth, Georg

Harries-Jones, Peter. Freedom and Labour: Mobilization and Political Control on the Zambian Copperbelt. Oxford: Basil Blackwell, 1975. Rev. by R. D. Grillo, Africa, 47(No. 3, 1977):327-9.

Harris, Charles H. III. A Mexican Family Empire: The Latifundio of the Sanchez Navarros 1765-1867. Austin: U Tex Press, 1975. Rev. by A. T. Bryan, AHR, 82(Feb 1977):224; D. A. Brading, JLAS, 9(May 1977):156-9.

Harris, Charles W., ed. and Buck Rainey, ed. The Cowboy: Six Shooters, Songs and Sex. Norman: U Ok Press, 1976. Rev. by J. Griffith, JAriH, 18(Spr 1977):111-2.

Harris, James E. and Kent R. Weeks. X-Raying the Pharaohs. New York: Charles Scribner's Sons, 1975. Rev. by D. Mueller, JNES, 36(Jan 1977):72-3.

131   HARRIS

Harris, Nigel. Competition and the Corporate Society: British Con-
    servatives, the State, and Industry, 1945-1964. London:
    Methuen, 1972. Rev. by C. K. Harley, Jeh, 37(Je 1977):
    518-9.

Harris, R. Cole and John Warkentin. Canada Before Confederation.
    Toronto: Ox U Press, 1974. Rev. by J. M. S. Coreless,
    CHR, 58(Mar 1977):68-70.

Harris, Richard. Freedom Spent. n. l.: Little, Brown, n. d. Rev.
    by J. W. Bishop, Comm, 63(Jan 1977):86-8.

Harrison, John P. see Ulibarri, George S.

Harrison, Margaret A. L., ed. Handbook of Middle American
    Indians. Austin: UT Press, 1976. Rev. by S. A. Colston,
    TAm, 33(Apr 1977):679-80.

Harriss, G. R. King, Parliament, and Public Finance in Medieval
    England to 1369. London: Ox U Press, 1975. Rev. by C.
    R. Young, AHR, 82(Feb 1977):77.

Hart, C. R. The Early Charters of Northern England and the North
    Midlands. Leicester U Press, 1975. Rev. by M. Roper,
    Archives, 13(Spr 1977):48-9.

Hart, Robert. The I. G. in Peking: Letters of Robert Hart,
    Chinese Maritime Customs, 1868-1907. Ed. by John King
    Fairbank, Katherine Frost Bruner, and Elizabeth MacLeod
    Matheson. Cambridge: Harvard U Press, 1975. Rev. by
    S. M. Jones, CQ, No. 69(Mar 1977):162-3.

Hart, Robert A. The Eccentric Tradition: American Diplomacy in
    the Far East. New York: Scribners, 1976. Rev. by M. H.
    Hunt, AHR, 82(Je 1977):772.

Hart, Roger L. Redeemers, Bourbons and Populists: Tennessee,
    1870-1896. Baton Rouge: LSU Press, 1975. Rev. by T. B.
    Alexander, AHR, 82(Feb 1977):185-6.

Hartman, David. Maimonides: Torah and Philosophic Quest. n. l.:
    Jewish Publication Society, n. d. Rev. by D. Singer, Comm,
    64(Dec 1977):90-3.

Harvey, A. McGehee. Adventures in Medical Research: A Century
    of Discovery at Johns Hopkins. Baltimore: JHU Press, 1976.
    Rev. by J. Duffy, AHR, 82(Apr 1977):463-4.

_____ see Bordley, James III

Harvey, Horace, Katherine Harvey Roger and Louise Destrehan
    Roger D'Oliveira. To Reach Afar: Memoirs and Biography
    of the Destrehan and Harvey Families of Louisiana. Clear-

water, Fla.: Hercules Publishing, 1974. Rev. by M. K. Gaupp, LaH, 18(Spr 1977):252.

Harvey, John. The Black Prince and His Age. Totowa, N.J.: Rowman and Littlefield, 1976. Rev. by M. Altschul, AHR, 82(Apr 1977):341-2.

Harvey, Nancy Lenz. The Rose and the Thorn: The Lives of Mary and Margaret Tudor. New York: Macmillan, 1975. Rev. by R. G. Eaves, AHR, 82(Feb 1977):92-3.

Harwell, Richard, ed. see Cumming, Kate

Harwell, Richard B. The Mint Julep. Charlottesville: U Virginia Press, 1977. Rev. by E. J. Kahn, Jr., GHQ, 51(Win 1977): 359-61.

Hasan, Parvez. Korea: Problems and Issues in a Rapidly Growing Economy. Baltimore and London: JHU Press, 1976. Rev. by K. Chao, JEH, 37(Sep 1977):811-2.

Haskins, Ralph W., ed. see Graf, LeRoy P., ed.

_____, ed. see Jackson, Andrew

Hatfield, Joseph T. William Claiborne: Jeffersonian Centurion in the American Southwest. Lafayette, La.: U Southwestern Louisiana, 1976. Rev. by F. L. Owsley, Jr., JMiH, 39 (Nov 1977):381-2; R. H. Pulley, JSH, 43(Nov 1977):614-5.

Hatje, Ann-Katrin. The Population Question and Public Welfare: The Public Debate on Family Policies and Increased Fertility during the 1930s and 1940s. Stockholm: Almanna Forlaget, 1974. Rev. by S. Koblik, AHR, 82(Feb 1977):122.

Hattaway, Herman. General Stephen D. Lee. Jackson: U Press Miss, 1976. Rev. by H. B. Hammett, AHR, 82(Feb 1977): 184; R. T. Connally, CWH, 23(Je 1977):179-81; R. A. Wooster, ETHJ, 15(Spr 1977):52-3; W. M. Drake, JSH, 43 (May 1977):300-1.

Hatton, Ragnild, ed. Louis XIV and Absolutism. London: Macmillan, 1976. Rev. by R. Mettam, History, 62(Feb 1977): 127-9.

_____, ed. Louis XIV and Europe. London: Macmillan, 1976. Rev. by R. Mettam, History, 62(Feb 1977):127-9.

Hauptman, La Vonne Siegel, ed. see De Pauw, Linda Grant, ed.

Haupts, Leo. Deutsche Friedenspolitik, 1918-1919: Eine Alternative zur Machtpolitik des Ersten Weltkrieges. Düsseldorf: Droste Verlag, 1976. Rev. by W. Jannen, Jr., AHR, 82(Je 1977):666.

Havens, Thomas R. Farm and Nation in Modern Japan: Agrarian
  Nationalism, 1870-1940. Princeton: Prin U Press, 1974.
  Rev. by K. I. Choi, JEH, 37(Je 1977):519-20.

Hawes, Lilla Mills and Albert S. Britt, Jr., ed. The Search for
  Georgia's Colonial Records. Savannah: Georgia Historical
  Society, 1976. Rev. by F. Harrold, GHQ, 51(Spr 1977):89-90.

_____, and Karen Elizabeth Osvald. Checklist of Eighteenth
  Century Manuscripts in the Georgia Historical Society. Savan-
  nah, Ga.: Georgia Historical Society, 1976. Rev. by P.
  Spalding, GHQ, 51(Fall 1977):283-4.

Hawke, David Freeman. Franklin. New York: Harper & Row,
  1976. Rev. by M. Hall, NEQ, 50(Mar 1977):153-5; J. K.
  Martin, WMH, 60(Sum 1977):343-4.

Hawke, G. R. Between Governments and Banks: A History of the
  Reserve Bank of New Zealand. Wellington: A. R. Shearer,
  1973. Rev. by J. C. Murdock, JEH, 37(Je 1977):520-2.

Hawkes, C. see Dwall, P. M.

Hawkes, Jacquetta. The Atlas of Early Man. Concurrent Develop-
  ments across the Ancient World 35000 BC-AD 500. London:
  Macmillan, 1976. Rev. by R. C. Whitehouse, Antiquity, 51
  (Jl 1977):169.

Hay, Douglas, Peter Linebaugh, and E. P. Thompson, ed. Albion's
  Fatal Tree: Crime and Society in Eighteenth Century England.
  London: Allen Lane, 1975. Rev. by J. Styles, HJ, 20(No. 4,
  1977):977-81.

Hay, Richard L. Geology of the Olduvai Gorge: A Study of Sedi-
  mentation in a Semiarid Basin. Berkeley: U California Press,
  1976. Rev. by W. W. Bishop, Antiquity, 51(Nov 1977):246-7.

Hayami, Yijiro. A Century of Agricultural Growth in Japan: Its
  Relevance to Asian Development. Minneapolis: U MINN Press,
  1975. Rev. by J. R. Gehrman, AgH, 51(Apr 1977):473-5.

Hayden, Dolores. Seven American Utopias: The Architecture of
  Communitarian Socialism, 1790-1975. Cambridge: MIT Press,
  1976. Rev. by H. R. Grant, AHR, 82(Oct 1977):1086-7; D. J.
  Coolidge, NEQ, 50(Sep 1977):533-5; A. D. Roberts, UHQ, 45
  (Win 1977):100-1.

Hayes, Robert A., ed. see Keith, Henry H., ed.

Hayne, David M., and Andre Vachon, eds. Dictionary of Canadian
  Biography. Volume II: 1701-1740. Toronto: U Tor Press,
  1974. Rev. by G. T. Stewart, WMQ, 34(Jan 1977):138-40.

Haynes, Robert V. The Natchez District and the American Revolution.
Jackson: U Press Miss., 1976. Rev. by J. L. Wright, Jr.,
AHR, 82(Feb 1977):174; A. H. DeRosier, Jr., AlaR, 30(Jan
1977):71-2; G. C. Din, JMiH, 39(Feb 1977):90-1; J. B.
Starr, JSH, 43(Feb 1977):112-4.

_____. A Night of Violence: The Houston Riot of 1917. Baton
Rouge: LSU Press, 1976. Rev. by R. A. Calvert, A&W, 19
(Sum 1977):185-6; W. H. Leckie, Historian, 39(May 1977):
582; C. H. Martin, JNH, 62(Jan 1977):109-10; J. P. Maddex,
Jr., JSH, 43(Aug 1977):474-5.

Hayter, William. Spooner: A Biography. n.l.: W. H. Allan,
n.d. Rev. by M. Latey, HTo, 27(Je 1977):408-9.

Hazan, Baruch A. Soviet Propaganda: A Case Study of the Middle
East Conflict. New Brunswick, N.J.: Transaction Books,
1976. Rev. by A. Z. Rubinstein, CurH, 72(Jan 1977):28; G.
Ginsburgs, CurH, 73(Oct 1977):128.

Hazard, Harry W., ed. see Setton, Kenneth M., ed.

Headlee, Thomas J., Jr., ed. Journal of the Senate of Virginia,
November Session, 1796. Journal of the Senate of Virginia,
Session of 1797/98. Richmond: Virginia State Library, 1976.
Rev. by W. K. Winfree, VMHB, 85(Jl 1977):374.

Headley, Owen. Queen Charlotte. Levittown, N.Y.: Transatlantic
Arts, 1976. Rev. by E. A. Reitan, AHR, 82(Feb 1977):99.

Healy, Ann Erickson. The Russian Autocracy in Crisis, 1905-1907.
Hamden, Conn.: Archon, 1976. Rev. by E. Edelman, AHR,
82(Feb 1977):152-3.

Healy, David. Gunboat Diplomacy in the Wilson Era: The U. S.
Navy in Haiti, 1915-1916. Madison: U Wis Press, 1976.
Rev. by L. D. Langley, AGR, 81(Dec 1976):1266-67; E.
Rosenberg, HAHR, 57(Feb 1977):134-5; R. E. Bunselmeyer,
PNQ, 68(Oct 1977):195-6; K. J. Grieb, TAm, 33(Apr 1977):
695-6.

Healy, George W. A Lifetime on Deadline: Self Portrait of a
Southern Journalist. Gretna: Pelican Publishing Company,
1976. Rev. by F. E. Hebert, LaH, 18(Sum 1977):378-81.

Heard, Kenneth A. General Elections in South Africa 1943-1970.
New York: Ox U Press, 1974. Rev. by O. Geyser, AfAf,
76(Jan 1977):122.

Hearn, Charles R. The American Dream in the Great Depression.
Westport, Conn.: Greenwood, 1977. Rev. by J. Braeman,
AS, 18(Fall 1977):109.

Hearsey, John E. Voltaire. New York: Harper & Row, 1976.
Rev. by P. F. Riley, Historian, 39(May 1977):552-3.

Heath, Jim F. Decade of Disillusionment: The Kennedy-Johnson
Years. Bloomington: Indiana U Press, 1975. Rev. by F.
R. Peterson, PNQ, 68(Jan 1977):42.

Heaton, E. W. Solomon's New Men. New York: Pica Press,
1974. Rev. by D. Pardee, JNES, 36(Jl 1977):218-9.

Hebert, Rev. Donald J. A Guide to Church Records in Louisiana:
1720-1975. Eunice, La.: n. p., 1975. Rev. by C. R.
Maduell, Jr., LaH, 18(Win 1977):119-20.

Heck, Frank H. Proud Kentuckian: John C. Breckinridge, 1821-
1875. Lexington: U Press Kentucky, 1976. Rev. by W. C.
Davis, WVH, 38(Jl 1977):326-7.

Heick, Welf H., ed. History and Myth: Arthur Lower and the
Making of Canadian Nationalism. Vancouver: U Brit Columbia Press, 1975. Rev. by L. S. Fallis, AHR, 82(Feb 1977):
218-9.

Heilman, Samuel. Synagogue Life. Chicago: U Chi Press, n. d.
Rev. by D. Singer, Comm, 63(Je 1977):92-4.

Heim, Ralph D., ed. see Bream, Howard N., ed.

Hein, Norvin. The Miracle Plays of Mathura. New Haven: Yale
U Press, 1972. Rev. by B. L. Smith, JAS, 36(Aug 1977):
780-1.

Heinze, R. W. The Proclamations of the Tudor Kings. New York:
Cam U Press, 1976. Rev. by S. E. Lehmberg, AHR, 82(Je
1977):629-31; D. M. Loades, HJ, 20(No. 4, 1977):1013-4; A.
Rosen, HT, 10(May 1977):489-90.

Heizer, Robert F., ed. A Collection of Ethnographical Articles on
the California Indians. Ramona, Calif.: Bellena Press, 1976.
Rev. by R. N. Ellis, NMHR, 52(Oct 1977):337-43.

_____, ed. The Costanoan Indians. Cupertino, Calif.: Califor-
nia History Center, De Anza College, 1974. Rev. by R. N.
Ellis, NMHR, 52(Oct 1977):337-43.

_____. The Indians of California: A Critical Bibliography.
Bloomington: Ind U Press, 1976. Rev. by R. N. Ellis,
NMHR, 52(Oct 1977):337-43.

_____, ed. Narrative of the Adventures and Sufferings of John
R. Jewitt While Held as a Captive of the Nootka Indians of
Vancouver Island, 1803-1805. Ramona: Ballena Press, 1975.
Rev. by J. H. Nottage, JOW, 16(Jan 1977):86.

_____, Karen M. Nissen, and Edward D. Castillo. California
Indian History, a Classified and Annotated Guide Source Materials. Ramona, Calif.: Ballena Press, 1975. Rev. in InHi,
10(Sum 1977):47-8; R. N. Ellis, NMHR, 52(Oct 1977):337-43.

Heller, Celia S. On the Edge of Destruction: Jews of Poland Between the Two World Wars. New York: Col U Press, 1977.
Rev. by A. Z. Rubinstein, CurH, 73(Nov 1977):175.

Hellmann, Donald C., ed. China & Japan: A New Balance of
Power. Lexington, Mass.: Lexington Books, 1976. Rev.
by H. Sato, JAS, 37(Nov 1977):90-2.

Helmreich, William B. Wake Up, Wake Up, to Do the Work of
Creator. n.l.: Harper & Row, n.d. Rev. by J. H. Lehmann, Comm, 64(Aug 1977):72-4.

Helms, Mary W. Middle America. A Culture History of Heartland and Frontiers. Englewood Cliffs: Prentice-Hall, 1975.
Rev. by A. Littlefield, TAm, 33(Jan 1977):545-6.

Hemery, Daniel. Révolutionnaires vietnamiens et pouvoir colonial
en Indochine: Communistes, Trotskystes, Nationalistes à
Saigon de 1932 à 1937. Paris: Francois Maspero, 1975.
Rev. by M. Osborne, JAS, 36(Feb 1977):382-3.

Hemphill, W. Edwin, ed. see Calhoun, John C.

Henderson, Dan Fenno. Village "Contracts" in Tokugawa Japan:
Fifty Specimens with English Translations and Comments.
Seattle: U Wash Press, 1975. Rev. by W. B. Hauser, JAS,
36(Feb 1977):356-7.

Henderson, H. James. Party Politics in the Continental Congress.
New York: McGraw-Hill, 1974. Rev. by C. Bonwick, JAmS,
11(Dec 1977):404-5.

Henderson, W. O. The Life of Friedrich Engels. London: Frank
Cass, 1976. Rev. by A. W. Coats, BH, 19(Jan 1977):96-8.

_____. The Rise of German Industrial Power, 1834-1914.
Berkeley: U Cal Press, 1976. Rev. by R. Cameron, AHR,
82(Feb 1977):124-5; E. Schremmer, BH, 19(Jl 1977):219-20;
L. D. Schwarz, History, 62(Feb 1977):158.

Hendricks, J. Edwin, ed. see Fries, Adelaide, ed.

Henri, Florette. Black Migration: Movement North, 1900-1920.
Garden City, N.Y.: Anchor Press/Doubleday, 1976. Rev.
by D. V. Taylor, MinnH, 45(Sum 1977):252-3.

Henson, Margaret Swett. Samuel May Williams: Early Texas
Entrepreneur. College Station: Texas A&M U Press, 1976.
Rev. by M. Darst, ETHJ, 15(Spr 1977):47-8.

Hentschel, Volker. Die Deutschen Freihändler und der volkswirt-
    schaftliche Kongress, 1858 bis 1885. Stuttgart: Ernst Klett
    Verlag, 1975. Rev. by W. O. Shanahan, AHR, 82(Oct 1977):
    997-8.

Herbert, Eugina W. see Lopez, Claude-Anne

Herity, Michael and George Eogan. Ireland in Prehistory. London:
    Routledge and Kegan Paul, 1977. Rev. by S. Piggott, Anti-
    quity, 51(Nov 1977):255-6.

Herman, A. L. An Introduction to Indian Thought. Englewood
    Cliffs, N. J.: Prentice-Hall, 1976. Rev. by J. B. Long,
    JAS, 36(Aug 1977):777-9.

Hermann, A. H. A History of the Czechs. Totowa, N. J.: Row-
    man and Littlefield, 1976. Rev. by S. B. Kimball, AHR, 82
    (Apr 1977):395-6.

Hermann, Georgina see Mallowan, Max

Hero, Alfred O., Jr., ed. see Fox, Annette Baker, ed.

Hersh, Jacques see Brun, Ellen

Hershkowitz, Leo. Tweed's New York: Another Look. Garden
    City, N.Y.: Anchor Press/Doubleday, 1977. Rev. by J.
    Muskrat, AHR, 82(Oct 1977):1085; S. Weaver, Comm, 63
    (Mar 1977):83-6; J. F. Richardson, CWH, 23(Je 1977):185-7.

Herwig, Holger H. Politics of Frustration: The United States in
    German Naval Planning, 1889-1941. Boston: Little, Brown,
    1976. Rev. by K. W. Bird, AHR, 82(Oct 1977):1005.

Herzog, Chaim. The War of Atonement, October, 1973. Boston:
    Little, Brown, 1975. Rev. by A. Z. Rubinstein, CurH, 72
    (Apr 1977):177.

Herzog, James H. Closing the Open Door: American-Japanese
    Diplomatic Negotiations, 1936-1941. Annapolis: Naval Insti-
    tute Press, 1973. Rev. by I. H. Anderson, PHR, 46(Feb
    1977):146-7.

Hessen, Robert. Steel Titan: The Life of Charles M. Schwab.
    New York: Ox U Press, 1975. Rev. by R. D. Simon, PH,
    45(Oct 1977):371-2.

Hewes, James E., Jr. From Roots to McNamara: Army Organi-
    zation and Administration, 1900-1963. Washington, D. C.:
    U.S. Army Center for Military History, 1975. Rev. by D. C.
    James, AHR, 82(Oct 1977):1092.

Hewitt, John. Out of My Time: Poems 1967-74. Belfast: Blackstaff
    Press, 1974. Rev. by E. Grennan, E-I, 12(Sum 1977):143-51.

_____. Time Enough: Poems New and Revised. Belfast: Blackstaff Press, 1976. Rev. by E. Grennan, E-I, 12(Sum 1977):143-51.

Heyck, Thomas William. The Dimensions of British Radicalism: The Case of Ireland, 1874-95. Urbana: U Illinois, 1974. Rev. by M. R. Temmel, AHR, 82(Oct 1977):970; G. Boyce, CHR, 58(Mar 1977):97-9.

Heymann, C. David. Ezra Pound, the Last Rower: A Political Profile. London: Faber and Faber, 1976. Rev. by D. Monk, JAmS, 11(Apr 1977):154-5.

Hibben, Frank C. Kiva Art of the Anasazi at Pottery Mound. Las Vegas: KC Publications, 1975. Rev. by M. H. Hall, ETHJ, 15(Spr 1977):46-7.

Hibbert, Christopher. The Rise and Fall of the House of Medici. London: Allen Lane, 1974. Rev. by P. McNair, History, 62 (Feb 1977):108.

Hickerson, H. Thomas, et al. Spindex II at Cornell University and a Review of Archival Automation in the United States. Ithaca, N.Y.: Cor U Lib, 1976. Rev. by R. H. Lytle, AmArc, 40 (Apr 1977):244-5.

Hiernaux, Jean. The People of Africa. London: Weidenfeld and Nicolson, 1974. Rev. by G. A. Harrison, Africa, 47(No. 1, 1977):111-12.

Hietala, Marjatta. Der Neue Nationalismus: In der Publizistik Ernst Jüngers und des Kreises um ihn, 1920-1933. Helsinki: Suomalainen Tiedeakatemia, 1975. Rev. by A. Dorpalen, AHR, 82(Je 1977):668-9.

Higginbotham, Don, ed. see Iredell, James

Higgins, Hugh. Vietnam. London: Heinemann, 1975. Rev. by P. J. Honey, History, 62(Je 1977):300-1.

Higgs, E. S., ed. Palaeoeconomy. New York and London: Cam U Press, 1975. Rev. by D. D. Simons, AgH, 51(Jan 1977): 281-3; J. M. Renfrew, Antiquity, 51(Mar 1977):82.

Higgs, Robert. Competition and Coercion: Blacks in the American Economy. New York: Cam U Press, 1977. Rev. by L. O. Christensen, History, 6(Oct 1977):6.

Higham, John. Send These to Me: Jews and Other Immigrants in Urban America. New York: Atheneum, 1975. Rev. by R. J. Vecoli, AHR, 82(Je 1977):755-6; W. Toll, PNQ, 58(Jan 1977): 41.

Higham, Robin. A Guide to the Sources of United States Military
    History. Hamden, Conn.: Shoestring Press, 1975. Rev. by
    D. E. Floyd, AmArc, 39(Jl 1976):362.

_____, ed. Intervention or Abstention: The Dilemma of Amer-
    ican Foreign Policy. Lexington: U Press Ky, 1975. Rev.
    by J. D. Doenecke, AHR, 81(Dec 1976):1265.

Highwater, Jamake. Fodor's Indian America. New York: David
    McKay, 1975. Rev. by D. M. Hufhines, JOW, 16(Jan 1977):
    84.

Higman, B. W. Slave Population and Economy in Jamaica, 1807-
    1834. New York: Cambridge U Press, 1976. Rev. by W.
    A. Green, AHR, 82(Oct 1977):1104-5; D. B. Gaspar, JEH,
    37(Sep 1977):813-5.

Hill, B. W. The Growth of Parliamentary Parties, 1689-1742.
    Hamden, Conn.: Archon Books, 1976. Rev. by H. Horowitz,
    AHR, 82(Oct 1977):962-3; S. R. Smith, 10(Aug 1977):637-8;
    H. T. Dickinson, History, 62(Je 1977):324-5.

Hill, Beth and Ray Hill. Indian Petroglyphs of the Pacific North-
    west. Seattle: U Washington Press, 1974. Rev. by A. E.
    Hippler, AIQ, 3(Aut 1977):257-9.

Hill, Francis. Victorian Lincoln. New York: Cambridge U Press,
    1975. Rev. by L. G. Bailey, AHR, 82(Je 1977):639-40.

Hill, Marvin S. see Oaks, Dallin H.

Hill, Patricia Kneas. The Oglethorpe Ladies and the Jacobite Con-
    spiracies. Atlanta: Cherokee Pub. Co., 1977. Rev. by C.
    Crowe, GHQ, 51(Sum 1977):196-7.

Hill, Ralph Nading. Lake Champlain: Key to Liberty. Taftsville,
    Vt.: Countryman Press, 1977. Rev. by J. H. G. Pell, VH,
    45(Sum 1977):178-9.

Hill, Ray see Hill, Beth

Hill, Robert T. Father of Texas Geology: Robert T. Hill. Dallas,
    SMU Press, 1976. Rev. by A. P. McDonald, ETHJ, 15(No.
    1, 1977):60-1.

Hiller, Hilde. Ionische Grabreliefs Der Ersten Hälfte Des 5. Jah-
    rhunderts v. Chr. Tubingen: Verlag Ernst Wasmuth, 1975.
    Rev. by B. S. Ridgway, AJA, 81(Win 1977):117-8.

Hillgarth, J. N. The Spanish Kingdoms, 1250-1516. Vol. 1: 1250-
    1410: Precarious Balance. New York: Ox U Press, 1976.
    Rev. by R. I. Burns, AHR, 82(Apr 1977):344; J. F. Powers,
    HAHR, 57(May 1977):323-4.

Hilton, Rodney H., ed. Peasants, Knights and Heretics: Studies in Medieval Social History. New York and London: Cam U Press, 1976. Rev. by S. Epstein, JEH, 37(Sep 1977):815-6.

Hilton, Stanley E. Brazil and the Great Powers, 1930-1939: The Politics of Trade Rivalry. Austin: U Tex Press, 1975. Rev. by D. M. Pletcher, AHR, 82(Feb 1977):39-59; J. D. Wirth, PHR, 46(Feb 1977):143-4.

Himmelberg, Robert F. The Origins of the National Recovery Administration: Business, Government, and the Trade Association Issue, 1921-1933. New York: Fordham U Press, 1976. Rev. by R. D. Cuff, AHR, 82(Feb 1977):208; W. Graebner, JEH, 37(Je 1977):523-4.

Himmelfarb, Gertrude. On Liberty and Liberalism: The Case of John Stuart Mill. London: Secker and Warburg, 1975. Rev. by K. Fielden, History, 62(Feb 1977): 142-3; S. Collini, HJ, 20(No. 1, 1977):237-54.

Hindley, Geoffrey. Saladin. New York: Barnes and Noble, 1976. Rev. by R. S. Humphreys, AHR, 82(Je 1977):706.

Hines, Thomas S. Burnham of Chicago: Architect and Planner. New York: Ox U Press, 1974. Rev. by J. D. Haeger, PH, 45(Jan 1977):93-5; D. Gebhard, PHR, 46(Aug 1977):518-9.

Hinton, Harold C. The Sino-Soviet Confrontation: Implications for the Future. New York: Crane, Russak, 1977. Rev. by O. E. S., CurH, 72(Sep 1977):85.

_____. Three and a Half Powers: The New Balance in Asia. Bloomington: Ind U Press, 1975. Rev. by C. Lee, JAS, 36 (May 1977):535-7.

Hinton, James and Richard Hyman. Trade Unions and Revolution: The Early Industrial Politics of the Communist Party. London: Pluto Press, 1975. Rev. by A. Reid & S. Tolliday, HJ, 20(No. 4, 1977):1001-12.

Hipkiss, Robert A. Jack Kerouac, Prophet of the New Romanticism. Kansas: Regents Press of Kansas, 1976. Rev. by J. M. Bailey, JAmS, 11(Dec 1977):413-14.

Hirschman, Charles. Ethnic and Social Stratification in Peninsular Malaysia. Washington: American Sociological Association, 1975. Rev. by J. C. Spores, JAS, 36(May 1977):593-4.

Hirschmeier, Johannes and Tsunehiko Yui. The Development of Japanese Business, 1600-1973. Cambridge: Har U Press, 1975. Rev. by W. B. Hauser, JAS, 36(Aug 1977):748-50.

Hirst, Derek. The Representative of the People? Voters and

Voting in England under the Early Stuarts. New York: Cam
U Press, 1975. Rev. by K. L. Sprunger, Historian, 39(May
1977):540-1; C. C. Ward, JMH, 49(Mar 1977):128-30.

Hisamatsu, Sen'ichi. Biographical Dictionary of Japanese Literature.
Tokyo: Kodansha International, 1976. Rev. by Yoshio Iwamoto,
JAS, 36(Aug 1977):760-1.

Hiskett, Mervyn. A History of Hausa Islamic Verse. London:
School of Oriental and African Studies, 1975. Rev. by P. M.
Ryan, Africa, 47(No. 3, 1977):322-3.

Hitching, Francis. Earth Magic. London: Cassell, 1976. Rev.
by R. J. C. Atkinson, Antiquity, 51(Jl 1977):156.

Hitchins, Keith. Orthodoxy and Nationality: Andreiu Saguna and
the Rumanians of Transylvania, 1846-1873. Cambridge, Mass.:
Har U Press, 1977. Rev. by S. A. Zenkovsky, History, 6
(Oct 1977):18.

Ho, Ping-ti. The Cradle of the East: An Inquiry Into the Indigenous Origins of Techniques and Ideas of Neolithic and Early
Historic China, 5000-1000 B.C. Chicago: U Chicago Press,
1976. Rev. by L. J. Bilsky, AHR, 82(Je 1977):716; D.
Dohrenwend, Archaeology, 30(Sep 1977):354; W. Gungwu, CQ,
71(Sep 1977):628-30.

Hoak, D. E. The King's Council in the Reign of Edward VI. New
York: Cam U Press, 1976. Rev. by M. Levine, AHR, 82
(Apr 1977):352.

Hoar, Joy S. New England's Lost Civil War Veterans. Arlington,
Texas: Seacliffe Press, 1976. Rev. by R. D. Hoffsommer,
CWTI, 16(Aug 1977):49.

Hobbs, Thomas Hubbard. The Journals of Thomas Hubbard Hobbs:
A Contemporary Record of an Aristocrat from Athens, Alabama. Written Between 1840, When the Diarist was Fourteen Years Old, and 1862, When He Died Serving the Confederate States of America. Ed. by Faye Acton Axford.
University, Alabama: U Alabama Press, 1976. Rev. by J.
H. Boore, VMHB, 85(Jan 1977):119-20.

Hobsbawm, E. J. The Age of Capital, 1848-1875. New York:
Charles Scribner's Sons, 1975. Rev. by R. Cameron, His-
torian, 39(Feb 1977):331-2; J. A. S. Grenville, History, 62
(Feb 1977):157-8; M. E. Fletcher, JEH, 37(Je 1977):524-6;
E. Shorter, JIH, 8(Sum 1977):155-7; W. R. Allen, Mankind,
5(No. 11, 1977):58.

Hockin, Thomas A. Government in Canada. New York: Norton,
1975. Rev. by O. E. S., CurH, 72(Apr 1977):176.

Hodas, Daniel. The Business Career of Moses Taylor: Merchant, Finance Capitalist, and Industrialist. New York: N Y U Press, 1976. Rev. by G. Browne, AHR, 82(Oct 1977):1073.

Hodge, William. A Bibliography of Contemporary North American Indians. New York: Interland Publishing, 1976. Rev. by R. N. Ellis, PHR, 46(Feb 1977):127-8.

Hodges, Donald C. Argentina, 1943-1976: The National Revolution and Resistance. Albuquerque: U NMex Press, 1976. Rev. by P. B. Goodwin, Jr., AHR, 82(Oct 1977):1111-12; C. E. Solberg, HT, 10(Aug 1977):635-6; CurH, 72(Feb 1977):80.

Hodgett, Gerald A. J. Tudor Lincolnshire. Lincoln: History of Lincolnshire Committee, 1975. Rev. by D. M. Palliser, History, 62(Feb 1977):112.

Hodgson, Godfrey. America in Our Time. Garden City, N.Y.: Doubleday, 1976. Rev. by A. L. Hamby, AHR, 82(Je 1977): 774-5; E. Abrams, Comm, 63(Feb 1977):72-4; M. Dunne, JAmS, 11(Dec 1977):383-4.

Hodgson, Marshall, G. S. The Venture of Islam. London: U Chi Press, 1974. Rev. by M. E. Yapp, History, 62(Je 1977): 279-80.

Hodson, F. R. see Doran, J. E.

Hoehling, A. A. Thunder at Hampton Roads. Englewood Cliffs, N.J.: Prentice-Hall, 1976. Rev. by M. B. Lucas, CWH, 23(Je 1977):181-2; E. M. Thomas, JSH, 43(Aug 1977):462.

Hoffecker, Carol E. Delaware: A Bicentennial History. New York: Norton, 1977. Rev. by G. S. Rowe, History, 6(Oct 1977):12-3.

Hoffman, Michael J. Gertrude Stein. London: George Prior Publishers, 1976. Rev. by A. T. K. Crozier, JAmS, 11(Dec 1977):400-1.

Hofmeister, Burkhard. Bundesrepublik Deutschland und Berlin. Vol. 1, Berlin: Eine geographische Strukturanalyse der zwölf westlichen Bezirke. Darmstadt: Wissenschaftliche Buchgesellschaft, 1975. Rev. by R. Wiedenhoeft, AHR, 82(Je 1977): 671-2.

Hofsommer, Donovan. Katy Northwest: The Story of the Branch Line Railroad. Boulder, Colorado: Pruett, 1976. Rev. by L. L. Graves, A&W, 19(Spr 1977):89-90; H. R. Grant, ChOk, 55(Spr 1977):109-10.

Hogrefe, Pearl. Tudor Women: Commoners and Queens. Ames: Iowa St U Press, 1975. Rev. by M. Levine, Historian, 39 (Feb 1977):327.

143 HOGREFE

_____. Women of Action in Tudor England: Nine Biographical Sketches. Ames: Io St U Press, 1977. Rev. by P. Lee, History, 6(Oct 1977):18-9.

Hoig, Stan. The Battle of the Washita: The Sheridan-Custer Indian Campaign of 1867-69. Garden City, N.Y.: Doubleday, 1976. Rev. by R. M. Utley, AHI, 11(Jan 1977):50; E. J. Danziger, Jr., CWH, 23(Mar 1977):90-3.

Hokkanen, Kari. Krieg und Frieden in der politischen Tagesliteratur Deutschlands zwischen Baseler und Lunéviller Frieden (1795-1801). Jyväskylä: Jyväskylän Yliopisto, 1975. Rev. by O. Connelly and P. Becker, AHR, 82(Oct 1977):996-7.

Holden, Jonathan. The Mark To Turn: A Reading of William Stafford's Poetry. Lawrence: U Press of Kansas, 1976. Rev. by L. Andrews, JAmS, 11(Dec 1977):414-15.

Holden, William Curry. A Ranching Saga: The Lives of William Electious Halsell and Ewing Halsell. San Antonio: Trinity U Press, 1976. Rev. by R. L. Davis, NMHR, 52(Oct 1977): 346-7.

Holderness, B. A. Pre-Industrial England: Economy and Society from 1500-1750. London: J. M. Dent, 1976. Rev. by R. M. Berger, JEH, 37(Sep 1977):785-6.

Holl, Brigitte. Hofkammerpräsident Gundaker Thomas Graf Starhemberg und die österreichische Finanzpolitik der Barockzeit (1703-1715). Vienna: Verlag der Östereichischen Akademie der Wissenschaften, 1976. Rev. by H. P. Liebel, JEH, 37 (Sep 1977):816-7.

Hollander, John. Reflections on Espionage. New York: Atheneum, 1976. Rev. by A. Corn, GR, 31(Sum 1977):533-41.

Hollenberg, Günter. Englisches Interesse am Kaiserreich. Die Attraktivität Preussen-Deutschlands für Konservative und Liberale Kreise in Gross-Brittanien 1860-1914. Wiesbaden: Franz Steiner Verlag, 1974. Rev. by V. R. Berghahn, JMH, 49(Sep 1977):502-4.

Holley, Donald. Uncle Sam's Farmers: The New Deal Communities in the Lower Mississippi Valley. Urbana: U Ill Press, 1975. Rev. by O. W. Miller, AgH, 51(Jl 1977):629-30; T. Badger, JAmS, 11(Apr 1977):152-3; H. C. Dethloff, LaH, 18(Sum 1977): 361-2; G. C. Fite, MinnH, 45(Win 1977):158-9.

Holloway, R. Ross. Influences and Styles in the Late Archaic and Early Classical Greek Sculpture of Sicily and Magna Graecia. Louvain: Institut Supérieur d'Archéologie et d'Histoire de l'Art, 1975. Rev. by B. S. Ridgway, AJA, 81(Win 1977): 123-4.

Holloway, Thomas H. The Brazilian Coffee Valorization of 1906: Regional Politics and Economic Dependence. Madison: Wisconsin History Foundation, 1976. Rev. by T. C. Wright, AgH, 51(Jl 1977):608.

Holm, Bill and Bill Reid. Indian Art of the Northwest Coast: A Dialogue on Craftsmanship and Aesthetics. Seattle: U Washington Press, 1975. Rev. by M. Cohodas, AIQ, 3(Sum 1977): 162-4.

Holman, C. Hugh see Rubin, Louis D. , Jr.

Holmes, George. The Good Parliament. New York: Ox U Press, 1975. Rev. by T. Callahan, Jr., AHR, 82(Feb 1977):77-8; A. L. Brown, History, 62(Feb 1977):106.

Holmes, Graeme M. Britain and America: A Comparative Economic History, 1850-1939. Newton Abbot: David & Charles, 1976. Rev. by B. W. E. Alford, JAmS, 11(Dec 1977):406-7; R. B. Du Boff, JEH, 37(Sep 1977):817-8.

Holmes, James. "Dr. Bullie's" Notes. Ed. by Delma E. Presley. Atlanta: Cherokee Pub. Co., 1976. Rev. by J. Whitehead, GHQ, 51(Spr 1977):88-9.

Holzman, Robert S. Adapt or Perish: The Life of General Roger A. Pryor, C. S. A. Hamden, Conn.: Archon, 1976. Rev. by L. J. Graybar, AHR, 82(Feb 1977):184-5; J. A. Carpenter, JSH, 43(May 1977):301-2; J. H. Bailey, VMHB, 85(Apr 1977): 210-11.

Homberger, Eric. The Art of the Real. London: Everyman's University Library, 1977. Rev. by C. E. Nicholson, JAmS, 11(Dec 1977):380-2.

Hong, Wontack, and Anne O. Krueger, eds. Trade and Development in Korea. New York and London: Col U Press for the National Bureau of Economic Research, 1975. Rev. by K. M. Langley, JEH, 37(Je 1977):482-5.

Hood, Miriam. Gunboat Diplomacy, 1895-1905: Great Power Pressure in Venezuela. London: George Allen & Unwin, 1975. Rev. by J. A. Rayfield, HAHR, 57(Feb 1977):136-7.

Hoogenboom, Ari and Olive Hoogenboom. A History of the ICC: From Panacea to Palliative. New York: Norton, 1976. Rev. by G. D. Nash, AHR, 81(Dec 1976):1271-72; W. O. Wagnon, JEH, 37(Je 1977):527.

Hoogenboom, Olive see Hoogenboom, Ari

Hook, Andrew. Scotland and America: A Study of Cultural Relations, 1750-1835. Glasgow: Blackie, 1975. Rev. by D. Sloan, WMQ, 34(Jan 1977):142-3.

Hook, Judith. The Baroque Age in England. Levittown, N.Y.:
  Transatlantic Arts, 1976. Rev. by H. J. Jensen, AHR, 82
  (Apr 1977):355-6.

Hoole, Addie S. see Taylor, Thomas Jones

Hoole, W. Stanley, ed. Confederate Foreign Agent: The European
  Diary of Major Edward C. Anderson. Baton Rouge: LSU
  Press, 1976. Rev. by L. Gara, CWH, 23(Je 1977):174-5;
  T. F. Armstrong, JSH, 43(Aug 1977):460-1.

_____, ed. see also Taylor, Thomas Jones

Hoopes, Alban W. The Road to the Little Big Horn--And Beyond.
  New York: Vantage, 1975. Rev. by H. T. Hoover, AIQ, 3
  (Sum 1977):152-3; J. W. Bailey, WHQ, 8(Jan 1977):77-8.

Hoover, Dwight W. The Red and the Black. Chicago: Rand
  McNally, 1976. Rev. by T. F. Gossett, AHR, 82(Je 1977):
  726; W. B. Weare, JSH, 43(Aug 1977):484-5.

Hoover, John P. Sucre, soldado y revolucionario. Cumana: Editorial de la Universidad de Oriente, 1975. Rev. by T.
  Blossom, AHR, 82(Apr 1977):480-1.

Hopkins, Joseph G. E., ed. Concise Dictionary of American Biography. New York: Charles Scribner's Sons, 1977. Rev. by
  S. W. Higginbotham, JSH, 43(Aug 1977):478-9.

Hopper, R. J. The Early Greeks. New York: Barnes and Noble,
  1977. Rev. by C. G. Thomas, AHR, 82(Oct 1977):926.

Horan, James D. The Authentic Wild West: The Gunfighters. New
  York: Crown Publishers, 1976. Rev. by L. J. White, JOW,
  16(Jan 1977):88.

Horecky, Paul L. and David E. Kraus, eds. East Central and Southeast Europe: A Handbook of Library and Archival Resources
  in North America. Santa Barbara, California: CLIO Press,
  1976. Rev. by O. V. Johnson, AHR, 82(Oct 1977):1013.

Horgan, Paul. Lamy of Sante Fe: His Life and Times. New York:
  Farrar, Straus and Giroux, 1975. Rev. by E. B. Adams,
  WHQ, 8(Jan 1977):59.

Horn, Pamela. The Rise and Fall of the Victorian Servant. Dublin:
  Gill and MacMillan; New York: St. Martin's Press, 1975.
  Rev. by N. A. Ferguson, Historian, 39(May 1977):541-3.

Horne, John C. Van, ed. The Correspondence of William Nelson
  as Acting Governor of Virginia, 1770-1771. Charlottesville,
  U Press Va, published for the Virginia Historical Society,
  1975. Rev. by M. L. Nicholls, WMQ, 34(Jan 1977):174-5.

Hornsby, Alton, Jr. The Black Almanac, from Involuntary Servitude (1619-1860) to the Age of Disillusionment (1964-1973). New York: Barron's Educational Series, 1975. Rev. by P. E. Murray, JNH, 62(Jl 1977):306-7.

Horowitz, Helen Lefkowitz. Culture and the City: Cultural Philanthropy in Chicago from the 1880s to 1917. Lexington: U Kentucky Press, 1976. Rev. by L. B. Miller, AHR, 82(Oct 1977):1088-9.

Horton, Loren N., ed. The Character of the Country: The Iowa Diary of James L. Broderick. Iowa City: Iowa State Historical Department, 1976. Rev. by J. K. Cowger, JISHS, 70 (Nov 1977):336.

Horton, Louise. Samuel Bell Maxey: A Biography. Austin: U Tx Press, 1974. Rev. by A. Barr, AHR, 81(Dec 1976):1253-54.

Horwitz, Henry. Parliament, Policy and Politics in the Reign of William III. Newark: U Del Press, 1976. Rev. by S. R. Smith, HT, 10(Aug 1977):637-8.

Horwitz, James. They Went Thataway. New York: E. P. Dutton and Company/Thomas Congdon, 1976. Rev. by J. C. Porter, WHQ, 8(Oct 1977):476-7.

Horwitz, Morton J. The Transformation of American Law, 1780-1860. Cambridge: Har U Press, 1977. Rev. by K. Newmyer, AHR, 82(Oct 1977):1067-8; R. H. Pear, JAmS, 11(Dec 1977):385-6; J. H. Kettner, JIH, 8(Aug 1977):390-2; D. F. Henderson, JSH, 43(Aug 1977):442-4.

Hosford, David H. Nottingham, Nobles, and the North: Aspects of the Revolution of 1688. Hamden, Conn.: Archon Books, 1976. Rev. by G. M. Straka, AHR, 82(Oct 1977):960-1; J. P. Kenyon, History, 62(Feb 1977):124; J. S. Morrill, HJ, 20(No. 4, 1977):961-70.

Hostetler, John A. Hutterite Society. Baltimore: Johns Hopkins U Press, 1974. Rev. by J. H. Smylie, AHR, 82(Je 1977): 778.

Hotmann, Francois. Francogallia. Latin text by Ralph Giesey, tr. by J. H. M. Salmon. London: Cambridge U Press, 1972. Rev. by H. M. Höpfl, ESR, 7(Apr 1977):233-9.

Houghton, Samuel G. A Trace of Desert Waters: The Great Basin Story. Glendale, Calif.: Arthur H. Clark, 1976. Rev. by D. J. Pisani, PNQ, 68(Oct 1977):194; R. H. Jackson, UHQ, 45(Win 1977):93-4; W. D. Rowley, WHQ, 8(Jl 1977):354-5.

Houtart, Francois. Religion and Ideology in Sri Lanka. Bangalore: Theological Publications, 1974. Rev. by M. S. Robinson, JAS, 36(May 1977):583-4.

Hovi, Kalervo. Cordon sanitaire or Barrière de l'Est? The Emergence of the New French Eastern European Alliance Policy,
1917-1919. Turku, Finland: Turun Yliopisto, 1975. Rev. by
W. A. McDougall, JMH, 49(Mar 1977):122-5.

Howard, Deborah. Jacopo Sansovino: Architecture and Patronage in
Renaissance Venice. London: Yale U Press, 1975. Rev. by
B. Pullan, History, 62(Feb 1977):109-10.

Howard, Elizabeth S. The Vagabond Dreamer. Huntsville, Alabama:
Strode Publishers, 1976. Rev. by P. Morgan, AlaR, 30(Oct
1977):317.

Howard, Michael. War in European History. Oxford: Ox U Press,
1976. Rev. by N. J. Padgett, Historian, 39(May 1977):539-40;
D. S. Birn, JIH, 8(Sum 1977):151-2.

Howard, Perry H., ed. see Carleton, Mark T., ed.

Howarth, Thomas. Charles Rennie Mackintosh and the Modern
Movement. n.l.: Routledge & Kegan Paul, n.d. Rev. by J.
Richardson, HTo, 27(Oct 1977):682-3.

Howe, Daniel Walker, ed. Victorian America. Philadelphia: U
Pa Press, 1976. Rev. by T. Bender, AHR, 82(Je 1977):
748-9; C. Bush, JAmS, 11(Dec 1977):412-3.

Howe, Irving. The Immigrant Jews of New York: 1881 to the Present. London: Routledge & Kegan Paul, 1976. Rev. by E.
Homberger, JAmS, 11(Aug 1977):281-2.

_____. World of Our Fathers. New York: Harcourt Brace
Jovanovich, 1976. Rev. by E. Alexander, AHR, 82(Feb 1977):
189-90.

Howe, K. R. The Loyalty Islands: A History of Culture Contacts
1840-1900. Honolulu: U Press Hawaii, 1977. Rev. by P.
J. Coleman, History, 6(Nov/Dec 1977):39.

Howell, David. British Social Democracy: A Study in Development
and Decay. New York: St. Martin's Press, 1976. Rev. by
C. A. Cline, AHR, 82(Oct 1977):974.

Howson, Colin, ed. Method and Appraisal in the Physical Sciences:
The Critical Background to Modern Science, 1800-1905. New
York: Cambridge U Press, 1976. Rev. by A. Thackray, JIH,
8(Aut 1977):352-4.

Hoyt, William Graves. Lowell and Mars. Tucson: U Ariz Press,
1976. Rev. by G. E. Webb, A&W, 19(Spr 1977):96-97; O. R.
Norton, JAriH, 18(Spr 1977):108-11.

Hözle, Erwin. Die Selbstentmachtung Europas: Das Experiment

des Friedens vor und im Ersten Weltkrieg. Göttingen: Mus-
terschmidt, 1975. Rev. by S. Wank, AHR, 82(Je 1977):626-7.

Hsu, Kai-yu. The Chinese Literary Scene: A Writer's Visit to the
People's Republic. New York: Vintage Books, 1975. Rev. by
P. Link, CQ, No. 69(Mar 1977):181-4; D. W. Fokkema, JAS,
36(May 1977):550-1.

Hsuan-Chih, Tai. Hung-ch'iang-hui (1916-1949) (The Red Spears
1916-1949). Taipei: Shih-huo ch'u-pan she, 1973. Rev. by
D. D. Buck, JAS, 36(Aug 1977):729-31.

Hsüeh-wen, Wang. Legalism and Anti-Confucianism in Maoist Politics. Taipei: Institute of International Relations, 1975. Rev.
by H. Rosemont, Jr., CQ, No. 70(Je 1977):425-8.

Hubatsch, Walther. Frederick the Great of Prussia: Absolutism
and Administration. Levittown, N.Y.: Transatlantic Arts,
1975. Rev. by H. G. Koenigsberger, AHR, 82(Oct 1977):
946-8.

Hubbell, John T., ed. Battles Lost and Won: Essays from "Civil
War History". Westport, Conn.: Greenwood, 1976. Rev.
by D. Kealey, JAmS, 11(Dec 1977):398-400.

Huch, Ronald K. The Radical Lord Radnor: The Public Life of
Viscount Folkstone, Third Earl of Radnor (1779-1869). Minneapolis: U Minn Press, 1977. Rev. by S. Manft, History,
6(Oct 1977):19.

Huddlestun, J. R. and Charles O. Walker. From Heretics to Heroes: A Study of Religious Groups in Georgia with Primary
Emphasis on the Baptists. Jasper, Ga.: Pickens Tech Press,
1976. Rev. by B. Davis, GHQ, 51(Sum 1977):203-4.

Hudgins, Carolyn S., ed. see Akioka, Lorena M., ed.

Hudson, Charles. The Southeastern Indians. Knoxville: U Tenn
Press, 1976. Rev. by F. Jennings, AHR, 82(Oct 1977):
1057-8; M. Z. Searcy, AlaR, 30(Jl 1977):235-6; H. T. Hoover,
GHQ, 51(Sum 1977):185-7; N. S. Furman, JSH, 43(Nov 1977):
639-40.

Hudson, Charles M. Four Centuries of Southern Indians. Athens:
U Ga Press, 1975. Rev. by L. DeVorsey, Jr., WMQ, 34(Oct
1977):685-7.

Hudson, Kenneth. The Archaeology of Industry. New York: Charles
Scribner's Sons, 1976. Rev. by E. S. Rutsch, Archaeology,
30(Sep 1977):356-7; P. Riden, Antiquity, 51(Jl 1977):159-60.

Huemer, Peter. Sektionschef Robert Hecht und die Zerstörung der
Demokratie in Österreich: Ein historischpolitische Studie.

Munich: R. Oldenbourg Verlag, 1975. Rev. by R. J. Rath, AHR, 82(Je 1977):676.

Huetz de Lemps, Christian. Géographie du commerce de Bordeaux à la fin du règne de Louis XIV. Paris: Mouton, 1975. Rev. by R. W. Unger, AHR, 82(Apr 1977):365-6.

Huff, Archie Vernon, Jr. Langdon Cheves of South Carolina. Columbia: U SC Press, 1977. Rev. by R. A. Brown, History, 6(Nov/Dec 1977):31.

Huger, Mary Esther. The Recollection of a Happy Childhood. Ed. by Mary Stevenson. Pendleton, S. C.: Foundation for Historic Restoration in Pendleton Area, 1976. Rev. by M. Watson, SCHM, 78(Apr 1977):150.

Hugg, Lawrence, ed. see Ernst, Robert T. , ed.

Huggett, Frank E. The Land Question and European Society. New York: Neale Watson Academic Publications, 1975. Rev. by A. Plakans, AHR, 82(Feb 1977):81-3; B. A. Holderness, History, 62(Feb 1977):80.

Huggins, Nathan I. , ed. Voices from the Harlem Renaissance. New York: Ox U Press, 1976. Rev. by C. F. Cooney, AHI, 11(Jan 1977):49-50.

Hughes, J. Donald. Ecology in Ancient Civilizations. Albuquerque: U NMex Press, 1975. Rev. by R. A. Padgug, AHR, 81(Dec 1976):1078-9.

Hughes, J. R. T. Social Control in the Colonial Economy. Charlottesville: U Press Virginia, 1976. Rev. by C. Brooks, EHR, 92(Oct 1977):910-11; A. Tully, JEH, 37(Je 1977):528; A. H. Jones, JIH, 8(Sum 1977):170-1; A. C. Land, JSH, 43 (Feb 1977):105-6; D. H. Flaherty, WMQ, 34(Apr 1977):338-9.

Hughes, Michael. The small towns of Hampshire: the archaeological and historical implications of development. Southampton: Hampshire Archaeological Committee, 1976. Rev. by P. V. Addyman, Antiquity, 51(Jl 1977):165.

Hughson, Lois. Thresholds of Reality: George Santayana and Modernist Poetics. New York: Kennikat Press, 1977. Rev. by I. F. A. Bell, JAmS, 11(Dec 1977):428-30.

Hui-Min, Lo see Morrison, G. E.

Huitron, Jacinto. Origenes e historia del movimiento obrero en México. México: Editores Mexicanos Unidos, 1974. Rev. by J. Womack, Jr. , HAHR, 57(Aug 1977):539-40.

Hull, Roger H. The Irish Triangle: Conflict in Northern Ireland.

Princeton: Princeton U Press, 1976. Rev. by D. W. Miller,
AHR, 82(Je 1977):646-7.

Humble, Richard. Marco Polo. New York: G. P. Putnam's Sons,
1975. Rev. by M. Rossabi, JAS, 36(May 1977):557.

Humphrey, David C. From King's College to Columbia, 1746-1800.
New York: Columbia U Press, 1976. Rev. by F. Rudolph,
AHR, 82(Feb 1977):172-3; D. W. Robson, WMQ, 34(Jan 1977):
143-5.

Humphrey, Hubert H. The Education of a Public Man: My Life
and Politics. Ed. by Norman Sherman. Garden City, N.Y.:
Doubleday, 1976. Rev. by S. Sayles, AI, 44(Fall 1977):
152-4; H. Berman, MinnH, 45(Win 1977):158.

Hundley, Norris, Jr., ed. The Chicano. Santa Barbara: Clio
Books, 1975. Rev. by G. I. Seligmann, Jr., AHR, 81(Dec
1976):1269.

_____. Water and the West: The Colorado River Compact and
the Politics of Water in the American West. Berkeley: U
Cal Press, 1975. Rev. by E. Pomeroy, PNQ, 68(Apr 1977):
98-9.

Hunt, E. H. Regional Wage Variations in Britain, 1850-1914. New
York: Ox U Press, 1973. Rev. by T. Mallier, JEH, 37(Je
1977):529.

Hunt, John Dixon. The Figure in the Landscape: Poetry, Painting,
and Gardening During the Eighteenth Century. Baltimore: JHU,
Press, 1977. Rev. by J. V. Mirallo, GR, 31(Fall 1977):
703-8.

Hunt, Michael H. Frontier Defense and the Open Door: Manchuria
in Chinese-American Relations, 1895-1911. New Haven: Yale
U Press, 1973. Rev. by J. H. Boyle, JAAS, 12(Jan/Oct 1977):
309-12.

Hunt, William R. Alaska: A Bicentennial History. New York:
Norton, 1976. Rev. by R. A. Burchell, JAmS, 11(Dec 1977):
411-12; T. C. Hinckley, WHQ, 8(Oct 1977):462-3.

_____. Arctic Passage: The Turbulent History of the Land and
People of the Bearing Sea, 1697-1975. New York: Charles
Scribner's Sons, 1975. Rev. by B. D. Lain, WHQ, 8(Jan
1977):63.

_____. North of 53°: The Wild Days of the Alaska-Yukon
Mining Frontier, 1870-1914. New York: Macmillan, 1974.
Rev. by S. Haycox, AHR, 81(Dec 1976):1249-50.

Hunter, J. Paul. Occasional Form: Henry Fielding and the Chains of Circumstance. Baltimore: JHU Press, 1976. Rev. by E. L. Steeves, GR, 31(Fall 1977):759-62.

Huppert, George. Les Bourgeois Gentilshommes: An Essay on the Definition of Elites in Renaissance France. Chicago: U Chi Press, 1977. Rev. by D. J. Wilcox, History, 6(Nov/Dec 1977):45.

Huq, Muhammad Shamsul. Education, Manpower, and Development. New York: Praeger, 1975. Rev. by P. Hackett, JAS, 36 (May 1977):538-9.

Hurst, G. Cameron, III. Insei: Abdicated Sovereigns in the Politics of Late Heian Japan, 1086-1185. New York: Columbia U Press, 1976. Rev. by T. H. Mesner, AHR, 82(Je 1977):720.

Hus, Alain. Les siècles d'or de l'histoire étrusque (675-475 avant J.-C.). Brussels: Latomus, 1976. Rev. by J. J. Reich, AHR, 82(Feb 1977):68-9.

Huskinson, Janet. Roman Sculpture from Cyrenaica Imperii Romani, Vol. II, Fascicule I. London: British Museum Publications, Ltd., 1975. Rev. by M. Vickers, Antiquity, 51(Mar 1977): 69-70.

Hutchinson, Alan. China's African Revolution. Boulder, Colorado: Westview Press, 1976. Rev. by R. F. Grow, JAS, 37(Nov 1977):130-1.

Hutchison, William R. The Modernist Impulse in American Protestantism. Cambridge: Harvard U Press, 1976. Rev. by D. W. Howe, AHR, 82(Feb 1977):199; C. A. Holbrook, NEQ, 50 (Sep 1977):544-6.

Huttenback, Robert A. Racism and Empire--White Settlers and Colored Immigrants in the British Self-Governing Colonies, 1830-1910. Ithaca: Cornell U Press, 1976. Rev. by C. Newbury, EHR, 92(Oct 1977):918-19; B. Porter, History, 62 (Je 1977):338.

Hyam, Ronald. Britain's Imperial Century, 1815-1914: A Study of Empire and Expansion. New York: Barnes and Noble, 1976. Rev. by H. R. Winkler, AHR, 82(Apr 1977):361-2; R. F. Holland, EHR, 92(Oct 1977):915-6; P. M. Kennedy, HJ, 20(No. 3, 1977):761-9.

_____, and Ged Martin. Reappraisals in British Imperial History. London: Macmillan, 1975. Rev. by D. K. Fieldhouse, History, 62(Feb 1977):89-91.

Hyde, George E. see Will, George F.

Hyman, Harold M. Union and Confidence: The 1860s. New York:

Crowell, 1976. Rev. by F. L. Klement, AHR, 82(Oct 1977): 1076.

Hyman, Richard see Hinton, James

Hynding, Alan A. California Historymakers. Dubuque, Iowa: Kendal/Hunt, 1976. Rev. by E. Staniford, CHQ, 56(Spr 1977): 83-4.

Hynes, Samuel. The Auden Generation: Literature and Politics in the 1930's. n.l.: Viking, n.d. Rev. by R. Berman, Comm, 64(Sep 1977):78-82.

Ichiko, Chūzō see Kamachi, Noriko

Idema, W. L. Chinese Vernacular Fiction: The Formative Period. Leiden: E. J. Brill, 1974. Rev. by W. L. Y. Yang, JAS, 36(Aug 1977):735-6.

Iggers, Georg G. New Directions in European Historiography. Middletown, Conn.: Wes U Press, 1975. Rev. by P. H. Reill, HT, 10(Feb 1977):340-1.

Ikime, Obaro, ed. Leadership in 19th Century Africa: Essays from Tarikh. London: Longman, 1974. Rev. by A. H. M. Kirk-Greene, Africa, 47(No. 2, 1977):226.

Illick, Joseph E. Colonial Pennsylvania: A History. New York: Charles Scribner's Sons, 1976. Rev. by F. S. Klein, AHI, 12(Je 1977):50; A. Tully, AHR, 82(Apr 1977):430; E. B. Bronner, Historian, 39(May 1977):570-1; J. E. Selby, VMHB, 85(Jan 1977):100-1; N. B. Wainwright, WHQ, 8(Apr 1977): 208-9; O. S. Ireland, WMQ, 34(Apr 1977):334-6.

Imhof, Arthur Erwin. Aspekte der Bevölkerungsentwicklung in den nordischen Ländern, 1720-1750. 2 vols. Bern: Franke Verlag, 1976. Rev. by H. Moller, AHR, 82(Oct 1977):992; M. W. Flinn, EHR, 92(Oct 1977):907.

The Impact of the American Revolution Abroad: Papers Presented at the Fourth Symposium, May 8 and 9, 1975. Library of Congress Symposia on the American Revolution. Washington, D.C.: Library of Congress, 1976. Rev. by H. M. Ward, JSH, 43(May 1977):283-4; A. Henderson, NEQ, 50(Je 1977): 366-8.

Ingle, Harold N. Nesselrode and the Russian Rapprochement with Britain, 1836-1844. Berkeley: U Cal Press, 1976. Rev. by J. C. Zacek, AHR, 82(Feb 1977):149-50.

Inglis, Brian. The Opium War. London: Hodder and Stoughton, 1976. Rev. by I. Nish, History, 62(Je 1977):291-2.

153   INGLIS

_____. Roger Casement. New York: Harcourt Brace Jovano-
vich, 1973. Rev. by N. Jenckes, E-I, 12(Spr 1977):141-3.

Ingram, K. E. Manuscripts Relating to Commonwealth Caribbean
Countries in United States and Canadian Repositories. New
York: Bowker, 1975. Rev. by A. Caiger, AHR, 82(Apr
1977):478-9; R. M. L. Bowe, AmArc, 40(Jan 1977):87-8.

Ingram, O. Kelly, ed. Methodism Alive in North Carolina: A
Volume Commemorating the Bicentennial of the Carolina Cir-
cuit. Durham, N.C.: Divinity School of Duke U, 1976.
Rev. by H. Y. Warnock, JSH, 43(May 1977):333-4.

International Commission of Jurists. Racial Discrimination and
Repression in Southern Rhodesia. Catholic Institute for International Relations, 1976. Rev. by E. Windrich, AfAf, 76(Jan
1977):119-22.

_____. The Trial of Beyers Naudé: Christian Witness and the
Rule of Law. London: Search Press, 1975. Rev. by H. B.
Hansen, AfAf, 76(Jan 1977):123-4.

Iredell, James. The Papers of James Iredell. Ed. by Don Higginbotham. Raleigh, N.C.: Division of Archives and History,
1976. Rev. by P. D. Chase, AHR, 82(Oct 1977):1061-2; C.
H. Bowman, Jr., GHQ, 51(Fall 1977):286-7.

Ireland, Robert M. Little Kingdoms: The Counties of Kentucky,
1850-1891. Lexington: U Press Ken, 1977. Rev. by H.
Sitkoff, History, 6(Nov/Dec 1977):30.

Iriye, Akira, ed. Mutual Images: Essays in American-Japanese
Relations. Cambridge, Mass.: Har U Press, 1975. Rev.
by R. Dingman, PHR, 46(Feb 1977):144-6.

Irving, David. Hitler's War. n.l.: Viking, n.d. Rev. by L.
Bushkoff, Comm, 64(Sep 1977):76-8.

Irving, R. E. M. The First Indo-China War: French and American
Policy 1945-1954. London: Croom Helm, 1975. Rev. by A.
Short, CQ, No. 71(Sep 1977):619-20; M. Caldwell, History, 62
(Je 1977):299-300.

Irwin, John T. Doubling and Incest, Repetition and Revenge: A
Speculative Reading of Faulkner. Baltimore: Johns Hopkins
U Press, 1975. Rev. by D. Tallack, JAmS, 11(Dec 1977):
408-9.

Isaac, Rael Jean. Isreal Divided: Ideological Politics in the Jewish
State. Baltimore: JHU Press, 1976. Rev. by A. Z. Rubinstein, CurH, 72(Jan 1977):28.

Isaacman, Allen F. The Tradition of Resistance in Mozambique:

The Zambesi Valley, 1850-1921. Berkeley: U Cal Press, 1977. Rev. by D. Chanaiwa, AHR, 82(Je 1977):713-14.

Isherwood, Robert M. Music in the Service of the King: France in the Seventeenth Century. Ithaca: Cornell U Press, 1973. Rev. by D. Koenigsberger, ESR, 7(Oct 1977):454-6.

Ishida, Eiichiro. Japanese Culture: A Study of Origins and Characteristics. Honolulu: U Press Hawaii, 1974. Rev. by R. K. Beardsley, JAS,` 36(May 1977):561-4.

Isichei, Elizabeth. A History of the Igbo People. London: Macmillan, 1975. Rev. by A. J. H. Latham, History, 62(Je 1977):269-70.

Israel, J. I. Race, Class, and Politics in Colonial Mexico: 1610-1670. Oxford: Ox U Press, 1975. Rev. by F. Morales, TAm, 33(Jan 1977):552-4.

Israel, John and Donald W. Klein. Rebels and Bureaucrats: China's December 9ers. Berkeley: U Cal Press, 1976. Rev. by R. B. Jeans, JAS, 37(Nov 1977):125-6.

Ivry, Alfred L. Al-Kindi's Metaphysics: A Translation of Ya qub ibn Ishaq al-Kindi's Treatis "On First Philosophy" (fi al-Falsafah al-Ula). Albany: SUNY, 1974. Rev. by W. Madelung, JNES, 36(Oct 1977):322-4.

Izenberg, Gerald N. The Existentialist Critique of Freud: The Crisis of Autonomy. Princeton: Prin U Press, 1976. Rev. by M. Poster, AHR, 82(Je 1977):625-6.

Jackson, Andrew. The Papers of Andrew Johnson, Volume 4, 1860-1861. Ed. by Leroy P. Graf, Ralph W. Haskins, and Patricia P. Clark. Knoxville: U Tenn Press, 1976. Rev. by R. N. Current, FHQ, 55(Jan 1977):384-5.

Jackson, Anthony. A Place Called Home: A History of Low-Cost Housing in Manhattan. Cambridge: MIT Press, 1976. Rev. by R. Lubove, AHR, 82(Oct 1977):1085-6.

Jackson, Blyden. The Waiting Years: Essays on American Negro Literature. Baton Rouge: LSU Press, 1976. Rev. by D. Dance, JNH, 62(Apr 1977):189-91.

Jackson, D. see Epstein, T. S.

Jackson, Donald, ed. see Washington, George

Jackson, Richard L. The Black Image in Latin American Literature. Albuquerque: U NM Press, 1976. Rev. by G. Cardoso, TAm, 34(Oct 1977):297-9.

Jackson, W. H. with Ethel Dassow. Handloggers. Anchorage: Alaska Northwest Publishing Company, 1974. Rev. by T. B. Colbert, JOW, 16(Jl 1977):98.

Jacob, Margaret C. The Newtonians and the English Revolution, 1689-1720. Ithaca: Cor U Press, 1976. Rev. by R. S. Westfall, AHR, 82(Apr 1977):353-5.

Jacobs, Donald M., ed. Antebellum Black Newspapers. Westport, Conn.: Greenwood Press, 1976. Rev. by H. Altschull, AHR, 82(Oct 1977):1068-9.

Jacobs, Louis. Theology in the Responsa. n.l.: Routledge and Kegan Paul, n.d. Rev. by D. Singer, Comm, 64(Dec 1977): 90-3.

Jacobsen, Phebe R. see Stiverson, Gregory A.

Jaenen, Cornelius J. Friend and Foe: Aspects of French-Amerindian Cultural Contact in the Sixteenth and Seventeenth Centuries. New York: Columbia U Press, 1976. Rev. by E. P. Patterson, AHR, 82(Apr 1977):474-5; D. Cole, Historian, 39(May 1977):591-2.

_____. The Role of the Church in New France. Toronto: McGraw-Hill Ryerson, 1976. Rev. by J. S. Moir, WMQ, 34 (Apr 1977):341-2.

Jaffe, Philip J. The Rise and Fall of American Communism. New York: Horizon Press, 1975. Rev. by D. A. Shannon, AHR, 82(Feb 1977):213-14.

Jager, Nita, ed. Charles Abrams: Papers and Files. A Guide to the Microfilm Publication. Ithaca, N.Y.: Cor U Libraries, 1975. Rev. by E. McKay, AmArc, 40(Jl 1977):354-5.

Jahoda, Gloria. Florida: A Bicentennial History. New York: Norton, 1976. Rev. by L. Collins, FHQ, 55(Jan 1977):364-6.

_____. The Trail of Tears. New York: Holt, Rinehart, and Winston, 1975. Rev. by M. R. Blaine, AIQ, 3(Spr 1977): 61-2; A. H. DeRosier, Jr., FHQ, 55(Jan 1977):378-80; R. Halliburton, JSH, 43(Feb 1977):123-4.

Jahrbuch fur Wirtschaftsgeschichte, 1975. East Berlin: Akademie Verlag, 1975. Rev. by L. Schofer, JEH, 37(Je 1977):529-31.

Jakes, John. The Titans. New York: Pyramid Publications, 1976. Rev. by R. Ashley, CWTI, 16(Apr 1977):47-8.

James, Coy Hilton. Silas Deane: Patriot or Traitor. East Lansing: Michigan St U Press, 1975. Rev. by E. E. Berger, Historian, 39(Feb 1977):367-8.

James, D. Clayton. The Years of MacArthur, Volume II: 1941-1945. Boston: Houghton Mifflin, 1975. Rev. by L. S. Wittner, PHR, 46(Feb 1977):147-8.

James, Don. Butte's Memory Book. Caldwell, Idaho: Caxton, 1975. Rev. by S. R. Davison, JOW, 16(Jan 1977):77-8.

James, Hunter. The Quiet People of the Land: A Story of the North Carolina Moravians in Revolutionary Times. Chapel Hill: Published for Old Salem, Inc. by the UNC Press, 1976. Rev. by R. S. Klein, JSH, 43(Nov 1977):645-7.

James, Sydney V. Colonial Rhode Island: A History. New York: Charles Scribner's Sons, 1975. Rev. by B. C. Daniels, NEQ, 50(Je 1977):364-5; J. P. Greene, JIH, 8(Aut 1977):385-7.

Jansen, Marius B. Japan and China: From War to Peace, 1894-1972. Chicago: Rand McNally, 1975. Rev. by A. Feurwerker, CQ, No. 69(Mar 1977):176-7.

Janson, Lone E. The Copper Spike. Anchorage: Alaska Northwest Publishing, 1975. Rev. by R. A. Stearns, 68(Apr 1977): 102.

Jao, Y. C. Banking and Currency in Hong Kong. London: Macmillan, 1974. Rev. by J. Cohen, JAS, 36(May 1977):559-60.

Jaramillo, Cleofas M. et al. The New Mexican Hispano. New York: Arno Press, 1974. Rev. by D. J. Weber, HAHR, 57 (May 1977):371-2.

Jaynes, Gregory. Sketches from a Dirt Road. Garden City, N.Y.: Doubleday, 1977. Rev. by B. Abney, GHQ, 51(Fall 1977): 284-6.

Jean, S. Les jachères en Afrique tropicale: interprétation technique et foncière. Paris: Institut d'Ethnologie, 1975. Rev. by R. Fardon, Africa, 47(No. 1, 1977):121-2.

Jeanneney, Jean-Noël. François de Wendel en Republique: L'argent et le pouvoir, 1914-1940. Paris: Editions du Seuil, 1976. Rev. by G. Silvestri, AHR, 82(Je 1977):655; M. J. Rust, JEH, 37(Je 1977):531-3.

Jeffery, L. H. Archaic Greece. The City-States c. 700-500 BC. London: Ernest Benn, 1976. Rev. by A. Andrewes, Antiquity, 51(Nov 1977):249-51.

Jeier, Thomas. Die Letzten Soehne Manitours: Das Schicksal der Indianer Nordamerikas. Dusseldorf-Vienna: Econ Verlag, 1976. Rev. by A. L. Makuck, A&W, 19(Spr 1977):93-94.

Jelliff, Theodore B. see Tweton, D. Jerome

Jellison, Richard M., ed. Society, Freedom, and Conscience: The American Revolution in Virginia, Massachusetts and New York. New York: Norton, 1976. Rev. by L. R. Gerlach, AHR, 82 (Apr 1977):433.

Jenkins, John H. Audobon and Other Capers, Confessions of a Texas Bookmaker. Austin: Pemberton Press, 1976. Rev. by M. A. Stevens, ETHJ, 15(Spr 1977):63-4.

Jennings, Francis. The Invasion of America: Indians, Colonialism, and the Cant of Conquest. Chapel Hill: U North Carolina Press, 1975. Rev. by J. P. Ronda, AHR, 82(Feb 1977): 168-9; L. E. Pennington, Historian, 39(May 1977):567-8; G. H. Phillips, PHR, 46(Aug 1977):489-91; W. C. Sturtevant, WMQ, 34(Apr 1977):312-4.

Jennings, Lawrence C. France and Europe in 1848: A Study in French Foreign Affairs in Time of Crisis. Oxford: Clarendon Press, 1973. Rev. by R. Magraw, ESR, 7(Jan 1977):113-14.

Jensen, Dean. The Biggest, the Smallest, the Longest, the Shortest: A Chronicle of the American Circus from Its Heartland. Madison: Wisconsin House, 1975. Rev. by P. Bouissac, WMH, 60(Sum 1977):348-9.

Jensen, Merrill, ed. The Documentary History of the Ratification of the Constitution. Madison: State Historical Society of Wisconsin, 1976. Rev. by D. F. Hawke, AmArc, 40(Jan 1977):78-9; W. U. Solberg, JSH, 43(Aug 1977):441-2; R. F. Cambell, NEQ, 50(Mar 1977):181-4; D. Gordon, VMHB, 85 (Apr 1977):203-5; R. K. Newmyer, WVH, 38(Jan 1977):173-5; R. A. Rutland, WMQ, 34(Jl 1977):479-81.

_____, and Robert A. Becker, ed. The Documentary History of the First Federal Elections, 1788-1790. Vol. I. Madison: U Wisconsin Press, 1976. Rev. by K. Coleman, GHQ, 51(Spr 1977):100; J. S. Pancake, JSH, 43(May 1977):288-90; N. E. Cunningham, Jr., WMQ, 36(Jl 1977):481-2.

Jensen, Ronald J. The Alaska Purchase and Russian-American Relations. Seattle: U Wash Press, 1975. Rev. by R. P. Browder, AHR, 81(Dec 1976):1249; T. C. Hinckley, PHR, 46 (May 1977):299-300.

Jenswold, John R. see Carter, Hilda R.

Jequier, Marie-Claude, ed. see Biaudet, Jean-Charles, ed.

Jessup, Ronald. Man of Many Talents: An Informal Biography of James Douglas 1753-1819. London: Phillimore, 1975. Rev. by G. Holleyman, Antiquity, 51(Jl 1977):158.

Jewell, Carey C. Harvest of Death. Hicksville, New York: Expo-

sition Press, 1976. Rev. by C. F. C., CWTI, 16(Oct 1977):
49.

Jewsbury, George F. The Russian Annexation of Bessarabia, 1774-
1828. New York: Columbia U Press, 1976. Rev. by B.
Jelavich, AHR, 82(Apr 1977):393-4.

Jick, Leon A. The Americanization of the Synagogue, 1820-1870.
Hanover, N.H.: Brandeis U Press, 1976. Rev. by L. Din-
nerstein, AHR, 82(Feb 1977):189.

Jin-Bee, Ooi. Peninsular Malaysia. London: Longman, 1976. Rev.
by J. A. Hafner, JAS, 36(Aug 1977):794.

Jiryis, Sabri. The Arabs in Israel. London: Monthly Review
Press, 1976. Rev. by P. J. Baram, AHR, 82(Je 1977):708-9.

Jocano, F. Landa. Slum as a Way of Life: A Study of Coping
Behavior in Urban Environment. Quezon City: U Philippines
Press, 1975. Rev. by J. J. Green, JAS, 36(Feb 1977):388-
90.

Johannes Schwalm Historical Association. Johannes Schwalm the
Hessian. Millville, Pa.: Precision Printers, 1976. Rev.
by K. J. R. Arndt, CHIQ, 50(Sum 1977):91-3.

Johansons, Andrejs. History of the Culture of Latvia, 1710-1800.
Stockholm: Daugava, 1975. Rev. by E. Anderson, AHR, 82
(Oct 1977):1023.

John, Elizabeth A. H. Storms Brewed in Other Men's Worlds: The
Confrontation of Indians, Spanish, and French in the Southwest,
1540-1795. College Station: Texas A & M U Press, 1975.
Rev. by D. E. Worcester, AIQ, 3(Spr 1977):53-4; H. C.
Porter, JAmS, 11(Dec 1977):391; C. L. Kenner, ChOk, 55
(Spr 1977):115-6; T. D. Watson, LaH, 18(Sum 1977):355-8;
R. H. Vigil, TAm, 33(Apr 1977):680-2.

Johnson, Broderick H., ed. Navajo Stories of the Long Walk Period. Tsaile, Navajo Nation, Ariz.: Navajo Community
College Press, 1974. Rev. by V. E. Tiller, PHR, 46(Feb
1977):128-30.

_____, comp. see also Roessel, Ruth, comp.

Johnson, Edward C. Walker River Paiutes: A Tribal History. Salt
Lake City: U Utah Printing Service, 1975. Rev. by W. R.
Jacobs, AIQ, 3(Sum 1977):156-8.

Johnson, Gordon. Provincial Politics and Indian Nationalism. Cambridge: Cam U Press, 1973. Rev. by P. Kolenda, JAAS, 12
(Jan/Oct 1977):279-81.

Johnson, Hildegard Binder. Order upon the Land: The U. S. Rec-
tangular Land Survey and the Upper Mississippi Country. New
York: Ox U Press, 1976. Rev. by M. L. Olsen, AgH, 51
(Apr 1977):464-6; T. G. Manning, AHR, 82(Apr 1977):451.

Johnson, James Turner. Ideology, Reason, and the Limitation of
War: Religious and Secular Concepts, 1200-1740. Princeton:
Prin U Press, 1975. Rev. by P. Paret, AHR, 82(Feb 1977):
88-9; H. G. Koenigsberger, EHR, 92(Oct 1977):898-9.

Johnson, Jerah. Africa and the West. Hinsdale, Ill.: Dryden
Press, 1974. Rev. by S. E. Fridie, LaH, 18(Spr 1977):
248-9.

Johnson, John Janney. John Kobler's Dream: A History of the
Fredericksburg United Methodist Church, 1802-1975. Fredericksburg, Va.: Fredericksburg United Methodist Church,
1975. Rev. by J. D. Neville, VMHB, 85(Apr 1977):209-10.

Johnson, Leland R. The Falls City Engineers: A History of the
Louisville District Corps of Engineers United States Army.
Louisville: Louisville District, U.S. Army Corps of Engineers,
1975. Rev. by C. E. Kramer, FCHQ, 51(Oct 1977):366-8.

Johnson, Patricia Givins. William Preston and the Allegheny
Patriots. Pulaski, Va.: B. D. Smith & Bros., Printers,
1976. Rev. by D. S. Brown, VMHB, 85(Apr 1977):207-8.

Johnson, Paul. A History of Christianity. New York: Atheneum,
1976. Rev. by J. E. Groh, AHR, 82(Apr 1977):332-3.

Johnson, Paul S. The Economics of Invention and Innovation, with
a Case Study of the Development of the Hovercraft. London:
Martin Robertson, 1975. Rev. by P. Uselding, JEH, 37(Je
1977):533-4.

Johnson, Sherman E. From the St. Croix to the Potomac--Reflec-
tions of a Bureaucrat. Bozeman: Montana State U, 1974.
Rev. by R. C. Tetro, AgH, 51(Apr 1977):460-2.

Johnson, Stephen. The Roman Forts of the Saxon Shore. New
York: St. Martin's Press, 1976. Rev. by J. W. Eadie,
AHR, 82(Je 1977):613-14; London: Paul Elek, 1976. Rev.
by B. Cunliffe, Antiquity, 51(Mar 1977):72-3.

Johnson, Steven L. Guide to American Indian Documents in the
Congressional Serial Set: 1817-1899. New York: Clearwater
Publishing, 1977. Rev. by R. N. Ellis, NMHR, 52(Oct 1977):
337-43.

Johnson, Walter, ed. see Stevenson, Adlai

Johnston, Leah Carter. San Antonio, St. Anthony's Town. San

Antonio: Naylor, 1976. Rev. by A. E. Heslop, ETHJ, 15
(No. 2, 1977):63-4.

Johnston, William B. see Levitan, Sar A.

Johnstone, Frederick A. Class, Race and Gold: A Study of Class
Relations and Racial Discrimination in South Africa. London:
Routledge & Kegan Paul, 1976. Rev. by P. Richardson, AfAf,
76(Apr 1977):249-58.

Joines, Karen Randolph. Serpent Symbolism in the Old Testament.
Haddonfield, N.J.: Haddonfield House, 1974. Rev. by D.
Pardee, JNES, 36(Oct 1977):318.

Jonasson, Gustaf. Per Edvin Sköld, 1946-1951. Stockholm: Almquist and Wiksell International, 1976. Rev. by A. W. Anderson, AHR, 82(Apr 1977):378-9.

Jones, Allen H. Bronze Age Civilization: The Philistines and the
Danites. Washington: Public Affairs Press, 1975. Rev. by
G. K. Sams, AHR, 82(Feb 1977):67-8.

Jones, Arthur F. The Art of Paul Sawyier. Lexington: U Press
of Kentucky, 1976. Rev. by M. Hamel-Schwulst, FCHQ, 51
(Jl 1977):280-2.

Jones, Charles, ed. see Anderson, John M., ed.

Jones, Chris. Climbing in North America. Berkeley: U Cal
Press, 1976. Rev. by J. B. O'Brien, Jr., PHR, 46(Aug
1977):515-6.

Jones, Dave. The Western Horse: Advice and Training. Norman:
U Ok Press, 1974. Rev. by W. E. McFarland, ChOk, 54
(Win 1976-7):540.

Jones, David. Chartism and Chartists. New York: St. Martin's,
1975. Rev. by E. J. Evans, AHR, 82(Feb 1977):101.

Jones, Eldred D., ed. African Literature Today, No. 8, Drama
in Africa. Heinemann, 1976. Rev. by C. L. Innes, AfAf,
76(Jan 1977):125-7.

Jones, Eric L., ed. see Parker, William N., ed.

Jones, James Pickett. Yankee Blitzkrieg: Wilson's Raid Through
Alabama and Georgia. Athens: U Georgia Press, 1976. Rev.
by J. T. Hubbell, AHR, 82(Oct 1977):1074; H. E. Sterkx,
AlaR, 30(Jl 1977):237-8; R. M. McMurray, CWH, 23(Mar
1977):87-9; J. I. Robertson, Jr., GHQ, 51(Spr 1977):93-5;
J. T. Currie, JSH, 43(Aug 1977):463-4.

Jones, John Finbar and John Middlemist Herrick. Citizens in Ser-

vice: Volunteers in Social Welfare during the Depression,
1929-1941. East Lansing: Michigan State U Press, 1976.
Rev. by N. P. Weiss, AHR, 82(Apr 1977):464-5.

Jones, Kenneth W. Arya Dharm: Hindu Consciousness in Nineteenth-Century Punjab. Berkeley: U Cal Press, 1976. Rev.
by L. A. Gordon, AHR, 82(Apr 1977):421.

_____, ed. see also Gustafson, W. Eric, ed.

Jones, Oakah L., Jr., ed. The Spanish Border Lands: A First
Reader. Los Angeles: Lorrin L. Morrison, 1974. Rev. by
J. H. Thomas, ChOk, 55(Spr 1977):120-1.

Jones, Richard. L'ideologie de l'Action Catholique, 1917-1939.
Portland, Ore.: International Scholarly Book Services, 1974.
Rev. by J. Hellman, AHR, 82(Feb 1977):220.

Jones, Robert B. Tennessee at the Crossroads: The State Debt
Controversy, 1870-1883. Knoxville: U Tenn Press, 1977.
Rev. by J. V. Mering, History, 6(Nov/Dec 1977):30.

Jones, Stephen. Oklahoma Politics in State and Nation, Volume 1.
Enid, Ok.: Haymaker Press, 1974. Rev. by M. L. Cantrell,
ChOk, 55(Spr 1977):117.

Jordan, Donald A. The Northern Expedition: China's National Revolution of 1926-1928. Honolulu: U Press Hawaii, 1976. Rev.
by J. E. Sheridan, AHR, 82(Je 1977):719-20; D. S. Sutton,
JAS, 37(Nov 1977):121-3.

Josephson, Harold. James T. Shotwell and the Rise of International-
ism in America. Rutherford, N.J.: Fairleigh Dickinson U
Press, 1975. Rev. by B. W. Cook, AHR, 82(Feb 1977):210;
W. F. Kuehl, PHR, 46(May 1977):305-6;

Joshi, Nirmala. Foundations of Indo-Soviet Relations: A Study of
Non-Official Attitudes and Contacts 1917-1947. New Delhi:
Radiant Publishers, 1975. Rev. by B. N. Pandey, History,
62(Je 1977):289-90.

Jouanna, Arlette. L'ideé de race en France au XV lème siècle et
au début du XVIIeme siècle (1498-1614). Paris: Librarie
Honore Champion, 1976. Rev. by M. C. Horowitz, AHR, 82
(Je 1977):647-8.

Jowett, Garth. Film: The Democratic Art. Boston: Little, Brown,
1976. Rev. by T. Cripps, AHR, 82(Apr 1977):466.

Judd, Denis. Radical Joe: A Biography of Joseph Chamberlain.
n.l.: Hamish Hamilton, n.d. Rev. by J. Richardson, HTo,
27(Jl 1977):473-5.

Judt, Tony. Le reconstruction du Parti socialiste, 1921-1926. Paris:
     Presses de la fondation nationale des sciences politiques, 1976.
     Rev. by S. P. Kramer, AHR, 82(Apr 1977):373-4.

Juhnke, James C. A People of Two Kingdoms: The Political Accul-
     turation of the Kansas Mennonites. Newton, Kans.: Faith and
     Life Press, 1975. Rev. by P. K. Conkin, AHR, 81(Dec 1976):
     1282-83.

Jules-Verne, Jean. Jules Verne. n. l.: Macdonald & Jane's, n. d.
     Rev. by J. Richardson, HTo, 27(Jan 1977):56-7.

Julia, Dominique see Chartier, Roger

July, Robert W. Precolonial Africa: An Economic and Social His-
     tory. New York: Scribners, 1975. Rev. by S. Feierman,
     AHR, 82(Feb 1977):154-5; R. Floud, JIH, 7(Win 1977):553-5.

Junker, Detlef. Der unteilbare Weltmarkt: Das ökonomische Inter-
     esse in der Außenpolitik der USA, 1933-1941. Stuttgart:
     Ernst Klett Verlag, 1975. Rev. by K. Moss, PHR, 46(May
     1977):308-9.

Juzbasic, Dzevad. The Building of Railways in Bosnia and Herce-
     govina in Light of Austro-Hungarian Policy from the Occupation
     to the End of the Kállay Era. Sarajevo: Akademija Nauka i
     Umjetnosti Bosne i Hercegovine, 1974. Rev. by R. Donia,
     . AHR, 82(Oct 1977):1014-15.

Kagan, Richard L. Students and Society in Early Modern Spain.
     Baltimore: JHU Press, 1974. Rev. by M. D. Gordon, JMH,
     49(Je 1977):298-301.

Kaggia, Bildad. Roots of Freedom 1921-1963. The Autobiography
     of Bildad Kaggia. Nairobi: East African Publishing House,
     1975. Rev. by J. Murray, AfAf, 76(Jl 1977):412-13.

Kahl, Joseph A. Modernization, Exploration and Dependence in
     Latin America. New Brunswick, N. J.: Transaction Books,
     1976. Rev. by CurH, 72(Feb 1977):80.

Kahn, E. J., Jr. The China Hands: America's Foreign Service
     Officers and What Befell Them. New York: Viking Press,
     1975. Rev. by W. W. Tozer, PHR, 46(Aug 1977):529-31.

Kahn, Edgar Myron. Cable Car Days in San Francisco. Oakland:
     Friends of the San Francisco Public Library, 1976. Rev. by
     D. F. Myrick, CHQ, 56(Sum 1977):184-6.

Kale, Pramod. The Theatric Universe: A Study of the Natyasastra.
     Bombay: Popular Prakashan, 1974. Rev. by C. R. Jones,
     JAS, 36(May 1977):573-4.

163   KALICKI

Kalicki, J. H.   The Pattern of Sino-American Crises: Political-
Military Interactions in the 1950s.   London: Cambridge U
Press, 1975.   Rev. by J. H. Boyle, JAAS, 12(Jan/Oct 1977):
309-12.

Kalivoda, Robert.   Revolution und Ideologie: Der Hussitismus.
Cologne: Böhlau Verlag, 1976.   Rev. by J. Klassen, AHR,
82(Je 1977):623.

Kallner, Rudolf.   Herzl und Rathenau: Wege jüdischer Existenz an
der Wende des 20. Jahrhunderts.   Stuttgart: Ernst Klett Verlag, 1976.   Rev. by D. G. Sanford, AHR, 82(Oct 1977):1001.

Kamachi, Noriko, John K. Fairbank, and Chūzō Ichiko.   Japanese
Studies of Modern China Since 1953.   Rev. by R. H. Myers,
JAS, 36(Feb 1977):349.

Kamenka, Eugene, and R. S. Neale, eds.   Feudalism, Capitalism
and Beyond.   London: Edward Arnold, 1975.   Rev. by V. G.
Kiernan, History, 62(Feb 1977):78.

Kaminkow, Marion J., ed.   United States Local Histories in the
Library of Congress: A Bibliography.   Baltimore: Magna
Carta Book Company.   Rev. by J. Meehan, VMHB, 85(Apr
1977):216.

Kamínski, Franciszek.   Religione e chiesa in Polonia, 1945-1975:
Saggio storico-instituzionale.   Padua: CESEO, 1976.   Rev.
by R. Camp, AHR, 82(Je 1977):689-90.

Kammen, Michael.   Colonial New York.   New York: Charles
Scribner's Sons, 1975.   Rev. by A. Keller, AHI, 12(Jl 1977):
49.

_____.   see also   Greene, Jack P.

Kammler, Hans.   Die Feudalmonarchien: Politische und wirtschaft-
lichsoziale Faktoren ihrer Entwicklung und Funktionsweise.
Cologne: Böhlau Verlag, 1974.   Rev. by B. Lyon, AHR, 82
(Feb 1977):74-5.

Kann, Robert A.   Erzherzog Franz Ferdinand Studien.   Vienna:
Verlag für Geschichte und Politik, 1976.   Rev. by P. W.
Schroeder, AHR, 81(Feb 1977):136.

Kantner, John F. and Lee McCaffrey, eds.   Population and Development in Southeast Asia.   Lexington, Mass.:   Lexington Books,
1975.   Rev. by W. Flieger, JAS, 37(Nov 1977):174-6.

Kantowicz, Edward R.   Polish-American Politics in Chicago, 1888-
1940.   Chicago: U Chicago Press, 1975.   Rev. by H. S. Nelli,
AHR, 82(Feb 1977):195.

Kaplan, Joanna Overing. The Piaroa, a People of the Orinoco
    Basin: A Study in Kinship and Marriage. Oxford: Clarendon
    Press, 1975. Rev. by W. Shapiro, JLAS, 9(May 1977):179-81.

Kaplan, Lawrence. Politics and Religion during the English Revo-
    lution: The Scots and the Long Parliament, 1643-1645. New
    York: NYU Press, 1976. Rev. by P. Christianson, AHR, 82
    (Oct 1977):959.

Kaplan, S. Bread, politics, and political economy in the reign of
    Louis XV. The Hague: Nijhoff, 1976. Rev. by O. Hufton,
    HJ, 20(No. 4, 1977):971-6.

Kapur, Ashok. India's Nuclear Option: Atomic Diplomacy and
    Decision Making. New York: Praeger, 1976. Rev. by O.
    Marwah, JAS, 37(Nov 1977):167-8.

Karageorghis, Vassos. View from the Bronze Age: Mycenaean and
    Phoenician Discoveries at Kition. New York: Dutton, 1976.
    Rev. by M. M. Eisman, AHR, 82(Je 1977):611-12.

Karageorghis, Vassos and Des Gagniers, Jean. La Ceramique
    Chypriote De Style Figure, Age du Fer. Rome: Edizioni
    dell'Ateneo, 1974. Rev. by J. L. Benson, AJA, 81(Sum
    1977):394-6.

Karff, Samuel E., ed. Hebrew Union College--Jewish Institute of
    Religion at One Hundred Years. New York: Hebrew Union
    College Press, 1976. Rev. by S. C. Berrol, AHR, 82(Apr
    1977):463.

Karier, Clarence J., ed. Shaping the American Educational State:
    1900 to the Present. New York: Free Press, 1975. Rev.
    by V. W. Shapiro, HT, 10(May 1977):496-7.

Karkala, John A. and Leena Karkala. Bibliography of Indo-English
    Literature: A Checklist of Works by Indian Authors in English,
    1800-1966. Bombay: Nirmala Sadanand, 1974. Rev. by C.
    Coppola, 36(May 1977):576.

Karkala, Leena see Karkala, John A.

Karl, Barry D. Charles E. Merriam and the Study of Politics.
    Chicago: U Chi Press, 1974. Rev. by R. Lowitt, AHR, 82
    (Oct 1977):1096-7.

Karlin, Jules A. Joseph M. Dixon of Montana. Part 1: Senator
    and Bull Moose Manager, 1867-1917. Part 2: Governor
    Versus the Anaconda, 1917-1934. Missoula: U Mon, 1974.
    Rev. by R. T. Ruetten, PNQ, 68(Oct 1977):194-5.

Karnes, Thomas L. The Failure of Union: Central America, 1824-
    1975. Tempe: Arizona St U, 1976. Rev. in CurH, 72(Feb 1977):
    80.

165   KARNI

Karni, Michael G. , Matti E. Kaups, and Douglas J. Ollila, Jr. , eds.
The Finnish Experience in the Western Great Lakes Region:
New Perspectives. Turku, Finland, Institute for Migration,
and St. Paul, Immigration History Research Center, 1975.
Rev. by T. J. Sinks, MinnH, 45(Win 1977):162.

Karpat, Kemel H. , et al. Turkey's Foreign Policy in Transition,
1950-1974. Leiden: E. J. Brill, 1975. Rev. by J. C.
Campbell, AHR, 82(Feb 1977):154.

Karst, Kenneth L. and Keith S. Rosenn. Law and Development in
Latin America: A Case Book. Berkeley, Calif.: U Cal
Press, 1976. Rev. by K. J. Grieb, JEH, 37(Je 1977):534-5;
C. N. Ronning, HAHR, 57(Feb 1977):160-1; J. I. Dominguez,
TAm, 34(Jl 1977):137-9.

Kasson, John F. Civilizing the Machine: Technology and Republican
Values in America, 1776-1900. New York: Grossman, 1976.
Rev. by G. M. Ostrander, AHR, 82(Feb 1977):177.

Kater, Michael H. Studentenschaft und Rechtsradikalismus in Deutschland 1918-1933: eine sozialeschichtliche Studie zur Bildungskrise in der Weimarer Republik. Hamburg, 1975. Rev.
by G. J. Giles, HJ, 20(No. 2, 1977):519-21.

Kathona, Géza. Chapters from the History of the Hungarian Reformation during the Turkish Occupation. Budapest: Akadémiai
Kiadó, 1974. Rev. by J. Held, AHR, 82(Oct 1977):1019.

Katz, Michael B. The People of Hamilton, Canada West: Family
and Class in a Mid-Nineteenth-Century City. Cambridge:
Harvard U Press, 1975. Rev. by G. A. Stelter, AHR, 82
(Apr 1977):475-6; A. F. J. Artibise, CHR, 58(Je 1977):224-6.

Katzenstein, Peter J. Disjointed Partners: Austria and Germany
since 1815. Berkeley: U Cal Press, 1976. Rev. by A. D.
Low, AHR, 82(Feb 1977):134.

Kaufman, Harold F. , J. Kenneth Morland, and Herbert H. Fockler,
eds. Group Identity in the South: Dialogue Between the Technological and the Humanistic. Mississippi State, Miss.: Miss
St. U Dept. of Sociology, 1975. Rev. by E. M. Lander, Jr. ,
JSH, 43(May 1977):332-3.

Kaufman, Martin. American Medical Education: The Formative
Years, 1765-1910. Westport, Conn.: Greenwood Press,
1976. Rev. by J. F. Kett, AHR, 82(Je 1977):729-30.

Kaufman, Stephen A. The Akkadian Influences on Aramaic. Chicago:
U Chi Press, 1974. Rev. by D. Pardee, JNES, 36(Oct 1977):
318-9.

Kaufman, Stuart B. , ed. see Washington, Booker T.

KAUPS   166

Kaups, Matti E., ed. see Karni, Michael G., ed.

Kay, F. George. The Shameful Trade. London: White Lion Pub-
    lishers, 1976. Rev. by J. White, JAmS, 11(Apr 1977):149-52.

Kay, Terry. The Year the Lights Came On. Boston: Houghton
    Mifflin, 1976. Rev. by G. Owen, GR, 31(Sum 1977):525-8.

Kazhdan, A. P. The Social Composition of the Ruling Class of
    Byzantium. Moscow: Nauka, 1974. Rev. by C. Mango, EHR,
    92(Oct 1977):851-3.

Kealey, Gregory S. and Peter Warrian, ed. Essays in Canadian
    Working Class History. Toronto: McClelland and Stewart,
    1976. Rev. by A. R. McCormack, AHR, 82(Je 1977):776-7.

Kearns, Doris. Lyndon Johnson and the American Dream. New
    York: Harper and Row, 1976. Rev. by H. F. Graff, AHR,
    82(Je 1977):776; A. Rolle, PHR, 46(Aug 1977):535-7.

Keay, John. Into India. New York: Charles Scribner's Sons,
    1973. Rev. by L. A. Gordon, JAS, 36(Feb 1977):364-5.

Kedar, Benjamin Z. Merchants in Crisis: Genoese and Venetian
    Men of Affairs and the Fourteenth-Century Depression. New
    Haven: Yale U Press, 1976. Rev. by J. C. Davis, AHR,
    82(Oct 1977):941-2.

Kedourie, Elie. In the Anglo-Arab Labyrinth: The McMahon-
    Husayn Correspondence and the Interpretations, 1914-1939.
    New York: Cambridge U Press, 1976. Rev. by P. Jabber,
    AHR, 82(Feb 1977):109-10; A. Z. Rubinstein, CurH, 72(Jan
    1977):28; A. J. P. Taylor, History, 62(Je 1977):283.

Keegan, John. The Face of Battle. London: Jonathan Cape, 1976.
    Rev. by B. Bond, History, 62(Feb 1977):81-2.

Keep, John L. H. The Russian Revolution: A Study in Mass
    Mobilization. New York: W. W. Norton, 1977. Rev. by W.
    J. Lavery, History, 6(Oct 1977):14-15.

Kehoe, Thomas F. The Gull Lake Site: A Prehistoric Bison Drive
    in Southwestern Saskatchewan. Milwaukee: Milwaukee Public
    Museum, 1973. Rev. by E. A. Morris, Antiquity, 42(Jan
    1977):136-9.

Keir, Gillian see Brooke, Christopher

Keith, Henry H. and Robert A. Hayes, ed. Perspectives on Armed
    Politics in Brazil. Tempe: Arizona Center for Latin Ameri-
    can Studies, 1976. Rev. by F. D. McCann, AHR, 82(Je 1977):
    784; J. P. Soder, TAm, 34(Oct 1977):302-3.

Keith, Robert G.   Conquest and Agrarian Change: The Emergence of the Hacienda System on the Peruvian Coast.   Cambridge, Mass.: Har U Press, 1976. Rev. by J. V. Lombardi, AgH, 51(Jl 1977):612-4; J. Lockhart, AHR, 82(Oct 1977):1107-8; W. Borah, JEH, 37(Sep 1977):818-9; A. S. Tibesar, TAm, 34(Jl 1977):153-4.

Kelf-Cohen, R.   British Nationalization, 1945-1973.   New York: St. Martin's Press, 1974. Rev. by C. K. Harley, JEH, 37(Je 1977):518-9.

Kellenbenz, Hermann.   The Rise of the European Economy: An Economic History of Continental Europe from the Fifteenth to the Eighteenth Century.   New York: Holmes and Meier, 1976. Rev. by C. R. Phillips, AHR, 82(Feb 1977):83.

_____, and Klara van Eyll, eds.   Zwei Jahrtausende Kölner Wirtschaft.   Vol. 1, Von den Anfangen bis zum Ende des 17. Jahrhunderts.   Vol. 2, Vom 18. Jahrhundert bis zur Gegenwart.   Cologne: Greven Verlag for Rheinisch-Westfälischer Wirtschaftsarchiv zu Köln, 1975. Rev. by F. B. Tipton, JEH, 37(Sep 1977):819-21.

Keller, Morton.   Affairs of State: Public Life in Late Nineteenth Century America.   Cambridge: Har U Press, 1977. Rev. by G. W. McFarland, AHR, 82(Oct 1977):1083-4; J. F. Richardson, CWH, 23(Je 1977):185-7; A. H. Graham, JAmS, 11(Dec 1977):384-5; V. P. DeSantis, JSH, 43(Nov 1977):624-5.

Kelley, Allen C. and Jeffrey G. Williamson.   Lessons from Japanese Development: An Analytical Economic History.   Chicago: Chi U Press, 1974. Rev. by K. Yamamura, JEH, 37(Sep 1977): 821-2.

Kelley, David Hamiston.   Deciphering the Maya Script.   Austin: UT Press, 1976. Rev. by M. D. Coe, Archaeology, 30(Mar 1977):139-40; J. A. Graham, HAHR, 57(Aug 1977):530-1.

Kelley, Henry Ansgar.   The Matrimonial Trials of Henry VIII.   Stanford: Stan U Press, 1976. Rev. by R. H. Helmholz, Historian, 39(Feb 1977):328-9; J. Samaha, JMH, 49(Sep 1977):493-5.

Kellogg, Charles E.   Agricultural Development: Soil, Food, People, Work.   Madison, Wis.: Soil Science Society of America, 1975. Rev. by D. M. P. McCarthy, AgH, 51(Jl 1977):599-600.

Kelly, Angeline A.   Liam O'Flaherty, the Storyteller.   New York: Barnes and Noble, 1976. Rev. by N. Jenckes, E-I, 12(Win 1977):140-2.

Kemble, C. Robert. The Image of the Army Officer in America: Background for Current Views. Westport, Conn.: Greenwood Press, 1974. Rev. by E. Ranson, JAmS, 11(Apr 1977):147-9.

Kennedy, Kieran A. and Brendan R. Dowling. Economic Growth in Ireland: The Experience Since 1974. Dublin: Gill and Macmillan, 1975. Rev. by D. J. Daly, JEH, 37(Sep 1977):822-3.

Kennedy, Paul M. The Rise and Fall of British Naval Mastery. New York: Scribners, 1976. Rev. by C. J. Bartlett, AHR, 82(Apr 1977):356; P. M. Hayes, EHR, 92(Oct 1977):912.

Kenney, Alice P. Stubborn for Liberty: The Dutch in New York. Syracuse: Syracuse U Press, 1975. Rev. by T. J. Condon, Historian, 39(May 1977):568-9.

Kenney, W. Howland. Laughter in the Wilderness: Early American Humor to 1783. Kent, Ohio: Kent St U Press, 1976. Rev. by G. A. Caldwell, NEQ, 50(Je 1977):341-4; E. G. Breslaw, WMQ, 34(Oct 1977):682-4.

Kenny, Herbert A. Literary Dublin. New York: Taplinger Publishing Co., 1974. Rev. by M. H. Begnal, E-I, 12(Win 1977): 153-5.

Kent, Marian. Oil and Empire: British Policy and Mesopotamian Oil, 1900-1920. London: Macmillan, 1976. Rev. by E. Penrose, BH, 19(Jan 1977):105-6; B. C. Busch, AHR, 82(Apr 1977):406; D. C. M. Platt, EHR, 92(Oct 1977):928-9; R. Heussler, Historian, 39(May 1977):549-50; M. Wilkins, JEH, 37(Sep 1977):823-4; G. G. Jones, HJ, 20(No. 2, 1977):516-18.

Kent, Sherman. The Election of 1827 in France. Cambridge: Har U Press, 1975. Rev. by T. D. Beck, JMH, 49(Mar 1977): 140-1.

Kenyon, Walter A. see Wheeler, Robert C.

Kepler, J. S. The Exchange of Christendom: The International Entrepôt at Dover, 1622-1651. Atlantic Highlands, N.J.: Humanities Press, 1976. Rev. by J. T. Evans, AHR, 82(Je 1977):633; G. D. Ramsay, History, 62(Je 1977):323.

Kerig, Dorothy Pierson. Luther T. Ellsworth: U. S. Consul on the Border during the Mexican Revolution. El Paso: Texas Western Press, 1975. Rev. by L. L. Blaisell, PHR, 46 (May 1977):306-7.

Kern, Stephen. Anatomy and Destiny: A Cultural History of the Human Body. New York: Bobbs-Merrill, 1975. Rev. by D. P. Verene, JMH, 49(Sep 1977):488-9.

Kerr, Homer, L. Fighting with Ross' Texas Cavalry Brigade,

C. S. A. : The Diary of George L. Griscom, Adjutant, 9th
Texas Cavalry Regiment. Hillsboro, Texas: Hill Jr. College
Press, 1976. Rev. by C. W. King, JSH, 43(Aug 1977):461-2.

Kerr, W. G. Scottish Capital on the American Credit Frontier.
Austin: Texas State Historical Association, 1976. Rev. by
W. T. Jackson, A&W, 19(Spr 1977):98-100; J. E. King, AgH,
51(Jl 1977):623-4; M. Rothstein, AHR, 82(Je 1977):750-1; D.
E. Green, ETHJ, 15(No. 1, 1977):55; S. G. Checkland, HJ,
20(No. 3, 1977):776-7; J. A. James, JEH, 37(Je 1977):535-6;
A. G. Bogue, JSH, 43(May 1977):310-11.

Kersey, Harry A. , Jr. Pelts, Plumes, and Hides: White Traders
among the Seminole Indians, 1870-1930. Gainesville: U
Presses Fla. , 1976. Rev. by M. Zanger, AHR, 81(Dec 1976):
1263; H. G. Jordan, WHQ, 8(Jan 1977):67.

Kessell, John L. Friars, Soldiers, and Reformers: Hispanic
Arizona and the Sonora Mission Frontier, 1767-1856. Tucson:
U Ariz Press, 1976. Rev. by B. E. Bobb, A&W, 19(Sum
1977):169-170; J. F. Bannon, AHR, 82(Apr 1977):439; C.
Polzer, HAHR, 57(May 1977):337-8; W. E. Derrick, JOW,
16(Jl 1977):96; T. E. Treutlein, NMHR, 52(Apr 1977):162-3;
B. M. Fireman, WHQ, 8(Jl 1977):339-40.

Kessler, Lawrence D. K'ang-hsi and the Consolidation of Ch'ing
Rule, 1661-1684. Chicago: U Chi Press, 1976. Rev. by S.
Wu, AHR, 82(Oct 1977):1044-5; J. P. Dennerline, JAS, 37
(Nov 1977):114-6.

Kessner, Thomas. The Golden Door: Italian and Jewish Immigrant
Mobility in New York City, 1880-1915. New York: Ox U
Press, 1977. Rev. by P. A. M. Taylor, JAmS, 11(Dec 1977):
432.

Kett, Joseph F. Rites of Passage; Adolescence in America 1790 to
the Present. New York: Basic Books, 1977. Rev. by D. W.
Noble, History, 6(Oct 1977):9.

Keylor, William R. Academy and Community: The Foundation of
the French Historical Profession. Cambridge, Mass.: Har
U Press, 1975. Rev. by S. Kinser, JMH, 49(Sep 1977):482-5.

Keynes, Milo, ed. Essays on John Maynard Keynes. Cambridge:
Cam U Press, 1975. Rev. by P. F. Clarke, History, 62(Feb
1977):146-7.

Kharbas, Datta Shankarrao. Maharashtra and the Marathas, Their
History and Culture: A Bibliographic Guide to Western Language Materials. Rev. by F. F. Conlon, JAS, 37(Nov 1977):
160-1.

Kibler, James E. , Jr. Pseudonymous Publications of William

Gilmore Simms. Athens, Ga.: U Georgia Press, 1976. Rev. by D. Moltke-Hansen, SCHM, 78(Apr 1977):152-3.

Kieckhefer, Richard. European Witch Trials: Their Foundations in Popular and Learned Culture. London: Routledge and Kegan Paul, 1976. Rev. by H. Kamen, History, 62(Je 1977):315-6.

Kierman, Frank A., Jr. and John K. Fairbank, ed. Chinese Ways in Warfare. Cambridge: Harvard U Press, 1974. Rev. by W. W. Whitson, CQ, No. 70(Je 1977):430-2.

Kiernan, Thomas. Arafat: The Man and the Myth. New York: Norton, 1976. Rev. by A. Z. Rubinstein, CurH, 72(Jan 1977): 28.

Kileff, C. and W. C. Pendleton. Urban Man in Southern Africa. Gwele and Salisbury, Rhodesia: Mambo Press, 1975. Rev. by R. M. Bronsen, JAAS, 12(Jan/Oct 1977):286-7.

Kilian, Klaus. Fibeln in Thessalien. München: C. H. Beck'sche Verlagsbuchhandlung, 1975. Rev. by H. L. Thomas, AJA, 81 (Win 1977):115-16.

Kilson, Martin L. and Robert I. Rotberg, ed. The African Diaspora: Interpretive Essays. Cambridge: Harvard U Press, 1976. Rev. by R. Anstey, JAmS, 11(Aug 1977):295-6.

Kim, Hee-Jin. Dōgen Kigen--Mystical Realist. Tucson: U Arizona Press, 1975. Rev. by R. J. Corless, JAS, 36(Aug 1977): 743-5.

Kim, Joungwon Alexander. Divided Korea: The Politics of Development, 1945-72. Cambridge: Har U Press, 1975. Rev. by D. Tretiak, CQ, No. 70(Je 1977):435-7.

Kim, Kwang Suk see Frank, Charles R., Jr.

Kimber, Edward. A Relation or Journal of a late Expedition to the Gates of St. Augustine, on Florida. Gainesville: U Presses of Florida, 1976. Rev. by R. F. A. Fabel, AlaR, 30(Jan 1977):69-71.

Kimmich, Christoph M. Germany and the League of Nations. Chicago: U Chi Press, 1976. Rev. by M. M. Lee, AHR, 82(Oct 1977):1006.

Kinder, A. Gordon. Casiodoro de Reina: Spanish Reformer in the Sixteenth Century. London: Tamesis Books, 1975. Rev. by J. C. Nieto, AHR, 82(Je 1977):656.

King, C. Richard. Suzanna Dickinson: Messenger of the Alamo. Austin: Shoal Creek Publishers, 1976. Rev. by M. S. Henson, ETHJ, 15(No. 2, 1977):57-8.

King, Francis P. see Greenough, William C.

King, Kenneth M. Mission to Paradise. Chicago: Franciscan
Herald Press, 1975. Rev. by J. B. Romney, JOW, 16(Jan
1977):81.

King, Mackenzie. Mackenzie King Diaries, 1893-1931. Toronto:
U Tor Press, 1974. Rev. by C. P. Stacey, CHR, 58(Je
1977):234-6.

Kinkade, M. Dale, Kenneth L. Hale, and Oswald Werner, ed.
Linguistics and Anthropology: In Honor of C. F. Voegelin.
Lisse: Peter De Ridder Press, 1975. Rev. by W. Bright,
AIQ, 3(Sum 1977):164-5.

Kinsella, Thomas. The Good Fight: A Poem for the Tenth Anniversary of the Death of John F. Kennedy. Dublin: Peppercanister, 1973. Rev. by J. Sisson, E-I, 12(Fall 1977):139-43.

_____. A Technical Supplement. Dublin: Peppercanister, 1976.
Rev. by F. Skloot, E-I, 12(Fall 1977):143-7.

_____, ed. see also Clarke, Austin

Kinsley, Michael E. Outer Space and Inner Sanctums: Government,
Business and Satellite Communication. New York: John
Wiley, 1976. Rev. by L. J. Mercer, JEH, 37(Je 1977):536-7.

Kinsman, Robert S., ed. The Darker Vision of the Renaissance:
Beyond the Fields of Reason. Berkeley: U Cal Press, 1975.
Rev. by J. E. Bullard, AHR, 82(Feb 1977):85; P. Burke,
EHR, 92(Oct 1977):893-4; J. Larner, History, 62(Feb 1977):
109.

Kiple, Kenneth F. Blacks in Colonial Cuba, 1774-1899. Gainesville, Fla.: U Presses of Florida, 1976. Rev. by C. N.
Degler, JLAS, 9(May 1977):150-2; J. E. & T. J. Eblen, JSH,
43(Feb 1977):119-30; G. D. Inglis, TAm, 34(Oct 1977):306-7.

Kirby, D. G., ed. Finland and Russia, 1808-1920: From Autonomy
to Independence. New York: Barnes and Noble, 1975. Rev.
by P. K. Hamalainen, AHR, 82(Apr 1977):379.

Kirby, E. Stuart. Russian Studies of China: Progress and Problems of Soviet Sinology. London: Macmillan, 1975. Rev.
by J. Fogel, CQ, No. 71(Sep 1977):620-3.

Kirby, R. G. and E. A. Munson. The Voice of the People: John
Doherty, 1798-1854, Trade Unionist, Radical and Factory Reformer. Totowa, N.J.: Rowman & Littlefield, 1976. Rev.
by R. K. Huch, AHR, 82(Feb 1977):101-2.

Kirchner, Walter. Studies in Russian-American Commerce, 1820-

1860. Leiden: E. J. Brill, 1975. Rev. by J. T. Alexander, AHR, 82(Feb 1977):148-9.

Kirk, G. S. Myth: Its Meaning and Functions in Ancient and Other Cultures. Cambridge: Cam U Press, 1970. Rev. by B. Alster, JNES, 36(Jl 1977):224-6.

Kirkman, James. Fort Jesus: A Portuguese Fortress on the East African Coast. London: Ox U Press, 1974. Rev. by G. S. P. Freeman-Grenville, AHR, 82(Apr 1977):407-8.

Kirschbaum, J. M. Slovak Language and Literature. Cleveland: U Manitoba, 1975. Rev. by S. B. Kimball, AHR, 82(Apr 1977):396.

Kirstein, Peter N. Anglo Over Bracero: A History of the Mexican Worker in the United States from Roosevelt to Nixon. San Francisco: R&E Research Associates, 1977. Rev. by C. Wollenberg, CHQ, 56(Fall 1977):282.

Kirsten, Ernst. Süditalienkunde. Ein Führer zu klassischen Stätten. Bd. 1: Campanien und seine Nachbarlandschaften. Heidelberg: Carl Winter Universitätsverlag, 1975. Rev. by R. R. Holloway, AJA, 81(Spr 1977):253.

Kistiakowsky, George B. A Scientist at the White House: The Private Diary of President Eisenhower's Special Assistant for Science and Technology. Cambridge, Mass.: Har U Press, 1976. Rev. by G. W. Reichard, AHR, 82(Oct 1977):1100-1.

Klaits, Joseph. Printed Propaganda under Louis XIV: Absolute Monarchy and Public Opinion. Princeton: Prin U Press, 1977.

Klein, Donald W. see Isreal, John

Klingaman, David C. and Richard K. Veddes, eds. Essays in Nineteenth Century Economic History: The Old Northwest. Athens: Ohio U Press, 1975. Rev. by R. P. Swierenga, CWH, 23(Je 1977):175-7.

Klingenstein, Grete. Der Aufstieg des Hauses Kaunitz: Studien zur Herkunft und Bildung des Staatskanzlers Wenzel Anton. Gottingen: Vandenhoeck and Ruprecht, 1975. Rev. by W. J. McGill, AHR, 82(Feb 1977):135.

_____, ed. see also Engel-Janosi, Friedrich, ed.

Klinghoffen, Arthur Jay. The Soviet Union and International Politics. New York: Col U Press, 1977. Rev. by A. Z. Rubinstein, CurH, 73(Oct 1977):128.

Klingman, David C. and Richard K. Vedder. Essays in Nineteenth

Century Economic History: The Old Northwest. Athens: Ohio U Press, 1975. Rev. by R. E. Shaw, PHR, 46(Aug 1977): 498-9.

Klingman, Peter D. Josiah Walls: Florida's Black Congressman of Reconstruction. Gainesville: U Presses Fla, 1976. Rev. by C. Vincent, AHR, 82(Apr 1977):446-7; J. H. Shofner, AlaR, 30(Apr 1977):152-3; E. L. Thornbrough, FHQ, 55(Jan 1977): 363-4; R. S. Alexander, JSH, 43(May 1977):309.

Kluge, Ulrich. Soldatenräte und Revolution. Studien zur Militär-politik in Deutschland, 1918/19. Gottingen: Vandenhoeck & Ruprecht, 1975. Rev. by M. Nolan, JNH, 49(Sep 1977):507-12.

Kluger, Richard. Simple Justice: The History of Brown v. Board of Education and Black America's Struggle for Equality. New York: Knopf, 1976. Rev. by A. M. Burns, III, FHQ, 55 (Apr 1977):506-8; J. C. Duram, Historian, 39(Feb 1977):380-1.

Knabe, Bernd. Die Struktur der russischen Posadgemeinden und ker Katalog der Beschwerden und Forderungen der Kaufman-nschaft (1762-1767). Berlin: Osteuropa-Institut, 1975. Rev. by C. S. Leonard, AHR, 82(Je 1977):693-4.

Knapp, Vincent J. Europe in the Era of Social Transformation: 1700-Present. Englewood Cliffs, N.J.: Prentice-Hall, 1976. Rev. by A. Plakans, AHR, 82(Feb 1977):81-3; E. L. Jones, JEH, 37(Je 1977):537-8.

Knechtges, David R. The Han Rhapsody: A Study of the Fu of Yang Hsiung (53 B.C.-A.D. 18). Cambridge: Cam U Press, 1976. Rev. by F. A. Bischoff, JAS, 37(Nov 1977):102-3.

Knight, David. Sources for the History of Science 1660-1914. London: Sources of History, 1975. Rev. by R. Fox, History, 62 (Feb 1977):75-6.

Knight, Russell W., ed. General John Glover's Letterbook, 1776-1777. Salem: Essex Institute, 1976. Rev. by G. A. Billias, NEQ, 50(Mar 1977):163-4.

Knoke, David. Change and Continuity in American Politics: The Social Bases of Political Parties. Baltimore & London: JHU Press, 1976. Rev. by N. V. Bartley, JSH, 43(Aug 1977): 477-8.

Knowles, David. Bare Ruined Choirs: The Dissolution of the English Monasteries. New York: Cam U Press, 1976. Rev. by B. D. Hill, AHR, 82(Feb 1977):93.

Knowlton, Robert J. Church Property and the Mexican Reform,

1856-1910. De Kalb: No Ill U Press, 1976. Rev. by D. J.
Mabry, AHR, 82(Je 1977):780-1; T. G. Powell, HAHR, 57
(May 1977):342-3.

Knudsen, Dean D. see Earle, John R.

Kobayashi, José María. La educación como conquista: Empresa
franciscana en Mexico. Mexico: El Colegio de Mexico, 1974.
Rev. by I. A. Leonard, HAHR, 57(May 1977):334-5.

Kohl, Herbert. On Teaching. New York: Schocken Books, 1976.
Rev. by J. L. Browne, HT, 10(Aug 1977):627.

Kohlstedt, Sally Gregory. The Formation of the American Scien-
tific Community. Urbana: U Ill Press, 1976. Rev. by R.
V. Bruce, AHR, 82(Feb 1977):187; H. D. Shapiro, AS, 18
(Fall 1977):113; H. W. Becker, Historian, 39(May 1977):575-6.

Kohn, Richard H. Eagle and Sword: The Federalists and the Crea-
tion of the Military Establishment in America 1783-1802. New
York: Free Press, 1975. Rev. by M. Blumenson, AHI, 11
(Feb 1977):50; F. C. Mevers, PHR, 46(Aug 1977):495-7.

Kolko, Gabriel. Main Currents in Modern American History. New
York: Harper and Row, 1976. Rev. by J. Braeman, AHR,
82(Apr 1977):427-8; R. S. Kirkendall, JSH, 43(May 1977):318-
20.

Komjathy, Anthony Tihamer. The Crises of France's East Central
European Diplomacy, 1933-1939. New York: Col U Press,
1976. Rev. by P. S. Wandycz, AHR, 82(Oct 1977):985.

Konnz, Claudia, ed. see Bridenthal, Renate, ed.

Korbel, Josef. Twentieth-Century Czechoslovakia: The Meanings of
its History. New York: Col U Press, 1977. Rev. by G. Kish,
History, 6(Oct 1977):17.

Korey, Marie Elena. The Books of Isaac Norris (1701-1766) at
Dickinson College. Carlisle, Pa.: Dickinson College, 1976.
Rev. by N. S. Fiering, WMQ, 34(Jl 1977):513-6.

Kornweibel, Theodore, Jr. No Crystal Stair: Black Life and the
Messenger, 1917-1928. Westport, Conn.: Greenwood Press,
1976. Rev. by L. Finkle, AHR, 82(Feb 1977):204-5; S. M.
Miller, Historian, 39(May 1977):582-3.

Kors, Alan Charles. D'Holbach's Coterie: An Enlightenment in
Paris. Princeton: Prin U Press, 1976. Rev. by I. F.
Knight, AHR, 82(Je 1977):649-50.

Korshin, Paul J., ed. The Widening Circle: Essays on the Circulation of Literature in Eighteenth Century Europe. Philadelphia:

U Pa Press, 1976. Rev. by F. A. Kafker, AHR, 82(Oct 1977):948-9; N. S. Fiering, WMQ, 34(Jl 1977):513-6.

Korson, J. Henry, ed. Contemporary Problems of Pakistan. Leiden: E. J. Brill, 1974. Rev. by H. Alavi, JAS, 36(Aug 1977):784-6.

Kortepeter, C. Max. Ottoman Imperialism During the Reformation: Europe and the Caucasus. New York: NYU Press, 1972. Rev. by A. Bennigsen, JNES, 36(Jl 1977):237-8.

Koss, Stephen. Asquith. London: Allen Lane, 1976. Rev. by K. O. Morgan, History, 62(Je 1977):341-2.

_____. Nonconformity in Modern British Politics. Hamden, Conn.: Archon Books, 1975. Rev. by D. M. Thompson, AHR, 82(Oct 1977):972; J. V. Crangle, Historian, 39(Feb 1977):337-8; B. B. Gilbert, JMH, 49(Mar 1977):138-40.

Kostianovsky, Olinda Massare de. La instrucción pública en la época colonial. Asuncion: n. p., 1975. Rev. by J. H. Williams, TAm, 33(Jan 1977):551-2.

Kostof, Sprio, ed. The Architect: Chapters in the History of the Profession. New York: Ox U Press, 1976. Rev. by R. Wiedenhoeft, AHR, 82(Oct 1977):924-5; C. E. Clark, Jr., JIH, 8(Aut 1977):354-6.

Kotel'nikova, L. A. Mondo contadino e citta in Italia dall' CI al XIV secolo, dalle fonti dell' Italia centrale Settentrionale. Bologna: Il Mulino, 1975. Rev. by J. K. Laurent, AgH, 51 (Jl 1977):602-4.

Kotze, D. A. African Politics in South Africa 1964-1974. London: Hurst, 1975. Rev. by I. Hexham, Africa, 47(No. 1, 1977): 113.

Kovács, Sándor, ed. Janus Pannonius Opera Latine et Hungarice. Vivae Memoriae Iani Pannonii Qvingentesimo Mortis Svae Anniversario Dedicatum. Budapest: Tankonyvkiado, 1972. Rev. by T. Kachinske, EEQ, 11(Je 1977):376-7.

Kozik, Zenobiusz. Political Parties in Cracow, 1945-1947. Cracow: Wydawnictwo Literackie, 1975. Rev. by T. Swietochowski, AHR, 82(Je 1977):688-9.

Kraay, Colin M. Archaic and Classical Greek Coins. Berkeley: U Cal Press, 1976. Rev. by R. R. Holloway, AHR, 82(Oct 1977):926-7; A. Walker, Archaeology, 30(May 1977):210.

Krader, Lawrence. The Asiatic Mode of Production: Sources Development and Critique in the Writings of Karl Marx. Assen, Netherlands: Van Gorcum, 1975. Rev. by N. Levine, JAS, 36 (May 1977):540-1.

Kraft, Barbara S., ed. see Washington, Booker T.

Kranzler, David. Japanese, Nazis and Jews: The Jewish Refugee Community of Shanghai, 1938-1945. Brooklyn: Sifria Distributors, 1976. Rev. by L. S. Forman, AHR, 82(Je 1977): 714-15.

Krasheninnikov, Stepan Petrovich. Explorations of Kamchatka: North Pacific Scimitar. Portland: Oregon Historical Society, 1972. Rev. by B. M. Marley, WHQ, 8(Jl 1977):342-3.

Krasuski, Jerzy. Polish-German Relations, 1919-1932. Poznań: Instytut Zachodni, 1975. Rev. by A. M. Cienciala, AHR, 82 (Apr 1977):397-8.

Kraus, David E., ed. see Horecky, Paul L., ed.

Kraus, Richard A. see Han-Sheng Chuan.

Krauskopf, Robert W., ed. see O'Neill, James E., ed.

Kren, George M. and Leon H. Rappoport, ed. Varieties of Psychohistory. New York: Springer Publishing, 1976. Rev. by R. L. Schoenwald, AHR, 82(Feb 1977):62-3.

Kretschmar, Robert S. and Robin Foor. The Potential for Joint Ventures in Eastern Europe. New York: Praeger, 1972. Rev. by A. J. Simon, EEQ, 11(Je 1977):371-6.

Kretzer, Hartmut. Calvinismus und französische Monarchie im 17. Jahrhundert: Die politische Lehre der Akademien Sedan und Saumur. Berlin: Duncker and Humblot, 1975. Rev. by R. Kleinman, AHR, 82(Oct 1977):977.

Kreuter, Gretchen, ed. see Stuhler, Barbara, ed.

Kreuzer, Georg. Die Honoriusfrage im Mittelalter und in der Heuzeit. Stuttgart: Hiersemann, 1975. Rev. by H. Chadwick, EHR, 92(Oct 1977):881-2.

Krick, Robert K. Neale Books, an Annotated Bibliography. Dayton, Ohio: Morningside Press, 1977. Rev. by D. Evans, GHQ, 51(Sum 1977):205-6.

_____. Parker's Virginia Battery, C.S.A. Berryville, Va.: Virginia Book Company, 1975. Rev. by J. I. Robinson, Jr., CWA, 23(Mar 1977):85-7.

Krickus, Richard. Pursuing the American Dream. White Ethics and the New Populism. Garden City: Anchor Books, 1976. Rev. by B. K. Martin, AI, 44(Sum 1977):68-70.

Kriegel, Abraham D., ed. The Holland House Diaries, 1831-1840:

The Diary of Henry Richard Vassall Fox, Third Lord Holland.
Boston: Routledge and Kegan Paul, 1977. Rev. by J. Clive,
AHR, 82(Oct 1977):965-6.

Kroeber, A. L. Yurok Myths. Berkeley: U Cal Press, 1976.
Rev. by J. Vandergriff, AIQ, 3(Aut 1977):256-7.

Kroeker, Marvin E. Great Plains Command: William B. Hazen in
the Frontier West. Norman: U Oklahoma Press, 1976. Rev.
by W. H. Leckie, AHR, 82(Feb 1977):192; R. W. Richmond,
AIQ, 3(Spr 1977):59-60; P. J. Scheips, A&W, 19(Spr 1977):
97-8; G. E. Moulton, JOW, 16(Jan 1977):84; R. Wilson, UHQ,
45(Spr 1977):208-9; R. Broades, WHQ, 8(Apr 1977):222.

Krueger, Anne O., ed. see Hong, Wontack, ed.

Krueger, Max Amadeus Paulus. Second Fatherland: The Life and
Times of a German Immigrant. College Station: Texas A&M
U Press, 1976. Rev. by V. L. Haskins, ChOk, 55(Sum
1977):234-5; D. G. Muckelroy, ETHJ, 15(No. 2, 1977):59-60;
F. H. Schapsmeier, JOW, 16(Jan 1977):76.

Kula, Witold. An Economic Theory of the Feudal System: Towards
a Model of the Polish Economy 1500-1800. London: New
Left Books, 1976. Rev. by F. Spooner, History, 62(Feb
1977):139.

Kulczykowski, Mariusz. Peasant Cotton Weaving in the Center of
Andrychow in the XIX Century. Wroclaw: Polska Akademia
Nauk, 1976. Rev. by R. D. Lewis, AHR, 82(Oct 1977):
1022-3.

Kunckel, Hille. Der römische Genius. Heidelberg: F. H. Kerle
Verlag, 1974. Rev. by D. E. E. Kleiner and F. S. Kleiner,
AJA, 81(Spr 1977):260.

Kunitz, Stephen J. see Levy, Jerrold E.

Kunkel, Mabel. Abraham Lincoln: Unforgettable American. Charlotte, N.C.: Delmar Co., 1976. Rev. by J. E. Suppiger,
JISHS, 70(Feb 1977):91.

Kunz, Merle H., ed. see Glauert, Earl T., ed.

Kunzle, David. History of the Comic Strip. Volume 1: The Early
Comic Strip: Narrative Strips and Picture Stories in the European Broadsheet from 1450 to 1825. Berkeley and London: U
Cal Press, 1973. Rev. by K. Wellman, JMH, 49(Je 1977):
301-3.

Kuo, Thomas C. Ch'en Tu-hsiu (1879-1942) and the Chinese Communist Movement. South Orange, N.J.: Seton Hall U Press,
1975. Rev. by K. Yip, CQ, No. 71(Sep 1977):612-14.

Kushner, David. The Rise of Turkish Nationalism, 1876-1908.
Totowa, N.J.: Frank Cass & Co., 1977. Rev. by R. H.
Davison, History, 6(Nov/Dec 1977):37.

Kushner, Howard I. Conflict on the Northwest Coast: American-
Russian Rivalry in the Pacific Northwest, 1790-1867. Westport, Conn.: Greenwood Press, 1975. Rev. by M. Sherwood,
PHR, 46(Feb 1977):120-2; R. J. Jensen, PNQ, 68(Jan 1977):
34-5.

Kusmer, Kenneth. A Ghetto Takes Shape: Black Cleveland, 1870-
1930. Urbana: U Ill Press, 1976. Rev. by H. P. Chudacoff,
AHR, 82(Feb 1977):190-1; W. W. Giffin, Historian, 39(May
1977):579-81; M. W. Homel, MichH, 61(Sum 1977):173-6.

Küther, Carsten. Räuber und Gauner in Deutschland: Das organ-
isierte Bandenwesen im 18. und frühen 19. Jahrhundert.
Göttingen: Vandenhoeck and Ruprecht, 1976. Rev. by M. W.
Gray, AHR, 82(Je 1977):661-2.

Kutscher, E. Y. The Language and Linguistic Background of the
Isaiah Scroll (1 Q Isa^a). Leiden: E. J. Brill, 1974. Rev.
by D. Pardee, JNES, 36(Jan 1977):64-5.

Kuykendall, James R., et al. Profiles of Alabama Pharmacy.
Birmingham, Ala.: Alabama Pharmaceutical Assn., 1974.
Rev. by M. C. McMillan, AlaR, 30(Jl 1977):240.

Kvasnicka, Robert M., ed. see Smith, Jane F., ed.

Kvetko, Martin and Miroslav Ján Licko, eds. Anthology of Personal
Recollections of the Slovak National Uprising. Toronto: Stála
Konferencia Slovenských Demokratických Exulantov, 1976. Rev.
by Y. Jelinek, AHR, 82(Je 1977):687.

Kynaston, David. King Labour: The British Working Class, 1850-
1914. London: Allen and Unwin, 1976. Rev. by H. Pelling,
JEH, 37(Sep 1977):824-5.

Kyrou, Alexis, ed. Dreams and Reality: Forty-five Years of
Diplomatic Life. Athens: P. Kleisiounes, 1972. Rev. by S.
V. Papacosma, AHR, 82(Apr 1977):392.

Labande-Maifert, Yvonne. Charles VIII Et Son Milieu (1470-1498):
La Jeunesse Au Pouvoir. Paris: Klincksieck, 1975. Rev.
by R. J. Knecht, History, 62(Je 1977):318.

Labaree, Benjamin W. see Christie, Ian R.

Labedz, Leopold, ed. Survey: A Journal of East and West Studies.
Cambridge, Mass.: Ox U Press, n.d. Rev. by C. Gershman,
Comm, 63(May 1977):86-8.

Labrousse, Ernest, ed. see Braudel, Fernand, ed.

Lach, Donald F. and Edmund S. Wehrle. International Politics in East Asia since World War II. New York: Praeger, 1975. Rev. by G. R. Hess, PHR, 46(May 1977):313-4.

Lacina, Vlastislav. The Crisis of Czechoslovak Agriculture, 1928-1934. Prague: Ústav Ceskoslovenskych a Svetových dejin CSAV, 1974. Rev. by Z. Pryor, AHR, 82(Feb 1977):144-5.

Lackner, E. E. From Tyranny to Texas: A German Pioneer in Harris County. San Antonio: Naylor Co., 1975. Rev. by G. T. Grubb, ETHJ, 15(Spr 1977):57-8.

Ladan, U. and D. Lyndersay. Shaihu Umar. Longman, 1975. Rev. by H. Dinwiddy, AfAf, 76(Jan 1977):127-9.

Ladurie, E. LeRoy. Times of Feast, Times of Famine: A History of Climate Since the Year 1000. London: Allen and Unwin, 1973. Rev. by J. Thirsk, History, 62(Feb 1977):77-8.

Ladurie, Emmanuel LeRoy. Le territoire de l'historien. Paris: Gallimard, 1975. Rev. by F. F. Mendels, JEH, 37(Je 1977): 540-1.

_____. Montaillow, Village Occitan de 1294 a 1324. n.l.: Gallimard, n.d. Rev. by P. Q., HTo, 27(Je 1977):405-6.

Lafaye, Jacques. Quetzalcoatl and Guadalupe: The Formation of Mexican National Consciousness 1531-1813. Chicago: U Chi Press, 1976. Rev. by I. W. Engstrand, JOW, 16(Jl 1977): 94-5; J. S. Cummins, HTo, 27(Aug 1977):543-4; W. Taylor, NMHR, 52(Jl 1977):252-3.

La Hood, Charles G., Jr. and Robert C. Sullivan. Reprographic Services in Libraries: Organization and Administration. Chicago: American Library Association, 1975. Rev. by A. H. Leisinger, Jr., AmArc, 40(Apr 1977):243-4.

Lake, Anthony. The 'Tar Baby' Option: American Policy toward Southern Rhodesia. New York: Columbia U Press, 1976. Rev. by E. Windrich, AfAf, 76(Apr 1977):260-1.

Lake, Marilyn. A Divided Society: Tasmania During World War I. Melbourne: Melbourne U Press, 1975. Rev. by F. P. King, AHR, 82(Feb 1977):166.

Lamb, Helen B. Studies on India and Vietnam. New York: Monthly Review Press, 1976. Rev. by R. Diwan, JAS, 36 (Aug 1977):711. Ed. by Corliss Lamont.

Lambert, M. E., ed. see Medlicott, W. N., ed.

Lambert, Malcolm. Medieval Heresy: Popular Movements from
    Bogomil to Hus. New York: Holmes & Meier, 1977. Rev.
    by F. L. Cheyette, History, 6(Oct 1977):22-3.

Lamont, Corliss, ed. Studies on India and Vietnam. New York
    and London: Monthly Review Press, 1976. Rev. by M.
    McAlpin, JEH, 37(Sep 1977):825.

Lamphear, John. The Traditional History of the Jie of Uganda.
    New York: Ox U Press, 1976. Rev. by D. W. Cohen, AHR,
    82(Oct 1977):1035-6; O. W. Furley, History, 62(Je 1977):279.

Lancaster, Robert Bolling. A Sketch of the Early History of
    Hanover County, Virginia, and Its Large and Important Con-
    tributions to the American Revolution. Richmond: Whittet
    and Shepperson, 1976. Rev. by W. A. Mabry, VMHB, 85
    (Jan 1977):110-11.

Land, Aubrey C. , Lois Green Carr, and Edward C. Papenfuse, eds.
    Law, Society and Politics in Early Maryland. Baltimore:
    JHU Press, 1977. Rev. by J. Levin, History, 6(Nov/Dec
    1977):30-1.

Lander, Ernest M. , Jr., and Richard J. Calhoun, eds. Two
    Decades of Change: The South Since the Supreme Court De-
    segregation Decision. Columbia, S. C.: Published for Clem-
    son University by the U SC Press, 1975. Rev. by G. P.
    Antone, JSH, 43(Nov 1977):633-4.

Landes, David S. , ed. Western Europe: The Trails of Partner-
    ship. Lexington: D. C. Heath, 1977. Rev. by O. E. S.,
    CurH, 73(Nov 1977):174.

Landreth, Harry. History of Economic Theory: Scope, Method,
    and Content. Boston: Houghton Mifflin, 1976. Rev. by J.
    J. Spengler, JEH, 37(Je 1977):538-40.

Landrum, Larry N. , Pat Browne, and Ray B. Browne, ed. Di-
    mensions of Detective Fiction. Bowling Green, Ohio: Pop-
    ular Press, 1976. J. Whitley, JAmS, 11(Aug 1977):284-6.

Landuyt, Ariane. Le Sinistre E L'Aventino. Milan: Franco
    Angeli, 1973. Rev. by A. Lyttelton, History, 62(Feb 1977):
    165-6; C. F. Dellzell, JMH, 49(Je 1977):321-6.

Lane, James B. Jacob A. Riis and the American City. New York:
    Kennikat, 1974. Rev. by J. F. Bauman, PH, 45(Jan 1977):
    90-1.

Lang, D. M. The Bulgarians: From Pagan Times to the Ottoman
    Conquest. London: Thames and Hudson, 1976. Rev. by R.
    Browning, History, 62(Je 1977):310; R. F. Hoddinott, Anti-
    quity, 51(Mar 1977):80-1.

Lange, Charles H., and Carroll L. Riley and Elizabeth M. Lange, eds. Southwest Journals of Adolph F. Bandolier, 1885-1888. Albuquerque: UNM, 1975. Rev. by D. A. Miller, A & W, 19(Spr 1977):86-87; W. A. Beck, WHQ, 8(Apr 1977):229-30.

Lange, Elizabeth M., ed. see Lange, Charles H., ed.

Langford, P. The First Rockingham Administration 1765-1766. London: Ox U Press, 1973. Rev. by J. Dinwiddy, HJ, 20(No. 4, 1977):983-9.

Langford, Paul. The Eighteenth Century, 1688-1815. New York: St. Martin's Press, 1976. Rev. by I. K. Steele, AHR, 82 (Oct 1977):963-4.

Langley, Lester D. Struggle for the American Mediterranean: United States-European Rivalry in the Gulf-Caribbean, 1776-1904. Athens: U Ga Press, 1976. Rev. by D. M. Pletcher, AHR, 82(Feb 1977):39-59; T. Schoonover, ETHJ, 15(No. 2, 1977):56-7; R. M. Malek, HAHR, 57(Feb 1977):195-6; W. LaFeber, TAm, 34(Jl 1977):147-8.

Langlois, Claude. Un diocèse breton au début du XIXe siècle. Rennes: Université de Haute-Bretagne, 1974. Rev. by G. D. Balsama, AHR, 82(Apr 1977):370-1.

Langlois, W. J., ed. A Guide to Aural History Research. Victoria: Provincial Archives of British Columbia, 1976. Rev. by W. W. Moss, AmArc, 40(Jan 1977):91-2.

Langlotz, Ernst. Studien Zur Nordostgriechischen Kunst. Mainz: Philipp von Zabern, 1975. Rev. by B. S. Ridgway, AJA, 81 (Sum 1977):396-7.

Lansdowne, J. F. Birds of the West Coast. Boston: Houghton Mifflin, 1976. Rev. by G. J. Pearson, PNQ, 68(Jl 1977): 149.

Laquer, Walter. Guerrilla. n. l.: Little, Brown, n. d. Rev. by S. Cropsey, Comm, 63(Je 1977):81-2.

Laran, Michel and Jean Saussay, eds. La Russie ancienne, IXe-XVIIe siecles. Paris: Masson et Cie, 1975. Rev. by L. Langer, AHR, 82(Feb 1977):147.

Large, Brian. Marinu. New York: Holmes and Meier, 1976. Rev. by W. M. Johnston, AHR, 82(Feb 1977):146.

Larkin, Emmet. The Roman Catholic and the Creation of the Modern Irish State, 1878-1886. Philadelphia: American Philosophical Society, 1975. Rev. by D. H. Akenson, AHR, 82(Feb 1977):113-4; P. Buckland, History, 62(Je 1977):337-8; J. Phillips, HJ, 20(No. 2, 1977):515-6.

Larsen, Knud. Defense and the League of Nations. A Study in the Formation of Opinion in the Defense Policies of the Liberal and Conservative Parties, 1918-22. Aarhus: Universitetsforlaget, 1976. Rev. by W. D. Andersen, AHR, 82(Feb 1977): 121.

Lash, Joseph P. Roosevelt and Churchill, 1939-1941: The Partnership that Saved the West. New York: Norton, 1976. Rev. by W. F. Kimball, AHR, 82(Oct 1977):1098-9; D. C. Watt, JAmS, 11(Aug 1977):290-1.

Lasky, Melvin J. Utopia and Revolution. Chicago: U Chi Press, n. d. Rev. by P. Hollander, Comm, 63(May 1977):74-6.

Lasky, Victor. It Didn't Start with Watergate. n. l.: Dial, n. d. Rev. by M. F. Plattner, Comm, 64(Oct 1977):78-80.

Latorre, Dolores L. see Latorre, Felipe A.

Latorre, Felipe A. and Dolores L. Latorre. The Mexico Kickapoo Indians. Austin: U Texas Press, 1976. Rev. by D. E. Worcester, AIQ, 3(Spr 1977):58-9; E. J. Hindman, ChOk, 54 (Win 1976-7):542-4; C. R. McClure, ETHJ, 15(No. 1, 1977): 46.

Lau, Joseph S. M. and Timothy A. Ross, eds. Chinese Stories from Taiwan, 1960-1970. New York: Columbia U Press, 1976. Rev. by L. Dong, and M. K. Hom, JAS, 36(Aug 1977):738-41.

Lauer, J. Ph. and J. Leclant. Le Temple haut du complexe funeraire du roi Teti. Cairo: Institut Francais d'Archeologie Orientale du Caire, 1972. Rev. by H. Goedicke, JNES, 36 (Oct 1977):313-4.

Lauer, Jean-Philippe. Saqqara: The Royal Cemetary of Memphis-- Excavations and Discoveries since 1850. London: Thames and Hudson, 1976. Rev. by B. J. Kemp, Antiquity, 51(Jl 1977): 162-3; B. Williams, Archaeology, 30(Jan 1977):63-4.

Lauren, Paul Gordon. Diplomats and Bureaucrats. Stanford: Hoover Institution Press, 1976. Rev. by L. L. Farrar, Jr., AHR, 82(Apr 1977):351-2.

Laurens, Henry. The Papers of Henry Laurens. Edited by George C. Rogers, Jr., David R. Chesnutt, and Peggy J. Clark. Columbia, S. C.: Published for the South Carolina Historical Society by the University of South Carolina Press, 1976. Rev. by H. H. Johnson, GHQ, 51(Win 1977):362-3; J. J. McCusker, JAmS, 11(Dec 1977):424-5; J. P. Greene, JSH, 43(Nov 1977): 605-6; C. L. Ver Steeg, SCHM, 78(Jan 1977):74-5; R. M. Weir, WMQ, 34(Oct 1977):666-8.

Laux, James M. In First Gear: The French Automobile Industry
   to 1914. Montreal: McGill-Queen's U Press, 1976. Rev. by
   H. D. Peiter, AHR, 82(Oct 1977):984.

Lavender, David. California: A Bicentennial History. New York:
   Norton, and Nashville: American Association for State and
   Local History, 1976. Rev. by J. E. Moss, WHQ, 8(Jl 1977):
   332-3.

_____. Nothing Seemed Impossible: William C. Ralston and
   Early San Francisco. Palo Alto, Calif. : American
   West, 1975. Rev. by R. W. Lotchin, PHR, 46(Feb
   1977):132-3.

Lawrence, Alan, ed. China's Foreign Relations Since 1949. London: Routledge and Kegan Paul, 1975. Rev. by R. Simmons,
   CQ, No. 69(Mar 1977):174-5.

Lawrence, Patricia see Amyx, D. A.

Lawrence-Dow, Elizabeth. Autographs, 1701/2: Charles City/
   Prince George and Surrey Counties. Richmond: Dietz
   Press, 1976. Rev. by J. C. Van Horne, VMHB, 85(Jan
   1977):103-4.

Lawson, Merlin P. see Blouet, Brian W.

Lawson, Steven F. Black Ballots: Voting Rights in the South,
   1944-1969. New York: Columbia U Press, 1976. Rev. by
   I. A. Newby, AHR, 82(Oct 1977):1101; J. M. Matthews, JSH,
   43(Nov 1977):632-3.

Leander, Brigitta, comp. see Silva, Raul

LeBar, Frank M. , ed. Ethnic Groups of Insular Southeast Asia.
   New Haven: Human Relations Area Files, 1975. Rev. by M.
   D. Zamora, JAS, 36(Aug 1977):797-8.

Lebeaux, Richard. Young Man Thoreau. Amherst: U Massachusetts Press, 1977. Rev. by E. W. Carlson, AS,
   18(Fall 1977):108.

Lebow, Richard Ned. White Britain and Black Ireland: The Influence of Stereotypes on Colonial Policy. Philadelphia: Institute for the Study of Human Issues, 1976. Rev. by R. E.
   Burns, AHR, 82(Apr 1977):364-5.

Lebra, Joyce C. , ed. Japan's Greater East Asia Co-Prosperity
   Sphere in World War II. New York: Ox U Press, 1975. Rev.
   by W. I. Cohen, PHR, 46(May 1977):311-2.

LEBRA   184

_____, Joy Paulson, and Elizabeth Powers, eds. Women in
    Changing Japan. Boulder: Westview Press, 1976. Rev. by
    S. J. Pharr, JAS, 36(Aug 1977):756-8.

Lebra, Takie Sugiyama, and William P. Lebra, eds. Japanese
    Culture and Behavior: Selected Readings. Honolulu: U
    Press Hawaii, 1974. Rev. by C. Caldarola, JAS, 36(Feb
    1977):358-9.

Lebra, William P., ed. see Lebra, Takie Sugiyama, ed.

Leclant, J. see Lauer, J. Ph.

Ledbetter, Rosanna. A History of the Malthusian League, 1877-
    1927. Columbus: Ohio St. U Press, 1976. Rev. by P.
    Branca, AHR, 82(Je 1977):640.

Ledeen, Michael A. The First Duce: D'Annunzio at Fiume. Balti-
    more, JHU Press, n.d. Rev. by J. Shattan, Comm, 64(Dec
    1977):93-5; F. J. Coppa, History, 6(Nov/Dec 1977):46.

Lee, Arthur T. see Thomas, W. Stephen

Lee, Chae-Jin. Japan Faces China: Political and Economic Rela-
    tions in the Postwar Era. Baltimore: JHU Press, 1976.
    Rev. by A. W. Burks, AHR, 82(Je 1977):715-6.

Lee, Katie. Ten Thousand Goddam Cattle: A History of the Amer-
    ican Cowboy in Song, Story and Verse. Flagstaff: Northland,
    1976. Rev. by J. Roach, JAriH, 18(Sum 1977):223-4.

Leff, Gordon. William of Ockham: The Metamorphosis of Scho-
    lastic Discourse. Totowa, N.J.: Rowman and Littlefield,
    1975. Rev. by R. Mather, AHR, 82(Je 1977):618-9.

Legum, Colin. Vorster's Gamble for Africa: How the Search for
    Peace Failed. Rex Collings, 1976. Review by R. Blausten,
    AfAf, 76(Jl 1977):416-18.

Lehman, John. The Executive, Congress and Foreign Policy:
    Studies of the Nixon Administration. New York: Praeger,
    1976. Rev. by A. Z. Rubinstein, CurH, 72(Jan 1977):42.

Lehmann, Winfred P., ed. Language and Linguistics in the People's
    Republic of China. Austin: U Texas Press, 1975. Rev. by
    P. Kratochvil, CQ, No. 69(Mar 1977):184-6.

Lehning, Arthur, ed. Archives Bakounine, V, Michel Bakowunine
    et ses relations slaves, 1870-1875. Leiden: E. J. Brill,
    1974. Rev. by A. Kelly, EHR, 92(Oct 1977):864-6.

Lehovich, Dmitry B. White Against Red: The Life of General Anton
    Denikin. New York: Norton, 1974. Rev. by A. Levin, Histo-
    rian, 39(Feb 1977):358-9.

Leibundgut, Annalis. Die Rkomischen Bronzen Der Schweig, II,
    Avenches. Mainz am Rhein: Philipp von Zabern, 1976. Rev.
    by D. K. Hill, AJA, 81(Sum 1977):405-6.

Leichter, Howard M. Political Regime and Public Policy in the
    Philippines: A Comparison of Bacolod and Iloilo Cities.
    DeKalb: No Ill U Center for Southeast Asian Studies, 1975.
    Rev. by J. J. Green, JAS, 36(Feb 1977):389-90.

Leigh, Michael. Mobilizing Consent: Public Opinion and American
    Foreign Policy, 1937-1947. Westport, Conn.: Greenwood
    Press, 1976. Rev. by G. Q. Flynn, AHR, 82(Je 1977):763-4.

Leith, J. Clark. Ghana. New York and London: Col U Press for
    the National Bureau of Economic Research, 1974. Rev. by
    K. M. Langley, JEH, 37(Je 1977):482-5.

Leland, Joy. Firewater Myths: North American Indian Drinking
    and Alcohol Addiction. New Brunswick, N.J.: Rutgers Center
    of Alcohol Studies, 1976. Rev. by W. R. Jacobs, WHQ, 8
    (Oct 1977):468.

Lemay, J. A. Leo, ed. The Oldest Revolutionary: Essays on
    Benjamin Franklin. Philadelphia: U Penn Press, 1976. Rev.
    by R. Ketcham, WMQ, 34(Oct 1977):684-5.

Lenon, Robert see Young, Otis E., Jr.

Lensing, George S. and Ronald Moran. Four Poets and the Emotive
    Imagination. Baton Rouge: LSU Press, 1976. Rev. by L.
    Andrews, JAmS, 11(Dec 1977):414-15.

Leon, George B. Greece and the Great Powers, 1914-1917.
    Salonika: Institute for Balkan Studies, 1974. Rev. by S. V.
    Papacosma, AHR, 82(Apr 1977):391-2.

Leonard, Glen M. see Allen, James B.

Lerner, Ralph. Averroes on Plato's "Republic." Ithaca and Lon-
    don: Cor U Press, 1974. Rev. by A. L. Ivry, JNES, 36
    (Jl 1977):238-9.

Lesky, Erna, ed. A System of Complete Medical Policy: Selections
    from Johann Peter Frank. Baltimore: JHU Press, 1976. Rev.
    by R. C. Maulitz, AHR, 82(Apr 1977):381-2.

Lesser, Charles H., ed. The Sinews of Independence: Monthly
    Strength Reports of the Continental Army. Chicago: U Chi
    Press, 1976. Rev. by R. A. Brown, WMQ, 34(Jan 1977):
    154-7.

Lester, Jim. A Man for Arkansas: Sid McMath and the Southern
    Reform Tradition. Little Rock: Rose Pub. Co., 1976. Rev.
    by R. L. Muncy, JMiH, 39(Nov 1977):382-4.

Lester, Richard I. Confederate Finance and Purchasing in Great Britain. Charlottesville: U Press Va, 1975. Rev. by M. Lester, AHR, 81(Dec 1976):1254.

Leuchtenburg, W. E. see Morison, S. E.

Leuschner, Joachim. Deutschland Im Spaten Mittelalter ('Deutsche Geschicte'). Gottingen: Vandenhoeck und Reprecht, 1975. Rev. by H. J. Cohn, History, 62(Je 1977):314.

Leventhal, Herbert. In the Shadow of the Enlightenment: Occultism and Renaissance Science in Eighteenth Century America. New York: NYU Press, 1976. Rev. by C. Hansen, AHR, 82(Apr 1977):431; J. A. Sokolow, MiA, 59(Oct 1977):203.

Levering, Ralph B. American Opinion and the Russian Alliance, 1939-1945. Chapel Hill: U NC Press, 1976. Rev. by M. Small, AHR, 82(Je 1977):764-5.

Lévesque, Jacques. L'URSS et la révolution cubaine. Montreal: Presses de la fondation nationale des sciences politiques, 1976. Rev. by J. E. Fagg, AHR, 82(Je 1977):704-5.

Levi, Fabio see Bongiovanni, Bruno

Levine, David Allan. Internal Combustion: The Races in Detroit, 1915-1926. Westport, Conn.: Greenwood Press, 1976. Rev. by K. L. Kusmer, AHR, 82(Apr 1977):461-2.

Levine, Donald N. Greater Ethiopia: The Evolution of a Multiethnic Society. Chicago: U Chi Press, 1974. Rev. by H. J. Schultz, JAAS, 12(Jan/Oct 1977):302-3.

Le Vine, Victor T. Political Corruption: The Ghana Case. Stanford: Hoover Institution Press, 1975. Rev. by J. P. Smaldone, JAAS, 12(Jan/Oct 1977):276-8.

Levins, Lynn Gartrell. Faulkner's Heroic Design: The Yoknapatawpha Novels. Athens: U Georgia Press, 1976. Rev. by D. Tallack, JAmS, 11(Dec 1977):308-9.

Levitan, Sar A. and William B. Johnston. Indian Giving: Federal Programs for Native Americans. Baltimore: Johns Hopkins U Press, 1975. Rev. by K. R. Philp, AIQ, 3(Spr 1977):64-5.

Levy, David W., ed. see Brandeis, Louis D.

Levy, Jacques E. César Chávez: Autobiography of La Causa. New York: Norton, 1975. Rev. by L. L. Arroyo, HAHR, 57(Feb 1977):107-108; O. J. Martinez, WHQ, 8(Jan 1977): 60-1.

Levy, Jerrold E. and Stephen J. Kunitz. Indian Drinking: Navajo

Practices and Anglo-American Theories. New York: John
Wiley, 1974. Rev. by M. E. F. Mathur, AIQ, 3(Aut 1977):
249-51.

Levy, Richard S. The Downfall of the Anti-Semitic Political Parties
in Imperial Germany. New Haven: Yale U Press, 1975. Rev.
by M. A. Meyer, AHR, 82(Feb 1977):127; P. Pulzer, History,
62(Feb 1977):160-1.

LeWarne, Charles Pierce. Utopias on Puget Sound, 1885-1915.
Seattle: U Wash Press, 1975. Rev. by H. H. Quint, PHR,
46(May 1977):297-9.

Lewicki, Tadeusz. West African Food in the Middle Ages, according
to Arabic Sources. London: Cambridge U Press, 1974. Rev.
by A. H. M. Kirk-Greene, Africa, 47(No. 2, 1977):226-7.

Lewin, Bernhard. Notes on Cabali: The Arabic Dialect Spoken by
the Alawis of "Jebel Ansariye." Goteborg, Sweden: Acta
Universitatis Gothoburgensis, 1974. Rev. by C. G. Killean,
JNES, 36(Jan 1977):63-4.

Lewis, Bernard, ed. Islam and the Arab World: Faith, People,
Culture. n.l.: Knopf, n.d. Rev. by W. M. Brinner, Comm,
63(Apr 1977):86-8.

Lewis, David L. District of Columbia: A Bicentennial History.
New York: Norton, 1976. Rev. by R. A. Burchell, JAmS,
11(Dec 1977):411-12; M. H. Ebner, History, 6(Oct 1977):12;
F. C. Rosenberger, JSH, 43(Nov 1977):648-9.

_____. The Public Image of Henry Ford, an American Folk
Hero and His Company. Detroit: Wayne State U Press, 1976.
Rev. by W. V. Hill, MichH, 61(Spr 1977):91-3; M. Klein,
AHI, 12(May 1977):50.

Lewis, Ralph H. Manual for Museums. Washington: National Park
Service, 1976. Rev. by F. Voss, AmArc, 40(Jl 1977):352.

Lewis, Willie Newbury. Between Sun and Sod: An Informal History
of the Texas Panhandle. College Station: Texas A&M U
Press, 1976. Rev. by B. D. Ledbetter, JOW, 16(Jl 1977):
95.

Leyda, Jay. Dianying: An Account of Films and the Film Audience
in China. Cambridge, Mass.: MIT Press, 1972. Rev. by R.
Witke, AHR, 82(Apr 1977):417.

Lhotsky, Alphons. Aus dem Nachlass. Munich: R. Oldenbourg
Verlag, 1976. Rev. by H. Gross, AHR, 82(Feb 1977):80.

Li, Dun J., trans. The Civilization of China: From the Formative
Period to the Coming of the West. New York: Scribners,
1975. Rev. by C. Leban, AHR, 82(Feb 1977):157. 8.

LI   188

Li, Lincoln. The Japanese Army in North China, 1937-1941: Prob-
      lems of Political and Economic Control. Tokyo: Ox U Press,
      1975. Rev. by W. Whitson, AHR, 82(Apr 1977):418; I. Nish,
      EHR, 92(Oct 1977):933-4.

Licko, Miroslav Jan, ed. see Kvetko, Martin, ed.

Lieberman, Jethro K. Milestones! 200 Years of American Law:
      Milestones in Our Legal History. New York: Ox U Press,
      1976. Rev. by J. W. Ely, Jr., JSH, 43(Aug 1977):444-5; G.
      W. Gawalt, NEQ, 50(Sep 1977):539-41.

Lieberthal, Kenneth. A Research Guide to Central Party and Gov-
      ernment Meetings in China, 1949-1975. White Plains, N.Y.:
      International Arts & Sciences Press, 1976. Rev. by D. S. G.
      Goodman, CQ, No. 71(Sep 1977):609-10.

Limbrey, Susan. Soil Science and Archaeology. New York: Aca-
      demic Press, 1975. Rev. by J. G. Evans, Antiquity, 51(Mar
      1977):70-1.

Lind, L. R. Studies in Pre-Vesalian Anatomy. Philadelphia:
      American Philosophical Society, 1975. Rev. by G. B. Risse,
      AHR, 82(Apr 1977):382-3.

Lindberg, David C. Theories of Vision from Al-Kindi to Kepler.
      Chicago: U Chi Press, 1976. Rev. by B. Eastwood, AHR,
      82(Apr 1977):334.

Lindberg, Staffan see Djurfeldt, Goran

Linden, Glenn M. Politics or Principle: Congressional Voting on
      the Civil War Amendments and Pro-Negro Measures, 1838-69.
      Seattle: U Wash Press, 1976. Rev. by L. P. Curry, AHR,
      82(Oct 1977):1077-8.

_____, and Matthew T. Downey, eds. Teaching American History:
      Structured Inquiry Approaches. Boulder: ERIC Clearinghouse,
      1975. Rev. by L. D. Stephens, HT, 10(May 1977):486-7.

Linden, Rolf. The Inevitable Equation: The Antithetic Pattern of
      Theodore Dreiser's Thought and Art. Upsala: Studia Angli-
      stica Upsaliensia, 1973. Rev. by M. Leaf, JAmS, 11(Aug
      1977):291-3.

Lindquist, Emory. Bethany in Kansas: The History of a College.
      Lindsborg, Kan.: Bethany College, 1975. Rev. by J. F.
      Hopkins, AHR, 82(Feb 1977):187-8.

Linebaugh, Peter, ed. see Hay, Douglas, ed.

Lineberry, Robert L., ed. see Bonjean, Charles M., ed.

Link, Arthur S., et al. The Papers of Woodrow Wilson. Princeton: Prin U Press, 1974. Rev. by E. D. Cronon, JSH, 43(May 1977):316-8.

Linkh, Richard M. American Catholicism and European Immigrants, 1900-1924. New York: Center for Migration Studies, 1975. Rev. by J. P. Dolan, AHR, 82(Apr 1977):460.

Lipke, William C. and Philip N. Grime, ed. Vermont Landscape Images 1776-1976. Brattleboro, Vt.: Stephen Greene Press, 1976. Rev. by R. J. Hefner, VH, 45(Win 1977):47-8.

Lipp, Solomon. Three Chilean Thinkers. Waterloo, Ontario: Wilfrid Laurier U Press, 1975. Rev. by S. Collier, JLAS, 9 (May 1977):162-3.

Lippit, Victor D. Land Reform and Economic Development in China. New York: International Arts and Science Press, 1975. Rev. by R. H. Myers, CQ, No. 70(Je 1977):420-2.

Lipset, Seymour Martin and David Riesman. Education and Politics at Harvard. New York: McGraw-Hill, 1975. Rev. by S. Diamond, AHR, 81(Dec 1977):1277-78.

Liss, Peggy K. Mexico Under Spain, 1521-1556: Society and Origins of Nationality. Chicago: U Chi Press, 1975. Rev. by M. M. Smith, JOW, 16(Jl 1977):94; R. E. Greenleaf, NMHR, 52(Jl 1977):343.

Lissak, Moshe. Military Roles in Modernization: Civil-Military Relations in Thailand and Burma. Beverly Hills: Sage Publications, 1976. Rev. by D. A. Wilson, JAS, 36(May 1977): 589.

Little, A. J. Deceleration in the Eighteenth-Century British Economy. London: Croom Helm, 1976. Rev. by J. R. Harris, History, 62(Feb 1977):135-6.

Little, Bryan. Sir Christopher Wren: A Historical Biography. London: Robert Hale, 1975. Rev. by S. J. Greenblatt, AHR, 82(Feb 1977):98.

Littlejohn, Bruce, photography and Wayland Drew, text. Superior: The Haunted Shore. Toronto: Gage Publishing, 1975. Rev. by R. C. Wheeler, MinnH, 45(Spr 1977):205.

Litvin, Martin. The Young Mary, 1817-1861. Galesburg, Ill.: Log City Books, 1976. Rev. by R. D. Hoffsommer, CWTI, 16(Aug 1977):49.

Liu, James J. Y. Chinese Theories of Literature. Chicago: U Chi Press, 1975. Rev. by P. Link, CQ, No. 69(Mar 1977): 181-4.

Liversidge, Joan. Everyday Life in the Roman Empire. New York:
   Putnam, n.d. Rev. by R. J. A. Wilson, Antiquity, 51(Nov
   1977):247-8.

Livet, Georges. L'équilibre européen de la fin du XVe a là fin du
   XVIIIe siècle. Paris: Preses Universitaires de France,
   1976. Rev. by W. Roosen, AHR, 82(Oct 1977):948.

Loades, D. M. Politics and the Nation, 1450-1660: Obedience,
   Resistance and Public Order. Atlantic Highlands, N.J.:
   Humanities Press, 1975. Rev. by R. M. Warnicke, AHR,
   82(Feb 1977):91.

Lobel, M. D. and W. H. Johns, ed. The Atlas of Historic Towns,
   vol. II. London: Scholar Press, 1977. Rev. by B. Harvey,
   EHR, 92(Oct 1977):879-80.

Locke, John. The Correspondence of John Locke. Vols. 1 & 2.
   Oxford: Ox U Press, 1976. Rev. by E. J. Hundert, AHR,
   82(Oct 1977):960.

Locke, R. R. French Legitimists and the Politics of Moral Order
   in the Early Third Republic. Princeton: Prin U Press, 1974.
   Rev. by R. Gibson, ESR, 7(Oct 1977):458-64; W. H. Sewell,
   Jr., JIH, 7(Win 1977):542-4.

Lockhart, James and Enrique Otte, trans. and eds. Letters and
   People of the Spanish Indies: Sixteenth Century. New York:
   Cam U Press, 1976. Rev. by J. L. Phelan, AHR, 81(Dec
   1976):1284; R. C. Padden, HAHR, 57(May 1977):328-9; N. F.
   Martin, Historian, 39(May 1977):593-4.

_____, ed. see Anderson, Arthur J. O., ed.

Lockwood, Stephen Chapman. Augustine Heard and Company, 1858-
   1862: American Merchants in China. Cambridge, Mass.:
   Harvard U Press, 1971.

Lodge, Henry Cabot. As It Was: An Inside View of Politics and
   Power in the '50s and '60s. New York: Norton, 1976. Rev.
   by J. G. Hurstfield, JAmS, 11(Dec 1977):392-3; F. Russell,
   NEQ, 50(Je 1977):380-1.

Loebl, Eugen. My Mind on Trial. n.l.: Harcourt Brace Jovanovich, n.d. Rev. by S. Cropsey, Comm, 63(Apr 1977):84-6.

Loehr, Max. Ancient Chinese Jades from the Grenville L. Winthrop
   Collection in the Fogg Art Museum, Harvard University. Cam-
   bridge: Fogg Art Museum, Harvard U, 1975. Rev. by W.
   Trousdale, JAS, 36(May 1977):545-7.

Loewe, Michael. Crisis and Conflict in Han China, 104 B.C. to
   A.D. 9. Totowa, N.J.: Rowman and Littlefield, 1975. Rev.
   by Ying-shih yu, AHR, 82(Je 1977):717-8.

Loewenberg, Robert J. Equality on the Oregon Frontier: Jason
   Lee and the Methodist Mission, 1834-43. Seattle: U Wash
   Press, 1976. Rev. by J. F. Cocks, III, AHR, 82(Je 1977):
   742; J. A. Hussey, OrHQ, 78(Je 1977):86-8; F. Somkin, PHR,
   46(Aug 1977):500-2.

Logan, Ben. The Land Remembers: The Story of a Farm and Its
   People. New York: Viking, 1975. Rev. by L. Woiwode,
   WMH, 60(Spr 1977):235-6.

Lomax, Bill. Hungary 1956. New York: St. Martin's Press,
   1977. Rev. by B. K. Kiraly, History, 6(Oct 1977):17-8.

Lombard, Maurice. Etudes d'économie médiévale. Paris and the
   Hague: Mouton, 1974. Rev. by A. R. Lewis, JEH, 37(Je
   1977):541-2.

Lombard-Jourdan, Anne. Paris-Genèse de la 'ville': La rive
   droite de la Seine des origines a 1223. Paris: Editions du
   Centre National de la Recherche Scientifique, 1975. Rev. by
   S. Reynolds, EHR, 92(Oct 1977):882-3.

Lombardi, John V. People and Places in Colonial Venezuela.
   Bloomington: Ind U Press, 1976. Rev. by W. Borah, AHR,
   82(Je 1977):782-3; S. Blank, WMQ, 34(Oct 1977):312-3.

Long, John Hamilton, ed. see Cappon, Lester J., ed.

Longacre, Edward G. Mounted Raids of the Civil War. South
   Brunswick, N.J.: A. S. Barnes, 1975. Rev. by A. R. Sunseri, AHR, 81(Dec 1976):1252.

Longeon, Claude. Une province française à la Renaissance: La
   vie intellectuelle en Forez au XVIe siècle. Saint-Etienne:
   Centre d'Etudes Foréziennes, 1975. Rev. by E. Schalk, AHR,
   82(Oct 1977):976-7.

Loomis, Albertine. For Whom Are the Stars? Honolulu: U Press
   Hawaii, 1976. Rev. by G. Barrett, WHQ, 8(Oct 1977):477-8.

Lopez, Adalberto. The Revolt of the Comuneros, 1721-1735: A
   Study in the Colonial History of Paraguay. Cambridge, Mass.:
   Schenkman, 1976. Rev. by J. S. Saeger, AHR, 82(Oct 1977):
   1110.

Lopez, Carlos V., ed. see Beilharz, Edwin A., ed.

Lopez, Claude-Anne and Eugenia W. Herbert. The Private Franklin:
   The Man and His Family. New York: Norton, 1975. Rev. by
   E. Cometti, WVH, 38(Jan 1977):163-5.

Lopez, E. Pareja see Gonzales, F. Molina

Lopez-Soria, Jose Ignacio. Des-Composicion de la dominacion
hispánica en el Perú. Lima, Peru: Editorial Arica, n.d.
Rev. by D. Gleason, HAHR, 57(Feb 1977):158-9.

Lorton, David. The Juridical Terminology of International Relations
in Egyptian Texts through Dynasty XVIII. Baltimore and London: JHU Press, 1974. Rev. by T. J. Logan, JNES, 36(Jl
1977):220.

Lottinville, Savoie. The Rhetoric of History. Norman: U Ok
Press, 1976. Rev. by T. W. Dillard, ArkHQ, 36(Spr 1977):
92-4; W. Rundell, Jr., PHR, 46(May 1977):279-80; R. A.
Billington, WHQ, 8(Jan 1977):68-9.

Louis, William Roger. Imperialism: The Robinson and Gallagher
Controversy. New York: New Viewpoints, 1976. Rev. by
P. M. Kennedy, HJ, 20(No. 3, 1977):761-9.

Lovelock, Yann see Bandopadhyaya, Manik

Lovell, Broward. Gone with the Hickory Stick: School Days in
Marion County, 1845-1960. Ocala, Florida: Green's Printing,
1975. Rev. by E. R. Ott, FHQ, 55(Jan 1977):370-1.

Loveman, Brian. Struggle in the Countryside. Bloomington: Ind
U Press, 1976. Rev. by O. E. S., CurH, 72(Feb 1977):79;
A. J. Bauer, HAHR, 57(May 1977):356-8; T. L. McCoy, TAm,
34(Oct 1977):303-4.

Lovett, Robert W., ed. Documents from the Harvard University
Archives, 1638-1750. Parts 4 and 5. Boston: Colonial
Society of Massachusetts, 1975. Rev. by R. Middlekauff,
AHR, 82(Feb 1977):171-2.

Lovoll, Odd Sverre. A Folk Epic: The Bygdelag in America.
Boston: Twayne, 1975. Rev. by C. H. Chrislock, AHR,
82(Dec 1976):1264-65.

Low, D. A. and Alison Smith, eds. History of East Africa. Volume III. Oxford: Ox U Press, 1976. Rev. by T. Ranger,
History, 62(Je 1977):276-9; M. Twaddle, Africa, 47(No. 3,
1977):331.

Lowance, Mason I., Jr. Increase Mather. New York: Twayne
Pub., 1974. Rev. by E. R. Fingerhut, WMQ, 34(Jan 1977):
168-9.

Lowe, C. J. and F. Mazari. Italian Foreign Policy 1870-1940.
London: Routledge & Kegan Paul, 1975. Rev. by E. Robertson, ESR, 7(Jan 1977):125-8.

Lowenkopf, Martin. Politics in Liberia: The Conservative Road to
Development. Hoover Institution Press, n.d. Rev. by R.

Jefferies, AfAf, 76(Apr 1977):265-7; C. Fyfe, AHR, 82(Je 1977):710-1.

Lowens, Irving. A Bibliography of Songsters Printed in America Before 1821. Worcester, Mass.: The American Antiquarian Society, 1976. Rev. by N. E. Tawa, NEQ, 50(Je 1977): 378-80.

Lowenthal, Abraham F., ed. The Peruvian Experiment: Continuity and Change under Military Rule. Princeton, N.J.: Prin U Press, 1975. Rev. by R. E. Scott, HAHR, 57(Feb 1977): 170-2.

Lowrance, Mason I., and Georgia B. Bumgardner, eds. Massachusetts Broadsides of the American Revolution. Amherst: U Mass Press, 1976. Rev. by J. D. Haskell, Jr., NEQ, 50 (Je 1977):358-9.

Loy, William G., producer. Atlas of Oregon. Eugene: U Ore Books, 1976. Rev. by H. M. Dole, OrHQ, 78(Je 1977):178-9.

Lucas, Homer C. see Dickson, Brenton H.

Lucas, Marion Brunson. Sherman and the Burning of Columbia. College Station: Tex A&M U Press, 1975. Rev. by R. M. McMurry, AHR, 82(Je 1977):747; J. G. Barrett, CWH, 23(Je 1977):183; A. Costel, CWTI, 16(Aug 1977):50; A. R. Sunseri, JSH, 43(Aug 1977):464-5.

Lucas, Paul R. Valley of Discord: Church and Society along the Connecticut River, 1636-1725. Hanover, N.H.: U Press New England, 1976. Rev. by A. T. Vaughan, AHR, 82(Je 1977): 730-1; S. Bercovitich, WMQ, 34(Jan 1977):136-8.

Lucas, S. Emmett, Jr. The Alstons and Allstons of North and South Carolina with Supplementary Material on the La Bruce, Pawley, and Ward Families of Waccamaw. Easley, S.C.: Southern Historical Press, 1976. Rev. by D. T. Lawson, SCHM, 78 (Apr 1977):150-2.

Luckert, Karl W. Olmec Religion, a Key to Middle America and Beyond. Norman: U Ok Press, 1976. Rev. by W. Bray, JLAS, 9(May 1977):152-3; J. D. L. Holmes, TAm, 33(Apr 1977):682.

Luckham, R. see D. Austin, ed.

Ludz, Peter Christian, ed. Soziologie Und Sozialgeschichte. Opladen: Westdeutscher Verlag, 1972. Rev. by K. G. Faber, H&T, 16(Feb 1977):51-66.

Lumpkin, Katherine DuPre. The Emancipation of Angelina Grimke. Chapel Hill: U North Carolina Press, 1974. Rev. by C. Crowe, FCHQ, 51(Apr 1977):208-10.

Lundstrom, John B. The First South Pacific Campaign: Pacific
    Fleet Strategy, Dec. 1941-June 1942. Annapolis: Naval
    Institute Press, 1976. Rev. by E. B. Potter, AHR, 82(Oct
    1977):1099-1100.

Lunt, James. John Burgoyne of Saratoga. New York: Harcourt
    Brace Jovanovich, 1975. Rev. by J. G. Rossie, WMQ, 34
    (Apr 1977):333-4.

Lutinen, Pertti. The Baltic Question, 1903-1908. Helsinki:
    Suomalainen Tiedeakatemia, 1975. Rev. by E. Anderson,
    AHR, 82(Apr 1977):399-400.

Luraghi, Raimondo. Gli Stati Uniti. Turin: Unione Tipografico-
    Editrice Torinese, 1974. Rev. by E. M. Thomas, AHR, 82
    (Feb 1977):168.

Luttwak, Edward N. The Grand Strategy of the Roman Empire:
    From the First Century A. D. to the Third. Baltimore: JHU
    Press, 1977. Rev. by R. MacMullen, AHR, 82(Oct 1977):
    930-1; B. Brodie, Comm, 64(Sep 1977):73-6.

Lutz, Heinrich, ed. see Engel-Janosi, Friedrich, ed.

Luza, Radomir. Austro-German Relations in the Anschluss Era.
    Princeton: Prin U Press, 1975. Rev. by K. Von Klemperer,
    AHR, 82(Apr 1977):380-1; R. J. Crampton, History, 62(Feb
    1977):167-8; F. Stambrook, Historian, 39(May 1977):559-60.

Lykes, Richard Wayne. Higher Education and the United States
    Office of Education (1867-1953). Washington, D.C.: U.S.
    Office of Education, 1975. Rev. by W. Rudy, AHR, 82(Feb
    1977):203-4.

Lynch, Joseph H. Simoniacal Entry into Religious Life from 1000
    to 1260: A Social, Economic and Legal Study. Columbus:
    Ohio St. U Press, 1976. Rev. by L. K. Little, AHR, 82
    (Oct 1977):934-5.

Lyndersay, D. see Ladan, U.

Lyon, David see Preston, Antony

Lyons, Charles H. To Wash an Aethiop White: British Ideas about
    Black African Educability, 1530-1690. New York: Columbia
    U Press, 1975. Rev. by G. Stepperson, AfAf, 76(Apr 1977):
    262-3; W. H. Pease, AHR, 82(Feb 1977):92.

Lyons, F. S. L. Charles Stewart Parnell. New York: Ox U
    Press, 1977. Rev. by G. Costigan, History, 6(Nov/Dec
    1977):45.

Lyttleton, Margaret. Baroque Architecture in Classical Antiquity.

Ithaca, N.Y.: Cor U Press; London: Thames and Hudson, 1974. Rev. by R. Scranton, JNES, 36(Jl 1977):228-30.

Maamagi, V., et al., eds. History of the Estonian SSR; from March 1917 to the Beginning of the 1950s. Tallinn: Kirjastus "Eesti Raamat," 1971. Rev. by T. Raun, AHR, 82(Feb 1977):146-7.

Mabro, Robert and Samir Radwan. The Industrialization of Egypt, 1939-1973: Policy and Performance. New York: Ox U Press, 1976. Rev. by R. L. Tignor, AHR, 82(Je 1977):707.

Macaulay, Neill. The Prestes Column: Revolution in Brazil. New York: New Viewpoints, 1974. Rev. by T. E. Skidmore, AHR, 82(Feb 1977):229-30.

McBride, Paul. Culture Clash: Immigrants and Reformers, 1880-1920. San Francisco: R&E Research Associates, 1975. Rev. by M. G. Karni, A&W, 19(Sum 1977):176-77.

McBride, Theresa M. The Domestic Revolution: The Modernisation of Household Service in England and France, 1820-1920. New York: Holmes and Meier, 1976. Rev. by J. W. Scott, AHR, 82(Je 1977):625; N. A. Ferguson, Historian, 39(May 1977): 541-3; E. Glass, History, 62(Je 1977):337.

McCaffrey, Lawrence J. The Irish Diaspora in America. Bloomington: Ind U Press, 1976. Rev. by W. D. Griffin, NEQ, 50 (Je 1977):356-8.

McCaffrey, Lee, ed. see Kantner, John F., ed.

McCall, Daniel F. and Edna G. Bay, ed. Essays in African Iconology. New York: Holmes & Meier, 1975. Rev. by R. Kauenhoven-Janzen, JAAS, 12(Jan/Oct 1977):287-8.

McCamant, John F. see Duff, Ernest A.

McCarty, Clara S. Duels in Virginia and Nearby Bladensburg. Richmond: Dietz Press, 1976. Rev. by J. T. Moore, VMHB, 85(Jan 1977):120-1.

McCarty, Kieran. Desert Documentary: The Spanish Years, 1767-1821. Tucson: Arizona Historical Society, 1976. Rev. by R. L. Ives, A&W, 19(Spr 1977):90-92.

Macciocchi, Maria Antonietta. Daily Life in Revolutionary China. New York: Monthly Review Press, 1972. Rev. by J. Maier, JAAS, 12(Jan/Oct 1977):268-9.

McClelland, Peter D. Causal Explanation and Model Building in History, Economics, and the New Economic History. Ithaca, N.Y.: Cor U Press, 1975. Rev. by D. Braybrooke, H&T,

16(Oct 1977):337-54; H. D. Woodman, JIH, 7(Win 1977):549-51.

Maccoby, Michael. The Gamesman. n.l.: Simon & Schuster, n.d. Rev. by S. Rothman, Comm, 63(Je 1977):94-6.

MacColl, E. Kimbark. The Shaping of a City: Business and Politics in Portland, Oregon, 1885-1915. Portland: Georgian Press, 1976. Rev. by M. Clark, OrHQ, 78(Je 1977):89-90; G. Barth, WHQ, 8(Oct 1977):474-5.

McConal, Jon see Stricklin, Al

McCormack, A. R., and Ian Macpherson, eds. Aties in the West. Ottawa: National Museum of Man, 1975. Rev. by T. Copp, CHR, 58(Mar 1977):70-2.

McCormmach, Russell, ed. Historical Studies in the Physical Sciences, vol. 4. Princeton: Prin U Press, 1975. Rev. by A. L. Norberg, AHR, 82(Feb 1977):66; J. Z. Fullmer, AHR, 82(Oct 1977):922-3.

_____, and Lewis Pyenson, eds. Historical Studies in the Physical Sciences, vol. 8. Baltimore: JHU Press, 1977. Rev. by R. E. Filner, History, 6(Nov/Dec 1977):41.

McCorry, Jesse J. see Barker, Lucius J.

McCoy, Ralph E., comp. Theodore Schroeder, a Cold Enthusiast: A Bibliography. Carbondale: So Ill U Libraries, 1973. Rev. by T. Walch, JISHS, 70(Aug 1977):254.

McCreary, Guy Weddington. From Glory to Oblivion: The Real Truth about the Mexican Revolution. New York: Vantage Press, 1974. Rev. by R. E. Ruiz, NMHR, 52(Jl 1977):259-60.

McCullough, David. The Path Between the Seas: The Creation of the Panama Canal 1870-1914. New York: Simon and Schuster, 1977. Rev. by M. Baker, History, 6(Oct 1977):2.

McDaniel, Ferris L. A Reader's Hebrew-English Lexicon of the Old Testament. Dallas: privately published, 1975. Rev. by D. Pardee, JNES, 36(Oct 1977):319-20.

McDermott, John Francis, ed. The Spanish in the Mississippi Valley, 1762-1804. Urbana: U Ill Press, 1974. Rev. by J. A. Carrigan, LaH, 18(Win 1977):111-3.

Mac Donagh, Oliver. Early Victorian Government, 1830-1870. New York: Holmes & Meier, 1977. Rev. by P. McCandless, History, 6(Oct 1977):19-20.

McDonald, Archie P. Travis. Austin, Texas: Jenkins Publishing;
Pemberton Press, 1976. Rev. by W. P. Vaughn, JSH, 43
(Nov 1977):619-20.

McDonald, Forest. The Presidency of Thomas Jefferson. Lawrence:
U Press of Kansas, 1976. Rev. by R. M. Calhoon, FHQ, 55
(Apr 1977):493-5; E. L. Schapsmeier, JOW, 16(Jan 1977):79;
P. W. Brewer, JSH, 43(Aug 1977):448-50; R. S. Klein, WMH,
60(Sum 1977):344-6; S. H. Hochman, WVH, 38(Apr 1977):237-
9; C. E. Prince, WMQ, 34(Jl 1977):505.

McDowell, R. B. The Church of Ireland 1869-1969. London:
Routledge and Kegan Paul, 1975. Rev. by O. Chadwick, History, 62(Feb 1977):145.

McElderry, Andrea Lee. Shanghai Old-Style Banks (Ch'ien-Chuang),
1800-1935. Ann Arbor: Center for Chinese Studies, U Mich,
1976. Rev. by S. M. Jones, JAS, 36(May 1977):557-8.

McFadden, Cyra. The Serial. n.l.: Knopf, n.d. Rev. by D.
Merkin, Comm, 64(Oct 1977):76-8.

McFarland, Gerald W. Mugwumps, Morals and Politics, 1884-1920.
Amherst: U Mass Press, 1975. Rev. by J. M. Dobson, AHR,
82(Apr 1977):459; T. C. Hinckley, PNQ, 68(Jan 1977):38-9.

McFarland, Keith D. Harry H. Woodring: A Political Biography
of FDR's Controversial Secretary of War. Lawrence: U
Press Kan, 1975. Rev. by G. E. Wheeler, AHR, 82(Apr
1977):468-9; F. W. Schrauben, Historian, 39(May 1977):587-
8; J. D. Elenbaas, MichH, 61(Sum 1977):168-70.

MacFarlane, Alan, ed. The Diary of Ralph Josselin, 1616-1683.
London: Ox U Press, 1976. Rev. by M. Lee, Jr., AHR,
82(Oct 1977):959-60.

McGee, J. Sears. The Godly Man in Stuart England: Anglicans,
Puritans, and the Two Tables, 1620-1670. New Haven: Yale
U Press, 1976. Rev. by Tai Liu, AHR, 82(Je 1977):631-2.

McGiffert, Michael, ed. God's Plot: The Paradoxes of Puritan
Piety, being the Autobiography & Journal of Thomas Shepard.
Amherst: U Mass Press, 1972. Rev. by F. J. Bremer,
WMQ, 34(Oct 1977):678-81.

MacGillivray, Royce. Restoration Historians and the English Civil
War. Hague: Martinus Nijhoff, 1974. Rev. by J. W. Daly,
CHR, 58(Je 1977):240-1.

McGovern, James R. The Emergence of a City in the Modern
South: Pensacola 1900-1945. Pensacola, Fla.: Author,
1976. Rev. by H. L. Platt, JSH, 43(Nov 1977):643-4.

McGowan, Don C. Grassland Settlers: The Swift Current Region during the Era of the Ranching Frontier. Regina: U Regina, 1975. Rev. by D. Breen, CHR, 58(Mar 1977):74-5.

McGrath, Partick. The Merchant Venturers of Bristol. Bristol: Society of Merchant Venturers of Bristol, 1975. Rev. by G. D. Ramsay, History, 62(Feb 1977):86.

MacGregor, James G. Father Lacombe. Edmonton: Hurtig, 1975. Rev. by P. Crunican, CHR, 58(Je 1977):228-30.

McGuire, Brian Partick. Conflict and Continuity at Øm Abbey: A Cistercian Experience in Medieval Denmark. Copenhagen: Museum Tusculanum, 1976. Rev. by J. H. Lynch, AHR, 82 (Je 1977):621; C. Morris, History, 62(Feb 1977):105-6.

Machaliński, Zbigniew. Maritime Economic Thought in the Second Republic, 1919-1939. Wroclaw: Ossolineum, 1975. Rev. by S. M. Horack, AHR, 82(Apr 1977):397.

Macias, Anna. Genesis de Gobierno Constitucional en México: 1808-1820. Mexico: SepSetentas, 1973. Rev. by H. M. Hamill, HAHR, 57(Feb 1977):118-21.

Maciel, David, comp. and Patricia Bueno, comp. Aztlán: Historia contemporánea de pueblo chicano. Mexico: SepSetentas, 1976. Rev. by F. D. Almaraz, Jr., HAHR, 57(Aug 1977):565-6.

McIntosh, James T., ed. The Papers of Jefferson Davis. Baton Rouge: LSU Press, 1974. Rev. by H. P. Jones, LaH, 18 (Win 1977):113-4.

Mack, Arien, ed. Death in American Experience. New York: Schocken Books, 1973. Rev. by T. N. Tentler, CSSH, 19 (Oct 1977):511-22.

McKay, John P. Tramways and Trolleys: The Rise of Urban Mass Transport in Europe. Princeton: Prin U Press, 1976. Rev. by C. L. Gilb, AHR, 82(Apr 1977):349-50; A. D. Anderson, JIH, 8(Aut 1977):372-3.

McKenzie, George W. The Economics of the Euro-Currency System. New York: John Wiley, 1976. Rev. by H. McRae, JEH, 37 (Sep 1977):827-8.

McKenzie, Robert H., ed. The Rising South, Volume II: Southern Universities and the South. University, Alabama: U Alabama Press, 1976. Rev. by L. N. Allen, AlaR, 30(Jl 1977):238-9.

McKeown, T. The Modern Rise of Population. London: Edward Arnold, 1976. Rev. by R. Mitchison, EHR, 92(Oct 1977): 907-8.

Mackie, Euan W. Science and Society in Prehistoric Britain. New
    York: St. Martin's Press, 1977. Rev. by K. A. R. Kennedy,
    History, 6(Oct 1977):20.

Mackie, J. A. C., ed. The Chinese in Indonesia. Honolulu: U
    Press Hawaii, 1976. Rev. by M. F. Somers Heidhues, JAS,
    36(Aug 1977):796.

McKusick, Marshall. The Iowa Northern Border Brigade. Iowa
    City: Office of the State Archaeologist, 1975. Rev. by T. N.
    Hyde, AI, 44(Fall 1977):147-9.

MacLachlan, Colin M. Criminal Justice in Eighteenth Century Mex-
    ico: A Study of the Tribunal of the Acordada. Berkeley: U
    Cal Press, 1974. Rev. by C. Gibson, AHR, 81(Dec 1977):
    1284-85; M. P. Costeloe, JLAS, 9(May 1977):154-6.

McLaurin, Melton see Thomason, Michael

McLean, Iain. Keir Hardie. New York: St. Martin's Press, 1975.
    Rev. by E. Moritz, Jr., Historian, 39(May 1977):546-7.

McLean, Malcolm D., ed. Papers Concerning Robertson's Colony
    in Texas. Fort Worth, Texas: TCU Press, 1976. Rev. by
    M. S. Henson, JSH, 43(Aug 1977):453-4.

Maclean, Norman. A River Runs Through It and Other Stories.
    Chicago: U Chi Press, 1976. Rev. by E. H. Eby, PNQ,
    68(Jan 1977):45-6.

McLeish, Kenneth, comp. see Nichols, Roger, comp.

McLellan, David S. Dean Acheson: The State Department Years.
    New York: Dodd, Mead, 1976. Rev. by A. DeConde, AHR,
    82(Je 1977):771-2.

Macleod, Duncan J. Slavery, Race and the American Revolution.
    London: Cam U Press, 1974. Rev. by R. C. Reinders,
    CHR, 58(Mar 1977):91-2; H. F. Rankin, LaH, 18(Sum 1977):
    364-5.

McLeod, Hugh. Class and Religion in the Late Victorian City.
    London: Croom Helm, 1974. Rev. by R. Currie, EHR, 92
    (Oct 1977):920.

Macleod, R. C. The Northwest Mounted Police and Law Enforce-
    ment, 1873-1905. Toronto: U Tor Press, 1975. Rev. by D.
    Morton, CHR, 58(Je 1977):230-1; J. A. Boudreau, WHQ, 8(Jl
    1977):348-9.

McLoughlin, Denis. Wild and Wooly: An Encyclopedia of the Old
    West. New York: Doubleday, 1975. Rev. by W. Parker,
    JOW, 16(Jan 1977):77.

McManus, Edgar J. Black Bondage in the North. Syracuse: Syracuse U Press, 1973. Rev. by P. L. Silver, AI, 44(Sum
1977):70-1.

MacMaster, Richard K. see Copeland, Pamela C.

McMath, Robert C., Jr. Populist Vanguard: A History of the
Southern Farmers' Alliance. Chapel Hill: U NC Press,
1976. Rev. by T. Saloutos, AHR, 82(Apr 1977):449-50; G.
Clanton, PNQ, 68(Jan 1977):45.

MacMullen, Ramsay. Roman Government's Response to Crisis.
A.D. 235-337. New Haven: Yale U Press, 1976. Rev. by
S. I. Oost, AHR, 82(Je 1977):614.

McNally, Raymond T. see Florescu, Radu

McNeal, Robert H., ed. Resolutions and Decisions of the Communist
Party of the Soviet Union. Toronto: U Tor Press, 1974. Rev.
by R. Pipes, CHR, 58(Mar 1977):105.

McNeill, William H. Plagues and Peoples. Garden City, N.Y.:
Anchor Press, 1976. Rev. by N. J. G. Pounds, AHR, 82
(Je 1977):604-5; K. F. Kiple, JSH, 43(Aug 1977):488-9.

MacNeish, Richard S. and Melvin L. Fowler, et al. The Prehistory
of the Tehuacan Valley. Vol. 5: Excavations and Reconnais-
sance. Austin: U Tex Press, 1975. Rev. by C. Gabel, AHR,
82(Feb 1977):223; D. A. Freidel, HAHR, 57(Feb 1977):111-3.

Macon, Nathaniel see Silverstein, Martin Elliot

Macpherson, Ian, ed. see McCormack, A. R., ed.

McPherson, James Alan and Miller Williams, eds. Railroad:
Trains and Train People in American Culture. New York:
Random House, 1976. Rev. by L. Carranco, JOW, 16(Jan
1977):73.

McPherson, James M. The Abolitionist Legacy: From Reconstruction to the NAACP. Princeton: Prin U Press, 1976. Rev.
by G. M. Fredrickson, AHR, 81(Dec 1976):1256-57; C. Crowe,
JSH, 43(Feb 1977):136-7; P. Kolchin, WMH, 60(Spr 1977):
251-2.

McReynolds, Edwin C. see Morris, John W.

McWilliams, Carey. California: The Great Exception. Salt Lake
City: Peregrine Smith, 1976. Rev. by C. Wollenberg, CHQ,
55(Win 1976/77):371.

Madan, T. N., ed. Muslim Communities of South Asia: Culture
and Society. New Delhi: Vikas Publishing House, 1976. Rev.
by M. Mines, JAS, 37(Nov 1977):170-1.

_____, ed. see also Beteille, Andre, ed.

Maddex, Jack P., Jr. The Reconstruction of Edward A. Pollard:
A Rebel's Conversion to Postbellum Unionism. Chapel Hill:
U NC Press, 1974. Rev. by J. M. Wiener, JSH, 43(May
1977):304-5.

Magnou-Nortier, Elisabeth. La société laïque et l'église dans la
province ecclésiastique de Narbonne (zone cispyrénéenne) de
la fin du VIIIe à la fin du XIe siècle. Toulouse: Association
des Publications de l'Université de Toulouse-Le Mirail, 1974.
Rev. by K. G. Madison, AHR, 82(Oct 1977):937-8.

Maguire, Doris D., ed. see Mahan, Alfred Thayer

_____, ed. see Seager, Robert, II, ed.

Maguire, Jane. On Shares: Ed Brown's Story. New York: Norton,
1975. Rev. by D. Lee, GHQ, 51(Sum 1977):188-90.

Mahan, Alfred Thayer. Letters and Papers of Alfred Thayer Mahan.
3 vols. (Robert Seager, II and Doris D. Maguire, eds.)
Annapolis: Naval Institute Press, 1976. Rev. by P. Karsten,
AHR, 82(Apr 1977):454.

Mahmood, Safdar. A Political Study of Pakistan. Lahore: Sh.
Muhammed Ashraf, 1972. Rev. by K. B. Sayeed, AHR, 82
(Oct 1977):1054-5.

Mahon, John K., ed. Indians of the Lower South: Past and Present.
Pensacola, Florida: Gulf Coast History and Humanities Conference, 1975. Rev. by A. H. DeRosier, Jr., AIQ, 3(Sum
1977):155-6.

Maiberger, Paul, ed. "Das Buch der Kostbaren Perle" von Severus
ibn al-Mugaffa. Wiesbaden: Franz Steiner Verlag, 1974. Rev.
by A. S. Ativa, JNES, 36(Oct 1977):325-6.

Maiello, Adele Massardo. Laburismo e Russia Sovietica, 1917-1924.
Milan: Dott. A. Giuffre, 1974. Rev. by R. Stites, AHR, 82
(Feb 1977):108.

Maier, Charles S. Recasting Bourgeois Europe: Stabilization in
France, Germany, and Italy in the Decade after World War I.
Princeton: Prin U Press, 1975. Rev. by H. A. Winkler,
JMH, 49(Mar 1977):125-8.

Maimann, Helene. Politik im Wartesaal: Osterreichische Exilpolitik
in Grossbritannien, 1938-1945. Vienna: Hermann Bohlaus
Nachf, 1975. Rev. by J. Haag, AHR, 82(Feb 1977):137-8.

Mair, Margaret Granville. The Papers of Harriet Beecher Stowe.
Hartford: Stowe-Day Foundation, 1977. Rev. by L. Buell,
NEQ, 50(Sep 1977):557-8.

Maitan, Livio. Party, Army and Masses in China: A Marxist
     Interpretation of the Cultural Revolution and Its Aftermath.
     London: NLB: Atlantic Highlands: Humanitites Press,
     1976. Rev. by C. A. Weiss, JAS, 36(Aug 1977):731-2.

Majno, Guido. The Healing Hand: Man and Wound in the Ancient
     World. Cambridge, Mass.: Har U Press, 1975. Rev. by
     J. Scarborough, AHR, 82(Feb 1977):66-7; R. D. Biggs, JNES,
     36(Oct 1977):302-3; M. C. Sigman, Mankind, 5(No. 11, 1977):
     58-9.

Mak, James see Haites, Erik F.

Makarova, Raisa V. Russians on the Pacific, 1743-1799. Kingston,
     Ont.: Limestone Press, 1975. Rev. by M. E. Wheeler,
     AHR, 82(Apr 1977):401; M. C. Mangusso, PNQ, 68(Jl 1977):
     150.

Makinson, Randell L. Greene & Greene: Architecture as a Fine
     Art. Salt Lake City: Peregrine Smith, 1977. Rev. by D.
     Gebhard, CHQ, 56(Fall 1977):278-9.

Makkreel, Rudolf A. Dilthey, Philosopher of the Human Studies.
     Princeton: Prin U Press, 1975. Rev. by R. A. M., H&T,
     16(Feb 1977):81.

Malalgoda, Kitsiri. Buddhism in Sinhalese Society, 1750-1900.
     Berkeley: U Cal Press, 1976. Rev. by M. Adas, AHR, 82
     (Apr 1977):423-4.

Maleczynski, Karol. Boteslaw III Krzywousty. Wroclaw: Ossolineum,
     1975. Rev. by P. W. Knoll, AHR, 82(Oct 1977):943.

Malettke, Klaus. Opposition und Konspiration unter-Ludwig XIV.
     Göttingen: Vandenhoeck and Ruprecht, 1976. Rev. by L.
     Rothkrug, AHR, 82(Oct 1977):979.

Mallon, Richard D. with Juan V. Sourrouille. Economic Policy-
     making in a Conflict Society: The Argentine Case. Cam-
     bridge: Har U Press, 1975. Rev. by J. H. Street, HAHR,
     57(Feb 1977):169-70.

Mallowan, Max and Georgina Herrmann. Furniture from SW7,
     Fort Shalmaneser: Ivories from Nimrud (1949-1963), fascicule
     III. London: British School of Archaeology in Iraq, 1974.
     Rev. by D. Stronach, Antiquity, 51(Mar 1977):67-8.

Malloy, James M., ed. Authoritarianism and Corporation in Latin
     America. Pittsburgh: U Pitt Press, 1977. Rev. by R. H.
     Chilcote, AHR, 82(Oct 1977):1102-3.

Malone, Dumas. Jefferson the President: Second Term, 1805-1809.
     Boston: Little, Brown, 1974. Rev. by D. P. Peeler, WMH,
     60(Spr 1977):249-50.

Malone, Michael P. and Richard B. Roeder. Montana: A History of Two Centuries. Seattle: U Wash Press, 1976. Rev. by S. R. Davison, JOW, 16(Jan 1977):88; T. A. Larson, PHR, 46(Aug 1977):508-9; J. L. Bates, PNQ, 68(Oct 1977):191-2; K. R. Toole, WHQ, 8(Apr 1977):212-3.

Mamdani, Mahmood. Politics and Class Formation in Uganda. New York: Monthly Review Press, 1976. Rev. by M. C. Young, AHR, 82(Je 1977):714; O. E. S., CurH, 72(Apr 1977):177.

Mandel, Neville J. The Arabs and Zionism Before World War I. Berkeley: U Cal Press, 1977. Rev. by B. C. Busch, AHR, 82(Oct 1977):1031-2; W. B. Bishai, History, 6(Oct 1977):13.

Mandel, William M. Soviet Women. Garden City, N.Y.: Anchor Books, 1975. Rev. by B. E. Clements, AHR, 82(Oct 1977): 1028-9.

Mandrou, Robert. Introduction to Modern France, 1500-1640. An Essay in Historical Psychology. New York: Holmes and Meier, 1976. Rev. by J. R. Major, Historian, 39(May 1977): 551-2.

Manfred, Frederick. The Golden Bowl. Albuquerque: U NM Press, 1976. Rev. by T. D. Isern, ChOk, 55(Sum 1977):232-3.

Manglapus, Raul S. Japan in Southeast Asia: Collision Course. New York: Carnegie Endowment for International Peace, 1976. Rev. by H. Sato, JAS, 37(Nov 1977):92-3.

Mani, Vettam. Purānic Encyclopedia: A Comprehensive Dictionary with Special Reference to the Epic and Purānic Literature. Delhi: Motilal Banarsidass, 1975. Rev. by R. Saloman, JAS, 36(Feb 1977):368-9.

Manis, Douglas R. Colonial New England: A Historical Geography. New York: Ox U Press, 1975. Rev. by R. C. Lemire, Jr., WMQ, 34(Jan 1977):159-60.

Mann, Bernhard. Die Württemberger und die deutsche National-versammlung, 1848-49. Düsseldorf: Droste Verlag, 1975. Rev. by F. Eyck, AHR, 82(Je 1977):662.

Mann, Galo. Wallenstein. n.l.: Andre Deutsch, n.d. Rev. by F. Watson, HTo, 27(Jan 1977):55-6.

Mann, Jacob. Texts and Studies in Jewish History and Literature. New York: Ktav Publishing House, 1972. Rev. by M. Harris, JNES, 36(Oct 1977):320.

Mannari, Hiroshi see Marsh, Robert M.

Manning, Brian. The English People and the English Revolution,

1640-1649. London: Heinemann, 1976. Rev. by C. Holmes,
AHR, 82(Feb 1977):96-7; B. Worden, EHR, 92(Oct 1977):902-
3; A. Woolrych, History, 62(Feb 1977):120-1; J. S. Merrill,
HJ, 20(No. 1, 1977):229-36.

Mansergh, N. and P. Moon, eds. Constitutional Relations Between
Britain and India, 1942-47. London: HMSO, 1976. Rev. by
J. M. Brown, EHR, 92(Oct 1977):936-7.

Mansergh, Nicholas, ed. The Transfer of Power, 1942-7, Volume
V: September 1944-28 July 1945. London: HMSO, 1975.
Rev. by W. Golant, History, 62(Je 1977):287-8.

Manton, Jo. Mary Carpenter and the Children of the Streets. London: Heinemann Educational Books, 1976. Rev. by M. Vic-
inus, AHR, 82(Apr 1977):358-9.

Manvell, Roger. International Encyclopedia of Film. London:
Michael Joseph, 1972. Rev. by D. J. Wenden, EHR, 92
(Oct 1977):930-2.

Maravall, Jose Antonio. La Cultura del barroco: Analisis de una
Estructura historica. Barcelona: Editorial Ariel, 1975. Rev.
by A. R. Vizzur, AHR, 82(Apr 1977):374; J. Casey, History,
62(Feb 1977):116-7.

_____. Estado Moderno y Mentalidad Social. Madrid: Ediciones
de la Revista de Occidente, 1972. Rev. by M. D. Gordon,
HAHR, 57(Feb 1977):113-4.

_____. Estudios de historia del pensamiento español. Madrid:
Ediciones Cultura Hispánica, 1975. Rev. by A. R. Vizzier,
AHR, 82(Apr 1977):374.

March, Andrew L. The Idea of China: Myth and Theory in Geographic Thought. New York: Praeger, 1974. Rev. by H. J.
Lamley, JAAS, 12(Jan/Oct 1977):304-7.

Marchetti, Valerio. Gruppi ereticali senesi del cinquecento.
Florence: La Nuova Italia, 1975. Rev. by D. Nugent, AHR,
82(Apr 1977):383-4.

Marcridis, Roy C., ed. Foreign Policy in World Politics. Englewood Cliffs, N.J.: Prentice-Hall, 1976. Rev. by O. E. S.,
CurH, 72(Apr 1977):177.

Marcus, G. J. Heart of Oak: A Survey of British Sea Power in
the Georgian Era. New York: Ox U Press, 1975. Rev. by
R. A. Courtemanche, AHR, 82(Feb 1977):99-100; J. S.
Bromley, History, 62(Feb 1977):131-2.

Marcus, Harold G., ed. Proceedings of the First United States
Conference on Ethiopian Studies, 1973. East Lansing: Michigan
St U, 1975. Rev. by C. Clapham, AfAf, 76(Jan 1977):116-17.

Marder, Arthur. Operation "Menace": The Dakar Expedition and the Dudley North Affair. New York: Ox U Press, 1976. Rev. by D. Stafford, AHR, 82(Feb 1977):110-1.

Marin, Joseph. Journal of Joseph Marin, French Colonial Explorer and Military Commander in the Wisconsin Country, August 7, 1753-June 20, 1754. Ed. by Kenneth P. Bailey. Irvine, California: Kenneth P. Bailey, 1975. Rev. by D. Chaput, WMH, 60(Spr 1977):236-7.

Markova, Zina. The Bulgarian National Ecclesiastical Movement Before the Crimean War. Sofia: Izdatelstvo na B'lgarskata Akademiia na Naukite, 1976. Rev. by J. D. Bell, AHR, 82 (Oct 1977):1017-8.

Markovitch, Tihomir J. Histoire des industries francaises. Geneva: Librairie Droz, 1976. Rev. by J. J. Hurt, AHR, 82(Je 1977):649.

Marks, Ellen and Mark Norton Schatz, eds. Between North and South: A Maryland Journalist Views the Civil War. Rutherford, N.J.: Fairleigh Dickinson U Press, 1976. Rev. by R. R. Duncan, CWH, 23(Je 1977):173-4.

Marks, Geoffrey and William K. Beatty. Epidemics. New York: Scribners, 1976. Rev. by N. J. G. Pounds, AHR, 82(Je 1977):604-5; D. B. Weiner, JIH, 8(Aut 1977):363-4.

Marlatt, Daphne, ed. Steveston Recollected: A Japanese-Canadian History. Victoria: Aural History, Provincial Archives of British Columbia, 1975. Rev. by H. H. Sugimoto, PNQ, 68 (Oct 1977):195.

Marlow, H. Carleton and Harrison M. Davis. The American Search for Woman. Santa Barbara, Cal.: Clio Books, 1976. Rev. by M. C. Davis, AHR, 82(Apr 1977):473.

Marlow, Joyce. Mr. and Mrs. Gladstone: An Intimate Biography. n.l.: Weidenfeld and Nicolson, n.d. Rev. by I. Bradley, HTo, 27(Sep 1977):615-7.

Marney, John. Liang Chien-wen Ti. New York: Twayne Publishers, 1976. Rev. by P. W. Kroll, JAS, 36(Aug 1977):736-8.

Marquand, David. Ramsay MacDonald. n.l.: Cape, n.d. Rev. by J. Richardson, HTo, 27(May 1977):339-42; R. J. Plowman, History, 6(Nov/Dec 1977):42.

Marquart, Frank. An Auto Worker's Journal: The UAW from Crusade to One-Party Union. University Park: Pennsylvania State U Press, 1975. Rev. by H. J. Harris, JAmS, 11(Aug 1977):286-9; M. Dubofsky, JISHS, 70(May 1977):170.

Marquis, Arnold. A Guide to America's Indians. Norman: U OK
    Press, 1974. Rev. by B. Satcher, ChOk, 54(Win 1976-7):541-2.

Marquis, Thomas B. Keep the Last Bullet for Yourself: The True
    Story of Custer's Last Stand. New York: Two Continents Pub.
    Group, 1976. Rev. by R. M. Utley, AHI, 11(Jan 1977):50.

Marrin, Albert. Nicholas Murray Butler. Boston: Twayne, 1976.
    Rev. by B. G. Rader, AHR, 82(Feb 1977):204.

Marriott, Alice and Carol K. Rachlin. Plains Indian Mythology.
    New York: Thos. Y. Crowell, 1975. Rev. by L. S. Theisen,
    ChOk, 54(Win 1976-7):534-5.

Marsden, Peter. The Wreck of Amsterdam. New York: Stein and
    Day, 1974. Rev. by N. Stavrolakes, Archaeology, 30(Mar
    1977):139.

Marsh, Robert M. and Hiroshi Mannari. Modernization and the
    Japanese Factory. Princeton: Prin U Press, 1976. Rev.
    by R. C. Clark, JAS, 36(Aug 1977):752-4.

Marshall, Douglas W. and Howard H. Peckham. Campaigns of the
    American Revolution: An Atlas of Manuscript Maps. Ann
    Arbor: U Mich Press, 1976. Rev. by J. R. Sellers, JSH,
    43(Feb 1977):111-2; R. A. Brown, WMQ, 34(Jan 1977):154-7.

Marshall, George C. Memoirs of My Services in the World War,
    1917-1918. Boston: Houghton Mifflin, 1976. Rev. by F. C.
    Pogue, AHI, 12(Nov 1977):47-8.

Marshall, John. The Papers of John Marshall, Volume I: Corres-
    pondence and Papers, November 10, 1775-June 23, 1788 and
    Account Book, September 1783-June 1788. Ed. by Herbert A.
    Johnson. Chapel Hill: U NC Press, 1974. Rev. by R. G.
    Seddig, PH, 45(Jan 1977):89-90.

Marshall, P. J. East India Fortunes: The British in Bengal in the
    Eighteenth Century. Oxford: Ox U Press, 1976. Rev. by C.
    R. Boxer, History, 62(Je 1977):322-3.

Martí, José. Inside the Monster: Writings on the United States
    and American Imperialism. New York: Monthly Review
    Press, 1975. Rev. by R. E. Ruiz, PHR, 46(Feb 1977):141.

Martin, Albro. James J. Hill and the Opening of the Northwest.
    New York: Ox U Press, 1976. Rev. by S. Salsbury, AHR,
    82(Je 1977):751-2; W. Parker, JOW, 16(Jan 1977):83; J. C.
    Spychalski, MiA, 59(Apr-Jl 1977):127-8; R. G. Athearn,
    MinnH, 45(Spr 1977):200-1.

Martin, Charles H. The Angelo Herndon Case and Southern Justice.
    Baton Rouge: LSU Press, 1976. Rev. by J. Kitchens, GHQ,

51(Sum 1977):202-3; R. L. Zangrando, JNH, 62(Jan 1977):
107-8; A. Meier, JSH, 43(Feb 1977):142-3.

Martin, David. General Amin. Faber & Faber, n.d. Rev. by I.
Opuk, pseud., AfAf, 76(Jl 1977):404-7.

Martin, F. X., ed. see Moody, T. W., ed.

Martin, Ged see Hyam, Ronald

Martin, Geoffrey Thorndike. The Royal Tomb of El-Amarna. Vol.
1. The Objects. London: Egypt Exploration Society, 1974.
Rev. by W. J. Murnane, JNES, 36(Oct 1977):306-8.

Martin, George. Madam Secretary: Frances Perkins. Boston:
Houghton Mifflin Co., 1976. Rev. by B. Bellush, AHR, 82
(Feb 1977):209-10; J. A. Imler, WMH, 60(Sum 1977):352-3.

Martin, H. J. see Febvre, L.

Martin, Harold H. Georgia. A Bicentennial History. New York:
Norton, 1977. Rev. by E. M. Coulter, GHQ, 51(Win 1977):
356-7.

Martin, James Kirby, ed. The Human Dimensions of Nation Making:
Essays on Colonial and Revolutionary America. Madison, Wis.:
State Historical Society of Wisconsin, 1976. Rev. by I. D.
Gruber, JSH, 43(May 1977):279-80; J. A. Henretta, WMH,
60(Spr 1977):341-2; P. L. White, WMQ, 34(Jl 1977):482-5.

Martin, John Bartlow. Adlai Stevenson of Illinois. Garden City,
N.Y.: Doubleday, 1976. Rev. by R. A. Lee, AHR, 82(Apr
1977):471.

Martin, Marie-Louise. Kimbange: An African Prophet and His
Church. Tr. by D. M. Moore. Oxford: Blackwell, 1975.
Rev. by L. Mair, Africa, 47(No. 2, 1977):222.

Martin, Tony. Race First: The Ideological and Organizational
Struggles of Marcus Garvey and the Universal Negro Improve-
ment Association. Westport, Conn.: Greenwood Press, 1976.
Rev. by A. Meier, AHR, 82(Feb 1977):205-6; R. G. Weis-
bord, Historian, 39(May 1977):583-4; R. E. Perdue, JSH, 43
(Feb 1977):140-1.

Martínez C., Pedro Santos. Repercusiones de Pavón en Mendoza
a través del periodismo (1861-1863). Mendoza: Universidad
Nacional de Cuyo, 1973. Rev. by J. T. Criscenti, AHR, 82
(Apr 1977):483-4.

Marwick, Arthur. War and Social Change in the Twentieth Century:
A Comparative Study of Britain, France, Germany, Russia and
the United States. London: Macmillan, 1974. Rev. by C. W.
Humphries, CHR, 58(Je 1977):241-2.

Marwil, Jonathon. The Trials of Counsel: Francis Bacon in 1621.
    Detroit: Wayne St. U Press, 1976. Rev. by R. Howell, Jr.,
    AHR, 82(Feb 1977):97; C. Russel, EHR, 92(Oct 1977):897-8.

Marz, Eduard. Einfuhrung in die Marxsche Theorie der wirtschaft-
    liche Entwicklung. Vienna: Europa Verlag, 1976. Rev. by
    E. F. Good, JEH, 37(Sep 1977):825-7.

Marzio, Peter C. The Art Crusade: An Analysis of American
    Drawing Manuals, 1820-1860. Washington, D.C.: Smithsonian
    Institution Press, 1976. Rev. by P. R. Baker, AHR, 82(Oct
    1977):1070-1.

Mason, F. Van Wyck. Trumpets Sound No More. Toronto: Little,
    Brown & Co., 1975. Rev. by R. Ashley, CWTI, 16(Apr 1977):
    47-8.

Mason, Otis Tufton. Aboriginal American Indian Basketry: Studies
    in a Textile Art Without Machinery. Santa Barbara and Salt
    Lake City: Peregrine Smith, 1976. Rev. by H. A. Howard,
    JOW, 16(Jl 1977):93.

Mason, Timothy W. Sozialpolitik im Dritten Reich: Arbeiterklasse
    und Volksgemeinschaft. Wiesbaden: Westdeutscher Verlag,
    1977. Rev. by W. Jannen, Jr., AHR, 82(Oct 1977):1008-9.

Mass, Jeffrey P. Warrior Government in Early Medieval Japan.
    London: Yale U Press, 1975. Rev. by R. Storry, History,
    62(Feb 1977):101.

Masselos, J. C. Toward Nationalism: Group Affiliations and the
    Politics of Public Associations in 19th Century Western India.
    Bombay: Popular Prakashan, 1974. Rev. by T. R. Metcalf,
    AHR, 82(Feb 1977):163-4.

Masser, L. and W. T. S. Gould. Inter-Regional Migration in
    Tropical Africa. London: Institute of British Geographers,
    1975. Rev. by H. G. J. Knoop, Africa, 47(No. 1, 1977):
    119-20.

Masui, Shigeo see Bereday, George Z. F.

Mata, Hector Malavé. Formación historica del antidesarrollo de
    Venezuela. Havana, Cuba: Casa de los Americas, 1974.
    Rev. by D. E. Blank, HAHR, 57(Aug 1977):555-6.

Matheson, Elizabeth Macleod, ed. see Fairbank, John King, ed.

_____, ed. see Hart, Robert

Mathews, Byron H., Jr. The McCook-Stoneman Raid. Philadelphia:
    Dorrance, 1976. Rev. by J. I. Robertson, Jr., GHQ, 51(Spr
    1977):93-5; J. H. DeBerry, JSH, 43(Aug 1977):462-3.

Mathews, John. Western Aristocracies and the Imperial Court A.D.
    364-425. New York: Ox U Press, 1975. Rev. by W. G.
    Sinnigen, AHR, 82(Feb 1977):72.

Mathiez, Albert. Etudes sur Robespierre (1758-1794). Paris:
    Editions sociales, 1973. Rev. by J. I. Shulim, AHR, 82
    (Feb 1977):20-38.

Mathurin, Owen Charles. Henry Sylvester Williams and the Origins
    of the Pan-African Movement, 1869-1911. Westport, Conn.:
    Greenwood Press, 1976. Rev. by J. A. Casada, Historian,
    39(May 1977):564-5.

Matson, Robert W. William Mulholland: A Forgotten Forefather.
    Stockton: U Pacific, 1976. Rev. by W. L. Kahrl, CHQ, 55
    (Win 1976/77):369-70; D. A. Williams, NMHR, 52(Jl 1977):
    260-1.

Matute, Alvaro, ed. La Teoría de la historia en México (1940-
    1973). Mexico: SepSetentas, 1974. Rev. by C. A. Hale,
    HAHR, 57(Feb 1977):127-8.

Matz, Friedrich. Die dionysischen Sarkophage. Berlin: Deutsches
    Archäologisches Institut, Gebr. Mann Verlag, 1968-75. Rev.
    by M. Lawrence, AJA, 81(Win 1977):127-34.

Maude, George. The Finnish Dilemma: Neutrality in the Shadow
    of Power. New York: Ox U Press, 1976. Rev. by A. Z.
    Rubinstein, CurH, 72(Feb 1977):80.

Maurice, E. Grace. Union List of Manuscripts in Canadian Repos-
    itories. Ottawa: Public Archives of Canada, 1975. Rev. by
    E. Jones, CHR, 58(Mar 1977):87-8.

Mauskopf, Seymour H. Crystals and Compounds: Molecular
    Structure and Composition in Nineteenth Century French
    Science. Philadelphia: American Philosophical Society,
    1976. Rev. by L. P. Williams, AHR, 82(Oct 1977):983-4.

May, Dean L. see Arrington, Leonard J.

May, Ernest R. The Making of the Monroe Doctrine. Cambridge,
    Mass.: Har U Press, 1975. Rev. by I. C. Nichols, Jr.,
    PHR, 46(Feb 1977):122-3; K. J. Grieb, TAm, 34(Oct 1977):
    301-2.

_____. The Truman Administration and China, 1945-1949.
    Philadelphia: J. B. Lippincott, 1975. Rev. by R. D. Buhite,
    PHR, 46(May 1977):316-7.

May, George S. A Most Unique Machine: The Michigan Origins of
    the American Automobile Industry. Grand Rapids, Mich.:
    Eerdmans, 1975. Rev. by J. J. Flink, AHR, 82(Feb 1977):
    200.

May, Harry S. The Tragedy of Erasmus: A Psychohistoric Approach. St. Charles, MO.: Piraeus Publishers, 1975. Rev. by W. K. Ferguson, AHR, 82(Apr 1977):376-7.

May, Henry F. The Enlightenment in America. New York: Ox U Press, 1976. Rev. by J. Appleby, AHR, 82(Je 1977):722-3; J. Zvesper, HJ, 20(No. 4, 1977):1015-7; H. Brogan, JAmS, 11(Apr 1977):160; N. C. Gillespie, JSH, 43(Aug 1977):439-40; D. R. McCoy, WMQ, 34(Apr 1977):314-6.

May, Virginia A. A Plantation Called Petapawag: Some Notes on the History of Groton, Massachusetts. Groton: Groton Historical Society, 1976. Rev. by T. F. Glick, NEQ, 50(Je 1977):353-6.

Mayet, Françoise see Delgado, Manuela

Mazari, F. see Lowe, C. J.

Mazlish, Bruce. James and John Stuart Mill: Father and Son in the Nineteenth Century. London: Hutchinson, 1975. Rev. by K. Fielden, History, 62(Feb 1977):142-3; R. W. Krouse, JMH, 49(Mar 1977):133-6.

_____. The Revolutionary Ascetic: Evolution of a Political Type. New York: Basic Books, 1976. Rev. by J. I. Shulim, AHR, 82(Feb 1977):20-38; P. Loewenberg, AHR, 82(Apr 1977):336-7.

Mazzolani, Lidia Storoni. Empire without End. New York: Harcourt Brace Jovanovich, 1976. Rev. by H. W. Benario, AHR, 82(Je 1977):612.

Meacham, Standish. A Life Apart: The English Working Class 1890-1914. Cambridge, Mass.: Har U Press, 1977. Rev. by O. E. S., CurH, 73(Nov 1977):175.

Meade, C. Wade. Road to Babylon: Development of U. S. Assyriology. Leiden: E. J. Brill, 1974. Rev. by R. D. Biggs, JNES, 36(Oct 1977):306.

Meaker, Gerald H. The Revolutionary Left in Spain, 1914-1923. Stanford, Calif.: Stan U Press, 1974. Rev. by J. B. McKenna, JMH, 49(Sep 1977):504-5.

Medlicott, W. N., ed. Documents on British Foreign Policy, 1919-1939. London: HMSO, 1976. Rev. by K. Robbins, History, 62(Feb 1977):147-8.

Medvedev, Roy A. and Zhores A. Medvedev. Khrushchev: The Years in Power. New York: Columbia U Press, 1976. Rev. by A. Dallin, AHR, 82(Oct 1977):1028; J. Rubinstein, Comm, 63(Feb 1977):74-6.

Medvedev, Zhores A. see Medvedev, Roy A.

Meek, Forest. Michigan's Timber Background: A History of Clare
County, 1674-1900. Clare, Michigan: Clare County Bicentennial Commission, 1976. Rev. by H. Kelsey, MichH, 61(Fall
1977):261-3.

Meek, R. L. Social Science and the Ignoble Savage. Cambridge:
Cam U Press, 1976. Rev. by N. Hampson, History, 62(Feb
1977):136.

Meer, Fernando de. La Cuestión religiosa en las Cortes Constituyentes de la II República Española. Pamplona: Ediciones
Universidad de Navarra, 1975. Rev. by J. O'Connell, TAm,
33(Jan 1977):540-1.

Mehlman, Jeffrey. A Structural Study of Autobiography, Proust,
Leiris, Sartre, Levi-Strauss. Ithaca: Cor U Press, 1974.
Rev. by W. A. Morris, GR, 31(Spr 1977):264-7.

Mehra, Parshotam. The McMahon Line and After: A Study of the
Triangular Contest on India's North-Eastern Frontier between
Britain, China and Tibet, 1904-47. Columbia, Mo.: South
Asia Books, 1976. Rev. by L. E. Rose, JAS, 36(Aug 1977):
711-2; G. J. Alder, History, 62(Je 1977):290.

Mehta, Ved. Mahatma Gandhi and His Apostles. n.l.: Andre
Deutsch, n.d. Rev. by F. Watson, HTo, 27(Oct 1977):679-81.

Meier, August and Elliott Rudwick. Along the Color Line: Explo-
rations, in the Black Experience. Urbana: U Ill Press, 1976.
Rev. by N. Lederer, GHQ, 51(Win 1977):366-7; G. H. Watson,
JISHS, 70(Aug 1977):254-5; V. P. Franklin, JNH, 62(Jl 1977):
294-301; H. N. Rabinowitz, JSH, 43(Nov 1977):636-7; D. C.
Smith, WVH, 38(Jl 1977):333-4.

Meillassoux, Claude. Femmes, Greniers et Capitaux. Paris:
Maspero, 1975. Rev. by M. M. Mackintosh, AfAf, 76(Jan
1977):113-14.

Meintjes, Johannes. President Paul Kruger: A Biography. London:
U Cal Press, 1975. Rev. by S. Marks, History, 62(Je 1977):
271-2.

Meisner, Maurice and Rhoads Murphey, eds. The Mozartian Historian: Essays on the Works of Joseph R. Levenson. Berkeley: U Cal Press, 1976. Rev. by A. Feuerwerker, AHR,
82(Feb 1977):157.

Melis, Federigo. Origini e sviluppi delle assicurazioni in Italia
(secoli XIV-XVI). Roma: Istituto Nazionale delle assicurazione,
1975. Rev. by T. Blomquist, JEH, 37(Sep 1977):829-30.

MELLAART   212

Mellaart, James. The Neolithic of the Near East. New York:
    Charles Scribner's, 1976. Rev. by P. S. De Jesus, Archae-
    ology, 30(Jan 1977):62-3.

Mellafe, Rolando. Negro Slavery in Latin America. Berkeley: U
    Cal Press, 1975. Rev. by C. N. Degler, JLAS, 9(May 1977):
    150-2.

Meller, H. E. Leisure and the Changing City, 1870-1914. Boston:
    Routledge and Kegan Paul, 1976. Rev. by L. L. Shiman,
    AHR, 82(Oct 1977):969; B. Cowell, JEH, 37(Sep 1977):830; D.
    Cannandine, HJ, 20(No. 3, 1977):777-82; F. M. Leventhal,
    JIH, 8(Aut 1977):364.

Mello, Jose Antonio. Gonsolve de Diario de Pernambuco e a His-
    toria Social do Nordeste. Recife: Diario de Pernambuco,
    1975. Rev. by R. M. Levine, HAHR, 57(Aug 1977):549-50;
    F. Azevedo, TAm, 33(Apr 1977):684-5.

Mello, Ronald. Thea Romĭ: The Worship of the Goddess Roma in
    the Greek World. Göttingen: Vandenhoeck and Ruprecht, 1975.
    Rev. by J. R. Fears, AHR, 82(Apr 1977):339.

Mendelssohn, Kurt. The Riddle of the Pyramids. London: Thames
    and Hudson, 1974. Rev. by K. R. Weeks, JNES, 36(Jan 1977):
    69-71.

Mendenhall, George E. The Tenth Generation: The Origins of the
    Biblical Tradition. Baltimore and London: JHU Press, 1973.
    Rev. by K. A. Kitchen, JNES, 36(Jan 1977):68-9.

Menier, Marie-Antoinette, et al., ed. Correspondance à l'arrivée
    en provenance de la Louisiane. vol. 1. Paris. Archives
    Nationales, 1976. Rev. by F. Stielow, AHR, 82(Je 1977):
    733-4.

Menozzi, Daniele. "Philosophes" e "Chrétiens éclairés". Brecia:
    Paideia Editrice, 1976. Rev. by W. H. Williams, AHR, 82
    (Oct 1977):949-50.

Menzel, Dorothy. Pottery Style and Society in Ancient Peru: Art
    as a Mirror of Society in the Ica Valley, 1350-1570. Berkeley:
    U Cal Press, 1976. Rev. by B. Orlove, AgH, 51(Jl 1977):
    611-2.

Mercer, Eric. English Vernacular Houses. London: HMSO, 1975.
    Rev. by C. R. J. Currie, EHR, 92(Oct 1977):880-1.

Merkl, Peter H. Political Violence Under the Swastika: 581 Early
    Nazis. Princeton: Prin U Press, 1975. Rev. by R. A. Pois,
    AHR, 82(Je 1977):669-71; B. F. Smith, JIH, 10(Win 1977):
    545-6.

Merkley, Paul. Reinhold Niebuhr: A Political Account. Montreal:
    McGill-Queen's U Press, 1975. Rev. by F. M. Szasz, AHR,
    81(Dec 1976):1278-79.

Merrens, H. Roy, ed. The Colonial South Carolina Scene: Con-
    temporary Views, 1697-1774. Columbia: U SC Press, 1977.
    Rev. by J. L. Wakelyn, History, 6(Nov/Dec 1977)31.

Merrill, Boynton, Jr. Jefferson's Nephews: A Frontier Tragedy.
    Princeton: Prin U Press, 1976. Rev. by F. M. Brodie,
    AHR, 82(Je 1977):741; J. R. Bentley, FCHQ, 51(Oct 1977):
    363-4; R. P. Hay, JSH, 43(Aug 1977):451-2; S. H. Hochman,
    VMHB, 85(Jl 1977):375-6; R. McColley, WMQ, 34(Oct 1977):
    689-91.

Merrill, Richard, ed. Radical Agriculture. New York: Harper
    Colophon Books, 1976. Rev. by L. K. Dyson, AgH, 51(Jl
    1977):617-8.

Merrill, Walter M. and Louis Ruchames, eds. From Disunionism
    to the Brink of War, 1850-1860. Cambridge: Har U Press,
    n.d. Rev. by A. Zilversmith, NEQ, 50(Mar 1977):156-8.

Meyer, Donald H. The Democratic Enlightenment. New York: G.
    Putnam's Sons, 1976. Rev. by W. D. Liddle, WMQ, 34(Apr
    1977):317-8.

Meyer, Jean. La Cristiada. Mexico: Siglo Venituno Editories,
    1974. Rev. by W. H. Beezley, TAm, 33(Jan 1977):558-9.

Meyer, Jean A. The Cristero Rebellion: The Mexican People
    Between Church and State, 1926-1929. Cambridge: Cam U
    Press, 1976. Rev. by L. Meyer, EHR, 92(Oct 1977):871-2.

Meyer, Larry L. Shadow of a Continent: The Prize that Lay to
    the West--1776. Palo Alto, Calif.: American West Publishing,
    1975. Rev. by M. Sprague, LaH, 18(Sum 1977):365-6.

Meyer, Michael C., ed. see Wilkie, James W., ed.

Meyer, S. L., ed. see Preston, Antony

Meyerowitz, E. L. R. The Early History of the Akan States of
    Ghana. London: Red Candle Press, 1974. Rev. by I. Wilks,
    Africa, 47(No. 1, 1977):108-9.

Miale, Florence R. and Michael Selzer. The Nuremberg Mind: The
    Psychology of the Nazi Leaders. New York: Quadrangle/New
    York Times Book, 1976. Rev. by R. Hilberg, AHR, 82(Oct
    1977):952-4.

Michaely, Michael. Israel. New York and London: Col U Press
    for the National Bureau of Economic Research, 1975. Rev. by
    K. M. Langley, JEH, 37(Je 1977):482-5.

Michel, Bernard. Banques et banquiers en Autriche au debut du 20e siècle. Paris: Presses de la fondation nationale des sciences politiques, 1976. Rev. by L. Schofer, AHR, 82(Je 1977):674-5.

Miguelez, Roberto. Sujet et Histoire. Ottawa: Editions de l' Universite d'Ottawa/U Ottawa Press, 1973. Rev. by J. Lawler, CHR, 58(Je 1977):217-8.

Milazzo, Matteo J. The Chetnik Movement and the Yugoslav Resistance. Baltimore and London: JHU Press, 1975. Rev. by W. H. McNeill, JMH, 49(Mar 1977):147-51.

Miles, Douglas. Cutlass and Crescent Moon: A Case Study of Social and Political Change in Outer Indonesia. Sydney: U of Sydney Centre for Asian Studies, 1976. Rev. by A. B. Hudson, JAS, 37(Nov 1977):176-8.

Miles, Elton. Tales of the Big Bend. College Station: Texas A&M Press, 1976. Rev. by G. R. Cruz, JOW, 16(Jl 1977):95-6.

Military History of the Spanish-American Southwest: A Seminar. Fort Huachuca, Arizona: n.p., 1976. Rev. by C. Beamer, JOW, 16(Jl 1977):96-7.

Millar, Fergus. The Emperor in the Roman World. New York: Cor U Press, 1977. Rev. by J. E. Rexine, History, 6(Oct 1977):13-4; M. Grant, HTo, 27(Sep 1977):615.

Miller, D. B. From Hierarchy to Stratification: Changing Patterns of Social Inequality in a North Indian Village. Delhi: Ox U Press, 1975. Rev. by M. Marriott, JAS, 36(Feb 1977):372-3.

Miller, Derek, ed. see Oddy, Derek, ed.

Miller, Donald C. Ghost Towns of Idaho. Boulder: Pruett Publishing Company, 1976. Rev. by D. E. Livingston-Little, JOW, 16(Jl 1977):100.

Miller, Floyd J. The Search for a Black Nationality: Black Emigration and Colonization, 1787-1863. Urbana: U Ill Press, 1975. Rev. by W. H. Pease, CWH, 23(Mar 1977):84-5; J. White, JAmS, 11(Apr 1977):149-52.

Miller, Helen Hill. George Mason: Gentlemen Revolutionary. Chapel Hill: U NC Press, 1975. Rev. by D. W. Jordan, AHR, 82(Apr 1977):433-4; P. H. Smith, FHQ, 55(Jan 1977): 375-6; L. Banning, Historian, 39(Feb 1977):366-7; K. R. Bowling, WMH, 60(Spr 1977):242-3.

Miller, Howard. The Revolutionary College: American Presbyterian Higher Education, 1707-1837. New York: NYU Press, 1976. Rev. by D. C. Humphrey, AHR, 82(Oct 1977):1062-3; J. I. Copeland, JSH, 43(Nov 1977):603-4.

Miller, J. Popery and Politics in England 1660-1688. Cambridge: Cam U Press, 1973. Rev. by R. Clifton, History, 62(Feb 1977):123.

Miller, J. D. B. Survey of Commonwealth Affairs: Problems of Expansion and Attrition. Cambridge: Ox U Press, 1974. Rev. by D. Harkness, History, 62(Feb 1977):91-2.

Miller, James E. T. S. Eliot's Personal Waste Land. University Park: Penn St U Press, 1977. Rev. by D. L. Eder, GR, 31(Fall 1977):755-9.

Miller, Joseph C. Equatorial Africa. Washington, D.C.: American Historical Association, 1976. Rev. by J. R. Smaldone, HT, 10(May 1977):633-4.

_____. Kings and Kinsmen: Early MBundu States in Angola. Oxford: Ox U Press, 1976. Rev. by D. Birmingham, History, 62(Je 1977):270-1.

Miller, Lucien. Masks of Fiction in Dream of the Red Chamber. Tucson: U Arizona Press, 1975. Rev. by F. P. Brandauer, JAS, 36(May 1977):554-7.

Miller, Nyle H. Kansas: The Thirty-Fourth Star. Topeka: Kansan State Historical Society, 1976. Rev. by P. Johnson, WHQ, 8(Oct 1977):458-9.

Miller, Orlando W. The Frontier in Alaska and the Matanuska Colony. New Haven: Yale U Press, 1975. Rev. by S. Haycox, AHR, 81(Dec 1976):1249-50; F. J. Rader, Al, 44(Fall 1977):150-2.

Miller, Richard G. Philadelphia--The Federalist City: A Study of Urban Politics, 1789-1801. Port Washington, N.Y.: Kennikat Press, 1976. Rev. by P. Goodman, AHR, 82(Apr 1977):437-8; G. W. Geib, WMQ, 34(Jl 1977):492-4.

Miller, V. I. Soldier Committees in the Russian Army in 1917: Their Origin and the Beginning Period of Their Activity. Moscow: Izdatel'stvo "Nauka", 1974. Rev. by A. Wildman, AHR, 82(Je 1977):702-3.

Miller, Zell. The Mountains Within Me. Toccoa, Ga.: Commercial Printing Company, 1976. Rev. by P. Spalding, GHQ, 51 (Spr 1977):92-3.

Milsom, S. F. C. The Legal Framework of English Feudalism. New York: Cam U Press, 1976. Rev. by S. S. Walker, AHR, 82(Je 1977):619.

Miner, H. Craig. The Corporation and the Indian: Tribal Sovereignty and Industrial Civilization in Indian Territory, 1865-

1907. Columbia: U Mo Press, 1976. Rev. by W. G. Robbins, AHR, 82(Feb 1977):192-3; M. L. Tate, AIQ, 3(Aut 1977):245-7; R. D. Edmunds, JSH, 43(May 1977):307-9; A. Morgan Gibson, WHQ, 8(Apr 1977):218-20.

Mingay, G. E., ed. Arthur Young and His Times. Toronto: Macmillan, 1975. Rev. by R. C. Loehr, AgH, 51(Apr 1977):476-7.

_____. The Gentry: The Rise and Fall of a Ruling Class. New York: Longman, 1976. Rev. by E. A. Wasson, AHR, 82 (Oct 1977):963.

Minge, Ward Alan. Acoma: Pueblo in the Sky. Albuquerque: U NM Press, 1976. Rev. by S. L. Tyler, AHR, 82(Feb 1977): 207; B. L. Fontana, HAHR, 57(Feb 1977):161-2; V. E. Tiller, NMHR, 52(Oct 1977):347-9.

Minger, Ralph Eldin. William Howard Taft and United States Foreign Policy: The Apprenticeship Years, 1900-1908. Urbana: U Ill Press, 1975. Rev. by K. J. Clymer, PHR, 46(May 1977):303-5.

Minogue, Martin and Judith Molloy. African Aims and Attitudes. London: Cam U Press, 1974. Rev. by A. H. M. Kirk-Greene, Africa, 47(No. 1, 1977):114.

Mintz, Sidney W., ed. Working Papers in Haitian Society and Culture. New Haven: Yale U, 1975. Rev. by T. O. Ott, HAHR, 57(Feb 1977):164-6.

Miranda, Jose. Vida colonial y albores de la independencia. Mexico: SepSetentas, 1972. Rev. by H. M. Hamill, HAHR, 57 (Feb 1977):118-21.

Mirsky, Jeannette. Sir Aurel Stein: Archaeological Explorer. Chicago: U Chi Press, 1977. Rev. by P. D. Rhomas, History, 6(Nov/Dec 1977):40.

Misgeld, Klaus. Die "Internationale Gruppe demokratischer Sozialisten" in Stockholm, 1942-1945. Stockholm: Almquist and Wiksell, 1976. Rev. by D. K. Buse, AHR, 82(Oct 1977):954-5.

Misner, Paul. Papacy and Development: Newman and the Primacy of the Pope. Leiden: E. J. Brill, 1976. Rev. by H. A. MacDougall, AHR, 82(Je 1977):639.

Misra, Girish K. see Sen, Lalit K.

Mitchell, Arthur. Labour in Irish Politics, 1890-1930. Dublin: Irish U Press, 1974. Rev. by J. C. Beckett, EHR, 92(Oct 1977):870-1.

Mitchell, B. R. European Historical Statistics 1750-1970. London: Macmillan, 1975. Rev. by R. A. H. Robinson, History, 62 (Feb 1977):153-4.

Mitchell, Broadus. Alexander Hamilton: A Concise Biography. New York: Ox U Press, 1976. Rev. by G. S. Wood, AHI, 12(Jl 1977):50.

Mitchell, Frank. The Irish Landscape. London: Collins, 1976. Rev. by R. E. Glasscock, Antiquity, 51(Jl 1977):168-9.

Mitchell, Richard H. Thought Control in Prewar Japan. Ithaca: Cornell U Press, 1976. Rev. by G. M. Berger, AHR, 82 (Je 1977):721; G. D. Allinson, JAS, 37(Nov 1977):142-4.

Mitchell, Thorton W. Norton on Archives: The Writings of Margaret Cross Norton on Archival and Records Management. Carbondale, Ill.: So Ill U Press, 1975. Rev. by R. C. Berner, AmArc, 39(Jl 1976):354-5; T. Walch, JISHS, 70(Aug 1977):250-1.

Mitchell, Virgil L. The Civil Works Administration in Louisiana: A Study in New Deal Relief, 1933-1934. Lafayette: U Southwestern Louisiana, 1976. Rev. by D. H. Culbert, LaH, 18 (Sum 1977):354-5.

Mitteilungen des osterreichischen Staatsarchivs. Vol. 28, Festschrift: Walter Goldinger. Vienna: Ferdinand Berger and Sons, 1975. Rev. by M. L. Brown, Jr., AHR, 82(Feb 1977):134-5.

Mitteis, H. The State in the Middle Ages: A Comparative Constitutional History of Feudal Europe. Amsterdam and Oxford: North Holland Publishing, 1975. Rev. by T. Reuter, History, 62(Feb 1977):95-6.

Mitten, David Gordon. Museum of Art, Rhode Island School of Design. Catalogue of the Collection. Providence: Rhode Island School of Design, 1975. Rev. by D. K. Hill, AJA, 81 (Win 1977):120-1.

Moggridge, D. E. British Monetary Policy, 1924-1931: The Norman Conquest of $4.86. Cambridge: Cam U Press, 1972. Rev. by J. Hughes, JEH, 37(Sep 1977):830-1.

Mohr, James C., ed. Radical Republicans in the North: State Politics During Reconstruction. Baltimore: JHU Press, 1976. Rev. by R. O. Curry, AHR, 81(Dec 1976):1255-56; A. R. Sunseri, Al, 44(Fall 1977):154-5; L. P. Curry, JISHS, 70 (May 1977):169-70; P. Levine, MichH, 61(Fall 1977):263-6.

Molloy, Anne. Wampum. New York: Hastings House, n.d. Rev. in InHi, 10(Sum 1977):47.

Molloy, Judith see Minogue, Martin

Mommsen, Wolfgang J. Imperialismustheorien: Ein Überblick über
die neuren Imperialismusinterpretationen. Gottingen: Band-
enhoeck und Rupprecht, 1977. Rev. by P. M. Kennedy, HJ,
20(No. 3, 1977):761-9.

Monach, Jorge. Frontiers in the Americas: A Global Perspective.
New York: Col U, 1975. Rev. by G. A. Brubaker, HAHR,
57(Feb 1977):106-7.

Monaco, Paul. Cinema and Society: France and Germany during
the Twenties. New York: Elsevier, 1976. Rev. by T. L.
Sakmyster, AHR, 82(Feb 1977):90-1.

Monfasani, John. George of Trebizond: A Biography and a Study
of His Rhetoric and Logic. Leiden: E. J. Brill, 1976. Rev.
by R. C. Dales, AHR, 82(Feb 1977):80-1; Alan Haynes, HTo,
27(Apr 1977):266-7.

Monkkonen, Eric H. The Dangerous Class: Crime and Poverty in
Columbus, Ohio, 1860-1885. Cambridge: Har U Press, 1975.
Rev. by L. J. Iorizzo, AHR, 81(Dec 1976):1257-58.

Monnig, Herman see Barratt, John

Monod, Th., ed. Pastoralism in Tropical Africa: Studies Pre-
sented and Discussed at the XIIIth International African Seminar,
Miamey, December 1972. London: Oxford U Press, 1975.
Rev. by T. Ingold, Africa, 47(No. 2, 1977):220-1.

Monroe, James T. Hispano-Arabic Poetry: A Student Anthology.
Los Angeles and London: U Cal Press, 1974. Rev. by A. G.
Chejne, JNES, 36(Jl 1977):241-2.

Monsagrati, Giuseppe. Federalismo e unità nell'azione di Enrico
Cernuschi (1848-1851). Pisa: Nistri-Lischi, 1976. Rev. by
K. J. Kirkland, AHR, 82(Apr 1977):385; H. Header, EHR,
92(Oct 1977):921-2.

Montaigne, Sanford H. Blood Over Texas. The Truth about Mexico's
War with the United States. New Rochelle: Arlington House,
1976. Rev. by F. Rader, AI, 44(Sum 1977):73-4; D. Stuart,
ETHJ, 15(No. 2, 1977):58-9; O. B. Faulk, LaH, 18(Sum 1977):
375.

Montana Historical Society. Not in Precious Metals Alone: A
Manuscript History of Montana. Helena: Montana Historical
Society Press, 1976. Rev. by M. Wells, WHQ, 8(Jl 1977):
337-8.

Monter, E. William. Witchcraft in France and Switzerland: The
Borderlands During the Reformation. London: Cornell U
Press, 1976. Rev. by P. Burke, History, 62(Je 1977):318-9.

Montgomery, Leslie Alexander. Ballygullion by Lynn Doyle, pseud. Belfast: Blackstaff Press, 1976. Rev. by C. W. Barrow, E-I, 12(Fall 1977):147-9.

Moodie, T. Dunbar. The Rise of Afrikanerdom: Power, Apartheid and the Afrikaner Civil Religion. Berkeley: U Cal Press, 1975. Rev. by S. Paterson, AfAf, 76(Jan 1977):108-11; S. Marks, History, 62(Je 1977):271-2.

Moody, Eric N. Southern Gentleman of Nevada Politics: Vail M. Pittman. Reno: U Nevada Press, 1974. Rev. by L. B. Chan, PHR, 46(Aug 1977):514-5.

Moody, Joseph N., ed. see Carter, Edward C., II, ed.

Moody, T. W., et al., eds. A New History of Ireland. Vol. 3: Early Modern Period, 1534-1691. New York: Ox U Press, 1976. Rev. by K. S. Bottigheimer, AHR, 82(Apr 1977): 364; B. Bradshaw, HJ, 20(No. 1, 1977):258-9; J. J. N. McGark, HTo, 27(Apr 1977):267-9.

Mookerjee, Amalendu Prasad. Social and Political Ideas of Bipin Chandra Pal. Calcutta: Minerva Associates, 1974. Rev. by C. Furedy, JAS, 36(May 1977):572-3.

Moon, P., ed. see Mansergh, N., ed.

Moore, Carey, A., ed. see Bream, Howard, N., ed.

Moore, D. M., tr. see Martin, Marie-Louise

Moore, Donald, ed. Wales in the Eighteenth Century. Swansea: Christopher Davies, 1976. Rev. by B. E. Howells, History, 62(Je 1977):325-6.

Moore, James Tice. Two Paths to the New South: The Virginia Debt Controversy, 1870-1883. Lexington: U Press of Kentucky, 1974. Rev. by M. V. Woodward, FCHQ, 51(Apr 1977): 206-8.

Moore, Joan W. Mexican Americans. Englewood Cliffs, N.J.: Prentice Hall, 1976. Rev. by R. H. Vigil, HAHR, 57(Feb 1977):108-9.

Moore, John Hammond. Albemarle: Jefferson's County, 1727-1976. Charlottesville: Published for the Albemarle County Historical Society by the University Press of Virginia, 1976. Rev. by G. L. Browne, JSH, 43(Aug 1977):494-6; G. G. Shackelford, VMHB, 85(Apr 1977):202-3.

Moore, John Preston. Revolt in Louisiana: The Spanish Occupation, 1766-1770. Baton Rouge: LSU Press, 1976. Rev. by J. Sosin, AHR, 82(Je 1977):734-5; A. Henderson, JISHS, 70(Aug

1977):256; J. D. L. Holmes, JMiH, 39(Aug 1977):281-2; M. Boyd, JSH, 43(Nov 1977):604-5; A. P. McDonald, WHQ, 8(Jl 1977):355-6.

Moore, Mary B. and Dietrich von Bothmer. Corpus Vasorum Antiquorum, U.S.A. 16, The Metropolitan Museum of Art 4. New York: Metropolitan Museum of Art, 1976. Rev. by C. G. Boulter, AJA, 81(Win 1977):122-3.

Moore, Robert see Ellis, Joseph

Moore, William Howard. The Kefauver Committee and the Politics of Crime, 1950-1952. Columbia: U Mo Press, 1974. Rev. by R. Griffith, AHR, 82(Apr 1977):471-2.

Moorhead, Max L. The Presidio: Bastion of the Spanish Borderlands. Norman: U Ok Press, 1975. Rev. by B. E. Bobb, PHR, 46(Feb 1977):119-20; J. L. Kessell, PHR, 46(Aug 1977): 492-4.

Mora, Manuel Arguello. La trinchera y otras páginas históricas. San Jose, C. R.: Editorial Costa Rica, 1975. Rev. by C. L. Stansifer, HAHR, 57(Aug 1977):545-6.

Morales, Waltraud Q. see Duff, Ernest A.

Moran, Ronald see Lensing, George S.

Moreno, Christiana Renate. Kaufmannschaft und Handelskapitalismus in der Stadt Mexiko (1759-1778). Bonn: Rheinische Freidrich - Wilhelms - Universitat. Rev. by W. Borah, HAHR, 57(Feb 1977):121-3.

Morenz, Siegfried. Religion und Geschicte des alten Agypten: gesammelte Aufsatze. Weimar: Hermann Bohlaus Nachfolger, 1975. Rev. by D. Mueller, JNES, 36(Oct 1977):314-5.

Moret, Jean-Marc. L'llioupersis Dans La Ceramique Italiote. Les Mythes et Leur Expression Figuerev Au IVe siecle. Geneva: Imprimerie du "Journal de Geneve", 1975. Rev. by M. I. Davies, AJA, 81(Sum 1977):404-5.

Morgan, Cecil, comp. The First Constitution of the State of Louisiana. Baton Rouge: LSU Press, 1975. Rev. by J. T. Hatfield, LaH, 18(Sum 1977):371-2.

Morgan, David. Suffragists and Liberals: The Politics of Woman Suffrage in England. Oxford: Basil Blackwell, 1975. Rev. by G. R. Searle, History, 62(Feb 1977):143-4.

Morgan, David T. and William J. Schmidt. North Carolinians in the Continental Congress. Winston Salem: John F. Blair, 1976. Rev. by M. R. Williams, CHQ, 51(Sum 1977):208-9.

Morgan, David W.   The Socialist Left and the German Revolution:
   A History of the German Independent Social Democratic Party,
   1917-1922.   Ithaca: Cornell U Press, 1975.   Rev. by W.
   Struve, AHR, 82(Je 1977):666-7; G. Eley, HJ, 20(No. 2,
   1977):521-4; M. Nolan, JMH, 49(Sep 1977):507-12.

Morgan, Edmund S.   American Slavery, American Freedom: The
   Ordeal of Colonial Virginia.   New York: W. W. Norton,
   1975.   Rev. by M. Mullin, AgH, 51(Jl 1977):618-20; J. R. Ple,
   HJ, 20(No. 2, 1977):503-13; W. M. Billings, VMHB, 85(Jan
   1977):98-100; A. Zilversmit, WMH, 60(Spr 1977):243-5.

_____. The Challenge of the American Revolution.   New York:
   W. W. Norton, 1976.   Rev. by D. L. Ammerman, NEQ, 50
   (Mar 1977):149-50.

_____. The Meaning of Independence: John Adams, George
   Washington, Thomas Jefferson.   Charlottesville: U Press Va,
   1976.   Rev. by C. Jackson, JSH, 607-8.

Morgan, Janet P.   The House of Lords and the Labour Government,
   1964-1970.   New York: Ox U Press, 1975.   Rev. by A. F.
   Havighurst, AHR, 82(Feb 1977):111.

Morgan, Neil and Tom Blair.   Yesterday's San Diego.   Miami: E.
   A. Seemann, 1976.   Rev. by R. Pourade, CHQ, 55(Win 1976/
   77):375; B. Luckinham, JOW, 16(Jan 1977):71.

Morgan, William James, ed.   Naval Documents of the American
   Revolution: Volume 7 American Theatre: Nov. 1, 1776-Dec.
   31, 1776.   European Theatre: Oct. 6, 1976-Dec. 31, 1776.
   American Theatre: Jan. 1, 1777-Feb. 28, 1777.   Washington,
   D.C.: Government Printing Office, 1976.   Rev. by W. B.
   Kennedy, GHQ, 51(Spr 1977):99-100; S. G. Morse, NEQ, 50
   (Sep 1977):551-4.

Morison, Elizabeth Forbes and Elting E. Morison.   New Hampshire:
   A Bicentennial History.   New York: Norton, 1976.   Rev. by
   J. B. Armstrong, NEQ, 50(Sep 1977):521-523.

Morison, Elting E.   see   Morison, Elizabeth Forbes

Morison, S. E., H. S. Commanger, W. E. Leuchtenburg.   A Concise History of the American People.   New York: Ox U Press,
   1977.   Rev. by P. A. M. Taylor, JAmS, 11(Dec 1977):379-80.

Morland, J. Kenneth, ed.   see   Kaufman, Harold F., ed.

Morningstar, Connie.   Early Utah Furniture.   Logan: Utah St U,
   Press, 1976.   Rev. by N. H. Richards, UHQ, 45(Spr 1977):
   204-5.

Morrill, J. S.   The Revolt of the Provinces: Conservatives and

Radicals in the English Civil War, 1630-1650. New York:
Barnes and Noble, 1976. Rev. by P. Zagorin, AHR, 82(Apr
1977):353; F. D. Don, History, 62(Feb 1977):120.

Morris, John W., Charles R. Goins, and Edwin C. McReynolds.
Historical Atlas of Oklahoma. Norman: U Ok Press, 1976.
Rev. by S. D. Nichol, ChOk, 55(Sum 1977):231-2.

Morris, Lucy Leavenworth Wilder, ed. Old Rail Fence Corners:
Frontier Tales Told by Minnesota Pioneers. St. Paul: Minnesota Historical Society Press, 1976. Rev. by J. T. Flanagan, MinnH, 45(Spr 1977):200.

Morris, Margaret. The General Strike. London: Penguin Books,
1976. Rev. by R. Bean, BH, 19(Jl 1977):224-6; A. Reid &
S. Tolliday, HJ, 20(No. 4, 1977):1001-12.

Morris, R. J. Cholera 1832: The Social Response to an Epidemic.
London: Croom Helm, 1976. Rev. by M. A. Crowther, HJ,
20(No. 4, 1977):991-9.

Morris, Richard B., and Floyd M. Shumway, eds. John Jay: The
Making of a Revolutionary. Volume I: Unpublished Papers,
1745-1780. New York: Harper & Row, 1975. Rev. by D.
Roper, WMQ, 34(Jan 1977):134-6.

Morrison, George E. The Correspondence of G. E. Morrison.
Vol. I: 1895-1912. New York: Cam U Press, 1976. Rev.
by H. Z. Schiffrin, AHR, 82(Apr 1977):413; E. P. Young,
CQ, 69(Mar 1977):160-2; E. W. Edwards, EHR, 92(Oct 1977):
926-7; I. Nish, History, 62(Je 1977):293-4; H. J. Wood, JAS,
36(Aug 1977):721-2.

Morrison, Theodore. Middlebury College Breadloaf Writers' Conference: The First Thirty Years (1926-1955). Middlebury:
Middlebury College Press, 1976. Rev. by J. J. Duffy, VH,
45(Fall 1977):249-52.

Morrow, Mable. Indian Rawhide: An American Folk Art. Norman:
U Oklahoma Press, 1975. Rev. by C. L. Tanner, AIQ, 3(Aut
1977):261-3; J. S. Ballard, JOW, 16(Jl 1977):92; J. C. Ewers,
NMHR, 52(Jl 1977):255-7.

Morton, David. The Traditional Music of Thailand. Berkeley: U
Cal Press, 1976. Rev. by M. J. Kartomi, JAS, 36(Aug 1977):
791-2.

Morton, Harry. The Wind Commands: Sailors and Sailing Ships in
the Pacific. Vancouver: U Brit Col Press, 1975. Rev. by
W. A. B. Douglas, CHR, 58(Mar 1977):101-2.

Morton, James. In the Sea of Sterile Mountains: The Chinese in
British Columbia. Vancouver: J. J. Douglas, 1974. Rev. by
R. L. Worden, JAS, 36(Feb 1977):347-9.

Moscotti, Albert D. British Policy and the Nationalist Movement in
    Burma, 1917-1937. Honolulu: U Press Hawaii, 1974. Rev.
    by M. Caldwell, History, 62(Je 1977):299.

Moser, Harold D., ed. see Wiltse, Charles M., ed.

Moses, John A. The Politics of Illusion: The Fischer Controversy
    in German Historiography. New York: Barnes and Noble,
    1975. Rev. by J. Remak, AHR, 82(Feb 1977):129-30.

Mosley, Leonard. Lindbergh: A Biography. New York: Doubleday,
    1976. Rev. by A. Keller, AHI, 11(Jan 1977):49; R. A. Lee,
    AHR, 82(Apr 1977):471; N. Eubank, MinnH, 45(Win 1977):159.

Mosley, Nicholas. Julian Grenfell: His Life and the Times of His
    Death, 1888-1915. New York: Holt, Rinehart and Winston,
    1976. Rev. by S. Hynes, AHR, 82(Je 1977):640-1.

Moss, Bernard H. The Origins of the French Labor Movement,
    1830-1914. Berkeley: U Cal Press, 1976. Rev. by C. H.
    Johnson, AHR, 82(Apr 1977):371-2; J. H. Smith, JEH, 37(Sep
    1977):832-3; W. H. Sewell, Jr., JIH, 8(Sum 1977):158-60.

Moss, R. P. and R. J. A. R. Rathbone. The Population Factor
    in African Studies. London: U London Press, 1975. Rev.
    by J. C. Caldwell, Africa, 47(No. 1, 1977):117-18.

Moss, Rosalind L. B. see Porter, Bertha

Mossiker, Frances. Pocahontas: The Life and the Legend. New
    York: Knopf, 1976. Rev. by W. S. Robinson, VMHB, 45(Jl
    1977):363-4.

Motley, Mary Penick. The Invisible Soldier: The Experience of the
    Black Soldier, World War II. Detroit: Wayne St U Press,
    1975. Rev. by R. W. Thomas, MichH, 61(Sum 1977):176-9;
    R. C. Reinders, JAmS, 11(Apr 1977):157-9.

Mott, Michael. Absence of Unicorns, Presence of Lions. Boston:
    Little, Brown, 1976. Rev. by M. G. Cooke, GR, 31(Fall
    1977):718-29.

Moureaux, Philippe. Les Préoccupations statistiques du gouvern-
    ment des Pays-Bas autrichiens et la denombrement des indus-
    tries dressé en 1764. Brussels: Editions de l'Université de
    Bruxelles, 1971. Rev. by F. F. Mendels, AHR, 82(Apr 1977):
    376.

Mousnier, Roland. Recherches sur la stratification sociale à Paris
    aux XVIIe siècles. Paris: Editions A. Pedone, 1976. Rev.
    by C. C. Lougee, AHR, 82(Je 1977):648-9.

Movius, Hallam L., Jr. Excavation of the Abri Patand, Les Eyzies

MOZINGO 224

(Dordogne). Cambridge: Harvard, 1975. Rev. by G. Clark, Antiquity, 51(Mar 1977):78-9.

Mozingo, David. Chinese Policy toward Indonesia, 1949-1967. Ithaca: Cornell U Press, 1976. Rev. by P. V. Ness, JAS, 37(Nov 1977):93-5.

Mueller, Peter G. and Douglas A. Ross. China and Japan--Emerging Global Powers. New York: Praeger, 1975. Rev. by R. Simmons, CQ, No. 69(Mar 1977):174-5.

Mugnier, Francois. Louisiana Images 1880-1920: A Photographic Essay. Baton Rouge: LSU Press, 1975. Rev. by L. V. Huber, LaH, 18(Win 1977):123-4.

Mugno, John F. see Rustow, Dankwort A.

Mukherji, Probhat Kumar. Life of Tagore. Tr. by Sisirkumar Ghosh. Thompson, Conn.: InterCulture Associates, 1976. Rev. by M. Lago, JAS, 37(Nov 1977):151-2.

Müller, Dirk H. Idealismus und Revolution: Zur Opposition der Jungen gegen den sozial demokratischen Parteivorstand, 1890 bis 1894. Berlin: Colloquium Verlag, 1975. Rev. by R. F. Wheeler, AHR, 82(Feb 1977):126-7.

Muller, Kurt, et al. Tiryns. Forschungen und Berichte. Mainz Am Rhein: Verlag Philipp von Zabern, 1975. Rev. by J. B. Rutter, AJA, 81(Sum 1977):392-4.

Muller, M. S. Action and Interaction: Social Relationships in a Low-Income Housing Estate in Itale, Kenya. Leiden: Afr. Studiecentrum, 1976. Rev. by R. D. Grillo, Africa, 47(No. 3, 1977):327-9.

Mullin, Michael, ed. American Negro Slaver: A Documentary History. Columbia: USC Press, 1976. Rev. by B. I. Wiley, AHI, 11(Feb 1977):49; R. Holland, JSH, 43(May 1977):295-6.

Munro, Dana G. The United States and the Caribbean Republics, 1921-1933. Princeton: Prin U Press, 1974. Rev. by D. M. Pletcher, AHR, 82(Feb 1977):39-59.

Munro, J. Forbes. Africa and the International Economy, 1800-1960. Totowa, N.J.: Rowman and Littlefield, 1976. Rev. by P. Manning, AHR, 82(Oct 1977):1032; P. D. Curtin, JEH, 37(Sep 1977):833-5.

_____. Colonial Rule and the Kamba: Social Change in the Kenya Highlands 1889-1939. Oxford: Clarendon Press, 1975. Rev. by G. W. B. Huntingford, Africa, 47(No. 2, 1977):227; C. Ehrlich, History, 62(Je 1977):278-9.

Munson, Charlie. Mister Charlie: Memoir of a Texas Lawman,
    1902-1910. Edited by Kenneth E. Munson. Austin: Madrona
    Press, 1975. Rev. by G. L. Roberts, A&W, 19(Sum 1977):
    186-7.

Munson, Kenneth E., ed. see Munson, Charlie

Muraskin, William Alan. Middle-Class Blacks in a White Society:
    Prince Hall Freemasonry in America. Berkeley: U Cal
    Press, 1976. Rev. by R. C. Reinders, JAmS, 11(Apr 1977):
    146-7.

Murfield, Doug, ed. see Williams, James H., ed.

Muria, Jose Marie. Bartolome de las Casas ante la historiografia
    mexicano. Mexico: SepSetentas, 1974. Rev. by H. R.
    Parish, HAHR, 57(Feb 1977):123-4.

Muriel, Josefina. Los recogimientos de mujeres: Respuesta a una
    problematica social novohispana. Mexico: Universidad Auto-
    noma de Mexico, 1974. Rev. by A. Lavrin, HAHR, 57(May
    1977):338-9.

Murphey, Rhoads, ed. see Basu, Dilip

_____, ed. see Meisner, Maurice, ed.

Murphree, M. W., ed. Education, Race and Employment in Rho-
    desia. Salisbury: Association of Round Tables in Africa,
    1975. Rev. by L. Mair, Africa, 47(No. 1, 1977):115-16.

Murphy, James. An Archeological History of the Hocking Valley.
    Athens: Ohio U Press, 1975. Rev. by B. H. Butler, AIQ,
    3(Sum 1977):153-5.

Murphy, Joseph F. Tenacious Monks: The Oklahoma Benedictines,
    1875-1975. Shawnee: Benedictine Color Press, 1974. Rev.
    by G. H. Shirk, ChOk, 55(Sum 1977):243.

Murray, Alton J. South Georgia Rebels, the True Wartime Exper-
    iences of the 26th Regiment Georgia Volunteer Infantry Lawton-
    Gordon-Evans Brigade Confederate States Army 1861-1865.
    St. Marys, Ga.: author, 1976. Rev. by D. Evans, GHQ, 51
    (Spr 1977):95-6.

Murray, Robert A. Fort Laramie: "Visions of a Grand Old Post."
    Ft. Collins, Colorado: Old Army Press, 1974. Rev. by P.
    D. Riley, A&W, 19(Spr 1977):88-89.

_____. Military Posts of Wyoming. Ft. Collins, Colorado:
    Old Army Press, 1974. Rev. by P. D. Riley, A&W, 19
    (Spr 1977):88-89.

_____. The 103rd Ballot: Democrats and the Disaster in Madison Square Garden. New York: Harper & Row, 1976. Rev. by B. Noggle, AHR, 82(Feb 1977):202-3; T. H. Smith, WVH, 38(Apr 1977):242-3.

Musset, Lucien. The Germanic Invasions: The Making of Europe A. D. 400-600. London: Elek, 1975. Rev. by R. A. Markus, History, 62(Feb 1977):94-5.

Mutiso, Gideon-Cyrus M. and S. W. Rohio, ed. Readings in African Political Thought. London: Heinemann, 1975. Rev. by A. H. M. Kirk-Greene, Africa, 47(No. 1, 1977):114.

Mutswairo, S. M., et al. Zimbabwe: Prose and Poetry. Washington, D.C.: Three Continents Press, 1974. Rev. by E. Windrich, AfAf, 76(Jan 1977):119-22.

Myers, Richmond E. Northampton County in the American Revolution. Easton, Pa.: Northampton County Historical Society, 1976. Rev. by H. J. Young, PH, 45(Jl 1977):283.

Myers, Robert Manson, ed. A Georgian at Princeton. New York: Harcourt, Brace, Jovanovich, 1976. Rev. by B. I. Wiley, CWTI, 16(Apr 1977):47; J. Rabun, FHQ, 55(Apr 1977):498-500; D. D. Bruce, Jr., JSH, 43(Feb 1977):129-30.

Myers, William A. and Ira L. Swett. Trolleys to the Surf: The Story of the Los Angeles Pacific Railway. Glendale: Interurban Publications, 1976. Rev. by S. Crump, CHQ, 56(Sum 1977):186-7.

Nachtigal, Gustav. Sahara and Sudan. Vol. 1: Tripoli and Fezzan, Tibesti or Tu. Tr. and ed. by Allan G. B. Fisher and Humphrey J. Fisher. London: C. Hurst, 1974. Rev. by A. H. M. Kirk-Greene, Africa, 47(No. 1, 1977):108.

Nackman, Mark E. A Nation Within a Nation: The Rise of Texas Nationalism. Port Washington, N.Y.: Kennikat Press, 1975. Rev. by A. Barr, WHQ, 8(Jl 1977):331.

Nadeau, Remi. The Real Joaquin Murieta: Robin Hood Hero or Gold Rush Gangster? Corona del Mar: Trans-Anglo Books, 1974. Rev. by L. Pitt, CHQ, 56(Spr 1977):86-7.

Nagel, Gunther W. Jane Stanford: Her Life and Letters. Stanford: Stanford Alumni Assoc., 1975. Rev. by G. R. Lothrop, PHR, 46(Aug 1977):507-8; F. L. Beach, WHQ, 8(Jan 1977):57-8.

Najita, Tetsuo. Japan. Englewood Cliffs, N.J.: Prentice-Hall, 1974. Rev. by G. L. Bernstein, JAS, 36(Aug 1977):754-6.

Nam, Koon Woo. The North Korean Communist Leadership, 1945-65. University, Alabama: U Alabama Press, 1974. Rev. by D. Tretiak, CQ, No. 70(Je 1977):435-7.

227 NAOHIRO

Naohiro, Goi. Kindai Nihon to Tōyō shigaku. Tokyo: Aoki shoten, 1976. Rev. by J. A. Fogel, JAS, 37(Nov 1977):145-6.

Napoleoni, Claudio. Smith, Ricardo, Marx. New York: Halsted Press, 1975. Rev. by J. E. Seigel, AHR, 82(Feb 1977):63.

Nardi, Paolo. Mariano Sozzini: Giureconsulto senese del quattrocento. Milan: Dott. A. Giuffre Editore, 1974. Rev. by M. P. Gilmore, AHR, 82(Feb 1977):139-40.

Narkiewicz, Olga A. The Green Flag: Polish Populist Politics, 1867-1970. Totowa, N.J.: Rowman and Littlefield, 1976. Rev. by W. W. Soroka, AHR, 82(Apr 1977):396-7.

Nasatir, Abraham P. Borderland in Retreat: From Spanish Louisiana and to the Far Southwest. Albuquerque: UNM Press, 1976. Rev. by D. Tyler, A&W, 19(Sum 1977):189-91; D. J. Weber, AHR, 82(Apr 1977):439; S. L. Myres, JSH, 43(Feb 1977):117-8; G. C. Din, LaH, 18(Sum 1977):377-8; C. I. Archer, NMHR, 52(Apr 1977):159-61; D. C. Cutter, PHR, 46 (Aug 1977):491-2; L. Kinnaird, WHQ, 8(Jan 1977):70-1.

Nash, George H. The Conservative Intellectual Movement in America since 1945. New York: Basic Books, 1976. Rev. by A. Guttman, AHR, 82(Feb 1977):215; F. D. Mitchell, JSH, 43(Feb 1977):143-4.

Nathan, Andrew J. Peking Politics, 1918-1923: Factionalism and the Failure of Constitutionalism. Berkeley: U Cal Press, 1976. Rev. by F. G. Chan, AHR, 82(Feb 1977):161-2; V. G. Kiernan, History, 62(Je 1977):294; H. Ch'i, JAS, 36(Aug 1977):723-4.

Nathan, Leonard, tr. The Transport of Love: The Meghaduta of Kalidasa. Berkeley: U Cal Press, 1976. Rev. by E. Gerow, JAS, 37(Nov 1977):150-1.

Naujoks, Eberhard. Die parlamentarische Entstehung des Reichpressegesetzes in der Bismarckzeit (1848/74). Düsseldorf: Droste Verlag, 1975. Rev. by E. J. C. Hahn, AHR, 82(Oct 1977): 999-1000.

Nava, Julian and Bob Barger. California: Five Centuries of Cultural Contrasts. Beverly Hills: Glencoe Press, 1976. Rev. by E. Staniford, CHQ, 56(Spr 1977):83-4; S. C. Olin, Jr., PHR, 46(Aug 1977):511-2.

Neale, Gay. Brunswick County, Virginia, 1720-1975. Brunswick County, Va.: Brunswick County Bicentennial Committee, 1975. Rev. by S. H. Short, III, VMHB, 85(Jl 1977):364-5.

Neale, R. S., ed. see Kamenka, Eugene, ed.

Neale, Walter C. Monies in Societies. San Francisco, Calif.:
Chandler & Sharp, 1976. Rev. by R. K. Davidson, JEH,
37(Je 1977):542-3.

Nechkina, M. V. Vasilii Osipovich Kliuchevskii: A History of
His Life and Creative Work. Moscow: Izdatel'stvo "Nauka",
1974. Rev. by T. P. Dilkes, AHR, 82(Je 1977):697.

Needham, Joseph. Science and Civilisation in China. Vol. 5.,
Chemistry and Chemical Technology, part 3. New York:
Cam U Press, 1976. Rev. by E. Samuel, AHR, 82(Apr 1977):
409-10; N. Sivin, AHR, 82(Oct 1977):1041-3.

Neher, Clark D., ed. Modern Thai Politics: From Village to
Nation. Cambridge, Mass.: Schenkman Pub. Co., 1976.
Rev. by F. C. Darling, JAS, 37(Nov 1977):178-9.

Nehring, Karl. Matthias Corvinus, Kaiser Friedrich III, und das
Reich: Zum hunyadisch-habsburgischen Gegensatz im Donauraum. Munich: R. Oldenbourg Verlag, 1975. Rev. by L.
S. Domonkos, AHR, 82(Apr 1977):394; H. J. Cohn, History,
62(Je 1977):314.

Neidle, Cecycle S. America's Immigrant Women. New York:
Hippocrene Books, 1976. Rev. by A. K. Harris, AHR, 82
(Je 1977):756-7.

Nelson, Daniel. Managers and Workers: Origins of the New Factory System in the United States, 1880-1920. Madison: U
Wis Press, 1975. Rev. by P. Uselding, AHR, 81(Dec 1976):
1261-62; A. D. Chandler, Jr., JEH, 37(Je 1977):543-4.

Nelson, Douglas W. Heart Mountain: The History of an American
Concentration Camp. Madison: U Wis Press, 1976. Rev. by
J. Modell, AHR, 82(Apr 1977):469-70; M. P. Malone, A&W,
19(Sum 1977):187-8; E. Uno, CHQ, 55(Win 1976/77):367-8; S.
Tanaka, PNQ, 68(Jl 1977):146-7; R. S. Uno, UHQ, 45(Win
1977):95-7; A. R. Page, WHQ, 8(Jl 1977):350-1.

Nelson, Keith L. Victors Divided: America and the Allies in Ger-
many, 1918-1923. Berkeley: U Cal Press, 1975. Rev. by
L. E. Gelfand, Historian, 39(Feb 1977):353-4; W. A. Mc-
Dougall, JMH, 49(Mar 1977):122-5.

Nelson, Paul David. General Horatio Gates: A Biography. Baton
Rouge: LSU Press, 1976. Rev. by J. L. Stokesbury, AHI,
12(Oct 1977):50; G. A. Billias, AHR, 82(Feb 1977):174-5; C.
W. Keller, AS, 18(Fall 1977):111; M. M. Klein, JSH, 43(Feb
1977):114-5; J. Catanzariti, WMQ, 34(Apr 1977):331-3; M. K.
Bushong, WVH, 38(Jan 1977):162-3.

Nelson, William. The Correspondence of William Nelson as Acting
Governor of Virginia, 1770-1771. Ed. by John C. Van Horne.

Charlottesville: U Press Virginia, 1975. Rev. by E. G.
Evans, VMHB, 85(Apr 1977):200-1.

Nelson, William E. Americanization of the Common Law: The
Impact of Legal Change on Massachusetts Society, 1760-1830.
Cambridge, Mass.: Harvard U Press, 1975. Rev. by H.
Belz, AHR, 82(Feb 1977):175; C. T. Cullen, WMQ, 34(Apr
1977):318-20.

Neruda, Pablo. Memoirs. n.l.: Farrar, Straus & Giroux, n.d.
Rev. by M. Falcoff, Comm, 63(May 1977):84-6.

Nesbit, Robert C. Wisconsin: A History. Madison: U Wis Press,
1973. Rev. by L. Gara, Historian, 39(Feb 1977):377-8.

Neubrech, Walt see Williams, C. H.

Neuenschwander, John A. Kenosha County in the Twentieth Century.
Kenosha County Bicentennial Commission, 1976. Rev. by N.
C. Burckel, HT, 10(May 1977):497-8.

Nevakivi, Jukka. The Appeal That Was Never Made: The Allies,
Scandinavia and the Finnish Winter War, 1939-1940. Montreal:
McGill-Queen's University, 1977. Rev. by K. Forster, His-
tory, 6(Nov/Dec 1977):42-3.

Neville, John Davenport. Bacon's Rebellion: Abstracts of Materials
in the Colonial Records Project. Jamestown: Jamestown
Foundation, 1976. Rev. by R. B. Davis, VMHB, 85(Jan 1977):
101-3.

Newcomb, Horace. TV: The Most Popular Art. New York: Anchor
Books, 1974. Rev. by D. Thorburn, GR, 31(Fall 1977):775-8.

Newell, Gordon. Rogues, Buffoons and Statesmen. Seattle: Hangman Press, Superior Publishing, 1975. Rev. by G. W. Scott,
PNQ, 68(Jan 1977):44-5.

Newman, Eric P. The Early Paper Money of America. Racine:
Western Pub. Co., 1976. Rev. by K. Bressett, WMH, 60
(Sum 1977):340-1.

Newman, Simon. March 1939: The British Guarantee to Poland,
a Study in the Continuity of British Foreign Policy. Oxford:
Clarendon Press, 1976. Rev. by D. Lammers, AHR, 82(Je
1977):642-3.

Niatum, Duane, ed. Carrier of the Dream Wheel: Contemporary
Native American Poetry. New York: Harper & Row, 1975.
Rev. by M. G. Cooke, AIQ, 3(Spr 1977):51-3.

Nibbi, Alessandra. The Sea Peoples and Egypt. Park Ridge, N.J.:
Noyes Press, 1975. Rev. by D. Lorton, JNES, 36(Oct 1977):
315-8.

Nicholas, H. G. The United States and Britain. Chicago: U Chi Press, 1975. Rev. by C. S. Campbell, PHR, 46(May 1977): 301-2.

Nichols, Roger and Kenneth McLeish, comps. Through Roman Eyes: Roman Civilisation in the Words of Roman Writers. Cambridge: Cam U Press, 1976. Rev. by J. P. Zaccano, Jr., HT, 10 (May 1977):631.

Nickerson, Jane Soames. Homage to Malthus. Folkstone: Bailey Bros. and Swinfen for Kennikat Press, 1975. Rev. by R. Smith, History, 62(Feb 1977):80.

Nickey, Louise K. Cookery of the Prairie Homesteader. Beaverton, Oregon: The Touchstone Press, 1976. Rev. by J. C. Carey, JOW, 16(Jan 1977):76.

Nicolo, Mario San. Die Schlussklauseln der altbabylonischen Kauf und Tauschvertrage. Munich: C. H. Becksche Verlag, 1974. Rev. by R. D. Biggs, JNES, 36(Jan 1977):160.

Nicolson, John, ed. The Arizona of Joseph Pratt Allyn: Letters from a Pioneer Judge. Tucson: U Arizona Press, 1974. Rev. by C. Trafzer, ChOk, 54(Win 1976-77):530-1.

Nicolson, Nigel, ed. The Question of Things Happening; The Letters of Virginia Woolf, 1912-1922. n.l.: Hogarth, n.d. Rev. by J. Richardson, HTo, 27(Apr 1977):269-71.

Nie, Norman H., et al. The Changing American Voter. Cambridge, Mass.: Harvard U Press, 1976. Rev. by E. C. Ladd, Jr., AHR, 82(Apr 1977):762-3.

Nielsen, David Gordon. Black Ethos: Northern Urban Negro Life and Thought, 1890-1930. Westport, Conn.: Greenwood Press, 1977. Rev. by K. W. Goings, History, 6(Nov/Dec 1977):29.

Nipperdey, Thomas. Gesellschaft, Kultur, Theorie: Gesammelte Aufsätze zur neueren Geschichte. Göttingen: Vendenhoeck and Ruprecht, 1976. Rev. by H. M. Ermarth, AHR, 82(Je 1977):665-6.

Nishihara, Masahi. The Japanese and Sukarno's Indonesia: Tokyo-Jakarta Relations, 1951-1966. Honolulu: U Press of Hawaii, 1976. Rev. by G. K. Goodman, JAS, 37(Nov 1977):95-6.

Nishimura, Eshin. Unsui: A Diary of Zen Monastic Life. Ed. by Bardwell Smith. Honolulu: U Press of Hawaii, 1973. Rev. by C. S. Prebish, JAAS, 12(Jan/Oct 1977):272-3.

Nissen, Karen M. see Heizer, Robert F.

Noble, Donald R. and Joab L. Thomas, ed. The Rising South, Vol-

ume I: Changes and Issues. University, Alabama: U Alabama Press, 1976. Rev. by L. N. Allen, AlaR, 30(Jl 1977):
238-9.

Noble, Harold Joyce. Embassy at War: An Account of the Early
Weeks of the Korean War and U. S. Relations with South
Korean President Syngman Rhee. Seattle: U Wash Press,
1975. Rev. by G. Henderson, JAS, 36(Feb 1977):362-3; B.
C. Koh, PHR, 46(May 1977):317-8.

Nock, L. Floyd, III. Drummondtown, "A One Horse Town,"
Accomac Court House, Virginia. Verona, Va.: McClure
Press, 1976. Rev. by J. W. Edmonds, III, VMHB, 85(Jan
1977):115-16.

Noether, E. P., ed. see Tannenbaum, E. R., ed.

Noggle, Burl. Into the Twenties, the United States from Armistice
to Normalcy. Urbana: U Ill Press, 1974. Rev. by L. L.
Murray, PH, 45(Jl 1977):279-80.

Nolan, Alan T. The Iron Brigade: A Military History. Madison:
State Historical Society of Wisconsin, 1975. Rev. by J. I.
Robinson, Jr., CWH, 23(Mar 1977):85-7.

Nolan, Charles E. A Southern Catholic Heritage, Volume I, 1704-
1813. New Orleans: Archdiocese of New Orleans, 1976.
Rev. by G. C. Din, JMiH, 39(Aug 1977):282-3.

Nomikos, Eugenia V. and Robert C. North. International Crisis:
The Outbreak of World War I. Montreal: McGill-Queen's U
Press, 1976. Rev. by P. G. Halpern, AHR, 82(Je 1977):
626.

Nordin, D. Sven. Rich Harvest: A History of the Grange, 1867-
1900. Jackson: U Press Miss, 1974. Rev. by V. Carstensen, PNQ, 68(Jan 1977):38.

Norman, Benjamin Moore. Norman's New Orleans and Environs.
Baton Rouge: LSU Press, 1976. Rev. by J. Belsom, LaH,
18(Sum 1977):375-7.

Norman, E. R. Church and Society in England, 1770-1970. New
York: Ox U Press, 1976. Rev. by P. Marsh, AHR, 82(Oct
1977):966-7; K. Robbins, EHR, 92(Oct 1977):860-1; H. Mc-
Leod, History, 62(Je 1977):332-3.

Norman, Hans, ed. see Runblom, Harald, ed.

Northedge, F. S. The International Political System. London:
Faber & Faber, 1976. Rev. by C. B. Navari, History, 62
(Feb 1977):93.

Norton, Mary Beth. The British-Americans: The Loyalist Exiles
in England 1774-1789. London: Constable, 1974. Rev. by
C. C. Bonwick, JAmS, 11(Apr 1977):155-6.

Norton, Thomas Elliot. The Fur Trade in Colonial New York 1686-
1776. Madison: U Wisconsin Press, 1974. Rev. by R. S.
Nelson, Jr., PH, 45(Jan 1977):81-2.

Notestein, Lucy Lillian. Wooster of the Middle West. Vol. 2.
1911-1944. Kent: Kent St U Press, n.d. Rev. by G. J.
Clifford, AHR, 81(Dec 1976):1270-71.

Notovny, Anne. The Life and Photography of an American Original:
Alice Austin, 1866-1952. Old Greenwich, Conn.: Chattam
Press, 1976. Rev. by S. G. L., AS, 18(Fall 1977):112.

Novák, Petr. Die Schwerter in Der Tschechoslowakei I. München:
Becksche Verlagsbuchhandlung, 1975. Rev. by H. L. Thomas,
AJA, 81(Win 1977):115-6.

Novotny, Ann, ed. Picture Sources 3: Collections of Prints and
Photography in the U. S. and Canada. New York: SLA,
1975. Rev. by M. Peters, AmArc, 39(Jl 1976):363-4.

Nugent, Walter T. K. From Centennial to World War: American
Society, 1876-1917. Indianapolis: Bobbs-Merrill, 1976. Rev.
J. G. Sproat, AHR, 82(Oct 1977):1083; R. Jeffreys-Jones,
JAmS, 11(Dec 1977):427-8.

Numbers, Ronald L. Prophetess of Health: A Study of Ellen G.
White. New York: Harper & Row, 1976. Rev. by J. H.
Young, AHR, 82(Apr 1977):464; G. N. Grob, NEQ, 50(Je
1977):361-3; J. B. Blake, WMH, 60(Spr 1977):250-1.

Nuñez Muñoz, Maria F. La iglesia y la restauración, 1875-1881.
Santa Cruz de Tenerife: Caja General de Ahorros, 1976.
Rev. by N. A. Rosenblatt, AHR, 82(Oct 1977):989-990.

Nunn, Frederick M. The Military in Chilean History: Essays on
Civil-Military Relations, 1810-1973. Albuquerque: U NM
Press, 1976. Rev. by R. Oppenheimer, AHR, 82(Je 1977):
784; B. Loveman, HAHR, 57(Feb 1977):151-3; F. B. Pike,
Historian, 39(May 1977):596-7; W. F. Sater, TAm, 33(Apr
1977):685-7.

Nunn, Louie B. The Public Papers and Governor Louie B. Nunn,
1967-1971. Ed. by Robert F. Sexton and Lewis Bellardo, Jr.
Lexington: U Press of Kentucky, 1975. Rev. by M. F.
Mitchell, FCHQ, 51(Apr 1977):204-5.

Nurel-Din, M. A. A. The Demotic Ostraca in the National Museum
of Antiquities at Leiden. Leiden: E. J. Brill, 1974. Rev.
by J. H. Johnson, JNES, 36(Jl 1977):219.

Nye, Joseph S., Jr., ed. see Fox, Annette Baker, ed.

O, Jamie E. Rodriguez. The Emergence of Spanish America.
Vicente Rocafuerte and Spanish Americanism 1808-1832.
Berkeley: U Cal Press, 1975. Rev. by F. B. Pike, TAm,
33(Jan 1977):543-5.

Oakley, Kenneth P. Decorative and Symbolic Uses of Vertebrate
Fossils. Oxford: Ox U Press, 1975. Rev. by W. R. Trotter,
Antiquity, 51(Mar 1977):74-5.

Oaks, Dallin H. and Marvin S. Hill. Carthage Conspiracy: The
Trial of the Accused Assassins of Joseph Smith. Urbana: U
Ill Press, 1975. Rev. by M. Feldberg, AHR, 81(Dec 1976):
1248-49; M. S. DePillis, PHR, 46(Aug 1977):499-500.

Oates, Stephen B. With Malice Toward None: The Life of Abraham
Lincoln. New York: Harper and Row, 1977. Rev. by C. F.
Cooney, AHI, 12(Aug 1977):49; R. N. Current, AHR, 82(Oct
1977):1074-5; H. L. Trefousse, CWH, 23(Je 1977):170-2; R.
P. Basler, CWTI, 16(Jl 1977):49.

Obelkevich, James. Religion and Rural Society: South Lindsey,
1825-1875. Oxford: Ox U Press, 1976. Rev. by J. F. C.
Harrison, AHR, 82(Oct 1977):967-8.

O'Brien, Donal Cruise. Saints and Politicians: Essays in the
Organization of a Senegalese Peasant Society. Oxford, 1975.
Rev. by R. W. Johnson, AfAf, 76(Jan 1977):115-16; M. Gil-
senan, Africa, 47(No. 1, 1977):112-13; A. Hughes, History,
62(Je 1977):267.

O'Brien, Joseph V. William O'Brien and the Course of Irish Politics, 1881-1918. Berkeley: U Cal Press, 1976. Rev. by
D. W. Miller, AHR, 82(Je 1977):646-7; P. S. L. Lyons,
EHR, 92(Oct 1977):924-5; L. J. McCaffrey, Historian, 39(May
1977):544-5.

O'Brien, Philip. Allende's Chile. New York: Praeger, 1976.
Rev. by O. E. S., CurH, 72(Feb 1977):79.

O'Broin, Leon. Revolutionary Underground: The Story of the Irish
Republican Brotherhood, 1858-1924. Totowa, N.J.: Rowman
and Littlefield, 1976. Rev. by L. J. McCaffrey, AHR, 82
(Oct 1977):975-6.

O'Connell, Marvin R. The Counter Reformation, 1559-1610. New
York: Harper and Row, 1974. Rev. by E. Cochrane, AHR,
82(Feb 1977):86-8.

O'Connell, Maurice R., ed. The Correspondence of Daniel O'Connell.
Shannon: Irish U Press, 1972-4. Rev. by A. D. MacIntire,
EHR, 92(Oct 1977):862-4.

O'Day, Rosemary and Felicity Heal, eds. Continuity and Change:
  Personnel and Administration of the Church in England, 1500-
  1642. Atlantic Highlands, N.J.: Humanities Press, 1976.
  Rev. by S. Lehmberg, AHR, 82(Feb 1977):94-5.

Oddy, Derek and Derek Miller, eds. The Making of the Modern
  British Diet. London: Croom Helm, 1976. Rev. by R.
  Perren, History, 62(Je 1977):329.

O'Farrell, Patrick. England and Ireland Since 1800. Oxford: Ox
  U Press, 1975. Rev. by P. J. Buckland, History, 62(Feb
  1977):144-5.

Ogelsby, J. C. M. Gringos from the Far North. Essays in the
  History of Canadian-Latin American Relations 1866-1968.
  Toronto: Macmillan of Canada, McLean-Hunter Press, 1976.
  Rev. by M. Savelle, TAm, 34(Oct 1977):295-7.

O'Gorman, Frank. The Rise of Party in England: The Rockingham
  Whigs 1760-82. London: George Allen & Unwin, 1975. Rev.
  by J. Dinwiddy, HJ, 20(No. 4, 1977):983-9.

Oldenburg, Philip. Big City Government in India: Councilor, Administrator, and Citizen in Delhi. Tucson: U Arizona Press,
  1976. Rev. by D. B. Rosenthal, JAS, 37(Nov 1977):165-6.

Oleson, Alexandra and Sanborn C. Brown, eds. The Pursuit of
  Knowledge in the Early American Republic: American Scien-
  tific and Learned Societies from Colonial Times to the Civil
  War. Baltimore and London: JHU Press, 1976. Rev. by
  T. L. Haskell, JSH, 43(Feb 1977):126-8; R. E. Welch, Jr.,
  NEQ, 50(Mar 1977):158-60; R. N. Lokken, WMQ, 34(Apr
  1977):345-77.

Oliveira Lima, M. de. Pernambuco: Seu Desenvolvimento Histórico.
  Recife: Secretaria de Educacao e Cultura, 1975. Rev. by R.
  M. Levine, HAHR, 57(Aug 1977):549-50.

Oliver, Roland and Brian M. Fagan. Africa in the Iron Age: ca.
  500 B. C. to A. D. 1400. New York: Cam U Press, 1975.
  Rev. by J. H. Atherton, Archaeology, 30(Jan 1977):64; J.
  Alexander, Antiquity, 51(Jl 1977):155-6.

Ollard, Richard. This War Without an Enemy. A History of the
  English Civil Wars. n.l.: Hodder & Stoughton, n.d. Rev.
  by B. Pool, HTo, 27(Feb 1977):130-1.

Ollila, Douglas J., ed. see Karni, Michael G., ed.

Olmstead, Alan L. New York City Mutual Savings Banks, 1819-1861.
  Chapel Hill: U NCar Press, 1976. Rev. by H. Cohen, AHR,
  82(Je 1977):743.

Olmsted, R. R. see Watkins, T. H.

Olsen, Donald J. The Growth of Victorian London. New York:
    Holmes and Meier, 1976. Rev. by M. Wolff, AHR, 82(Oct
    1977):968; D. Cannandine, HJ, 20(No. 3, 1977):777-82.

Olson, Russell L. The Electric Railways of Minnesota. Hopkins,
    Minn.: Minnesota Transportation Museum, Inc., 1976. Rev.
    by A. J. Larsen, MinnH, 45(Fall 1977):301.

Olson, Sigurd F. Reflections from the North Country. New York:
    Knopf, 1976. Rev. by N. Searle, MinnH, 45(Sum 1977):255-6.

Olteanu, Stefan. Les Pays rounains à l'époque de Michel le Brave
    (l'Union de 1600). Bucharest: Editura Academiei Republicii
    Socialiste Romania, 1975. Rev. by K. Hitchins, JMH, 49(Je
    1977):339-41.

One Canada: Memoirs of the Right Honourable John G. Diefenbaker:
    The Crusading Years 1895-1965. Toronto: Macmillan, 1975.
    Rev. by H. B. Neathy, CHR, 58(Mar 1977):82-3.

O'Neal, William Bainter. Jefferson's Fine Arts Library: His Se-
    lections for the University of Virginia Together with His Own
    Architectural Books. Charlottesville: U Press Virginia,
    1976. Rev. by W. H. Adams, VMHB, 85(Jan 1977):111-12.

O'Neill, James E. and Robert W. Krauskopf, eds. World War II:
    An Account of its Documents. Washington: Howard Univer-
    sity Press, 1976. Rev. by R. D. Frederick, AmArc, 40(Apr
    1977):241.

Onon, Urgunge, tr. see Brown, William A., tr.

Ooms, Herman. Charismatic Bureaucrat: A Political Biography
    of Matsudaira Sadanobu, 1758-1829. Chicago: U Chi Press,
    1975. Rev. by J. W. Hall, JAS, 36(Aug 1977):741-3.

Oppler, Alfred C. Legal Reform in Occupied Japan: A Participant
    Looks Back. Princeton: Princeton U Press, 1976. Rev. by
    R. M. Spaulding, JAS, 37(Nov 1977):144-5; J. Williams, PHR,
    46(Aug 1977):531-2.

Orleans, Leo. Health Policies and Services in China, 1974. Wash-
    ington, D.C.: Government Printing Office, 1974. Rev. by P.
    S. Heller, CQ, No. 69(Mar 1977):179-81.

Orme, Nicholas. Education in the West of England, 1066-1548.
    Exeter: U Exeter Press, 1976. Rev. by J. M. McCarthy,
    AHR, 82(Je 1977):629; A. L. Rowse, HTo, 27(Aug 1977):
    548-9.

Orr, Linda. Jules Michelet: Nature, History, and Language.

Ithaca: Cornell U Press, 1976. Rev. by C. Rearick, AHR, 82(Je 1977):651-2; H. Kellner, H&T, 16(May 1977):217-29.

Ortega Y Medina, Juan A. Estudios de Tema Mexicano. Mexico: SepSetentas, 1973. Rev. by W. D. Root, HAHR, 57(Feb 1977): 110-11.

Ortí, Vicente Carcel. Política Eclesial de los Gobiernos Liberales Españoles, 1833-1840. Pamplona, Spain: Ediciones Universidad de Navarra, 1975. Rev. by J. C. Ullman, TAm, 34(Oct 1977):299-300.

Ortiz, Simon J. Going for the Rain. New York: Harper and Row, 1977. Rev. by J. H. C., InHi, 10(Sum 1977):48.

Osborne, Alfred E., Jr. see Bobo, Benjamin F.

Osfosu-Appiah, L. H. The Encyclopaedia Africana Dictionary of African Biography. Rev. by O. E. S. CurH, 73(Dec 1977): 223.

Oshinsky, David M. Senator Joseph McCarthy and the American Labor Movement. Columbia: U Mo Press, 1976. Rev. by A. Theoharis, AHR, 81(Dec 1976):1281.

Osthaus, Carl R. Freedman, Philanthropy, and Fraud: A History of the Freedman's Savings Bank. Urbana: U Ill Press, 1976. Rev. by W. S. McFeely, AHR, 82(Apr 1977):445-6; J. M. Richardson, FHQ, 55(Apr 1977):502-3; W. Hanchett, JISHS, 70(Feb 1977):92-3; L. Grossman, JSH, 43(May 1977):306-7.

Osvald, Karen Elizabeth see Hawes, Lilla Mills

Otte, Enrique, ed. see Lockhart, James, ed.

Otto, Volker. Das Staatsverstandnis des Parlamentarischen Rates. Dusseldorf: Droste Verlag, 1971. Rev. by C. G. Anthon, AHR, 82(Feb 1977):133-34.

Overmyer, Daniel. Folk Buddhist Religion: Dissenting Sects in Late Traditional China. Cambridge, Mass.: Har U Press, 1976. Rev. by M. Gasster, AHR, 82(Oct 1977):1047-8; R. Thaxton, JAS, 37(Nov 1977):105-7; E. C. Carlson, JIH, 8(Aut 1977):397-8.

Overy, R. J. William Morris, Viscount Nuffield. London: Europa Publications, 1976. Rev. by P. N. Davies, BH, 19(Jan 1977): 107.

Owens, Harry P., ed. Perspectives and Irony in American Slavery. Jackson: U Press Mississippi, 1976. Rev. by J. M. Richardson, JMiH, 39(May 1977):185-6; V. B. Howard, JSH, 43(Aug 1977):456-7.

Owens, Leslie Howard. This Species of Property: Slave Life and
    Culture in the Old South. New York: Ox U Press, 1976.
    Rev. by B. I. Wiley, AHI, 11(Feb 1977):49; J. W. Blassingame,
    AHR, 82(Feb 1977):180-1; J. F. Smith, FHQ, 55(Apr 1977):
    497-8; J. D. Anderson, JNH, 62(Jl 1977):389-93.

Owens, William A. A Fair and Happy Land. New York: Scribner's
    1975. Rev. by A. E. Henderson, FCHQ, 51(Jl 1977):286-7.

Oxborrow, John see Glynn, Sean

Packard, David W. Minoan Linear A. Berkeley: U Cal Press,
    1974. Rev. by G. Nagy, AJA, 81(Spr 1977):243-4.

Paget, Julian. The Story of the Guards. n. l.: Osprey, n. d.
    Rev. by T. Prittie, HTo, 27(Je 1977):401-2.

Paget, Roger K. , ed. Indonesia Accuses! Soekarno's Defense
    Oration in the Political Trial of 1930. Kuala Lumpur: Ox U
    Press, 1975. Rev. by W. H. Frederick, JAS, 36(Feb 1977):
    386-7.

Painter, Nell Irvin. Exodusters: Black Migration to Kansas after
    Reconstruction. New York: Knopf, 1977. Rev. by W. I.
    Hair, AHR, 82(Oct 1977):1079.

Palic, Vladmir M. Government Publications: A Guide to Biblio-
    graphic Tools. Washington, D. C.: Library of Congress,
    1975. Rev. by H. Q. Schroyer, AmArc, 40(Jan 1977):91.

Palij, Michael. The Anarchism of Nesor Makhno, 1918-1921: An
    Aspect of the Ukrainian Revolution. Seattle: U Wash, 1977.
    Rev. by D. Reinhartz, History, 6(Oct 1977):16.

Palmer, Alan. Bismarck. New York: Scribners, 1976. Rev. by
    J. J. Johnson, Jr. , AHR, 82(Je 1977):663; F. B. M. Holly-
    day, Historian, 39(May 1977):556-7.

Palmer, Colin A. Slaves of the White God: Blacks in Mexico,
    1570-1650. Cambridge, Mass.: Har U Press, 1976. Rev.
    by H. S. Klein, AHR, 82(Apr 1977):477-8; P. Carroll, HAHR,
    57(May 1977):332-4; G. W. Graff, TAm, 34(Jl 1977):145-7; C.
    Gibson, JIH, 8(Aut 1977):396-7.

Palmer, Dave Richard. The Way of the Fox: American Strategy
    in the War for America, 1775-1783. Westport, Conn.:
    Greenwood Press, 1975. Rev. by J. M. Coleman, AHR, 82
    (Apr 1977):435-6.

Palmquist, Peter E. Fine California Views: The Photography of
    A. W. Ericson. Eureka: Interface California Corp. , 1975.
    Rev. by B. T. Hamilton, OrHQ, 78(Sep 1977):287.

_____ . With Nature's Children: Emma B. Freeman (1880-1928),
Camera and Brush. Eureka: Interface California Corp. , 1976.
Rev. by L. M. Dicker, CHQ, 56(Fall 1977):282-3.

Paludan, Phillip S. A Covenant with Death: The Constitution, Law,
and Equality in the Civil War Era. Urbana: U Ill Press,
1975. Rev. by D. M. Roper, NYHSQ, 61(Jan/Apr 1977):
94-5.

Paluka, Frank. The Three Voyages of Captain Cook. Pittsburgh:
Beta Phi Mu, 1974. Rev. by A. N. Ryan, History, 62(Je
1977):302-3.

Pancake, John S. 1777: The Year of the Hangman. University,
Ala.: U Ala Press, 1977. Rev. by L. R. Gerlach, History,
6(Oct 1977):3.

Pandey, B. N. Nehru. N.Y.: Stein and Day, 1976. Rev. by G.
Douds, HTo, 27(Mar 1977):197-8.

Pane, Luigi Dal. Industria e commercio nel Granducato di Toscana
nell'Eta del Risorigimento. Bologna: Il Mutino, 1971. Rev.
by I. A. Glazier, JEH, 37(Je 1977):504-5.

Pang-Yuan, Chi, ed. , et al. An Anthology of Contemporary Chinese Literature. Taipei: National Institute for Compilation
and Translation, 1975. Rev. by L. Dong and M. K. Hom,
JAS, 36(Aug 1977):738-41.

Panitch, Leo. Social Democracy and Industrial Militancy: The
Labour Party, the Trade Unions, and Incomes Policy, 1945-
1974. Cambridge and New York: Cam U Press, 1976. Rev.
by H. Pelling, JEH, 37(Sep 1977).

Paoli, Maria Céla Pinheiro Machado. Desenvolvimento e Margenalidade: Um Estudo de Caso. São Paulo: Livraria Peoneira
Editôra, 1974. Rev. by R. H. Chilcote, HAHR, 57(May
1977):373-4.

Papanikolas, Helen Z. , ed. The Peoples of Utah. Salt Lake City:
Utah State Historical Society, 1976. Rev. by W. H. Lyon,
JOW, 16(Jl 1977):93; C. S. Peterson, NMHR, 52(Jan 1977):
74-5; J. B. Romney, WHQ, 8(Jl 1977):336-7.

Papenfuse, Edward C. In Pursuit of Profit: The Annapolis Merchants in the Era of the American Revolution, 1763-1805.
Baltimore: JHU Press, 1975. Rev. by K. S. Kutolowski,
Historian, 39(May 1977):571-3; P. G. E. Clemens, NYHSQ,
61(Jan/Apr 1977):81-2.

_____ , et al. The Era of the American Revolution 1775-1789.
Annapolis: Hall of Records Commission, 1977. Rev. by J.
L. Harwood, AmArc, 40(Jl 1977):351-2.

_____, ed. see also Land, Aubrey C., ed.

Paranjpe, A. C. In Search of Identity. New York: Halsted Press,
1976. Rev. by P. N. Desai, JAS, 36(Aug 1977):774-5.

Parch, Geace D., ed. Directory of Newspaper Libraries in the U.
S. and Canada. New York: Special Libraries Assoc., 1976.
Rev. by H. Altschull, AHR, 82(Oct 1977):1068-9.

Paret, Peter. Clausewitz and the State. New York: Ox U Press,
1976. Rev. by R. B. M. Hollyday, AHR, 82(Feb 1977):
89-90.

Parker, John, ed. Journals of Jonathan Carver and Related Documents, 1766-1770. Rev. by O. W. Holmes, MinnH, 45(Win
1977):157.

Parker, Joseph B., ed. see Carleton, Mark T., ed.

Parker, Mattie Erma Edwards. North Carolina Higher-Court Records, 1697-1701. Raleigh, N.C.: State Department of
Archives and History, 1971. Rev. by H. A. Johnson, WMQ,
34(Jl 1977):501-3.

Parker, R. A. C. Coke of Norfolk: A Financial and Agricultural
Study, 1707-1842. New York: Ox U Press, 1975. Rev. by
B. H. Sexauer, AgH, 51(Apr 1977):477-8; R. G. Wilson, History, 62(Je 1977):329-30; R. A. Smith, JEH, 37(Je 1977):
544-6.

Parker, T. H. L. John Calvin: A Biography. London: J. M.
Dent, 1975. Rev. by A. Duke, History, 62(Je 1977):320.

Parker, William N. and Eric L. Jones, eds. European Peasants
and Their Markets: Essays in Agrarian Economic History.
Princeton: Prin U Press, 1975. Rev. by J. P. Huttman,
AgH, 51(Jan 1977):278-9; K. F. Drew, AHR, 82(Feb 1977):
83-4; M. P. Gutmann, JIH, 8(Sum 1977):152-4; R. B. Outhwaite, HJ, 20(No. 2, 1977):497-502.

Parkin, David, ed. Town and Country in Central and Eastern
Africa: Studies Presented and Discussed at the Twelfth International African Seminar, Lusaka, September 1972. London:
Ox U Press, 1975. Rev. by R. D. Grillo, Africa, 47(No. 3,
1977):327-9.

Parkinson, F. Latin America, the Cold War & the World Powers,
1945-1973, a Study in Diplomatic History. Beverly Hills:
Sage Publications, 1974. Rev. by D. M. Pletcher, AHR, 82
(Feb 1977):39-59.

Parkinson, J. R. see Faaland, Just

Parkinson, Roger. The Fox of the North: The Life of Kutuzov--
General of War and Peace. n.l.: Peter Davies, n.d. Rev.
by I. Grey, HTo, 27(Mar 1977):197.

Parkman, Aubrey. David Jayne Hill and the Problem of World
Peace. Lewisburg: Bucknell U Press, 1975. Rev. by R.
Stone, AHR, 81(Dec 1976):1265-66.

Parks, Joseph H. Joseph E. Brown of Georgia. Baton Rouge:
LSU Press, 1977. Rev. by P. D. Escott, GHQ, 51(Sum
1977):183-5.

Parks, Stephen. John Dunton and the English Book Trade: A
Study of His Career with a Checklist of His Publications.
New York: Garland, 1976. Rev. by N. S. Fiering, WMQ,
34(Jl 1977):513-6.

Parman, Donald L. The Navajos and the New Deal. New Haven:
Yale U Press, 1976. Rev. by L. K. Kelly, AHR, 82(Feb
1977):206-7; G. Thompson, Historian, 39(Feb 1977):383-4;
R. A. Trennert, NMHR, 52(Apr 1977):161-2; W. T. Hagan,
PHR, 46(Aug 1977); 513-4; L. M. Hauptman, WHQ, 8(Apr
1977):221-2.

Parmet, Herbert S. The Democrats: The Years Since FDR. New
York: Macmillan, 1976. Rev. by R. A. Divine, Historian,
39(May 1977):588-89.

Parmiter, G. de C. Elizabethan Popish Recusancy in the Inns of
Court. London: U London Institute of Historical Research,
1976. Rev. by C. Cross, History, 62(Je 1977):321.

Parrot, André. Mari Capitale Fabuleuse. Paris: Payot, 1974.
Rev. by M. J. Mellink, AHA, 81(Win 1977):115; M. J. Mellink, AHA, 81(Win 1977):115.

Parry, Noel and José Parry. The Rise of the Medical Profession:
A Study of Collective Social Mobility. London: Croom Helm,
1976. Rev. by M. A. Crowther, HJ, 20(No. 4, 1977):991-9.

Parry, V. J. and M. E. Yapp, eds. War, Technology and Society
in the Middle East. Oxford: Ox U Press, 1975. Rev. by J.
S. F. Parker, History, 62(Je 1977):281-2.

Parsons, F. V. The Origins of the Morocco Question, 1880-1900.
n.l.: Duckworth, n.d. Rev. by A. Boyle, HTo, 27(Jl 1977):
479-80.

Parsons, William Barclay. Engineers and Engineering in the Renaissance. Cambridge, Mass.: MIT Press, 1976. Rev. by
B. Hansen, AHR, 82(Je 1977):678-9.

Partner, Peter. Renaissance Rome 1500-1559: A Portrait of a

241   PASQUINUCCI

Society. Berkeley, Ca.: U Cal Press, 1977. Rev. by F. L. Cheyette, History, 6(Oct 1977):22.

Pasquinucci, Marinella see Boitani, Francesca

Pastor, Peter. Hungary between Wilson and Lenin: The Hungarian Revolution of 1918-1919 and the Big Three. New York: Columbia U Press, 1976. Rev. by E. S. Balogh, AHR, 82(Oct 1977):1020-21.

Patinkin, Don. Keynes' Monetary Thought: A Study of Its Development. Durham, N.C.: Duke U Press, 1976. Rev. by H. P. Minsky, JEH, 37(Je 1977):546-8.

Patrick, Hugh, ed. with assistance of Larry Meissner. Japanese Industrialization and Its Social Consequences. Berkeley: U Cal Press, 1976. Rev. by R. M. Marsh, JAS, 36(Aug 1977): 750-2.

Patschovsky, Alexander. Die Anfänge Einer Städigen Inquisition im Böhmen. Berlin: DeGruyter, 1975. Rev. by G. Leff, EHR, 92(Oct 1977):888.

Patterson, David S. Toward a Warless World: The Travail of the American Peace Movement, 1887-1914. Bloomington: Ind U Press, 1976. Rev. by R. Marchand, AHR, 82(Je 1977):758; A. E. Campbell, JAmS, 11(Aug 1977):296.

Patterson, James T., ed. Paths to the Present: Intrepretive Essays on American History since 1930. Minneapolis, Minn.: Burgess Publ. Co., 1975. Rev. by R. T. Ruetten, AHR, 81 (Dec 1976):1273.

Patterson, Sheila see Fortes, Meyer, ed.

Paul, Virginia. This Was Sheep Ranching Yesterday and Today. Seattle: Superior, 1976. Rev. by C. M. Sypolt, UHQ, 45 (Spr 1977):206-7.

Paulson, Joy, ed. see Lebra, Joyce, ed.

Paulson, Ronald. The Art of Hogarth. New York: Praeger, 1975. Rev. by J. D. Hunt, GR, 31(Sum 1977):517-22.

_____. Emblem and Expression: Meaning in English Art of the Eighteenth Century. Cambridge: Har U Press, 1975. Rev. by J. D. Hunt, GR, 31(Sum 1977):517-22.

Pauw, B. A. Christianity and Xhosa Tradition. Oxford U Press, 1975. Rev. by S. Marks, AfAf, 76(Apr 1977):273-4.

Pawson, Michael and David Buisseret. Port Royal, Jamaica. Oxford: Clarendon Press, 1975. Rev. by E. L. Farley, AHR, 82(Feb 1977):227-8; M. Craton, WMQ, 34(Apr 1977):343-5.

Payne, Harry C. The Philosophes and the People. New Haven, Conn.: Yale U Press, 1976. Rev. by R. Anchor, AHR, 82 (Feb 1977):90; N. Hampson, History, 62(Je 1977):327; O. Hufton, HJ, 29(No. 4, 1977):971-6.

Pearce, Ian and Clare Cowling. Guide to the Public Records of Tasmania: Section Four, Records Relating to Free Immigration. Hobart: Archives Office of Tasmania, 1975. Rev. by M. Fraser, AmArc, 40(Jan 1977):86-7.

Pearse, Andrew. The Latin American Peasant. London: Frank Cass, 1975. Rev. by E. Hansen, HAHR, 57(May 1977):316-7.

Pearson, Michael Naylor. Merchants and Rulers in Gujarat: The Response to the Portuguese in the Sixteenth Century. Berkeley: U Cal Press, 1976. Rev. by D. Alden, JEH, 37(Je 1977):549-50.

Pease, Theodore Calvin. The Story of Illinois. Chicago: U Chi Press, 1975. Rev. by J. L. Tevebaugh, MichH, 61(Fall 1977):270-2.

Peattie, Mark R. Ishiwara Kanji and Japan's Confrontation with the West. Princeton: Prin U Press, 1975. Rev. by R. Storry, History, 62(Je 1977):296-7.

Peck, H. Daniel. A World by Itself: The Pastoral Moment in Cooper's Fiction. New Haven: Yale U Press, 1977. Rev. by M. Ewart, JAmS, 11(Dec 1977):421-2.

Peckham, Howard, ed. The Fall of Independence, Engagements and Battle Casualities of the American Revolution. Chicago: U Chi Press, 1974. Rev. by L. G. Bowman, Historian, 39(Feb 1977):368-9.

Peckham, Howard H. see Marshall, Douglas W.

Peek, Walter W., ed. see Sanders, Thomas E., ed.

Peele, Gillian, and Chris Cook, eds. The Politics of Reappraisal 1918-1939. New York: St. Martin's Press, 1975. Rev. by N. Thompson, Historian, 39(May 1977):550-1; K. O. Morgan, History, 62(Feb 1977):146.

Peirce, Neal R. The New England States: People, Politics, and Power in the Six New England States. New York: W. W. Norton, 1976. Rev. by J. E. Fell, NEQ, 50(Je 1977):344-6.

Pena, Jose Enrique de la. With Santa Anna in Texas: A Personal Narrative of the Revolution. College Station: Texas A & M U Press, 1975. Rev. by S. V. Connor, AHR, 81(Dec 1976): 1247-48; R. E. Ruiz, NMHR, 52(Jan 1977):75-7; F. D. Almaraz, Jr., PHR, 46(Feb 1977):124-5.

Pendleton, W. C. see Kileff, C.

Penick, James Jr. The New Madrid Earthquakes of 1811-1812.
Columbia: U Mo Press, 1976. Rev. by W. E. Parrish,
AHR, 82(Apr 1977):440; J. E. Fickle, JSH, 43(May 1977):
290-1; A. H. Mattingly, JOW, 16(Jl 1977):100-1.

Penney, Sherry. Patrician in Politics: Daniel Dewey Bernard of
New York. Port Washington, N.Y.: Kennikat Press, 1974.
Rev. by E. Barkan, NYHSQ, 61(Jan/Apr 1977):89-90.

Pennock, Lee. Brothers in Arms. Taftsville, Vt.: Countryman
Press, 1976. Rev. by C. True, VH, 45(Win 1977):49.

Penrose, E. F., ed. European Imperialism and the Partition of
Africa. London: Frank Cass, 1975. Rev. by P. M. Kennedy, HJ, 20(No. 3, 1977):761-9.

Penton, M. James. Jehovah's Witnesses in Canada: Champions of
Freedom of Speech and Worship. Toronto: Macmillan of
Canada, 1976. Rev. by J. S. Moir, AHR, 82(Je 1977):778-9.

Percival, John. The Roman Villa: An Historical Introduction.
Berkeley: U Cal Press, 1977. Rev. by L. Richardson, Jr.,
AHR, 82(Oct 1977):929-30.

Perdue, Charles L, Jr., Thomas E. Barden, and Robert K. Phillips,
eds. Weevils in the Wheat: Interviews with Virginia Ex-
slaves. Charlottesville: U Press Va, 1976. Rev. by T.
Kornweibel, Jr., JSH, 43(Nov 1977):618-9; F. N. Boney,
VMHB, 85(Apr 1977):211-12.

Pereia, João Baptista Borges. Italianos no Mundo Rural Paulista.
São Paulo: Livraria Pioneira Editôra, 1974. Rev. by J. L.
Tigner, HAHR, 57(May 1977):375-7.

Pereira, Luiz. Ensaios de Sociologia do Desenvolvimento. Pioneira/
Ministerio da Educacão e Cultura, 1975. Rev. by R. H. Chilcote,
HAHR, 57(May 1977):373-4.

_____. Estudos sôbre o Brasil Contemporâneo. São Paulo:
Pioneira/Ministerio da Educacão e Cultura, 1975. Rev. by
R. H. Chilcote, HAHR, 57(May 1977):373-4.

Perham, Margery. African Apprenticeship, an Autobiographical
Journey. Faber, 1974. Rev. by A. Smith, AfAf, 76(Jan
1977):114.

Peri, Vittorio. Ricerche sull'Editio Princeps degli Atti Greci del
Consilio di Firenze. Vatican: Biblioteca Apostolica Vaticana,
1975. Rev. by J. Gill, EHR, 92(Oct 1977):896.

Perkins, David and Norman Tanis. Native Americans of North

America: A Bibliography Based on Collections in the Libraries
of California State University, Northridge. Metuchen, N.J.:
Scarecrow, 1975. Rev. by R. N. Ellis, PHR, 46(Feb 1977):
127-8.

Perkins, Dwight H., ed. China's Modern Economy in Historical
Perspective. Stanford: Stanford U Press, 1975. Rev. by
Tzong-shian Yu, AHR, 82(Apr 1977):414-15.

Perkins, Edwin J. Financing Anglo-American Trade. The House of
Brown, 1800-1880. Cambridge: Harvard U Press, 1975. Rev.
by J. R. Killick, BH, 19(Jan 1977):94-6; H. Jones, Historian,
39(Feb 1977):374-5.

Perlmutter, Amos. The Military and Politics in Modern Times:
On Professionals, Praetorians and Revolutionary Soldiers.
New Haven: Yale U Press, 1977. Rev. by O. E. S., CurH,
73(Sep 1977):89.

Perry, George Sessions. Texas: A World in Itself. Louisiana:
Pelican, 1975. Rev. by A. Bush, ETHJ, 15(Spr 1977):57.

Perry, Rosalie Sandra. Charles Ives and the American Mind.
Kent: Kent St U Press, 1974. Rev. by A. Stoutamire, AHR,
81(Dec 1976):1264.

Pescatelo, Ann M. Power and Pawn: The Female in Iberian
Families, Societies, and Cultures. Westport, Conn.: Greenwood Press, 1976. Rev. by C. E. Lida, AHR, 82(Oct 1977):
944-5.

Pessen, Edward, ed. Jacksonian Panorama. Indianapolis: Bobbs-
Merrill Co., 1976. Rev. by F. H. Schapsmeier, JOW, 16
(Jan 1977):78-9.

Petchenik, Barbara B., ed. see Cappon, Lester J., ed.

Peters, Thelma. Lemon City: Pioneering on Biscayne Bay, 1850-
1925. Miami: Banyan, 1976. Rev. by J. D. Pennekamp,
FHQ, 55(Apr 1977):483-4.

Peterson, Charles S. Look to the Mountains: Southeastern Utah
and the La Sal National Forest. Provo: Brigham Young
Press, 1975. Rev. by T. G. Alexander, PHR, 46(Feb 1977):
135-6.

Peterson, F. Ross. Idaho: A Bicentennial History. New York:
Norton and Nashville: American Association for State and Local
History, 1976. Rev. by M. P. Malone, WHQ, 8(Jl 1977):
333-4.

Peterson, Harold F. Diplomat of the Americas: A Biography of
William I. Buchanan (1852-1909). Albany, N.Y.: U NY Press,
1977. Rev. by P. S. Holbo, History, 6(Oct 1977):2.

Peterson, Merrill D. Adams and Jefferson: A Revolutionary Dia-
logue. Athens, Ga.: U GA Press, 1976. Rev. by R. A.
Rutland, GHQ, 51(Sum 1977):192-3; J. Zvesper, JAmS, 11
(Dec 1977):393-4; M. K. Tachau, JSH, 43(Nov 1977):606-71;
J. H. Moore, WVH, 38(Jl 1977):331-2.

Petit, Paul. Pax Romana. Berkeley and Los Angeles: U Cal
Press, 1976. Rev. by T. S. Burns, JEH, 37(Je 1977):550-1.

Petras, James and Morris Morley. The United States and Chile:
Imperialism and the Overthrow of the Allende Government.
New York: Monthly Review Press, 1975. Rev. by J. Rybáček-
Mlýnková, AHR, 82(Apr 1977):481-2.

Petrement, Simone. Simone Weil: A Life. n.l.: Pantheon, n.d.
Rev. by E. Grossman, Comm, 63(Je 1977):76-81.

Petrovich, Michael Boro. A History of Modern Serbia, 1804-1918.
2 vols. New York: Harcourt Brace Jovanovich, 1976. Rev.
by P. Auty, AHR, 82(Oct 1977):1014.

Pevsner, Nikolaus. A History of Building Types. n.l.: Thames
& Hudson, n.d. Rev. by M. Greenhalgh, HTo, 27(Feb 1977):
129-30.

Pfeiffer, Rudolf. History of Classical Scholarship from 1300 to
1850. New York: Ox U Press, 1976. Rev. by D. Sullivan,
AHR, 82(Je 1977):610.

Pfister, Christian. Agrarkonjunktur und Witterungsverlauf im
westlichen Schweizer Mittelland zur Zeit der Okonomischen
Patrioten, 1755-1797. Bern: Land Druck, 1975. Rev. by
J. G. Gagliardo, AHR, 82(Feb 1977):138.

Pflueger, Donald H., ed. Charles C. Chapman: The Career of a
Creative Californian, 1853-1944. Los Angeles: Anderson,
Ritchie & Simon, 1976. Rev. by J. Caughey, CHQ, 55(Win
1976/77):371-3.

Phares, Ross. Cavalier in the Wilderness: The Story of the
Explorer and Trader Louis Juchereau de St. Denis. Gretna,
La.: Pelican Publishing Co., 1976. Rev. by E. J. Gum,
ETHJ, 15(No. 2, 1977):55.

Philp, Kenneth R. John Collier's Crusade for Indian Reform,
1920-1954. Tucson: U Ari Press, 1977. Rev. by J. F.
Sefcik, History, 6(Nov/Dec 1977):28.

_____, and Elliot West, eds. Essays on Walter Prescott Webb.
Austin: UT Press, 1976. Rev. by N. S. Furman, HT, 10
(May 1977):498-9; R. W. Etulain, JOW, 16(Jl 1977):102.

_____ and _____, eds. The Walter Prescott Webb Memorial

Lectures: Essays on Walter Prescott Webb. Austin: UT Press, 1976. Rev. by C. C. Spence, A&W, 19(Sum 1977): 179-80; W. R. Jacobs, AHR, 82(Feb 1977):193-4; F. E. Vandiver, WHQ, 8(Apr 1977):206.

Phillips, Cabell. The 1940s: Decade of Triumph and Trouble. New York: Macmillan Publishing Co., 1975. Rev. by R. R. Haynes, LaH, 18(Win 1977):125-6.

Phillips, G. A. The General Strike: The Politics of Industrial Conflict. New York: Holmes and Meier, 1976. Rev. by J. H. M. Laslett, AHR, 82(Oct 1977):973-4; A. Reid & S. Tolliday, HJ, 20(No. 4, 1977):1001-12.

Phillips, George Harwood. Chiefs and Challengers: Indian Resistance and Cooperation in Southern California. Berkeley: U Cal Press, 1975. Rev. by J. F. Bannon, AIQ, 3(Spr 1977):63-4; R. N. Ellis, JOW, 16(Jan 1977):87.

Phillips, Robert K., ed. see Perdue, Charles L., Jr., ed.

Piault, Colette, ed. Prophétisme et Thérapeutique. Albert Atcho et la Communatué de Bregbo. Paris: Collection Savoir/ Hermann, 1976. Rev. by D. C. O'Brien, AfAf, 76(Apr 1977): 268-9.

Picott, J. Rupert and Walter N. Ridley. History of the Restitution Fund Commission of the Episcopal Diocese of Pennsylvania. Washington, D.C.: Restitution Fund Commission of the Episcopal Diocese of Pennsylvania, 1976. Rev. by L. Suggs, JNH, 62(Apr 1977):18-6.

Pieper, Thomas I. and James G. Gidney. Fort Laurens, 1778-1779: The Revolutionary War in Ohio. Kent, Ohio: Kent State U Press, 1976. Rev. by K. B. West, MichH, 61(Fall 1977): 273-5.

Pieri, Piero and Giorgio Rochat. Pietro Badoglio. Turin: L'-Unione Tipografico-Editrice Torinese, 1974. Rev. by C. F. Delzell, AHR, 82(Je 1977):682-3.

Pierson, Peter. Philip II of Spain. Levittown, N.Y.: Transatlantic Arts, 1975. Rev. by H. G. Koenigsberger, AHR, 82 (Oct 1977):946-8; W. D. Phillips, Jr., HAHR, 57(May 1977): 325-6; G. Parker, History, 62(Feb 1977):116.

Pieterse, C. and G. Hallett. Present Lives Future Becoming: South African Landscape in Words. Hickey Press, 1974. Rev. by H. Dinwiddy, AfAf, 76(Jan 1977):127-9.

Pieterse, Wilhelmina C. Inventory of the Archives of the Holland Company, 1789-1869. Amsterdam: Municipal Archives of Amsterdam, 1976. Rev. by J. B. Riggs, AmArc, 40(Jan 1977):84-5.

Pigeaud, Theodore G. Th. and H. J. De Graaf. Islamic States in Java, 1500-1700: A Summary, Bibliography and Index. Hague: Martinus Nijhoff, 1976. Rev. by J. R. W. Small, JAS, 36(Aug 1977):796-7.

Pigeot, Jacqueline. Historie de Yokobue (Yokobue no sōshi): Etudes sur les recits de l'epoque muromachi. Paris: Presses Universitaires de France, 1972. Rev. by B. Ruch, JAS, 36(Feb 1977):354-6.

Pike, Frederick B. and Thomas Stritch, eds. The New Corporatism: Social-Political Structures in the Iberian World. Notre Dame: U Notre Dame Press, 1974. Rev. by J. F. Petras, AHR, 82 (Feb 1977):231-2.

Ping-Ti, Ho. The Cradle of the East: An Inquiry into the Indigenous Origins of Techniques and Ideas of Neolithic and Early Historic China, 5000-1000 B.C. Hong Kong: Chinese U of Hong Kong Press; Chicago: U Chi Press, 1975. Rev. by E. G. Pulleyblank, JAS, 36(Aug 1977):715-7; J. Rawson, Antiquity, 51(Nov 1977):244-5.

Pinheiro, Paulo Sérgio De M. S. Politica e Trabalho no Brasil: Dos Años Vinte a 1930. Rio de Janeiro: Editora Paz e Terra S. A., 1975. Rev. by H. Spalding, HAHR, 57(Aug 1977):553-4.

Pini, Antonio Ivan. La popolazione di Imola e del suo territorio nel XIII e XIV secolo. Bologna: Pàtron Editore, 1976. Rev. by S. R. Blanshei, AHR, 82(Oct 1977):940-1.

Pinkney, Alphonso. Red, Black, and Green: Black Nationalism in the United States. New York: Cam U Press, 1976. Rev. by W. M. Tuttle, Jr., AHR, 81(Dec 1976):1268-69.

Pinkowski, Edward. Pills, Pen & Politics: The Story of General Leon Jastremski, 1843-1907. Wilmington, Del.: Capt. S. Mlotkowski Memorial Brigade Society, 1974. Rev. by E. F. Haas, AHR, 81(Dec 1976):1260.

Pino, Frank. Mexican Americans, a Research Bibliography. East Lansing: Mich St U, 1974. Rev. by E. Long, JLAS, 9(May 1977):145-7.

Pisney, Raymond F., ed. Historical Resources: Finding, Preserving, and Using. Verona, Va.: McClure Press, 1976. Rev. by R. A. Murdock, VMHB, 85(Jl 1977):378-9.

Pitkin, Thomas Monroe. Keepers of the Gate: A History of Ellis Island. New York: NYU Press, 1975. Rev. by R. Ernst, AHR, 81(Dec 1976):1267.

Pizer, Donald. The Novels of Theodore Dreiser: A Critical Study.

Minneapolis: U Minnesota Press, 1976. Rev. by M. Leaf, JAmS, 11(Aug 1977):291-3.

Plaks, Andrew H. Archetype and Allegory in the Dream of the Red Chamber. Princeton: Prin U Press, 1976. Rev. by F. P. Brandauer, JAS, 36(May 1977):554-7.

Planchart, Alejo see Fernández, Anibal

Plant Studies in the People's Republic of China: A Trip Report of the American Plant Studies Delegation. Washington, D.C.: National Academy of Sciences, 1975. Rev. by A. W. Galston, JAS, 36(May 1977):550.

Plantation Societies, Race Relations, and the South: The Regimentation of Populations. Selected Papers of Edgar T. Thompson. Durham: Duke U Press, 1975. Rev. by C. Vincent, Historian, 39(May 1977):577-8.

Plante, Julian G. Checklist of Manuscripts Microfilmed for the Monastic Microfilm Library, St. John's University, Collegeville, Minnesota. Collegeville, Minn.: Monastic Manuscript Microfilm Library, 1974. Rev. by Sis. M. L. McDonald, AmArc, 39(Jl 1976):361.

Platt, Colin. The English Medieval Town. n.l.: Secker & Warburg, n.d. Rev. by A. R. Myers, HTo, 27(Mar 1977):201-2.

Platter, Felix. Tagebuch (Lebensbeschreibung), 1536-1567. Basel: Schwabe Verlag, 1976. Rev. by E. W. Monter, AHR, 82(Je 1977):676-7.

Plessen, Marie-Louise. Die Wirksamkeit des Vereins für Socialpolitik von 1872-1890. Berlin: Duncker und Humblot, 1975. Rev. by C. Landauer, AHR, 82(Je 1977):663-4.

Plimpton, George. Writers at Work: The Paris Review Interviews. n.l.: Viking Press, n.d. Rev. by J. Wilson, Comm, 63(Feb 1977):76-8.

Plowden, Alison. Marriage with My Kingdom: The Courtship of Elizabeth I. n.l.: Macmillan, n.d. Rev. by A. Haynes, HTo, 27(Oct 1977):683-5.

Plumly, Stanley. Giraffe. Baton Rouge: LSU Press, 1974. Rev. by P. Stitt, GR, 31(Fall 1977):762-71.

Pocock, J. G. A. The Machiavellian Movement. Florentine Political Thought and Atlantic Republican Tradition. Princeton: Prin U Press, 1975. Rev. by J. H. Hexter, H&T, 16(Oct 1977):306-37.

Pois, Robert A. The Bourgeois Democrats of Weimar Germany.

Philadelphia: American Philosophical Society, 1976. Rev. by
E. L. Evans, AHR, 82(Oct 1977):1007; M. Eksteins, Historian, 39(May 1977):558.

Polakoff, K. I., et al. Generations of Americans: A History of
the United States. London: St. James Press, 1977. Rev.
by P. A. M. Taylor, JAmS, 11(Dec 1977):379-80.

Polk, James K. Correspondence of James K. Polk: Vol. 3, 1835-
1836. (Herbert Weaver and Kermit L. Hall, eds.) Nashville: Vanderbilt U Press, 1975. Rev. by M. G. Baxter,
AHR, 81(Dec 1976):1247.

Polley, Joseph B. Hood's Texas Brigade. Dayton, Ohio: Press
of Morningside Bookshop, 1976. Rev. by R. D. Hoffsommer,
CWTI, 16(Aug 1977):50.

Polonsky, Anthony, ed. The Great Powers and the Polish Question
1941-45: A Documentary Study in Cold War Origins. London:
Orbis Books for L. S. W. , 1976. Rev. by R. S. Leslie,
History, 62(Feb 1977):170.

Polzer, Charles W. Rules and Precepts of the Jesuit Missions of
Northwestern New Spain. Tucson: U Arizona Press, 1976.
Rev. by D. Chipman, WHQ, 8(Jl 1977):341.

Pombeni, Paolo. Le "Cronache Sociali" di Dossetti, 1947-1951:
Geografia di un movimento di opinione. Florence: Vallecchi
Editore, 1976. Rev. by P. V. Cannistraro, AHR, 82(April
1977):389-90.

Pomerance, Leon. The Phaistos Disc. Goteborg, Sweden: Paul
Astroms Forlag, 1976. Rev. by S. Gibbs, Archaeology, 30(Jl
1977):283-5.

Pong, David. A Critical Guide to the Kwangtung Provincial Ar-
chives, Deposited at the Public Record Office of London.
Cambridge, Mass. : Har U Press, 1975. Rev. by L. J.
Stout, Am Arc, 40(Apr 1977):236.

Port, M. H. , ed. The House of Parliament. New Haven: Yale U
Press, for Paul Mellon Centre for Studies in British Art,
n. d. Rev. by M. Greenhalgh, HTo, 27(Jan 1977):59-60.

Porter, Bernard. The Lion's Share: A Short History of British
Imperialism, 1850-1970. New York: Longman, 1976. Rev.
by H. R. Winkler, AHR, 82(April 1977):361-2; P. J. Cain,
History, 62(Je 1977):338-9; P. M. Kennedy, HJ, 20(No. 3,
1977):761-9.

Porter, Bertha and Rosalind L. B. Moss. Topographical Bibliog-
raphy of Ancient Egyptian Hieroglyphic Texts, Reliefs, and
Paintings. Oxford: Clarendon Press, 1972. Rev. by C. F.
Nims, JNES, 36(Jan 1977):74-5.

Porter, Gareth. A Peace Denied: The United States, Vietnam, and the Paris Agreement. Bloomington: Ind U Press, 1975. Rev. by W. J. Duiker, JAS, 36(Feb 1977):383-4.

Porter, Katherine A. The Never Ending Wrong. n. l. : Atlantic-Little, Brown, n. d. Rev. by R. Starr, Comm, 64(Dec 1977): 95-6.

Post, Gaines, Jr. The Civil-Military Fabric of Weimar Foreign Policy. Princeton: Prin U Press, 1973. Rev. by A. Thimme, CHR, 58(Je 1977):243-6.

Post, John D. The Last Great Subsistence Crisis in the Western World. Baltimore: JHU Press, 1977. Rev. by G. C. Fite, History, 6(Oct 1977):18; T. C. Smout, JEH, 37(Sep 1977): 816-7.

Post, Robert C. Physics, Patents, and Politics: A Biography of Charles Grafton Page. New York: Science History Publications, 1976. Rev. by C. Pursell, AS, 18(Fall 1977):113.

Postan, M. M. Essays on Medieval Agriculture and General Problems of the Medieval Economy. Cambridge: Cambridge U Press, 1973. Rev. by F. A. Cazel, Jr. , JIH, 7(Winter 1977):537-9.

_____. Medieval Trade and Finance. Cambridge: Cambridge U Press, 1973. Rev. by F. A. Cazel, Jr. , JIH, 7(Winter 1977):537-9.

Poster, Mark. Existential Marxism in Postwar France: From Sartre to Althusser. Princeton: Prin U Press, 1976. Rev. by M. Hilton, History, 62(Feb 1977):171-2.

Potter, David M. Freedom and Its Limitations in American Life. Ed. by Don E. Fehrenbacher. Stanford: Stanford U Press, 1976. Rev. by S. L. Engerman, JIH, 8(Autumn 1977):383-5.

_____. The Impending Crisis, 1848-1861. N. Y. : Harper and Row, 1976. Rev. by H. Hamilton, AHR, 82(Feb 1977): 182-3; R. W. Johannsen, JSH, 43(Feb 1977):103-5.

Potter, E. B. Nimitz. Annapolis: Naval Institute Press, 1976. Rev. by C. G. Reynolds, AHR, 82(June 1977):766.

Potter, Jack M. That Peasant Social Structure. Chicago: U Chicago Press, 1976. Rev. by L. M. Hanks, JAS, 37(Nov 1977):179-81.

Potter, K. R. , ed. Gesta Stephani. Oxford: Ox U Press, 1976. Rev. by E. King, History, 62(Feb 1977):99-100.

Potter, Miles F. Oregon's Golden Years: Bonanza of the West.

Caldwell: Caxton Printers, 1976. Rev. by L. Carranco,
JOW, 16(Jan 1977):75.

Potts, E. Daniel and Annette Potts. Young America and Australian
Gold: Americans and the Gold Rush of the 1850s. St. Lucia,
Queensland: U Queensland Press, 1974. Rev. by R. W.
Paul, PNQ, 68(Apr 1977):100-1; J. Monaghan, AHR, 82(Feb
1977):167.

Pouillon, Jean. Fetiches sans fetichisme. Paris: Maspero, 1975.
Rev. by E. Gillies, Africa, 47(No. 2, 1977):221-2.

Pouilloux, J. Fouilles De Delphes, Tome III, Epigraphie, Fascicule IV. Paris: Editions de Boccard, 1976. Rev. by D. M.
Lewis, AJA, 81(Sum 1977):399.

Poulter, S. Family Law and Litigation in Basotho Society. Oxford
U Press, 1976. Rev. by P. Sanders, AfAf, 76(July 1977):
415-16.

Powell, Anthony. Hearing Secret Harmonies. Boston: Little,
Brown, 1975. Rev. by H. McAlexander, GR, 31(Spr 1977):
248-52.

Powell, Edith Hopps, ed. San Francisco's Heritage in Art Glass.
Seattle: Salisbury Press, 1976. Rev. by K. M. Johnson,
JOW, 16(Jan 1977):80.

Powell, Lawrence Clark. Arizona: A Bicentennial History. New
York: W. W. Norton, 1976. Rev. by S. B. Brinckerhoff,
A&W, 19(Sum 1977):163-164; W. H. Lyon, WHQ, 8(Apr 1977):
209-10.

_____. From the Heartland: Profiles of People and Places of
the Southwest and Beyond. Flagstaff: Northland, 1977. Rev.
by J. P. Schaefer, JAriH, 18(Sum 1977):219-20.

Powell, T. G. El liberalismo y el campesinado en el centro de
México (1850-1876). Mexico: SepSetentas, 1974. Rev. by R.
J. Knowlton, HAHR, 57(May 1977):350-1.

Powers, Barry D. Strategy Without Slide-Rule: British Air Strategy, 1914-1939. London: Croom Helm 1976. Rev. by M.
Smith, History, 62(Je 1977):343.

Powers, Elizabeth, ed. see Lebra, Joyce, ed.

Powers, Stephen. The Northern California Indians. n.l.: University of Cal Archaeological Research Facility, 1975. Rev. by
R. N. Ellis, NMHR, 52(Oct 1977):337-43.

Prang, Margaret. N. W. Powell: Ontario Nationalist. Toronto:
U Tor Press, 1975. Rev. by J. English, CHR, 58(Mar
1977):78-81; J. A. Boudreau, PHR, 46(May 1977):307-8.

Pratt, Cranford.   The Critical Phase in Tanzania, 1945-1968:
Nyerere and the Emergence of a Socialist Strategy.   N. Y.:
Cam U Press, 1976.   Rev. by J. G. Liebenow, AHR, 82(Oct
1977):1037-8.

Press, Irwin,   Tradition and Adaptation: Life in a Modern Yucatan
Maya Village.   Westport, Conn.:   Greenwood Press, 1975.
Rev. by R. Adams, TAm, 33(Jan 1977):560-1.

Preston, Antony, David Lyon, and John H. Batchelor.   Navies of
the American Revolution.   Ed. by S. L. Meyer.   Englewood
Cliffs, N. J.:   Prentice-Hall, 1975.   Rev. by N. R. Stout,
VH, 45(Spring 1977):125-7.

Preston, Paul, ed.   Spain in Crisis: The Evolution and Decline of
the Franco Regime.   N. Y.:   Barnes and Noble, 1976.   Rev.
by V. R. Pilapil, AHR, 82(Feb 1977):119.

Price, Don C.   Russia and the Roots of the Chinese Revolution,
1896-1911.   Cambridge, Mass.:   Harvard U Press, 1974.
Rev. by T. Ganschow, AHR, 82(Apr 1977):413-14; V. G.
Kiernan, History, 62(Je 1977):293.

Price, Richard.   The Guiana Maroons: A Historical and Bibliographical Introduction.   Baltimore: JHU Press, 1976.   Rev. by J.
Postma, AHR, 82(Oct 1977):1106.

Price, Roger.   The Economic Modernisation of France, 1730-1880.
New York: Halsted Press, 1975.   Rev. by S. F. Scott,
Historian, 39(Feb 1977):345-7; L. D. Schwarz, History, 62(Feb
1977):158.

_____, ed.   Revolution and Reaction: 1848 and the Second French
Republic.   New York: Barnes and Noble, 1976.   Rev. by D.
H. Pinkney, AHR, 81(Dec 1976):1130-1; S. F. Scott, Historian,
39(Feb 1977):345-7; R. Magraw, History, 62(Feb 1977):156-7.

Price, Warren C.   The Eugene Register-Guard: A Citizen of Its
Community.   Portland: Binford & Mort, 1976.   Rev. by M.
Clark, OrHQ, 78(Sep 1977):286-7.

Price, William S. , Jr.   North Carolina Higher-Court Records,
1702-1708.   Raleigh, N. C.: Department of Cultural Resources,
Division of Archives and History, 1974.   Rev. by H. A. Johnson, WMQ, 34(Jl 1977):501-3.

Prideaux, Gwynn Cochran.   Summerhouses of Virginia.   Richmond:
William Byrd Press, 1976.   Rev. by C. Loth, VMHB, 85(July
1977):377-8.

Proctor, Samuel, ed.   Eighteenth-Century Florida and the Caribbean.   Gainesville: U Presses of Florida, 1976.   Rev. by
R. R. Rea, AlaR, 30(July 1977):234-5; R. K. Murdoch, FHQ,

55(Jan 1977):368-9; J. L. Wright, Jr., FHQ, 55(Apr 1977):
484-5; M. R. Bradley, JSH, 43(May 1977):280-1; J. D. L.
Holmes, LaH, 18(Sum 1977):369-70.

_____, ed. Eighteenth-Century Florida: Life on the Frontier.
Gainesville: U Presses of Florida, 1974. Rev. by R. R.
Rea, AlaR, 30(July 1977):234-5.

Prucha, Francis P. A Bibliographical Guide to the History of
Indian-White Relations in the United States. Chicago: U Chi
Press, Center for the History of the American Indian, n.d.
Rev. in InHi, 10(Sum 1977):48; R. N. Ellis, NMHR, 52(Oct
1977):337-43.

Prucha, Francis Paul. American Indian Policy in Crisis: Christian Reformers and the Indian, 1865-1900. Norman: U Ok
Press, 1976. Rev. by R. White, WHQ, 8(Oct 1977):463-4.

_____, ed. Documents of United States Indian Policy.
Lincoln: U Nebraska Press, 1975. Rev. by H. G. Jordan,
AIQ, 3(Spring 1977):68-9.

Pryce-Jones, David. Unity Mitford: An Enquiry Into Her Life and
the Frivolity of Evil. n.l.: Dial Press, n.d. Rev. by H.
Maccoby, Comm, 64(Jl 1977):76-80.

Pugh, R. B., ed. Calendar of London Trailbaston Trails Under
Commissions of 1305-1306. London: HMSO, 1975. Rev. by
J. R. Maddicott, EHR, 92(Oct 1977):887-8.

Pullapilly, Cyriac K. Caesar Baronius: Counter-Reformation Historian. Notre Dame: U Notre Dame Press, 1975. Rev. by
R. Bireley, AHR, 82(Feb 1977):88.

Punekar, S. D. and Alkar R. Golwalkar. Rural Change in Maha-
rashtra: An Analytical Study of Change in Six Villages in
Konkan. Bombay: Popular Prakashan, 1973. Rev. by D.
W. Attwood, JAS, 36(Feb 1977):378-9.

Punekar, Vijaya B. Assimilation: A Study of North Indians in
Bangalore. Bombay: Popular Prakashan, 1974. Rev. by H.
E. Ullrich, JAS, 36(May 1977):580-1.

Punjab Disturbances, 1919-20. vol. 1. Indian Perspective. vol.
2. British Perspective. New Delhi: Deep Publications, 1976.
Rev. by J. Barrier, AHR, 82(Oct 1977):1053-4.

Puntila, L. A. The Political History of Finland, 1809-1966.
Helsinki: n.p., 1974. Rev. by A. F. Upton, EHR, 92(Oct
1977):939-9.

Purchell, L. Edward, ed. see Grant, H. Roger

Puryear, Pamela Ashworth and Nath Winfield, Jr. <u>Sandbars and</u>
<u>Sternwheelers: Steam Navigation on the Brazos.</u> College
Station, Texas: Texas A&M U Press, 1976. Rev. by D. H.
Winfrey, A&W, 19(Sum 1977):188-9; H. L. Sandefer, ETHJ,
15(Spr 1977):49; T. H. Baker, JSH, 43(Feb 1977):122-3.

Pyenson, Lewis, ed. <u>see</u> McCormmach, Russell, ed.

Quarles, Benjamin. <u>Allies for Freedom: Blacks and John Brown.</u>
New York: Oxford U Press, 1974. Rev. by F. C. Campbell,
WMH, 60(Summer 1977):339-40.

Quazza, Guido. <u>Resistenza e storia d'Italia: Problemi e ipotesi di</u>
<u>ricerca.</u> Milan: Feltrinelli Editore, 1976. Rev. by A.
deGrand, AHR, 82(June 1977):683.

Quigley, W. G. H. and E. D. F. Roberts, eds. <u>Registrum</u>
<u>Iohannis Mey: The register of John Mey archbishop of</u>
<u>Armagh, 1443-1456.</u> Belfast: HMSO, 1972. Rev. by J. A.
Watt, EHR, 92(Oct 1977):853-5.

Quinn, D. B. <u>The Hakluyt Handbook.</u> London: Hakluyt Society,
1974. Rev. by W. A. Kenyon, CHR, 58(Mar 1977):89-90.

Quinn, David B. , ed. <u>The Last Voyage of Thomas Cavendish,</u>
<u>1591-1592.</u> Chicago: U Chi Press, 1975. Rev. by L. C.
Allin, JEH, 38(Sep 1977):837-8; U. Lamb, HAHR, 57(Feb
1977):124-6.

Raat, William D. <u>El Positivismo Durante el Porfiriato.</u> Mexico:
Sep-Setentas, 1975. Rev. by H. E. Davis, TAm, 33(Apr
1977):689-90.

Rabb, T. K. <u>The Struggle for Stability in Early Modern Europe.</u>
Oxford: Ox U Press, 1975. Rev. by G. Parker, History,
62(Je 1977):316-7.

Rabb, Theodore K. <u>The Struggle for Stability in Early Modern</u>
<u>Europe.</u> N. Y. : Ox U Press, 1975. Rev. by A. Plakans,
AHR, 82(Feb 1977):81-3; G. Parker, History, 62(Je 1977):
316-7.

Rabinow, P. <u>Symbolic Domination: Cultural Form and Historical</u>
<u>Change in Morocco.</u> Chicago: U Chicago Press, 1975. Rev.
by J. R. Tallman, JAAS, 12(Jan. /Oct. 1977):307-8.

Rabinowitch, Alexander. <u>The Bolsheviks Come to Power: The</u>
<u>Revolution of 1917 in Petrograd.</u> N. Y. : Norton, 1976. Rev.
by R. G. Suny, AHR, 82(Je 1977):701-2.

Rachlin, Carol K. <u>see</u> Marriott, Alice

Radkau, J. <u>see</u> Hallgarten, G.

Radkey, Oliver H. The Unknown Civil War in Soviet Russia: A
Study of the Green Movement in the Tambov Region, 1920-
1921. Stanford: Hoover Institution, 1976. Rev. by P.
Kenez, AHR, 82(Je 1977):703-4.

Radosh, Ronald, ed. The New Cuba: Paradoxes and Potentials.
New York: William Morrow, 1976. Rev. by L. A. Perez,
Jr., HAHR, 57(Feb 1977):133-4.

_____. Prophets on the Right: Profiles of Conservative Critics
of American Globalism. New York: Simon and Schuster,
1975. Rev. by T. L. Kennedy, PHR, 46(Aug 1977):528-9.

Radwan Samir see Mabro, Robert

Raftis, J. Ambrose. Warboys: Two Hundred Years in the Life of
an English Mediaeval Village. Toronto: Pontifical Institute of
Mediaeval Studies, 1974. Rev. by C. R. Young, CHR, 58(Mar
1977):88-9.

Ragsdale, Kenneth Baxter. Quicksilver: Terlingua and the Chisos
Mining Company. College Station: Tex A&M U Press, 1976.
Rev. by J. B. Allen, AHR, 82(Oct 1977):1095-6; J. L.
Bernardi, JEH, 37(Sep 1977):838; L. S. Theisen, JSH,
43(May 1977):315-6.

Raina, Peter. Polish-German Relations, 1937-1939: The True
Character of Józef Beck's Foreign Policy. London: Oficyna
Poetów i Malarzy, 1975. Rev. by W. Jedrzejewicz, AHR,
82(June 1977):688.

Rainey, Buck, ed. see Harris, Charles W. , ed.

Raistrick, Arthur. The Lead Industry of Wensleydale and Swaledale.
Buxton: Moorland, 1975. Rev. by J. R. Harris, BH, 19(July
1977):231.

Rallo, Antonia. Lasa. Iconografia e esegesi. Florence: G. C.
Sansoni Editore, 1974. Rev. by L. Bonfante, AJA, 81(Winter
1977):125.

Ramelli, Agostino. The Various and Ingenious Machines of Agostino
Ramelli (1588). Baltimore: JHU Press, 1976. Rev. by R.
Hall, AHR, 82 (Je 1977):679-80.

Rampersad, Arnold. The Art and Imagination of W. E. B. Du Bois.
Cambridge, Mass. : Har U Press, 1976. Rev. by L. C.
Lamon, JSH, 43(Aug 1977):485-6; J. White, JAmS, 11(Dec
1977):390.

Ramsay, G. D. The City of London in International Politics at the
accession Elizabeth Tudor. n. l. : Manchester U Press, 1975.
Rev. by C. E. Challis, History, 62(Feb 1977):115-6.

Ramsdell, Charles. San Antonio: A Historical and Pictorial Guide. Austin: U Texas Press, 1976. Rev. by A. E. Heslop, ETHJ, 15(No. 2, 1977):63-4.

Rangel, Domingo Alberto. Gómez, el amo del poder. Caracas: Yadell Hermanos, 1975. Rev. by J. Ewell, HAHR, 57(Feb 1977):137-8.

Ransel, David L. The Politics of Catherinian Russia: The Panin Party. London: Yale U Press, 1975. Rev. by R. P. Bartlett, History, 62(Feb 1977):138.

Ranum, Orest, ed. Jacques-Bénigne Bossuet: Discourse on Universal History. London: U Chi Press, 1976. Rev. by R. M. Hatton, History, 62(Feb 1977):129.

Raphael, Morris. The Battle in Bayou Country. Detroit: Harlo Press, 1975. Rev. by R. J. Sommers, CWTI, 16(Apr 1977):48.

Rapp, Richard Tilden. Industry and Economic Decline in 17th Century Venice. Cambridge: Har U Press, 1976. Rev. by E. Muir, AHR, 82(Feb 1977):140-1; Billington, EHR, 92(Oct 1977): 901-2; J. Kirshner, JMH, 49(Je 1977):319-21.

Rasmussen, Wayne D. Agriculture in the United States: A Documentary History. New York: Random House, 1975. Rev. by J. H. Shideler, AGH, 51(Jan 1977):259-60; J. D. Reid, JEH, 37(Je 1977):552-4.

Rathbone, R. J. A. R. see Moss, R. P.

Rathje, William L. see Sabloff, Jeremy A. , ed.

Ratkevich, Ronald Paul. Dinosaurs of the Southwest. Albuquerque: U NM Press, 1976. Rev. by J. M. Nixon, JOW, 16(Jan 1977):79-80.

Rauch, Günter. Pröpste, Propstei und Stift von Sankt Barthol mäus in Frankfurt: 9. Jahrhundert tis 1802. Frankfurt: Waldemar Kramer, 1975. Rev. by J. B. Freed, AHR, 82(Oct 1977):919.

Ray, Dorothy Jean. The Eskimos of Bering Strait, 1650-1898. Seattle: U Wash Press, 1976. Rev. by R. A. Pierce, AHR, 82(Feb 1977):169; J. Bockstoce, AIQ, 3(Summer 1977):170-1; O. W. Miller, WHQ, 8(Apr 1977):230-1.

Rayfield, Donald. The Dream of Lhasa: The Life of Nikolay Przhevalsky (1839-88), Explorer of Central Asia. London: Paul Elek, 1976. Rev. by D. S. M. Williams, History, 62(Je 1977):288-9.

Raynor, Henry. Music and Society Since 1815. n. l. : Schocken, n. d. Rev. by E. Rothstein, Comm, 64(Oct 1977):80-4.

Read, Jan. War in the Peninsula. n. l. : Faber, n. d. Rev. by
A. Haynes, HTo, 27(Aug 1977):546-7.

Read, Oliver and Walter L. Welch. From Tin Foil to Stereo:
Evolution of the Phonograph. Indianapolis: Howard W. Sams,
1976. Rev. by T. H. Peterson, Am Arc, 40(Jan 1977):76-7.

Ready, Milton, ed. see Coleman, Kenneth, ed.

Reardon, John J. Edmund Randolph: A Biography. New York:
Macmillan, 1975. Rev. by R. Leffler, WMH, 60(Spring
1977):248-9.

Rebentisch, Dieter. Ludwig Landmann: Frankfurter Oberbürgermeister der Weimarer Republik. Wiesbaden: Steiner Verlag,
1975. Rev. by A. Dorpalen, AHR, 82(June 1977):668-9.

Record of the Thirteenth International Conference of the Archival
Round Table, Bonn 1971. Paris: International Council on
Archives, 1974. Rev. by L. K. Aun, Am Arc, 39(Jl
1976):353-4.

Reddaway, Peter see Bloch, Sidney

Redford, Donald B. , ed. see Grayson, A. K. , ed.

Reece, R. H. W. Aborigines and Colonists: Aborigines and Colo-
nial Society in New South Wales in the 1830s and 1840s.
Sydney: Sydney U Press, 1974. Rev. by W. E. Unrau,
Historian, 39(Feb 1977):364-5.

Reed, John R. Victorian Conventions. Athens: Ohio U Press,
1975. Rev. by J. Mazzaro, GR, 31(Fall 1977):739-42.

Reed, M. C. Investment in Railways in Britain, 1820-1844: A
Study in the Development of the Capital Market. N. Y. : Ox U
Press, 1975. Rev. by D. N. McCloskey, AHR, 82(Feb
1977):102; D. H. Aldcroft, BH, 19(Jan 1977):101-2; T. C.
Barker, History, 62(Je 1977):335.

Reed, T. J. Thomas Mann: The Uses of Tradition. New York &
London: Clarendon Press, 1974. Rev. by H. Eichner, JMH,
49(Je 1977):335-7.

Rees, Una, ed. The Cartulary of Shrewsbury Abbey. Aberystwyth:
National Library of Wales, 1975. Rev. by R. H. C. Davis,
History, 62(Feb 1977):99.

Rees, William, ed. Calendar of Ancient Petitions Relating to Wales.
Cardiff: U Wales Press, 1975. Rev. by R. R. Davies,
History, 62(Feb 1977):101-2.

Reese, M. M. The Royal Office of the Master of the House. n. l. :

Threshold Books, n. d.   Rev. by A. Haynes, HTo, 27(Feb
1977):131-2.

Reese, W. S.   Six Score: The 120 Best Books on the Range Cattle
Industry.   Austin: Kenkins, 1976.   Rev. by A. C. Ashcraft,
JOW, 16(Jl 1977):101.

Reeves, P. D. , B. D. Graham, and J. M. Goodman.   A Handbook
to Elections in Uttar Pradesh, 1920-1951.   Delhi: Manohar
Book Service, 1975.   Rev. by H. W. Blair, JAS, 37(Nov
1977):166.

Reeves, Richard.   Convention.   n. l. :   Harcourt Brace Jovanovich,
n. d.   Rev. by N. W. Polsby, Comm, 64(Sep 1977):70-3.

Regmi, Mahesh C.   Landownership in Nepal.   Berkeley: U Cal
Press, 1976.   Rev. by L. Caplan, JAS, 36(Aug 1977):786-7.

Regnery, Dorothy F.   An Enduring Heritage: Historic Buildings of
the San Francisco Peninsula, 1850-1920.   Stanford: Stanford
U Press, 1976.   Rev. by G. Ehrlich, AS, 18(Fall 1977):112;
F. Egan, CHQ, 56(Sum 1977):180-1; K. M. Johnson, JOW,
16(Jan 1977):73.

Regueiro, Helen.   The Limits of Imagination: Wordsworth, Yeats,
and Stevens.   Ithaca: Cor U. Press, 1976.   Rev. by F.
Ferguson, GR, 31(Sum 1977):511-6.

Reichard, Gary W.   The Reaffirmation of Republicanism: Eisenhower and the Eighty-Third Congress.   Knoxville: U Tenn
Press, 1975.   Rev. by H. S. Parmet, Historian, 39(Feb
1977):379-80.

Reichel-Dolmatoff, G.   The Shaman and the Jaguar: A Study of
Narcotic Drugs Among the Indians of Colombia.   Philadelphia:
Temple U Press, 1975.   Rev. by W. T. Vickers, HAHR,
57(May 1977):370-1.

Reichert, William O.   Partisans of Freedom: A Study in American
Anarchism.   Bowling Green, Ohio: Bowling Green U Popular
Press, 1976.   Rev. by L. Perry, AHR, 82(Apr 1977):452-3.

Reid, Alfred Sandlin.   Furman University: Toward a New Identity,
1925-1975.   Durham, N. C. :   Duke U Press, 1976.   Rev. by
R. F. Durden, JSH, 43(Aug 1977):492-3.

Reid, B. L.   The Lives of Roger Casement.   New Haven: Yale U
Press, 1976.   Rev. by V. E. Glandon, AHR, 82(Feb 1977):114.

Reid, Bill see Holm, Bill

Reid, John Phillip.   A Better Kind of Hatchet: Law, Trade, and
Diplomacy in the Cherokee Nation During the Early Years of

European Contact. University Park: Pa St U Press, 1976.
Rev. by B. Graymont, AHR, 82(Apr 1977):429; R. L.
Munkres, JOW, 16(Jan 1977):78; A. M. Gibson, WMQ,
18(Oct 1977):465-6; J. P. Ronda, WMQ, 34(Jl 1977):498-9.

Reid, W. Stanford. Trumpeter of God: A Biography of John Knox.
New York: Charles Scribner's Sons, 1974. Rev. by I. B.
Cowan, History, 62(Je 1977):321.

Reill, Peter Hans. The German Enlightenment and the Rise of
Historicism. Berkeley: U Cal Press, 1975. Rev. by G. G.
Iggers, HT, 10(Feb 1977):339-40; T. C. W. Blanning, History,
62(Feb 1977):136-7.

Reinharz, Jehuda. Fatherland or Promised Land: The Dilemma of
the German Jew, 1893-1914. Ann Arbor: U Mich Press,
1975. Rev. by R. Hilberg, AHR, 82(Oct 1977):952-4; L.
Kochan, History, 62(Feb 1977):162-3.

Reischauer, Edwin O. The Japanese. Cambridge: Har U Press,
n. d. Rev. by C. Horner, Comm, 64(Sep 1977):87-8.

Reisler, Mark. By the Sweat of Their Brow: Mexican Immigrant
Labor in the United States, 1900-1940. Westport, Conn.:
Greenwood Press, 1976. Rev. by A. Hoffman, AHR, 82(Je
1977):757-8; M. S. Meier, CHQ, 56(Sum 1977):184; T. H.
Kreneck, ETHJ, 15(No. 2, 1977):60-1; R. N. Ellis, JOW,
16(Jan 1977):89; N. Lederer, TAm, 34(Oct 1977):311-2.

Reisman, David A. Adam Smith's Sociological Economics. London:
Croom Helm, 1976. Rev. by E. McKinley, JEH, 37(Je
1977):555-6.

Reitt, Barbara B., ed. Georgia Women: A Celebration. Atlanta:
Atlanta Branch, American Association of University Women,
1976. Rev. by D. Roth-White, GHQ, 51(Summer 1977):195-6.

Remini, Robert V. The Revolutionary Age of Andrew Jackson.
New York: Harper & Row, 1976. Rev. by A. Castel, AHI,
11(Jan 1977):50; F. N. Stites, AHR, 82(Feb 1977):178-9.

Remley, David A. Crooked Road: The Story of the Alaska Highway. New York: McGraw-Hill, 1976. Rev. by A. R. C.
Helms, PHR, 46(Feb 1977):138-9; C. M. Naske, PNQ, 68(Oct
1977):196.

Rendell, Sir William. The History of the Commonwealth Development Corporation. London: Heinemann, 1976. Rev. by J.
D. Hargreaves, History, 62(Feb 1977):263-4.

Renshaw, Patrick. The General Strike. London: Eyre Methuen,
1975. Rev. by A. Reid & S. Tolliday, HJ, 20(No. 4,
1977):1001-12.

REPS   260

Reps, John W.   Cities on Stone: Nineteenth Century Lithograph
    Images of the Urban West.   Fort Worth: Amon Carter Muse-
    um, 1976. Rev. by R. A. Weinstein, A&W, 19(Sum 1977):
    175-76; B. Luckingham, NMHR, 52(Apr 1977):166-7; R. E.
    Kibbey, UHQ, 45(Win 1977):99-100.

Resnick, Stephen A.   see Birnberg, Thomas B.

Rest, Mathias.   Die Russische Judengesesetzgebung Von Der Ersten
    Polnischen Teilung Bis Zum "Polozenie Dlja Evreev" 1804.
    Wiesbaden: Otto Harrassowitz Verlag, 1975. Rev. by R. F.
    Leslie, History, 62(Feb 1977):139-40.

Reuther, Victor G.   The Brothers Reuther and the Story of the
    UAW: A Memoir.   Boston: Houghton Mifflin, 1976. Rev. by
    M. Dubofsky, AHR, 82(Feb 1977):208-9.

Revel, Jean-Francois.   The Totalitarian Temptation. n. l. : Double-
    day, n. d. Rev. by S. Haseler, Comm, 64(Aug
    1977):79-80.

Reynolds, Lloyd G. , ed.   Agriculture in Development Theory.   New
    Haven: Yale U Press, 1975. Rev. by O. V. Wells, AgH,
    51(Jan 1977):263-4; G. E. Schuh, JEH, 37(Je 1977):556-7.

Riasanovsky, Nicholas V.   A Parting of Ways: Government and the
    Educated Public in Russia, 1801-1855.   N. Y. : Ox U Press,
    1977. Rev. by W. B. Lincoln, AHR, 82(Oct 1977):1024-5;
    S. A. Zenkovsky, History, 6(Oct 1977):15.

Rice, C. Duncan.   The Rise and Fall of Black Slavery.   N. Y. :
    Harper and Row, 1975. Rev. by W. D. Jordan, AHR,
    82(Feb 1977):180; H. Temperly, History, 62(Feb 1977):87-8;
    A. Meier, WMQ, 34(Jan 1977):171-2. Also London: Macmil-
    lan, 1975. Rev. by D. Kealey, JAmS, 11(April
    1977):145-6.

Rice, E. B.   Extension in the Andes: An Evaluation of Official
    U. S. Assistance to Agricultural Extension Services in Central
    and South America.   Cambridge, Mass. : MIT Press, 1974.
    Rev. by M. Redclift, JLAS, 9(May 1977):184-6.

Rice, Howard C. , Jr.   Thomas Jefferson's Paris.   Princeton:
    Princeton U Press, 1976. Rev. by W. M. Whitehill, VMHB,
    85(April 1977):205-6.

Rich, J. W.   Declaring War in the Roman Republic in the Period
    of Transmarine Expansion.   Brussels: Latomus, 1976. Rev.
    by J. E. Phillips, AHR, 82(Oct 1977):930.

Richards, J. F.   Mughal Administration in Golconda.   London: Ox
    U Press, 1975. Rev. by G. R. G. Hambly, AHR, 82(Apr
    1977):420-1.

Richards, Paul, ed. African Environment; Problems and Perspectives. London: International African Institute, 1975. Rev. by A. Warren, Africa, 47(No. 1, 1977):121.

Richardson, Emeline Hill. The Etruscans: Their Art and Civilization. Chicago: U Chi Press, 1976. Rev. by T. A. Fabiano, 10(Aug 1977):629-30.

Richardson, H. Edward. Cassius Marcellus Clay: Firebrand of Freedom. Lexington: U Press Ken, 1976. Rev. by R. E. Luker, JSH, 43(Feb 1977):125-6.

Richardson, John. The Local Historian's Encyclopedia. New Barnet, Herts.: Historical Publications, 1975. Rev. by F. A. Youngs, Jr., AHR, 82(Oct 1977):956-7.

Richardson, W. C., ed. The Report of the Royal Commission of 1552. Morgantown, W. Va.: West Virginia U Library, 1974. Rev. by G. R. Elton, HJ, 20(No. 3, 1977):737-40.

Richey, Elinor. Eminent Women of the West. Berkeley: Howell-North Books, 1975. Rev. by L. B. Donovan, CHQ, 56(Spr 1977):85-6.

Rickey, Don, Jr. $10 Horse, $40 Saddle: Cowboy Clothing, Arms, Tools and Horse Gear of the 1880s. Fort Collins, Colorado: Old Army Press, 1976. Rev. by M. H. Brown, WHQ, 8(Oct 1977):475-6.

Ricklefs, M. C. Jogjakarta under Sultan Mangkubumi, 1749-1792: A History of the Division of Java. London: Ox U Press, 1974. Rev. by B. R. Anderson, JAS, 36(May 1977):596-7.

Rickover, H. G. How the Battleship "Maine" Was Destroyed. Washington: Department of Navy, 1976. Rev. by R. E. Johnson, AHR, 82(Apr 1977):454-5; L. L. Gould, PHR, 46(Aug 1977):523-4.

Ridley, Jasper. The Roundheads. n.l.: Constable, n.d. Rev. by M. Ashley, HTo, 27(Jan 1977):58-9.

Ridley, Walter N. see Picott, J. Rupert

Riesman, David see Lipset, Seymour Martin

Riess, Suzanna, ed. Julie Morgan Architectural History Project. Berkeley: Bancroft Library, 1976. Rev. by S. H. Boutelle, CHQ, 56(Fall 1977):279-80.

Rigler, Edith. Frauenleitbild und Frauenarbeit in Österreich vom ausgehenden 19. Jahrhundert bis zum Zweiten Weltkrieg.

Vienna: Verlag fur Geschichte und Politik, 1976. Rev. by
P. Branca, JMH, 49(Sep 1977):491-3.

Riley, Carroll L., ed. <u>see</u> Lange, Charles H., ed.

Ringelblum Emanuel. <u>Polish-Jewish Relations During the Second
World War.</u> N.Y.: Howard Fertig, 1976. Rev. by E. D.
Wynot, Jr., AHR, 82(Apr 1977):399.

Ripley, C. Peter. <u>Slaves and Freedmen in Civil War Louisiana.</u>
Baton Rouge: LSU Press, 1976. Rev. by L. S. Gerteis,
AHR, 82(Je 1977):747-8.

Rissel, Maria. <u>Rezeption antiker und patristischer Wissenschaft
bei Hrabanus Maurus.</u> Bern/Frankfurt: Lang, 1976. Rev.
by J. M. Wallace-Hadrill, EHR, 92(Oct 1977):882.

Ritter, Ernst. <u>Das Deutsch Ausland-Institut in Stuttgart, 1917-1945.</u>
Wiesbaden: Franz Steiner Verlag, 1976. Rev. by J. W.
Baird, AHR, 82(Oct 1977):1006-7.

Roark, James L. <u>Masters Without Slaves: Southern Planters in
the Civil War and Reconstruction.</u> New York: W. W. Norton,
1977. Rev. by J. H. Pease, History, 6(Oct 1977):4-5.

Robb, P. G. <u>The Government of India and Reform: Policies
toward Politics and the Constitution, 1916-1921.</u> N.Y.: Ox U
Press, 1976. Rev. by B. C. Busch, AHR, 82(Oct 1977):1053;
A. P. Kammsky, History, 6(Nov/Dec 1977):38.

Robbins, Keith. <u>The Abolition of War: The "Peace Movement" in
Britain, 1914-1919.</u> Cardiff: U Wales, 1975. Rev. by T. C.
Kennedy, AHR, 82(Oct 1977):972-3.

Robbins, Lord. <u>Political Economy Past and Present: A Review of
Leading Theories of Economic Policy.</u> New York: Col U
Press, 1976. Rev. by C. D. Goodwin, JEH, 37(Sep 1977):
838-9.

Robbins, Roy M. <u>Our Landed Heritage: The Public Domain, 1776-
1970.</u> Lincoln: U Neb Press, 1976. Rev. by J. W. Whitaker, AgH, 51(Jl 1977):630-1.

Roberts, Andrew. <u>A History of Zambia.</u> New York: Africana
Pub., 1976. Rev. by J. P. Smaldone, HT, 10(Aug 1977):
633-4.

Roberts, E. D. F., ed. <u>see</u> Quigley, W. G. H., ed.

Roberts, John. <u>Revolution and Improvement: The Western World,
1775-1847.</u> Berkeley and Los Angeles: U Cal Press, 1976.
Rev. by C. H. Johnson, JEH, 37(Je 1977):557-8.

Roberts, Laurance P.   A Dictionary of Japanese Artists: Painting, Sculpture, Ceramics, Prints, Lacquer. New York: Weather- hill, 1976. Rev. by J. Cahill, JAS, 37(Nov 1977):146-8.

Roberts, Walter R.   Tito, Mihailović and the Allies, 1941-1945. New Brunswick, N. J.: Rutgers U Press, 1973. Rev. by W. H. McNeill, JMH, 49(Mar 1977):147-51.

Roberts, William.   An Account of the First Discovery and Natural History of Florida. Gainesville: U Presses of Florida, 1976. Rev. by R. R. Rea, AlaR, 30(July 1977):234-5.

Robertson, Martin.   A History of Greek Art. Cambridge: Univer- sity Press, 1975. Rev. by J. Boardman, Antiquity, 51(March 1977):71-2.

Robertson, Pauline Durrett and R. L. Robertson.   Panhandle Pil- grimage: Illustrated Tales Tracing History in the Texas Pan- handle. Canyon: Staked Plains Press, 1976. Rev. by D. W. Whisenhunt, NMHR, 52(Apr 1977):163-4.

Robertson, R. L.   see Robertson, Pauline Durrett

Robinson, David.   Chiefs and Clerics: The History of Abdul Bokar Kan and Futa Toro 1853-1891. Oxford: Ox U Press, 1975. Rev. by D. C. O'Brien, History, 62(Je 1977):266-7.

Robinson, Glen O.   The Forest Service: A Study in Public Land Management. Baltimore: JHU Press, 1975. Rev. by V. Wiser, AHR, 81(Dec 1976):1271; J. A. Miller, A&W, 19(Sum 1977):165-7; R. S. Maxwell, ETHJ, 15(No. 2, 1977):66-7.

Robinson, J. Cordell.   El movimiento gaitanista en Colombia: 1930-1948. Bogotá: Ediciones Tercer Mundo, 1976. Rev. by J. L. Payne, HAHR, 57(Aug 1977):556-7.

Robinson, M. E.   The New South Wales Wheat Frontier, 1851 to 1911. Canberra, Australia: Australian National University, 1976. Rev. by P. Perry, AgH, 51(Apr 1977):479-80.

Robinson, Marguerite S.   Political Structure in a Changing Sinhalese Village. Cambridge: Cam U Press, 1975. Rev. by H. L. Seneviratne, JAS, 36(May 1977):582-3.

Robles, Bob see Dedera, Don

Rocha, Nogueira Arlinda.   A Imigração Japonêsa para a Lovaura Cafeeira Paulista, 1908-1922. São Paulo: Instituto de Estudios Brasileiros-Universidade de São Paulo, 1973. Rev. by J. L. Tigner, HAHR, 57(May 1977):375-7.

Rochat, Giorgio see Pieri, Piero

Rock, David, ed. Argentina in the Twentieth Century. Pittsburgh:
U Pittsburgh Press, 1975. Rev. by T. F. McGann, AHR,
82(Oct 1977):1111; J. R. Scobie, JLAS, 9(May 1977):167-70;
W. Schiff, TAm, 33(Jan 1977):548-9.

_____ . Politics in Argentina 1890-1930: The Rise and Fall of
Radicalism. New York: Cam U Press, 1975. Rev. by C.
Solberg, AHR, 81(Dec 1976):1285-86; M. Falcoff, HAHR,
57(Feb 1977):146-9; J. R. Scobie, JLAS, 9(May 1977):167-70;
W. Schiff, TAm, 34(Jl 1977):139-40.

Rodes, Robert E., Jr. Ecclesiastical Administration in Medieval
England: The Anglo-Saxons to the Reformation. Notre Dame:
U Notre Dame Press, 1977. Rev. by T. Callahan, Jr.,
History, 6(Oct 1977):23.

Rodewald, Cosmo. Money in the Age of Tiberius. Totowa, N.J.:
Rowman and Littlefield, 1976. Rev. by R. L. Hohlfelder,
AHR, 82(Feb 1977):70-1.

Rodnitzky, Jerome L. Minstrels of the Dawn: The Folk-Protest
Singer as a Cultural Hero. Chicago: Nelson-Hall, 1976.
Rev. by C. Smith, AHR, 82(Je 1977):775.

Rodríguez, Raúl Palacios. La Chilenización de Tacna y Arica
1883-1929. Lima: Editorial Arica S. A., 1975. Rev. by W.
F. Sater, HAHR, 57(May 1977):359-60.

Rodriguez O, Jaime E. The Emergence of Spanish America: Vin-
cente Rocafuerte and Spanish Americanism, 1808-1832.
Berkeley: U Cal Press, 1975. Rev. by C. A. Hale, AHR,
82(Feb 1977):224-5; G. A. Brubaker, HAHR, 57(Feb 1977):
116-7.

Roeder, Richard B. see Malone, Michael P.

Roelker, Jack R. Mathu of Kenya: A Political Study. Stanford:
Hoover Inst. Press, 1976. Rev. by J. Spencer, AHR, 82(Oct
1977):1038-9.

Roessel, Ruth, comp. and Broderick H. Johnson, comp. Navajo
Livestock Reduction: A National Disgrace. Chinle, Ariz.:
Navajo Community College Press, 1974. Rev. by V. E.
Tiller, PHR, 46(Feb 1977):128-30.

Roff, William R. Kelantan: Religion, Society and Politics in a
Malay State. Juala Lumpur: Oxford U Press, 1974. Rev.
by P. Pederson, JAAS, 12(Jan./Oct. 1977):312-14.

Roffman, Howard. Understanding the Cold War: A Study of the
Cold War in the Interwar Period. Cranbury, N.J.: Fairleigh
Dickinson U Press, 1977. Rev. by R. R. Trask, History,
6(Oct 1977):7.

Roger, Katherine Harvey see Harvey, Horace

Rogers, Barbara. White Wealth and Black Poverty: American Investments in Southern Africa. Westport, Conn. : Greenwood
Press, 1976. Rev. by R. Blausten, AfAf, 76(July 1977):416-18.

Rogers, George C. , Jr. , ed. , David R. Chesnutt, ed. and Peggy J.
Clark, ed. The Papers of Henry Laurens. Columbia, S. C. :
Published for the South Carolina Historical Society by the
University of South Carolina Press, 1976. Rev. by J. P.
Greene, JSH, 43(Nov 1977):605-6; R. M. Weir, WMQ, 34(Oct
1977):666-8.

_____ , ed. see also Laurens, Henry

Rogin, Michael Paul. Fathers and Children, Andrew Jackson and
the Subjugation of the American Indian. New York: Alfred A.
Knopf, 1975. Rev. by D. Brown, AHI, 12(Oct 1977):50; L.
Perry, H&T, 16(May 1977):174-95; R. V. Remini, PNQ,
68(Jan 1977):36.

Rohio, S. W. see Mutiso, Gideon-Cyrus M.

Röhl, John C. G. , ed. Philipp Eulenburgs Politische Korrespondenz.
Volume I: Von der Reichsgründung bis zum Neuen Kurs, 1866-
1891. Boppard: Harald Boldt, 1976. Rev. by V. E. Berghahn, HJ, 20(No. 3, 1977):773-6.

Roland, Charles P. The Improbable Era: The South Since World
War II. Lexington: U Press Ken, 1975. Rev. by N. V.
Bartley, ETHJ, 15(Spr 1977):63-4; D. Buice, LaH, 18(Spr
1977):253-4; W. D. Barnard, AlaR, 30(Jan 1977):73-4.

Romero, Fernando. Rodriguez de Mendoza: Hombre de lucha.
Lima, Peru: Editorial Arica, n. d. Rev. by D. Gleason,
HAHR, 57(Feb 1977):158-9.

Roosen, William James. The Age of Louis XIV: The Rise of
Modern Diplomacy. Cambridge, Mass. : Schenkman, 1976.
Rev. by J. T. O'Connor, AHR, 82(Je 1977):624-5.

Root, Waverley and Richard de Rochemont. Eating in America, A
History. New York: William Morrow, 1976. Rev. by M.
Kreidberg, MinnH, 45(Fall 1977):299-300.

Roper, Laura Wood. FLO: A Biography of Frederick Law Olmsted.
Baltimore: Johns Hopkins U Press, 1974. Rev. by D. W.
Marcell, PH, 45(Jan 1977):92-3.

Rose, C. B. , Jr. Arlington County, Virginia: A History. Baltimore: Port City Press, 1976. Rev. by J. H. Moore, VMHB,
85(Jan 1977):116-17.

Rose, Lisle A. Roots of Tragedy: The United States and the Struggle for Asia, 1945-1953. Westport, Conn.: Greenwood Press,
1976. Rev. by R. D. Buhite, PHR, 46(Aug 1977):532-3; J. A.
Thompson, JAmS, 11(Dec 1977):416.

Rose, Richard. Managing Presidential Objectives. London: Macmillan, 1977. Rev. by D. J. S. Morris, JAmS, 11(Dec
1977):394-5.

Rose, Willie Lee. A Documentary History of Slavery in North
America. New York: Oxford U Press, 1976. Rev. by J. H.
Moore, FHQ, 55(Jan 1977):382-4.

Rosecrance, Richard, ed. America as an Ordinary Country: U. S.
Foreign Policy and the Future. Ithaca: Cornell U Press,
1976. Rev. by W. R. Barker, JAmS, 11(Dec 1977):391-2.

Rosen, Andrew. Rise up, Women! The Militant Campaign of the
Women's Social and Political Union, 1903-1914. London:
Routledge & Kegan Paul, 1974. Rev. by C. Rover, CHR,
58(Mar 1977):99-100.

Rosen, Elliot A. Hoover, Roosevelt, and the Brains Trust: From
Depression to New Deal. New York: Col U Press, 1977.
Rev. by A. A. Ekirch, Jr., History, 6(Nov/Dec 1977):26.

Rosenberg, Bruce A. Custer and the Epic of Defeat. University
Park: Penn St U Press, 1974. Rev. by R. C. Carriker,
PHR, 46(Aug 1977):504-6.

Rosenberg, Charles E., ed. The Family in History. Philadelphia:
U Penn Press, 1975. Rev. by A. MacFarlane, History,
62(Feb 1977):79; P. Branca, JMH, 49(Mar 1977):118-20.

Rosenberg, Charles E. No Other Gods: On Science and American
Social Thought. Baltimore: Johns Hopkins U Press, 1976.
Rev. by G. N. Grob, JIH, 8(Autumn 1977):394-6.

_____ . The Trial of the Assassin Guiteau: Psychiatry and Law
in the Gilded Age. Chicago: U Chi Press, 1968. Rev. by
A. Peskin, CWH, 23(Je 1977):183-5.

Rosenberg, Nathan. Perspectives on Technology. Cambridge: Cam
U Press, 1976. Rev. by W. P. Strassmann, JEH, 37(Je
1977):559-60.

Rosenberger, Homer Tope. The Philadelphia and Erie Railroad:
Its Place in American Economic History. Potomac, Maryland:
Fox Hills Press, 1975. Rev. by R. E. Carlson, PH, 45(April
1977):188-9.

Rosenbloom, Noah. Tradition in an Age of Reform. n. l. : Jewish
Publication Society, n. d. Rev. by D. Singer, Comm, 64(Dec
1977):90-3.

Rosenblum, Illith see Esh, Tina

Rosengarten, Frederic, Jr. Freebooters Must Die! The Life and
Death of William Walker, the Most Notorious Filibuster of the
Nineteenth Century. Wayne, Pa. : Haverford House Pub.,
1976. Rev. by D. E. Livingston-Little, JOW, 16(Jl 1977):100;
David E. Meerse, JSH, 43(Feb 1977):130; C. J. Bussey,
FCHQ, 51(July 1977):287-8.

Rosenman, Dorothy see Rosenman, Samuel

Rosenman, Samuel and Dorothy Rosenman. Presidential Style:
Some Giants and a Pygmy in the White House. N. Y. : Harper
and Row, 1976. Rev. by W. H. Harbaugh, AHR, 82(Oct
1977):1091-2.

Rosenn, Keith S. see Karst, Kenneth L.

Rosenof, Theodore. Dogma, Depression, and the New Deal: The
Debate of Political Leaders Over Economic Recovery. Port
Washington, N. Y. : Kennikat Press, 1975. Rev. by J. B.
Gilbert, AHR, 81(Dec 1976):1273.

Rosenthal, Harry Kenneth. German and Pole: National Conflict and
Modern Myth. Gainesville, Fla. : U Presses Fla, 1976. Rev.
by F. G. Cambell, AHR, 82(Oct 1977):1000.

Rosenthal, Joel T. Nobles and the Noble Life, 1295-1500. New
York: Barnes and Noble Books, 1976. Rev. by J. J.
Contreni, HT, 10(May 1977):488-9.

Rosnek, Carl and Joseph Stacy. Skystone and Silver: The Collec-
tor's Book of Southwest Indian Jewelry. Englewood Cliffs:
Prentice Hall, 1976. Rev. by B. L. Fontana, JAriH, 18(Spr
1977):104-6.

Ross, C. D. The Wars of the Roses. n. l. : Thames & Hudson,
n. d. Rev. by A. R. Myers, HTo, 27(Jan 1977):57-8.

Ross, Douglas A. see Mueller, Peter G.

Ross, Jack C. An Assembly of Good Fellows: Voluntary Associations in History. Westport, Conn. : Greenwood Press, 1976.
Rev. by R. K. McClure, AHR, 82(Je 1977):609.

Ross, Michael. The Reluctant King. Joseph Bonaparte, King of
the Two Sicilies and Spain. Sidgwick & Jackson, n. d. Rev.
by C. Hope, HTo, 27(Jan 1977):61.

Ross, Ronald J. Beleaguered Tower: The Dilemma of Political
Catholicism in Wilhelmine Germany. Notre Dame: U Notre
Dame, 1976. Rev. by G. M. Kren, Historian, 39(Feb 1977):
351-2; J. Sperber, JMH, 49(Je 1977):333-5.

Ross, Timothy A. , ed. see Lau, Joseph S. M. , ed.

Rossabi, Morris. China and Inner Asia: From 1368 to the Present
Day. N. Y. : Universe Books, 1975. Rev. by F. Michael,
AHR, 82(Apr 1977):410; G. J. Alder, History, 62(Je 1977):
290-1.

Rossie, Jonathan Gregory. The Politics of Command in the American Revolution. Syracuse, N. Y. : Syracuse U Press, 1975.
Rev. by D. R. Gerlach, WMQ, 34(Apr 1977):327-9.

Rossiter, Frank R. Charles Ives and His America. New York:
Liveright, 1975. Rev. by A. Stoutamire, AHR, 81(Dec
1976):1264.

Rossiter, Margaret. The Emergence of Agricultural Science:
Justus Liebig and the Americans, 1840-1880. New Haven:
Yale U Press, 1975. Rev. by C. Pursell, AgH, 51(Apr
1977):467-9; E. E. Lampard, AHR, 81(Dec 1976):1244-45;
H. D. Shapiro, AS, 18(Fall 1977):114.

Rotberg, R. I. , ed. see Chittick, H. N. , ed.

Roth, Martin. Comedy and America: The Lost World of Washington Irving. Port Washington, NY: Kennikat Press, 1976.
Rev. by G. A. Cardwell, NEQ, 50(Je 1977):341-4.

Rothenberg, Gunther E. The Army of Francis Joseph. West
Lafayette, Ind. : Purdue U Press, 1976. Rev. by W. A.
Jenks, AHR, 82(Feb 1977):136.

Rothwell, Harry, ed. English Historical Documents. vol. 3.
N. Y. : Ox U Press, 1975. Rev. by J. S. Beckerman, AHR,
82(Feb 1977):75-6.

Rotondo, Antonio. Studi e ricerche di storia ereticale italiana del
cinquecento. Vol. I. Turin: Edizioni Giappichell, 1974.
Rev. by D. Nugent, AHR, 82(Apr 1977):383-4.

Rout, Leslie R. , Jr. The African Experience in Spanish America:
1502 to the Present Day. N. Y. : Cam U Press, 1976. Rev.
by J. V. Lombardi, AHR, 82(Apr 1977):476-7; C. Gibson,
JIH, 8(Autumn 1977):396-7.

Routh, Guy. The Origin of Economic Ideas. White Plains, N. Y. :
International Arts and Sciences Press, 1975. Rev. by J. J.
Spengler, JEH, 37(Je 1977):538-40.

Rowe, John Carlos. Henry Adams and Henry James: The Emergence of a Modern Consciousness. Ithaca: Cor U Press,
1976. Rev. by W. Michaels, GR, 31(Spr 1977):258-64; J. W.
Crowley, NEQ, 50(Mar 1977):184-6.

Rowell, John W. Yankee Artillerymen. Knoxville: U Tennessee
Press, 1975. Rev. by J. D. Smith, FCHQ, 51(Oct 1977):
369-71; W. L. Burton, JISHS, 70(Feb 1977):95-6.

Rowland, A. Ray and Helen Callahan. Yesterday's Augusta. Miami, Florida: Seeman Pub. Co., 1976. Rev. by O. P.
Mackie, GHQ, 51(Summer 1977):199-200.

Rowland, Marie B. Masters and Men in the West Midlands Metalware Trades before the Industrial Revolution. Manchester:
Manchester U Press, 1975. Rev. by J. R. Harris, BH,
19(July 1977):218-19.

Rowley, Trevor and Mike Breakell, ed. Planning and the historic
environment. Oxford: U Oxford, 1975. Rev. by J. Alexander, Antiquity, 51(July 1977):160-1.

Roy, Asish Kumar. The Spring Thunder and After: A Survey of
the Maoist and Ultra-Leftist Movements in India, 1962-75.
Columbia, Mo.: South Asia Books, 1975. Rev. by M. F.
Franda, JAS, 36(Aug 1977):771-2.

Roy, Jean P. The Diary of a Dead Man. N. P.: Jean P. Roy,
1976. Rev. by R. D. Hoffsommer, CWTI, 16(Aug 1977):49-50.

Roy, Manisha. Bengali Women. Chicago: U Chi Press, 1976.
Rev. by M. H. Beech, JAS, 36(Feb 1977):374-5.

Roy, Ramashray. The Uncertain Verdict: A Study of the 1969
Elections in Four Indian States. Berkeley: U Cal Press,
1975. Rev. by N. D. Palmer, JAS, 36(Feb 1977):372.

Royal Commission on Historical Monuments (England). An inventory
of historical monuments in the County of Dorset: Vol. V:
East. London: H. M. S. O., 1975. Rev. by B. Cunliffe,
Antiquity, 51(March 1977):66-7; D. Dymond, Antiquity, 51(Nov
1977):248-9.

Royal Commission on the Ancient and Historical Monuments of Scotland. Argyll: an inventory of the ancient monuments. Vol.
II: Lorn. Edinburgh: 1975. Rev. by R. Feachem, Antiquity,
51(March 1977):73-4.

Roxborough, Ian, et al. Chile: The State and Revolution. N. Y.:
Holmes and Meier, 1977. Rev. by P. W. Drake, AHR,
82(Oct 1977):1108-9.

Rubeinstein, Alvin Z., ed. Soviet and Chinese Influence in the
Third World. New York: Praeger, 1975. Rev. by T. M.
Shaw, JAAS, 12(Jan/Oct 1977):296-7.

Rubin, Louis D., Jr. William Elliott Shoots a Bear: Essays on
the Southern Literary Imagination. Baton Rouge: LSU Press,
1976. Rev. by R. King, GR, 31(Fall 1977):743-6.

_____, and C. Hugh Holman. Southern Literary Study: Problems and Possibilities. Chapel Hill: UNC Press, 1975. Rev. by R. King, GR, 31(Fall 1977):743-6; R. Gray, JAmS, 11(Dec 1977):402-4.

Rubin, Vera, ed. and Richard P. Schaedel, ed. The Haitian Potential: Research and Resources of Haiti. New York: Teachers College Press, Col U, 1975. Rev. by T. O. Ott, HAHR, 57(Feb 1977):164-6.

Ruchames, Louis, ed. see Merrill, Walter M., ed.

Rudolph, Richard L. Banking and Industrialization in Austria-Hungary: The Role of Banks in the Industrialization of the Czech Crownlands, 1873-1914. Cambridge: Cam U Press, 1976. Rev. by A. B. Baker, JEH, 37(Sep 1977):840-1.

Rudwick, Elliott see Meier, August

Ruffin, Edmund. The Diary of Edmund Ruffin. Volume II: The Years of Hope, April 1861-June 1863. Ed. by William Kauffman Scarborough. Baton Rouge: Louisiana St U Press, 1976. Rev. by W. T. Doherty, Jr., WVH, 38(July 1977):327-9.

Ruiz, Ramón Eduardo. Labor and the Ambivalent Revolutionaries: Mexico, 1911-1923. Baltimore: JHU Press, 1976. Rev. by J. Womack, Jr., HAHR, 57(May 1977):345-6; K. J. Grieb, JEH, 37(Je 1977):560-1; M. D. Berstein, PHR, 46(Aug 1977):524-6; J. M. Hart, TAm, 33(Apr 1977):690-1.

Rummel, Leo. History of the Catholic Church in Wisconsin. Madison: Wisconsin State Council, Knights of Columbus, 1976. Rev. by B. T. Mackin, WMH, 60(Summer 1977):346-7.

Runblom, Harald, ed. and Hans Norman, ed. From Sweden to America: A History of the Migration. Minneapolis: U Minn Press, 1976. Rev. by R. C. Ostergren, MinnH, 45(Spr 1977):202-3; C. Erickson, JAmS, 11(Aug 1977):289-90.

Rürup, Reinhard, ed. Arbeiter-und Soldatenräte im rheinischwestfälischen Industriegebiet. Studien zur Geschichte der Revolution 1918/1919. Wuppertal: Peter Hammer Verlag, 1975. Rev. by M. Nolan, JMH, 49(Sep 1977):507-12.

_____. Emanzipation und Antisemitismus: Studien zur "Judenfrage" der bürgerlichen Gesellschaft. Gottingen: Vandenhoeck & Ruprecht, 1975. Rev. by J. Katz, JMH, 49(Je 1977):326-8.

Rusco, Elmer R. "Good Time Coming?" Black Nevadans in the Nineteenth Century. Westport, Conn.: Greenwood Press, 1975. Rev. by L. B. de Graaf, Historian, 39(May 1977):578-9; E. H. Berwanger, PHR, 46(May 1977):292-4.

Rusho, W. L. and C. Gregory Crampton. Desert River Crossing: Historic Lee's Ferry on the Colorado River. Salt Lake City and Santa Barbara: Peregrine Smith, 1975. Rev. by R. E. Levinson, JOW, 16(Jan 1977):87.

Russell, Francis. Adams: An American Dynasty. New York: American Heritage, 1976. Rev. by G. Parkinson, WVH, 38(Jan 1977):175-6.

_____. The President Makers: From Mark Hanna to Joseph P. Kennedy. Boston: Little, Brown, 1976. Rev. by J. N. Giglio, Historian, 39(May 1977):590-1; J. D. Buenker, NEQ, 50(Je 1977):346-8.

Russell, Howard S. A Long, Deep Furrow; Three Centuries of Farming in New England. Hanover: U Press New England, 1976. Rev. by A. A. Spielman, NEQ, 50(Mar 1977):155-6; M. M. True, VH, 45(Spring 1977):113-14.

Russett, Bruce M. and Alfred Stepan, ed. Military Force and American Society. New York: Harper & Row, 1973. Rev. by E. Ranson, JAmS, 11(April 1977):147-9.

Russett, Cynthia Eagle. Darwin in America: The Intellectual Response, 1865-1912. San Francisco: Freeman, 1976. Rev. by P. F. Baller, Jr., Historian, 39(May 1977):576-7; M. M. Vance, JSH, 43(Aug 1977):466-7.

Rustin, Bayard. Strategies for Freedom: The Changing Patterns of Black Protest. New York: Col U Press, 1976. Rev. by R. L. Zangrando, JSH, 43(Feb 1977):141-2.

Rutherford, Ward. The Russian Army in World War I. London: Gordon Cremonesi, 1975. Rev. by J. W. Long, Historian, 39(May 1977):561-3.

Ryan, Alan. J. S. Mill. London: Routledge and Kegan Paul, 1975. Rev. by S. Collini, HJ, 20(No. 1, 1977):237-54.

Ryan, Marleigh Grayer. The Development of Realism in the Fiction of Tsubouchi Shoyo. Seattle: U Wash Press, 1975. Rev. by R. Epp, JAS, 36(Aug 1977):758-60.

Ryan, Mary E. see Cochrane, Willard W.

Rystad, Göran. Ambiguous Imperialism: American Foreign Policy and Domestic Politics at the Turn of the Century. Stockholm: Scandinavian U Books, 1975. Rev. by R. W. Sellen, Historian, 39(Feb 1977):375-6.

Sachar, Howard M. A History of Israel: From the Rise of Zionism to Our Time. n.l.: Knopf, n.d. Rev. by J. Shattan, Comm, 63(Feb 1977):68-72.

Saes, Décio.   Classe Média e Política na Primera Republica
  Brasileira, 1889-1930.   Petropolis: Editora Vozes, 1975.
  Rev. by E. Pang, HAHR, 57(Aug 1977):550-1.

Safford, Frank.   The Ideal of the Practical: Colombia's Struggle
  to Form a Technical Elite.   Austin: U T Press, 1976.   Rev.
  by H. Delpar, HAHR, 57(Feb 1977):131-3;   L. Lewin, TAm,
  33(Apr 1977):687-9.

Sagan, Carl.   The Dragons of Eden: Speculations on the Evolution
  of Human Intelligence.   n. l. :   Random House, n. d.   Rev. by
  R. J. Herrnstein, Comm, 64(Aug 1977):66-70.

Saldern Axel von et al.   Glaser der Antike: Sammlung Erwin
  Oppenlander.   Mainz: Philip von Zabern, 1974.   Rev. by J.
  D. Cooney, JNES, 36(Jan 1977):159-60.

Sale, Roger.   Seattle: Past to Present.   Seattle: U Wash Press,
  1976.   Rev. by N. Clark. PNQ, 68(Oct 1977):190-1.

Salmon, J. H. M.   Society in Crisis: France in the Sixteenth Century.   New York: St. Martin's Press, 1975.   Rev. by O.
  Ranum, Historian, 39(Feb 1977):340-2;   H. M. Solomon, JMH,
  49(Je 1977):314-5.

Samaha, Joel.   Law and Order in Historical Perspective: The Case
  of Elizabethan Essex.   New York: Academic Press, 1974.
  Rev. by C. Holmes, JMH, 49(Sep 1977):495-500.

Sambuccetti, Susana Rato De.   Avellaneda y la nación versus
  laprovinica de Buenos Aires: Crisis económica y política,
  1873-1880.   Buenos Aires: Editorial La Pleyade, 1975.   Rev.
  by D. J. Guy, HAHR, 57(Aug 1977):547-9.

Samuels, Harold see Samuels, Peggy

Samuels, Peggy and Harold Samuels.   The Illustrated Biographical
  Encyclopedia of Artists of the American West.   Garden City,
  N. Y. :   Doubleday, 1976.   Rev. by J. A. Stout, Jr. , NMHR,
  52(Jl 1977):257-8.

Sande, Theodore Anton.   Industrial Archeology: A New Look at the
  American Heritage.   Brattleboro, Vt. :   Stephen Greene Press,
  1976.   Rev. by V. P. Packard, MinnH, 45(Fall 1977):300.

Sanders, Thomas E. , ed. and Peek, Walter W. , ed.   Literature of
  the American Indian.   Beverly Hills, Calif. :   Glencoe Press,
  1976.   Rev. by H. A. Howard, JOW, 16(Jan 1977):76-7.

Sanderson, Kenneth M. , ed.   see Anderson, Frederick, ed.

Sanford, Robinson Rojas.   The Murder of Allende and the End of
  the Chilean Way to Socialism.   New York: Harper & Row,
  1975.   Rev. by P. E. Sigmund, HAHR, 57(Feb 1977):153-5.

Satz, Ronald N. American Indian Policy in the Jacksonian Era.
Lincoln: U Neb Press, 1975. Rev. by W. T. Hagan, PHR,
46(May 1977):287-8; R. J. Loewenberg, PNQ, 68(Jan 1977):
36-7.

Sauer, Franz A. von. The Alienated "Loyal" Opposition: Mexico's
Partido Accion Nacional. Albuquerque: U NM Press, 1974.
Rev. by T. Schooner, JLAS, 9(May 1977):175-8.

Savage, W. Sherman. Blacks in the West. Westport, Conn.:
Greenwood Press, 1976. Rev. by N. G. Brinhurst, UHQ,
45(Sum 1977):315-7.

Savage, William W., Jr. Cowboy Life: Reconstructing an American Myth. Norman: U Ok Press, 1975. Rev. by J. B.
Frantz, PHR, 469(May 1977):296-7.

Sayers, R. S. The Bank of England, 1891-1944. New York: Cam
U Press, 1976. Rev. by D. B. Graddy, JEH, 37(Sep 1977):
841-3.

Scalapino, Robert A. Asia and the Road Ahead: Issues for the
Major Powers. Berkeley: U Cal Press, 1975. Rev. by C.
Lee, JAS, 36(May 1977):535-7.

Scally, Robert J. The Origins of the Lloyd George Coalition: The
Politics of Social-Imperialism, 1900-1918. Princeton: Prin
U Press, 1975. Rev. by B. B. Gilbert, JMH, 49(Mar 1977):
138-40.

Scamehorn, H. Lee. Pioneer Steelmaker in the West: The Colorado
Fuel and Iron Company 1892-1903. Boulder, Colorado: Pruett,
1976. Rev. by T. G. Alexander, WHQ, 8(Oct 1977):471.

Scarano, Julita. Devocāo e Escravidāo. A Irmandale de Nossa
Senhora do Rosário dos Pretos no Distrito Diamantino no
Século XVIII. Sao Paulo: Companhia Editora Nacional, 1976.
Rev. by A. J. R. Russell Wood, HAHR, 57(May 1977):339-40.

Scarborough, John. Facets of Hellenic Life. Boston: Houghton
Mifflin, 1976. Rev. by S. B. Pomeroy, Historian, 39(May
1977):533-4.

Scarr, Deryck. The Majesty of Colour: A Life of Sir John Bates
Thurston, Volume 1: I, The Very Bayonet. Canberra:
Australian National University Press, 1973. Rev. by G.
Jackson, History, 62(Je 1977):303-4.

Schaedel, Richard P., ed. see Rubin, Vera, ed.

Schafer, Roy. A New Language For Psychoanalysis. New Haven:
Yale U Press, 1976. Rev. by R. H. King, GR, 31(Spr
1977):252-8.

Schandler, Herbert Y. The Unmaking of a President: Lyndon Johnson and Vietnam. Princeton, N.J.: Prin U Press, 1977. Rev. by N. W. Polsby, Comm, 64(Dec 1977):87-90.

Schapsmeier, Edward L. and Frederick H. Schapsmeier. Encyclopedia of American Agricultural History. Westport, Conn.: Greenwood Press, 1975. Rev. by J. H. Shideler, AgH, 51(Jan 1977):269-70.

Schapsmeier, Frederick H. see Schapsmeier, Edward L.

Scharfstein, Ben-Ami. The Mind of China: The Culture, Customs, and Beliefs of Traditional China. New York: Basic Books, 1974. Rev. by J. K. Riegel, JAS, 37(Nov 1977):108-10; H. J. Lamley, JAAS, 12(Jan/Oct 1977):304-7.

Scheick, William J. The Writings of Jonathan Edwards: Theme, Motif, and Style. College Station: Texas A&M U Press, 1975. Rev. by D. L. Parker, WMQ, 34(Jan 1977):169-70.

Scheper, Burchard. Frühe bürgerliche Institutionen norddeutscher Hansestädte: Beiträge zu einer vergleichenden Verfassungsgeschichte Lübecks, Bremens, Lüneburgs and Hamburgs im Mittelalter. Koln: Bohlau Verlag, 1975. Rev. by W. Kirchner, JEH, 37(Je 1977):561-2.

Scherer, Lester B. Slavery and the Churches in Early America, 1619-1819. Grand Rapids, Mich.: William B. Eerdmans, 1975. Rev. by M. Drimmer, WMQ, 34(Jl 1977):499-501.

Schiefel, Werner. Bernhard Dernburg, 1865-1937: Kolonialpolitiker und Bankier im Wilhelminischen Deutschland. Zurich: Atlantis Verlag, 1975. Rev. by L. Cecil, JMH, 49(Je 1977):329-33.

Schleier, Hans. Die Bürgerliche deutsch Geschichtsschreibung der Weimarer Republik. Berlin, GDR: Akademie-Verlag, 1975. Rev. by G. G. Iggers, JMH, 49(Mar 1977):144-7.

Schlumbohm, Jürgen. Freiheit: Die Anfänge der bürgerlichen Emanzipationsbewegung in Deutschland im Spiegel ihres Leitwortes (ca 1760-ca 1800). Düsseldorf: Padogogischer Verlag Schwann, 1975. Rev. by M. Gray, JMH, 49(Mar 1977):143-4.

Schneider, Jane and Peter Schneider. Culture and Political Economy in Western Sicily. New York: Academic Press, 1976. Rev. by R. Grew, JIH, 8(Autumn 1977):377-9.

Schneider, Jürgen. Handel und Unternehmer im französischen Brasiliengeschaft, 1815-1848. Köln: Böhlau Verlag, 1975. Rev. by C. Medalen, HAHR, 57(May 1977):355-6.

Schneider, Louis, ed. see Bonjean, Charles M. , ed.

Schneiderman, Jeremiah. Sergei Zubatov and Revolutionary Marx-
ism: The Struggle for the Working Class in Tsarist Russia.
Ithaca and London: Cornell U Press, 1976. Rev. by K. E.
McKenzie, JEH, 37(Je 1977):563-4.

Schnore, Leo F. , ed. The New Urban History: Quantitative Explorations by American Historians. Princeton: Prin U Press,
1975. Rev. by W. G. Robbins, PHR, 46(Aug 1977):488-9.

Schob, David E. Hired Hands and Plowboys: Farm Labor in the
Midwest, 1815-60. Urbana: U Ill Press, 1975. Rev. by A.
G. Bogue, PHR, 46(Feb 1977):125-6.

Scholem, Gershom. On Jews and Judaism in Crisis: Selected Essays. n. l. : Schocken, n. d. Rev. by C. Raphael, Comm,
63(Mar 1977):78-83.

Schuker, Stephen A. The End of French Predominance in Europe:
The Financial Crisis and the Adoption of the Dawes Plan.
Chapel Hill: U NC Press, 1976. Rev. by C. P. Kindleber-
ger, JEH, 37(Sep 1977):843-5; R. O. Paxton, JIH, 8(Autumn
1977):373-5.

Schulz, Gerhard. Geschichte Heute. Positionen, Tendenzen und
Probleme. Gottingen: Vandenhoeck & Ruprecht, 1973. Rev.
by K. G. Faver, H&T, 16(Feb 1977):51-66.

Schulzinger, Robert D. The Making of the Diplomatic Mind: The
Training, Outlook and Style of the United States Foreign Service Officers, 1908-1931. Middletown, Ct. : Wes U Press,
1975. Rev. by M. Small, Historian, 39(Feb 1977):376-7.

Schusky, Ernest L. The Forgotten Sioux: An Ethnohistory of the
Lower Brule Reservation. Chicago: Nelson Hall, 1975. Rev.
by W. R. Jacobs, PHR, 46(Feb 1977):118-9.

Schuster, Kurt G. P. Der Rote Frontkämpferbund, 1924-1929.
Beiträge zur Geschichte und Organisationsstruktur eines
politischen Kampfbundes. Düsseldorf: Drost Verlag, 1975.
Rev. by M. Nolan, JMH, 49(Sep 1977):507-12.

Schustereit, Hartmut. Linksliberalismus und Sozialdemokratie in
der Weimarer Republik. Düsseldorf: Padagogischer Verlag
Schwann, 1975. Rev. by M. Nolan, JMH, 49(Sep 1977):507-12.

Schwartz, Michael. Radical Protest and Social Structure: The
Southern Farmer's Alliance and Cotton Tenancy, 1880-1890.
New York, San Francisco, & London: Academic Press, 1976.
Rev. by R. C. McMath, JSH, 43(Nov 1977):627-8.

Schwieder, Dorothy see Schwieder, Elmer

Schwieder, Elmer and Dorothy Schwieder. A Peculiar People: Iowa's Old Order Amish. Ames: Iowa St U Press, n. d. Rev. by D. Crosson, Historian, 39(Feb 1977):381-2.

Scobie, James R. Buenos Aires, Plaza to Suburb 1870-1910. Oxford: Ox U Press, 1975. Rev. by J. C. Crossley, JLAS, 9(May 1977):166-7.

Scott, Stanley H. and Levi H. Davis. A Giant in Texas: A History of the Dallas-Ft. Worth Regional Airport Controversy, 1911-1974. Quannah, Texas: Nortex, 1974. Rev. by D. McComb, ETHJ, 15(Spr 1977):64-5.

Scribner, Robert L. and Brent Tarter, ed. Revolutionary Virginia: The Road to Independence. Volume III. The Breaking Storm and the Third Convention, 1775; A Documentary Record. Charlottesville: U Press of Virginia, 1977. Rev. by G. M. Herndon, GHQ, 51(Winter 1977):365-6.

Scruggs, Charles G. The Peaceful Atom and the Deadly Fly. Austin: Pemberton Press, 1975. Rev. by J. H. Perkins, AgH, 51(Jan 1977):262-3.

Scully, Vincent. Pueblo: Mountain, Village, Dance. New York: Viking, 1972. Rev. by R. C. Euler, NMHR, 52(Jan 1977): 87-8.

Seabury, Paul, ed. Universities in the Western World. New York: Free Press, n. d. Rev. by C. M. Selkin, Mankind, 5(No. 12, 1977):64.

Seager, Robert, II, ed. and Doris D. Maguire, ed. Letters and Papers of Alfred Thayer Mahan. Annapolis: Naval Institute Press, 1975. Rev. by G. E. Wheeler, PHR, 46(Aug 1977): 522-3.

Sealsfield, Charles. The Making of an American: An Adaptation of Memorable Tales. Dallas: SMU Press, 1974. Rev. by S. Cox, ETHJ, 15(Spr 1977):62.

Sedlak, Michael W. see Church, Robert L.

Seelye, John. Prophetic Waters: The River in Early American Life and Literature. New York: Ox U Press, 1977. Rev. by P. F. Gura, NEQ, 50(Sep 1977):529-31.

Seibert, Ilse. Women in the Ancient Near East. New York: Abner Schram, 1974. Rev. by J. S. Cooper, JNES, 36(Jl 1977):231-3.

Seidman, Laurence J. The Fools of '49: The California Gold Rush 1848-1856. New York: Knopf, 1976. Rev. by D. A. Smith, JOW, 16(Jan 1977):81-2.

Selby, John. The Conquest of the American West. Totowa, N.J.:
    Rowman and Littlefield, 1976. Rev. by M. H. Brown, WHQ,
    8(Oct 1977):475-6.

Selleck, George A. Quakers in Boston, 1656-1964. Cambridge:
    Friends Meeting, 1976. Rev. by E. S. Gaustad, NEQ, 50(Sep
    1977):536-7.

Seminaro de Historia de América. Estudios sobre política
    indigenista española en América. Valladolid, Spain:
    Universidad de Valladolid, 1975. Rev. by B. Keen, HAHR,
    57(May 1977):329-31.

Sen, Lalit K., R. N. Tripathy, Girish K. Misra, and Abdul L.
    Thaha. Growth Centres in Raichur: An Integrated Area De-
    velopment Plan for a District in Karnataka. Hyderabad:
    National Institute of Community Development, 1975. Rev. by
    S. G. Hadden, JAS, 37(Nov 1977):162-3.

Sen, S. P., ed. Dictionary of National Biography. Calcutta:
    Institute of Historical Studies, 1972. Rev. by M. Yanuck,
    JAS, 37(Nov 1977):154-6.

_____, ed. Historians and Historiography in Modern India.
    Calcutta: Institute of Historical Studies, 1973. Rev. by R.
    P. Tucker, JAS, 36(Aug 1977):767-8.

_____, ed. History in Modern Indian Literature. Calcutta:
    Institute of Historical Studies, 1975. Rev. by U. S. Nilsson,
    JAS, 37(Nov 1977):153-4.

_____. Modern Bengal: A Socio-economic Survey. Calcutta:
    Institute of Historical Studies, 1973. Rev. by G. Forbes,
    JAS, 36(Aug 1977):782-3.

_____, ed. The Sino-Indian Border Question: A Historical
    Review. Calcutta: Institute of Historical Studies, 1971. Rev.
    by L. E. Rose, JAS, 37(Nov 1977):96-7.

Sennett, Richard. The Fall of Public Man. n.l.: Knopf, n.d.
    Rev. by S. Miller, Comm, 63(Apr 1977):81-4.

Serjeant, R. B., ed. and R. L. Bidwell. Arabian Studies I. Lon-
    don: C. Hurst & Co., 1974. Rev. by G. L. Geddes, JNES,
    36(Jan 1977):59-60.

Sernett, Milton C. Black Religion and American Evangelicalism:
    White Protestants, Plantation Missions, and the Flowering of
    Negro Christianity, 1787-1865. Metuchen, N.J.: Scarecrow
    Press, 1975. Rev. by S. A. Ayatey, LaH, 18(Sum 1977):
    358-61.

Sewall, Rufus K. Sketches of St. Augustine. Gainesville: U

Presses of Florida, 1976.   Rev. by R. F. A. Fabel, AlaR,
30(Jan 1977):69-71.

Sewell, Richard H.   Ballots for Freedom: Antislavery Politics in
the United States, 1837-1860.   New York: Ox U Press, 1976.
Rev. by M. Fellman, PNQ, 68(Oct 1977):193; L. C. Perry,
JSH, 43(Feb 1977):124-5; D. B. Davis, WMH, 60(Summer
1977):338-9.

Shaban, M. A.   The Abbasid Revolution.   Cambridge: Cam U
Press, 1970.   Rev. by W. Madelung, JNES, 36(Jl 1977):235-6.

_____.   Islamic History: A New Interpretation, 2 A. D.
750-1055 (A. H. 132-448).   Cambridge: Cam U Press, 1976.
Rev. by R. B. Serjeant, History, 62(Je 1977):280-1.

_____.   Islamic History A. D. 600-750 (A. H. 132):   A New
Interpretation.   Cambridge: Cam U Press, 1971.   Rev. by
W. Madelung, JNES, 36(Jl 1977):235-6.

Shadily, Hassan see Echols, John M.

Shaffer, Arthur H.   The Politics of History: Writing the History
of the American Revolution, 1783-1815.   Chicago: Precedent
Publishing, 1975.   Rev. by J. T. Main, PNQ, 68(Jan 1977):
33.

Shah, Ghanshyam.   Caste Association and Political Process in
Gujarat: A Study of Gujarat Kshatriya Sabha.   Bombay: Popular Prakashan, 1975.   Rev. by R. W. Jones, JAS, 36(Aug
1977):773-4.

Shah, U. P. and M. A. Dhaky, ed.   Aspects of Jaina Art and
Architecture.   Ahmedabad: L. D. Institute of Indology, 1975.
Rev. by M. W. Meister, JAS, 37(Nov 1977):158-9.

Shahane, Vasant A.   Ruth Prawer Jhabvala.   New Delhi: Arnold
Heinemann, 1976.   Rev. by M. Fisher, JAS, 36(Aug 1977):
782.

Shang-jen, K'ung.   The Peace Blossom Fan.   Tr. by Ch'en Shih-
Hsiang and Harold Acton.   Berkeley: U California Press,
1976.   Rev. by C. Liu, JAS, 37(Nov 1977):97-9.

Sharar, Abdul Halim.   Lucknow: The Last Phase of an Oriental
Culture.   London: Paul Elek, 1975.   Rev. by M. H. Fisher,
JAS, 36(Feb 1977):366-7.

Sharp, William Frederick.   Slavery on the Spanish Frontier: The
Colombian Choco, 1680-1810.   Norman: U Ok Press, 1976.
Rev. by W. P. McGreevey, JEH, 37(Sep 1977):845.

Shaw, Peter.   The Character of John Adams.   Chapel Hill: U

North Carolina Press, 1976. Rev. by P. K. Conkin, WMH,
60(Spring 1977):245-6; J. Howe, WMQ, 34(Jan 1977):133-4.

Sheehan, Edward R. F. The Arabs, Israelis, and Kissinger: A
Secret History of American Diplomacy in the Middle East.
Pleasantville, N. Y.: Reader's Digest Press, n. d. Rev. by
E. Grossman, Comm, 63(Jan 1977):78-82.

Shepherd, Jack. The Forest Killers: The Destruction of the Amer-
ican Wilderness. New York: Weybright and Talley, 1975.
Rev. by J. A. Miller, A&W, 19(Sum 1977):165-167; T. R.
Cox, PNQ, 68(Jan 1977):40-1.

Sheridan, James E. China in Disintegration: The Republican Era
in Chinese History, 1912-1949. New York: Free Press,
1975. Rev. by L. P. Van Slyke, JAS, 36(Aug 1977):728-9.

Sheridan, Richard B. Sugar and Slavery: An Economic History of
the British West Indies, 1623-1775. Baltimore: JHU Press,
1974. Rev. by K. J. Grieb, TAm, 33(Jan 1977):539-40.

Sheridan, T. Mindful Militants: The Amalgamated Engineering
Union in Australia, 1920-1972. New York: Cam U Press,
1976. Rev. by E. A. Beever, JEH, 37(Sep 1977):845-7.

Shibley, Ronald E. Historic Fredericksburg: A Pictorial History.
Norfolk, Va.: Donning Co., 1976. Rev. by D. F. Riggs,
VMHB, 85(April 1977):212-13.

Shideler, James H., ed. Agriculture in the Development of the
Far West. Washington, D. C.: Agricultural History Society,
1975. Rev. by G. E. Wheeler, PNQ, 68(Jan 1977):39-40.

Shih, Chung-wen. The Golden Age of Chinese Drama: Yüan Tsa-
chü. Princeton: Princeton U Press, 1976. Rev. by C.
Mackerras, JAS, 37(Nov 1977):99-100.

Shilhan, Michael J. When I Think of Hingham. Hingham: Hingham Historical Society, 1976. Rev. by T. F. Glick, NEQ,
50(Je 1977):353-6.

Shimazaki, Toson. The Family. Tr. by Cecilia Segawa Seigle.
Tokyo: U Tokyo Press, 1976. Rev. by J. Rubin, JAS,
37(Nov 1977):149-50.

Shimpo, Mitsuru. Three Decades in Shiwa: Economic Development
and Social Change in a Japanese Farming Community. Vancouver: U British Columbia Press, 1976. Rev. by E. H.
Johnson, JAS, 37(Nov 1977):140-1.

Shivji, Issa G. Class Struggles in Tanzania. New York and London: Monthly Review, 1976. Rev. by D. M. P. McCarthy,
JEH, 37(Je 1977):486-9.

Shklar, Judith N. Freedom and Independence: A Study of the Political Ideas of Hegel's Phenomenology of Mind. Cambridge:
Cam U Press, 1976. Rev. by K. Brinkman, History, 62(Feb
1977):71-2.

Shofner, Jerrell H. History of Jefferson County. Tallahassee:
Sentry Press, 1976. Rev. by O. W. Taylor, 43(May 1977):
329-30.

Short, Anthony. The Communist Insurrection in Malaya 1948-60.
London: Frederick Muller, 1975. Rev. by M. Caldwell,
History, 62(Je 1977):299-300.

Shorter, Edward. The Making of the Modern Family. New York:
Basic Books, 1975. Rev. by P. Branca, JMH, 49(Mar 1977):
118-20.

Shoufani, Elias. Al-Riddah and the Muslim Conquest of Arabia.
Toronto: U Tor Press, 1973. Rev. by W. Madelung, 36(Jan
1977):58-9.

Shover, John L. First Majority--Last Minority: The Transforming
of Rural Life in America. De Kalb, Ill: N ILL U Press,
1976. Rev. by J. H. Shideler, AgH, 51(Apr 1977):463-4; A.
O'Rourke, JISHS, 70(Nov 1977):333-4; W. Reid, MichH,
61(Fall 1977):266-70.

Showman, Richard K. , ed. The Papers of General Nathanael
Greene. Chapel Hill: U NC Press, 1976. Rev. by R. Buel,
NEQ, 50(Sep 1977):548-551; P. D. Nelson, WMQ, 34(Oct
1977):668-70.

Shriver, Donald W. , Jr. see Earle, John R.

Shumate, Albert. The California of George Gordon and the 1849
Sea Voyages of his California Association: A San Francisco
Pioneer Rescued from the Legend of Gertrude Atherton's First
Novel. Glendale, Calif. : Arthur H. Clark, 1976. Rev. by
W. A. Beck, WHQ, 18(Jl 1977):345.

Shumway, Floyd M. , ed. see Morris, Richard B. , ed.

Shy, John. A People Numerous and Armed: Reflections on the
Military Struggle for American Independence. New York: Ox
U Press, 1976. Rev. by F. B. Wickwire, WMQ, 34(Apr
1977):325-6.

Shyllon, F. O. Black Slaves in Britain. Cambridge: Ox U Press,
1974. Rev. by H. Temperley, History, 62(Feb 1977):87-8.

Siegel, Jay H. see Stanbury, W. T.

Silin, Robert H. Leadership and Values: The Organization of

Large-Scale Taiwanese Enterprises. Cambridge: Harvard U Press, 1976. Rev. by M. K. Whyte, JAS, 37(Nov 1977):131-3.

Silva, Raul, Brigitta Leander, and Sun Axelsson. Evidence on the Terror in Chile. London: Merlin Press, 1974. Rev. by P. E. Sigmund, HAHR, 57(Feb 1977):153-5.

Silva Dias, J. S. da. O'Erasmismo e a Inquisicão em Portugal: O processo de Fr. Valentim da Luz. Coimbra: Universidade de Coimbra, 1975. Rev. by J. L. Vogt, HAHR, 57(May 1977):326-7.

Silverman, Kenneth. A Cultural History of the American Revolution: Painting, Music, Literature, and the Theatre in the Colonies and the United States from the Treaty of Paris to the Inauguration of George Washington. New York: Thomas Y. Crowell, 1976. Rev. by S. S. Cohen, JSH, 43(Aug 1977):437-8; P. Shaw, WMQ, 34(Oct 1977):654-5.

Silverman, Sydel. Three Bells of Civilization: The Life of An Italian Hill Town. New York: Columbia U Press, 1975. Rev. by D. H. Bell, JIH, 8(Autumn 1977):375-6.

Simmonds, A. J. The Gentile Comes to Cache Valley: A Study of the Logan Apostasies of 1894 and the Establishment of Non-Mormon Churches in Cache Valley, 1873-1913. Logan: Utah St U Press, 1976. Rev. by L. Coates, UHQ, 45(Spr 1977): 203-4.

Simmons, R. C. The American Colonies: From Settlement to Independence. New York: David McKay Co., 1976. Rev. by L. H. Harrison, AHI, 12(Jl 1977):50.

Simpson, Donald. Dark Companions: The African Contribution to The European Exploration of East Africa. London: Elek, 1976. Rev. by K. Ingham, History, 62(Je 1977):275-6.

Simpson, Harold B. Audie Murphy: American Soldier. Hillsboro: Hill Jr. College Press, 1975. Rev. by R. L. Wagner, ETHJ, 15(Spr 1977):65-6.

Simpson, John Eddins, comp. Georgia History: A Bibliography. Metuchen, N.J.: Scarecrow, 1976. Rev. by K. Coleman, GHQ, 51(Summer 1977):190-1.

Simpson, William Kelly. The Terrace of the Great God at Abydos: The Offering Chapels of Dynasties 12 and 13. New Haven and Philadelphia: The Peabody Museum of Natural History of Yale University and the University Museum of the University of Pennsylvania, 1974. Rev. by D. P. Silverman, JNES, 36(Jl 1977):221-2.

_____ see also Dunham, Dows

Sinclair, Bruce. Philadelphia's Philosopher Mechanics: A History
    of the Franklin Institute, 1824-1865. Baltimore: JHU Press,
    1974. Rev. by D. Knight, NYHSQ, 61(Jan/Apr 1977):86-7.

Sinclair, Robert A. Winds Over Lake Huron: Chronicles in the
    Life of a Great Lakes Mariner. Hicksville, N. Y. : Exposition
    Press, 1977. Rev. by W. P. Strauss, MichH, 61(Fall 1977):
    276-7.

Singh, Harbans, ed. Perspectives on Guru Nanak: Seminar Papers.
    Patiala: Guru Govind Singh Department of Religious Studies,
    Punjabi University, 1975. Rev. by N. G. Barrier, JAS, 37
    (Nov 1977):161.

Singh, Harjinder. Authority and Influence in Two Sikh Villages.
    New Delhi: Sterling Publishers, 1976. Rev. by M. J. Leaf,
    JAS, 37(Nov 1977):161-2.

Singh, Purushottam. Neolithic Cultures of Western Asia. London
    and New York: Seminar Press, 1974. Rev. by L. S.
    Braidwood, JNES, 36(Jan 1977):157-9.

Singleton, Fred. Twentieth-century Yugoslavia. New York: Col U
    Press, 1976. Rev. by G. Stokes, Historian, 39(Feb 1977):
    356-7.

Sinks, Julia Lee. The Chronicles of Fayette. La Grange: Bicen-
    tennial Commission, City Hall, 1975. Rev. by A. Lowman,
    ETHJ, 15(Spr 1977):49-50.

Skard, Sigmund. The United States in Norwegian History. Westport,
    Conn. : Greenwood, 1977. Rev. by S. P. Oakley, JAmS,
    11(Dec 1977):415-16.

Sked, Alan, ed. and Chris Cook, ed. Crisis and Controversy:
    Essays in Honour of A. J. P. Taylor. London: Macmillan,
    1976. Rev. by P. F. Clarke, History, 62(Je 1977):340-1; D.
    R. Stevenson, Historian, 39(May 1977):531-2.

Skelley, Jeffrey, ed. The General Strike, 1926. London: Law-
    rence and Wishart, 1976. Rev. by A. Reid & S. Tolliday,
    HJ, 20(No. 4, 1977):1001-12.

Skinner, Andrew S. , ed. and Thomas Wilson, ed. Essays on Adam
    Smith. Oxford: Ox U Press, 1975. Rev. by N. T. Phillip-
    son, History, 62(Je 1977):326.

Sklar, Robert. Movie-Made America: A Cultural History of Amer-
    ican Movies. New York: Random House, 1975. Rev. by D.
    G. Nielson, Historian, 39(Feb 1977):382-3.

Sky, Alison and Michelle Stone. Unbuilt America: Forgotten
    Architecture in the United States From Thomas Jefferson to

283   SLACK

the Space Age. New York: McGraw-Hill, 1976. Rev. by M.
Hollander, GR, 31(Fall 1977):746-51.

Slack, Paul see Clark, Peter

Slaughter, Frank G. The Stonewall Brigade. Garden City, New
York: Doubleday, 1975. Rev. by R. Ashley, CWTI, 16(Apr
1977):47-8.

Slavery and Serfdom in the Middle Ages: Selected Papers by Marc
Block. London: U Cal Press, 1975. Rev. by R. H. Hilton,
History, 62(Feb 1977):95.

Slavitt, David R. Vital Signs: New and Selected Poems. New
York: Doubleday, 1975. Rev. by M. G. Cooke, GR, 31(Fall
1977):718-29.

Smart, James G., ed. A Radical View: The "Agate": Dispatches
of Whitelaw Reid, 1861-1865. Memphis: Memphis St U Press,
1976. Rev. by L. G. Lindley, JSH, 43(Feb 1977):133-4.

Smethurst, Richard J. A Social Basis for Prewar Japanese Militarism: The Army and the Rural Community. London: U
Cal Press, 1975. Rev. by R. Storry, History, 62(Je 1977):
296-7.

Smith, A. Hassell. County and Court: Government and Politics in
Norfolk, 1558-1603. Oxford: Clarendon Press, 1974. Rev.
by C. Holmes, JMH, 49(Sep 1977):495-500.

Smith, Alice E. The History of Wisconsin. Volume I, From Exploration to Statehood. Madison: State Historical Society of
Wisconsin, 1973. Rev. by L. Gara, Historian, 39(Feb 1977):
377-8.

Smith, Bardwell L., ed. Hinduism: New Essays in the History of
Religions. Leiden: E. J. Brill, 1976. Rev. by S. Lavan,
JAS, 37(Nov 1977):157-8.

Smith, Canfield F. Vladivostok Under Red and White Rule: Revolu-
tion and Counter-revolution in the Russian Far East 1920-1922.
London: University of Wash Press, 1976. Rev. by D. S. M.
Williams, History, 62(Je 1977):294-5.

Smith, Colin. Carlos: Portrait of a Terrorist. N. Y.: Holt,
Rinehart & Winston, 1977. Rev. by E. M. Reindel, Comm,
64(Nov 1977):71-5.

Smith, Denis Mack. Mussolini's Roman Empire. New York:
Viking, 1976. Rev. by G. Baer, JIH, 8(Summer 1977):163-4.

Smith, Dorothy Blakey, ed. The Reminiscences of Doctor John
Sebastian Helmcken. Vancouver, B. C.: U Brit Col Press,
1975. Rev. by D. McNab, PNQ, 68(Oct 1977):197.

Smith, Duane A.   Colorado Mining: A Photographic History.
    Albuquerque: U NM Press, 1977. Rev. by W. T. Jackson,
    NMHR, 52(Oct 1977):343-5.

Smith, Dwight L.   Indians of the United States and Canada: A Bib-
    liography. Santa Barbara, Calif. : Clio Press, 1974. Rev.
    by R. N. Ellis, PHR, 46(Feb 1977):127-8.

Smith, Elbert B.   The Presidency of James Buchanan.   Lawrence:
    U Press Kan, 1975. Rev. by R. W. Johannsen, PNQ, 68(Jan
    1977):37.

Smith, Jane F. , ed. and Robert M. Kvasnicka, ed.   Indian-White
    Relations: A Persistent Paradox. Washington, D. C. : How-
    ard U Press, 1976. Rev. by W. Corbett, JOW, 16(Jl 1977):
    92; W. L. Williams, JSH, 43(Aug 1977):482-4; B. W. Sheehan,
    WHQ, 8(Jl 1977):328-9.

Smith, Merritt Roe.   Harpers Ferry Armory and the New Technol-
    ogy. Ithaca, N. Y. : Cor U Press, 1977. Rev. by H. L.
    Peterson, CWTI, 16(Aug 1977):50.

Smith, Myron J.   American Civil War Navies: A Bibliography.
    Metuchen, N. J. : Scarecrow Press, 1972. Rev. by R.
    Lurachi, VMHB, 85(July 1977):376-7.

Smith, Page.   A New Age Now Begins: A People's History of the
    American Revolution. New York: McGraw-Hill, 1976. Rev.
    by J. J. Zimmerman, JSH, 43(Feb 1977):110-1; E. J. Fergu-
    son, WMQ, 34(Apr 1977):322-5.

_____. Jefferson: A Revealing Biography. New York: Ameri-
    can Heritage Pub. Co. , 1976. Rev. by R. S. Klein, WMH,
    60(Summer 1977):344-6.

Smith, Paul, ed.   The Historian and Film. Cambridge: Cam U
    Press, 1976. Rev. by A. J. P. Taylor, History, 62(Feb
    1977):74-5.

Smith, Peter C. , ed. see Flieger, Wilhelm, ed.

Smith, Peter Seaborn.   Oil and Politics in Modern Brazil. Toronto:
    Maclean - Hunter Press, 1976. Rev. by J. D. Wirth, HAHR,
    57(Feb 1977):142-3.

Smith, Sidonie.   Where I'm Bound: Patterns of Slavery and Free-
    dom in Black American Autobiography. Westport, Conn. :
    Greenwood Press, 1974. Rev. by M. V. Woodward, FCHQ,
    51(Oct 1977):371-3.

Smith, T. Lynn.   Brazilian Society. Albuquerque: U NM Press,
    1974. Rev. by R. F. Colson, JLAS, 9(May 1977):178-9.

_____. The Race Between Population and Food Supply in Latin America. Albuquerque: U NM Press, 1976. Rev. by I. S. Wiarda, HAHR, 57(May 1977):315-6.

Smith, Thomas H. , ed. An Ohio Reader: 1750 to the Civil War and An Ohio Reader: Reconstruction to the Present. Grand Rapids: William B. Eerdmans Publishing Co. , 1975. Rev. by R. M. Miller, JOW, 16(Jan 1977):90-1.

Smole, William J. The Yanoama Indians. A Cultural Geography. Austin: UT Press, 1976. Rev. by D. Sweet, AgH, 51(Jl 1977):608-10; R. C. West, HAHR, 57(Feb 1977):166-7.

Smyly, Carolyn see Smyly, John

Smyly, John and Carolyn Smyly. The Totem Poles of Skedans. Seattle: University of Washington Press, 1975. Rev. by H. J. Calkins, PNQ, 68(Oct 1977):197-8.

Smyth, Alfred P. Scandinavian York and Dublin: The History and Archaeology of Two Related Viking Kingdoms. Dublin: Templekieran Press, 1975. Rev. by H. R. Lyon, History, 62(Je 1977):309-10.

Smyth, Paul. Conversions: Poems. Athens: U Ga Press, 1974. Rev. by P. Stitt, GR, 31(Fall 1977):762-71.

Sōbin, Yamada see Covell, Jon

Soboul, Albert. The French Revolution 1787-1799: From the Storming of the Bastille to Napoleon. New York: Vintage Books, 1975. Rev. by E. L. Newman, 18(Win 1977):116-8.

Sokoloff, Michael. The Targum to Job from Qumran Cave XI. Ramat-Gan, Israel: Bar Ilan U, 1974. Rev. by D. Pardee, JNES, 36(Jl 1977):216-7.

Solberg, Carl. Oil Power: The Rise and Imminent Fall of an American Empire. New York: Mason/Charter, 1976. Rev. by G. D. Nash, PHR, 46(May 1977):318-20.

Solberg, Winton U. Redeem the Time: The Puritan Sabbath in Early America. Cambridge: Har U Press, 1977. Rev. by E. Emerson, 50(Sep 1977):537-9.

Sorenson, Jerold G. see Studt, Ward B.

Sourrouille, Juan V. see Mallon, Richard D.

Spalding, Phinizy. Oglethorpe in America. Chicago: U Chicago Press, 1977. Rev. by P. H. Wood, GHQ, 51(Fall 1977): 281-3.

Spence, Clark C. Territorial Politics and Government In Montana, 1864-89. Urbana: U ILL Press, 1975. Rev. by T. A. Larson, A&W, 19(Spr 1977):92-93; E. Pomeroy, PHR, 46(Feb 1977):133-5.

Spiegel, Joachim. Das Auferstehungsritual der Unas-Pyramide. Wiesbaden: Otto Harrossowitz, 1971. Rev. by M. Gilula, JNES, 36(Oct 1977):314.

Spiller, Robert E. et al. Four Makers of the American Mind: Emerson, Thoreau, Whitman, and Melville. Durham: Duke U Press, 1976. Rev. by R. D. Gozzl, NEQ, 50(Sep 1977):546-8.

Spink, Walter M. The Axis of Eros. New York: Penguin Books, 1975. Rev. by J. D. La Plante, JAS, 36(Feb 1977):370-2.

Sprague, Kurth. The Promise Kept. Austin: Encino Press, 1975. Rev. by D. S. Gaus, TAm, 33(Jan 1977):538-9.

Sprague, Marshall. Colorado: A Bicentennial History. New York: Norton, 1976. Rev. by M. F. Taylor, WHQ, 8(Apr 1977):211.

Springhall, John. Youth, Empire and Society: British Youth Movements. London: Croom Helm, 1977. Rev. by M. A. Crowther, HJ, 20(No. 4, 1977):991-9.

Spuler, Bertold. History of the Mongols Based on Eastern and Western Accounts of the Thirteenth and Fourteenth Centuries. Berkeley and Los Angeles: U Cal Press, 1972. Rev. by J. E. Woods, JNES, 36(Oct 1977):324-5.

Srinivasan, T. N. see Bhagwati, Jagdish N.

Stadelmann, Rudolph. Social and Political History of the German 1848 Revolution. Athens, Ohio: Ohio St U Press, 1975. Rev. by J. J. Cahill, Historian, 39(Feb 1977):349-50.

Stagg, Albert. The First Bishop of Sonora: Antoñio de los Reyes, O. F. M. Tucson: U Arizona Press, 1976. Rev. by C. R. De Murrieta, HAHR, 57(Aug 1977):532; L. R. Murphy, WHQ, 8(Apr 1977):226-7.

Stairs, Denis. The Diplomacy of Constraint: Canada, the Korean War, and the United States. Toronto: U Tor Press, 1974. Rev. by R. J. Caridi, PHR, 46(Feb 1977):149-50.

Stanbury, W. T., assisted by Jay H. Siegel. Success and Failure: Indians in Urban Society. Vancouver: U Brit Col Press, 1975. Rev. by J. G. Jorgensen, WHQ, 8(Jan 1977):64-5.

Stanley, Harold. Senate vs. Governor, Alabama 1971: Referents for Opposition in a One-Party Legislature. University, Ala-

bama: U Alabama Press, 1975.   Rev. by W. H. Stewart, Jr.,
AlaR, 30(April 1977):151-2.

Stanton, William. The Great United States Exploring Expedition of
1838-1842. Berkeley and Los Angeles: U Cal Press, 1975.
Rev. by S. G. Kohlstedt, NEQ, 50(Mar 1977):176-8.

Stave, Bruce M., ed. Socialism and the Cities.   Port Washington:
Kennikat Press, 1975. Rev. by H. A. Levenstein, Historian,
39(May 1977):589-90.

Steeg, Clarence L. Ver. Origins of a Southern Mosaic: Studies of
Early Carolina and Georgia.   Athens: U Ga Press, 1975.
Rev. by W. W. Abbot, WMQ, 34(Jan 1977):140-1.

Steen, Harold K. The U.S. Forest Service: A History.   Seattle:
U Wash Press, 1976. Rev. by R. W. Chandler, OrHQ,
78(Sep 1977):280; C. B. Coulter, WHQ, 8(Jl 1977):330-1.

Steffen, Jerome O. William Clark: Jeffersonian Man on the Frontier.   Norman: U Ok Press, 1977. Rev. by W. E. Larsen,
JSH, 43(Nov 1977):613-4; W. E. Foley, MHR, 71(Jl 1977):
468-9; F. P. Prucha, WHQ, 8(Oct 1977):455-6.

Stegmaier, Harry I., Jr. et al. Allegany County: A History.
Parsons, W. Va.: McClain Printing Co., 1976. Rev. by J.
C. Klotter, JSH, 43(Nov 1977):647-8.

Stein, Burton, ed. Essays on South India.   Honolulu: U Press
Hawaii, 1975. Rev. by S. Lewandowski, JAS, 36(Aug 1977):
770-1.

Steiner, George. After Babel. New York: Ox U Press, 1975.
Rev. by B. Weller, GR, 31(Spr 1977):267-73.

Steiner, Stan. The Vanishing White Man. New York: Harper &
Row, 1976. Rev. by B. W. Dippie, WHQ, 8(Oct 1977):469-70.

Steinsaltz, Adin. The Essential Talmud. n.l.: Basic Books, n.d.
Rev. by D. Singer, Comm, 63(Jan 1977):84-6.

Stekl, Hannes. Österreichs Aristokratie im Vormärz. Herr-
schaftsstil und Lebensformen der Fürstenhäuser Liechtenstein
und Schwarzenberg.   Munich: R. Oldenbourg Verlag, 1973.
Rev. by J. A. Vann, JMH, 49(Sep 1977):517-9.

Steneck, Nicholas H. Science and Creation in the Middle Ages:
Henry of Langenstein (d. 1397) on Genesis. Notre Dame: U
Notre Dame Press, 1976. Rev. by M. McVaugh, Historian,
39(May 1977):537-8.

Stensel, Franz. James Madison Alden: Yankee Artist of the Pacific Coast, 1854-1860. Ft. Worth: Amon Carter Museum,
1975. Rev. by R. W. Winter, PHR, 46(May 1977):294-5.

Stepan, Nancy. Beginnings of Brazilian Oswaldo Cruz, Medical Research and Policy, 1890-1920. New York: Neale Watson Academic Publications, 1976. Rev. by D. Cooper, HAHR, 57(May 1977):352-3.

Stephan, John J. The Kuril Islands: Russo-Japanese Frontier in the Pacific. Oxford: Ox U Press, 1975. Rev. by E. W. Edwards, History, 62(Je 1977):295-6.

Stephenson, Jill. Women in Nazi Society. New York: Barnes & Noble, 1975. Rev. by H. J. Schmeller, Historian, 39(Feb 1977):354-5; P. D. Stachura, JMH, 49(Je 1977):337-9.

Sterling, Dorothy, ed. The Trouble They Seen: Black People Tell the Story of Reconstruction. Garden City, N.Y.: Doubleday, 1976. Rev. by D. V. Taylor, MinnH, 45(Sum 1977):252-3; B. I. Wiley, AHI, 11(Feb 1977):49; W. Hanchett, JISHS, 70(Feb 1977):92.

Stern, Fritz. Gold and Iron: Bismarck, Bleichroder, and the Building of the German Empire. n.l.: Knopf, n.d. Rev. by E. N. Luttwak, Comm, 63(May 1977):72-4.

Stevens, Holly. Souvenirs and Prophecies: The Young Wallace Stevens. New York: Alfred Knopf, 1977. Rev. by L. Leary, NEQ, 50(Sep 1977):523-6.

Stevenson, Adlai. The Papers of Adlai Stevenson. Vol. 5: Visit to Asia, the Middle East, and Europe, March-August 1953. Ed. by Walter Johnson. Boston: Little, Brown, 1975. Rev. by H. G. Nicholas, AHR, 82(Feb 1977):216-17.

Stevenson, Mary, ed. The Recollection of A Happy Childhood By Mary Esther Huger Daughter of Francis Kinloch Huger of Long House Near Pendleton, South Carolina, 1826-1848. Pendleton, S.C.: Research and Publication Committee Foundation for Historic Restoration in Pendleton Area, n.d. Rev. by W. Edgar, GHQ, 51(Summer 1977):207-8.

Stewart, James Brewer. Holy Warriors: The Abolitionists and American Slavery. New York: Hill and Wang, 1976. Rev. by B. L. Fladeland, JSH, 43(Aug 1977):458-9; F. J. Blue, WMH, 60(Summer 1977):336-8.

Stivers, Rueben Elmore. Privateers and Volunteers, The Men and Women of Our Reserve Naval Forces: 1766 to 1866. Annapolis: Naval Institute Press, 1975. Rev. by L. C. Allin, Historian, 39(May 1977):574-5.

Stiverson, Gregory A. and Phebe R. Jacobsen. William Paca: A Biography. Baltimore: Maryland Historical Society, 1976. Rev. by F. A. Cassell, WMQ, 34(Jl 1977):504.

Stoddard, Ellwyn R. Mexican Americans. New York: Random
    House, 1973. Rev. by R. H. Vigil, HAHR, 57(Feb 1977):
    108-9.

Stoeffler, Ernest F. , ed. Continental Pietism and Early American
    Christianity. Grand Rapids, Mich. : William B. Eerdmans,
    1976. Rev. by J. B. Frantz, WMQ, 34(Apr 1977):348-50.

Stoehr, C. Eric. Bonanza Victorian: Architecture and Society in
    Colorado Mining Towns. Albuquerque: UNM Press, 1975.
    Rev. by R. A. Weinstein, A&W, 19(Sum 1977):175-76.

Stoessinger, John G. Henry Kissinger: The Anguish of Power.
    New York: Norton, 1976. Rev. by H. G. Nicholas, JAmS,
    11(April 1977):159-60.

Stoianovich, Teaian. French Historical Method: The Annales Para-
    digm. Ithaca and London: Cor U Press, 1976. Rev. by J.
    N. Moody, Historian, 39(May 1977):555-6.

Stone, Lawrence, ed. The University in Society. Princeton: Prin
    U Press, 1974. Rev. by M. D. Gordon, JMH, 49(Je 1977):
    298-301.

Stone, Michelle see Sky, Alison

Stone, Norman. The Eastern Front 1914-1917. New York: Charles
    Scribner's Sons, 1975. Rev. by J. W. Long, Historian,
    39(May 1977):561-3.

Stone, Sharman N. , ed. Aborigines in White Australia: A Docu-
    mentary History of the Attitudes Affecting Official Policy and
    the Australian Aborigine, 1697-1973. London: Heinemann,
    1974. Rev. by S. Glynn, History, 62(Je 1977):304-5.

Stookey, Robert W. America and the Arab States: An Uneasy En-
    counter. New York: John Wiley, 1975. Rev. by R. L.
    Daniel, PHR, 46(May 1977):320-1.

Stork, Joe. Middle East Oil and the Energy Crisis. New York:
    Monthly Review Press, 1975. Rev. by G. D. Nash, PHR,
    46(May 1977):318-20.

Stover, John F. History of the Illinois Central Railroad. New
    York: Macmillan Publishing Co. , 1975. Rev. by M. S.
    Legan, LaH, 18(Sum 1977):366-8.

Stover, Leon E. and Takeko K. Stover. China: An Anthropological
    Perspective. Pacific Palisades, Calif. : Goodyear Publishing
    Co. , 1975. Rev. by L. L. Mark, JAS, 36(Aug 1977):734-5.

Stover, Takeko K. see Stover, Leon E.

Straub, Eberhard. Das Bellum Iustum des Hernán Cortés in Mexico.
    Cologne: Bohlau Verlag, 1976. Rev. by E. J. Burrus, HAHR,
    57(May 1977):331-2.

Strickland, Rennard. Fire and the Spirits: Cherokee Law from
    Clan to Court. Norman: U Ok Press, 1975. Rev. by M. D.
    Green, WHQ, 8(Jan 1977):65-6.

Stuart, Reginald Ray. Kassai, The Story of Raoul De Premorel,
    African Trader. Stockton, Calif.: Pacific Center for Western
    Historical Studies, U Pacific, 1975. Rev. by L. Kaufman,
    JOW, 16(Jan 1977):91.

Studt, Ward B., Jerold G. Sorensen, and Beverly Burge. Medicine
    in the Intermountain West: A History of Health Care in Rural
    Areas of the West. Salt Lake City: Olympus, 1976. Rev.
    by C. W. Bodemer, UHQ, 45(Spr 1977):205-6.

Stuhler, Barbara, ed. and Gretchen Kreuter, ed. Women of Min-
    nesota: Selected Biographical Essays. St. Paul: Minnesota
    Historical Society Press, 1977. Rev. by A. Hinding, MinnH,
    45(Fall 1977):297.

Sturhahn, Joan. Carvalho: Artist, Photographer, Adventurer,
    Patriot; Portrait of a Forgotten American. Merrick, N. Y.:
    Richwood, 1976. Rev. by P. J. Broder, WHQ, 8(Jan 1977):
    56-7.

Sturtevant, David R. Popular Uprisings in the Philippines, 1840-
    1940. London: Cornell U Press, 1976. Rev. by M. Cald-
    well, History, 62(Je 1977):301-2; D. J. Steinberg, JIH,
    8(Summer 1977):179-81.

Sullivan, Walter. A Requiem for the Renascence: The State of
    Fiction in the Modern South. Athens, Ga.: U Ga Press,
    1976. Rev. by M. K. Spears, JSH, 43(May 1977):325-6; R.
    Gray, JAmS, 11(Dec 1977):402-4.

Summersell, Charles G., ed. see Hamilton, Peter J.

Sundkler, Bengt. Zulu Zion and Some Swazi Zionists. Oxford:
    Ox U Press, 1976. Rev. by M. Newitt, History, 62(Je
    1977):273-4.

Surtees, Virginia. Charlotte Canning: Lady-in-Waiting to Queen
    Victoria and Wife of the First Viceroy of India, 1817-1861.
    Levittown, N. Y.: Transatlantic, 1976. Rev. by C. Coppola,
    JAS, 36(Aug 1977):781-2.

Sutton, Imre. Indian Land Tenure: Bibliographical Essays and A
    Guide to the Literature. New York: Clearwater Publishing,
    1975. Rev. by G. H. Phillips, PHR, 46(Feb 1977):117-8; M.
    D. Green, PNQ, 68(Apr 1977):99-100.

Sutton, Robert P. , ed. The Prairie State: A Documentary History
of Illinois. Grand Rapids, Mich. : Wm. B. Eerdmans, 1976.
Rev. by D. B. Center, JISHS, 70(May 1977):166-7.

Sutton, William A. , ed. Newdick's Season of Frost: An Interrupted
Biography of Robert Frost. Albany, New York: State U NY
Press, 1976. Rev. by R. F. Fleissner, NEQ, 50(Je 1977):
351-3; J. J. Duffy, VH, 45(Fall 1977):249-52.

Swanber, W. A. Norman Thomas: The Last Idealist. New York:
Scribner's, 1976. Rev. by M. Q. Sibley, MinnH, 45(Spr
1977):202; R. Starr, Comm, 63(Feb 1977):78-80.

Sweet, Leonard I. Black Images of America, 1784-1870. New
York: W. W. Norton, 1976. Rev. by C. E. Wynes, JSH,
43(Feb 1977):120.

Swetz, Frank. Mathematics Education in China: its growth and
development. Cambridge: MIT Press, 1974. Rev. by R. F.
Price & N. Shelley, JAAS, 12(Jan/Oct 1977):299-302.

Swierenga, Robert P. Acres for Cents: Delinquent Tax Auctions in
Frontier Iowa. Westport, Conn: Greenwood Press, 1976.
Rev. by M. B. Husband, JOW, 16(Jan 1977):89-90; W. D.
Aeschbacher, AgH, 51(Jl 1977):620-1; B. J. Williams, WMQ,
8(Jl 1977):349-50; D. Kealey, JAmS, 11(Dec 1977):398-400.

_____, ed. Beyond the Civil War Synthesis: Political Essays of
the Civil War Era. Westport, Conn. : Greenwood Press, 1975.
Rev. by P. Hubbard, Historian, 39(Feb 1977):371-2; J. Logs-
don, LaH, 18(Sum 1977):351-2.

Swift, Esther Munroe. Vermont Place-Names: Footprints of History. Brattleboro, Vt. : Stephen Greene Press, 1977. Rev.
by H. G. Barnum, VH, 45(Fall 1977):252-4.

Syrett, David, ed. see Balderston, Marion, ed.

Syrett, Harold C. , ed. et al. The Papers of Alexander Hamilton.
New York: Col U Press, 1976. Rev. by F. McDonald, WMQ,
34(Oct 1977):670-1; N. E. Cunningham, Jr. , JSH, 43(Aug
1977):447-8.

Szasz, Thomas. Karl Kraus and the Soul Doctors. Baton Rouge:
LSU, n. d. Rev. by P. H. Schuck, Comm, 64(Jl 1977):71-3.

_____. Psychiatric Slavery. n. l. : Free Press, n. d. Rev. by
P. H. Schuck, Comm, 64(Jul 1977):71-3.

_____. Schizophrenia: The Sacred Symbol of Psychiatry. n. l. :
Basic Books, n. d. Rev. by P. H. Schuck, Comm, 64(Jl
1977):71-3.

Tagliaferri, Amelio. Relazioni dei Rettori Veneti in Terraferma. Milan: Dott. A. Giuffre Editore, 1976. Rev. by L. B. Robbert, JEH, 37(Je 1977):564.

Tal, Uriel. Christians and Jews in Germany. Ithaca: Cor U Press, 1974. Rev. by P. R. Duggan, Historian, 39(Feb 1977):352-3.

Tambiah, S. J. World Conqueror and World Renouncer: A Study of Buddhism and Polity in Thailand against a Historical Background. New York: Cam U Press, 1976. Rev. by M. E. Spiro, JAS, 36(Aug 1977):789-91.

Tanner, Annie Clark. A Biography of Ezra Thompson Clark. Salt Lake City: Tanner Trust Fund, U Utah Library, 1975. Rev. by S. J. Layton, JOW, 16(Jan 1977):74; B. D. Blumell, PNQ, 68(Jl 1977):144-5.

Tanner, Faun McConkie. The Far Country: A Regional History of Moab and LaSal, Utah. Salt Lake City: Olympus Publishing Co., 1976. Rev. by A. R. Mortensen, A&W, 19(Sum 1977): 182-83.

Tanner, Robert G. Stonewall in the Valley. Garden City, N.Y.: Doubleday, 1976. Rev. by J. I. Robertson, CWTI, 16(Apr 1977):48; D. Evans, GHQ, 51(Summer 1977):204-5.

Tarbell, Ida M. The Early Life of Abraham Lincoln. New York: A. S. Barnes, 1974. Rev. by R. D. Rietveld, JISHS, 70(Feb 1977):90-1.

Tarling, Nicholas. Imperial Britain in South-East Asia. Oxford: Ox U Press, 1975. Rev. by I. G. Brown, History, 62(Je 1977):298.

Tatum, George B. Philadelphia Georgian: The City House of Samuel Powel and Some of its Eighteenth-Century Neighbors. Middletown, Conn.: Wesleyan U Press, 1976. Rev. by G. W. Geib, WMQ, 34(Jl 1977):492-4.

Tavares, Luís Henrique Dias. História de Sedicão Intentada no Bahia em 1798: A Conspiracão dos Alfaiates. São Paulo: Pioneirof MEC. Rev. by M. Cordozo, HAHR, 57(Aug 1977): 533-4.

Tavernier, K. see Wee, H. Van der

Taylor, Arnold H. Travail and Triumph: Black Life and Culture in the South Since the Civil War. P. B. Scott, JSH, 43(Nov 1977):623-4.

Taylor, Benjamin J., ed. and Thurman J. White, ed. Issues and Ideas in America. Norman: U Ok Press, 1976. Rev. by W. Rundell, Jr., JSH, 43(Nov 1977):637-8.

Taylor, Charles. Hegel. Cambridge: Cam U Press, 1975. Rev. by K. Brinkman, History, 62(Feb 1977):71-2.

Taylor, Claire, ed. British and American Abolitionists: An Episode on Transatlantic Understanding. Edinburgh: Edin U Press, 1974. Rev. by J. B. Stewart, Historian, 39(Feb 1977):329-31.

Taylor, Geoffrey W. Timber: History of the Forest Industry in B. C. Vancouver: J. J. Douglas, 1975. Rev. by T. R. Cox, WHQ, 8(Apr 1977):225-6.

Taylor, Joe Gray. Louisiana: A Bicentennial History. New York: W. W. Norton, 1976. Rev. by G. B. Mills, JSH, 43(Aug 1977):489-90.

_____. Louisiana Reconstructed, 1863-1877. Baton Rouge: LSU Press, 1974. Rev. by O. E. Cunningham, ETHJ, 15(Spr 1977):54.

Taylor, Lonn and David B. Warren. Texas Furniture: The Cabinetmakers and Their Work, 1840-1880. Austin: UT Press, 1975. Rev. by B. H. Green, ETHJ, 15(Spr 1977):48-9.

Taylor, Richard. The Drama of W. B. Yeats: Irish Myth and the Japanese No. New Haven: Yale U Press, 1976. Rev. by R. Schleifer, GR, 31(Fall 1977):736-9.

Taylor, Robert. Lord Salisburg. New York: St. Martin's Press, 1975. Rev. by P. Stansky, Historian, 39(Feb 1977):332-4.

Taylor, Samuel W. The Kingdom or Nothing: The Life of John Taylor, Militant Mormon. New York: Macmillan, 1976. Rev. by R. W. Sadler, WHQ, 8(Jl 1977):353-4.

Taylor, Thomas Jones. A History of Madison County and Incidentally of North Alabama 1732-1840. Ed. by W. Stanley Hoole and Addie S. Hoole. University, Alabama: Confederate Pub. Co., 1976. Rev. by H. Marks, AlaR, 30(Oct 1977):316-17.

Teaford, Jon C. The Municipal Revolution in America: Origins of Modern Urban Government, 1650-1825. Chicago: U Chi Press, 1975. Rev. by R. C. Wade, WMQ, 34(Jan 1977):162-5; J. E. Cooke, PH, 45(July 1977):282-3.

Tebeau, Charlton W. The University of Miami: A Golden Anniversary History, 1926-1976. Coral Gables, Fla.: U Miami Press, 1976. Rev. by J. D. Wright, Jr., JSH, 43(Aug 1977):493-4.

Tello, Pilar Leon. Documentos relativos a la independencia de norteamérica existentes en archivos españoles. Madrid: Ministerio de Asuntos Exteriores, 1976. Rev. by D. Bushnell, HAHR, 57(Aug 1977):535-6.

Temin, Peter. Did Monetary Forces Cause the Great Depression?
    New York: W. W. Norton, 1976. Rev. by M. E. Sushka,
    JEH, 37(Je 1977):565-6; J. C. Moody, WMH, 60(Summer
    1977):350-1.

Terrell, John Upton. The Plains Apache. New York: Thomas Y.
    Crowell, 1975. Rev. by D. E. Worcester, NMHR, 52(Jan
    1977):77-8.

Terrell, Lloyd P. and Marguerite S. C. Terrell. Blacks in Augus-
    ta: A Chronology 1741-1977. Augusta, Ga.: Preston Publi-
    cations, 1977. Rev. by G. J. Smith, GHQ, 51(Winter 1977):
    361.

Thane, James L., ed. A Governor's Wife on the Mining Frontier:
    The Letters of Mary Edgerton from Montana, 1863-1865.
    Salt Lake City: Tanner Trust Fund, U Utah Library, 1976.
    Rev. by K. R. Toole, UHQ, 45(Sum 1977):315.

Tharpe, Jac, ed. Frost: Centennial Essays II. Jackson, Miss.:
    U Press Miss, 1976. Rev. by J. F. Sears, NEQ, 50(Sep
    1977):531-3.

Thayer, Theodore. Colonial and Revolutionary Morris County.
    Morristown, N. J.: The Morris County Heritage Commission,
    1975. Rev. by L. R. Gerlach, WMQ, 34(Jan 1977):153-4.

Thimm, Alfred L. Business Ideologies in the Reform-Progressive
    Era, 1880-1914. University, Alabama: U Ala Press, 1976.
    Rev. by M. N. Rothbard, JEH, 37(Sep 1977):847.

Thirsk, Joan, ed. The Restoration. London: Longmans, 1976.
    Rev. by J. S. Morrill, HJ, 20(No. 4, 1977):961-70.

Tholfsen, Trygve. Working Class Radicalism in Mid-Victorian
    England. New York: Col U Press, 1977. Rev. by J. E.
    Cronin, JEH, 37(Sep 1977):848-9.

Thomas, Lewis G., ed. The Prairie West to 1905: A Canadian
    Sourcebook. Toronto: Ox U Press, 1975. Rev. by J. W.
    Bailey, JOW, 16(Jan 1977):90.

Thomason, Michael and Melton McLaurin. Mobile: American River
    City. Mobile: Easter Pub. Co., 1975. Rev. by R. G.
    Mitchell, AlaR, 30(Jan 1977):68-9.

Thomis, Malcolm I. The Town Labourer and the Industrial Revolu-
    tion. New York: Barnes and Noble, 1974. Rev. by A.
    Briggs, JMH, 49(Sep 1977):500-2.

Thompson, Dorothy Burr. Ptolemaic Oinochoai and Portraits in
    Faience: Aspects of the Ruler Cult. Oxford: Clarendon
    Press, 1973. Rev. by W. H. Peck, JNES, 36(Jan 1977):73-4.

295 THOMPSON

Thompson, E. P. Whigs and Hunters: The origin of the Black Act.
London: Allen Lane, 1975. Rev. by J. Styles, HJ, 20(No. 4,
1977):977-81.

Thompson, George H. Arkansas and Reconstruction: The Influence
of Geography, Economics and Personality. Port Washington:
N. Y.: Kennikat Press, 1976. Rev. by M. Perman, JSH,
43(May 1977):305-6.

Thompson, Gerald. The Army and the Navajo: The Bosque Redon-
do Reservation Experiment, 1863-1868. Tucson: U Arizona
Press, 1976. Rev. by E. C. Bearss, JOW, 16(Jan 1977):85;
D. A. Miller, NMHR, 52(Jan 1977):73-4; J. D. Sylvester,
UHQ, 45(Win 1977):97-8; R. W. Delaney, WHQ, 8(Apr 1977):
217-8.

Thompson, Hildegard. The Navajos' Long Walk for Education: A
History of Navajo Education. Tsaile, Navajo Nation, Ariz.:
Navajo Community College, 1975. Rev. by V. E. Tiller, PHR,
46(Feb 1977):128-30.

Thompson, Lawrence and R. H. Winnick. Robert Frost: The Later
Years 1938-1963. n. l.: Holt, Rinehart & Winston, n. d. Rev.
by E. Hirsch, Comm, 63(Mar 1977):86-90.

Thompson, Leonard. Survival in Two Worlds: Moshoeshoe of
Lesotho 1786-1870. Oxford: Ox U Press, 1976. Rev. by F.
Harcourt, History, 62(Je 1977):272-3.

_____, and Jeffrey Butler, ed. Change in Contemporary South
Africa. Berkeley: U California Press, n. d. Rev. by C. L.
Geshekter, JAAS, 12(Jan/Oct 1977):314-16.

Thompson, Paul. The Edwardians: The Remaking of British Society. Bloomington and London: Ind U Press, 1975. Rev. by
H. Pelling, JMH, 49(Je 1977):311-4.

Thompson, Roger, ed. see Allen, H. C., ed.

Thompson, Thomas L. The Historicity of the Patriarchal Narra-
tives: The Quest for the Historical Abraham. Berlin and
New York: Walter de Gruyter, 1974. Rev. by D. Pardee,
JNES, 36(Jl 1977):222-4.

Thonoff, Robert H. see Weddle, Robert S.

Tiely, Charles, ed. The Formation of National States in Western
Europe. Princeton: Prin U Press, 1975. Rev. by P.
Sonnino, Historian, 39(Feb 1977):339-40; G. R. Elton, JMH,
49(Je 1977):294-8.

Tilden, Richard. Industry and Economic Decline in Seventeenth
Century Venice. Cambridge: Har U Press, 1976. Rev. by
J. C. Brown, JEH, 37(Je 1977):551-2.

TILLETT 296

Tillett, Leslie, ed. Wind on the Buffalo Grass: The Indians' Own
Account of the Battle at the Little Big Horn River, and the
Death of their Life on the Plains. New York: Thomas Y.
Crowell, 1976. Rev. by A. B. Sageser, JOW, 16(Jan 1977):75.

Tindall, George Brown. The Ethnic Southerners. Baton Rouge:
LSU Press, 1976. Rev. by M. S. Legan, JSH, 43(Nov 1977):
602; F. N. Boney, GHQ, 51(Summer 1977):203.

Tindall, George Brown. The Persistent Tradition in New South
Politics. Baton Rouge, LSU Press, 1975. Rev. by E. C.
Williamson, AlaR, 30(April 1977):150-1.

Ting, Lee-Hsie Hsu, comp. see Ting, Nai-Tung, comp.

Ting, Nai-Tung, comp. and Ting, Lee-Hsie Hsu, comp. Chinese
Folk Narratives: A Bibliographical Guide. San Francisco:
Chinese Materials and Research Aids Service Center, 1975.
Rev. by A. Yen, JAS, 36(May 1977):557.

Tipton, Frank B., Jr. Regional Variations in the Economic Development of Germany During the Nineteenth Century. Middletown, Conn.: Wesleyan U Press, 1976. Rev. by C. Trebilcock, HJ, 20(No. 3, 1977):751-60.

Titus, David Anson. Palace and Politics in Prewar Japan. New
York: Col U Press, 1974. Rev. by A. E. Tiedemann, JAS,
36(Aug 1977):745-8.

Tobin, Gregory M. The Making of a History: Walter Prescott
Webb and the Great Plains. Austin: UT Press, 1976. Rev.
by W. T. Jackson, AgH, 51(Jl 1977):621-3; D. W. Noble,
JSH, 43(Aug 1977):475-6; G. Wolfskill, WHQ, 18(Jl 1977):346.

Toland, John. Adolf Hitler. Garden City, N.Y.: Doubleday, 1976.
Rev. by G. L. Mosse, WMH, 60(Summer 1977):353-4; V. Cox,
Mankind, 5(No. 12, 1977):64-6.

Tomasevich, Jozo. War and Revolution in Yugoslavia, 1941-1945:
The Chetniks. Stanford, Calif.: Stan U Press, 1975. Rev.
by W. H. McNeill, JMH, 49(Mar 1977):147-51.

Tomlinson, B. R. The Indian National Congress and the Raj 1929-
1942. London: Macmillan, 1976. Rev. by J. M. Brown,
History, 62(Je 1977):285-6.

Tomlinson, Juliette, ed. The Paintings and Journal of Joseph
Whiting Stock. Middletown, Conn.: Wesleyan U Press, 1976.
Rev. by C. C. Sellers, NEQ, 50(Je 1977):372-4.

Tredway, G. R. Democratic Opposition to the Lincoln Administration in Indiana. Indianapolis: Indiana Historical Bureau,
1973. Rev. by V. B. Howard, JISHS, 70(Aug 1977):249-50.

Trefousse, Hans L. Impeachment of a President: Andrew Johnson, the Blacks, and Reconstruction. Knoxville: U Tenn Press, 1975. Rev. by J. L. Barnidge, LaH, 18(Sum 1977):353-4.

Trennert, Robert A. , Jr. Alternative to Extinction: Federal Indian Policy and the Beginnings of the Reservation System, 1846-51. Philadelphia: Temple U Press, 1975. Rev. by D. J. Berthrong, PHR, 46(May 1977):288-9.

Treue, Wolfgang. Die Jaluit-Gesellschaft auf den Marshall-Insein, 1887-1914: Ein Beitrag zur Kolonial-und Verwaltungsgeschichte in der Epoche des deutschen Kaiserreichs. Berlin: Duncker & Humblot, 1976. Rev. by T. K. Nugent, JEH, 37(Sep 1977): 849-50.

Trevor, John C. Scrolls From Qumran Cave I: The Great Isaiah Scroll, The Order of the Community, the Pesher to Habakkuk from Photographs. Jerusalem: Albright Institute of Archaeological Research and The Shrine of the Book, 1972. Rev. by J. C. Greenfield, JNES, 36(Jl 1977):215-6.

Trevor-Roper, Hugh. Edward Hyde, Earl of Clarendon. Oxford: Clarendon U Press, 1975. Rev. by J. S. Morrill, HJ, 20(No. 4, 1977):961-70.

Trilling, Diana. We Must March My Darlings. n. l. : Harcourt, Brace, Jovanovich, n. d. Rev. by H. Kramer, Comm, 64(Jul 1977):66-70.

Trilling, Richard J. Party Image and Electoral Behavior. Chichester, Sussex: John Wiley, 1976. Rev. by P. Calvert, JAmS, 11(Dec 1977):422-3.

Tripathi, Amales. Vidyasagar: The Traditional Moderniser. Bombay: Orient Longman, 1974. Rev. by D. Kopf, JAS, 36(May 1977):573.

Tripathl, Chandrabhal. Catalogue of the Jaina Manuscripts at Strasbourg. Leiden: E. J. Brill, 1975. Rev. by P. S. Jaini, JAS, 36(May 1977):577-8.

Tucker, Robert W. The Inequality of Nations. n. l. : Basic Books, n. d. Rev. by M. Ledeen, Comm, 64(Aug 1977):74-5.

Tung, William L. Revolutionary China, A Personal Account, 1926-1949. New York: St. Martin's Press, 1973. Rev. by S. C. Chu, JAAS, 12(Jan/Oct 1977):308-9.

Turner, R. L. Collected Papers, 1912-1973. London: Ox U Press, 1975. Rev. by G. H. Fairbanks, JAS, 36(May 1977): 578-9.

Tuska, Jon. The Filming of the West. New York: Doubleday and

Company, 1976. Rev. by R. Anderson, NMHR, 52(Oct 1977):
349-50; C. L. Sonnichsen, A&W, 19(Spr 1977):87-88.

't Veld, N. K. C. A. in, ed. De SS en Nederland: Documenten
uit SS-Archieven, 1935-1945. 2 vols. 's-Gravenhage:
Martinus Nijhoff, 1976. Rev. by E. L. Presseisen, AHR,
82(June 1977):657.

Tweton, D. Jerome and Theodore B. Jelliff. North Dakota: The
Heritage of A People. Fargo: North Dakota Institute for
Regional Studies, 1976. Rev. by J. W. Carson, JOW, 16(Jan
1977):88-9.

Twohig, Dorothy, ed. see Jackson, Donald, ed.

Tyler, Daniel, ed. Red Men and Hat Wearers: Viewpoints in
Indian History. Boulder: Pruett Publishing, 1976. Rev. by
P. Iverson, NMHR, 52(Jan 1977):78-9.

Tyler, Ron. The Cowboy. New York: William Morrow, 1975.
Rev. by D. D. Walker, WHQ, 8(Jan 1977):76.

Tyrrell, R. Emmett, ed. The Future That Doesn't Work: Social
Democracy's Failures in Britain. n. l. : Doubleday, n. d.
Rev. by M. Novak, Comm, 64(Sep 1977):82-4.

Uekusa, Masu see Caves, Richard E.

Ulibarri, George S. and John P. Harrison. Guide to Materials on
Latin America in the National Archives of the United States.
Washington, D. C. : U. S. Government Printing Office, 1974.
Rev. by M. T. Hamerly, TAm, 33(Apr 1977):678-9.

Ullman, Hans-Peter. Der Bund der Industriellen. Gottingen:
Vandenhoeck & Ruprecht, 1976. Rev. by F. B. Tipton, JEH,
37(Sep 1977):850-1.

Ullrich, Helen E. , ed. Competition and Modernization in South Asia.
New Delhi: Abhinav, 1975. Rev. by M. Davis, JAS, 36(Aug
1977):772-3.

Urlsperger, Samuel, ed. Detailed Reports on the Salzburger Emigrants Who Settled in America. Athens, Ga. : U Ga Press,
1976. Rev. by M. Rubincam, JSH, 43(Aug 1977):430-1.

Vachon, Andre, ed. see Hayne, David M. , ed.

Valdes, Herman. Diary of a Chilean Concentration Camp. London:
Victor Gollancz, 1975. Rev. by J. N. Goodsell, HAHR,
57(Feb 1977):155-6.

Vanderstappen, Harrie A. , ed. The T. L. Yuan Bibliography of
Western Writings on Chinese Art and Archaeology. London:

Mansell, 1975. Rev. by K. M. Linduff, JAS, 37(Nov 1977): 104-5.

Vandiver, Frank E. The Southwest: South or West? College Station: Texas A&M University, 1975. Rev. by S. Peterson, JOW, 16(Jl 1977):102.

Van Kley, Dale. The Jansenists and the Expulsion of the Jesuits from France 1757-1765. New Haven: Yale U Press, 1975. Rev. by H. S. Vsyverberg, Historian, 39(Feb 1977):342-3; J. M. J. Rogister, History, 62(Je 1977):327-8; O. Hufton, HJ, 20(No. 4, 1977):971-6.

Vanloon, Antonia. For Us the Living. New York: St. Martin's Press, 1976. Rev. by R. Ashley, CWTI, 16(Apr 1977):47-8.

Van Schreeven, William J. and Robert L. Scribner. Revolutionary Virginia: The Road to Independence. Volume II: The Committees and the Second Convention, 1773-1775: A Documentary Record. Charlottesville: U Press Virginia, 1975. Rev. by E. G. Evans, WVH, 38(Jan 1977):166-8.

Van Zwanenberg, R. M. A. An Economic History of Kenya and Uganda 1800-1970. London: Macmillan, 1975. Rev. by C. Ehrlich, History, 62(Je 1977):278-9.

Varona, Alberto J. Francisco Bilbao. Revolucionario de América. Panama and Buenos Aires: Ediciones Excelsior, 1973. Rev. by S. Collier, JLAS, 9(May 1977):162-3.

Vatter, Harold G. The Drive to Industrial Maturity: The U. S. Economy, 1860-1914. Westport, Conn.: Greenwood Press, 1975. Rev. by P. Perry, Historian, 39(May 1977):584-5; M. E. Reed, JSH, 43(Feb 1977):132-3; R. E. Shaw, WMH, 60(Spring 1977):253-4.

Vaughan, Thomas, ed. The Western Shore: Oregon Country Essays Honoring the American Revolution. Portland: Oregon Historical Society and American Revolution Bicentennial Commission of Oregon, 1975 (?). Rev. by E. Pomeroy, PNQ, 68(Jl 1977):143.

Vedder, Richard K. see Klingman, David C.

Veeder, William. Henry James--The Lessons of the Master: Popular Fiction and Personal Style in the Nineteenth Century. Chicago: U Chi Press, 1975. Rev. by W. Michaels, GR, 31(Spr 1977):258-64; B. Roberts, JAmS, 11(Apr 1977):153-4.

Veit, Lawrence A. India's Second Revolution: The Dimensions of Development. New York: McGraw-Hill, 1976. Rev. by U. Lele, JAS, 37(Nov 1977):169-70.

Vella, Walter, ed. Aspects of Vietnamese History. Honolulu: U Press of Hawaii, 1974. Rev. by W. J. Duiker, JAAS, 12(Jan/ Oct 1977):274-6.

Vernam, Glenn R. The Rawhide Years: A History of the Cattle- men and the Cattle Country. Garden City: Doubleday, 1976. Rev. by R. W. Richmond, NMHR, 52(Jan 1977):79-81; M. H. Brown, WHQ, 8(Oct 1977):475-6.

Vicuna, Francisco Orrego. Chile, The Balanced View. Santiago: Universidad de Chile, 1975. Rev. by J. N. Goodsell, HAHR, 57(Feb 1977):155-6.

Viel, Benjamin. The Demographic Explosion: The Latin American Experience. New York: Irvington, 1976. Rev. by R. L. Clinton, HAHR, 57(May 1977):314-5.

Vieira, Francisca Isabel Schurig. O Japonês na Frente de Expansão Paulista: O Processo de Absorcão do Japonês em Marília. São Paulo: Livraria Pioneira Editôra, 1973. Rev. by J. L. Tigner, HAHR, 57(May 1977):375-7.

Vigneras, Louis - Andre. The Discovery of South America and the Andalusian Voyages. Chicago: U Chi Press, 1976. Rev. by M. Obregon, HAHR, 57(Aug 1977):524-6; A. R. Lewis, JEH, 37(Je 1977):567-8; B. W. Diffie, WMQ, 34(Oct 1977):662-4.

Villamarin, Juan A. and Judith E. Villamarin. Indian Labor in Mainland Colonial Spanish America. Newark, Del.: U Del Press, 1975. Rev. by G. M. Riley, JEH, 37(Sep 1977):852-3.

Villamarin, Judith E. see Villamarin, Juan A.

Villanueva, Victor, El Apra en busca de poder, 1930-1940. Lima: Editorial Horizonte, 1975. Rev. by T. M. Davies, Jr., HAHR, 57(May 1977):361-2.

Villena, Guillermo Lohmann. Los ministros de la audiencia de Lima en el reinado de los Borbones (1700-1821): Esquema de un estudio sobre un nucleo diregente. Sevilla: Escuela de Estudios Hispano-Americanos, 1974. Rev. by D. S. Chandler, HAHR, 57(Aug 1977):534-5.

Vincent, Charles. Black Legislators in Louisiana During Recon- struction. Baton Rouge: LSU Press, 1976. Rev. by L. S. Gerteis, JNH, 62(Jan 1977):110-2; A. W. Trelease, JSH, 43(Feb 1977):135-6.

Viola, Herman J. The Indian Legacy of Charles Bird King. Washington: Smithsonian Institution Press, 1976. Rev. by W. N. Banks, GHQ, 51(Summer 1977):187-8.

_____. Thomas L. McKenney, Architect of America's Early

Indian Policy, 1816-1830.   Chicago: Swallow Press, 1974.
Rev. in JISHS, 70(Aug 1977):252-3.

Voigt, David Q.   America Through Baseball.   Chicago: Nelson-
Hall, 1976.   Rev. by B. Whitney, JISHS, 70(May 1977):166.

Vorys, Karl Von.   Democracy Without Consensus: Communalism
and Political Stability in Malaysia.   Princeton: Prin U Press,
1975.   Rev. by R. Peritz, JAS, 36(Aug 1977):794-5.

Wacker, Peter O.   Land and People: A Cultural Geography of Pre-
industrial New Jersey: Origins and Settlement Patterns.   New
Brunswick: Rutgers U Press, 1975.   Rev. by R. D. Mitchell,
WMQ, 34(Oct 1977):661-2.

Wade, Michael S.   The Bitter Issue: The Right to Work Law in
Arizona.   Tucson: Arizona Historical Society, 1976.   Rev.
by G. E. Hansen, NMHR, 52(Jl 1977):262-3.

Wadley, Susan Snow.   Shakti: Power in the Conceptual Structure of
Karimpur Religion.   Chicago: U Chi Studies in Anthropology,
1975.   Rev. by S. S. Bean, JAS, 36(Feb 1977):375-7.

Wagley, Charles, ed.   Man in the Amazon.   Gainesville: U Presses
of Florida, 1974.   Rev. by S. L. Forman, HAHR, 57(Feb
1977):167-8.

Wagoner, Jay J.   Early Arizona: Prehistory to Civil War.   Tucson:
U Arizona Press, 1975.   Rev. by A. Wallace, PHR, 46(May
1977):290-1.

Wahab, Farouk Abdel.   Modern Egyptian Drama.   Minneapolis &
Chicago: Bibliotheca Islamica, 1974.   Rev. by R. Allen,
JNES, 36(Jan 1977):61-3.

Waite, Robert G. L.   The Psychopathic God: Adolf Hitler.   n. l. :
Basic Books, n. d.   Rev. by L. Bushkoff, Comm, 64(Sep
1977):76-8.

Wakelyn, Jon L.   Biographical Dictionary of the Confederacy.   Westport, Conn. : Greenwood Press, 1977.   Rev. by C. F. C. ,
CWTI, 16(Aug 1977):49; E. Thomas, GHQ, 51(Summer 1977):
206-7.

Wakeman, Frederic, Jr.   The Fall of Imperial China.   New York:
The Free Press, 1975.   Rev. by J. H. Cole, JAS, 36(Feb
1977):342-3.

_____, and Carolyn Grant, eds.   Conflict and Control in Late
Imperial China.   Berkeley: U Cal Press, 1976.   Rev. by
E. S. Rawski, JAS, 36(Feb 1977):343-5.

Walker, Joseph E. , ed. Pleasure and Business in Western Pennsylvania: The Journal of Joshua Gilpin, 1809. Harrisburg: Pennsylvania Historical and Museum Commission, 1975. Rev. by R. E. Smith, PH, 45(April 1977):186-7.

Walker, James W. St. G. The Black Loyalists: The Search for a Promised Land in Nova Scotia and Sierra Leone, 1783-1870. New York: Holmes and Maiers Publishing, 1976; and New York: Africana Publishing, 1976. Rev. by M. B. Norton, JNH, 62(Apr 1977):186-7; P. J. Duignan, JSH, 43(May 1977):287-8.

Wallace, William A. Causality and Scientific Explanation. Ann Arbor: U Mich Press, 1972. Rev. by W. R. Shea, JMH, 49(Mar 1977):116-7.

Wallace-Hadrill, J. M. Early Medieval History. Oxford: Blackwell, 1975. Rev. by W. Davies, History, 62(Feb 1977):94.

Waller, Bruce. Bismarck at the Crossroads: The Reorientation of German Foreign Policy after the Congress of Berlin, 1878-1880. London: Athlone Press, 1974. Rev. by O. Planze, Historian, 39(May 1977):557-8.

Waller, George M. The American Revolution in the West. Chicago: Nelson-Hall, 1976. Rev. by J. L. Harper, WMH, 60(Summer 1977):342-3.

Wallerstein, I. The Modern World-System: Capitalist Agriculture and the Origins of the European World-Economy in the Sixteenth Century. New York: Academic Press, 1974. Rev. by R. B. Outhwaite, HJ, 20(No. 2, 1977):497-502.

Walters, Ronald G. The Antislavery Appeal: American Abolitionism After 1830. Baltimore & London: JHU Press, 1976. Rev. by A. S. Kraditor, JSH, 43(Nov 1977):616-8; J. A. Andrew, MiA, 59(Oct 1977):204.

Walton, Gary M. see Haites, Erik F.

Wandel, Eckhard. Hans Schaffer: Steuermann in wirtschaftlichen und politischen Krisen. Stuttgart: Deutsch Verlags-Anstalt, 1974. Rev. by L. Cecil, JMH, 49(Je 1977):329-33.

Ward, John Manning. Colonial Self-Government: The British Experience 1759-1856. London: Macmillan, 1976. Rev. by D. K. Fieldhouse, History, 62(Feb 1977):89-91.

Ware, Gilbert. From the Black Bar: Voices for Equal Justice. New York: G. P. Putnam's Sons, 1976. Rev. by G. R. McNeil, JNH, 62(Apr 1977):192-4.

Warman, Arturo.   ... Y venimos a Contradecir.   Los Campesinos
de Morelos y el Estado Nacional.   Mexico: Ediciones de la
casa chata, 1976.   Rev. by J. M. Hart, TAm, 33(Jan 1977):
554-6.

Warner, Ezra J. and W. Buck Yearns.   Biographical Register of
the Confederate Congress.   Baton Rouge: LSU Press, 1975.
Rev. by H. Hattaway, LaH, 18(Sum 1977):32-4.

Warren, David B.   see Taylor, Lonn

Warren, Robert Penn.   Selected Poems, 1923-1975.   N. Y. :   Random House, n. d.   Rev. by J. Romano, Comm, 63(Apr 1977):
76-8.

Washington, George.   The Diaries of George Washington.   Ed. by
Donald Jackson and Dorothy Twohig.   Charlottesville: U Press
Virginia, 1976.   Rev. by G. M. Curtis III, AHR, 82(Oct 1977):
1060; L. H. Harrison, JSH, 43(Aug 1977):431-2; D. Higginbotham, VMHB, 85(July 1977):362-3.

Watanabe, Kazuo, ed.   see Ebato, Akira, ed.

Watson, Andrew.   Living in China.   Totowa, N. J. :   Rowman and
Littlefield, 1975.   Rev. by D. G. White, JAS, 36(May 1977):
549-50.

Watson, Charles S.   Antebellum Charleston Dramatists.   University,
Ala. :   U Ala. Press, 1976.   Rev. by G. R. Mathis, JSH,
43(May 1977):293-4.

Watson, Francis.   A Concise History of India.   New York: Charles
Scribner's Sons, 1975.   Rev. by L. A. Gordon, JAS, 36(Feb
1977):364-5.

Watson, Robert.   Selected Poems.   New York: Atheneum, 1974.
Rev. by Sister B. Quinn, GR, 31(Fall 1977):752-5.

Watts, S. J.   From Border to Middle Shire: Northumberland 1586-
1625.   Atlantic Highlands, N. J. :   Humanities Press, 1975.
Rev. by D. M. Palliser, Historian, 39(May 1977):540.

Waugh, Dorothy.   Emily Dickinson's Beloved, A Surmise.   New
York: Vantage Press, 1976.   Rev. by R. Miller, NEQ,
50(Mar 1977):169-70.

Webber, Bert.   Retaliation: Japanese Attacks and Allied Countermeasures on the Pacific Coast in World War II.   Corvallis:
Oregon St U Press, 1975.   Rev. by G. E. Wheeler, PNQ,
68(Jan 1977):40.

Webber, Irving L. and Alfredo Ocampo Zamorano.   Valores,
desarrollo e historia: Popajan, Medellin, Cali y el valle del

Cauca. Bogota, Colombia: Ediciones Tercer Mundo, 1975. Rev. by C. Bergquist, HAHR, 57(Feb 1977):163-4.

Weber, David J. El México perdido: ensayos sobre el antiguo norte de México, 1540-1821. Mexico City: Secretaría de Educación Publica, 1976. Rev. by E. D. Jones, WHQ, 8(Jl 1977):341-2.

_____. Northern Mexico on the Eve of the United States Invasion: Rare Imprints Concerning California, Arizona, New Mexico and Texas, 1821-1846. New York: Arno Press, 1976. Rev. by A. L. Campa, JAriH, 18(Sum 1977):228-9.

Weber, Eugen. Peasants into Frenchman: The Modernization of Rural France, 1870-1914. Stanford, Cal.: Stanford U Press, 1976. Rev. by P. M. Hohenberg, JEH, 37(Je 1977):568-9.

Weber, Michael P. Social Change in an Industrial Town: Patterns of Progress in Warren, Pennsylvania, from Civil War to World War I. University Park: Penn State U Press, 1976. Rev. by W. G. Shade, PH, 45(Oct 1977):372-3.

Weber, William A., ed. Theodore D. A. Cockerell: Letters from West Cliff, Colorado, 1887-1889. Boulder: Colorado Associated University Press, 1976. Rev. by F. H. Hayes, WHQ, 8(Oct 1977):457-8.

Webster, Daniel. The Papers of Daniel Webster: Correspondence, Volume 2, 1825-1829. Ed. by Charles M. Wiltse. Hanover, N.H.: University Press New England, 1976. Rev. by R. N. Current, WVH, 38(Jan 1977):165-6.

Webster, Mary. Johan Zoffany, 1733-1810. London: National Portrait Gallery, 1977. Rev. by R. Paulson, GR, 31(Sum 1977):502-11.

Webster, Richard A. Industrial Imperialism in Italy, 1908-1915. Berkeley: U Cal Press, 1975. Rev. by R. Albrecht-Carrie, JEH, 37(Je 1977):570-1; C. Trebilcock, HJ, 20(No. 3, 1977): 751-60.

Weddle, Robert S. and Robert H. Thonhoff. Drama & Conflict: The Texas Saga of 1776. Austin: Madrona Press, 1976. Rev. by F. D. Almaraz, Jr., A&W, 19(Sum 1977):170-171; J. Dykes, ETHJ, 15(Spr 1977):45-6; D. E. Worcester, JSH, 43(Feb 1977):118-9.

Wee, H. Van der and K. Tavernier. La Banque Nationale de Belgique et l'histoire monetaire entre les deux guerres Mondiales. Brussels: Banque Nationale de Belgique, 1975. Rev. by D. E. Moggridge, JEH, 37(Sep 1977):851-2.

Weems, John Edward. Death Song, The Last of the Indian Wars.

New York: Doubleday, 1976. Rev. by D. Brown, AHI,
12(Oct 1977):50.

Wehler, Hans-Ulrich. Der Deutsche Bauernkrieg, 1524-1526.
Göttengen: Vandenhoeck und Ruprecht, 1975. Rev. by H. J.
Cohn, History, 62(Je 1977):319.

_____. Der Aufstieg des amerikanischen Imperialismus: Studien
zur Entwicklung des Imperium Americanum, 1865-1900.
Göttingen: Vandenhoeck und Ruprecht, 1974. Rev. by P. M.
Kennedy, PHR, 46(Feb 1977):139-40.

_____, ed. Geschichte Und Okonomie. Cologne: Kiepenheuer &
Witsch, 1973. Rev. by K. G. Faber, H&T, 16(Feb 1977):
51-66.

_____, ed. Geschichte und Soziologie. Cologne: Kiepenheuer &
Witsch, 1972. Rev. by K. G. Faber, H&T, 16(Feb 1977):
51-66.

Wehrle, Edmund S. see Lach, Donald F.

Weidman, Bette S. , ed. see Black, Nancy B. , ed.

Weigle, Marta. Brothers of Light, Brothers of Blood: The
Penitentes of the Southwest. Albuquerque: U NM Press,
1976. Rev. by C. J. Bayard, WHQ, 8(Jan 1977):61-2.

Wei-ming, Tu. Neo-Confucian Thought in Action: Wang Yang-
ming's Youth (1472-1509). Berkeley: U California Press,
1976. Rev. by T. A. Metzger, JAS, 37(Nov 1977):112-4.

Weinstein, Jay A. Madras: An Analysis of Urban Ecological
Structure in India. Beverly Hills: Sage Research Papers in
the Social Sciences, 1974. Rev. by W. E. Reed, JAS, 37(Nov
1977):163-4.

Weinstein, Martin. Uruguay: The Politics of Failure. Westport,
Conn. : Greenwood Press, 1975. Rev. by M. H. J. Finch,
JLAS, 9(May 1977):176-7.

Weiskel, Thomas. The Romantic Sublime: Studies in the Structure
and Psychology of Transcendence. Baltimore: JHU Press,
1976. Rev. by D. M. Wyatt, GR, 31(Sep 1977):243-8.

Weisser, Henry. British Working Class Movements and Europe,
1815-48. Manchester: Man U Press, 1976. Rev. by R.
Tilly, JEH, 37(Je 1977):571-2.

Weitzman, David. Underfoot: An Everyday Guide to Exploring the
American Past. New York: Charles Scribner's Sons, 1976.
Rev. by M. Abrash, HT, 10(Aug 1977):639-40.

Wells, Robert V. The Population of the British Colonies in America
   Before 1776: A Survey of Census Data. Princeton, N. J. :
   Prin U Press, 1975. Rev. by A. Kulikoff, WMQ, 34(Apr
   1977):337-8.

Welter, Barbara. Dimity Convictions: The American Woman in
   the Nineteenth Century. Athens, Ohio: Ohio U Press, 1976.
   Rev. by M. A. Burgan, NEQ, 50(Sep 1977):526-8.

Welter, Rush. The Mind of America, 1820-1860. New York: Col
   U Press, 1975. Rev. by L. O. Saum, PNQ, 68(Jan 1977):35;
   W. J. Gates, PH, 45(April 1977):190-2.

Wennergren, E. Boyd and Morris D. Whitaker. The Status of
   Bolivian Agriculture. New York: Praeger Special Studies,
   1975. Rev. by D. A. Preston, JLAS, 9(May 1977):183-4.

Wenig, Steffen, ed. see Edel, Elmar, ed.

Wertz, Raanam, ed. Urbanization and the Developing Countries:
   Report on the Sixth Rehobot Conference. New York: Praeger,
   1973. Rev. by T. F. Barton, JAAS, 12(Jan/Oct 1977):269-72.

Weslager, C. A. The Stamp Act Congress: With an Exact Copy of
   the Complete Journal. Newark, Del. : U Del Press, 1976.
   Rev. by J. D. Neville, 43(Aug 1977):438-9.

West, Elliott, ed. see Philp, Kenneth R. , ed.

West, Philip. Yenching University and Sino-Western Relations,
   1916-1952. Cambridge: Harvard U Press, 1976. Rev. by
   J. Israel, JAS, 37(Nov 1977):117-19.

Westenholz, Aage. Old Sumerian and Old Akkadian Texts in Philadelphia Chiefly from Nippur. Malibu, Calif: Undena Publications, 1975. Rev. by B. J. Foster, JNES, 36(Oct 1977):
   299-302.

Westphal, Larry see Frank, Charles R. , Jr.

Westphal-Hellbusch, Sigrid and Ilse Bruns. Metallgefässe aus
   Buchara. Berlin: Veröffentlichungen des Museums für
   Völkerkunde, 1974. Rev. by C-J. Charpentier, JAS, 36(May
   1977):541-2.

Wheeler, Richard. Voices of the Civil War. New York: Thomas
   Y. Crowell, 1976. Rev. by B. I. Wiley, AHI, 12(Jl 1977):50.

Wheeler, Robert C. , Walter A. Kenyon, Alan R. Woolworth, and
   Douglas A. Birk. Voices from the Rapids: An Underwater
   Search for Fur Trade Artifacts, 1960-73. St. Paul, Minn. :
   Minnesota Historical Society, 1975. Rev. by J. R. Halsey,
   MichH, 61(Summer 1977):164-5; R. J. Mason, WMH,
   60(Spring 1977):238-40.

Whitaker, Morris D. see Wennergren, E. Boyd

White, G. Edward. The American Judicial Tradition: Profiles of
Leading American Judges. New York: Ox U Press, 1976.
Rev. by D. M. Roper, JSH, 43(Aug 1977):445-6.

White, Judy, ed. Chile's Days of Terror: Eyewitness Accounts of
the Military Coup. New York: Pathfinder Press, 1974. Rev.
by J. N. Goodsell, HAHR, 57(Feb 1977):155-6.

White, Thurman J., ed. see Taylor, Benjamin J., ed.

Whiteman, Maxwell. Gentlemen in Crisis: The First Century of
the Union League of Philadelphia, 1862-1962. Philadelphia:
Union Leage of Philadelphia, 1975. Rev. by A. Hoogenboom,
NYHSQ, 61(Jan/Apr 1977):95-6; C. M. Frank, PH, 45(July
1977):284-5.

Whiteside, Andrew G. The Socialism of Fools: Georg Ritter von
Schonerer and Austrian Pan-Germanism. Berkeley: U Cal
Press, 1975. Rev. by R. V. Luza, Historian, 39(Feb 1977):
355-6.

Whitfield, Stephen J. Scott Nearing: Apostle of American Radicalism. New York: Columbia U Press, 1974. Rev. by M. R.
Greco, PH, 45(April 1977):189-90.

Whiting, Allen S. The Chinese Calculus of Deterrence: India and
Indochina. Ann Arbor: U Mich Press, 1975. Rev. by K.
Gupta, JAS, 36(Aug 1977):713-5.

Widmer, Eric. The Russian Ecclesiastical Mission in Peking during
the Eighteenth Century. Cambridge: Har U Press, 1976.
Rev. by N. Chou, JAS, 36(Aug 1977):718-9.

Wiebe, Paul D. Social Life in an Indian Slum. Durham: Carolina
Academic Press, 1975. Rev. by K. L. Michaelson, JAS,
36(Feb 1977):373-4.

Wiebe, Robert H. The Segmented Society: An Historical Preface
to the Meaning of America. New York: Oxford U Press,
1975. Rev. by M. P. Weber, PH, 45(Jan 1977):86-8.

Wiethoff, Bodo. Introduction to Chinese History From Ancient
Times to 1912. London: Thames and Hudson, 1975. Rev.
by V. G. Kiernan, History, 62(Je 1977):291.

Wiggins, Sarah Woolfolk. The Scalawag in Alabama Politics, 1865-
1881. University, Alabama: U Alabama Press, 1977. Rev.
by R. Mathis, GHQ, 51(Winter 1977):364-5.

Wilbur, C. Martin. Sun Yat-sen: Frustrated Patriot. New York:
Columbia U Press, 1976. Rev. by L. E. Eastman, JAS,
37(Nov 1977):120-1.

Wilbur, Richard. The Mind-Reader: New Poems. New York:
Harcourt Brace Jovanovich, 1976. Rev. by M. G. Cooke, GR,
31(Fall 1977):718-29.

Wilder, Mitchell A. with Edgar Breitenbach. Santos: The Religious
Folk Art of New Mexico. New York: Hacker Art Books, 1976.
Rev. by R. Quinn, HAHR, 57(Aug 1977):560-1.

Wiley, Bell I. The Common Soldier of the Civil War. New York:
Charles Scribner's Sons, 1975. Rev. by B. H. Groene, LaH,
18(Spr 1977):246-7.

Wilkie, Edna Monzon de, ed. see Wilkie, James W., ed.

Wilkie, James W., Michael C. Meyer, and Edna Monzón De Wilkie.
Contemporary Mexico: Papers of IV International Congress of
Mexican History. Berkeley: U Cal Press, 1976. Rev. by
S. A. Soeiro, HAHR, 57(Aug 1977):520-2; P. J. Bakewell,
NMHR, 52(Jl 1977):258-9.

Wilkins, Mira. The Maturing of Multinational Enterprise: American Business Abroad from 1914 to 1970. Cambridge: Har U
Press, 1974. Rev. by R. W. Gronet, TAm, 33(Jan 1977):
542-3.

Wilkinson, David. Revolutionary Civil War: The Elements of Victory and Defeat. Palo Alto, Calif.: Page-Ficklin Publications,
1975. Rev. by P. Calvert, History, 62(Feb 1977):92-3.

Wilkinson, Ernest L., ed., Leonard J. Arrington, ed. and Bruce
C. Hafen, ed. Brigham Young University: The First One
Hundred Years. Provo, Utah: Brigham Young U Press,
1975-6. Rev. by T. S. Buchanan, UHQ, 45(Sum 1977):309-11.

Wilkinson, J. B. Laredo and the Rio Grande Frontier. Austin:
Pemberton Press, 1975. Rev. by J. R. Jameson, ETHJ,
15(Spr 1977):58-9; H. Gambrell, WHQ, 8(Jan 1977):74.

Wilks, Ivor. Asante in the Nineteenth Century: The Structure and
Evolution of a Political Order. Cambridge: Cam U Press,
1975. Rev. by J. D. Fage, History, 62(Je 1977):268-9.

Will, George F. and George E. Hyde. Corn Among the Indians of
the Upper Missouri. Lincoln: U Neb Press, 1964, 1976.
Rev. by W. C. Van Deventer, AgH, 51(Jl 1977):616-7.

Willan, T. S. The Inland Trade: Studies in English Internal Trade
in the Sixteenth and Seventeenth Centuries. Manchester: Man
U Press, 1976. Rev. by R. M. Berger, JEH, 37(Sep 1977):
853.

Willcox, William B. et al. The Papers of Benjamin Franklin.
New Haven: Yale U Press, 1972. Rev. by G. S. Wood, JSH,
43(May 1977):281-3.

Willeke, Frei Venâncio. Missões Franciscanas no Brasil.
    Petropolis: Editora Vozes Ltda. , 1974. Rev. by S. A.
    Soeiro, HAHR, 57(Aug 1977):523-4.

Willey, Gordon R. et al. Excavations at Seibal, Department of
    Peten, Guatemala. Cambridge: Harvard U, 1975. Rev. by
    W. Bray, JLAS, 9(May 1977):149.

Williams, Dorothy Hunt. Historic Virginia Gardens: Preservations
    by the Garden Club of Virginia. Charlottesville: U Press
    Virginia, 1975. Rev. by G. G. Shackelford, VMHB, 85(Jan
    1977):114-15.

Williams, Edward G. , ed. Bouquet's March to the Ohio: The
    Forbes Road. Pittsburgh, Pa. : Historical Society of Western
    Pennsylvania, 1975. Rev. by W. M. E. Rachal, VMHB,
    85(Jan 1977):105-6.

Williams, Edward J. and Freeman J. Wright. Latin American
    Politics: A Developmental Approach. Palo Alto, Calif. :
    Mayfield Publishing, 1975. Rev. by I. Roxborough, JLAS,
    9(May 1977):170-1.

Williams, George H. , et al. Thomas Hooker: Writings in England
    and Holland, 1626-1633. Cambridge, Mass. : Har U Press,
    1976. Rev. by E. B. Holifield, WMQ, 34(Jan 1977):166-8.

Williams, Glyn. The Desert and the Dream: A Study of Welsh
    Colonization in Churbut, 1865-1915. Cardiff: U Wales Press,
    1975. Rev. by R. C. Eidt, HAHR, 57(Feb 1977):145-6.

Williams, James H. and Doug Murfield, ed. Agricultural Atlas of
    Nebraska. Lincoln: U Nebraska Press, 1977. Rev. by L.
    Barnett, MichH, 61(Fall 1977):277-80.

Williams, John Alexander. West Virginia and the Captains of Indus-
    try. Morgantown, W. Va. : West Virginia University Library,
    1976. Rev. by P. J. Funigiello, JSH, 43(Mah 1977):328-9;
    M. W. Schlegel, JSH, 43(Aug 1977):491-2; J. E. Stealey, III,
    WVH, 38(April 1977):244-6.

Williams, John Lee. A View of West Florida. Gainesville: U
    Presses of Florida, 1976. Rev. by R. F. A. Fabel, AlaR,
    30(Jan 1977):69-71.

Williams, Joyce G. and Jill E. Farrelly. Diplomacy on the Indiana-
    Ohio Frontier, 1783-1791. Bloomington: Indiana U Bicenten-
    nial Committee, 1976. Rev. by N. C. Eggleston, FCHQ,
    51(Jl 1977):288-9.

Williams, Miller, ed. see McPherson, James Alan, ed.

Williamson, Jeffrey G. see Kelley, Allen C.

Wilson, Amy A., Sidney L. Greenblatt, and Richard W. Wilson.
    Deviance and Social Control in Chinese Society. New York:
    Praeger, 1977. Rev. by D. M. Raddock, JAS, 37(Nov 1977):
    128-30.

Wilson, Charles. The Transformation of Europe, 1558-1648.
    Berkeley and Los Angeles: U Cal Press, 1976. Rev. by A.
    Appleby, JEH, 37(Sep 1977):854.

Wilson, Derek. A History of South and Central Africa. Cambridge:
    Cam U Press, 1975. Rev. by D. L. Wheeler, History, 62(Je
    1977):270.

Wilson, Don W. Governor Charles Robinson of Kansas. Lawrence:
    U Press Kan, 1975. Rev. by H. E. Socolofsky, PHR, 46(May
    1977):295-6; J. A. Rawley, PNQ, 68(Jl 1977):145.

Wilson, Ellen Gibson. The Loyal Blacks. New York: Capricorn
    Books, 1976. Rev. by P. J. Duignan, JSH, 43(May 1977):
    287-8.

Wilson, Howard McKnight. Great Valley Patriots: Western Virginia
    in the Struggle for Liberty. Verona, Va.: McClure Press,
    1976. Rev. by R. S. Klein, JSH, 43(Nov 1977):645-7; G. M.
    Herndon, VMHB, 85(July 1977):365-6.

Wilson, Larmon C. see Davis, Harold Eugene

Wilson, Raymond see Brugge, David M.

Wilson, Thomas, ed. see Skinner, Andrew S., ed.

Wilson, Woodrow. The Papers of Woodrow Wilson. Volume 19:
    1909-1910. Ed. by Arthur S. Link, et al. Princeton:
    Princeton U Press, 1975. Rev. by V. A. Carrafiello, PH,
    45(July 1977):272-4.

_____. Volume 20: 1910. Rev. by V. A. Carrafiello, PH,
    45(Oct 1977):373-6.

_____. Volume 22: 1910-1911. Rev. by L. E. Gelfand, WVH,
    38(July 1977):329-31.

Wiltse, Charles M. The Papers of Daniel Webster, Correspondence,
    Volume 2, 1825-1829. Hanover, N.H.: U Press of New
    England, 1976. Rev. by I. H. Bartlett, NEQ, 50(Mar 1977):
    178-80; C. T. Cullen, NEQ, 50(Je 1977):348-51; N. D. Brown,
    JSH, 43(May 1977):291-2.

Wiltsee, Ernest A. The Pioneer Miner and the Pack Mule Express.
    Lawrence, Mass.: Quarterman Publications, 1976. Rev. by
    A. Probert, JOW, 16(Jan 1977):82.

Winfield, Nath, Jr. see Puryear, Pamela Ashworth

Winnick, R. H. see Thompson, Lawrence

Winstone, H. V. F. Captain Shakespear: A Portrait. London:
    Jonathan Cape, 1976. Rev. by M. E. Yapp, History, 62(Je
    1977):282.

Wintz, Julia. Kanawah County Marriages January 1, 1792, to
    December 31, 1869. Parsons, W. Va.: McClain Printing
    Co., 1975. Rev. by O. A. Jones, WVH, 38(April 1977):
    239-40.

Wiseman, D. J., ed. Peoples of Old Testament Times. Oxford:
    Ox U Press, 1973. Rev. by R. Harris, JNES, 36(Jl 1977):
    230-1.

Wiser, Vivian, ed. Two Centuries of American Agriculture.
    Washington, D. C.: Agricultural History Society, 1976. Rev.
    by R. V. Scott, WHQ, 8(Jl 1977):329-30.

Wistrich, Robert. Revolutionary Jews From Marx to Trotsky.
    N. Y.: Barnes & Noble, n.d. Rev. by H. Maccoby, Comm,
    63(Apr 1977):78-81.

Witke, Roxane, ed. see Wolf, Margery, ed.

Wittgenstein, Ludwig. Philosophical Grammar. Berkeley: U Cal
    Press, 1974. Rev. by K. Linnville, GR, 31(Fall 1977):772-5.

Wojcik, Donna M. The Brazen Overlanders of 1845. Portland:
    author, 1976. Rev. by E. W. Buehler, OrHQ, 78(Sep 1977):
    281.

Wolf, Eric R. The Valley of Mexico: Studies in Pre-Hispanic
    Ecology and Society. Albuquerque: UNM Press, 1976. Rev.
    by R. C. West, HAHR, 57(Aug 1977):526-7.

Wolf, Margery, ed. and Roxane Witke, ed. Women in Chinese
    Society. Stanford: Stan U Press, 1975. Rev. by J. Strauch,
    JAS, 36(Feb 1977):350-2.

Wolf, Stephanie Grauman. Urban Village: Population, Community,
    and Family Structure in Germantown, Pennsylvania, 1683-1800.
    Princeton, N.J.: Prin U Press, 1976. Rev. by D. H. Kent,
    WHQ, 8(Oct 1977):472-3.

Wolfe, George H., ed. Faulkner: Fifty Years after The Marble
    Faun. University, Alabama: U Alabama Press, 1976. Rev.
    by W. T. Gong, AlaR, 30(April 1977):154-5.

Wolfe, Tom. Mauve Gloves & Madmen, Clatter & Vine. n.l.:
    Farrar, Straus & Giroux, n.d. Rev. by D. Rabinowitz, Comm,
    63(May 1977):76-8.

Wolfe, Willard. From Radicalism to Socialism: Men and Ideas in the Formation of Fabian Socialist Doctrines, 1881-1889. New Haven: Yale U Press, 1975. Rev. by W. C. Wilbur, Historian, 39(Feb 1977):334-5; S. Collini, HJ, 20(No. 1, 1977): 237-54.

Wolters, O. W. , ed. see Cowan, C. D. , ed.

Wong, J. Y. Yeh Ming-Ch'en, Viceroy of Liang Kuang 1852-8. Cambridge: Cam U Press, 1976. Rev. by V. G. Kiernan, History, 62(Je 1977):292.

Wood, Robert L. Men, Mules and Mountains: Lieutenant O'Neil's Olympic Expeditions. Seattle: Mountaineers, 1976. Rev. by L. L. McArthur, OrHQ, 78(Sep 1977):281-2; F. H. Hayes, WHQ, 8(Oct 1977):457-8.

Wood, Robin. Personal Vieros: Explorations in Film. London: Gordon Fraser, 1976. Rev. by A. Sesonske, GR, 31(Fall 1977):729-32.

Woodhouse, Michael and Brian Pearce. Essays on the History of Communism in Britain. London: New Park, 1975. Rev. by A. Reid & S. Tolliday, HJ, 20(No. 4, 1977):1001-12.

Woodruff, William. America's Impact on the World: A Study of the Role of the United States in the World Economy, 1750-1970. New York: John Wiley, 1975. Rev. by W. LaFeber, PHR, 46(Aug 1977):485-6.

Woodside, Alexander B. Community and Revolution in Modern Vietnam. Boston: Houghton Mifflin, 1976. Rev. by W. J. Duiker, Historian, 39(May 1977):566-7; J. Werner, JAS, 37(Nov 1977):174.

Woodward, Ralph Lee, Jr. Central America: A Nation Divided. New York: Ox U Press, 1976. Rev. by M. J. Macleod, HAHR, 57(Feb 1977):104-5; T. L. Karnes, Historian, 39(May 1977):594-5; T. Schoonover, LaH, 18(Spr 1977):247-8; C. L. Stansifer, TAm, 34(Jl 1977):143-4.

Woolf, Leonard. The Village in the Jungle. Delhi: B. R. Publishing, 1975. Rev. by R. Obeyesekere, JAS, 36(May 1977): 581-2.

Wooster, Ralph A. Politicians, Planters, and Plain Folk: Courthouse and Statehouse in the Upper South, 1850-1860. Knoxville: U Tennessee Press, 1975. Rev. by J. C. Klotter, FCHQ, 51(Jan 1977):51-2.

Worcester, Donald E. , ed. Forked Tongues and Broken Treaties. Caldwell, Idaho: Caxton Printers, 1975. Rev. by L. J. White, A&W, 19(Spr 1977):85-86; R. L. Nichols, PHR, 46(May 1977):286-7; R. M. Benson, WHQ, 8(Oct 1977):464-5.

Wriggins, W. Howard, ed. Pakistan in Transition. Islamabad:
    University of Islamabad Press, 1975. Rev. by B. Metcalf,
    JAS, 37(Nov 1977):171-2.

Wright, Freeman J. see Williams, Freeman J.

Wright, J. Leitch, Jr. Britain and the American Frontier, 1783-
    1815. Athens: U Ga Press, 1976. Rev. by A. P. Nasatir,
    PHR, 46(Aug 1977):497-8; H. D. Abadie, JMiH, 39(Feb 1977):
    89-90; R. R. Alexander, WVH, 38(April 1977):236-7; J. H.
    O'Donnell, III, WMQ, 34(Jan 1977):151-2.

_____. Florida in the American Revolution. Gaines-
    ville: The U Presses of Florida, published for the
    American Bicentennial Commission of Florida, 1975. Rev.
    by J. H. O'Donnell, III, WMQ, 34(Jan 1977):151-2.

Wright, John D. Transylvania: Tutor to the West. Lexington,
    Ky.: Transylvania U, 1975. Rev. by W. L. Fox, JSH,
    43(Feb 1977):145-6.

Wright, Louis B. South Carolina: A Bicentennial History. New
    York: W. W. Norton, 1976. Rev. by W. Moore, JSH,
    43(Feb 1977):146-7.

Wrigley, Chris. David Lloyd Goerge and the British Labour Move-
    ment: Peace and War. New York: Barnes & Noble, 1976.
    Rev. by S. H. Palmer, Historian, 39(May 1977):547-8.

Wright, Stuart Thurman, ed. see Fries, Adelaide, ed.

Wu, Tien-wei. The Sian Incident: A Pivotal Point in Modern
    Chinese History. Ann Arbor: Center for Chinese Studies,
    1976. Rev. by J. H. Boyle, JAS, 37(Nov 1977):124-5.

Wuertele, Elizabeth. Bibliographical History of California Anthro-
    pological Research, 1850-1917. n.l.: U Cal Archaelogical
    Research Facility, 1975. Rev. by R. N. Ellis, NMHR,
    52(Oct 1977):337-43.

Wynn, Neil A. The Afro-American and the Second World War.
    London: Paul Elek, 1976. Rev. by R. C. Reinders, JAmS,
    11(April 1977):157-9.

Yang, Paul Fu-Mien. Chinese Linguistics: A Selected And Classi-
    fied Bibliography. Hong Kong: The Chinese U Hong Kong,
    1974. Rev. by J. Norman, JAS, 36(Feb 1977):349-50.

Yapp, M. E., ed. see Parry, V. J., ed.

Yearns, W. Buck see Warner, Ezra J.

Yergin, Daniel. Shattered Peace: The Origins of the Cold War

and the National Security Council. n. l. : Houghton Mifflin,
n. d. Rev. by E. N. Luttwak, Comm, 64(Aug 1977):64-6.

Yip, Wai-lim, ed. Chinese Poetry: Major Modes and Genres.
Berkeley: U California Press, 1976. Rev. by S. Owen, JAS,
37(Nov 1977):100-2.

Yokoi, Yūhō with the Assistance of Daizen Victoria. Zen Master
Dōgen: An Introduction with Selected Writings. New York:
John Weatherhill, 1976. Rev. by R. J. Corless, JAS,
36(Aug 1977):743-5.

Yoshino, M. Y. Japan's Multinational Enterprises. Cambridge:
Harvard U Press, 1976. Rev. by R. S. Ozaki, JAS, 37(Nov
1977):136-7.

Young, Alfred F. , ed. The American Revolution: Explorations in
the History of American Radicalism. DeKalb: Northern
Illinois U Press, 1976. Rev. by M. Egnal, JIH, 8(Autumn
1977):387-90.

Young, Frederic A. , Jr. The Proclamations of the Tudor Queens.
Cambridge: Cambridge U Press, 1976. Rev. by D. M.
Loades, HJ, 20(No. 4, 1977):1013-14.

Young, John Aubrey. Business and Sentiment in a Chinese Market
Town. Taipei: Orient Cultural Service, Asian Folklore and
Social Monographs 60, 1974. Rev. by C. F. Blake, JAS,
36(May 1977):560.

Young, Otis E. , Jr. Black Power and Hand Steel: Miners and
Machines on the Old Western Frontier. With the Technical
Assistance of Robert Lenon. Norman: U Ok Press, 1976.
Rev. by J. E. Niebur, A&W, 19(Sum 1977):191-2; M. Wells,
WHQ, 8(Apr 1977):224-5.

Youngdale, James M. Populism: A Psychohistorical Perspective.
Port Washington, N. Y. : Kennikat Press, 1975. Rev. by E.
C. Blackorby, AgH, 51(Jl 1977):625-7.

Youngs, J. William T. , Jr. , Frank S. Brewer, and Elizabeth D.
Brewer. God's Messengers: Religious Leadership in Colonial
New England, 1700-1750. Baltimore: JHU Press, 1976. Rev.
by R. Warch, WMQ, 34(Oct 1977):677-8.

Yui, Tsunehiko see Hirschmeier, Johannes

Yu-ning, Li, ed. The First Emperor of China: The Politics of
Historiography. White Plains: International Arts and Sciences Press, 1975. Rev. by L. A. Schneider, JAS, 36(Feb
1977):345-7.

Zall, Paul M. , ed. Comical Spirit of Seventy-Six: The Humor of

Francis Hopkinson. San Marino, Calif.: The Huntington Library, 1976. Rev. by W. H. Kenney, WMQ, 34(Apr 1977): 347-8.

Zamorano, Alfredo Ocampo see Webber, Irving L.

Zasloff, Joseph J., ed. and MacAlister Brown, ed. Communism in Indochina: New Perspectives. Lexington, Mass.: Lexington Books, 1975. Rev. by D. G. Marr, JAS, 36(Feb 1977): 384-5.

Zea, Leopoldo. Dependencia y liberación en la cultura latino - americana. Mexico: Editorial Joaquin Mortiz, 1974. Rev. by W. D. Raat, HAHR, 57(May 1977):317-9.

Zile, Judy Van. Dance in India: An Annotated Guide to Source Materials. Providence: Asian Music Publications, 1973. Rev. by J. Blank, JAS, 36(May 1977):574-5.

Zimmerling, Dieter. Die Hanse: Handelsmacht im Zeichen der Kogge. Düsseldorf and Vienna: Econ Verlag, 1976. Rev. by W. Kirchner, JEH, 37(Je 1977):561-2.

Zochert, Donald. Laura: The Life of Laura Ingalls Wilder. Chicago: Henry Regnery, 1976. Rev. by C. Flanagan, MinnH, 45(Spr 1977):205.

Zucker, Stanley. Ludwig Bamberger: German Liberal Politician and Social Critic, 1823-1899. Pittsburgh: U Pitt Press, 1975. Rev. by L. Cecil, JMH, 49(Je 1977):329-33.

Zumpe, Lotte. Wirschaft und Staat im Imperialismus: Beiträge zur Entwicklungsgeschichte des staatsmonopolistischen Kapitalismus in Deutschland. Berlin: Akademie-Verlag, 1976. Rev. by L. Schofer, JEH, 37(Sep 1977):807-8.

1400 A. D.   R. Oliver and B.
Fagan.

African Aims and Attitudes.   Martin
Minogue and Judith Molloy.

African Apprenticeship, An Autobiographical Journey.   Margery
Perham.

The African Dream: Martin R.
Delany and the Emergence of
Pan-African Thought.   Cyril E.
Griffith.

African Environment: Problems
and Perspectives.   Paul
Richards, ed.

African Experience in Spanish
America: 1502 to the Present
Day.   Leslie R. Rout, Jr.

African Literature in the 20th
Century.   O. R. Dathorne.

African Literature Today, No. 8.
Drama in Africa.   Eldred D.
Jones, ed.

African Music: A People's Art.
Francis Bebey.

African Politics in South Africa
1964-1974.   D. A. Kotze.

The African Slave in Colonial
Peru, 1524-1650.   Frederick P.
Bowser.

The Afro-American and the Second
World War.   Neil A. Wynn.

After Babel.   George Steiner.

Against the Specter of A Dragon:
The Campaign for American
Military Preparedness, 1914-1917.
John Patrick Finnegan.

The Age of Alignment: Electoral
Politics in Britain, 1922-1929.
Chris Cook.

The Age of Capital, 1848-1875.
E. J. Hobsbawm.

Age of Louis XIV: The Rise of
Modern Diplomacy.   William
James Roosen.

Agency of Fear.   Edward J. Epstein.

Agrarkonjunktur und Witterungsverlauf im westlichen Schweizer
Mittelland zur Zeit der Okonomischen Patrioten, 1755-1797.
Christian Pfister.

Agraverbände in der Weimarer
Republik: Wirtschaftliche und
soziale Voraussetzungen
agarkonservativer Politik vor
1933.   Dieter Gessner.

Agricultural Atlas of Nebraska.
James H. Williams Doug Murfield, ed.

The Agricultural Development of
Turkey.   Oddvar Aresvik.

Agricultural Development: Soil, Food,
People Work.   Charles E. Kellogg.

Agriculture in Development Theory.
Llody G. Reynolds, ed.

Agriculture in the Development of the
Far West.   James H. Shideler, ed.

Agriculture in the Postbellum South:
The Economics of Production and
Supply.   Stephen J. De Canio.

Agriculture in the United States: A
Documentary History.   Wayne D.
Rasmussen.

Akkadian Influences on Aramaic.
Stephen A. Kaufman.

The Alabama Claims: American Politics and Anglo-American Relations,
1865-1872.   Adrian Cook.

Alaska: A Bicentennial History.
William R. Hunt.

Alaska Purchase and Russian-American Relations.   Ronald J. Jensen.

Albemarle: Jefferson's County, 1727-
1976.   John Hammond Moore.

Alexander Hamilton.   Broadus Mitchell.

Alexander McDougall and the American
Revolution in New York.   Roger J.
Champagne.

Alienated "Loyal" Opposition: Mexico's Partido Accion Nacional.
Franz A. von Sauer.

Alienation, Praxis, and Techne in the
Thought of Karl Marx.   Kostas
Axelos.

Al-Kindi's Metaphysics: A Translation of Ya qub ibn Ishaq al-Kindi's
Treatis "On First Philosophy" (fi
al-Falsafah al-Ula).   Alfred L.
Ivry.

Allan Nevins on History.   Ray Allen
Billington, ed.

Alle origini del notariato italiano.
Mario Amelotti and Giorgia
Costamagna.

Allegany County: A History.   Harry I.
Stegmaier, Jr. , et al.

Les Allemands au Chili (1816-1945).
Jean-Pierre Blancpain.

Allende's Chile.   Philip O'Brien.

Allende's Chile: The Political Economy of the Rise and Fall of the
Unidad Popular.   Stefan DeVylder.

Allies for Freedom: Blacks and John
Brown.   Benjamin Quarles.

Along the Color Line: Explorations in
the Black Experience.   August
Meier and Elliott Rudwick.

Al-Riddah and the Muslim Conquest of Arabia. Elias Shoufani.

Alstons and Allstons of North and South Carolina with Supplementary Material on the La Bruce, Pawley and Ward Families of Waccamaw. S. Emmett Lucas, Jr.

Alternative to Extinction: Federal Indian Policy and the Beginnings of the Reservation System, 1846-51. Robert A. Trennert, Jr.

Altithermal Occupation of the Spring Sites in the Northern Great Basin. John Lee Fagan.

Altsumerische Wirtschaftstexte aus Lagasch. Josef Bauer.

Ambassador Du Luc und der Trücklibund von 1715. Fredy Gröbli.

Ambiguous Imperialism: American Foreign Policy and Domestic Politics at the Turn of the Century. Göran Rystad.

America and the Arab States: An Uneasy Encounter. Robert W. Stookey.

America as an Ordinary Country: U. S. Foreign Policy and the Future. Richard Rosecrance, ed.

America in Our Time. Godfrey Hodgson.

America Latina en el Mundo. J. M. Briceno Guerrero.

America Through Baseball. David Q. Voigt.

American and French Culture, 1800-1900: Interchange in Art, Science, Literature, and Society. Henry Blumenthal.

American Catholicism and European Immigrants, 1900-1924. Richard M. Linkh.

American Civil War Navies: A Bibliography. Myron J. Smith.

American Colonies: From Settlement to Independence. R. C. Simmons.

American Defense Policy from Eisenhower to Kennedy: The Politics of Changing Military Requirements, 1957-1961. Richard A. Aliano.

American Diplomatic Relations with the Middle East, 1784-1975: A Survey. Thomas A. Bryson.

American Education Through Japanese Eyes. George Z. F. Bereday and Shigeo Masui.

The American Farm: A Photographic History. Maisie Conrat and Richard Conrat.

American Farm Policy, 1948-1973. Willard W. Cochrane and Mary E. Ryan.

American Indian Policy in Crisis: Christian Reformers and the Indian, 1865-1900. Francis Paul Prucha.

American Indian Policy in the Jacksonian Era. Ronald N. Satz.

The American Journals of Lt. John Enys. John Enys.

American Judicial Tradition: Profiles of Leading American Judges. G. Edward White.

American Labor Songs of the Nineteenth Century. Philip S. Foner.

American Lawyers in a Changing Society, 1776-1876. Maxwell Bloomfield.

American Medical Education: The Formative Years, 1765-1910. Martin Kaufman.

American Negro Slavery: A Documentary History. Michael Mullin, ed.

American Opinion and the Russian Alliance, 1939-1945. Ralph B. Levering.

The American Revolution: Explorations in the History of American Radicalism. Alfred F. Young, ed.

The American Revolution in the West. George M. Waller.

American Search for Woman. H. Carleton Marlow and Harrison M. Davis.

American Slavery, American Freedom: The Ordeal of Colonial Virginia. Edmund S. Morgan.

An American Teacher in Early Meiji Japan. Edward R. Beauchamp.

American Welfare Capitalism, 1880-1940. Stuart D. Brandes.

Americanization of the Common Law: The Impact of Legal Change on Massachusetts Society, 1760-1830. William E. Nelson.

Americanization of the Synagogue, 1820-1870. Leon A. Jick.

America's Cultural Experiment in China, 1942-1949. Wilma Fairbank.

America's Exiles: Indian Colonization in Oklahoma. Arrell Morgan Gibson, ed.

America's Freedom Trail (Mas-
sachusetts, New York, New
Jersey, Pennsylvania): A Tour
Guide to Historical Sites of the
Colonial and Revolutionary War
Period.   M. Victor Alper.
America's Heritage Trail (South
Carolina, North Carolina, Vir-
ginia).   M. Victor Alper.
America's Immigrant Women.
Cecyle S. Neidle.
America's Impact on the World:
A Study of the Role of the
United States in the World
Economy, 1750-1970.   William
Woodruff.
Americo Castro y el origen de los
Espanoles: Historia de uno
polemica.   Jose Luis Gomez-
Martinez.
Amerikanuak: Basques in the New
World.   William A. Douglass
and Jon Bilbao.
Anarchism of Nesor Makhno, 1918-
1921: An Aspect of the Ukrain-
ian Revolution.   Michael Palij.
Ancient Chinese Jades From the
Grenville L. Winthrop Collec-
tion in the Fogg Art Museum,
Harvard University.   Max
Loehr.
Ancient Cosmologies.   Carmen
Blacker and Michael Loewe, ed.
Ancient Scilly: From the Farm-
ers to the Early Christians.
Paul Ashbee.
And They All Sang Hallelujah:
Plain-Folk Campmeeting Reli-
gion, 1800-1845.   Dickson D.
Bruce, Jr.
Andrew Jackson and the Search
for Vindication.   James C.
Curtis.
Die Anfänge Einer Ständigen In-
quisition im Böhmen.   Alex-
ander Patschovsky.
Angelo Herndon Case and Southern
Justice.   Charles H. Martin.
Anglo Over Bracero: A History
of the Mexican Worker in the
United States from Roosevelt
to Nixon.   Peter N. Kirstein.
Anglo-Saxon England, IV.   P.
Clemoes, ed.
Annan Parish Censuses, 1801-
1821.   George Gilchrist, ed.
Das Anniversarbuch des Basler
Comstifts, 1334/8-1610.   Paul
Bloesch.

Another Part of the Twenties.   Paul
A. Carter.
Antebellum Black Newspapers.
Donald M. Jacobs, ed.
Antebellum Charleston Dramatists.
Charles S. Watson.
Anthology of Contemporary Chinese
Literature.   Chi Pang-Yuan, ed.
et al.
Anthology of Personal Recollections of
the Slovak National Uprising.
Martin Kvetko, ed. and Miroslav
Jan Licko, ed.
The Anti-Lynching Movement: 1883-
1932.   Donald L. Grant.
Antislavery Appeal: American Aboli-
tionism After 1830.   Ronald G.
Walters.
Appeal That Was Never Made: The
Allies, Scandinavia and the Finnish
Winter War, 1939-1940.   Jukka
Nevakivi.
El Apra en busca de poder, 1930-
1940.   Victor Villanueva.
The Arab-Israeli Conflict: A Histori-
cal, Political, Social, and Military
Bibliography.   Ronald M. Devore.
Arabian Studies I.   R. B. Serjeant
and R. L. Bidwell, ed.
Arabs and Zionism Before World
War I.   Neville J. Mandel.
The Arabs in Israel.   Noam Chomsky.
Arabs in Israel.   Sabri Jiryis.
The Arabs, Israelis, and Kissinger:
A Secret History of American
Diplomacy in the Middle East.
Edward R. F. Sheehan.
Arafat: The Man and the Myth.
Thomas Kiernan.
Arbeiter-und Soldaternräte im rheini-
schwestfälischen Industriegebiet.
Reinhard Rürup, ed.
Archaeology at the National Greek
Orthodox Shrine, St. Augustine,
Florida: Microchange in Eighteenth
Century Spanish Colonial Material
Culture.   Kathleen A. Deagan.
The Archaeology of Industry.   Kenneth
Hudson.
Archaeology of the Boat.   Basil Green-
hill, et al.
Archaic and Classical Greek Coins.
Colin M. Kraay.
Archaic Greece.   The City-States c.
700-500 B.C.   L. H. Jeffery.
The Archaic Period: History of the
Hellenic World, vol. 2.   George A.
Christopoulos and John C. Bastias,
ed.

-B-

Bacon's Rebellion, 1676-1976. Jane Carson.

Badoglio: Un militare al potere. Giovanni De Luna.

Ballots for Freedom: Antislavery Politics in the United States, 1837-1860. Richard H. Sewell.

Ballygullion. Leslie Alexander Montgomery.

Baltic Question, 1903-1908. Pertti Luntinen.

Banca e industria in Italia, 1894-1906. Antonio Confalonieri.

Bangladesh: The Test Case for Development. Just Faaland and J. R. Parkinson.

Bank of England, 1891-1944. R. S. Sayers.

Bankiers, Kunstler und Gelehrte: Unveroffentlichte Briefe der Familie Mendelssohn aus dem 19. Jahrhundert. Felix Gilbert, ed.

Banking and Industrialization in Austria-Hungary: The Role of Banks in the Industrialization of the Czech Crownlands, 1873-1914. Richard L. Rudolph.

Banking and Currency in Hong Kong. Y. C. Jao.

La Banque Nationale de Belgique et l'histoire monetaire entre les deux guerres Mondiales. H. Van der Wee and K. Tavernier.

Banques et banquiers en Autriche au debut du 20e siècle. Bernard Michel.

The Barbary Slaves. Stephen Clissold.

Bare Ruined Choirs: The Dissolution of the English Monasteries. David Knowles.

The Baroque Age in England. Judith Hook.

Baroque Architecture in Classical Antiquity. Margaret Lyttleton.

The Barristers of Toulouse in the Eighteenth Century (1740-1793). Lenard R. Berlanstein.

Bartolome de las Casas ante la historiografia mexicano. Jose Maria Muria.

The Ba'th Party: A History from Its Origins to 1966. John F. Devlin.

Battle in Bayou Country. Morris Raphael.

The Battle of the Washita: The Sheridan-Custer Indian Campaign of 1867-69. Stan Hoig.

Battles Lost and Won: Essays from "Civil War History." John T. Hubbell.

Die Bauskultur des Heroons Von Limyra. Jurgen Borchardt.

Before the Industrial Revolution: European Society and Economy 1000-1700. Carlo M. Cipolla.

Beginnings of Brazilian Oswaldo Cruz, Medical Research and Policy, 1890-1920. Nancy Stepan.

The Beginnings of Russian-American Relations, 1775-1815. Nikolai N. Bolkhovitinov.

Beginnings on Market Street: Nashville and Her Jewry 1861-1901. Fedora Small Frank.

Beiträge zur Mediävistik: Ausgewählte Zufsätze. Heinrich Fichtenau.

Beleaguered Tower: The Dilemma of Political Catholicism in Wilhelmine Germany. Ronald J. Ross.

Das Bellum Iustum des Hernán Cortés in Mexico. Eberhard Straub.

Bengal: The Nationalist Movement, 1876-1940. Leonard A. Gordon.

Bengali Women. Manisha Roy.

Benjamin Franklin and the Zealous Presbyterians. Melvin H. Buxbaum.

Bernhard Dernburg, 1865-1937: Kolonialpolitiker und Bankier im Wilhelminischen Deutschland. Werner Schiefel.

The Best of Bob Edwards. Hugh A. Dempsey, ed.

Bethany in Kansas: The History of a College. Emory Lindquist.

Better Kind of Hatchet: Law, Trade, and Diplomacy in the Cherokee Nation during the Early Years of European Contact. John Phillip Reid.

Between North and South: A Maryland Journalist Views the Civil War. Ellen Marks, ed. and Mark Norton Schatz, ed.

Between Sun and Sod: An Informal History of the Texas Panhandle. Willie Newbury Lewis.

Beyond Belief: Essays on Religion in a Post-traditional World. Robert Bellah.

Beyond the Civil War Synthesis: Political Essays of the Civil War

Era. Robert P. Swierenga, ed.

Beyond the Codices: The Nahua View of Colonial Mexico. Arthur J. O. Anderson, et al.

Beyond the Furrow: Some Keys to Successful Farming in the Twentieth Century. Hiram M. Drache.

Bharuci's Commentary on the Manusmrti. J. Duncan M. Derrett, ed.

Bibliographical History of California Anthropological Research, 1850-1917. Elizabeth Wuertele.

Bibliographie du Nepal. L. Boulnois.

A Bibliography of Cameroon. Mark W. DeLancey and Virginia H. DeLancey.

A Bibliography of Contemporary North American Indians. William Hodge.

A Bibliography of English History to 1485. Edgar B. Graves, ed.

Bibliography of Indo-English Literature: A Checklist of Works by Indian Authors in English, 1800-1966. John A. Karkala and Leena Karkala.

A Bibliography of Songsters Printed in America Before 1821. Irving Lowens.

Big City Government in India: Councilor, Administrator and Citizen in Delhi. Philip Oldenburg.

Big Story: How the American Press and Television Reported and Interpreted the Crisis of Tet 1968 in Vietnam and Washington. Peter Braestrup.

Biggest, The Smallest, the Longest, the Shortest: A Chronicle of the American Circus from Its Heartland. Dean Jensen.

Biographical Dictionary of Japanese Literature. Sen'ichi Hisamatsu.

Biographical Dictionary of the Confederacy. Jon L. Wakelyn.

Biographical Register of the Confederate Congress. Ezra J. Warner and W. Buck Yearns.

A Biographical Register of the University of Oxford, A. D. 1501-1540. A. B. Emden.

The Biography of an African Society, Rwanda, 1900-1960, Based on Forty-Eight Twandan Autobiographies. Helen Codere.

Biography of Ezra Thompson Clark. Annie Clark Tanner.

Birds of the West Coast. J. F. Lansdowne.

Bismarck. Alan Palmer.

Bismarck at the Crossroads: The Reorientation of German Foreign Policy after the Congress of Berlin, 1878-1880. Bruce Waller.

The Bitter Issue: The Right to Work Law in Arizona. Michael S. Wade.

The Black Almanac, From Involuntary Servitude (1619-1860) to the Age of Disillusionment (1964-1973). Alton Hornsby Jr.

Black America: Geographic Perspective. Robert T. Ernst, ed. and Lawrence Hugg, ed.

Black Americans and the Political System. Lucius J. Barker and Jesse J. McCorry.

Black Americans and the White Man's Burden, 1898-1903. Werner Gauer.

Black Americans in Congress. Maurice Christopher.

Black Americans in World War II. A. Russell Buchanan.

Black Ballots: Voting Rights in the South, 1944-1969. Steven F. Lawson.

Black Bondage in the North. Edgar J. McManus.

Black Death to Industrial Revolution: A Social and Economic History of England. Pauline Gregg.

Black Ethos: Northern Urban Negro Life and Thought, 1890-1930. David Gordon Nielsen.

The Black Family in Slavery & Freedom, 1750-1925. Herbert G. Gutman.

Black Image in Latin American Literature. Richard L. Jackson.

Black Images of America, 1784-1870. Leonard I. Sweet.

Black Legislators in Louisiana During Reconstruction. Charles Vincent.

Black Loyalists: The Search for a Promised Land in Nova Scotia and Sierra Leone, 1783-1870. James W. St. G. Walker.

Black Migration: Movement North, 1900-1920. Florette Henri.

Black Ohio and the Color Line, 1860-1915. David A. Gerber.

Black Power and Hand Steel: Miners and Machines on the Old Western Frontier. Otis E. Young, Jr.

Black Protest: Issues and Tactics. Robert C. Dick.

Black Religion and American Evangelicalism: White Protestants, Plantation Missions, and the Flowering of Negro Christianity, 1787-1865. Milton C. Sernett.

Black Slaves in Britain. F. O. Shyllon.

Blacks in Augusta: A Chronology 1741-1977. Lloyd P. Terrell, and Marguerite S. C. Terrell.

Blacks in Colonial Cuba, 1774-1899. Kenneth F. Kiple.

Blacks in the American Revolution. Philip S. Foner.

Blacks in the West. W. Sherman Savage.

Blind Ambition. John Dean.

Blood over Texas. The Truth about Mexico's War with the United States. Sanford H. Montaigne.

Bolsheviks Come to Power: The Revolution of 1917 in Petrograd. Alexander Rabinowitch.

Bonanza Victorian: Architecture and Society in Colorado Mining Towns. C. Eric Stoehr.

The Bonds of Womanhood: "Woman's Sphere" in New England, 1780-1835. Nancy F. Cott.

The Book of Abigail and John: Selected Letters of the Adams Family, 1762-1784. L. H. Butterfield, ed., Marc Friedlaender, ed., and Mary Jo Kline, ed.

Books of Isaac Norris (1701-1766) at Dickinson College. Marie Elena Korey.

Books That Changed the South. Robert B. Downs.

Border Wars of Texas. James T. De Shields.

Borderland in Retreat: From Spanish Louisiana to the Far Southwest. Abraham P. Nasatir.

The Bosnian Church: A New Interpretation. John V. A. Fine, Jr.

Boteslaw III Krzywousty. Karol Maleczynski.

Botschafter Paul Graf von Hatzfeldt: Nachgelassene Papiere, 1838-1901. Gerhard Ebel and Michael Behnen, ed.

Bounder from Wales: Lloyd George's Career before the First World War. Don M. Cregier.

Bouquet's March to the Ohio: The Forbes Road. Edward G. Williams, ed.

Bourgeois Democrats of Weimar Germany. Robert A. Pois.

Les Bourgeois Gentilshommes: An Essay on the Definition of Elites in Renaissance France. George Huppert.

The BP Book of Industrial Archaeology. Neil Cossons.

Brazen Overlanders of 1845. Donna M. Wojcik.

Brazil and the Great Powers, 1920-1939: The Politics of Trade Rivalry. Stanley E. Hilton.

The Brazilian Coffee Valorization of 1906: Regional Politics and Economic Dependence. Thomas H. Holloway.

Brazilian Society. T. Lynn Smith.

Bread, Politics and Political Economy in the Reign of Louis XV. S. Kaplan.

Breckinridge: Statesman, Soldier, Symbol. William C. Davis.

Brian Moore. Jeanne Flood.

Brigham Young University: The First One Hundred Years. Ernest L. Wilkinson, ed., Leonard J. Arrington, ed. and Bruce C. Hafen, ed.

Britain and America: A Comparative Economic History, 1850-1939.

Britain and the American Frontier, 1783-1815. J. Leitch Wright, Jr.

Britain and the Origins of the New Europe 1914-1918. Kenneth J. Calder.

Britain in the Nineteen Twenties. Noreen Branson.

Britain's Imperial Century, 1815-1914: A Study of Empire and Expansion. Ronald Hyam.

The British-Americans: The Loyalist Exiles in England 1774-1789. Mary Beth Norton.

British and American Abolitionists: An Episode on Transatlantic Understanding. Claire Taylor, ed.

British China Policy 1933-37; Diplomacy and Enterprise. S. L. Endicott.

British Columbia Chronicle, 1778-
1846: Adventures by Sea and
Land. G. P. V. Akrigg and
Helen Akrigg.
The British Heroic Age. Nora
Chadwick.
The British Insurance Business,
1547-1970: An Introduction and
Guide to Historical Records in
the United Kingdom. H. A. L.
Cockerell and Edwin Green.
The British Machine Tool Industry,
1850-1914. Roderick Floud.
British Monetary Policy, 1924-
1931: The Norman Conquest of
$4.86. D. E. Moggridge.
British Nationalization, 1945-1973.
R. Kelf-Cohen.
British Nitrates and Chilean Poli-
tics 1866-1896: Balmaceda and
North. Harold Blakemore.
British Policy and the Nationalist
Movement in Burma, 1917-1937.
Albert D. Moscotti.
British Policy in Southeast Europe
in the Second World War.
Elisabeth Barker.
British Policy Towards Wartime
Resistance in Yugoslavia and
Greece. Phyllis Auty, ed. and
Richard Clogg, ed.
British Slave Emancipation: The
Sugar Colonies and the Great
Experiment, 1830-1865. Wil-
liam A. Green.
British Social Democracy: A
Study in Development and Decay.
David Howell.
British Working Class Movements
and Europe, 1815-48. Henry
Weisser.
Broadsides and Bayonets: The
Propaganda of the American
Revolution. Carl Berger.
The Broken Covenant: American
Civil Religion in Time of Trial.
Robert Bellah.
Bronze Age Civilization: The
Philistines and the Danites.
Allen H. Jones.
Brothers in Arms. Lee Pennock.
Brothers of Light, Brothers of
Blood: The Penitentes of the
Southwest. Marta Weigle.
Brothers Reuther and the Story of
the UAW: A Memoir. Victor
G. Reuther.
Brunswick County, Virginia, 1720-
1975. Gay Neale.

Buddhism in Sinhalese Society, 1750-
1900. Kitsiri Malalgoda.
"Das Buch der Kostbaren Perle" von
ibn al Mugaffa°. Paul Maiberger,
ed.
Buenos Aires, Plaza to Suburb 1870-
1910. James R. Scobie.
Building a Great Library: The Cool-
idge Years at Harvard. William
Bentinck-Smith.
Building the City of God: Community
and Cooperation Among the Mor-
mons. Leonard J. Arrington, et al.
Bulgarian National Ecclesiastical Move-
ment Before the Crimean War.
Zina Markova.
The Bulgarians: From Pagan Times
to the Ottoman Conquest. D. M.
Lang.
Bulgaro-Italian Political Relations,
1922-43. Ilcho Dimitrov.
Der Bund der Industriellen. Hans-
Peter Ullman.
Bundesrepublik Deutschland und Berlin.
Berlin: Eine geographische Struk-
turanalyse der zwolf westlichen
Bezirke. Burkhard Hofmeister.
Bureaucratic Politics and Administra-
tion in Chile. Peter S. Cleaves.
Die Bürgerliche deutsch Geschichts-
schreibung der Weimarer Republik.
Hans Schleier.
Bürgerliche Intelligenz um 1800: Zur
Soziologie des deutschen Frühliber-
alismus. Hans H. Gerth.
Burnham of Chicago: Architect and
Planner. Thomas S. Hines.
Business and Sentiment in a Chinese
Market Town. John Aubrey Young.
The Business Career of Moses Tay-
lor: Merchant, Finance Capitalist,
and Industrialist. Daniel Hodas.
Business Ideologies in the Reform-
Progressive Era, 1880-1914. Al-
fred L. Thimm.
Butch Cassidy, My Brother. Lula
Parker Betenson.
Butte's Memory Book. Don James.
By the Sweat of Their Brow: Mexican
Immigrant Labor in the United
States, 1900-1940. Mark Reisler.

-C-

Caesar Baronius: Counter-Reformation
Historian. Cyriac K. Pullapilly.

Calendar of Ancient Petitions Relating to Wales.   William Rees, ed.

Calendar of London Trailbaston Trials under Commissions of 1305-1306.   R. B. Pugh, ed.

California: A Bicentennial History. David Lavender.

California: Five Centuries of Cultural Contrasts.   Julian Nava and Bob Barger.

The California Gold Rush.   Gordon V. Axon.

California Historymakers.   Alan A. Hynding.

California Indian History, A Classified and Annotated Guide to Source Materials.   Robert F. Heizer, Karen M. Nissen and Edward D. Castillo.

California of George Gordon and the 1849 Sea Voyages of His California Association: A San Francisco Pioneer Rescued from the Legend of Gertrude Atherton's First Novel.   Albert Shumate.

California: The Great Exception. Carey McWilliams.

The Call to Seriousness: The Evangelical Impact on the Victorians.   Ian Bradley.

Calligraphy on the Spanish Borderland.   Gerald P. Doyle.

Calvinismus und frazösische Monarchie im 17. Jahrhundert: Die Politische Lehre der Akademien Seden und Saumur. Hartmut Kretzer.

The Cambridge History of Africa. Richard Gray, ed.

Campaigns of the American Revolution: An Atlas of Manuscript Maps.   Douglas W. Marshall and Howard H. Peckham.

Canada.   Barry Gough.

Canada and the United States: Transnational and Transgovernmental Relations.   Annette Baker Fox, ed. , Alfred O. Hero, Jr. , ed. and Joseph S. Nye, Jr. , ed.

Canada in the North Atlantic Triangle: Two Centuries of Social Change.   John L. Finlay.

Canadian-American Relations in Wartime: From the Great War to the Cold War.   R. D. Cuff and J. L. Granatstein.

A Canadian Indian Bibliography, 1960-1970.   Thomas S. Abler, Douglas Sanders, and Sally M. Weaver.

Canadian-Soviet Relations Between the World Wars.   Aloysius Balawyder.

Canning: Politician & Statesman. Peter Dixon.

Captain Shakespear: A Portrait.   H. V. F. Winstone.

Captains of Consciousness: Advertising and the Social Roots of the Consumer Culture.   Stuart Ewen.

Captive Americans: Prisoners during the American Revolution.   Larry G. Bowman.

The Car Culture.   James J. Flink.

Carlism and Crisis in Spain, 1931-1939.   Martin Blinkhorn.

Carlos: Portrait of a Terrorist. Colin Smith.

Carrier of the Dream Wheel: Contemporary Native American Poetry. Duane Niatum, ed.

Carteggi di Bettino Ricasoli.   Sergio Camerani, ed.

Carthage Conspiracy: The Trial of the Accused Assassins of Joseph Smith.   Dallin H. Oaks and Marvin S. Hill.

Cartulary of Shrewsbury Abbey.   Una Rees, ed.

Carvalho: Artist, Photographer, Adventurer, Patriot; Portrait of a Forgotten American.   Joan Sturhahn.

Casas Grandes: A Fallen Trading Center of the Gran Chichimeca. Charles C. Di Peso.

Casiodoro de Reina: Spanish Reformer in the Sixteenth Century.   A. Gordon Kinder.

The Casper Site: A Hell Gap Bison Kill on the High Plains.   George C. Frison, ed.

Cassius Marcellus Clay: Firebrand of Freedom.   H. Edward Richardson.

Caste Association and Political Process in Gujarat: A Study of Gujarat Kshatriya Sabha.   Ghanshyam Shah.

Castlereagh.   John W. Derry.

La Catalogne du milieu de X^e à la fin du XIe siècle: Croissance et mutations d'une société.   Pierre Bonnassie.

Catalogue of Panjabi Printed Books Added to the India Office Library, 1902-1964.   Ganesh Gaur, comp.

Coastal Resource Use: Decisions on Puget Sound. Robert L. Bish, et al.

Coke of Norfolk: A Financial and Agricultural Study, 1707-1842. R. A. C. Parker.

Collected Papers, 1912-1973. R. L. Turner.

Collected Poems. Austin Clarke.

Collected Poems, 1936-1976. Robert Francis.

A Collection of Documents on the Slave Trade of Eastern Africa. R. W. Beachey.

Collection of Ethnographical Articles on the California Indians. Robert F. Heizer, ed.

Colonel William Fleming of Botetcourt, 1728-1795. Edmund P. Goodwin.

Colonial and Revolutionary Morris County. Theodore Thayer.

Colonial Development: An Econometric Study. Thomas B. Birnberg and Stephen A. Resnick.

Colonial Georgia: A History. Kenneth Coleman.

Colonial New England: A Historical Geography. Douglas R. Manis.

Colonial New York. Michael Kammen.

A Colonial Pastor: Jonathan Edwards the Younger, 1745-1801. Robert L. Ferm.

Colonial Pennsylvania: A History. Joseph E. Illick.

The Colonial Physician & Other Essays. Whitfield J. Bell, Jr.

Colonial Records of the State of Georgia: Original Papers of Governors Reynolds, Ellis, Wright, and Others, 1757-1763. Kenneth Coleman, ed. and Milton Ready, ed.

Colonial Rhode Island: A History. Sydney V. James.

Colonial Rule and the Kamba: Social Change in the Kenya Highlands 1889-1939. J. Forbes Munro.

Colonial Russian America: Kyrill T. Khlebnikov's Reports, 1817-1832. Basil Dmytryshyn, ed., and E. A. P. Crownhart-Vaughn, ed.

Colonial Self-Government: The

British Experience 1759-1856. John Manning Ward.

Colonial South Carolina Scene: Contemporary Views, 1697-1774. H. Roy Merrens, ed.

Colonialism in Africa 1870-1960. Peter Guifnan, ed. and L. H. Gann, ed.

The Coloradans. Robert G. Athearn.

Colorado: A Bicentennial History. Marshall Sprague.

Colorado: A History of the Centennial State. Carl Abbott.

Colorado Mining: A Photographic History. Duane A. Smith.

Coloured Views on the Liverpool and Manchester Railway. T. T. Bury.

Comanche Days. Albert S. Gilles, tr.

Comedy and America: The Lost World of Washington Irving. Martin Roth.

Comical Spirit of Seventy-Six: The Humor of Francis Hopkinson. Paul M. Zall, ed.

The Coming of the Book: The Impact of Printing, 1450-1800. L. Febvre and H. J. Martin.

Coming Visible: Women in European History. Renate Bridenthal, ed.

Commerce exterieur et developpement economique de l'Europe au XIXe siecle. Paul Bairoch.

The Committee of One Million: "China Lobby" and Politics, 1953-1971. Stanley D. Bachrack.

Common Soldier of the Civil War. Bell I. Wiley.

Communism in Indochina: New Perspectives. Joseph J. Zasloff, ed. and MacAlister Brown, ed.

Communism in Italy and France. Donald L. M. Blackmer, ed. and Sidney Tarrow, ed.

Communist Insurrection in Malaya 1948-60. Anthony Short.

The Communist Movement: From Comintern to Cominform. Fernando Claudin.

The Communist Party of Poland. M. K. Dziewanowski.

Le Communità di valle in epoca signorile. Irma Valetti Bonini.

Community and Polity: The Organizational Dynamics of American Jewry. Daniel J. Elazar.

Community and Revolution in Modern Vietnam. Alexander B. Woodside.

Competition and Coercion: Blacks in

Copper Spike. Lone E. Janson.

Cordon sanitaire or Barriere de l'Est? The Emergence of the New French Eastern European Alliance Policy, 1917-1919. Kalervo Hovi.

Corinth VII, Part II, Archaic Pottery and the Anaploga Well. D. A. Amyx and Patricia Lawrence.

Corinth VII, Part III, Corinthian Hellenistic Pottery. G. Roger Edwards.

Corn Among the Indians of the Upper Missouri. George F. Will and George E. Hyde.

Cornelius Howatt: Superstar! Harry Baglole, ed. and David Weale, ed.

Corporation and the Indian: Tribal Sovereignty and Industrial Civilization in Indian Territory, 1865-1907. H. Craig Miner.

Corpus of Maya Hieroglyphic Inscriptions. Ian Graham.

Corpus Vasorum Antiquorum, Italy LV, Tarquinia, Museo Archeologico Nazionale III. Fulvio Canciani.

Corpus Vasorum Antiquorum, Poland 9, Warsaw, National Museum 6. Marie-Louise Bernhard.

Corpus Vasorum Antiquorum, U. S. A. 16. Mary B. Moore and Dietrich von Bothmer.

Correspondance à l'arrivée en provenance de la Louisiane. Marie-Antoinette Menier, et al.

Correspondence of Daniel O'Connell. Maurice R. O'Connell, ed.

Correspondence of G. E. Morrison. G. E. Morrison.

The Correspondence of G. E. Morrison, Volume 1: 1895-1912. Lo Hui-min, ed.

Correspondence of James K. Polk: Vol. 3, 1835-1836. James K. Polk.

The Correspondence of John Locke. John Locke.

The Correspondence of W. E. B. Du Bois. Herbert Aptheker, ed.

The Correspondence of W. E. B. DuBois. W. E. B. DuBois.

The Correspondence of William

Nelson as Acting Governor of Virginia, 1770-1771. John C. Van Horne.

The Cost of War, 1914-1919: British Economic War Aims and the Origins of Reparation. Robert E. Bunselmeyer.

Co-Traditions and Convergent Trends in Prehistoric California. Bert A. Gerow.

Count Hans Azel von Fersen: Aristocrat in the Age of Revolution. H. Arnold Barton.

Counter Reformation, 1559-1610. Marvin R. O'Connell.

The Country Life Movement in America, 1900-1920. William L. Bowers.

County and Court: Government and Politics in Norfolk, 1558-1603. A. Hassell Smith.

A County Community at Peace and War: Sussex 1600-1660. A. Fletcher.

County Court Records of Accomach-Northampton, Virginia, 1640-1645. Susie M. Ames, ed.

The Courts of Europe: Politics, Patronage and Royalty 1400-1800. A. G. Dickens, ed.

Covenant with Death: The Constitution, Law and Equality in the Civil War Era. Philip S. Paludan.

Cowboy. Ron Tyler.

Cowboy Life: Reconstructing an American Myth. William W. Savage, Jr.

Cradle of the East: An Inquiry into the Indigenous Origins of Techniques and Ideas of Neolithic and Early Historic China, 5000-1000 B. C. Ho Ping-Ti.

Crazy Horse and Custer: The Parallel Lives of Two American Warriors. Stephen E. Ambrose.

The Creation of Elizabethville, 1910-1940. Bruce Fetter.

Crime and Law Enforcement in the Colony of New York, 1691-1776. Douglas Greenberg.

Criminal Justice in Eighteenth Century Mexico. A Study of the Tribunal of the Acordada. C. M. MacLachlan.

Crise du féodalisme: Economie rurale et démographie en Normandie orientale du début du 14ᵉ siècle au milieu du 16ᵉ diècle. Guy Bois.

The Crises of France's East Central

European Diplomacy, 1933-1938. Anthony Tihamer Komjathy.

Crisis and Conflict in Han China, 104 B. C. to A. D. 9. Michael Loewe.

Crisis and Controversy: Essays in Honour of A. J. P. Taylor. Alan Sked and Chris Cook, ed.

The Crisis of Conservative Virginia: The Byrd Organization and the Politics of Massive Resistance. James W. Ely, Jr.

The Crisis of Czechoslovak Agriculture, 1928-1934. Vlastislav Lacina.

Cristero Rebellion: The Mexican People Between Church and State, 1926-1929. Jean A. Meyer.

La Cristiada. Jean Meyer.

Critical Guide to the Kwangtung Provincial Archives, Deposited at the Public Record Office of London. David Pong.

Critical Phase in Tanzania, 1945-1968: Nyerere and the Emergence of a Socialist Strategy. Cranford Pratt.

Cromwellian Ireland: English Government and Reform in Ireland, 1649-1660. T. C. Barnard.

Le "Cronache Sociali" di Dossetti, 1947-1951: Geografia di un movimento di opinione. Paolo Pombeni.

Crooked Paths: Reflections on Socialism, Conservatism, and the Welfare State. Peter Clecak.

Crooked Road: The Story of the Alaska Highway. David A. Remley.

Crown and Charter: The Early Years of the British South Africa Company. John S. Galgraith.

The Crucible of Europe: The Ninth and Tenth Centuries in European History. Geoffrey Barraclough.

Crusader Manuscript Illumination at Saint-Jean D'Acre, 1275-1291. Jaroslav Folda.

Crying of a Vision: A Rosebud Sioux Trilogy, 1886-1976. John A. Anderson, Eugene Buechel, and Don Doll.

Crystals and Compounds: Molecular Structure and Composition in Nineteenth Century French Science. Seymour H. Mauskopf.

La Cuestión religiosa en las Cortes Constituyentes de la II República Española. Fernando de Meer.

The Cult of Tara: Magic and Ritual in Tibet. Stephan Beyer.

La Cultura del barroco: Analisis de Una Estructura Historica. José Antonio Maravall.

Cultural Aspects of the Italian Renaissance: Essays in Honour of Paul Oskar Kristeller. Cecil H. Clough, ed.

Cultural Change and Continuity: Essays in Honor of James Bennett Griffin. Charles E. Cleland, ed.

A Cultural History of India. A. L. Basham, ed.

Cultural History of the American Revolution: Painting, Music, Literature, and the Theatre in the Colonies and the United States from the Treaty of Paris to the Inauguration of George Washington. Kenneth Silverman.

Cultural Regions of the United States. Raymond D. Gastil.

Cultural and Political Economy in Western Sicily. Jane Schneider and Peter Schneider.

Culture and the City: Cultural Philanthropy in Chicago from the 1880's to 1917. Helen Lefkowitz Horowitz.

Culture Clash: Immigrants and Reformers, 1880-1920. Paul McBride.

Curacao and Guzman Blanco. C. Ch. Goslinga.

The Currency of the American Colonies, 1700-1764: A Study in Colonial Finance and Imperial Relations. Leslie V. Brock.

Custer and the Epic of Defeat. Bruce A. Rosenberg.

Custer's Last Stand: The Anatomy of an American Myth. Brian W. Dippie.

-D-

Daily Life in Revolutionary China.
Maria Antonietta Macciocchi.
The Damnable Question: A Study
in Anglo-Irish Relations.
George Dangerfield.
The Damned and the Beautiful:
American Youth in the 1920's.
Paula S. Fass.
Damned Englishman: A Study of
Erskine Childers (1870-1922).
Tom Cox.
Dance in India: An Annotated
Guide to Source Materials.
Judy Van Zile.
Dangerous Class: Crime and
Poverty in Columbus, Ohio,
1860-1885. Eric H. Monkkonen.
Daniel Smith, Frontier Statesman.
Walter T. Surham.
Dans la tourmente: Les relations
hungaro-roumaines de 1940 à
1945. Daniel Csatári.
Dark Companions: The African
Contribution to the European
Exploration of East Africa.
Donald Simpson.
Darker Vision of the Renaissance:
Beyond the Fields of Reason.
Robert S. Kinsman, ed.
Darwin in America: The Intellec-
tual Response. Cynthia Eagle
Russett.
David Jayne Hill and the Problem
of World Peace. Aubrey Park-
man.
David Lloyd George and the
British Labour Movement:
Peace and War. Chris Wrigley.
Days at the Factories or the Manu-
facturing Industry of Britain
Described. G. Dodd.
The Deadly Innocents: Portraits
of Children Who Kill. Muriel
Gardiner.
Dean Acheson: The State Depart-
ment Years. David S. McLel-
lan.
Death and the Afterlife in Pre-
Columbian America. Elizabeth
P. Benson, ed.
Death, Disease and Famine in
Pre-Industrial England. Leslie
Clarkson.
Death in the American Experience.
Arien Mack, ed.

The Death of Stalin. Georges Bortoli.
Death Song, The Last of the Indian
Wars. John Edward Weems.
Deceleration in the Eighteenth Century
British Economy. A. J. Little.
December's Child: A Book of Chumash
Oral Narratives. Thomas C. Black-
burn, ed.
Deciphering the Maya Script. David
Hamiston Kelley.
The Decision to Relocate the Japanese
Americans. Roger Daniels.
Declaring War in the Roman Republic
in the Period of Trans-marine Ex-
pansion. J. W. Rich.
Decorative and Symbolic Uses of
Vertebrate Fossils. Kenneth P.
Oakley.
Defense and the League of Nations.
Knud Larsen.
Delaware: A Bicentennial History.
Carol E. Hoffecker.
Deliver Us from Evil: An Interpreta-
tion of American Prohibition.
Norman H. Clark.
Democracy and Organisation in the
Chinese Industrial Enterprise, 1948-
1953. William Brugger.
Democracy Without Consensus: Com-
munalism and Political Stability in
Malaysia. Karl Von Vorys.
Democratic Englightenment. Donald
H. Meyer.
The Democratic Left in Exile: The
Antidictatorial Struggle in the
Caribbean, 1945-1959. Charles D.
Ameringer.
Democratic Opposition to the Lincoln
Administration in Indiana. G. R.
Tredway.
The Democratic Party and the Negro:
Northern and National Politics,
1868-92. Lawrence Grossman.
Democratic Promise: The Populist
Moment in America. Lawrence
Goodwyn.
The Democrats: The Years Since
FDR. Herbert S. Parmet.
The Demographic Explosion: The
Latin American Experience.
Benjamin Viel.
A Demographic Path to Modernity:
Patterns of Early Transition in the
Philippines. Wilhelm Flieger, ed.
and Peter C. Smith, ed.
Demotic Ostraca in the National Muse-
um of Antiquities at Leiden. M. A.
A. Nurel-Din.

Dependencia y liberación en la Cultura latino-americana. Leopoldo Zea.

Desenvolvimento e Margenalidade: Um Estudo de Caso. Maria Célia Pinheiro Machado.

Desert and the Dream: A Study of Welsh Colonization in Churbut, 1865-1915. Glyn Williams.

Desert Documentary: The Spanish Years, 1767-1821. Kieran McCarty.

Desert River Crossing: Historic Lee's Ferry on the Colorado River. W. L. Rusho and C. Gregory Crampton.

Desideratum in Washington: The Intellectual Community in the Capital City, 1870-1900. J. Kirkpatrick Flack.

Desperate Diplomacy: William H. Seward's Foreign Policy, 1861. Norman B. Ferris.

Detailed Reports on the Salzburger Emigrants Who Settled in America. Samuel Urlsperger, ed.

Detente and the Democratic Movement in the USSR. Frederick C. Barghoorn.

La dette des collectivités publiques de Marseille au SVIIIe siecle. Marcel Courdurié.

Das Deutsch Ausland-Institut in Stuttgart, 1917-1945. Ernst Ritter.

Die Deutsch Sozialdemokratie, 1890-1933. Georg Fülberth and Jürgen Harrer.

Der Deutsche Bauernkrieg, 1524-1526. H. -U. Wehler.

Die Deutschen Freihandler und der volkswirtschaftliche Kongress, 1858 bis 1885. Volker Hentschel.

Deutschland Im Spaten Mittelalter ('Deutsche Geschicte'). Joachim Leuschner.

The Development of English Glassmaking 1560-1640. E. S. Godfrey.

The Development of Japanese Business, 1600-1973. Johannes Hirschmeier and Tsunehiko Yui.

Development of Realism in the Fiction Tsubouchi Shoyo. Marleight Grayer Ryan.

Deviance and Social Control in Chinese Society. Amy A. Wilson, Sidney L. Greenblatt, and Richard W. Wilson.

Devocão e Escravidão. A Irmandade de Nossa Senhora do Rosário dos Pretos no Distrito Diamantino no Século XVIII. Julita Scarano.

D'Holbach's Coterie: An Enlightenment in Paris. Alan Charles Kors.

Dianying: An Account of Films and the Film Audience in China. Jay Leyda.

The Diaries and Papers of Sir Edward Dering, 2nd Baronet, 1644-1684. Edward Dering.

The Diaries of a Cabinet Minister. Richard Crossman.

The Diaries of George Washington. George Washington.

Diary of a Chilean Concentration Camp. Herman Valdes.

Diary of a Dead Man. Jean P. Roy.

Diary of Charles Francis Adams. Marc Friedlaender, ed. and L. H. Butterfield, ed.

The Diary of Edmund Ruffin. Edmund Ruffin.

Diary of Ralph Josselin, 1616-1683. Alan MacFarlane, ed.

A Dictionary of Japanese Artists: Painting, Sculpture, Ceramics, Prints, Lacquer. Laurance P. Roberts.

Dictionary of National Biography. S. P. Sen, ed.

Did Monetary Forces Cause the Great Depression? Peter Temin.

Dilthey, Philosopher of the Human Studies. Rudolf A. Makkreel.

Dimensions of British Radicalism: The Case of Ireland, 1874-95. Thomas William Heyck.

Dimensions of Detective Fiction. Larry N. Landrum, Pat Browne, and Ray B. Browne, ed.

Dimity Convictions: The American Woman in the Nineteenth Century. Barbara Welter.

Dinosaurs of the Southwest. Ronald Paul Ratkevich.

Un diocèse breton au debut du XIXe siecle. Claude Langlois.

Die dionysischen Sarkophage. Friedrich Matz.

Diplomacy and Enterprise: British China Policy 1933-1937. Stephen Lyon Endicott.

Diplomacy of Constraint: Canada, the Korean War, and the United States. Denis Stairs.

Diplomacy on the Indiana-Ohio Frontier, 1783-1791. Joyce G. Williams and Jill E. Farrelly.

Diplomat of the Americas: A Biography of William I. Buchanan (1852-1909). Harold F. Peterson.

Diplomats and Bureaucrats. Paul Gordon Lauren.

Diplomats in Crisis: United States-Chinese-Japanese Relations, 1919-1941. Richard Dean Burns, ed. and Edward M. Bennett, ed.

Directory of Newspaper Libraries in the U. S. and Canada. Geace D. Parch, ed.

The Discontented Society: Interpretations of Twentieth Century American Protest. LeRoy Ashby, ed. and Bruce M. Stave, ed.

Discourse on Universal History. Jacques-Benique Bossuet.

Discovery of South America and the Andalusian Voyages. Louis-Andre Vigneras.

Disjoined Partners: Austria and Germany Since 1815. Peter J. Katzenstein.

Disraeli. Richard W. Davis.

The Disruption of the Pennsylvania Democracy, 1848-1860. John F. Coleman.

The Distorted Image: German Jewish Perceptions of Germans and Germany 1918-1935. Sidney M. Bolkosky.

District of Columbia: A Bicentennial History. David L. Lewis.

Dives and Pauper. Priscilla Heath Barnum, ed.

A Divided Society: Tasmania During World War I. Marilyn Lake.

The Divine Hierarchy: Popular Hinduism in Central India. Lawrence A. Babb.

"Dr. Bullie's" Notes. James Holmes.

Documentary History of Slavery in North America. Willie Lee Rose.

Documentary History of the First Federal Congress of the United States of America, March 4, 1789-March 3, 1791. Linda Grant De Pauw, Charlene Bangs Bickford, and La Vonne Siegel Hauptman, ed.

Documentary History of the First Federal Elections, 1788-1790. Merrill Jensen and Robert A. Becker, ed.

A Documentary History of the Indiana Decade of the Harmony Society, 1814-1824: Volume I: 1814-1819. Karl J. R. Arndt, ed.

Documentary History of the Ratification of the Constitution. Merrill Jensen, ed.

Documentos relativos a la independencia de norteamérica existentes en archivos españoles. Pilar Leon Tello.

Documents from the Harvard University Archives, 1638-1750. Robert W. Lovett, ed.

Documents of the American Revolution, 1770-1783. E. K. G. Davies, ed.

Documents of United States Indian Policy. Francis Paul Prucha, ed.

Documents on British Foreign Policy, 1919-1939. Medlicott, W. N. , ed.

Dogma, Depression, and the New Deal: The Debate of Political Leaders Over Economic Recovery. Theodore Rosenof.

Dokumnty Vneshney Politiki USSR, XIX and XX, 1936, 1937. A. Gromyko, chm. of editing Commission.

Domestic Revolution: The Modernisation of Household Service in England and France, 1820-1920. Theresa M. McBride.

Domestic Slavery in West Africa, with Particular Reference to the Sierra Leone Protectorate, 1896-1927. John Grace.

Donoso Cortés: Utopian Romanticist and Political Realist. John T. Graham.

Dissiers sur le commerce français en Méditerranée orientale au XVIIIe siècle. Jean-Pierre Filippini, et al, ed.

Dostoevsky: The Seeds of Revolt, 1821-1849. Joseph Frank.

Doubling and Incest, Repetition and Revenge: A Speculative Reading of Faulkner. John T. Irwin.

The Downfall of the Anti-Semitic Political Parties in Imperial Germany. Richard S. Levy.

Dracula: A Biography of Vlad the Impaler. Radu Florescu and Raymond T. McNally.

Dragons of Eden: Speculations on the

Evolution of Human Intelligence. Carl Sagan.

Drama & Conflict: The Texas Saga of 1776. Robert S. Weddle and Robert H. Thonhoff.

Drama of W. B. Yeats: Irish Myth and the Japanese No. Richard Taylor.

Le Drame de Byzance: Idéal et échec d'une société chrétienne. Alain Ducellier.

The Dream and the Destiny. Alexander Cordell.

Dream of Lhasa: The Life of Nikolay Przhevalsky (1839-88), Explorer of Central Asia. Donald Rayfield.

Dreams and Reality: Forty-Five Years of Diplomatic Life. Alexis ad. Kyrou.

Drei Volksdemokratien: Ein Konzept kommunistischer Machtstabilisierung und seine Verwirklichung in Polen, der Tschechoslowakei und der Swojetischen Besatzungszone Deutschlands, 1944-1948. Wolfgang Diepenthal.

Drive to Industrial Maturity: The U.S. Economy, 1860-1914. Harold G. Vatter.

Duel Between the First Ironclads. William C. Davis.

Duels in Virginia and Nearby Bladensburg. Clara S. McCarty.

The Duke of Newcastle. Reed Browning.

The Dukes of Durham, 1865-1929. Robert F. Durden.

The Dutch in America, 1609-1974. Gerald F. DeJong.

The Dynamics of Change in a Slave Society: A Sociopolitical History of the Free Coloreds of Jamaica, 1800-1865. Mavis Christin Campbell.

Dyrus E. Dallin: Let Justice Be Done. Rell G. Francis.

-E-

Eagle and Sword: The Federalists and the Creation of the Military Establishment in America, 1783-1802. Richard H. Kohn.

Early Arizona: Prehistory to Civil War. Jay J. Wagoner.

Early Chinese Civilization: Anthropological Perspectives. K. C. Chang.

The Early Greeks. R. J. Hopper.

Early History of the Akan States of Ghana. E. L. R. Meyerowitz.

The Early Life of Abraham Lincoln. Ida M. Tarbell.

Early Medieval History. J. M. Wallace-Hadrill.

Early Ming Government: The Evolution of Dual Capitals. Edward L. Farmer.

The Early Paper Money of America. Eric P. Newman.

Early Russian Principalities in the Tenth Through the Thirteenth Centuries. L. G. Beskrovnyi, et al, ed.

Early Utah Furniture. Connie Morningstar.

Early Victorian Government, 1830-1870. Oliver MacDonagh.

Early Years of the Republic from the End of the Revolution to the First Administration of Washington (1783-1793). Herbert Aptheker.

Earth Magic. Francis Hitching.

East Africa and the Orient: Cultural Syntheses in Pre-Colonial Times. H. Neville Chittick and Robert I. Rotberg, ed.

East Central and Southeast Europe: A Handbook of Library and Archival Resources in North America. Paul L. Horecky and David E. Kraus.

East India Fortunes: The British in Bengal in the Eighteenth Century. P. J. Marshall.

Eating in America, A History. Waverley Root and Richard de Rochemont.

Ebenezer Cooke: The Sot-Weed Canon. Edward H. Cohen.

Ecclesiastical Administration in Medieval England: The Anglo-Saxons to the Reformation. Robert E. Rodes, Jr.

Eclipse of an Aristocracy: An Investigation of the Ruling Elites of the City of Cordoba. Juan Carlos Agulla.

Ecology in Ancient Civilizations. J. Donald Mughes.

Economia E Politica Nell'itatia Liberale (1890-1915). Giuseppe Are.

Economic Change in Precolonial Africa. Phillip D. Curtin.

The Economic Growth of Seven-
teenth-Century New England: A
Measurement of Regional Income. Terry Lee Anderson.

An Economic History of Kenya and
Uganda 1800-1970. R. M. A.
Van Zwanenberg.

Economic History of the Jews.
Salo W. Baron, et al.

Economic History of the Jews.
Nachum Gross, ed.

Economic Modernisation of France,
1730-1880. Roger Price.

Economic Nationalism in Latin
America: The Quest for Eco-
nomic Independence. Shoshana
B. Fancer.

An Economic Theory of the Feudal
System: Towards a Model of the
Polish Economy 1500-1800.
Witold Kula.

Economics of the Euro-Currency
System. George W. McKenzie.

Economics of Invention and Innova-
tion, with a Case Study of the
Development of the Hovercraft.
Paul S. Johnson.

Economy of Europe in an Age of
Crisis, 1600-1750. Jan de
Vries.

The Economy of the Roman Empire. Richard Duncan-Jones.

Edmund Randolph: A Biography.
John J. Reardon.

Edouard Thouvenel et la diplomatie
du Second Empire. Lynn M.
Case.

La educación como conquista:
Empresa franciscana en Mexico.
José María Kobayashi.

Education and Politics at Harvard.
Seymour Martin Lipset and
David Riesman.

Education for Freedom: A History
of Lincoln University, Pennsylvania. Horace Mann Bond.

Education in France, 1848-1870.
R. D. Anderson.

Education in the United States: An
Interpretive History. Robert L.
Church and Michael W. Sedlak.

Education in the West of England,
1066-1548. Nicholas Orme.

Education, Manpower, and Development. Muhammad Shamsul Hug.

Education of a Public Man: My
Life and Politics. Hubert H.
Humphrey.

Education, Race and Employment in
Rhodesia. M. W. Murphree, ed.

Education, Society and Development:
New Perspectives from Kenya. David Court and Dharam P. Ghai, ed.

Edward Hyde, Earl of Clarendon.
Hugh Trevor-Roper.

Edward Kennedy and the Camelot
Legacy. James MacGregor Burnes.

Edward Sheriff Curtis: Visions of a
Vanishing Race. Florence Curtis
Graybill and Victor Boesen.

Edwardians: The Remaking of British
Society. Paul Thompson.

Eighteenth-Century Florida and the
Caribbean. Samuel Proctor, ed.

Eighteenth-Century Florida: Life on
the Frontier. Samuel Proctor, ed.

The Eighteenth Century, 1688-1815.
Paul Langford.

Einfuhrung in die Marxsche Theorie
der wirtschaftliche Entwicklung.
Eduard Marz.

Elbridge Gerry: Founding Father
and Republican Statesman. George
Athan Billias.

The Elder Pitt, Earl of Chatham.
Stanley Ayling.

Electoral Participation in a South
Indian Context. David J. Elkins.

Electric Railways of Minnesota.
Russell L. Olson.

The Elizabethan Conquest of Ireland:
A Pattern Established, 1565-76.
Nicholas P. Canny.

An Elizabethan in 1582: The Diary of
Richard Madox, Fellow of All Souls.
E. S. Donno, ed.

Elizabethan Popish Recusancy in the
Inns of the Court. G. de C.
Parmiter.

The Emancipation of Angelina Grimke.
Katherine DuPre Lumpkin.

Emancipation und Antisemitismus:
Studien zur "Jedenfrage" zer
bürgerlichen Gesellschaft.
Reinhard Rürup.

Embassy at War: An Account of the
Early Weeks of the Korean War
and U. S. Relations with South
Korean President Syngman Rhee.
Harold Joyce Noble.

Emblem and Expression: Meaning in
English Art of the Eighteenth Century. Ronald Paulson.

Emergence of a City in the Modern
South: Pensacola 1900-1945.
James R. McGovern.

Equatorial Africa. Joseph C. Miller.

L'équilibre européen de la fin du XVe a là fin du XVIIIe siècle. Georges Livet.

The Equity Side of the Exchequer: Its Jurisdiction, Administration, Procedures and Records. W. H. Bryson.

Era of the American Revolution. Edward C. Papenfuse et al.

Eresia e Riforma nell'Italia del Cinquecento. Albano Biondi, et al.

Erzherzog Franz Ferdinand Studien. Robert A. Kann.

Eskimos of Bering Strait, 1650-1898. Dorothy Jean Ray.

Essays in African Iconology. Daniel F. McCall and Edna G. Bay, ed.

Essays in Canadian Working Class History. Gregory S. Kealey and Peter Warrian, eds.

Essays in Nineteenth Century Economic History: The Old Northwest. David C. Klingman and Richard K. Vedder.

Essays in Population History: Mexico and the Caribbean. Sherburne F. Cook and Woodrow Borah.

Essays on Adam Smith. Andrew S. Skinner, ed. and Thomas Wilson, ed.

Essays on John Maynard Keynes. Milo Keynes, ed.

Essays on Medieval Agriculture and General Problems of the Medieval Economy. M. M. Postan.

Essays on South India. Burton Stein, ed.

Essays on the American West, 1974-1975. Thomas G. Alexander.

Essays on the History of Communism in Britain. Michael Woodhouse and Brian Pearce.

Essays on Walter Prescott Webb. Kenneth Philp, ed. and Elliot West, ed.

Essential Talmud. Adin Steinsaltz.

Estado Moderno y Mentalidad Social. José Antonio Maravall.

Estudios de historia del pensamiento espanol. José Antonio Maravall.

Estudios de Teme Mexicano. Juan A. Ortega Y Medina.

Estudios sobre la hacienda colonial en Mexico. Ursula Ewald.

Estudios sobre política indigenista española en América. Seminaro De Historia De América.

Estudios sôbre o Brasil Contemporâneo. Luiz Pereira.

Ethnic and Social Stratification in Peninsular Malaysia. Charles Hirschman.

Ethnic Groups of Insular Southeast Asia. Frank M. Lebar, ed.

Ethnic Southerners. George Brown Tindall.

Etruscan Cities. Francesca Boitani, Maria Cataldi, and Marinella Pasquinucci.

Etruscan Dress. Larissa Bonfante.

Etruscans: Their Art and Civilization. Emeline Hill Richardson.

Etudes d'économie médiévale. Maurice Lombard.

Etudes sur Robespierre (1758-1794). Albert Mathiez.

Eugene Register-Guard: A Citizen of Its Community. Warren C. Price.

Eugene V. Debs. Harold W. Currie.

Europe in the Era of Social Transformation: 1700-Present. Vincent J. Knapp.

The Europe Communities: The Social Policy of the First Phase. Doreen Collins.

European Historical Statistics 1750-1970. B. R. Mitchell.

European Imperialism and the Partition of Africa. E. F. Penrose, ed.

European Peasants and Their Markets: Essays in Agrarian Economic History. William N. Parker and Eric L. Jones, ed.

European Political Facts 1918-73. Chris Cook and John Paxton.

European Witch Trials: Their Foundations in Popular and Learned Culture. Richard Kieckhefer.

The Europecentric Historiography of Russia, An Analysis of the Contribution by Russian Emigre Historians in the U. S. A., 1925-1955 Concerning 19th Century Russian History. Elizabeth Beyerly.

Everyday Life in the Roman Empire. Joan Liversidge.

Everything in Its Path: Destruction of Community in the Buggalo Creek Flood. Kai T. Erikson.

Argentina. Ezequiel
Galdo.

Farming in Prehistory. Barbara
Bender.

Fat Mutton and Liberty of Conscience: Society in Rhode Island. Carl Bridenbaugh.

Father Lacombe. James G.
MacGregor.

Father of Texas Geology: Robert
T. Hill. Nancy Alexander.

Fatherland or Promised Land:
The Dilemma of the German
Jew, 1893-1914. Jehuda
Reinharz.

Fathers and Children, Andrew
Jackson and the Subjugation of
the American Indian. Michael
Paul Rogin.

The Fathers of the Towns: Leader-
ship and Community Structure in
Eighteenth-Century New England.
Edward M. Cook, Jr.

Faulkner: Fifty Years After the
Marble Faun. George H. Wolfe,
ed.

Faulkner's Heroic Design: The
Yoknapatawpha Novels. Lynn
Gartrell Levins.

The Feasibility of Fertility
Planning. T. S. Epstein and
D. Jackson.

A Feast of Snakes. Harry Crews.

Federalism e unità nell'azione di
Enrico Cernuschi (1848-1851).
Giuseppe Monsagrati.

The Female Hero in Folklore and
Legend. Tristram Potter
Coffin.

The Feminization of American
Culture. Ann Douglas.

Femmes, Greniers et Capitaux.
Claude Meillassoux.

Los Ferrocariles briticos y la
U. C. R. , 1916-1930. Paul B.
Goodwin.

Festivals in Classical China:
New Year and Other Annual
Observances During the Han
Dynasty, 206 B. C. -A. D. 220.
Derk Bodde.

Fetiches sans fetichisme. Jean
Pouillon.

Feudalism, Capitalism and
Beyond. Eugene Kamenka,
ed. and R. S. Neale, ed.

Die feudalmonarchien: Politische
und wirtschaftlichsoziale

Faktoren ihrer Entwicklund und
Funktionsweise. Hans Kammler.

Fibeln in Thessalien. Klaus Kilian.

Fields of the Tzotzil: The Ecological
Bases of Tradition in Highland
Chiapas. George A. Collier.

Figure in the Landscape: Poetry,
Painting, and Gardening During
the Eighteenth Century. John
Dixon Hunt.

Figures of Capable Imagination.
Harold Bloom.

Filming of the West. Jon Tuska.

Financing Anglo-American Trade.
Edwin J. Perkins.

Fine California Views: The Photography of A. W. Ericson. Peter E.
Palmquist.

Finland and Russia, 1808-1920: From
Autonomy to Independence. D. G.
Kirby, ed.

Finnish Dilemma: Neutrality in the
Shadow of Power. George Maude.

Finnish Experience in the Western
Great Lakes Region: New Perspec-
tives. Michael G. Karni, ed. and
Matti E. Kaups, ed. and Douglas
J. Ollila, Jr. , ed.

Fire and the Spirits: Cherokee Law
from Clan to Court. Rennard
Strickland.

Firewater Myths: North American
Indian Drinking and Alcohol Addic-
tion. Joy Leland.

The First Amendment and the Future
of American Democracy. Walter
Berns.

First Bishop of Sonora: Antonio de
los Reyes. Albert Stagg.

First Constitution of the State of
Louisiana. Cecil Morgan, comp.

The First Duce: D'Annunzio at Fiume.
Michael A. Ledeen.

First Emperor of China: The Politics
of Historiography. Li Yu-ning, ed.

The First Hundred Years of Wesleyan
College. Samuel Luttrell Akers.

First Images of America: The Impact
of the New World on the Old.
Fredi Chiapelli, ed.

First Indo-China War: French and
American Policy 1945-1954. R. E.
M. Irving.

The First Kuwait Oil Concession
Agreement: A Record of Negotia-
tions, 1911-34. Archibald H. T.
Chisholm.

First Majority--Last Minority: The

Foundation Sires of the American Quarter Horse. Robert M. Denhardt.

Foundations of Indo-Soviet Relations: A Study of Non-Official Attitudes and Contacts 1917-1947. Nirmala Joshi.

The Foundations of Newton's Alchemy or, "The Hunting of the Greene Lyon." Betty Jo Teeter Dobbs.

Four Centuries of Southern Indians. Charles M. Hudson.

Four Fine Gentlemen. Hester Chapman.

Four Makers of the American Mind: Emerson, Thoreau, Whitman, and Melville. Robert E. Spiller et al.

Four Poets and the Emotive Imagination. George S. Lensing and Ronald Moran.

Fox of the North: The Life of Kutuzov--General of War and Peace. Roger Parkinson.

Fran fred till krig: De finansiella problemen kring krigsutbrottet or 1700. James Cavallie.

Les Francais Et L'Armée Sous Louis XIV: D'Après Les Mémoires Des Intendants, 1687-1689. André Corvisier.

France and Europe in 1848: A Study in French Foreign Affairs in Time of Crisis. Lawrence C. Jennings.

France and Sherwood Anderson: "Paris Notebook, 1921." Michael Fanning, ed.

La France et l'Indépendance américaine: Le livre du bicentenaire de l'Indépendance. René de la Croix.

La France et l'Italie pendant la primere guerre mondiale. Grenoble University.

Francesco Guicciardini. Peter E. Bondanella.

Francisco Bilbao. Revolucionario de América. Alberto J. Varona.

Francogallia. Francois Hotmann.

François de Wendel en Republique: L'argent et le pouvoir, 1914-1940. Jean-Noël Jeanneney.

Frank Murphy: The Detroit Years. Sidney Fine.

Franklin. David Freeman Hawke.

Frans Blom, Maya Explorer. Robert L. Brunhouse.

Frauenleitbild und Frauenarbeit in Österreich von ausgehenden 19. Jahrhundert bis zum Zweiten Weltkrieg. Edith Rigler.

Fred Rosenstock: A Legend in Books & Art. Donald E. Bower.

Frederick the Great of Prussia: Absolutism and Administration. Walther Hubatsch.

The Free Soldiers, Third Party Politics, 1848-54. Frederick J. Blue.

Freebooters Must Die! The Life and Death of William Walker, the Most Notorious Filibuster of the Nineteenth Century. Frederic Rosengarten, Jr.

Freedmen, Philanthropy, and Fraud: A History of the Freedmen's Savings Bank. Carl R. Osthaus.

Freedom and Change: Essays in Honour of Lester B. Pearson. Michael G. Fry.

Freedom and Independence: A Study of the Political Ideas of Hegel's Phenomenology of Mind. Judith N. Shklar.

Freedom and Its Limitations in American Life. Don E. Fehrenbacker, ed.

Freedom and Its Limitations in American Life. David M. Potter.

The Freedom of the Poet. John Berryman.

Freiheit: Die Anfänge der bürgerlichen Emanzipationsbewegung in Deutschland im Spiegel ihres Leitwortes (ca 1760-ca 1800). Jurgen Schlumbohm.

Frémont: Explorer for a Restless Nation. Ferol Egan.

French Historical Method: The Annales Paradigm. Teaian Stoianovich.

French Legislators 1800-1834: A Study in Quantitative History. Thomas D. Bick.

French Legitimists and the Politics of Moral Order in the Early Republic. R. R. Locke.

The French Navy and American Independence: A Study of Arms and Diplomacy, 1774-1787. Jonathan R. Dull.

French Revolution 1787-1799: From the Storming of the Bastille to Napoleon. Albert Soboul.

French Tragic Drama in the Sixteenth & Seventeenth Centuries.
Geoffrey Brereton.

Friars, Soldiers, and Reformers:
Hispanic Arizona and the Sonora
Mission Frontier, 1767-1856.
John L. Kessell.

Friend and Foe: Aspects of
French-Amerindian Cultural
Contact in the Sixteenth and
Seventeenth Centuries.
Cornelius J. Jaenen.

From Border to Middle Shire:
Northumberland 1586-1625.
S. J. Watts.

From Centennial to World War:
American Society, 1876-1917.
Walter T. K. Nugent.

From Cultural Rebellion to Counter-
revolution: The Politics of
Maurice Barres.   C. Stewart
Doty.

From Disunionism to the Brink of
War, 1850-1860.   Walter M.
Merrill, ed. and Louis
Ruchames, ed.

From Glory to Oblivion: The Real
Truth About the Mexican Revo-
lution.   Guy Weddington
McCreary.

From Heretics to Heroes: A
Study of Religious Groups in
Georgia with Primary Emphasis
on the Baptists.   J. R. Huddlestun and Charles O. Walker.

From Hierarchy to Stratification:
Changing Patterns of Social
Inequality in a Northern Indian
Village.   D. B. Miller.

From King's College to Columbia,
1746-1800.   David C. Humphrey.

From Parlor to Prison: Five
American Suffragists Talk About
Their Lives.   Sherna Gluck, ed.

From Quaker to Latter-Day Saint:
Bishop Edwin D. Woolley.
Leonard J. Arrington.

From Radicalism to Socialism:
Men and Ideas in the Formation
of Fabian Socialist Doctrines,
1881-1889.   Willard Wolfe.

From Roots to McNamara: Army
Organization and Administration,
1900-1963. James E. Hewes, Jr.

From Sweden to America: A History of the Migration.   Harald
Runblom, ed. and Hans Norman,
ed.

From the Black Bar: Voices for
Equal Justice.   Gilbert Ware.

From the Ghetto: The Fiction of
Abraham Cahan.   Jules Chametzky.

From the Heartland: Profiles of
People and Places of the Southwest
and Beyond.   Lawrence Clark
Powell.

From the St. Croix to the Potomac--
Reflections of a Bureaucrat.
Sherman E. Johnson.

From Tin Foil to Stereo: Evolution
of the Phonograph.   Oliver Read
and Walter L. Welch.

From Tobacco Road to Route 66: The
Southern Poor White in Fiction.
Sylvia Jenkins Cook.

From Tyranny to Texas: A German
Pioneer in Harris County.   E. E.
Lackner.

Frontier Defense and the Open Door:
Manchuria in Chinese-American
Relations, 1895-1911.   Michael H.
Hunt.

Frontier in Alaska and the Matanuska
Colony.   Orlando W. Miller.

Frontiers in the Americas: A Global
Perspective.   Jorge Monach.

Frost: Centennial Essays II.   Jac
Tharpe, ed.

Frühe bürgerliche Institutionen norddeutscher Hansestädte: Beiträge zu
einer vergleichenden Verfassungsgeschichte Lübecks, Bremens, Lune-
burgs and Hamburges im Mittelalter.
Burchard Scheper.

The Fur Trade in Colonial New York
1686-1776.   Thomas Elliot Norton.

Furman University: Toward a New
Identity, 1925-1975.   Alfred
Sandlin Reig.

Future That Doesn't Work: Social
Democracy's Failures in Britain.
R. Emmett Tyrrell, ed.

-G-

The Ga Family and Social Change.   D.
G. Azu.

Das Gabdeksgays der Runtinger zu
Regensburg.   Wiltrud Eikenberg.

Gambretta and the Making of the
Third Republic.   J. P. T. Bury.

Gamesman.   Michael Maccoby.

Ghandi and Civil Disobedience: The

Mahatma in Indian Politics, 1928-34. Judith M. Brown.

Die Geburt der Athena im Ostgiebel des Parthenon. Ernst Berger.

General Amin. David Martin.

General Burgoyne in Canada and America: Scapegoat for a System. Michael Glover.

General Horatio Gates: A Biography. Paul David Nelson.

General John Glover's Letterbook, 1776-1777. Russell W. Knight, ed.

General Report on the Gosford Estates in County Armagh, 1821. William Greig.

General Strike. Margaret Morris.

The General Strike. Patrick Renshaw.

The General Strike, 1926. Jeffrey Skelley, ed.

General Strike: The Politics of Industrial Conflict. G. A. Phillips.

Generations of Americans: History of the United States. K. I. Polakoff, et al.

Genesis de Gobierno Constitucional en México: 1808-1820. Anna Macias.

Gentile Comes to Cache Valley: A Study of the Logan Apostasies of 1894 and the Establishment of Non-Mormon Churches in Cache Valley, 1873-1913. A. J. Simmonds.

Gentlemen in Crisis: The First Century of the Union League of Philadelphia, 1862-1962. Maxwell Whiteman.

Gentry: The Rise and Fall of a Ruling Class. G. E. Mingay.

Geographie du commerce de Bordeaux a la fin du regne de Louis XIV. Christian Huetz de Lemps.

Geography III. Elizabeth Bishop.

George Jacob Holyoake: A Study in the Evolution of a Victorian Radical. Lee E. Grugel.

George Mason: Gentleman Revolutionary. Helen Hill Miller.

George of Trebizond: A Biography and a Study of His Rhetoric and Logic. John Monfasani.

George Walton Williams: The Life of a Southern Merchant and

Banker, 1820-1903. E. Merton Coulter.

Georgia: A Bicentennial History. Harold H. Martin.

Georgia History: A Bibliography. John Eddins Simpson, comp.

Georgia Statistical Abstract, 1976. Lorena M. Akioka and Carolyn S. Hudgins, ed.

Georgia Women: A Celebration. Barbara B. Reitt, ed.

Georgian at Princeton. Robert Manson Myers.

German and Pole: National Conflict and Modern Myth. Harry Kenneth Rosenthal.

The German Diplomatic Service, 1871-1914. Lamar Cecil.

German Enlightenment and the Rise of Historicism. Peter Hans Reill.

The German Evangelical Church and the Jews, 1879-1950. Richard Gutteridge.

German Foreign Policy, 1871-1914. Imanuel Geiss.

Germanic Invasions: The Making of Europe A. D. 400-600. Lucien Musset.

Germany and the League of Nations. Christoph M. Kimmich.

Geronimo, The Man, His Time, His Place. Angie Debo.

Gertrude Stein. Michael J. Hoffman.

Geschichte Heute. Positionen, Tendenzen und Probleme. Gerhard Schulz.

Geschichte Und Okonomie. Hans-Ulrich Wehler, ed.

Geschichte Und Soziologie. Hans-Ulrich Wehler, ed.

Gesellschaft, Kultur, Theorie: Gesammelte Aufsätze zur neueren Geschichte. Thomas Nipperdey.

Gesta Stephani. K. R. Potter, ed.

Gettysburg: A Journey in Time. William A. Frassanito.

Gewalt in der Politik. Gerhard Botz.

Ghana. J. Clark Leith.

Ghana and Nigeria, 1957-70: A Study in Inter-African Discord. Olajide Aluko.

A Ghetto Takes Shape: Black Cleveland, 1870 to 1930. Kenneth Kusmer.

Ghost Towns of Idaho. Donald C. Miller.

Giant in Texas: A History of the Dallas-Ft. Worth Regional Airport

Controversy, 1911-1974. Stanley H. Scott and Levi H. Davis.

Gibbon et Rome.... Pierre Ducrey.

Gilpin County Gold: Peter McFarlane, 1848-1929, Mining Entrepreneur in Central City, Colorado. H. William Axford.

Giraffe. Stanley Plumly.

Gladstone. E. J. Feuchtwanger.

Gladstone and Radicalism: The Reconstruction of Liberal Policy, 1835-94. Michael Barker.

The Gladstone Diaries. M. R. D. Foot and H. C. G. Matthew, ed.

Glaser der Antike: Sammlung Erwin Oppenlander. Axel von Saldern et al.

Gli Stati Uniti. Raimondo Luraghi.

Glossar zur fruhmittelalterlichen Geschichte im ostlichen Europa. Jadran Ferluga, et al. , ed.

Godly Man in Stuart England: Anglicans, Puritans, and the Two Tables, 1620-1670. J. Sears McGee.

God's Messengers: Religious Leadership in Colonial New England, 1700-1750. J. William T. Youngs, Jr. , Frank S. Brewer and Elizabeth D. Brewer.

God's Plot: The Paradoxes of Puritan Piety, Being the Autobiography & Journal of Thomas Shepard. Michael McGiffert, ed.

Going for the Rain. Simon J. Ortiz.

Gold and Iron: Bismarch, Bleichroder, and the Building of the German Empire. Fritz Stern.

The Golden Age of Chinese Drama: Yüan Tsa-chü. Chung-wen Shih.

Golden Bowl. Frederick Manfred.

Golden Door: Italian and Jewish Immigrant Mobility in New York City, 1880-1915. Thomas Kessner.

Gómez, el amo del poder. Domingo Alberto Rangel.

Gompers in Canada: A Study in American Continentalism Before the First World War. Robert H. Babcock.

Gone for a Soldier: The Civil War Memoirs of Private Alfred Bellard. David Herbert Donald, ed.

Gone with the Hickory Stick: School Days in Marion County, 1845-1960. Broward Lovell.

Gonsolve de Diário de Pernambuco e a História Social do Nordeste. José Antonio Mello.

Good Fight: A Poem for the Tenth Anniversary of the Death of John F. Kennedy. Thomas Kinsella.

The Good Parliament. George Holmes.

The Good Ships of Newport News: An Informal Account of Ships, Shipping and Shipbuilding in the Lower Chesapeake Bay Region Together with the Story of the Last Terrible Voyage of the Yarmouth Castle. Alexander Crosby Brown.

"Good Time Coming?" Black Nevadans in the Nineteenth Century. Elmer R. Rusco.

Goodbye, Garcia, Adios. Don Dedera and Bob Robles.

Goswin Kempgyn de Nussia Trivita studentium. M. Bernhard, ed.

The Goths in Ancient Poland: A Study on the Historical Geography of the Odervistula Region During the First Two Centuries of Our Era. Jan Czarnecki.

Government by Judiciary: The Transformation of the Fourteenth Amendment. Raoul Berger.

Government in Canada. Thomas A. Hockin.

Government of India and Reform: Policies Twoards Politics and the Constitution, 1916-1921. P. G. Robb.

The Government Policy of Protector Somerset. M. L. Bush.

Government Publications: A Guide to Bibliographic Tools. Vladmir M. Palic.

Governor Charles Robinson of Kansas. Don W. Wilson.

Governor's Wife on the Mining Frontier: The Letters of Mary Edgerton from Montana, 1863-1865. James L. Thane, ed.

Gran Bretaña y el Peru: Informes de los cónsules britanicos. Heradio Bonilla, comp.

Grand Strategy. N. H. Gibbs.

The Grand Strategy of the Roman Empire: From the First Century A. D. to the Third. Edward N. Luttwak.

Grassland Settlers: The Swift Current Region During the Era of the Ranching Frontier. Don C. McGowan.

The Great American Frontier: A Story of Western Pioneering. Thomas D. Clark, ed.

The Great Boer War. Byron Farwell.

The Great Great Salt Lake. Peter G. Czerny.

Great Plains Command: William B. Hazen in the Frontier West. Marvin E. Kroeker.

Great Powers and the Polish Question 1941-45: A Documentary Study in Cold War Origins. Anthony Polonsky, ed.

The Great Trek of the Russian Mennonites to Central Asia, 1880-1884. Fred Richard Belk.

Great United States Exploring Expedition of 1838-1842. William Stanton.

Great Valley Patriots: Western Virginia in the Struggle for Liberty. Howard McKnight Wilson.

Greater Ethiopia: The Evolution of a Multiethnic Society. Donald N. Levine.

Greece and the Great Powers, 1914-1917. George B. Leon.

The Greek Revival: Neo-Classical Attitudes in British Architecture 1760-1870. J. Mordaunt Crook.

The Greeks in Riverboating on the Lower Danube. Spyridonos G. Fokas.

Green Flag: Polish Populist Politics, 1867-1970. Olga A. Narkiewicz.

Greene & Greene: Architecture as a Fine Art. Randell L. Makinson.

Gringos from the Far North. Essays in the History of Canadian-Latin American Relations 1866-1968. J. C. M. Oglesby.

Group Identity in the South: Dialogue Between the Technological and the Humanistic. Harold F. Kaufman, ed., J. Kenneth Morland, ed. and Herbert H. Fockler, ed.

Growing Up in Minnesota: Ten Writers Remember Their Childhoods. Chester G. Anderson, ed.

The Growth and Fluctuation of the British Economy, 1790-1850: An Historical Statistical, and Theoretical Study of Britain's Economic Development. Arthur D. Gayer, et al.

Growth Centres in Raichur: An Integrated Area Development Plan for a District in Karnataka. Lalit K. Sen, et al.

Growth of Parliamentary Parties, 1689-1742. B. W. Hill.

Growth of Victorian London. Donald J. Olsen.

Gruppi ereticali senesi del cinquecento. Valerio Marchetti.

The Guard Movement, 1931-1935. Keith Amos.

Guerrilla. Walter Laquer.

Guiana Maroons: A Historical and Bibliographical Introduction. Richard Price.

Guide des Archives d'Enterprises Conserees dans les depots publics de la Belgique. H. Coppejans-Desmedt.

Guide des sources de l'histroie des Etats-Unis dans les Archives Francais. Madeline Astorquia, et al.

Guide to America's Indians. Arnold Marquis.

Guide to American Indian Documents in the Congressional Serial Set: 1817-1899. Steven L. Johnson.

A Guide to Aural History Research. W. J. Langlois, ed.

Guide to Materials on Latin America in the National Archives of the United States. George S. Ulibarri and John P. Harrison.

Guide to the Manuscript Collections of the Atlanta Historical Society. D. Louise Cook, comp.

Guide to the Public Records of Tasmania: Section Four, Records Relating to Free Immigration. Ian Pearce and Clare Cowling.

Guide to the Sources of United States Military History. Robin Higham.

Gull Lake Site: A Prehistoric Bison Drive in Southwestern Saskatchewan. Thomas F. Kehoe.

Gunboat Diplomacy, 1895-1905: Great Power Pressure in Venezuela. Miriam Hood.

Gunpowder and Galleys: Changing Technology and Mediterranean Warfare at Sea in the Sixteenth Century. John Francis Guilmartin, Jr.

-H-

Hagarism: The Making of the Islamic World. Patricia Crone and Michael Cook.

Haitian Potential: Research and Resources of Haiti. Vera Rubin, ed. and Richard P. Schaedel, ed.

Hakluyt Handbook. D. B. Quinn.

Han Rhapsody: A Study of the Fu of Yang Hsiung (53 B.C.-A.D. 18). David Knechtges.

A Handbook to Elections in Uttar Pradesh, 1920-1951. P. D. Reeves, B. D. Graham, and J. M. Goodman.

Handbuch der Keilschriftliteratur. Rykle Borger.

Handel und Unternehmer im französischen Brasiliengeschaft, 1815-1849. Jürgen Schneider.

Handloggers. W. H. Jackson with Ethel Dassow.

Hans Schaffer: Steuermann in wirtschaftlichen und politischen Krisen. Eckhard Wandel.

Die Hanse: Handelsmacht im Zeichen der Kogge. Dieter Zimmerling.

Har Dayal, Hindu Revolutionary and Rationalist. Emily C. Brown.

Harijan: Collected Issues of Gandhi's Journal, 1933-1955. Joan V. Bondurant, ed.

Harpers Ferry Armory and the New Technology. Merritt Roe Smith.

The Harrowing of Eden: White Attitudes Toward Native Americans. J. E. Chamberlin.

Harry H. Woodring: A Political Biography of FDR's Controversial Secretary of War. Keith D. McFarland.

Harvest of Death. Carey C. Jewell.

Harvest of the Palm: Ecological Change in Eastern Indonesia. James J. Fox.

The Healers: The Rise of the Medical Establishment. John Duffy.

Healing Hand: Man and Wound in the Ancient World. Guido Majno.

Health Care in the People's Republic of China: A Bibliography with Abstracts. Shahid Akhtar.

Health Policies and Services in China, 1974. Leo Orleans.

Hearing Secret Harmonies. Anthony Powell.

Heart Full of Horses. Florence Fenley.

Heart Mountain: The History of an American Concentration Camp. Douglas W. Nelson.

Heart of Oak: A Survey of British Sea Power in the Georgian Era. G. J. Marcus.

Heart of the Valley: A History of Knoxville, Tennessee. Lucile Deaderick, ed.

Heaven My Blanket, Earth My Pillow: Poems from Sung Dynasty China. Jonathan Chaves.

Hebrew Union College-Jewish Institute of Religion at One Hundred Years. Samuel E. Karff, ed.

Hecla II and III: An Interpretive Study of Archaeological Remains from the Lakeshore Project, South Central Arizona. Albert C. Goodyear, III.

Hegel. Charles Taylor.

Hell or Connaught!: The Cromwellian Colonisation of Ireland, 1652-1660. Peter Feresford Ellis.

Henry Adams and Henry James: The Emergence of a Modern Consciousness. John Carlos Rowe.

Henry James--The Lessons of the Master: Popular Fiction and Personal Style in the Nineteenth Century. William Veeder.

Henry Kissinger: The Anguish of Power. John G. Stoessinger.

Henry Sylvester Williams and the Origins of the Pan-African Movement, 1869-1911. Owen Charles Mathurin.

Hereditas: Essays and Studies Presented to Professor Seámus O Duilearga. Bo Almqvist, et al., ed.

The Heritage of Thai Sculpture. Jean Boisselier.

Herzen Against Autocracy: The Secret Political History of Russia in the

18th and 19th Centuries and the
Free Press. N. Ia. Eidelman.
Herzl und Rathenau: Wege jüdisch-
er Existenz an der Wende des
20. Jahrhunderts. Rudolf
Kallner.
Heute sprach ich mitt...: Tage-
bucher eines Berliner Publizis-
ten 1926-1932. Ernst Feder.
Higher Education and the United
States Office of Education (1867-
1953). Richard Wayne Lykes.
Hillforts of the Iron Age in Eng-
land and Wales. J. Forde-
Johnston.
Hincmar: Archeveque de Reims,
845-882. Jean Devisse.
Hinduism: New Essays in the His-
tory of Religions. Bardwell L.
Smith, ed.
Hired Hands and Plowboys: Farm
Labor in the Midwest, 1815-60.
David E. Schob.
The Hispanic Contribution to the
State of Colorado. José
DeOnis, ed. '
Hispano-Arabic Poetry: A Student
Anthology. James T. Monroe.
Histoire de la France. Georges
Duby and Armand Wallon, ed.
Histoire de Yokobue (Yokobue no
sōshi): Etudes sur les recits
de l'epoque muromachi.
Jacqualine Pigeot.
Histoire des industries francaises.
Tihomir J. Markovitch.
Histoire economique et sociale
contemporaine. Maurice
Flamant.
Histoire economique et sociale de
la France. Fernad Braudel
and Ernest Labrousse, ed.
Histoire et Historiens: Une muta-
tion idéologique des historiens
francais, 1865-1885. Charles-
Oliver Carbonell.
História de Sedicão Intentada no
Bahia em 1798: A Conspiracão
dos Alfaiates. Luís Henrique
Dias Tavares.
Historian and Film. Paul Smith,
ed.
Historians and Historiography in
Modern India. S. P. Sen, ed.
Historians and the Open Society.
A. R. Bridbury.
Historic Georgia Mothers, 1776-
1976. Georgia Mothers Asso-
ciation.

The Historic Indians of Ohio.
Randall Buchman, ed.
Historic Resources: Finding, Pre-
serving, and Using.
Historic Virginia Gardens: Preser-
vations by the Garden Club of
Virginia. Dorothy Hunt Williams.
Historical Atlas of Oklahoma. John
W. Morris, Charles R. Goins,
and Edwin C. McReynolds.
Historical Knowing. Leon J.
Goldstein.
Historical Linguistics. John M.
Anderson, ed. and Charles Jones,
ed.
Historical Studies in the Physical
Sciences. Russell McCormmach,
ed. and Lewis Pyenson, ed.
Historical Writing in England, c. 550
to c. 1307. Antonio Gransden.
Historicity of the Patriarchal Narra-
tives: The Quest for the Histori-
cal Abraham. Thomas L. Thomp-
son.
History in Modern Indian Literature.
S. P. Sen, ed.
A History of Augusta College. Ed-
ward J. Cashin.
History of Black Americans: From
Africa to the Emergence of the
Cotton Kingdom. Philip S. Foner.
History of Building Types. Nikolaus
Pevsner.
A History of Chinese Drama. Wil-
liam Dolby.
History of Christianity. Paul John-
son.
History of Classical Scholarship from
1300 to 1850. Rudolf Pfeiffer.
History of East Africa. D. A. Low,
ed. and Alison Smith, ed.
History of Economic Theory: Scope,
Method, and Content. Harry
Landreth.
History of Greek Art. Martin Robert-
son.
History of Hampden-Sydney College.
Herbert Clarence Bradshaw.
A History of Hausa Islamic Verse.
Mervyn Hiskett.
History of Israel: From the Rise of
Zionism to Our Time. Howard M.
Sachar.
History of Jefferson County. Jerrell
H. Shofner.
A History of Jefferson County, Texas,
from Wilderness to Reconstruction.
W. T. Block.
A History of Madison County and

Incidentally of North Alabama
1732-1840. Thomas Jones
Taylor.

A History of Modern Serbia, 1804-
1918. Michael Boro Petrovich.

A History of Northern Botswana,
1850-1910. J. Mutero Chirenje.

History of Persia Under Qajar
Rule: Translated from the
Persian of Hasan-e Fasa'i's
Farsnama-ye Naseri. Heribert
Busse.

History of Public Works in the
United States. Ellis L. Armstrong, ed.

A History of Russia. Basil
Dmytryshyn.

A History of South and Central
Africa. Derek Wilson.

History of the Atchison, Topeka
and Santa Fe Railway. Keith
L. Bryant, Jr.

History of the Catholic Church in
Wisconsin. Leo Rummel.

History of the Comic Strip.
David Kunzle.

History of the Commonwealth
Development Corporation. Sir
William Rendell.

History of the Culture of Latvia,
1710-1800. Andrejs Johansons.

History of the Czechs. A. H.
Hermann.

A History of the Daniel Boone
National Forest, 1770-1970.
Robert F. Collins.

History of the Estonian SSR.
V. Maamagi et al. , eds.

A History of the ICC: From
Panacea to Palliative. Ari
Hoogenboom and Olive Hoogen-
boom.

History of the Ibgo People.
Elizabeth Isichei.

History of the Illinois Central
Railroad. John F. Stover.

A History of the Lewis and Clark
Journals. Paul Russell Cutright.

A History of the Malthusian
League, 1877-1927. Rosanna
Ledbetter.

History of the Mongolian People's
Republic. William A. Brown
and Urgunge Onon, tr.

History of the Mongols Based on
Eastern and Western Accounts
of the Thirteenth and Four-

teenth Centuries. Bertold
Spuler.

A History of the Philippines: From
the Spanish Colonization to the
Second World War. Renato
Constantino.

A History of the Trade Union Move-
ment in the Hosiery and Knitwear
Industry, 1776-1976. Richard
Gurnham.

A History of Western Education.
James Bowen.

History of Wisconsin. Richard N.
Current.

History of Wisconsin. Alice E.
Smith.

History of Zambia. Andrew Roberts.

Hitler Among the Germans. Rudolph
Binion.

Hitler's Children: The Story of the
Baader-Meinhog Terrorist Gang.
Jillian Becker.

Hitler's Decision to Invade Russia,
1941. Robert Cecil.

Hitler's War. David Irving.

Hofkammerprasident Gundaker Thomas
Graf Starhemberg und die oster-
reichische Finanzpolitik der
Barockzeit (1703-1715). Brigitte
Holl.

Holding the Line: The Eisenhower
Era, 1952-1961. Charles C.
Alexander.

Holland House Diaries, 1831-1840:
The Diary of Henry Richard Vassall
Fox, Third Lord Holland. Abra-
ham D. Kriegel, ed.

Hollywood Costume Design. David
Chierichetti.

Hollywood's Canada: The Americanization of Our National Image. Pierre
Berton.

A Holocaust Reader. Lucy S.
Dawidowicz, ed.

Holy Warriors: The Abolitionists and
American Slavery. James Brewer
Stewart.

Homage to Malthus. Jane Soames
Nickerson.

Un hombre llamado Rómulo Betancourt. Rómulo Blanco, et al.

Homes of the Signers of the Declaration. Janet Perry Fairhurst.

Les Hommes et al peste en France
et dans les pays européens et méditerranéens. Jean-Noël Biraben.

Honor Thy Father and Mother.
Gerald Blidstein.

tungsgeschichte in der Epoche des deutschen Kaiserreichs. Wolfgang Treue.

James and John Stuart Mill: Father and Son in the Nineteenth Century. Bruce Mazlish.

James Ensor. John David Farmer.

James J. Hill and the Opening of the Northwest. Albro Martin.

James Madison Alden: Yankee Artist of the Pacific Coast, 1854-1860. Franz Stensel.

James T. Shotwell and the Rise of Internationalism in America. Harold Josephson.

Jane Stanford: Her Life and Letters. Gunther W. Nagel.

Jansenists and the Expulsion of the Jesuits from France 1757-1765. Dale Van Kley.

Janus Pannonius Opera Latine et Hungarice. Vivae Memoriae Iani Pannonii Ovingentesimo Mortis Svae Anniversario Dedicatum. Sándor Kóvacs, ed.

Japan. Tetsuo Najita.

Japan: An Economic Survey. Andrea Boltho.

Japan and China: From War to Peace, 1894-1972. Marius B. Jansen.

Japan Faces China: Political and Economic Relations in the Postwar Era. Chae-Jin Lee.

Japan in Southeast Asia: Collision Course. Raul S. Manglapus.

Japanese. Edwin O. Reischauer.

Japanese and Americans: Cultural Parallels and Paradoxes. Charles Grinnell Cleaver.

The Japanese and Peru, 1873-1973. C. Harvey Gardiner.

The Japanese and Sukarno's Indonesia: Tokyo-Jakarta Relations, 1951-1966. Masahi Nishihara.

The Japanese Army in North China, 1937-1941. Lincoln Li.

Japanese Culture: A Study of Origins and Characteristics. Eiichiro Ishida.

Japanese Culture and Behavior: Selected Readings. Takie Sugiyama Lebra and William P. Lebra, eds.

Japanese Industrialization and Its Social Consequences. Hugh Patrick, ed. with assistance of Larry Meissner.

Japanese, Nazis and Jews. The Jewish Refugee Community of Shanghai, 1938-1945. David Kranzler.

The Japanese Siege of Tsingtare: World War I in Asia. Charles B. Burdick.

Japanese Studies of Modern China Since 1953. Noriko Kamachi, John F. Fairbank, and Chūzō Ichiko.

Japanese Urbanism: Industry and Politics in Kariya, 1872-1972. Gary D. Allinson.

Japan's Greater East Asia Co-prosperity Sphere in World War II. Joyce C. Lebra, ed.

Japan's Multinational Enterprises. M. Y. Yoshino.

Japan's Parliament: An Introduction. Hans H. Baerwald.

Jawaharlal Nehru, A Biography. Sarvepalli Gopal.

Jean Bodin and the Rise of Absolutist Theory. Julian H. Franklin.

Jean de Brébeuf, 1593-1649. Joseph P. Donnelly.

Jefferson: A Revealing Biography. Page Smith.

Jefferson, Nationalism, and the Enlightenment. Henry Steele Commager.

The Jefferson Papers of the University of Virginia. Julian P. Boyd, ed.

Jefferson the President: Second Term, 1805-1809. Dumas Malone.

Jefferson's Fine Arts Library: His Selections for the University of Virginia Together with His Own Architectural Books. William Bainter O'Neal.

Jefferson's Louisiana: Politics and the Clash of Legal Traditions. George Dargo.

Jefferson's Nephews: A Frontier Tragedy. Boynton Merrill, Jr.

Jehovah's Witnesses in Canada: Champions of Freedom of Speech and Worship. M. James Penton.

Jesus. Michael Grant.

Jogjakarta Under Sultan Mangkubumi, 1749-1792: A History of the Division of Java. M. C. Ricklefs.

Johan Zoffany, 1733-1810. Mary Webster.

Johannes Schwalm the Hessian.

-K-

Kanawah County Marriages January 1, 1792, to December 31, 1869. Julia Wintz.

K'ang-hsi and the Consolidation of Ch'ing Rule, 1661-1684. Lawrence D. Kessler.

Kansas: A Bicentennial History. Kenneth S. Davis.

The Kansas Art Reader. Jonathan Wesley Bell, ed.

Kansas: The Thirty-Fourth Star. Nyle H. Miller.

Kant and the Problem of History. William A. Galston.

Karl Kraus and the Soul Doctors. Thomas Szasz.

Kassai, The Story of Raoul de Premorel, African Trader. Reginald Ray Stuart.

Kathy Northwest: The Story of the Branch Line Railroad. Donovan, Hofsommer.

Kaufmannschaft und Handelskapitalismus in der Stadt Mexiko (1759-1778). Christiana Renate Moreno.

Keats and the Sublime. Stuart A. Ende.

Keep the Last Bullet for Yourself: The True Story of Custer's Last Stand. Thomas B. Marquis.

Keepers of the Gate: A History of Ellis Island. Thomas Monroe Pitkin.

Kefauver Committee and the Politics of Crime, 1950-1952. William Howard Moore.

Keir Hardie. Iain McLean.

Kelantan: Religion, Society and Politics in a Malay State. William R. Roff.

Kenosha County in the Twentieth Century. John A. Neuenschwander.

Kentucky: Settlement and Statehood, 1750-1800. George M. Chinn.

Kenya: Into the Second Decade. John Burrows, ed.

Keynes' Monetary Thought: A Study of Its Development. Don Patinkin.

Kilwa: An Islamic Trading City on the East African Coast. H. Neville Chittick.

Kimbange: An African Prophet and His Church. Marie-Louise Martin.

Kindai Nihon to Tōyō shigaku. Goi Naohiro.

King Labour: The British Working Class, 1850-1914. David Kynaston.

King of Two Worlds: Philip II of Spain. Edward Grierson.

The Kingdom of John, 1641-1728. Leonard Y. Andaya.

The Kingdom of the Netherlands in the Second World War. L. De Jong.

Kingdom or Nothing: The Life of John Taylor, Militant Mormon. Samuel W. Taylor.

Kings and Kinsmen: Early Mbundu States in Angola. Joseph C. Miller.

The King's Council in the Reign of Edward VI. D. E. Hoak.

Kingston, Jamaica: Urban Development and Social Change, 1692-1962. Colin G. Clarke.

Kittitas Frontiersmen. Earl T. Glauert, ed. and Merle H. Kunz, ed.

Kiva Art of the Anasazi at Pottery Mound. Frank C. Hibben.

Klassenkampf in Der Diaspora: Geschichte Der Judischen Arbeiterbewengung. John Bunzl.

Die Kontorniat-Medaillons. Andreas Alfoldi and Elisabeth Alfoldi.

Kraal and Castle: Khoikhoi and the Founding of White South Africa. Richard Elphick.

Der Krieg der "achsenmachte" im Mittelmeer-Raum. Walter Baum and Eberhard Weichold.

Krieg und Frieden in der politischen Tagesliteratur Deutschlands zwischen Baseler und Luneviller Frieden (1795-1801). Kari Hokkanen.

Kristofer Janson in America. Nina Draxten.

Krushcheve: The Years in Power. Roy A. Medvedev and Zhores A. Medvedev.

Kunst der Ptolemäer- und Römerzeit im Ägyptischen Museum Kairo. Günter Grimm.

Kuril Islands: Russo-Japanese Frontier in the Pacific. John J. Stephan.

-L-

Labor and the Ambivalent Revolutionaries: Mexico, 1911-1923. Ramón Eduardo Ruiz.

Labor and the American Revolution. Philip S. Foner.

The Labour Aristocracy in Victorian Edinburgh. Robert Q. Gray.

Labour in Irish Politics, 1890-1930. Arthur Mitchell.

Labour, Race and Colonial Rule: The Copperbelt from 1924 to Independence. Elena L. Berger.

Laburism e Russia Sovietica, 1917-1924. Adele Massardo Maiello.

Lafayette. Peter Buckman.

Lafayette: Documents conservés en France. Chantal de Tourtier-Bonazzi, comp.

Lake Champlain: Key to Liberty. Ralph Nading Hill.

Lamy of Sante Fe: His Life and Times. Paul Horgan.

Land and People: A Cultural Geography of Preindustrial New Jersey: Origins and Settlement Patterns. Peter O. Wacker.

The Land and the People of Nineteenth-Century Cork: The Rural Economy and the Land Question. James S. Donnelly, Jr.

Land, People and Politics: A History of the Land Question in the United Kingdom, 1878-1952. Roy Douglas.

Land Question and European Society. Frank E. Huggett.

Land Reform and Economic Development in China. Victor D. Lippit.

The Land Remembers: The Story of a Farm and Its People. Ben Logan.

Landed Estates in the Colonial Philippines. Nicolas P. Cushner.

Landlocked Countries of Africa. Z. Cervenka.

Landownership in Nepal. Mahesh C. Regmi.

Langdon Cheves of South Carolina. Archie Vernon Huff, Jr.

Language and Interpretation in Psychoanalysis. Marshall Edelson.

The Language and Linguistic Background of the Isaiah Scroll (1 Q Isa^a). E. Y. Kutscher.

Language and Linguistics in the People's Republic of China. Winfred P. Lehman, ed.

Language & Time & Gertrude Stein. Carolyn Faunce Copeland.

Laredo and the Rio Grande Frontier. J. B. Wilkinson.

Lasa. Iconografia e esegesi. Antonia Rallo.

Last Chance in China: The World War II Despatches of John S. Service. Joseph W. Esherick, ed.

The Last Chopper: The Denouement of the American Role in Vietnam, 1963-1975. Weldon A. Brown.

The Last Days of United Pakistan. G. W. Choudhury.

Last Great Subsistence Crisis in the Western World. John D. Post.

Last Voyage of Thomas Cavendish. David B. Quinn, ed.

Late-Medieval England, 1377-1485. Delloyd J. Guth.

Latin America: An Economic and Social Geography. J. P. Cole.

Latin America, the Cold War & the World Powers, 1945-1973, A Study in Diplomatic History. F. Parkinson.

Latin American Foreign Policies: An Analysis. Harold Eugene Davis and Larmon C. Wilson.

Latin American Peasant. Andrew Pearse.

The Latin American Policy of Warren G. Harding. Kenneth J. Grieb.

Latin American Politics: A Developmental Approach. Edward J. Williams and Freeman J. Wright.

Laura Clay and the Woman's Rights Movement. Paul E. Fuller.

Laura: The Life of Laura Ingalls Wilder. Donald Zochert.

L'Austria-Ungheria nella politica Americana durante la prima guerra mondiale. Angelo Ara.

Law and Development in Latin America: A Case Book. Kenneth L. Karst and Keith S. Rosenn.

Law and Order in Historical Perspective: The Case of Elizabethan Essex. Joel Samaha.

Law and Politics. James G. Dickson, Jr.

Law, Society and Politics in Early Maryland. Aubrey C. Land, Lois Green Carr, and Edward C. Papenfuse, ed.

Lead Industry of Wensleydale and Swaledale. Arthur Raistrick.

Leadership and Values: The Organization of Large-Scale Taiwanese Enterprises. Robert H. Silin.

Leadership in 19th Century Africa: Essays from Tarikh. Obaro Ikime, ed.

Leaves Before the Wind. Consuelo Northrop Bailey.

Lebensfragen der Wirtschaft. Hermann J. Abs.

L'education en France du XVIᵉ au XVIIIᵉ siècle. Roger Chartier, Marie-Madeleine Compère, and Dominique Julia.

The Legacy of Malthus: The Social Costs of the New Scientific Racism. Allan Chase.

Legal Framework of English Feudalism. S. F. C. Milsom.

Legal Reform in Occupied Japan: A Participant Looks Back. Alfred C. Oppler.

Legalism and Anti-Confucianism in Maoist Politics. Wang Hsueh-wen.

Legislative and Political Development: Lebanon, 1842-1972. Abdo I. Baaklini.

Leisure and the Changing City, 1870-1914. H. E. Meller.

Lemon City: Pioneering on Biscayne Bay. Thelma Peters.

Lessons from Japanese Development: Allen C. Kelley and Jeffrey G. Williamson.

The Letters and Diaries of John Henry Newman. C. S. Dessain and T. Gornall, ed.

Letters and Notes on the North American Indians. George Catlin.

Letters and Papers of Alfred Thayer Mahan. Robert Seager, II, ed. and Doris D. Maguire, ed.

Letters and People of the Spanish Indies: Sixteenth Century. James Lockhart, ed. and Enrique Otte, ed.

The Letters and Poems of Fulbert of Chartres. Frederick Behrends, ed. and tr.

Letters from New England, The Massachusetts Bay Colony, 1629-1638. Everett Emerson, ed.

Letters from the Promised Land: Swedes in America, 1840-1914. H. Arnold Barton, ed.

Letters of Louis D. Brandeis, Volume IV (1916-1921): Mr. Justice Brandeis. Louis D. Brandeis.

Levi-Strauss: Structuralism and Sociological Theory. C. R. Badcock.

Lewis and Clark: Historic Places Associated with Their Transcontinental Exploration (1804-06). Roy E. Appleman with Robert G. Ferris.

L'hérésie de Jean Hus. Paul De Vooght.

Liam O'Flaherty, the Storyteller. Angeline A. Kelley.

Liang Chien-wen Ti. John Marney.

El Liberalism y el campesinado en el centro de Mexico (1850-1876). T. G. Powell.

Liberating Women's History: Theoretical and Critical Essays. Bernice A. Carroll, ed.

La libération de la France: Actes du Colloque International tenu à Paris du 28 au 31 octobre 1974. Centre National de la Recherche Scientifique.

Liberia and Sierra Leone: An Essay in Comparative Politics. Christopher Clapham.

L'ideologie de l'Action Catholique, 1917-1939. Richard Jones.

The Life and Photography of an American Original: Alice Austin, 1866-1952. Anne Notovny.

A Life Apart: The English Working Class 1890-1914. Standish Meacham.

The Life and Times of Chaucer. John Gardner.

The Life and Times of Robert F. W. Allston. Anthony Q. Devereux.

Life History and the Historical Moment. Erik H. Erickson.

The Life of Captain James Cook. J. C. Beaglehole.

Life of Freidrich Engels. W. O. Henderson.

Life of Tagore. Probhat Kumar Mukherji.

A Light Unto My Path: Old Testament Studies in Honor of Jacob M. Myers. Howard N. Bream, ed.,

The Lower Middle Class in Britain,
1870-1914.   Geoffrey Crossick,
ed.
Loyal Blacks.   Ellen Gibson Wilson.
The Loyalists in Revolutionary
America, 1760-1781.   Robert
McCluer Calhoon.
The Loyalty Islands: A History of
Culture Contacts 1840-1900.
K. R. Howe.
Lucknow: The Last Phase of an
Oriental Culture.   Abdul Halim
Sharar.
Ludwig Bamberger: German Lib-
eral Politician and Social Critic,
1823-1899.   Stanley Zucker.
Ludwig Landmann: Frankfurter
Oberbürgermeister der Weimarer
Republik.   Dieter Rebentisch.
Luis Maria Peralta and His Adobe.
Frances L. Fox.
The Lusitania Disaster: The Real
Answers Behind the World's
Most Controversial Sea Tragedy.
Thomas A. Bailey and Paul B.
Ryan.
Lyndon Johnson and the American
Dream.   Doris Kearns.
Lyon et les lyonnais au XVIIIe
siècle.   Maurice Garden.

-M-

M. S. Lunin: Catholic Decem-
brist.   Glynn Barratt.
Machiavellian Movement.   Floren-
tine Political Thought and
Atlantic Republican Tradition.
J. G. A. Pocock.
A Machiavellian Treatise by
Stephen Gardiner.   Peter Sam-
uel Donaldson.
Mackenzie King Diaries, 1893-
1931.   Mackenzie King.
Madam Secretary: Frances
Perkins.   George Martin.
Madison County Homes: A Col-
lection of Pre-Civil War Homes
and Family Heritages.   Vee
Dove.
Madras: An Analysis of Urban
Ecological Structure in India.
Jay A. Weinstein.
Maharashtra and the Marathas,

Their History and Culture: A Bib-
liographic Guide to Western Lan-
guage Materials.   Datta Shankarrao
Kharbas.
Mahatma Gandhi and His Apostles.
Ved Mehta.
Main Currents in Modern American
History.   Gabriel Kolko.
Mainsprings of Indian and Pakistani
Foreign Policies.   S. M. Burke.
The Majesty of Colour: A Life of
Sir John Bates Thurston, Volume 1:
The Very Bayonet.   Deryck Scarr.
Making of a History: Walter Prescott
Webb and the Great Plains.   Greg-
ory M. Tobin.
Making of an American: An Adapta-
tion of Memorable Tales.   Charles
Sealsfield.
The Making of Lloyd George.   W. R.
P. George.
The Making of Modern Belize:
Politics, Society and British
Colonialism in Central America.
C. H. Grant.
Making of the Diplomatic Mind: The
Training, Outlook and Style of the
United States Foreign Service Of-
ficers, 1908-1931.   Robert D.
Schulzinger.
The Making of the English Country
House 1500-1640.   Malcolm Airs.
Making of the Modern British Diet.
Derek Oddy, ed. and Derek Miller,
ed.
The Making of the Modern Family.
Edward Shorter.
Making of the Monroe Doctrine.
Ernest R. May.
The Making of the Third Republic:
Class and Politics in France,
1868-1884.   Sanford Elwitt.
Man and Land in the Far East.
Pierre Gourou.
A Man for Arkansas: Sid McMath and
the Southern Reform Tradition.
Jim Lester.
Man in the Amazon.   Charles Wagley,
ed.   .
Man of Many Talents: An Informal
Biography of James Douglas 1753-
1819.   Ronald Jessup.
Managers and Workers: Origins of
the New Factory System in the
United States, 1880-1920.   Daniel
Nelson.
Managing Presidential Objectives.
Richard Rose.

The Mansion of History. Carl G. Gustavson.

Manual for Museums. Ralph H. Lewis.

Manuscripts Guide to Collections at the University of Illinois at Urbana-Champaign. Maynard J. Brichford, et al.

Manuscripts Relating to Commonwealth Caribbean Countries in United States and Canadian Repositories. K. E. Ingram.

The Maoist Educational Revolution. Theodore Hsi-en Chen.

March 1939: The British Guarantee to Poland, A Study in the Continuity of British Foreign Policy. Simon Newman.

Marco Polo. Richard Humble.

Mari Capitale Fabuleuse. André Parrot.

Mariano Sozzini: Giureconsulto senese del quattrocento. Paolo Nardi.

Marinu. Brian Large.

Maritime Economic Thought in the Second Republic, 1919-1939. Zbigniew Machalinski.

The Mark to Turn: A Reading of William Stafford's Poetry. Jonathan Holden.

Mark Twain's Notebooks and Journals, Volume I: 1855-1873. Frederick Anderson, ed., Michael B. Frank, ed. and Kenneth M. Sanderson, ed.

Markets in Oaxaca. Scott Cook and Martin Diskin.

Marriage, Inheritance and Witchcraft: A Case Study of a Rural Ghanaian Family. W. Bleek.

Marriage with My Kingdom: The Courtship of Elizabeth I. Alison Plowden.

Mars and Minerva: World War I and the Uses of the Higher Learning in America. Carol S. Gruber.

Mary Carpenter and the Children of the Streets. Jo Manton.

Masks of Fiction in Dream of the Red Chamber. Lucien Miller.

Massachusetts Broadsides of the American Revolution. Mason I. Lowance, ed. and Georgia B. Bumgardner, ed.

Massenarmut und Hungerkrisen im vorindustriellen Europa: Versuch einer Synopsis. Wilhelm Abel.

The Mastaba of Queen Mersyankh III G 7530-7540. Dows Dunham and William Kelly Simpson.

Masters and Men in the West Midlands Metalware Trades Before the Industrial Revolution. Marie B. Rowland.

Masters Without Slaves: Southern Planters in the Civil War and Reconstruction. James L. Roark.

The Material Culture of Key Marco Florida. Marion Spjut Gilliland.

Mathematics and Computers in Archaeology. J. E. Doran and F. R. Hodson.

Mathematics Education in China: Its Growth and Development. Frank Swetz.

Mathu of Kenya: A Political Study. Jack R. Roelker.

The Matrimonial Trials of Henry VIII. Henry Ansgar Kelley.

Matteotti: Una vita per il socialismo. Antonio G. Casanova.

A Matter of Allegiances: Maryland from 1850 to 1861. William J. Evitts.

Matthias Corvinus, Kaiser Friedrich III, und das Reich: Zum hunyadisch-habsburgischen Gegensatz im Donauraum. Karl Nehring.

Maturing of Multinational Enterprise: American Business Abroad from 1914 to 1970. Mira Wilkins.

Mauve Gloves & Madmen, Clatter & Vine. Tom Wolfe.

Maya. Charles Gallenkamp.

Maya Cities: Place Making and Urbanization. G. F. Andrews.

McCook-Stoneman Raid. Byron H. Mathews, Jr.

McMahon Line and After. Parshotam Mehra.

Meaning of Independence: John Adams, George Washington, Thomas Jefferson. Edmund S. Morgan.

Medicine in Seventeenth Century England: A Symposium. Allen G. Debus, ed.

Medicine in the Intermountain West: A History Health Care in Rural Areas of the West. Ward B. Studt, Jerold G. Sorensen, and Beverly Burge.

Medicine Man to Missionary: Missionaries as Agents of Change Among the Indians of Southern Ontario, 1784-1867. Elizabeth Graham.

Medieval Heresy: Popular Movements

from Bogomil to Hus. Malvolm Lambert.

Medieval Learning and Literature. J. J. G. Alexander, ed. and M. T. Gibson, ed.

The Medieval Machine: The Industrial Revolution of the Middle Ages. Sean Gimpel.

The Medieval Vision: Essays in History and Perception. Carolly Erickson.

Megaliths, Myths, and Men: An Introduction. Peter Lancaster Brown.

Mei Yao-ch'en and the Development of Early Sung Poetry. Jonathan Chaves.

Melchor Ocampo: Textos Politicos. Raúl Arreola Cortes.

Mémoires du Landamman Monod pour servir à l'histoire de la Suisse en 1815. Jean-Charles Biaudet and Marie-Claude Jequier, ed.

Memoirs. Pablo Neruda.

Memoirs of My Services in the World War, 1917-1918. George C. Marshall.

Men Against McCarthy. Richard M. Fried.

Men and Brothers: Anglo-American Antislavery Cooperation. Betty Fladeland.

Men, Mules and Mountains, Lieutenant O'Neil's Olympic Expeditions. Robert L. Wood.

Mennonites in Canada, 1786-1920: The History of a Separate People. Frank H. Epp.

Merchant Venturers of Bristol. Patrick McGrath.

Merchants and Rulers in Gujarat: The Response to the Portuguese in the Sixteenth Century. Michael Naylor Pearson.

Merchants in Crisis: Genoese and Venetian Men of Affairs and the Fourteenth Century Depression. Benjamin Z. Kedar.

Metallgefasse aus Buchara. Sigrid Westphal-Hellbusch and Ilse Bruns.

Method and Appraisal in the Physical Sciences: The Critical Background to Modern Science, 1800-1905. Colin Howson.

Methodism Alive in North Carolina: A Volume Commemorating the Bicentennial of the Carolina Circuit. O. Kelly Ingram, ed.

Mexican Americans. Joan W. Moore.

Mexican Americans. Ellwyn R. Stoddard.

Mexican Americans, a Research Bibliography. Frank Pino.

The Mexico Kickapoo Indians. Felipe A. Latorre and Dolores L. Latorre.

El México perdido: ensayos sobre el antiguo norte de México, 1540-1821. David J. Weber.

Mexico State Papers, 1744-1843. Michael P. Costeloe.

Mexico Under Spain, 1521-1556: Society and Origins of Nationality. Peggy K. Liss.

Mexico Views Manifest Destiny, 1821-1846: An Essay on the Origin of the Mexican War. Gene M. Brack.

Michigan: A Bicentennial History. Bruce Catton.

Michigan's Timber Background: A History of Clare County, 1674-1900. Forest Meek.

Mid-Ch'ing Rice Markets and Trade: An Essay in Price History. Han-Sheng Chuan and Richard A. Kraus.

The Middle Ages in French Literature, 1851-1900. Janine R. Dakyns.

Middle America. A Culture History of Heartland and Frontiers. Mary W. Helms.

Middle-Class Blacks in a White Society: Prince Hall Freemasonry in America. William Alan Muraskin.

Middle East Oil and the Energy Crisis. Joe Stork.

Middlebury College Breadloaf Writers' Conference; The First Thirty Years (1926-1955). Theodore Morrison.

The Middlebury College Foreign Language Schools: The Story of a Unique Idea. Stephen A. Freeman.

Migrants of the Mountains: The Cultural Ecology of the Blue Miao (Hmong Njua) of Thailand. William Robert Geddes.

Milestones! 200 Years of American Law: Milestones in Our Legal History. Jethro K. Lieberman.

Military and Politics in Modern Times: On Professionals, Praetorians, and Revolutionary Soldiers. Amos Perlmutter.

Military Force and American Society. Bruce M. Russett and Alfred Stepan, ed.

Military in Chilean History: Essays on Civil-Military Relations, 1810-1973. Frederick M. Nunn.

The Military Intellectual and Battle: Raimondo Montecuccoli and the Thirty Years War. Thomas M. Barker.

Military Memoirs of a Confederate. Edward Porter Alexander.

Military Music of the American Revolution. Raoul F. Camus.

Military Necessity and Civil Rights Policy, Black Citizenship and Reconstruction, 1961-1968. Mary Francis Berry.

Military Posts of Wyoming. Robert A. Murray.

Military Roles in Modernization: Civil-Military Relations in Thailand and Burma. Moshe Lissak.

Mills and Markets: A History of the Pacific Coast Lumber Industry to 1900. Thomas R. Cox.

The Mind of America 1820-1860. Rush Welter.

The Mind of China: The Culture, Customs, and Beliefs of Traditional China. Ben-Ami Scharfstein.

The Mind-Reader: New Poems. Richard Wilbur.

Mindful Militants: The Amalgamated Engineering Union in Australia, 1920-1972. T. Sheridan.

Los ministros de la audiencia de Lima en el reinado de los Borbones (1700-1821): Esquema de un estudio sobre un nucleo diregente. Guillermo Lohmann Villena.

Minoan Linear A. David W. Packard.

Minstrels of the Dawn: The Folk-Protest Singer as a Cultural Hero. Jerome L. Rodnitzky.

The Minutemen and Their World. Robert A. Gross.

Miracle Plays of Mathura. Norvin Hein.

Mirza Malkum Khan: A Study in the History of Iranian Modernism. Hamid Algar.

Mission for Hammarskjold: The Congo Crisis. Rajeshwar Dayal.

Mission to Paradise. Kenneth M. King.

Missões Franciscanas no Brasil. Frei Venâncio Willeke.

Mr. and Mrs. Gladstone: An Intimate Biography. Joyce Marlow.

Mister Charlie: Memoir of a Texas Lawman, 1902-1910. Charlie Munson.

Mr. Roosevelt's Navy: The Private War of the U.S. Atlantic Fleet, 1939-1942. Patrick Abbazia.

Il mito americano nella Venezia del settecento. Piero Del Negro.

Die Mittlere Bronzezeit Ungaras und Ihre Sudestlichen Bezichungen. Istvan Bona.

Mobile: American River City. Michael Thomason and Melton McLaurin.

Mobilizing Consent: Public Opinion and American Foreign Policy, 1937-1947. Michael Leigh.

Modelo demo-econômico de Venezuela. Anibal Fernandez, Alejo Planchart, and Gene Bigler.

Modern Bengal: A Socio-economic Survey. S. P. Sen.

Modern Chinese Literature in Malaysia and Singapore: A Classified Bibliography of Books in Chinese. Goh Thean Chye.

Modern Egyptian Drama. Farouk Abdel Wahab.

Modern German Nationalism. Abraham Ashkenasi.

The Modern Japanese Military System. James H. Buck, ed.

Modern Manuscripts: A Practical Manual for Their Management, Care, and Use. Kenneth W. Duckett.

Modern Migrations in West Africa. Samir Amin, ed.

Modern Rise of Population. T. McKeown.

Modern Thai Politics: From Village to Nation. Clark D. Neher, ed.

The Modern World-System: Capitalist Agriculture and the Origins of the European World-Economy in the Sixteenth Century. I. Wallerstein.

Modernist Impulse in American Protestantism. William R. Hutchison.

Modernization and the Japanese Factory. Robert M. Marsh and Hiroshi Mannari.

-N-

N. W. Powell: Ontario National-
ist. Margaret Prang.
Narrative of the Adventures and
Sufferings of John R. Jewitt
While Held as a Captive of the
Nootka Indians of Vancouver
Island, 1803-1805. Robert F.
Heizer, ed.
Narrator and Character in Finne-
gans Wake. Michael H. Beg-
nal and Grace Eckley.
The Natchez District and the
American Revolution. Robert
V. Haynes.
Nathan Appleton: Merchant and
Entrepreneur, 1779-1861.
Francis W. Gregory.
Nathaniel Hawthorne: The Poetics
of Enchantment. Edgar A.
Dryden.
A Nation Within a Nation: The
Rise of Texas Nationalism.
Mark E. Nackman.
The Nationalisation of British
Industry 1945-51. Norman
Chester.
Native American Historical Demog-
raphy: A Critical Bibliography.
Henry F. Dobyns.
Native Americans of North Amer-
ica: A Bibliography Based on
Collections in the Libraries of
California State University,
Northridge. David Perkins and
Norman Tanis.
The Native Population of the Amer-
icas in 1492. William M.
Denevan, ed.
Navajo Livestock Reduction: A
National Disgrace. Ruth Roes-
sel, comp. and Broderick H.
Johnson, comp.
Navajo Rugs: How to Find, Eval-
uate, Buy and Care for Them.
Don Dedera.
Navajo Stories of the Long Walk
Period. Broderick H. Johnson,
ed.
Navajos and the New Deal. Donald
L. Parman.
Navajos' Long Walk for Education:
A History of Navajo Education.
Hildegard Thompson.
Naval Documents of the American
Revolution: Volume 7, Ameri-

can Theatre, November 1, 1776-
February 28, 1777. European
Theatre October 6, 1776-December
31, 1776. William James Morgan,
ed.
Navies of the American Revolution.
Antony Preston, David Lyon, and
John H. Batchelor.
Neale Books, An Annotated Bibliogra-
phy. Robert K. Krick.
Neglected Formosa: A Translation
from the Dutch of Frederic Coyett's
Verwaerloosde Formosa. Indez de
Beauclair, ed.
Negro Slavery in Latin America.
Rolando Mellafe.
Nehru. B. N. Pandey.
Nehru: A Political Biography.
Michael Edwardes.
Neither Slave nor Free: The Freed-
men of African Descent in the So-
cieties of the New Rodl. David W.
Cohen, ed. and Jack P. Greene, ed.
Neolithic Cultures of Western Asia.
Purushottam Singh.
The Neolithic of the Near East. James
Mellaart.
Nesselrode and the Russian Rapproche-
ment with Britain, 1836-1844.
Harold N. Ingle.
Der Neue Nationalismus: In der
Publizistik Ernst Jungers und des
Kreises um ihn, 1920-1933.
Marjatta Hietala.
Nevada: Land of Discovery. David
Beatty and Robert O. Beatty.
Never Ending Wrong. Katherine A.
Porter.
New Age Now Begins: A People's
History of the American Revolu-
tion. Page Smith.
New Approaches to Latin American
History. Richard Graham, ed. and
Peter H. Smith, ed.
A New Birth of Freedom: The Re-
publican Party and Freedmen's
Rights, 1861 to 1866. Herman
Belz.
New Corporatism: Social-Political
Structures in the Iberian World.
Frederick B. Pike and Thomas
Stritch, eds.
The New Country: A Social History
of the American Frontier, 1776-
1890. Richard A. Barlett.
New Cuba: Paradoxes and Potentials.
Ronald Radosh, ed.
The New Deal. John Braeman, ed.,

North Dakota: The Heritage of a People. D. Jerome Tweton and Theodore B. Jelliff.

North Korean Communist Leadership, 1945-65. Koon Woo Nam.

North of 53°: The Wild Days of the Alaska-Yukon Mining Frontier, 1870-1914. William R. Hunt.

The North, the South, and the Powers, 1861-1865. D. P. Crook.

Northampton County in the American Revolution. Richmond E. Myers.

Northeast Asia in Prehistory. Chester S. Chard.

Northern California Indians. Stephen Powers.

Northern Expedition: China's National Revolution of 1926-1928. Donald A. Jordan.

Northern Mexico on the Eve of the United States Invasion: Rare Imprints Concerning California, Arizona, New Mexico and Texas, 1821-1846. David J. Weber.

Northumbria in the Days of Bede. Peter Hunter Blair.

Northwest Mounted Police and Law Enforcement, 1873-1905. R. C. Macleod.

Norton on Archives: The Writings of Margaret Cross Norton on Archival and Records Management. Thornton W. Mitchell.

Not in Precious Metals Alone: A Manuscript History of Montana. Montana Historical Society.

Noted Guerrillas, or the Warfare of the Border. John N. Edwards.

Notes on Cabali: The Arabic Dialect Spoken by the Alawis of "Jebel Ansariye." Bernhard Lewin.

Nothing Seemed Impossible: William C. Ralston and Early San Francisco. David Lavender.

Nottingham, Nobles, and the North: Aspects of the Revolution of 1688. David H. Hosford.

Nouvelle histoire de Paris: De la fin du siège de 885-886 à la mort de Philippe Auguste. Jacques Boussard.

The Novels of Theodore Dreiser: A Critical Study. Donald Pizer.

Nuremberg Mind: The Psychology of the Nazi Leaders. Florence R. Miale and Michael Selzer.

-O-

O Diário de Pernambuco e a História Social do Nordeste. José Antonio Gonsalves de Mello.

O Japonês na Frente de Expasão Paulista: O Processo de Absorcão do Japonês em Marília. Francisca Isabel Shurig Vieira.

Occasional Form: Henry Fielding and the Chains of Circumstance. J. Paul Hunter.

The O'Conor Papers: A Descriptive Catalog and Surname Register of the Materials at Clonalis House. Gareth W. Dunleavy and Janet E. Dunleavy.

Octavious Brooks Frothingham: Gentle Radical. J. Wade Caruthers.

O'Erasmismo e a Inquisicão em Protugal: O Processo de Fr. Valentim da Luz. J. S. Da Silva Dias.

Off at Sunrise: The Overland Journal of Charles Glass Gray. Thomas D. Clark, ed.

Les officiers bleus dans la marine francaise au XVIIIe siècle. Jacques Aman.

Oglethorpe in America. Phinizy Spalding.

Oglethorpe Ladies and the Jacobite Conspiracies. Patricia Kneas Hill.

An Ohio Reader: 1750 to the Civil War and an Ohio Reader: Reconstruction to the Present. Thomas H. Smith, ed.

Oil and Politics in Modern Brazil. Peter Seaborn Smith.

Oil Power: The Rise and Imminent Fall of an American Empire. Carl Solberg.

Oklahoma Politics in State and Nation, Volume 1. Stephen Jones.

Old Rail Fence Corners: Frontier Tales Told by Minnesota Pioneers. Lucy Leavenworth Wilder Morris, ed.

Old Sumerian and Old Akkadian Texts in Philadelphia Chiefly from Nippur. Aage Westenholz.

Our Landed Heritage: The Public
Domain, 1776-1970. Roy M.
Robbins.
Out of My Time: Poems, 1967-
1974. John Hewitt.
Outcasts in Their Own Land:
Mexican Industrial Workers,
1906-1911. Rodney D. Ander-
son.
Outer Space and Inner Sanctums:
Government, Business and
Satellite Communication.
Michael E. Kinsley.
An Outline of the Late Egyptian
Verbal System. Paul John
Frandsen.
Oxford Companion to Film. Liz-
Anne Bawden, ed.

-P-

Padma River Boatman. Manik
Bandopadhyaya.
Painting and Sculpture in Minne-
sota, 1820-1914. Rena Neu-
mann Coen.
Paintings and Journal of Joseph
Whiting Stock. Juliette Tom-
linson, ed.
Pakistan in Transition. W.
Howard Wriggins, ed.
Palace and Politics in Prewar
Japan. David Anson Titus.
Palaeoeconomy. E. S. Higgs, ed.
Panhandle Pilgrimage: Illustrated
Tales Tracing History in the
Texas Panhandle. Pauline Dur-
rett Robertson and R. L.
Robertson.
La Pannonie sous Gallian. Jeno
Fitz.
Papacy and Development: Newman
and the Primary of the Pope.
Paul Misner.
Papers Concerning Robertson's
Colony in Texas. Malcolm D.
McLean, ed.
The Papers of Adlai Stevenson.
Adlai Stevenson.
Papers of Alexander Hamilton.
Harold C. Syrett, ed. et al.
The Papers of Andrew Johnson.
Leroy P. Graf, and Ralph W.
Haskins, eds.
The Papers of Andrew Johnson,

Volume 4, 1860-1861. Andrew
Johnson.
Papers of Benjamin Franklin. Wil-
liam B. Willcox, et al.
The Papers of Daniel Webster, Cor-
respondence: Volume I, 1798-
1824. Charles M. Wiltse, ed.
Papers of Daniel Webster, Corres-
pondence: Volume 2, 1825-1829.
Charles M. Wiltse.
Papers of General Nathanael Greene.
Richard K. Showman, ed.
Papers of Harriet Beecher Stowe.
Margaret Granville Mair.
Papers of Henry Laurens. George
C. Rogers, Jr., ed., David R.
Chestnutt, ed., and Peggy J.
Clark, ed.
Papers of Jefferson Davis. James T.
McIntosh, ed.
The Papers of John C. Calhoun.
John C. Calhoun.
The Papers of John C. Calhoun, 1824-
1825, Vol. IX. John C. Calhoun.
The Papers of John Marshall. John
Marshall.
The Papers of Nathanael Greene.
Nathanael Greene.
The Papers of the Order of Indian
Wars. John M. Carroll, ed.
The Papers of Ulysses S. Grant.
Ulysses S. Grant.
Papers of Woodrow Wilson. Arthur
S. Link.
Papers on the Archaeology of Black
Mesa, Arizona. George Gumerman,
ed. and Robert C. Euler, ed.
Das Papsttum und der Amtszölibat.
Georg Denzler.
Papyrus and Tablet. A. K. Grayson,
ed. and Donald B. Redford, ed.
Parade of Memories: A History of
Clay County, Florida. Arch
Frederic Blakey.
Paris and Its Provinces, 1792-1802.
Richard Cobb.
Paris-Genèse de la 'ville': La rive
droite de la Seine des origines
a 1223. Anne Lombard-Jourdan.
Parker's Virginia Battery, C.S.A.
Robert K. Krick.
Die Parlamentarische Entstehung des
Reichpressegesetzes in der Bis-
marckzeit (1848/74). Eberhard
Naujoks.
Parliament, Policy, and Politics in
the Reign of William III. Henry
Horwitz.

Peoples of Utah. Helen Z. Papanikolas, ed.

Per Edvin Skold, 1946-1951. Gustaf Jonasson.

The Permanent Collection. Erna Gunther.

Pernambuco: Seu Desenvolvimento Histórico. M. de Oliveira Lima.

Perpetual Dilemma: Jewish Religion in the Jewish State. S. Zalman Abramor.

The Persistent Tradition in New South Politics. George Brown Tindall.

Personal Vieros: Explorations in Film. Robin Wood.

Perspectives and Irony in American Slavery. Harry P. Owens, ed.

Perspectives on Armed Politics in Brazil. Henry H. Keith and Robert A. Hayes, eds.

Perspectives on Guru Nanak: Seminar Papers. Harbans Singh, ed.

Perspectives on Technology. Nathan Rosenberg.

Perspectives on the Social Sciences in Canada. T. N. Guinsburg and G. L. Renber.

Perspectives '76. Del Goodwin and Dorcas Chaffee, ed.

Peru: A Cultural History. Henry F. Dobyns and Paul L. Doughty.

Perugia, 1260-1340: Conflict and Change in a Medieval Italian Urban Society. Sarah Rubin Blanshei.

Peruvian Experiment: Continuity and Change Under Military Rule. Abraham F. Lowenthal, ed.

Peruvian Nationalism: A Corporatist Revolution. David Chaplin, ed.

Peter Dillon of Vanikoro: Chevalier of the South Seas. J. W. Davidson.

Phaistos Disc. Leon Pomerance.

Pharisee Among Philistines: The Diary of Judge Matthew P. Deady, 1871-1892. Malcolm Clark, Jr., ed.

The Philadelphia and Erie Railroad: Its Place in American Economic History. Homer Tope Rosenberger.

Philadelphia Georgian: The City House of Samuel Powell and Some of Its Eighteenth-Century Neighbors. George B. Tatum.

The Philadelphia Quakers in the Industrial Age, 1865-1920. Philip S. Benjamin.

Philadelphia--the Federalist City: A Study of Urban Politics, 1789-1801. Richard G. Miller.

Philadelphia's Philosopher Mechanics: A History of the Franklin Institute, 1824-1865. Bruce Sinclair.

Philipp Eulenburgs Politische Korrespondenz. John C. G. Rohl, ed.

Philip II of Spain. Peter Pierson.

The Philippines. Robert E. Baldwin.

The Philosophes and the People. H. G. Payne.

"Philosophes" e "Chrétiens éclairés." Daniele Menozzi.

Philosophical Chemistry in the Scottish Enlightenment: The Doctrines and Discoveries of William Cullen and Joseph Black. A. L. Donavon.

Philosophical Grammar. Ludwig Wittgenstein.

Photographs of the Southwest. Ansel Adams.

The Physician and Sexuality in Victorian America. John S. Haller, Jr. and Robin M. Haller.

Physics, Patents, and Politics: A Biography of Charles Crafton Page. Robert C. Post.

The Piano: A History. Cyril Ehrlich.

Piaroa, a People of the Orinoco Basin: A Study in Kinship and Marriage. Joanna Overing Kaplan.

Picture Sources 3: Collections of Prints and Photographs in the U. S. and Canada. Ann Novotny, ed.

Pierre Leroux and the Birth of Democratic Socialism, 1797-1848. Jack Bakunin.

Pietro Badoglio. Piero Pieri and Giorgio Rochat.

Pigtail War: American Involvement in the Sino-Japanese War of 1894-1895. Jeffery M. Dorwart.

Pills Against Poverty: A Study of the Introduction of Western Medicine in a Tamil Village. Goran Djurfeldt and Staffan Lindberg.

Pills, Pen & Politics: The Story of General Leon Jastremski, 1843-1907. Edward Pinkowski.

Pioneer Miner and the Pack Mule
Express. Ernest A. Wiltsee.
Pioneer Steelmaker in the West:
The Colorado Fuel and Iron
Company 1892-1903. H. Lee
Scamehorn.
Pipe Clay and Drill, John J.
Pershing: The Classic Ameri-
can Soldier. Richard Goldhurst.
Pistoia nell XIII secolo: Saggio
storico sulla stirpe dei
Cancellieri di Pistoia. Girol-
amo Ganucci Cancellieri.
A Place Called Home: A History
of Low-Cost Housing in Man-
hattan. Anthony Jackson.
Plagues and Peoples. William
H. McNeill.
Plains Apache. John Upton
Terrell.
Plains Indian Mythology. Alice
Marriott and Carol K. Rachlin.
Planning and the Historic Environ-
ment. Trevor Rowley, ed. and
Mike Breakell, ed.
A Plantation Called Petapawag:
Some Notes on the History of
Groton, Massachusetts. Vir-
ginia A. May.
The Plantation School. Anthony
Gerald Albanese.
Pleasure and Business in Western
Pennsylvania: The Journal of
Joshua Gilpin, 1809. Joseph E.
Walker. ed.
Pocahontas: The Life and the
Legend. Frances Mossiker.
The Poetry of Chaucer. John
Gardner.
A Point of Pride: The University
of Portland Story. James T.
Covert.
Poland and the Coming of the
Second World War: The Diplo-
matic Papers of A. J. Drexel
Biddle, Jr., United States
Ambassador to Poland, 1937-
1939. Philip F. Cannistraro,
et al, ed.
The Policy of the Emperor
Gallienus. Lukas de Blois.
Polish-American Politics in
Chicago, 1888-1940. Edward R.
Kantowicz.
Polish-German Relations, 1919-
1932. Jerzy Krasuski.
Polish-German Relations, 1937-
1939: The True Character of

Jozef Beck's Foreign Policy.
Peter Raina.
Polish-Jewish Relations During the
Second World War. Emanuel
Ringelblum.
Politica e Trabalho no Brasil: Dos
Años Vinte a 1930. Paulo Sérgio
De M. S. Pinheiro.
Política Eclesial de Los Gobiernos
Liberales Españoles, 1833-1840.
Vicente Carcel Ortí.
Political Corruption: The Ghana Case.
Victor T. Levine.
The Political Economy of Agrarian
Change: An Essay on the Green
Revolution. Keith Griffin.
Political Economy Past and Present:
A Review of Leading Theories of
Economic Policy. Lord Robbins.
Political History of Finland, 1809-
1966. L. A. Puntila.
Political Leadership in Korea. Suh
Dae-Sook and Chae-jin Lee.
Political Participation in a Developing
Nation: India. Madan Lal Goel.
Political Parties in Cracow, 1945-
1947. Zenobiusz Kozik.
Political Regime and Public Policy
in the Philippines: A Comparison
of Bacolod and Iloilo Cities.
Howard M. Leichter.
Political Structure in a Changing
Sinhalese Village. Marguerite S.
Robinson.
Political Study of Pakistan. Safdar
Mahmood.
The Political Thought of Hannah
Arendt. Margaret Canovan.
Political Violence Under the Swastika:
581 Early Nazis. Peter H. Merkl.
Politicians and Soldiers in Ghana,
1962-1972. D. Austin and R.
Luckham, ed.
Politicians, Planters, and Plain Folk:
Courthouse and Statehouse in the
Upper South, 1850-1860. Ralph A.
Wooster.
Politics and Class Formation in Uganda.
Mahmood Mamdani.
Politics and Religion During the Eng-
lish Revolution of the Scots and the
Long Parliament, 1643-1645.
Lawrence Kaplan.
Politics and the Migrant Poor in
Mexico City. Wayne A. Cornelius.
Politics and the Nation, 1450-1660:
Obedience, Resistance and Public
Order. D. M. Loades.

Politics in Argentina 1890-1930: The Rise and Fall of Radicalism. David Rock.

Politics in Liberia: The Conservative Road to Development. Martin Lowenkopf.

Politics in the Sudan: Parliamentary and Military Rule in an Emerging African Nation. Peter K. Bechtold.

The Politics of American Individualism: Herbert Hoover in Transition, 1918-1921. Gary Dean Best.

The Politics of Business in California, 1890-1920. Mansel G. Blackford.

Politics of Catherinian Russia: The Panin Party. David L. Ransel.

Politics of Command in the American Revolution. Jonathan Gregory Rossie.

Politics of Frustration: The United States in German Naval Planning. Holger H. Herwig.

Politics of History: Writing the History of the American Revolution, 1783-1815. Arthur H. Shaffer.

The Politics of Hostility--Castro's Revolution and United States Policy. Lynn Darrell Bender.

Politics of Illusion: The Fischer Controversy in German Historiography. John A. Moses.

Politics of Reappraisal 1918-1919. Gillian Peele and Chris Cook, eds.

Politics or Principle: Congressional Voting on the Civil War Amendments and Pro-Negro Measures, 1838-69. Glenn M. Linden.

Politik im Wartesaal: Osterreichische Exilpolitik in Grossbritannien, 1938-1945. Helene Maimann.

Popery and Politics in England 1660-1688. J. Miller.

La popolazione de Imola e del suo territorio nel XIII e XIV secolo. Antonio Iven Pini.

Popular Uprisings in the Philippines 1840-1940. David R. Sturtevant.

Population and Development in Southeast Asia. John Kantner and Lee McCaffrey, ed.

Population Factor in African Studies. R. P. Moss and R. J. A. R. Rathbone.

Population of the British Colonies in America Before 1776: A Survey of Census Data. Robert V. Wells.

The Population of the California Indians, 1769-1970. Sherburne F. Cook.

Populism: A Psychohistorical Perspective. James M. Youngdale.

Populism and Politics: William Alfred Peffer and the People's Party. Peter H. Argersinger.

Populist Vanguard: A History of the Southern Farmers' Alliance. Robert C. McMath, Jr.

Positivism in Bengal: A Case Study in the Transmission and Assimilation of an Ideology. Geraldine Hancock Forbes.

El Positivismo Durante el Porfiriato. William D. Raat.

Potential for Joint Ventures in Eastern Europe. Robert S. Kretschmar and Robin Foor.

Pottery Style and Society in Ancient Peru: Art as a Mirror of Society in the Ica Valley, 1350-1570. Dorothy Menzel.

Pouvoir royal et vie régionale en Provence au déclin de la monarchie. François-Xavier Emmanuelli.

Poverty and Charity in Aix-en-Provence, 1640-1789. Cissie C. Fairchilds.

Power and Pawn: The Female in Iberian Families, Societies, and Cultures. Ann M. Pescatelo.

Power and the Pulpit in Puritan New England. Emory Elliott.

Power in the Pacific: The Origins of Naval Arms Limitations, 1914-1922. Roger Dingman.

The Prairie State: A Documentary History of Illinois. Robert P. Sutton, ed.

Prairie West to 1905: A Canadian Sourcebook. Lewis G. Thomas, ed.

Prehistoric Maori Fortifications. Aileen Fox.

Prehistory of the Tehuacan Valley. Richard S. MacNeish.

Pre-Industrial England: Economy and Society from 1500-1750. B. A. Holderness.

Prelude to Disaster: The American Role in Vietnam, 1940-1963. Weldon A. Brown.

Prelude to Power: The Parisian Radical Press, 1789-1791. Jack Richard Censer.

Prelude to Protectorate in Morocco: Precolonial Protest and Resistance, 1860-1912. Edmund Burke III.

Les Préoccupations statistiques du gouvernement des Pays-Bas autrichiens et la denombrement des industries dressé en 1764. Philippe Moureaux.

Presencia Hispanica en La Florida, Ayer y Hoy: 1513-1976. Jose Agustin Balseiro, ed.

Present Lives Future Becoming: South African Landscape in Words. C. Pieterse and G. Hallett.

The Preservation of Australia's Aboriginal Heritage. Robert Edwards, ed.

Presidency of James Buchanan. Elbert B. Smith.

The Presidency of John Adams. Ralph Adams Brown.

Presidency of Thomas Jefferson. Forest McDonald.

President Makers: From Mark Hanna to Joseph P. Kennedy. Francis Russell.

President Paul Kurger: A Biography. Johannes Meintjes.

Presidential Spending Power. Louis Fisher.

Presidential Style: Some Giants and a Pygmy in the White House. Samuel Rosenman and Dorothy Rosenman.

Presidio: Bastion of the Spanish Borderlands. Max L. Moorhead.

Prestes Column: Revolution in Brazil. Neill Macaulay.

A Primer for Local Historical Societies. Dorothy Weyer Creigh.

La Primera Republica Federal de Mexico (1824-1835). Michael P. Costeloe.

The Private Franklin: The Man and His Family. Calude-Anne Lopez and Eugenia W. Herbert.

Private Theodore Ewert's Diary of the Black Hills Expedition of 1974. John M. Carroll, ed. and Lawrence A. Frost, ed.

Privateers and Volunteers, the Men and Women of Our Reserve Naval Forces: 1766 to 1866. Rueben Elmore Stivers.

The Problem of Slavery in the Age of Revolution 1770-1823. David Brion Davis.

Problemi di storia dell-Internazionale Comunista (1919-1939). Fernando Claudin, et al.

Proceedings of the First United States Conference on Ethiopian Studies, 1973. Harold G. Marcus, ed.

Processi politici del Senato Lombardo-Veneto, 1815-1851. Alfredo Grandi, ed.

Proclamations of the Tudor Kings. R. W. Heinze.

The Proclamations of the Tudor Queens. Frederic A. Youngs, Jr.

Profiles of Alabama Pharmacy. James R. Kuykendall, et al.

The Proletariat of Russia and Poland in Their Joint Revolutionary Struggle (1907-1912). S. M. Fal'kovich.

Prologue to Independence: New Jersey in the Coming of the American Revolution. Larry R. Gerlach.

Prologue to Peron: Argentina in Depression and War, 1930-1943. Mark Falcoff and Ronald H. Dolkart, ed.

The Promise Kept. Kurth Sprague.

Prophetess of Health: A Study of Ellen G. White. Ronald L. Numbers.

Prophetic Waters: The River in Early American Life and Literature. John Seelye.

Prophétisme et thérapeutique: Albert Atcho et la communauté de Bregbo. Marc Augé, et al.

Prophets on the Right: Profiles of Conservative Critics of American Globalism. Ronald Radosh.

Pröpste, Propstei und Stift von Sankt Barthol mäus in Frankfurt:9. Jarhundert tis 1802. Günter Rauch.

Protestantism and the New South: North Carolina Baptists and Methodists in Political Crisis, 1894-1903. Frederick A. Bode.

Une Province francaise à la Renaissance: La vie intellectuelle en Forez au XVIe siècle. Claude Longeon.

La Provincia Franciscana de Santa Cruz de Caracas. Lino Gomez Canedo.

British Self-Governing Colonies,
1830-1910. Robert A. Huttenback.

Radical Agriculture. Richard
Merrill, ed.

The Radical Lord Radnor: The
Public Life of Viscount Folkstone, Third Earl of Radnor
(1779-1869). Ronald K. Huch.

Radical Protest and Social Structure: The Southern Farmers'
Alliance and Cotton Tenancy,
1880-1890. Michael Schwartz.

Radical Republicans in the North:
State Politics During Reconstruction. James C. Mohr, ed.

Radical View: The "Agate": Dispatches of Whitelaw Reid, 1861-
1865. James G. Smart, ed.

I radicali in Italia (1849-1925).
Alessandro Galante Garrone.

Railroad: Trains and Train Peo-
ple in American Culture.
James Alan McPherson, ed. and
Miller Williams, ed.

Rain-Forest Collectors and Traders: A Study of Resource Utilization in Modern and Ancient
Malaya. F. L. Dunn.

The Raindance People: The Pueblo
Indians, Their Past and Present.
Richard Erdoes.

Ramsay Macdonald. David
Marquand.

A Ranching Saga: The Lives of
William Electious Halsell and
Ewing Halsell. William Curry
Holden.

Ras Shamra Parallels: The Texts
from Ugarit and the Hebrew
Bible. Loren R. Fisher, ed.

Räuber und Gauner in Deutschland:
Das organisierts Banden wesen
im 18. und fruhen 19.
Jahrhundert. Carsten Küther.

The Rawhide Years: A History of
the Cattlemen and the Cattle
Country. Glenn R. Vernam.

Reader's Hebrew-English Lexicon
of the Old Testament. Ferris
L. McDaniel.

Readings in African Political
Thought. Gideon-Cyrus M.
Mutiso and S. W. Rohio, ed.

Readings in Louisiana Politics.
Mark T. Carleton, ed. , Perry
H. Howard, ed. , and Joseph
B. Parker, ed.

Reaffirmation of Republicanism:
Eisenhower and the Eighty-Third
Congress. Gary W. Reichard.

Real Joaquin Murieta: Robin Hood
Hero or Gold Rush Gangster?
Remi Nadeau.

Reappraisals in British Imperial
History. Ronald Hyam and Ged
Martin.

Rebels and Bureaucrats: China's
December 9ers. John Israel and
Donald W. Klein.

Rebels Under Sail: The American
Navy During the Revolution.
William M. Fowler, Jr.

Rebuilding the Christian Commonwealth: New England Congregationalists and Foreign Missions, 1800-
1830. John A. Andrew, III.

Recasting Bourgeois Europe: Stabilization in France, Germany and Italy
in the Decade After World War I.
Charles S. Maier.

Recent Archaeological Excavations in
Europe. Rupert Bruce-Mitford.

Recent Work in Rural Archaeology.
P. J. Fowler.

Recherches sur la stratification
sociale à Paris aux XVIIe siècles.
Roland Mousnier.

The Reckless Breed of Men: The
Trappers and Fur Traders of the
Southwest. Robert Glass Cleland.

Reckoning With Slavery. Paul A.
David, et al.

Los recogimientos de mujeres:
Respuesta a una problematica
social novohispana. Josefina
Muriel.

The Recollection of a Happy Childhood
by Mary Esther Huger Daughter of
Francis Kinloch Huger of Long
House Near Pendleton, South Carolina, 1826-1848. Mary Stevenson,
ed.

Reconstruction of Edward A. Pollard:
A Rebel's Conversion to Postbellum
Unionism. Jack P. Maddex, Jr.

The Red and the Black. Dwight W.
Hoover.

Red, Black, and Green: Black Nationalism in the United States.
Alphonso Pinkney.

Red Children in White America. Ann
H. Beuf.

Red Men and Hat Wearers: Viewpoints
in Indian History. Daniel Tyler,
ed.

Redeem the Time: The Puritan
Sabbath in Early America.
Winton U. Solberg.
Rediscovering Hawthorne. Kenneth Dauber.
Reflections from the North
Country. Sigurd F. Olson.
Reflections on Espionage. John
Hollander.
Reform and Revolution in China:
The 1911 Revolution in Hunan
and Hubei. Joseph W.
Esherick.
Reform in Nineteenth-Century
China. Paul A. Cohen and
John E. Schrecker, ed.
Das Regigiöse Geschichtsbilt Der
Azteken. Anncharlott Eschmann.
Regional Variations in the Economic Development of Germany During the Nineteenth Century.
Frank B. Tipton, Jr.
Regional Wage Variations in
Britain, 1850-1914. E. H.
Hunt.
Registrum Iohannis Mey: The
Register of John Mey Archbishop of Armagh, 1443-1456.
W. G. H. Quigley and E. D.
F. Roberts, ed.
Reichsstädtekurie und Westfälischer
Friendenskongress. Günter
Buchstab.
Reinhold Niebuhr: A Political Account. Paul Merkley.
Relations Between the Autochthonous Population and the Migratory
Populations on the Territory of
Romania. Miron Constantinescu,
et al.
Relazioni dei Rettori Veneti in
Terraferma. Amelio Tagliaferri.
Religion and Ideology in Sri Lanka.
Francois Houtart.
Religion and Rural Society: South
Lindsey, 1825-1875. James
Obelkevich.
Religion and Society in Industrial
England: Church, Chapel and
Social Change, 1740-1914.
Alan D. Gilbert.
Religion and the Church in Russian History. E. F. Grekulov,
ed.
Religion in Antebellum Kentucky.
John B. Boles.
The Religion of the Chinese People. Marcel Granet.

The Religion of the Slaves: A Study
of the Religious Tradition and
Behavior of Plantation Slaves in
the United States 1830-1865.
Olli Alho.
Religion und Geschicte des alten
Agypten: gesammelte Aufsatze.
Siegfried Morenz.
Religione e chiesa in Polonia, 1945-
1975: Saggio storico-
instituzionale. Franciszek
Kaminski.
Religione e società dalle riforme
napoleoniche all'età liberale.
Angelo Gambasin.
Reluctant King: Joseph Bonaparte,
King of the Two Sicilies and
Spain. Michael Ross.
Remember the Ladies: New Perspectives on Women in American History. Carol V. R. George, ed.
The Reminiscences of Doctor John
Sebastian Helmcken. Dorothy
Blakey Smith, ed.
Renaissance Rome 1500-1559: A
Portrait of a Society. Peter
Partner.
Repercusiones de Pavón en Mendoza
a través del periodismo (1861-
1863). Pedro Sanots Martínez C.
A Report and Survey Presented to the
Pilgrim and Radcliffe Trustees.
The Central Records of the Church
of England.
The Report of the Royal Commission
of 1552. W. C. Richardson, ed.
The Representative of the People?
Voters and Voting in England Under
the Early Stuarts. Derek Hirst.
Reprographic Services in Libraries:
Organization and Administration.
Charles G. La Hood and Robert
C. Sullivan.
La république jacobine, 10 août 1792-
9 thermidor an 11. Marc
Bouloiseau.
Requiem for the Renascence: The
State of Fiction in the Modern
South. Walter Sullivan.
Research Guide to Central Party and
Government Meetings in China,
1949-1975. Kenneth Lieberthal.
Research Guide to the Chiao-bui-bsin-
pao (The Church News), 1868-1874.
Adrian A. Bennett, comp.
Researching, Writing and Publishing
Local History. Thomas E. Felt.
Resistenza e storia d'Italia: Problemi
e ipotesi di ricerca. Guido Quazza.

Resolutions and Decisions of the
Communist Party of the Soviet
Union. Robert H. McNeal, ed.
Respectable Folly: Millenarians
and the French Revolution in
England and France. Clarke
Garrett.
The Restoration. Joan Thirsk, ed.
Restoration Historians and the
English Civil War. Royce
MacGillivray.
Retaliation: Japanese Attacks and
Allied Countermeasures on the
Pacific Coast in World War II.
Bert Webber.
Retreat from Reform: The Prohi-
bition Movement in the United
States, 1890-1913. Jack S.
Blocker, Jr.
Retrospect at a Tenth Anniversary:
Southern Illinois University at
Edwardsville. David L. Butler.
Revolt in Louisiana: The Spanish
Occupation, 1766-1770. John
Preston Moore.
The Revolt of the Comuneros,
1721-1735: A Study in the
Colonial History of Paraguay.
Adalberto Lopez.
Revolt of the Provinces: Conserva-
tives and Radicals in the Eng-
lish Civil War, 1630-1650.
J. S. Morrill.
Revolts und Revolution in Europa.
Peter Blickle, ed.
A Revolucão por Dentro. Hernani
D'Aguiar.
Revolution. Jean Baechler.
Revolution. David Chaplin.
Revolution and Improvement: The
Western World, 1775-1847.
John Roberts.
Revolution and Mass Democracy:
The Paris Club Movement in
1848. Peter H. Amann.
Revolution and Reaction: 1848
and the Second French Repub-
lic. Roger Price, ed.
Revolution and Reaction in Cuba,
1933-1960: A Political Soci-
ology from Machado to Castro.
Samuel Farber.
Revolution and the Revolutionary
Ideal. Robert Blackey and
Clifford Paynton.
Revolution in Central Europe,
1918-1919. F. L. Carsten.
Revolution und Ideologie: Der

Hussitismus. Robert
Kalivoda.
Revolutionaries vietnamiens et
pouvoir colonial en Indochine:
Communistes, Trotskystes, National-
istes a Saigon de 1932-1937.
Daniel Hemery.
Revolutionary Age of Andrew Jackson.
Robert V. Remini.
Revolutionary Ascetic: Evolution of a
Political Type. Bruce Mazlish.
Revolutionary China, A Personal Ac-
count, 1926-1949. William L.
Tung.
Revolutionary Civil War: The Ele-
ments of Victory and Defeat.
David Wilkinson.
Revolutionary College: American
Presbyterian Higher Education,
1707-1837. Howard Miller.
Revolutionary Jews from Marx to
Trotsky. Robert Wistrich.
Revolutionary Left in Spain, 1914-
1923. Gerald H. Meaker.
Revolutionary Organization: Institu-
tion-Building Within the People's
Liberation Armed Forces. Paul
Berman.
Revolutionary Underground: The
Story of the Irish Republican
Brotherhood, 1858-1924. Leon
O'Broin.
Revolutionary Virginia: The Road to
Independence. Robert L. Scribner
and Brent Tarter, ed.
Revolution's Godchild: The Birth,
Death, and Regeneration of the
Society of the Cincinnati in North
Carolina. Curtis Carroll Davis.
Rezeption antiker und patristischer
Wissenschaft bei Hrabanus Maurus.
Maria Rissel.
The Rhetoric of History. Savoie
Lottinville.
Ricchata Quellccani, Pinturas Murales
Prehispanicas. Duccio Bonavia.
Ricerche Sull'Editio Princeps degli
Atti creci del Consilio di Firenze.
Vittorio Peri.
Rich Harvest: A History of the
Grange, 1867-1900. D. Sven
Nordin.
Richard Mather of Dorchester. B. R.
Burg.
Richard II in the Early Chronicles.
Louisa Desaussure Duls.
Richelieu and Reason of State. Wil-
liam F. Church.

Richmond: The Story of a City.
Virginius Dabney.
Riddle of the Pyramids.   Kurt
Mendelssohn.
Rio Claro: A Brazilian Plantation
System, 1820-1920.   Warren
Dean.
Rise and Fall of American Com-
munism.   Philip J. Jaffe.
Rise and Fall of Black Slavery.
C. Duncan Rise.
The Rise and Fall of the House of
Medici.   Christopher Hibbert.
The Rise and Fall of the Victorian
Servant.   Pamela Horn.
The Rise of Adventism.   Edwin
Scott Gaustad, ed.
Rise of Afrikanerdom: Power,
Apartheid and the Afrikaner
Civil Religion.   T. Dunbar
Moodie.
Rise of German Industrial Power,
1834-1914.   W. O. Henderson.
The Rise of Modern Japan.   Peter
Duus.
The Rise of Nationalism in Viet-
nam, 1900-1941.   William J.
Duiker.
The Rise of Party in England:
The Rockingham Whigs 1760-82.
Frank O'Gorman.
Rise of the European Economy:
An Economic History of Conti-
nental Europe from the Fifteenth
to the Eighteenth Century.
Hermann Kellenbenz.
The Rise of the Medical Profes-
sion: A Study of Collective
Social Mobility.   Noel Parry
and José Parry.
The Rise of Turkish Nationalism,
1876-1908.   David Kushner.
Rise Up, Women!   The Militant
Campaign of the Women's Social
and Political Union, 1903-1914.
Andrew Rosen.
The Rising South, Volume 1:
Changes and Issues.   Donald R.
Noble and Joab L. Thomas, ed.
The Rising South, Volume II:
Southern Universities and the
South.   Robert H. McKenzie,
ed.
Rites of Passage; Adolescence in
America 1790 to the Present.
Joseph F. Kett.
Rival Empires of Trade in the
Orient, 1600-1800.   Holden
Furber.

River Runs Through It and Other
Stories.   Norman Maclean.
Die Rkomischen Bronzen Der Schweig,
II, Avenches.   Annalis Leibundgut.
Road to Babylon: Development of U. S.
Assyriology.   C. Wade Meade.
The Road to 1945: British Politics
and the Second World War.   Paul
Addison.
The Road to the Little Big Horn--And
Beyond.   Alban W. Hoopes.
Robert Frost: The Later Years
1938-1963.   Lawrence Thompson
and R. H. Winnick.
Robert Laird Borden: A Bibliography.
Robert Craig Brown.
Robert Marion LaFollette.   Fred
Greenbaum.
Robert Potter: Founder of the Texas
Navy.   Ernest G. Fischer.
Robespierre the Incorruptible, A
Psycho-Biography.   Max Gallo.
The Rock Paintings of the Chumash:
A Study of the California Indian
Culture.   Campbell Grant.
Rocky Mountain Rendezvous: A His-
tory of the Fur Trade Rendezvous,
1825-1840.   Fred R. Gowans.
Rodriguez de Mendoza: Hombre de
lucha.   Fernando Romero.
Roger Casement.   Brian Inglis.
Rogues, Buffoons and Statesmen.
Gordon Newell.
Role of the Church in New France.
Cornelius J. Jaenen.
The Role of the Supreme Court in
American Government.   Archibald
Cox.
Roll, Jordan, Roll: The World the
Slaves Made.   Eugene D. Genovese.
The Roman Catholic and the Creation
of the Modern Irish State, 1878-
1886.   Emmet Larkin.
Roman Forts of the Saxon Shore.
Stephen Johnson.
Roman Government's Response to
Crisis.   Ramsay MacMullen.
Roman Sculpture from Cyrenaica
Imperii Romani, Vol. II, fascicule
I.   Janet Huskinson.
Roman Villa: An Historical Introduc-
tion.   John Percival.
Romantic Sublime: Studies in the
Structure and Psychology of Trans-
cendence.   Thomas Weiskel.
Der römische Genius.   Kunckel, Hille.
Die römischen Inshriften von Tarraco.
Gëza Alföldy.
Roosevelt and Churchill, 1939-1941:

Sektionschef Robert Hecht und die
Zerstorung der Demokratie in
Osterreich: Eine histori-
schpolitische Studie.   Peter
Huemer.
Die Selbstentmachtung Europas:
Das Experiment des Friedens
vor und im Ersten Weltkrieg.
Erwin Hozle.
Selected Poems.   Robert Watson.
Selected Poems, 1923-1975.
Robert Penn Warren.
The Seleucid Army: Organization
and Tactics in the Great Cam-
paigns.   Bezalel Bar-Kochva.
Senate vs. Governor, Alabama 1971:
Referents for Opposition in a
One-Party Legislature.   Harold
Stanley.
Senator Joseph McCarthy and the
American Labor Movement.
David M. Oshinsky.
Send These to Me: Jews and
Other Immigrants in Urban
America.   John Higham.
Sergei Zubatov and Revolutionary
Marxism: The Struggle for the
Working Class in Tsarist Rus-
sia.   Jeremiah Schneiderman.
Serial.   Cyra McFadden.
Serpent Symbolism in the Old
Testament.   Karen Randolph
Joines.
1777: The Year of the Hangman.
John S. Pancake.
Seventy Days to Singapore.
Stanley L. Falk.
Sexual Variance in Society and
History.   Vern L. Bulough.
Shadow of a Continent: The Prize
that Lay to the West--1776.
Larry L. Meyer.
The Shadow of the Telescope: A
Biography of John Herschel.
Gunther Buttmann.
Shaihu Umar.   U. Ladan and D.
Lyndersay.
Shakti: Power in the Conceptual
Structure of Karimpur Reli-
gion.   Susan Snow Wadley.
Shaman and the Jaguar: A Study
of Narcotic Drugs Among the
Indians of Columbia.   G.
Reichel-Dolmatoff.
Shameful Trade.   F. George Kay.
Shanghai Old-Style Banks (Ch'ien-
Chuang), 1800-1935.   Andrea
Lee McElderry.

The Shape of Hawthorne's Career.
Nina Baym.
Shaping of a City: Business and
Politics in Portland, Oregon, 1885-
1915.   E. Kimbark MacColl.
Shaping the American Educational
State: 1900 to the Present.
Clarence J. Karier, ed.
Shattered Peace: The Origins of the
Cold War and the National Security
Council.   Daniel Yergin.
Shen Pu-Hai: A Chinese Political
Philosopher of the Fourth Century
B. C.   Herrlee G. Creel.
Sherman and the Burning of Columbia.
Marion Brunson Lucas.
Shipbuilding in Colonial America.
Joseph A. Goldenberg.
Ships of the Great Lakes.   David T.
Glick.
The Sian Incident: A Pivotal Point in
Modern Chinese History.   Tien-
wei Wu.
Les siècles d'or de l'histoire étrusque
(675-475 avant J. -C.).   Alain Hus.
El siglo XIX en Panamâ.   Victor F.
Goytia.
Le Signe zodiacal du Scorpion dans
les traditions occidentales de
l'Antiquite greco-latine a la
Renaissance.   Luigi Aurigemma.
Silas Deane: Patriot or Traitor.
Coy Hilton James.
Silent Sisterhood: Middle Class
Women in the Victorian Home.
Patricia Branca.
Simone Weil: A Life.   Simone
Petrement.
Simoniacal Entry into Religious Life
from 1000 to 1260: A Social,
Economic and Legal Study.   Joseph
H. Lynch.
Simple Justice: The History of Brown
V. Board of Education and Black
America's Struggle for Equality.
Richard Kluger.
Sinews of Independence: Monthly
Strength Reports of the Continental
Army.   Charles H. Lesser, ed.
Le Sinistre E L'Aventino.   Ariane
Landuyt.
The Sino-Indian Border Question: A
Historical Review.   S. P. Sen, ed.
The Sino-Soviet Confrontation: Impli-
cations for the Future.   Harold C.
Hinton.
Sir Aurel Stein: Archaeological Ex-
plorer.   Jeannette Mirsky.

Sir Christopher Wren: A Histori-
cal Biography. Bryan Little.
Sir Frank Swettenhams' Malayan
Journals, 1874-1876. P. L.
Burns, and C. D. Cowan, ed.
Sir Robert Peel's Administration,
1841-1846. Travis L. Crosby.
Sir Samuel Hoare och Etiopienkon-
flikten, 1935. Lars Akerblom.
Sister Kenny: The Woman Who
Challenged the Doctors. Victor
Cohn.
Six Score: Thd 120 Best Books
on the Range Cattle Industry.
W. S. Reese.
Sixteenth Century European Printed
Works on the First Japanese
Mission to Europe: A Descrip-
tive Bibliography. Adriana
Boscaro.
A Sketch of the Early History of
Hanover County, Virginia, and
Its Large and Important Contri-
butions to the American Revolu-
tion. Robert Bolling Lancaster.
Sketches from a Dirt Road.
Gregory Jaynes.
Sketches of St. Augustine. Rugus
K. Sewall.
Skystone and Silver: The Collec-
tor's Book of Southwest Jewelry.
Carl Rosnek and Joseph Stacy.
Slave Population and Economy in
Jamaica, 1807-1834. B. W.
Higman.
The Slave Trade of Eastern Africa.
R. W. Beachey.
Slavery: A Problem in American
Institutional and Intellectual Life.
Stanley M. Elkins.
Slavery, Abolition and Emancipa-
tion: Black Slaves and the
British Empire. Michael
Carton, ed., James Walvin,
ed., and David Wright, ed.
Slavery and the Churches in Early
America, 1619-1819. Lester
B. Scherer.
Slavery and Serfdom in the Middle
Ages: Selected Papers by Marc
Block.
Slavery on the Spanish Frontier:
The Colombian Choco, 1680-
1810. William Frederick Sharp.
Slavery, Race and the American
Revolution. Duncan J.
MacLeod.
Slaves and Freedmen in Civil War
Louisiana. C. Peter Ripley.

Slaves and the White God: Blacks
in Mexico, 1570-1650. Colin A.
Palmer.
Slaves Without Masters: The Free
Negro in the Antebellum South.
Ira Berlin.
Slovak Language and Literature.
J. M. Kirschbaum.
The Slovak National Awakening: An
Essay in the Intellectual History
of East Central Europe. Peter
Brock.
Slow Fade to Black: The Negro in
American Film, 1900-1942.
Thomas Cripps.
Slum as a Way of Life: A Study of
Coping Behavior in Urban Environ-
ment. F. Landa Jocano.
Small Towns of Hampshire: The
Archaeological and Historical Im-
plications of Development.
Michael Hughes.
Smith, Ricardo, Marx. Claudio
Napoleoni.
Smuts: A Reappraisal. Bernard
Friedman.
A Social and Economic History of the
Near East in the Middle Ages.
E. Ashtor.
Social and Political History of the
German 1848 Revolution. Rudolph
Stadelmann.
Social and Political Ideas of Bipin
Chanra Pal. Amalendu Prasad
Mookerjee.
Social Basis for Prewar Japanese
Militarism: The Army and the
Rural Community. Richard J.
Smethurst.
Social Change in a Peripheral Society:
The Creation of a Balkan Colony.
Daniel Chirot.
Social Change in an Industrial Town:
Patterns of Progress in Warren,
Pennsylvania, from Civil War to
World War I. Michael P.
Weber.
Social Composition of the Ruling
Class of Byzantium. A. P.
Kazhdan.
Social Control in the Colonial Economy.
J. R. T. Hughes.
Social Democracy and Industrial
Militancy: The Labour Party, the
Trade Unions, and Incomes Policy,
1945-1974. Leo Panitch.
Social Gospel in Canada: Papers of
the Interdisciplinary Conference on
the Social Gospel in Canada, March

21-24, 1973 at the University of Regina. Richard Allen, ed.

The Social History of the Machine. John Ellis.

Social Life in an Indian Slum. Paul D. Wiebe.

The Social Milieu of Alexander Pope: Lives, Example and the Poetic Response. Howard Erskine-Hill.

Social Mobility Among the Professions: Study of the Professions in a Transitional Indian City. S. M. Dubey.

Social Science and the Ignoble Savage. R. L. Meek.

Social Science in America: The First Two Hundred Years. Charles M. Bonjean, ed., Louis Schneider, ed., and Robert L. Lineberry, ed.

Social Welfare: Legend and Legacy. S. D. Gokhale.

Socialism and the Cities. Bruce M. Stave, ed.

Socialism of Fools: Georg Ritter von Schonerer and Austrian Pan-Germanism. Andrew G. Whiteside.

Socialism Since Marx: A Century of the European Left. Leslie Derfler.

Socialist Korea: A Case Study in the Strategy of Economic Development. Ellen Brun and Jacques Hersh.

Socialist Left and the German Revolution: A History of the German Independent Social Democratic Party, 1917-1922. David W. Morgan.

La societé laique et l'église dans la province ecclesiastique de Narbonne (zone cispyrénéenne) de la fin du VIIIᵉ à la fin ou XIᵉ siècle. Elisabeth Magnou-Nortier.

Society and Politics in Revolutionary Bordeaux. Alan Forrest.

Society, Freedom and Conscience: The American Revolution in Virginia, Massachusetts and New York. Richard M. Jellison, ed.

Society in Crisis: France in the Sixteenth Century. J. H. M. Salmon.

Society Under Siege: A Psychology

of Northern Ireland. Rona M. Fields.

Sociology of Kinship: An Analytical Survey of Literature. Leela Dube.

Soil Science and Archaeology. Susan Limbrey.

Soldatenräte und Revolution. Studien zur Militärpolitik in Deutschland, 1918/19. Ulrich Kluge.

Soldier Committees in the Russian Army in 1917: Their Origin and the Beginning Period of Their Activity. V. I. Miller.

The Songs of Seydou Camara. C. Bird, et al, tr.

The Sound of Bells: The Episcopal Church in South Florida, 1892-1969. Joseph D. Cushman, Jr.

Sources for the History of Science 1660-1914. David Knight.

Sources in Punjab History. W. Eric Gustafson, ed. and Kenneth W. Jones, ed.

South Africa: A Modern History. T. R. H. Davenport.

South Carolina: A Bicentennial History. Louis B. Wright.

South Georgia Rebels, the True Wartime Experiences of the 26th Regiment Georgia Volunteer Infantry Lawton-Gordon-Evans Brigade Confederate States Army, 1861-1865. Alton J. Murray.

South Korea. Charles R. Frank, Jr., Kwang Suk Kim, and Larry Westphal.

Southeast Asian History and Historiography: Essays Presented to D. G. E. Hall. C. D. Cowan, ed. and O. W. Wolters, ed.

The Southeastern Indians. Charles Hudson.

Southern Africa: The New Politics of Revolution. Basil Davidson, Joe Slovo, and Anthony R. Wilkinson.

A Southern Catholic Heritage, Volume 1, 1704-1813. Charles E. Nolan.

Southern Gentleman of Nevada Politics: Vail M. Pittman. Eric N. Moody.

Southern Governors and Civil Rights: Racial Segregation as a Campaign Issue in the Second Reconstruction. Earl Black.

Southern Literary Study: Problems and Possibilities. Louis D. Rubin, Jr. and C. Hugh Holman.

A Southern Odyssey: Travelers in the Antebellum North. John Hope Franklin.

Southern Politics and the Second Reconstruction. Nunan V. Bartley and Hugh D. Graham.

Southwest Journals of Adolph F. Bandolier, 1885-1888. Charles H. Lange and Carroll L. Riley and Elizabeth Lange, eds.

Southwest: South or West? Frank E. Vandiver.

Souvenirs and Prophecies: The Young Wallace Stevens. Holly Stevens.

Soviet-American Academic Exchanges, 1958-1975. Robert F. Byrnes.

Soviet and Chinese Influence in the Third World. Alvin Z. Rubenstein, ed.

The Soviet Union and International Politics. Arthur Jay Klinghoffen.

Soviet Women. William M. Mandel.

Sozialpolitik im Dritten Reich: Arbeiterklasse und Volksgemeinschaft. Timothy W. Mason.

Soziologie Und Sozialgeschichte. Peter Christian Ludz, ed.

Spain in Crisis: The Evolution and Decline of Franco Regime. Paul Preston, ed.

The Spanish American Novel: A Twentieth Century Survey. John S. Brushwood.

Spanish-Americans as a Political Factor in New Mexico. E. B. Fincher.

The Spanish Anarchists: The Heroic Years, 1868-1936. Murray Bookchin.

Spanish Border Lands: A First Reader. Oakah L., Jr., ed.

Spanish Colonial Tucson: A Demographic History. Henry F. Dobyns.

Spanish in the Mississippi Valley, 1762-1804. John Francis McDermott, ed.

The Spanish Kingdoms, 1250-1516. 1250-1410: Precarious Balance. J. N. Hillgarth.

Spindex II at Cornell University and a Review of Archival Automation in the United States. H. Thomas Hickerson et al.

Spindles and Spires: A Re-study of Religion and Social Change in Gastonia. John R. Early,

Dean D. Knudsen, and Donald W. Shriver, Jr.

The Spirit of '76: The Growth of American Patriotism Before Independence. Carl Bridenbaugh.

Spring Thunder and After: A Survey of the Maoist and Ultra-Leftist Movements in India, 1962-75. Asish Kumar Roy.

Squatters and Oligarchs: Authoritarian Rule and Policy Change in Peru. David Collier.

The Squire's Memoirs. J. Winston Coleman, Jr.

The SR Party: From Petit-bourgeois Revolutionism to Counter-Revolution. K. V. Gusev.

De SS en Nederland: Documenten uit SS Archieven, 1935-1945. N. K. C. A. 't Veld, ed.

Der Staat des Deutschen Ordens in Preussen nach dem II, Thorner Frieden. Lothar Dralle.

Das Staatsverstandnis des Parlamentarischen Rates. Volker Otto.

Stadelmann, Rudolph. Social and Political History of the German 1848 Revolution. Rudolph Stadelmann.

Stamford from Puritan to Patriot: The Shaping of a Connecticut Community: 1641-1774. Estelle F. Feinstein.

Stamp Act Congress: With an Exact Copy the Complete Journal. C. A. Weslager.

The Standard-Vacumn Oil Company and United States East Asian Policy, 1933-1941. Irvine H. Anderson, Jr.

The State and Economic Development: Peru Since 1968. E. V. K. Fitzgerald.

State in the Middle Ages: A Comparative Constitutional History of Feudal Europe. H. Mitteis.

Statistical Abstract of Arizona. Nat De Gennaro, ed.

The Statistical Movement in Early Victorian Britain: The Foundations of Empirical Social Research. M. J. Cullen.

Status of Bolivian Agriculture. E. Boyd Wennergren and Morris D. Whitaker.

Steel Titan: The Life of Charles M. Schwab. Robert Hessen.

Steveston Recollected: A Japanese-

Canadian History. Daphne
Marlatt, ed.
Stonewall Brigade. Frank G.
Slaughter.
Stonewall in the Valley. Robert
G. Tanner.
Storms Brewed in Other Men's
Worlds: The Confrontation of
Indians, Spanish and French in
the Southwest. Elizabeth A. H.
John.
The Story of Illinois. Theodore
Calvin Pease.
Story of the Guards. Julian
Paget.
The Story of the Latter-Day Saints.
James B. Allen and Glen M.
Leonard.
Strain of Violence: Historical
Studies of American Violence
and Vigilantism. Richard
Maxwell Brown.
Strategies for Freedom: The
Changing Patterns of Black
Protest. Bayard Rustin.
Strategy for Development. John
Barratt, David S. Collier, Kurt
Glaser, and Herman Monnig, ed.
Strategy, Risk and Personality in
Coalition Politics: The Case of
India. Bruce Bueno de Mesquita.
Strategy Without Slide-Rule:
British Air Strategy, 1914-1939.
Barry D. Powers.
Structural Study of Autobiography,
Proust, Leiris, Sartre, Levi-
Strauss. Jeffrey Mehlman.
The Structure of Jewish History
and Other Essays. Heinrich
Graetz.
Struggle for Stability in Early
Modern Europe. Theodore K.
Rabb.
Struggle for the American Mediter-
ranean: United States-European
Rivalry in the Gulf-Caribbean,
1776-1904. Lester D. Langley.
Struggle in the Countryside.
Brian Loveman.
Die Struktur der russischen
Posadgemeinden und ker
Katalog der Beschwerden und
Forderungen der Kaufmann-
schaft (1762-1767). Bernd
Knabe.
Studentenschaft und Rechtsradi-
kalismus in Deutschland 1918-
1933: eine sozialeschichtliche

Studie zur Bildungskrise in der
Weimarer Republik. Michael H.
Kater.
Studi e ricerche di storia ereticale
italiana del cinquecento. Antonio
Rotondo.
Studien zur altorientalischen und
griechischen Heilkunde: Therapie--
Arzneibereitung--Rezeptstruktur.
Dietlinde Goltz.
Studien zur Frühgeschichte des
Deutschen Ordens. Marie-Luise
Favreau.
Studien Zur Nordostgriechieschen
Kunst. Ernst Langlotz.
Studies in African Social Anthropology.
Meyer Fortes and Sheila Patterson,
ed.
Studies in Arabic Literary Papyri,
III, Language and Literature.
Nabia Abbott.
Studies in Pre-Vesalian Anatomy.
L. R. Lind.
Studies in Roman Property. M. I.
Finley, ed.
Studies in Russian-American Com-
merce, 1820-1860. Walter
Kirchner.
Studies in Southeastern Indian Lan-
guages. James M. Crawford, ed.
Studies in the Colonial History of
Spanish America. Mario Gongora.
Studies in the Russian Economy Before
1914. Olga Crisp.
Studies in the Semantic Structure of
Hindi. Kali Charan Bahl.
Studies in the Short Stories of William
Carleton. Margaret Chesnutt.
Studies on India and Vietnam. Helen
B. Lamb.
Studies on India and Vietnam. Corliss
Lamont, ed.
Style in History. Peter Gay.
Success and Failure: Indians in Urban
Society. W. T. Stanbury assisted
by Jay H. Siegel.
Success in America: The Yeoman
Dream and the Industrial Revolution.
Rex Burns.
Sucre, soldado y revolucionario.
John P. Hoover.
Sudafrika in Geschichte und Gegenwart.
Harald R. Bilger.
Süditalienkunde. Ein Führer zu
klassischen Stätten. Ernst Kirsten.
Suffering to Silence, 29th Texas Caval-
ry CSA Regimental History. John
C. Grady and Bradford K. Felmly.

L'URSS et la révolution cubaine.
Jacque Levesque.
Uruguay: The Politics of Failure.
Martin Weinstein.
Utopia and Revolution. Melvin J.
Lasky.
Utopias on Puget Sound, 1885-
1915. Charles Pierce LeWarne.

-V-

V Was for Victory: Politics and
American Culture During World
War II. John Morton Blum.
The Vagabond Dreamer. Elizabeth
S. Howard.
Valley of Discord: Church and
Society Along the Connecticut
River, 1636-1725. Paul R.
Lucas.
Valley of Mexico: Studies in Pre-
Hispanic Ecology and Society.
Eric R. Wolf.
Valores, desarrollo e historia:
Popajan, Medellin, Cali y el
valle del Cauca. Irving L.
Webber and Alfredo Ocampo
Zamorano.
Vanishing White Man. Stan
Steiner.
Varieties of Psychohistory. George
M. Kren, ed. and Leon H.
Rappoport, ed.
Various and Ingenious Machines of
Agostino Ramelli (1588).
Agostino Ramelli.
Vasilii Osipovich Kliuchevskii: A
History of His Life and Creative
Work. M. V. Nechkina.
Vendetta: A True Story of the
Worst Lynching in America, the
Mass Murder of Italian-Ameri-
cans in New Orleans in 1891,
the Vicious Motivations Behind
It, and the Tragic Repercussions
That Linger to This Day.
Richard Gambino.
A Venetian Family and Its Fortune.
James C. Davis.
Venezuela Dueña de su petroleo.
Romulo Betancourt.
The Venture of Islam. Marshall
G. S. Hodgson.
Vermont Landscape Images 1776-
1976. William C. Lipke and
Philip N. Grime, ed.

Vermont Place-Names: Footprints of
History. Esther Munroe Swift.
Vermont: The State with the Story-
book Past. Cora Cheney.
Vico and Herder. Two Studies in the
History of Ideas. Isiah Berlin.
Victoria County History of Wiltshire,
Volume X. Elizabeth Critall, ed.
Victoria History of Stafford. M. W.
Greenslade, ed.
The Victoria History of the County of
York, East Riding. K. J. Allison,
ed.
Victorian America. Daniel Walker
Howe.
Victorian Clerks. Gregory Anderson.
Victorian Lincoln. Francis Hill.
Victors Divided: America and the
Allies in Germany, 1918-1923.
Keith L. Nelson.
Vida Colonial y albores de la
independencia. Jose Miranda.
La Vida y La Historia, Ensayos sobre
Personas, lugares y problemas.
Jorge Basadre.
Vidyasagar: The Traditional Modern-
iser. Amales Tripathi.
Vie et mort de nos ancêtres: Etude
démographique. Hubert Charbon-
neau.
Vietnam. Hugh Higgins.
View from the Bronze Age: Mycena-
ean and Phoenician Discoveries
at Kition. Vassos Karageorghis.
A View of West Florida. John Lee
Williams.
The Viking Road to Byzantium. H. R.
Ellis Davidson.
The Village Commune in Russia from
the Seventeenth to the Beginning
of the Nineteenth Century. V. A.
Aleksandrov.
Village "Contracts" in Tokugawa
Japan: Fifty Specimens with Eng-
lish Translations and Comments.
Dan Fenno Henderson.
Village in the Jungle. Leonard Woolf.
Villages of Vision. Gillian Darley.
La Ville de Quebec, 1800-1850: Un
Inventaire de Cartes et Plans.
Edward H. Dahl, ed. et al.
Violence and Repression in Latin
America: A Quantitative and His-
torical Analysis. Ernest A. Duff
and John F. McCamant.
The Virgin. Geoffrey Ashe.
Visions of Courtly India, The Archer
Collection of Pahari Miniatures.
W. G. Archer.

Vital Signs: New and Selected
Poems. David R. Slavitt.
Vladivostok Under Red and White
Rules: Revolution and Counter-
Revolution in the Russian Far
East, 1920-1922. Canfield F.
Smith.
Voice of the People: John Doherty,
1798-1854, Trade Unionist,
Radical and Factory Reformer.
R. G. Kirby and E. A. Munson.
Voices from the Harlem Renais-
sance. Nathan I. Huggins, ed.
Voices from the Rapids: An
Underwater Search for Fur
Trade Artifacts, 1960-73.
Robert C. Wheeler, et al.
Voices of America: The Nation's
Story in Slogans, Sayings and
Songs. Thomas A. Bailey.
Voices of the Civil War. Richard
Wheeler.
Vorster's Gamble for Africa: How
the Search for Peace Failed.
Colin Legum.

-W-

Waiting Years: Essays on Ameri-
can Negro Literature. Blyden
Jackson.
Wake Up, Wake Up, to Do the
Work of the Creator. William
B. Helmreich.
Wales in the Eighteenth Century.
Donald Moore, ed.
Walker River Paiutes: A Tribal
History. Edward C. Johnson.
Walking the Boundaries: Poems
1957-74. Peter Davison.
Wallenstein. Galo Mann.
Walter Prescott Webb: His Life
and Impact. Necah Stewart
Furman.
Walter Prescott Webb Memorial
Lectures: Essays on Walter
Prescott Webb. Kenneth R.
Philp, ed. and Elliott West, ed.
Wampum. Anne Molloy.
War and Revolution in Yugoslavia,
1941-1945: The Chetniks.
Jozo Tomasevich.
War and Social Change in the
Twentieth Century: A Compara-
tive Study of Britain, France,

Germany, Russia and the United
States. Arthur Marwick.
War Books: A Study in Historical
Criticism. Jean Norton Cru.
War, Business, and American Society:
Historical Perspectives on the
Military-Industrial Complex.
Benjamin Franklin Cooling, ed.
War in European History. Michael
Howard.
War in the Ancient World: A Social
History. Yvon Garlan.
War in the Peninsula. Jan Read.
War, Literature, and Politics in the
Late Middle Ages. C. T. Allmand,
ed.
The War of Atonement, October, 1973.
Chaim Herzog.
War, Technology and Society in the
Middle East. V. J. Parry, ed.
and M. E. Yapp, ed.
Warboys: Two Hundred Years in the
Life of an English Medieval Village.
J. Ambrose Raftis.
Warlord Politics in China, 1916-1928.
Hsi-sheng Ch'i.
Warrior Government in Early Medieval
Japan. Jeffrey P. Mass.
Wars of the Roses. C. D. Ross.
Wartime. Milovan Djilas.
Washington: A Bicentennial History.
Norman H. Clark.
Washington--Berlin, 1908-1917: Die
Tätigkeit des Botschafters Johann
Heinrich Graf von Bernstorff in
Washington. Reinhard R. Doerries.
Water and the West: The Colorado
River Compact and the Politics of
Water in the American West.
Norris Hundley, Jr.
Watermark 74. Colin Cohen.
Way of the Fox: American Strategy
in the War for America, 1775-1783.
Dave Richard Palmer.
We Must March My Darlings. Diana
Trilling.
We, the Other People. Philip S.
Foner.
We Were 49ers! Chilean Accounts of
the California Gold Rush. Edwin A.
Beilharz, ed. and Carlos U.
Lopez, ed.
We Were Not Summer Soldiers: The
Indian War Diary of Plympton J.
Kelly. William N. Bischoff.
Weathering the Storm: Women of
the American Revolution. Elizabeth
Evans.

Weevils in the Wheat: Interviews with Virginia Ex-Slaves. Charles L. Perdue, Jr., ed., Thomas E. Barden, ed. and Robert K. Phillips, ed.

Wellington's Surgeon General: Sir James McGrigor. Richard L. Blanco.

West African Food in the Middle Ages, According to Arabic Sources. Tadeusz Lewicki.

The West in the Life of the Nation. Arrell Morgan Gibson.

West Virginia: A Bicentennial History. John Alexander Williams.

West Virginia and the Captains of Industry. John Alexander Williams.

Western American Writing: Tradition and Promise. Jay Gurian.

Western Aristocracies and the Imperial Court A.D. 364-425. John Mathews.

Western Europe: The Trails of Partnership. David S. Landes, ed.

Western Horse: Advice and Training. Dave Jones.

Western Populism. Karel D. Bicha.

The Western Pyrenees: Differential Evolution of the French and Spanish Borderland. Daniel Alexander Gomez-Ibanez.

Western Shore: Oregon Country Essays Honoring the American Revolution. Thomas Vaughn, ed.

What's Going On? (In Modern Folklore). Francis Edward Abernethy, ed.

Wheat Flour Messiah: Eric Jansson of Bishop Hill. Paul Elmen.

When Farmers Voted Red: The Gospel of Socialism in the Oklahoma Countryside, 1910-1924. Garin Burbank.

When I Think of Hingham. Michael J. Shilhan.

Where and How the War Was Fought: An Armchair Tour of the American Revolution. William J. Casey.

Where I'm Bound: Patterns of Slavery and Freedom in Black

American Autobiography. Sidonie Smith.

Whigs and Hunters: The Origin of the Black Act. E. P. Thompson.

White Against Red: The Life of General Anton Denikin. Dmitry B. Lehovich.

White Britain and Black Ireland: The Influence of Stereotypes on Colonial Policy. Richard Ned Lebow.

White House Witness, 1942-45. Jonathan Daniels.

White on Red: Images of the American Indian. Nancy B. Black, ed. and Bette S. Wiedman, ed.

White Wealth and Black Poverty: American Investments in Southern Africa. Barbara Rogers.

Whitelaw Reid: Journalist, Politician, Diplomat. Bingham Duncan.

Whither India? G. S. Ghurye.

Whiteman's Journeys into Chaos: A Psychoanalytic Study of the Poetic Process. Stephen A. Black.

Whittier: A Comprehensive Annotated Bibliography. Albert J. von Frank.

Why They Give: American Jews and Their Philanthropies. Milton Goldin.

Widening Circle: Essays on the Circulation of Literature in Eighteenth Century Europe. Paul J. Korshin, ed.

Wild and Wooly: An Encyclopedia of the Old West. Denis McLoughlin.

Die "Wilden" und die "Zivilisierten." Urs Bitterli.

William Caxton: A Portrait in a Background. Edmund Childs.

William Claiborne: Jeffersonian Centurion in the American Southwest. Joseph T. Hatfield.

William Clark: Jeffersonian Man on the Frontier. Jerome O. Steffen.

William Elliott Shoots a Bear: Essays on the Southern Literary Imagination. Louis D. Rubin, Jr.

William Howard Taft and United States Foreign Policy: The Apprenticeship Years, 1900-1908. Ralph Eldin Minger.

William Morris, Viscount Nuffield. R. J. Overy.

William Mulholland: A Forgotten Forefather. Robert W. Matson.

William O'Brien and the Course of Irish Politics, 1881-1918. Joseph V. O'Brien.

The World History of the Jewish People. Michael AviYonah, ed.
World of Our Fathers. Irving Howe.
World War II: An Account of Its Documents. James E. O'Neill, ed. and Robert W. Krauskopf, ed.
Worship and Theology in England. Horton Davies.
Wreck of Amsterdam. Peter Marsden.
Writers at Work: The Paris Review Interviews. George Plimpton.
Writings of Jonathan Edwards: Theme, Motif, and Style. William J. Scheick.
Die Wurttemberger und die deutsche Nationalversammlung, 1848-49. Bernhard Mann.

-Y-

Y venimos a Contradecir. Los Campesinos de Morelos y el Estado Nacional. Arturo Warman.
Yankee Artillerymen. John W. Rowell.
Yankee Blitzkrieg: Wilson's Raid Through Alabama and Georgia. James Pickett Jones.
A Yankee Guerrillero: Frederick Funston and the Cuban Insurrection, 1896-1897. Thomas W. Crouch.
Yanoma Indians. A Cultural Geography. William J. Smole.
Yazoo: Its Legends and Legacies. Harriet DeCell and JoAnne Prichard.
Year Books of Richard II, 1378-9. Morris S. Arnold, ed.
Year the Lights Came On. Terry Kay.
Years of MacArthur, Volume II: 1941-1945. D. Clayton James.
The Years of Struggle: The Farm Diary of Elmer G. Powers, 1931-1936. H. Roger Grant, ed. and L. Edward Purcell, ed.
Yeh Ming-Ch'en, Viceroy of Liang Kuang 1852-8. J. Y. Wong.

Yenching University and Sino-Western Relations, 1916-1952. Philip West.
Yermak's Campaign in Siberia: A Selection of Documents. Terence Armstrong, ed.
Yesterday's Augusta. A. Ray Rowland and Helen Callahan.
Yesterday's Memphis. Charles W. Crawford.
Yesterday's Michigan. Frank Angelo.
Yesterday's San Diego. Neil Morgan and Tom Blair.
Yohannes IV of Ethiopia: A Political Biography. Dejjazmach Zewde Gabre-Sellassie.
Young America and Australian Gold: Americans and the Gold Rush of the 1850s. E. Daniel Potts and Annette Potts.
Young John Dewey: An Essay in American Intellectual History. Neil Coughlan.
The Young Lloyd George. John Grigg.
Young Man Thoreau. Richard Lebeaux.
The Young Mary, 1817-1861. Martin Litvin.
The Young Mazarin. Georges Dethan.
Youth, Empire and Society: British Youth Movements. John Springhall.
Yugoslavia Before the Roman Conquest. John Alexander.
Yurok Myths. A. L. Kroeber.

-Z-

Zen at Daitoku-ji. Jon Covell and Yamada Sōbin.
Zen Master Dōgen: An Introduction with Selected Writings. Yūhō Yokoi with Assistance of Daizen Victoria.
Zimbabwe: Prose and Poetry. S. M. Mitswairo, et al.
Zulu Zion and Some Swazi Zionists. Bengt Sundkler.
Zwei Jahrtausende Kölner Wirtschaft. Hermann Kellenbenz, ed. and Klara van Eyll, ed.

Le territoire de l'historien.
LeRoy Emmanuel Ladurie.
Territorial Governors of Oklahoma.
Leroy H. Fischer.
Territorial Politics and Govern-
ment in Montana, 1864-89.
Clark C. Spence.
Terror Out of Zion: Irgun Zvai
Leumi, LEHI, and the Palestine
Underground, 1929-1949. J.
Bowyer Bell.
Texas: A Bicentennial History.
Joe B. Frantz.
Texas: A World in Itself.
George Sessions Perry.
Texas Furniture: The Cabinet-
makers and Their Work, 1840-
1880.   Lonn Taylor and David
B. Warren.
Texas in 1776.   Seymour V. Con-
nor.
The Textile Revolution. John Addy.
Texts and Studies in Jewish His-
tory and Literature.   Jacob
Mann.
Thai Peasant Social Structure.
Jack M. Potter.
Thea Romi: The Worship of the
Goddess Roma in the Greek
World.   Ronald Mello.
Theodore D. A. Cockerell: Let-
ters from West Cliff, Colorado,
1887-1889.   William A. Weber,
ed.
Theodore Schroeder, A Cold En-
thusiast: A Bibliography. Ralph
E. McCoy, comp.
Theology in the Responsa. Louis
Jacobs.
Theories of Vision from Al-Kindi
to Kepler. David C. Lindberg.
They Came to the Mountain: The
Story of Flagstaff's Beginnings.
Platt Cline.
They Went Thataway. James
Horwitz.
Thinkers and Tinkers. Silvio A.
Bedini.
The Third World Revolution.
Fred J. Carrier.
This Affair of Louisiana. Alex-
ander De Conde.
This Island of Japan: Joao
Rodrigues' Account of 16th-
Century Japan.   Michael
Cooper, ed.
This Species of Property: Slave
Life and Culture in the Old
South.   Leslie Howard Owens.

This War Without an Enemy. A His-
tory of the English Civil Wars.
Richard Ollard.
This Was Sheep Ranching Yesterday
and Today.   Virginia Paul.
Thomas Hooker: Writings in England
and Holland, 1626-1633.   George
H. Williams et al.
Thomas Jefferson's Paris. Howard
C. Rice, Jr.
Thomas L. McKenney, Architect of
America's Early Indian Policy,
1816-1830. Herman J. Viola.
Thomas McKean: Forgotten Leader
of the Revolution.   John M.
Coleman.
Thomas Mann: The Uses of Tradition.
T. J. Reed.
Thought Control in Prewar Japan.
Richard H. Mitchell.
Three and a Half Powers: The New
Balance in Asia. Harold C.
Hinton.
Three Bells of Civilization: The Life
on an Italian Hill Town. Sydel
Silverman.
Three Chilean Thinkers. Solomon
Lipp.
Three Decades in Shiwa: Economic
Development and Social Change in
a Japanese Farming Community.
Mitsuru Shimpo.
Three Voyages of Captain Cook.
Frank Paluka.
Thresholds of Reality: George
Santayana and Modernist Poetics.
Lois Hughson.
Through Roman Eyes: Roman Civilisa-
tion in the Words of Roman Writers.
Roger Nichols and Kenneth
McLeish, comps.
Thunder at Hampton Roads. A. A.
Hoehling.
Timber: History of the Forest
Industry. Geoffrey W. Taylor.
Time Enough: Poems New and Re-
vised.   John Hewitt.
Times of Feast, Times of Famine:
A History of Climate Since the
Year 1000.   LeRoy E. Ladurie.
Tiryns.   Forschungen und Berichte.
Kurt Muller et al.
Titans.   John Jakes.
Tito, Mihailovíc and the Allies, 1941-
1945.   Walter R. Roberts.
To Wash an Aethiop White: British
Ideas about Black African Educabil-
ity, 1530-1690.   Charles H.
Lyons.

The Tobacco Lords: A Study of the Tobacco Merchants of Glasgow and Their Trading Activities c. 1740-90. T. M. Devine.

Tolandiana Materiali bibliografici per lo studio dell'opera e della fortuna di John Toland (1670-1722). Giancarlo Carbelli.

Tom Paine and Revolutionary America. Eric Foner.

Topographical Bibliography of Ancient Egyptian Hieroglyphic Texts, Reliefs, and Paintings. Bertha Porter and Rosalind L. B. Moss.

The Tory Crisis in Church and State, 1688-1730: The Career of Frances Atterbury, Bishop of Rochester. G. V. Bennett.

Total Revolution: A Comparative Study of Germany Under Hitler, the Soviet Union under Stalin and China under Mao. C. W. Cassinelli.

Totalitarian Temptation. Jean-Francois Revel.

Totem Poles of Skedans. John Smyly and Carolyn Smyly.

Tourism in Developing Countries-Trick or Treat? A Report from the Gambia. Tina Esh and Illith Rosenblum.

Toward a Planned Society: From Roosevelt to Nixon. Otis L. Graham, Jr.

Toward a Warless World: The Travail of the American Peace Movement 1887-1914. David S. Patterson.

Toward an Urban Vision: Ideas and Institutions in Nineteenth Century America. Thomas Bender.

Towards Nationalism: Group Affliations and the Politics of Public Associations in 19th Century Western India. J. C. Masselos.

Town and Country in Central and Eastern Africa:.... David Parkin, ed.

Town Labourer and the Industrial Revolution. Malcolm I. Thomis.

Trabalho Urbano e Conflito Social (1890-1920). Boris Fausto.

A Trace of Desert Waters: The Great Basin Story. Samuel G. Houghton.

Trade and Development in Korea. Wontack Hong and Anne O. Krueger.

Trade Unions and Revolution: The Early Industrial Politics of the Communist Party. James Hinton and Richard Hyman.

Trading in West Africa. P. N. Davies.

Tradition and Adaptation: Life in a Modern Yucatan Maya Village. Irwin Press.

Tradition in an Age of Reform. Noah Rosenbloom.

Tradition of Resistance in Mozambique: The Zambesi Valley, 1850-1921. Allen F. Isaacman.

The Traditional History of the Jie of Uganda. John Lamphear.

Traditional Music of Thailand. David Morton.

Traditions of American Education. Lawrence A. Cremin.

Tragedy of Erasmus: A Psychohistoric Approach. Harry S. May.

Trail of Tears. Gloria Jahoda.

Training the Nihilists: Education and Radicalism in Tsarist Russia. Daniel R. Brower.

Tramways and Trolleys: The Rise of Urban Mass Transport in Europe. John P. McKay.

Transfer of Power, 1942-7. Nicholas Mansergh, ed.

The Transformation of American Foreign Relations, 1865-1900. Charles S. Cambell.

The Transformation of American Law, 1780-1860. Morton J. Horwitz.

Transformation of Europe, 1558-1648. Charles Wilson.

The Transformation of Southern Politics: Social Change and Political Consequence Since 1945. Jack Bass and Walter DeVries.

The Transport of Love: The Meghaduta of Kalidasa. Leonard Nathan, tr.

Transylvania: Tutor to the West. John D. Wright.

The "Trattato Politico-Morale" of Giovanni Cavalcanti (1381-c. 1451). Marcella Grendler.

Travail and Triumph: Black Life and Culture in the South Since the Civil War. Arnold H. Taylor.

Travis. Archie P. McDonald.

Trial of Beyers Naude: Christian

-U-